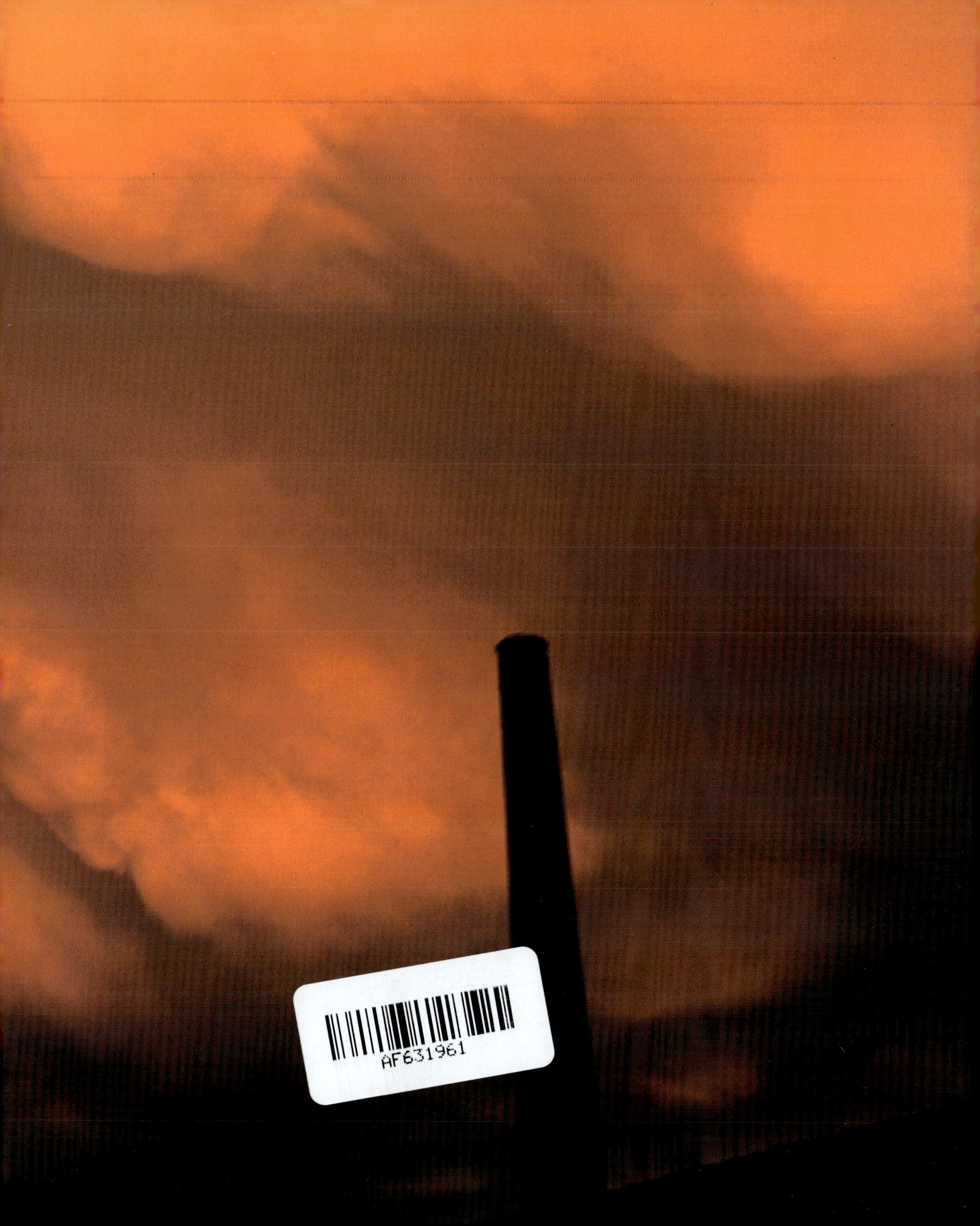

AF631961

DIE PARKETT-REIHE MIT GEGENWARTSKÜNSTLERN / THE PARKETT SERIES WITH CONTEMPORARY ARTISTS

Book Series with contemporary artists in English and German, published three times a year. Each volume is created in collaboration with artists, who contribute an original work specially made for the readers of Parkett. The works are reproduced in the regular edition and available in a limited and signed Special Edition.

Buchreihe mit Gegenwartskünstlern in deutscher und englischer Sprache, erscheint dreimal im Jahr. Jeder Band entsteht mit Künstlern oder Künstlerinnen, die eigens für die Leser von Parkett einen Originalbeitrag gestalten. Diese Werke sind in der gesamten Auflage abgebildet und zusätzlich in einer limitierten und signierten Vorzugsausgabe erhältlich.

PARKETT NR. 58 ENTSTEHT IN COLLABORATION MIT • SYLVIE FLEURY, JASON RHOADES, JAMES ROSENQUIST • WILL BE COLLABORATING ON PARKETT NO. 58

JAHRESABONNEMENT (DREI NUMMERN) / ANNUAL SUBSCRIPTION (THREE ISSUES) SFR. 108.– (SCHWEIZ), DM 130,– (BRD), SFR. 118.– (ÜBRIGES EUROPA), US$ 80 (USA AND CANADA ONLY)

Zürichsee Druckereien AG (Stäfa) Satz, Litho, Druck/Copy, Printing, Color Separations

No parts of this magazine may be reproduced without publisher's permission. We appreciate seeing any mention of Parkett in critical reviews.
Nachdrucke jeder Art sind nur mit Genehmigung des Verlags erlaubt, bei Besprechungen bitten wir um Belege.

Parkett does not assume any responsibility for unsolicited texts and pictures.
Für unaufgefordert eingesandte Texte und Bilder übernimmt der Verlag keine Verantwortung.

Copyright Parkett & Pro Litteris

PARKETT-VERLAG AG, ZÜRICH, DEZEMBER 1999 PRINTED IN SWITZERLAND ISBN 3-907582-07-1 ISSN 0256-0917

Special thanks to Edit deAk, John Marchant, Renee Padt & Christian Rattemeyer

HEFTRÜCKEN / SPINE 55–57: LOUISE BOURGEOIS

ODE A MA MERE, 1995, one of a series of 9 drypoint etchings, sheet: 12 x 12" / aus einer Serie von 9 Kaltnadelradierungen, Blattformat 30,4 x 30,4 cm.

Cover, front page / Umschlag vorn: DOUG AITKEN, BAD ANIMAL, 1996, video still (top/oben) & NAN GOLDIN, BRUCE IN THE SMOKE, POZZUOLI, ITALY, 1995. Flap & page 1 / Klappe & Seite 1: NAN GOLDIN, THE SKY ON THE TWILIGHT OF PHILIPPINE'S SUICIDE, WINTERTHUR, 1997. Inside cover page & flap / Umschlagklappe innen: DOUG AITKEN, DIAMOND SEA, 1997, production still. Back cover / Rückseite: THOMAS HIRSCHHORN, VDP—VERY DERIVED PRODUCTS, 1998, group exhibition / Gruppenausstellung "Premises," Guggenheim Museum Soho, New York, detail.

The editors of Parkett and Nan Goldin dedicate this issue to the memory of Philippine Lambert (1977–1997).

PARKETT Zürich New York Frankfurt

Bice Curiger Chefredaktorin/Editor-in-Chief; **Jacqueline Burckhardt** Redaktorin/Senior Editor; **Cay Sophie Rabinowitz** Redaktorin USA/Associated Editor US; **Susanne Schmidt** Textredaktion und Produktion/Editing and Production; **Trix Wetter · Hanna Koller** Graphik/Design; **Catherine Schelbert** Englisches Lektorat/Editorial Assistant for English; **Claudia Meneghini Nevzadi** Korrektorat/Proof Reading

Beatrice Fässler Vorzugsausgaben, Inserate/Special Editions, Advertising; **Brigitte Grüninger** Buchvertrieb, Administration/Distribution, Administration; **Conradin Bernoulli** Abonnemente/Subscriptions; **Ali Subotnick** Redaktionsassistenz, Vorzugsausgaben und Marketing USA/Assistant Editor, Editions and Marketing US; **Monika Condrea** Abonnemente USA/Subscriptions US; **Adrian Koerfer** Deutsche Verlagsvertretung/German Representative

Jacqueline Burckhardt – Bice Curiger – Dieter von Graffenried Herausgeber/Parkett Board; **Jacqueline Burckhardt – Bice Curiger – Dieter von Graffenried – Walter Keller – Peter Blum** Gründer/Founders

Dieter von Graffenried Verleger/Publisher

www.parkettart.com

PARKETT-VERLAG AG, QUELLENSTRASSE 27, CH-8031 ZURICH, TEL. 41-1-271 81 40, FAX 41-1-272 43 01
PARKETT, NEW YORK, 155 AV. OF THE AMERICAS, N.Y. 10013, PHONE (212) 673-2660, FAX (212) 271-0704
PARKETT-VERLAG AG, TANNENWALDALLEE 17, D-61348 BAD HOMBURG, FAX 06172-937 444

EDITORIAL *Die Ränder in uns*

Wo sind eigentlich die viel beschworenen Ränder der Gesellschaft, wie sehen sie aus? Gibt es überhaupt noch Ränder, wo es doch heisst, wir hätten das Zentrum verloren und seien eine einzige globalisierte Kultur? Wer die Werke der in diesem Parkett-Band vorgestellten Künstler, Doug Aitken, Nan Goldin und Thomas Hirschhorn, betrachtet, den befällt sofort das schnelle Wiedererkennen. Aus den Werken der drei Künstler spricht mit grosser Direktheit das, was Wirklichkeit genannt wird. Sie zeigen auch, wie stark besagte «Ränder» schon in uns selbst angelegt sind. In der Konfrontation mit Lebensbereichen, die unser aller Alltagserfahrung, wie immer sie sich gestaltet, gerade auch mit ihren eingeschriebenen Grenzlinien und Übergangsmomenten ausmacht.

Thomas Hirschhorn bedient sich der visuellen Sprache jener Aussenseiter, denen wir als Passanten in den Strassen der Städte begegnen. In Schildern und Signalisationen, die weder amtlich verordnet noch kommerziell indiziert sind, scheint er die Rauchzeichen einer armen, verlorenen Seele, in billigen, hinfälligen Materialien, in einem alles andere als stromlinienförmigen Ausdruck einzufangen. Zu dünn der Stift, zu emphatisch die Diktion – es manifestiert sich das Amateurtum in reinster, geballter Form. Doch Hirschhorns Verweise sind wissend und bewusst gesetzt, souverän und luzide zeigen sie in einem brisanten Paradox auf das grosse, zum Scheitern verurteilte Antiprogramm der Schwachen. Ihr Raffinement ist, dass sie sich auf das abseitige Dichterleben richten, aber eben auch auf das harte gesellschaftliche Kerngeschäft. Sie öffnen sozusagen Ritzen im Asphalt, während sie gleichsam unseren kunstbeflissenen Geist entzünden.

Auch wenn Nan Goldins Photos uns ein «Milieu» vor Augen führen, das nicht das der Betrachterin/des Betrachters sein mag, wird man niemals zum Voyeur. Hier liegt ein wichtiger Angelpunkt ihrer Kunst und der Grund, warum Nan Goldins Popularität so gross und so breit ist. Nan Goldin photographiert als Beteiligte. Ihr Blick ist immer ein liebender, ein warmer Blick. Deshalb wirken manchmal unbekleidete Menschen in ihren Photos mehr existenziell denn physisch nackt – es ist eine Frage der Blicke, der Haltung, der kommunikativen Aura und der diese Menschen umgebenden weiteren Hüllen im Raum, in denen sie Schutz zu suchen scheinen. Die Form, die Sorgfalt der Komposition, das Licht, die Farben bauen diesen unnachahmlich würdevollen Rahmen auf. In ihrem Essay schreibt Elisabeth Lebovici, dass die kommunikative Nähe auch in den neueren Photos auszumachen ist, Landschafts- und Naturbilder, die frei sind von Gefühlen der Ferne und Unendlichkeit (S. 65).

Während Nan Goldin Fiktionales herunterreissen will, wie sie sagt, im ungebrochenen Glauben, dass Photographie uns die Wirklichkeit näher bringen kann, schliessen uns die Werke von Doug Aitken mit einer Realität kurz, die wesentlich im Kopf stattzufinden scheint. In den einnehmenden Videoinstallationen sind seine Landschaften ebenso mental wie real. So die überbelichtete Wüste mit der Stacheldrahtabzäunung (DIAMOND SEA) und die vor und nach einem Vulkanausbruch geräumte Insel (ERASER). Bereits die Titel weisen die Richtung, etwa ELECTRIC EARTH oder 2-SECOND SEPARATION, oder – im Falle der Parkett-Edition – DECREASE THE MASS AND RUN LIKE HELL: Ein gleissend silberner Drachen steigt in die Luft um im Himmel als kollektives, aus den Köpfen der Erdenbürger gelöstes Psychogeschoss in blendend kalter Spiegelung einen physikalischen Prozess als Gemütszustand vorzuführen.

Das Titelblatt mit seinen beiden unterschiedlichen gesichtslosen Figuren verkörpert zwei nach innen gekehrte Welten, die aber gerade auch die Spannung zum Aussen aufrechterhalten. Ebenso wird die Museumstür auf der Rückseite durch persönliche Tags und Kleber aus Hirschhorns Fundus in den Bereich des anonymen persönlichen Ausdrucks gehoben.

Bleibt noch der Hinweis auf eine Besonderheit in diesem Band: In Abweichung zum Gewohnten hat Thomas Hirschhorn das Layout seiner Bildseiten selbst gestaltet.

EDITORIAL *The Margins Within*

Where can we actually find the much vaunted margins of society and what do they look like? Do they even exist inasmuch as we have supposedly lost our center and become one vast globalized culture? On studying the work of Doug Aitken, Nan Goldin, and Thomas Hirschhorn in this issue of Parkett, we are at once immersed in instant recognition. With striking immediacy, the works of all three artists bespeak what is commonly called reality. They demonstrate how firmly said "margins" are, in fact, rooted within ourselves, by confronting us with areas of life whose inevitably inscribed boundaries and points of transition define the everyday experiences of each and everyone of us, no matter how we conduct our lives.

Thomas Hirschhorn adopts the visual language of the outsiders that we encounter as pedestrians in urban conglomerations. He seems to capture the smoke signals of a poor, lost soul in signs and signals that are neither officially dictated nor commercially indicated, in cheap, dilapidated materials and in expressions that are anything but streamlined. Too thin the pencil stroke, too emphatic the diction—a manifestation of pure, unadulterated amateurism. But Hirschhorn's references are intentional and conscious; masterful and lucid, they are couched in a disquieting paradox that reveals the grand but inevitably doomed anti-program of the weak. Their subtlety lies in being directed at both the remove of the poet's life as well as the hard, core business of society. They make cracks in the asphalt, as it were, and inflame our eager, art-oriented minds.

Even though Nan Goldin's photographs display a "milieu" that may not coincide with our own, we are never placed in the position of being a voyeur. This pinpoints a salient feature of her art and explains why she enjoys such widespread popularity. Nan Goldin is a participant of the pictures she shoots; the gaze she directs at her subjects is always loving, always warm. For this reason, when she photographs people in the nude, the effect is an existential rather than a physical nudity. It is a question of the gaze, of an attitude that conveys a communicative aura, and of other wrappings in the space around her subjects, in which they seem to seek sanctuary. The form, the careful composition, the lighting, the coloring create this inimitably dignified framework. In her essay Elisabeth Lebovici writes that Goldin's more recent pictures of landscapes and nature are invested with the same communicative intimacy and do not describe feelings of distance or infinity (p. 69).

While Nan Goldin aims to demolish fiction with her unbroken faith in photography's ability to bring us closer to reality, the work of Doug Aitken fuses with a reality that essentially takes place in the mind. The landscapes in his captivating video installations are both mental and real—the overexposed desert enclosed in a barbed wire fence (DIAMOND SEA), the island evacuated before and after a volcanic eruption (ERASER). The titles themselves are signposts as well, like ELECTRIC EARTH or 2-SECOND SEPARATION, or the Parkett Edition, DECREASE THE MASS AND RUN LIKE HELL: a searing, silver kite that rises into the air, a collective psycho-missile, detached from the minds of earthlings, converting a physical process into an emotional state, mirrored in the sparkling cold of the skies.

The cover with its two different faceless figures embodies two introverted worlds that still sustain tension with the world outside. The museum door on the back cover has also been transported into the realm of anonymous personal expression with tags and stickers from Hirschhorn's own inventory.

In addition, this volume of Parkett has a surprise in store: Contrary to custom, the layout of Thomas Hirschhorn's section has been designed by the artist himself.

Bice Curiger

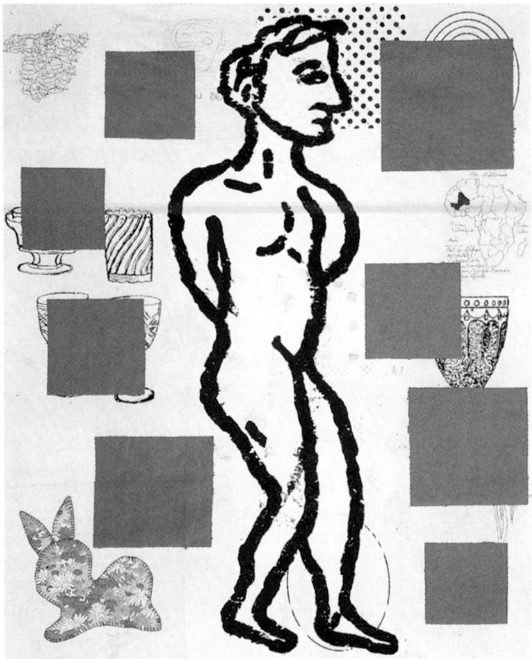

DONALD BAECHLER, RED ABSTRACTION WITH STANDING FIGURE, 1995, gouache, gesso, and collage on paper, 46 x 36" / ROTE ABSTRAKTION MIT STEHENDER FIGUR, Gouache, Kreidegrund und Collage auf Papier, 116,8 x 91,5 cm.

DONALD BAECHLER, MEMORY & ILLUSION (GLOBE), 1998, acrylic and fabric collage on canvas, 111 x 222" / ERINNERUNG & ILLUSION (GLOBUS), Acryl und Stoffcollage auf Leinwand, 282 x 564 cm. (PHOTO: BETH PHILLIPS)

DAVID GREENBERG

Surface to Air

When Roman sculptors wanted to create a patina for their bronzes to pass them off as Greek artifacts, they buried them in the sand and directed soldiers to piss in that specific spot. Unearthed months later, the sculptures had been aged to perfection. Perfect fakes. The surface of Donald Baechler's recent collage paintings has a slightly less sordid past, but the artist employs a similar ingenuity to create his own "false history."

Like an archeological site that has yet to be excavated, the surface of Baechler's paintings is rich with both the exotic and the banal. And as always when digging up the past, there is a great possibility for disappointment. No, that underwear collaged into the bottom of the canvas was not found on the studio floor, left behind by an overnight guest; it was bought in Chinatown, brand new. But sometimes the truth is ultimately more interesting than our fantasies. In the realm of art history, "just the facts" can be a revelation.

In theory, Baechler always stresses the lack of a narrative in his paintings. Yet, a typical conversation with him invariably involves some anecdote about a particular assistant's fuck-up or some shopping expedition for art materials gone humorously wrong. In fact, it may be safe to conclude that the true narrative in Donald Baechler's paintings rests in the story of their creation and specifically, the construction of

DAVID GREENBERG is a poet and musician. He is the author of *Feeling Gravity's Pull* (Soft Skull Press, New York), and two books in collaboration with Donald Baechler: *Crowd Paintings* (Lars Bohman Gallery, Stockholm) and *Gray Paintings* (Bernd Kluser Gallery, Munich). He lives and works in New York City.

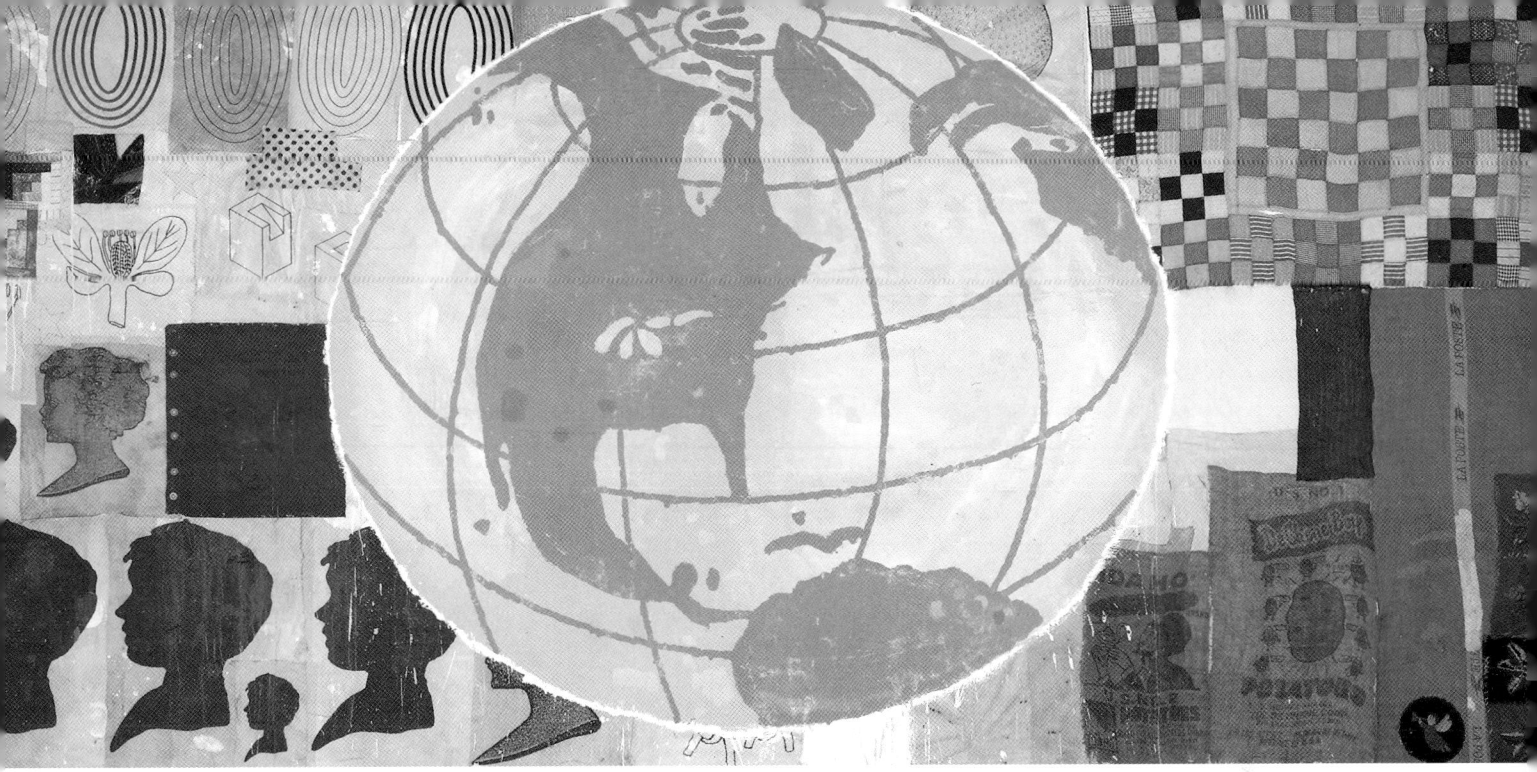

The Collage Paintings of Donald Baechler

their particular surfaces. Baechler's ever evolving modus operandi can be seen, like the rings of a tree, in the layers beneath the images: the pieces of fabric, the paint spills, the maps and ticket stubs, the fortune cookie fortunes, potato sacks, and airmail bags. The construction of a ground on which to paint is, for Baechler, a primary focus of his art. One might conclude that it is the very surface of his paintings which make them art, as distinct from the image we see painted on top.

So much has been made of Baechler's so-called vocabulary, which has included flowers, beach balls, crudely drawn human figures, globes and, more recently, ice cream. But on their own, these images are more or less the sum of their sources. Many are derived from non-art sources: third world barber shop signs and wall paintings, primitive commercial illustration. In a sense, they are what they represent. A beach ball is a beach ball. A flower, a flower. It's pretty safe to say that some guy in India painting an ice-cream cone on the wall is much more concerned with making it look like an actual ice-cream cone than in creating some kind of ironic icon. He just wants it to look good enough to eat. By using this same ice-cream cone for example, Baechler comes as close as he can to painting nothing. In other words, it is not so much what is painted but how. The painter's concerns are formal. Donald Baechler is an abstract painter. For him a flower is just something with a red top and a green stem. And an ice-cream cone is... well, you get the point.

It's easy to be distracted by Baechler's images. They're bright and colorful, almost playful. But don't be fooled. In the hand of the artist they are radically recontextualized. It is in the very act of painting where these simple pictographs are transformed into art. For Baechler, painting is a form of alchemy. But I won't get into that here. My concerns presently are with the ground, not with what's painted on top. Baechler on constructing a ground for his collage paintings:

What I'm trying to do at every stage… is to make something that could almost stop right there because for me it's difficult to approach. I'm very interested in the figure/ground relationship. If the ground is not complete, I can't paint the figure on top. A white wall, to me, is completely uninteresting to paint on. But something found on the street might be interesting because it has a completeness and a life of its own.

The need to construct a ground with such characteristics has both psychological and art-historical implications. The former I'll leave to the shrinks. The latter I'll take a stab at. But in order to understand the evolution of Baechler's ground, we first have to go back to his days as a student.

Baechler never much cared for thick paint. His earliest paintings were done with thin enamel. After years of breathing poisonous fumes, he smartly switched to acrylic. But his distaste for thick paint still posed a problem. The young artist liked to show his mistakes. By revealing previous attempts at painting a figure, what he'd later call "false starts," the canvas accumulated a history of erasure. Each "false start" was painted over, leaving the ghost of an image slightly visible. He wanted to imbue the surface with a kind of poetic pentimento as distinct from a palimpsest of brushstrokes. But in order to create this effect, more and more paint had to be applied. Eventually, Donald Baechler discovered a way to create these "ghosts" and avoid thick paint: He glued down thin pieces of fabric onto the canvas. This device would become intregal to the construction of a surface that was uniquely his own.

The gradual build-up of fabric on the canvas yielded much more than a fresh surface on which to paint a figure. Although editorial in origin, the scraps of fabric produced a roughed-up surface. The grounds had a beautifully impoverished feel to them. The accumulation of fabric contributed to an air of the ancient, the antique. It produced a sense of the artifact, the buried treasure. It also made the paintings look embossed. But perhaps the most profound effect was on the nature of Baechler's line. By obstructing the path of the brush, the new, unpredictable surface resulted in a ragged line. With the look of chewed string and the feel of a wandering dervish's tattered garments, this line would become synonymous with Baechler's work. It would be his trademark. Like Pollack's drip or Schnabel's broken plate. A new bumpy road had been constructed for the artist to travel. From this point forward, there would be no straight lines in a Baechler painting.

Eventually, Baechler came to depend more and more on the collage element in his paintings. What was once a convenient solution to a technical problem ultimately evolved into an aesthetic choice. To this day, in fact, it's almost impossible to think of a Baechler painting without scraps of fabric collaged into the ground.

Meanwhile, simultaneously a more complex collage was evolving on another surface: paper. Baechler's collage work on paper started off innocently enough—with a sort of waste-not-want-not approach. The artist explains:

I started making collages when I was traveling and I'd be drawing all these heads and making all these accumulations and I had all these scraps of paper left over. It seemed like a waste to throw all these beautiful scraps of paper away… so I glued them down. You know when traveling, one collects all sorts of bits of paper: receipts and travel documents. And I hate throwing things away. So I would just sort of stick something in the corner. And it went on and on from there. The collages became an almost autobiographical thing. My passage through time.

Soon all sorts of souvenirs would begin to show up in Baechler's collages: taxi receipts, museum ticket stubs, restaurant checks, children's homework. Gradually, he found himself going from a surplus of crap to a real drought. And so began yet another ingenious device of the artist's—the manufacturing of false documents. Through the use of what Baechler calls his "human Xerox machines," collage elements were manufactured in the studio by young apprentices, under the master's watchful eyes. One Egyptian assistant wrote homework assignments in Arabic and filled in maps—grammar school geography les-

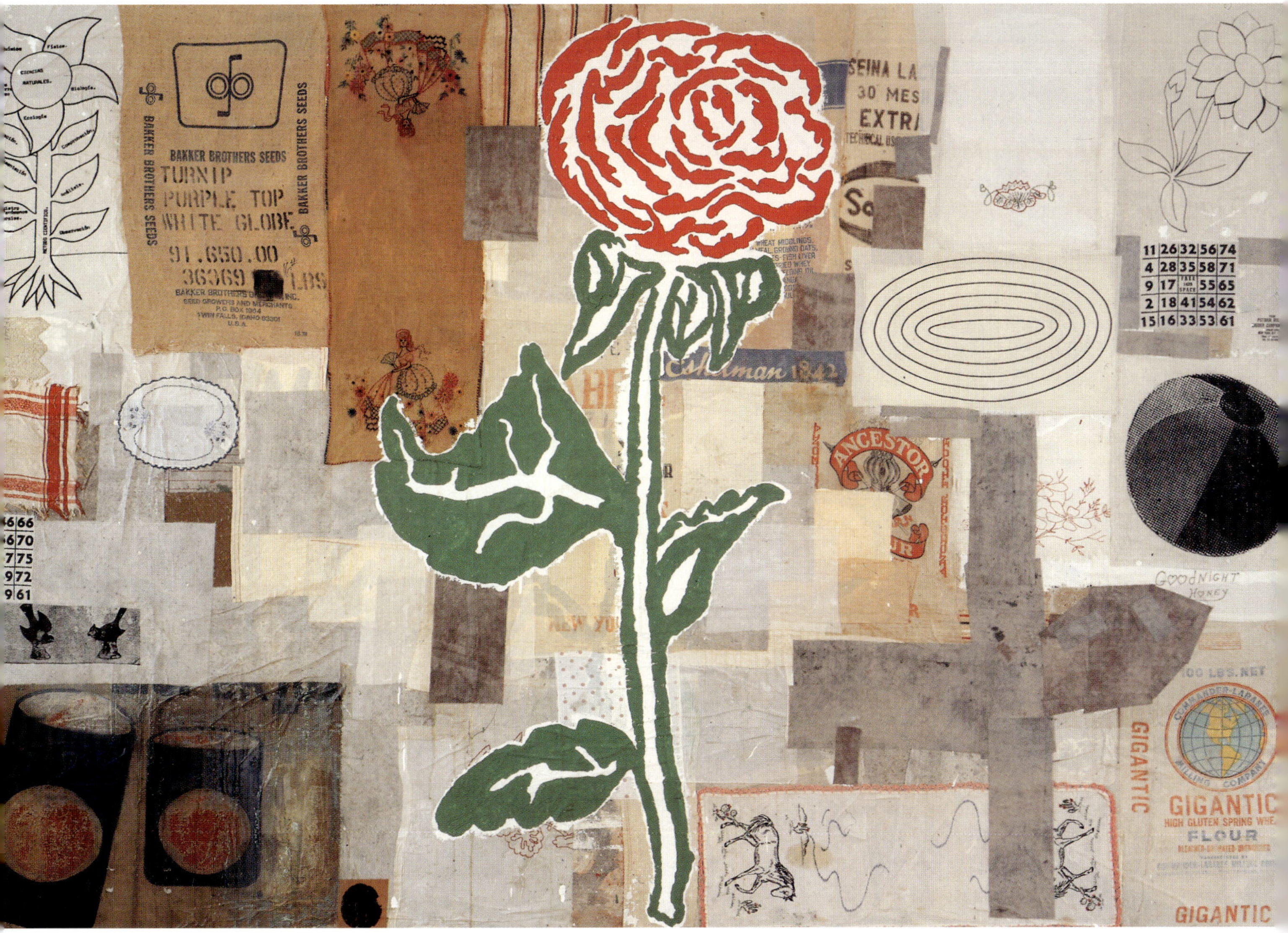

DONALD BAECHLER, ANCESTOR, 1994, acrylic, fabric collage, and Rhoplex on canvas, 90 x 130" /
VORGÄNGER, Acryl, Stoffcollage und Rhoplex-Lack auf Leinwand, 228,6 x 330,2 cm.

sons. Another assistant copied images out of a yoga handbook in a primitive, child-like style. Skilled silkscreeners were hired to print found images onto fabric, which yet another assistant would then meticulously stain. Baechler created a kind of cottage industry for himself with his own little army of "human Xerox machines" or as Philip Taaffe dubbed it: "The Baechler Home for Wayward Youth." It was an updated version of Roman soldiers pissing on buried sculpture. Like Andy Warhol before him, who actually had asked certain Factory employees and friends to piss on his paintings (for his *Oxidation Series*), Baechler surrounded himself with a swirl of creative—and sometimes volatile—people. And in effect, he created his own "fakes."

As Baechler approached a larger scale for his collages, the wealth of materials increased. Much more was required to fill the expansive space of a 5 by 6-foot canvas. Soon, more precious items began to pop up in Baechler's collages. Pieces of ancient Peruvian tapestries, burlap rice bags from Mexico, well-worn American jeans, and of course, the occasional pair of whities would reappear in a painting. But perhaps closest to the artist's heart were his mother's quilts. "She was a real artist," Baechler once explained. By incorporating her work into his own, Donald not only continued to bathe his paintings in the glow of autobiography, but made a deliberate, physical connection to his own past. Again, he was finding new ways to "age" his collages, and new recruits for the Baechler army of human Xerox machines.

Of course, the General does a lot of the strategic legwork himself, traveling to distant lands, surveying foreign cities like a benign conqueror. Baechler is the perpetual stranger in a strange land, constantly searching for raw materials to bring back to his studio in New York. A modern-day Marco Polo collecting the awkward remnants of culture. The not-so-accidental tourist returning from a business trip with a suitcase full of obscure detritus from second-hand bookstores and out-of-the-way flea markets. Mercenaries offer up their services, combing garage sales and grandparents' attics in the hope that one of their impoverished scraps will one day make a stunning debut in a Donald Baechler Production. And like an old Hollywood director casting extras for an epic, Donald sifts through his booty and arranges the collaged elements onto the silver screen, or in his case, a giant canvas.

To paraphrase an old cliché, one man's shit is another man's ice-cream painting. But Baechler is quick to explain:

The whole idea is to create a complete picture that I can then intrude upon with another image; it's kind of a violent act—to have an almost perfect found picture that I can paint on top of. It's the intervention that gives the work a charge. Without that, they would just be pretty backgrounds.

Abstract painters have been known to fall in love with Baechler's backgrounds. In fact, legend has it that Ross Bleckner once begged Donald to not paint over a certain background. I can just see him, recreating his cameo in AS GOOD AS IT GETS, where he picks up a male prostitute (played by Skeet Ulrich) for the grandiose purposes of art—"I need a pretty face. This is for a portrait."—picking out an unfinished work and cooing "It's soooo beautiful Donald. Don't touch it!" But Ross misses the whole

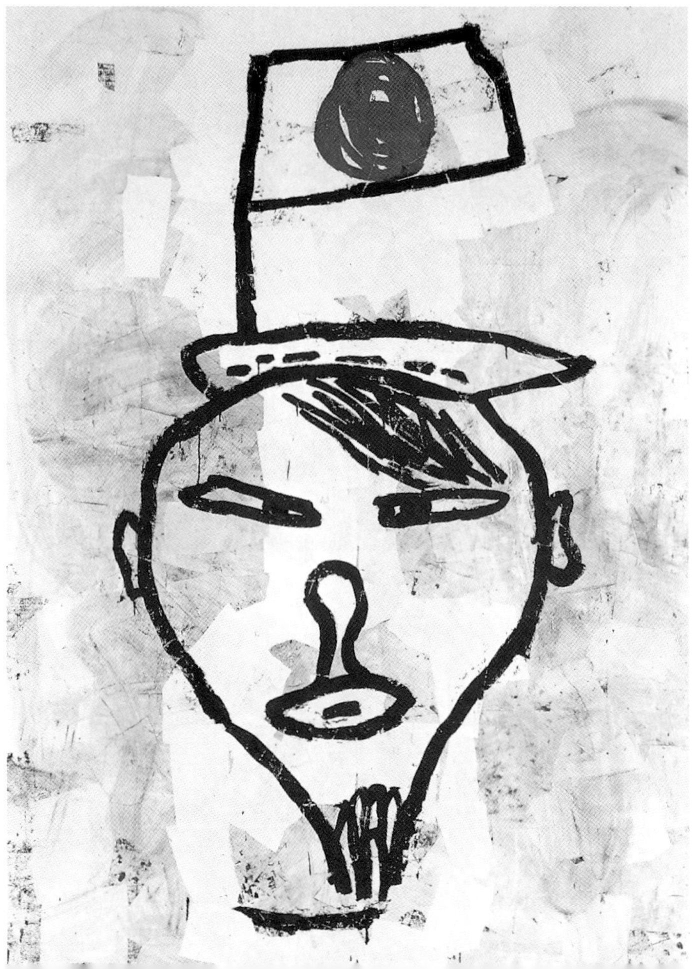

DONALD BAECHLER, DIE FAHNE HOCH, 1984, acrylic, acrylic medium, and paper on canvas, 97 x 64" / Acryl, Acrylmalmittel und Papier auf Leinwand, 264,4 x 162,6 cm.

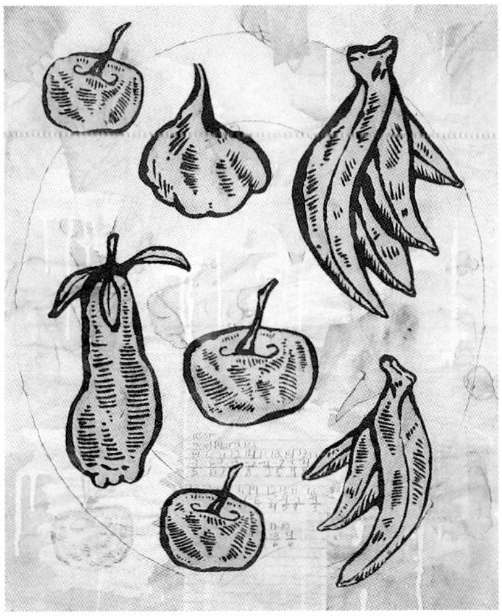

DONALD BAECHLER, FRUITS, 1989, ink, gesso, and collage on paper, 27 x 21" / FRÜCHTE, Tusche, Kreidegrund und Collage auf Papier, 68,6 x 53,4 cm.

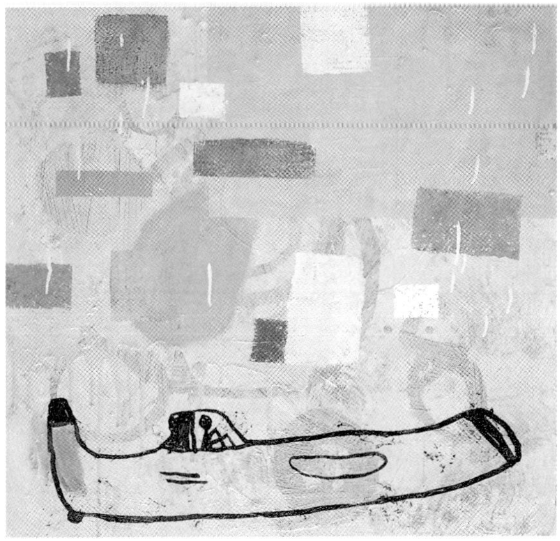

DONALD BAECHLER, ABSTRACT PAINTING WITH SPACESHIP, 1985, acrylic and polyurethane on canvas, 30 x 30" / ABSTRAKTES BILD MIT RAUMSCHIFF, Acryl und Polyurethan auf Leinwand, 76,2 x 76,2 cm.

point. For Baechler, it's not about making pretty pictures, it's about fucking them up.

Case in point. Baechler was preparing for an exhibition in Paris of large-scale flower collages. One particular horizontal work was giving him trouble. The composition of three flowers standing in a row was just not working. (It's interesting to note that he would attempt this particular composition again for Basel, finally getting it right by creating a kind of pyramid shape.) Something had to be done, so he directed an assistant to cover up two of the three flowers with fabric, leaving the center flower alone to hold the space. Amazingly, it worked. There was only one problem. One particular collage element, a hand-painted image on delicate fabric from Morocco, had been painted on. The paint had to be carefully scraped away from the image—a beautifully awkward blue can of some sort. The task assigned was a difficult one. And this particular assistant suspected it was all some kind of game. He was pissed. Donald, oblivious to his assistant's suspicions, yelled at him to scrape more paint off, like some cartoon of the big bad bossman. The whole thing was a surreal comedy of errors. I just happened to be there to witness it.

Donald left the back studio to greet a visitor at the front door. A collector? A celeb? Who cared—the real drama was happening on the surface of this colossal canvas, lying on the floor like a wounded racehorse. I stayed in the studio, trying in vain to assuage the furious assistant. It didn't work. He just kept muttering under his breath, cursing out his boss like a child sent to bed without dessert, all the while violently scraping paint from this exquisite piece of fabric. But I knew the real fireworks would erupt when Donald came back to the studio. "What are you doing! You're ruining that piece of fabric. I found it with Philip Taaffe in Morocco." Baechler was red-faced and screaming. Fast forward. I'm sitting in the same studio weeks after the scraping incident, leafing through the Paris catalogue. I flip to a reproduction of, what is to me, the now infamous painting. Feeling that enough time has passed, I lightheartedly point to the bruised area of the painting, half joking, "Remember that, Donald?"

Stone-faced, without the slightest hint of irony, Baechler responds: "You know, that turned out to be the most beautiful part of the painting."

I can almost hear some boy unzipping his pants...

At Donald Baechler's studio / In Donald Baechlers Atelier.

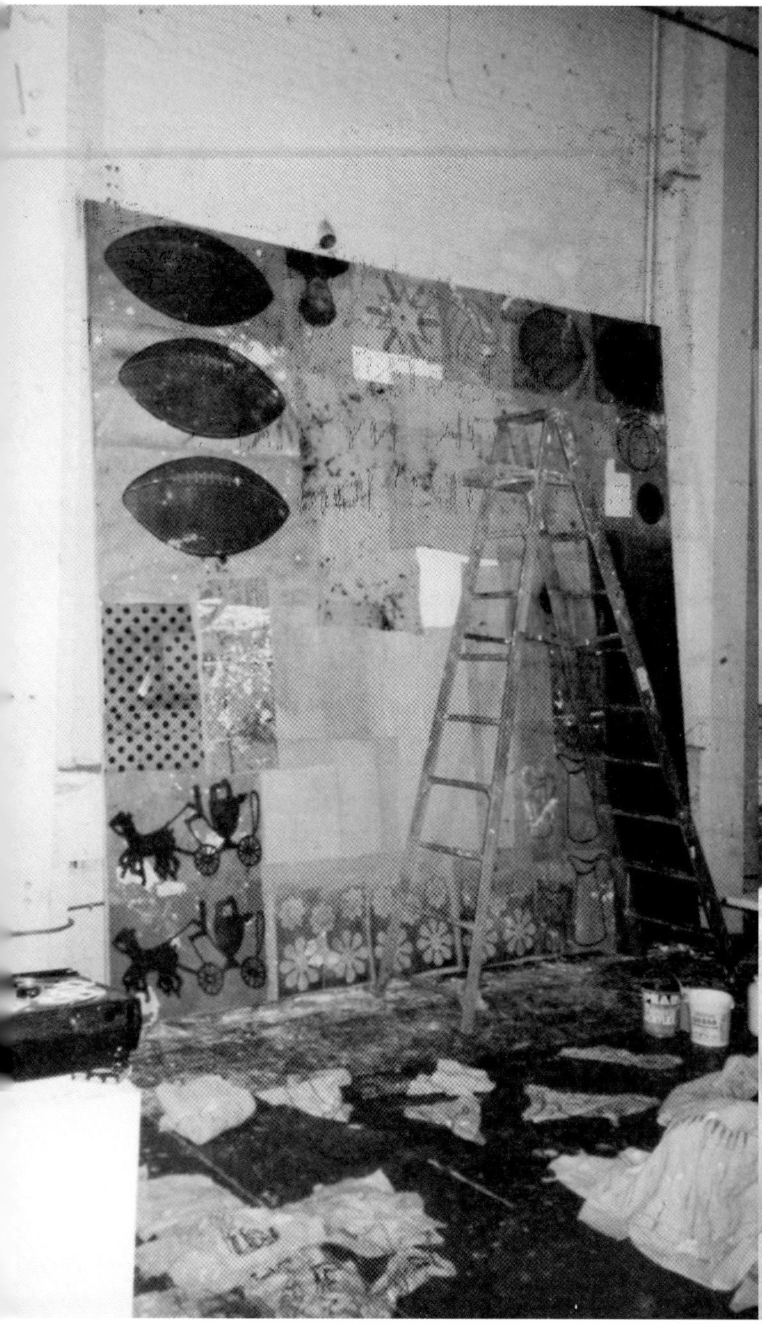

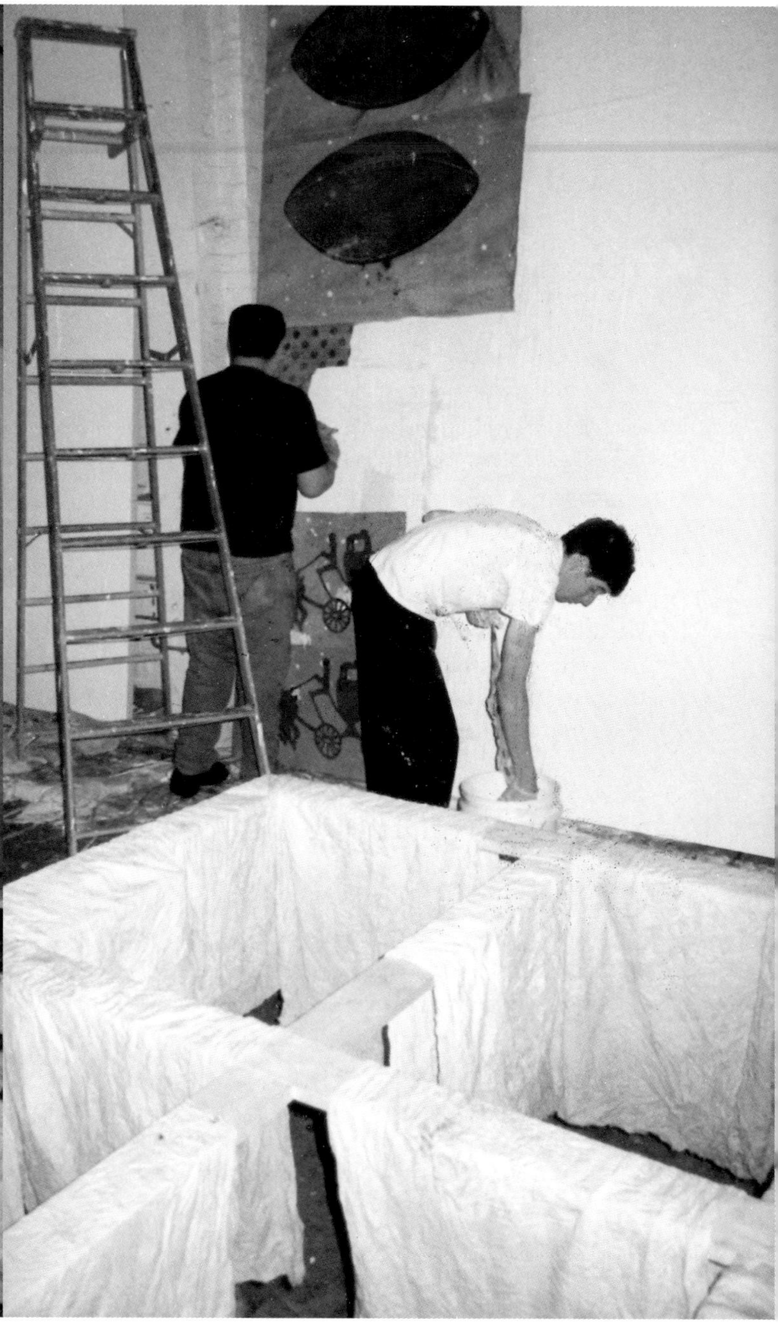

Oberflächenreize
Donald Baechlers Collagebilder

Wenn römische Bildhauer ihren Bronzen eine Patina verleihen wollten um sie als Werke griechischer Herkunft ausgeben zu können, vergruben sie sie im Sand und gaben Soldaten die Anweisung, an der betreffenden Stelle zu pinkeln. Wurden die Skulpturen dann Monate später wieder ausgegraben, waren sie aufs Vollkommenste gealtert. Perfekte Fälschungen. Die Oberfläche von Donald Baechlers neuesten Collagebildern hat zwar keine ganz so eklige Vorgeschichte, der Künstler bietet aber einen ähnlichen Einfallsreichtum auf, um seine eigene «falsche Vergangenheit» zu erfinden.

Wie eine archäologische Fundstätte, die noch der Ausgrabung harrt, birgt die Oberfläche von Baechlers Gemälden Exotisches und Banales zugleich. Und wie immer, wenn Vergangenes ausgegraben wird, ist die Wahrscheinlichkeit der Enttäuschung gross. Nein, die Unterwäsche, die unten auf der Leinwand klebt, wurde nicht etwa vom Atelierfussboden aufgelesen, sie ist kein Relikt eines über Nacht gebliebenen Gastes, sondern wurde nagelneu in Chinatown gekauft. Manchmal ist die Wahrheit letzten Endes doch interessanter als unsere Phantasien. Im Bereich der Kunstgeschichte können die «simplen Fakten» eine regelrechte Offenbarung sein.

Theoretisch betont Baechler zwar stets, dass in seinen Gemälden keinerlei erzählende Elemente enthalten seien. Dennoch vergeht in der Regel kaum ein Gespräch mit ihm, ohne dass er irgendeine Anekdote zum Besten gibt, etwa über einen Assistenten, der Mist gebaut hat, oder eine Expedition zum Einkauf von Künstlermaterialien, die auf erheiternde Weise in die Hosen ging. Tatsächlich liesse sich mit einigem Recht behaupten, dass das eigentliche erzählerische Moment der Gemälde Donald Baechlers in der Geschichte ihrer Entstehung, genauer, in der Konstruktion ihrer jeweiligen Oberfläche, zu finden ist. Baechlers ständig in Entwicklung begriffener Modus Operandi lässt sich wie bei den Wachstumsringen eines Baums an den Schichten ablesen, aus denen sich das fertige Bild zusammensetzt: die Stofffetzen, die Farbspritzer, die Landkarten und Ticket-Kontrollabschnitte, die Fortune-cookie-Papierstreifchen, die Kartoffel- und Luftpostsäcke. Der Aufbau des Malgrundes ist für Baechler ein wesentlicher Punkt seiner Kunst. Man könnte daraus schliessen, dass die Oberfläche selbst, und nicht etwa das darauf gemalte Bild seine Gemälde zu Kunst macht.

Es wurde viel Aufhebens gemacht um Baechlers sogenanntes Vokabular: Blumen, Wasserbälle, grob umrissene menschliche Figuren, Erdkugeln und in

DAVID GREENBERG ist Dichter und Musiker. Er ist Autor von *Feeling Gravity's Pull* (Soft Skull Press, New York) und hat den Text zu zwei in Zusammenarbeit mit Donald Baechler entstandenen Büchern verfasst: *Crowd Paintings* (Galerie Lars Bohman, Stockholm) und *Gray Paintings* (Galerie Bernd Klüser, München). Er lebt und arbeitet in New York City.

jüngerer Zeit auch Eiscreme. Für sich betrachtet sind diese Bilder jedoch mehr oder weniger eine Summe ihrer jeweiligen Vorbilder. Viele gehen auf nicht künstlerische Vorlagen zurück: Friseursalonschilder und Wandmalereien aus der Dritten Welt, Werbegrafik mit einfachen Mitteln. In gewisser Weise sind sie genau das, was sie darstellen. Ein Wasserball ist ein Wasserball, eine Blume eine Blume. Wenn irgendein Typ in Indien eine Eiscremetüte an die Wand malt, kann man getrost davon ausgehen, dass er sie vor allem möglichst echt aussehen lassen, und nicht eine Art ironischer Ikone schaffen möchte. Sie soll einfach Lust auf das Eis machen. Wenn sich nun Baechler ebendiese Eistüte vornimmt, kommt er dem Punkt nichts zu malen so nah wie nur möglich. Mit anderen Worten, es geht weniger darum, was als vielmehr wie gemalt wird. Donald Baechler interessieren formale Fragen. Er ist ein abstrakter Maler. Für ihn ist eine Blume einfach etwas, was oben rot ist und einen grünen Stengel hat. Und eine Eistüte ist... nun ja, es dürfte klar sein, was gemeint ist.

Man lässt sich von Baechlers Bildmotiven leicht Sand in die Augen streuen. Sie sind bunt und heiter, fast verspielt. Aber man lasse sich nicht täuschen. Die Künstlerhand rückt sie in einen radikal neuen Zusammenhang. Es ist der Akt des Malens selbst, der diese schlichten Piktogramme in Kunst verwandelt. Für Baechler ist die Malerei eine Form von Alchimie. Das soll an dieser Stelle jedoch nicht weiter vertieft werden. Was uns hier interessiert, ist der Malgrund, nicht, was darauf gemalt ist. Baechler selbst sagt über den Aufbau eines Malgrundes für seine Collagebilder:

Worum ich mich in jedem Stadium bemühe, ist..., etwas zu machen, was an dem betreffenden Punkt praktisch abgeschlossen sein könnte, weil ich nur schwer einen Zugang finde. Das Verhältnis von Figur und Grund ist mir sehr wichtig; wenn der Grund nicht abgeschlossen ist, kann ich darauf keine Figur malen. Eine weisse Wand zum Beispiel ist für mich völlig uninteressant als Malgrund. Ein Fundgegenstand von der Strasse kann dagegen sehr interessant sein, weil er in sich geschlossen ist und ein Eigenleben hat.

Das Bedürfnis, einen derart beschaffenen Grund aufzubauen, hat sowohl eine psychologische wie eine kunsthistorische Dimension. Erstere überlasse ich den Seelendoktoren. Letztere werde ich etwas unter die Lupe nehmen. Um jedoch die Entwicklung von Baechlers Malgrund besser zu verstehen, müssen wir zunächst in die Zeit seines Kunststudiums zurückblenden.

Baechler hat sich nie viel aus kräftigem Impasto gemacht. Seine ersten Bilder malte er in Email. Nach jahrelangem Einatmen giftiger Dämpfe stellte er klugerweise auf Acryl um. Seine Abneigung gegen jedes Impasto stellte aber weiterhin ein Problem dar. Dem jungen Künstler war daran gelegen, dass seine Fehlversuche sichtbar blieben. Durch die Blosslegung der gescheiterten Versuche eine Figur zu malen – der «Fehlstarts», wie er sie später nennen sollte –, wurde auf der Leinwand eine Geschichte der Tilgung sichtbar. Jeder «Fehlstart» wurde so übermalt, dass seine Spuren gerade noch schemenhaft zu erkennen waren. Er wollte die Oberfläche mit einer Art poetischem Pentimento sättigen, nicht zu verwechseln mit einem Palimpsest der Pinselstriche. Um aber diesen Effekt zu erzeugen, war es nötig, immer mehr Farbe aufzutragen. Schliesslich entwickelte Donald eine Methode diese «Schemen» ohne grosse Farbmengen auf die Leinwand zu bannen: Er klebte dünne Stofffetzen auf die Leinwand. Dieser Trick wurde ein wesentliches Element für den Aufbau seiner ganz eigenen Art von Oberfläche.

Das stufenweise Aufschichten von Stoff auf der Leinwand ergab nicht nur eine neue Grundfläche für die zu malende Figur, sondern hatte wesentlich weitreichendere Folgen. Trotz ihrer ursprünglich rein «redaktionellen» Funktion erzeugten die Stoffstreifen eine aufgerauhte Oberfläche. Die Bildgründe wirkten wunderbar ausgelaugt. Die Stoffschichten verliehen den Bildern eine Aura von Alter und Altertum; man fühlte sich an ein historisches Kunsterzeugnis oder einen vergrabenen Schatz erinnert. Gleichzeitig erhielt das Gemälde Reliefcharakter. Vielleicht am nachhaltigsten aber wirkte sich der Stoff auf den Strich des Künstlers aus. Da sie den Pinsel in seinem Lauf behinderte, entstand durch die neue, unberechenbare Oberfläche eine gezackte Linie. An zerkauten Bindfaden oder die abgerissenen Kleider eines wandernden Derwisches gemahnend, wurde dieser Strich zum Synonym für seine Kunst. Sie wurde sein Markenzeichen. Wie Pollocks

Farbspritzer oder Schnabels kaputtes Geschirr. Damit war ein neuer holpriger Weg angelegt, den der Künstler beschreiten konnte. Hinfort sollten ungebrochene Linien in Baechlers Bildern keinen Platz mehr haben.

Schliesslich wurde Baechler mehr und mehr vom Collageelement in seinen Gemälden abhängig. Was einst die bequeme Lösung für ein technisches Problem gewesen war, wurde am Ende zu einer grundlegenden ästhetischen Entscheidung. Tatsächlich ist ein Baechler-Bild ohne auf den Malgrund geklebte Stofffetzen bis heute nahezu undenkbar.

Unterdessen bildete sich eine komplexere Collageform auf einer anderen Oberfläche heraus, nämlich auf Papier. Baechlers Arbeit mit Collagen auf Papier fing denkbar unschuldig an, aus einer Art Sparsamkeit heraus. Der Künstler erklärt:

Ich fing mit den Collagen an, während ich auf Reisen war. Ich zeichnete dauernd diese Köpfe und es sammelte sich mehr und mehr Material an. Schliesslich hatte ich all die Papierfetzen übrig und hielt es für Verschwendung, sie einfach wegzuwerfen ..., also klebte ich sie auf. Du weisst schon, wenn man auf Reisen ist hebt man dieses ganze Papierzeug auf: Quittungen, Reisepapiere usw. Und ich werfe äusserst ungern Dinge weg. Also klebte ich einfach mal etwas in eine Ecke. Und von da gings weiter und immer weiter. Aus den Collagen wurde fast etwas Autobiographisches. Meine Reise durch die Zeit.

Bald tauchten in Baechlers Collagen alle möglichen Relikte auf: Taxiquittungen, Eintrittskarten für Museen, Restaurantrechnungen, Hausaufgaben für Schulkinder. Der anfangs überreiche Materialvorrat schrumpfte rapide und Baechler sah sich allmählich mit einem richtiggehenden Engpass konfrontiert. So kam es zu einem weiteren inspirierten Kunstgriff, der Herstellung gefälschter Dokumente. Mittels Rückgriff auf «menschliche Kopiermaschinen», so Baechler, stellten «Lehrlinge» unter Aufsicht des Meisters im Atelier die nötigen Collageelemente her. Ein ägyptischer Assistent schrieb Hausaufgaben auf Arabisch und beschrieb Landkarten – Lektionen aus dem Grundschulgeographieunterricht. Ein anderer Assistent zeichnete in primitiv kindlichem Stil Illustrationen aus einem Yoga-Handbuch ab. Siebdruckspezialisten wurden beauftragt, vorgefundene Bildmotive auf Stoff zu drucken, woraufhin wieder ein anderer Assistent diese Bilder sorgfältig einfärbte. Baechler schuf so eine Art Heimindustrie – seine eigene kleine Armee «menschlicher Kopiermaschinen» oder wie Philip Taaffe prophezeite: «Das Baechler-Heim für verwahrloste Jugendliche.» Es war eine moderne Entsprechung zu den römischen Soldaten, die auf vergrabene Skulpturen pinkelten. Wie Andy Warhol vor ihm, der tatsächlich gewisse Factory-Mitarbeiter und Freunde gebeten hatte, auf seine Gemälde zu pinkeln (für die Serie seiner OXYDATIONSBILDER), umgab sich Baechler mit einer Traube kreativer, mitunter flatterhafter Leute und schuf so in der Tat seine eigenen «Fälschungen».

Als Baechler sich bei seinen Collagen allmählich auf ein grösseres Format zubewegte, nahm der Reichtum der Materialien zu. Um die weite Fläche einer Leinwand von 1,5 auf 1,8 Meter zu füllen, war allerhand nötig. Bald tauchten kostbarere Elemente in den Collagen auf. Fragmente altperuanischer Tapisserien, Jutefetzen von Reissäcken aus Mexiko, Teile abgetragener amerikanischer Jeans und, wie gesagt, gelegentlich auch ein weisser Slip fanden sich auf einem Bild ein. Am meisten lagen dem Künstler jedoch die Quilts seiner Mutter am Herzen. «Sie war eine richtige Künstlerin», erklärte Baechler einmal. Indem er ihr Werk in sein eigenes einbaute, liess Baechler seine Gemälde nicht nur weiterhin in einem autobiographischen Licht erstrahlen, sondern stellte auch eine gezielte, ganz konkrete Verbindung zu seiner eigenen Vergangenheit her. Wieder hatte er neue Wege gefunden, seine Collagen «älter» aussehen zu lassen. Und neue Rekruten für die Baechler'sche Armee menschlicher Kopiermaschinen.

Selbstverständlich erledigt der General einen Grossteil der strategischen Laufarbeit selbst. Er reist in ferne Länder und besichtigt fremde Städte wie ein wohlgesinnter Eroberer. Baechler ist der ewige Fremde in einem fremden Land, ständig auf der Suche nach Rohmaterial für sein Atelier in New York. Ein moderner Marco Polo der schrägen Kulturabfälle. Der gar nicht so lustlose Geschäftsreisende, der mit einem Koffer voller Altmaterial aus Antiquariaten und von entlegenen Flohmärkten zurückkehrt. Söldner bieten ihre Dienste an und durchkämmen zum Verkauf angebotene Gerümpelsammlungen und

DONALD BAECHLER, RED SUNDAE (THE BLUE BOWL), 1998, acrylic and fabric collage on canvas, 144 x 144" /
ROTES FRUCHTEIS (DIE BLAUE SCHALE), Acryl und Stoffcollage auf Leinwand, 366 x 366 cm. (PHOTO: BETH PHILLIPS)

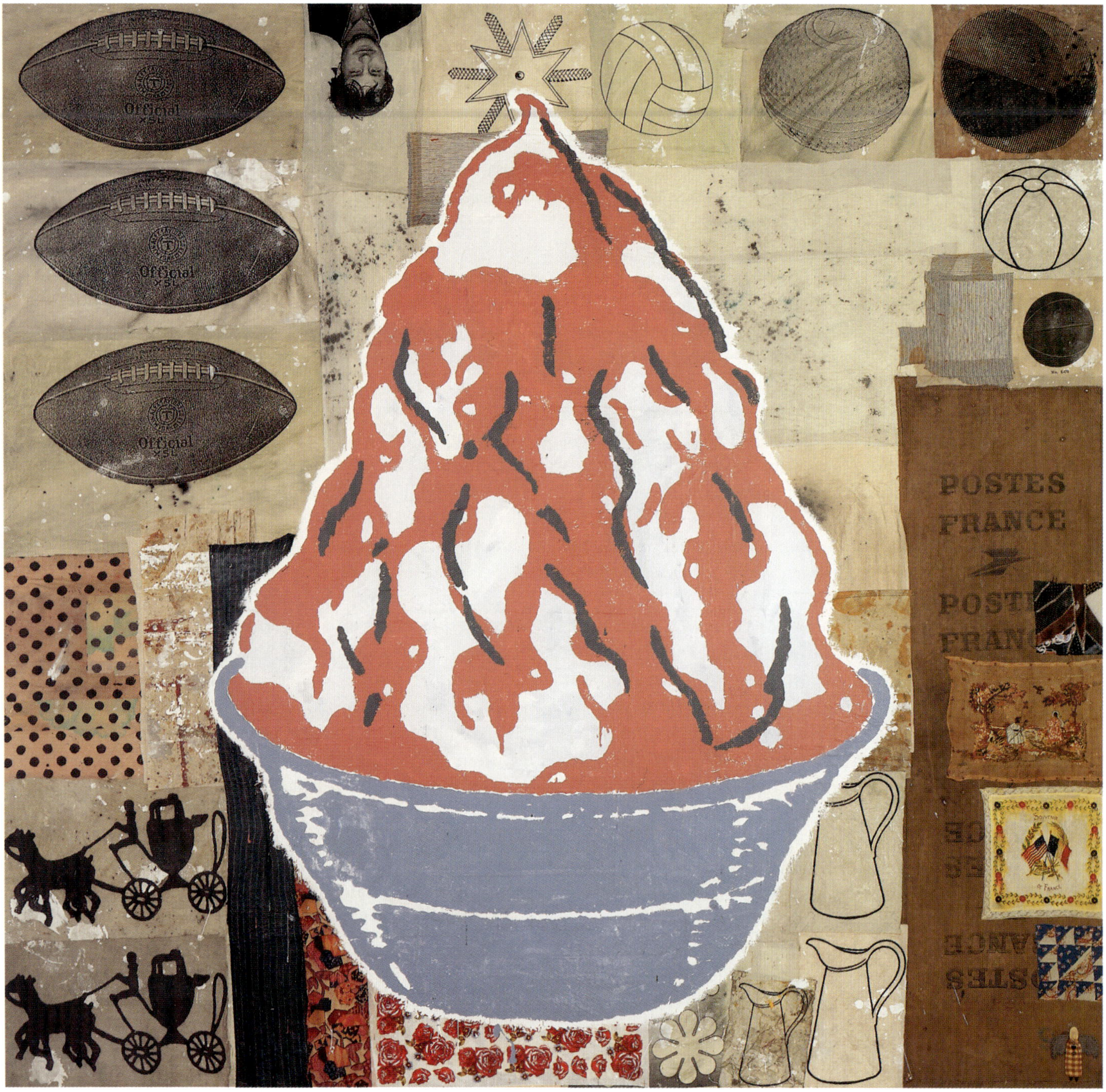

DONALD BAECHLER, SARANAC (CAMOUFLAGE SANDWICH), 1998, acrylic and fabric collage on canvas, 144 x 144" /
SARANAC (TARNSANDWICH), Acryl und Stoffcollage auf Leinwand, 366 x 366 cm. (PHOTO: BETH PHILLIPS)

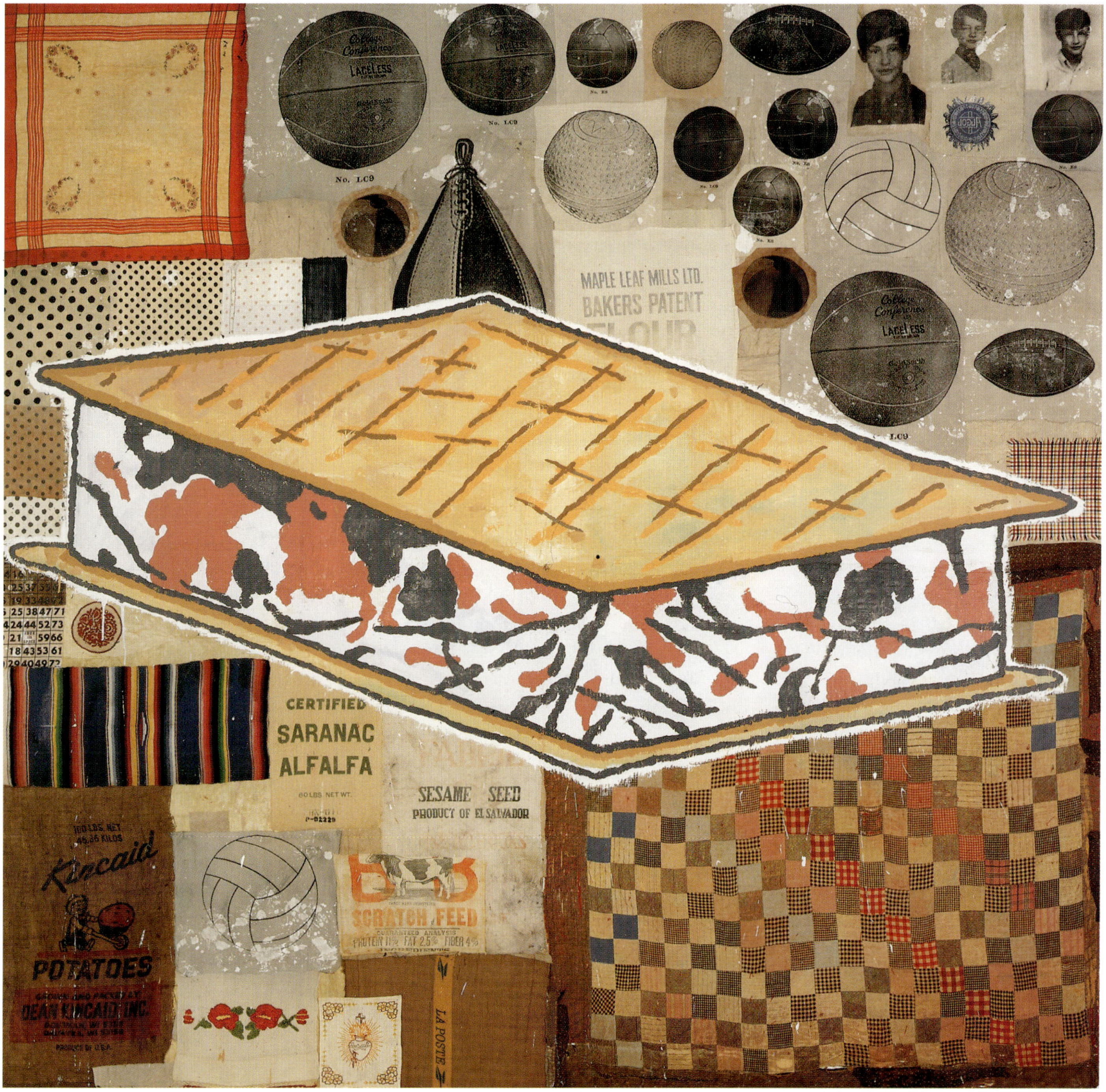

grosselterliche Dachböden in der Hoffnung, eines der Objekte, die sie vor dem Müllhaufen bewahrt haben, könnte eines Tages einen umwerfenden Einstand in einer Baechler-Inszenierung feiern. Und wie ein alter Hollywood-Regisseur, der Statisten für ein Filmepos besetzt, sichtet Donald seine Beute und arrangiert die Collageelemente auf der Grossleinwand.

Um eine alte Floskel abzuwandeln: Was dem einen Scheisse, ist dem anderen ein Eiscreme-Bild. Baechler beeilt sich jedoch klarzustellen:

Die Idee ist letztlich die, ein abgeschlossenes Bild zu schaffen, dem ich anschliessend ein anderes Bild aufdrängen kann. Es ist eine Art Gewaltakt – schon ein nahezu perfektes Bild zu haben um darauf zu malen. Es ist dieser Übergriff, der dem Werk seine Spannung verleiht. Ohne ihn wärens bloss nette Hintergründe.

Es ist bekannt, dass verschiedene abstrakte Maler ihr Herz an Baechlers Hintergründe verloren haben. So soll Ross Bleckner Donald einmal gebeten haben einen bestimmten Hintergrund nicht zu übermalen. Ich sehe Ross förmlich vor mir, wie er seinen Auftritt in *As Good As It Gets*, wo er einen (von Skeet Ulrich gespielten) Strichjungen zu hehren künstlerischen Zwecken aufgabelt, noch einmal durchspielt – «Ich brauche ein hübsches Gesicht. Es ist für ein Porträt» –, dann ein unfertiges Werk herauspickt und gurrt: «Es ist sooo schön, Donald. Rührs bloss nicht mehr an!» Ross liegt aber völlig falsch. Baechler geht es nicht darum, hübsche Bilder zu machen, sondern darum, sie zu versauen.

Typisches Beispiel. Donald bereitete eine Ausstellung grossformatiger Blumencollagen für Paris vor. Mit einem bestimmten, querformatigen Werk hatte er Probleme. Die Komposition mit drei nebeneinander stehenden Blumen haute einfach nicht hin. (Interessanterweise versuchte er sich für Basel erneut an einer solchen Komposition, wobei er das Problem dadurch löste, dass er eine pyramidenähnliche Anordnung wählte.) Es musste etwas geschehen, also wies er einen Assistenten an, zwei der drei Blumen mit Stoff zu bedecken, so dass am Ende die Blume in der Mitte allein den Raum beherrschte. Erstaunlicherweise funktionierte das. Es gab nur ein Problem. Ein bestimmtes Collageelement, ein Siebdruckmotiv auf einem feinen Stoff aus Marokko, war übermalt worden. Die Farbe musste vorsichtig von dem Bildmotiv – eine wunderschön plumpe, blaue Büchse – abgekratzt werden. Es war eine schwierige Aufgabe, und der damit betraute Assistent argwöhnte, das Ganze sei eine Art Spiel, das mit ihm getrieben werde. Er war sauer. Ohne dem Argwohn seines Assistenten Beachtung zu schenken, schrie ihn Donald wie die Karikatur eines übellaunigen Vorgesetzten an, mehr Farbe abzukratzen. Das Ganze war wie eine surreale Verwechslungskomödie und ich war zufällig als Zeuge zugegen.

Donald verliess das Atelier, das im hinteren Teil des Gebäudes gelegen war, um an der Vordertür einen Besucher zu begrüssen. Einen Sammler? Einen Promi? Und wenn schon: Das eigentliche Drama entrollte sich auf der Oberfläche dieser kolossalen Leinwand, die wie ein verletztes Rennpferd auf dem Boden lag. Ich blieb im Atelier und versuchte vergebens, den aufgebrachten Assistenten zu besänftigen. Nichts half. Wie ein Kind, das ohne Nachtisch ins Bett geschickt wurde, murmelte er, während er mit heftigen Handbewegungen Farbe von dem erlesenen Stück Stoff abkratzte, unentwegt Flüche gegen seinen Boss aus. Mir aber war klar, dass die Fetzen erst richtig fliegen würden, wenn Donald ins Atelier zurückkäme: «Was machst du da! Du machst ja den Stoff kaputt. Den habe ich mit Philip Taaffe in Marokko gefunden.» Baechler war ausser sich und schrie. Zeitsprung. Einige Wochen nach diesem Vorfall sitze ich im gleichen Atelier und blättere im Pariser Ausstellungskatalog, bis ich auf eine Abbildung des für mich inzwischen berüchtigten Gemäldes stosse. In der Überzeugung, dass das alles lange genug zurückliege, zeige ich unbeschwert auf die arg zugerichtete Partie des Bildes und sage halb im Scherz: «Erinnerst du dich noch, Donald?»

Mit steinerner Miene und ohne jede Spur von Ironie erwidert Baechler: «Weisst du, dies ist eigentlich die schönste Stelle des ganzen Bildes geworden.»

Irgendwo, ich höre es förmlich, wird jetzt ein junger Mann seinen Hosenschlitz öffnen.

(Übersetzung: Bram Opstelten)

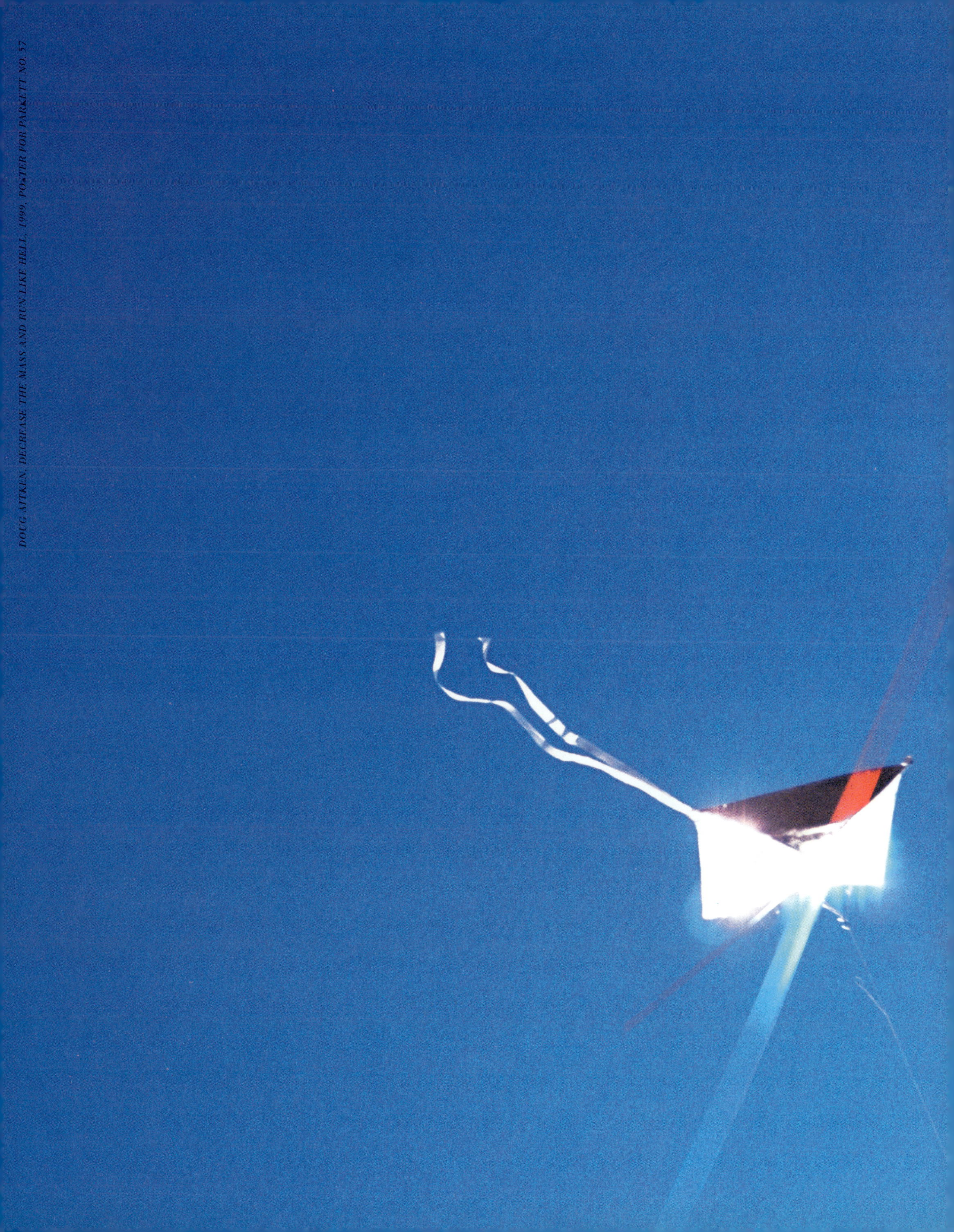

DOUG AITKEN, DECREASE THE MASS AND RUN LIKE HELL, 1999, POSTER FOR PARKETT NO. 57

Doug Aitken, born 1968 in Redondo Beach, California, lives and works in New York City and Los Angeles / geboren 1968 in Redondo Beach, Kalifornien, lebt und arbeitet in New York und Los Angeles.

Nan Goldin, born 1953 in Washington, lives and works in New York City / geboren 1953 in Washington, lebt und arbeitet in New York.

Thomas Hirschhorn, born 1957 in Berne, Switzerland, lives and works in Paris / geboren 1957 in Bern, lebt und arbeitet in Paris.

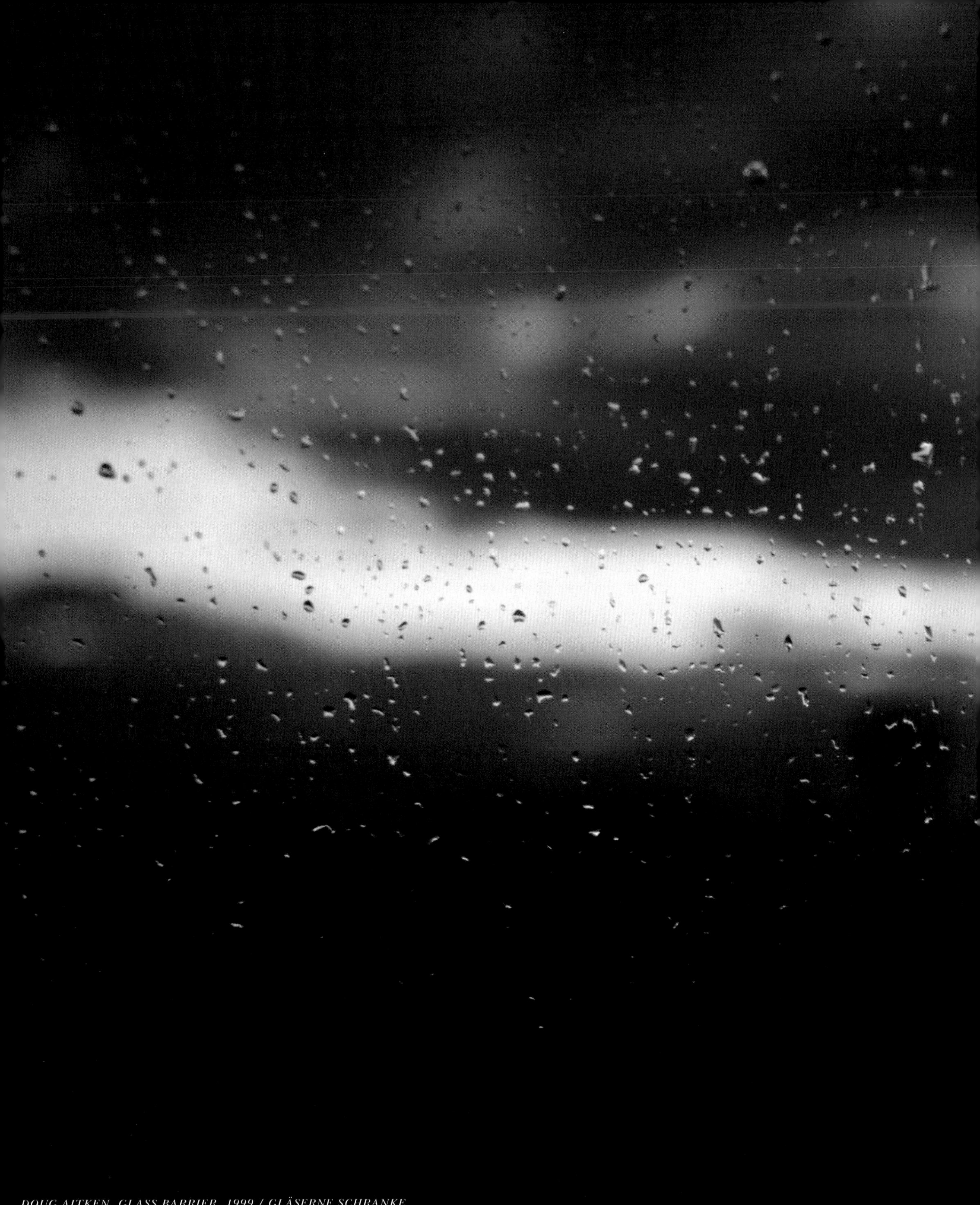

DOUG AITKEN, GLASS BARRIER, 1999 / GLÄSERNE SCHRANKE.

DOUG AITKEN

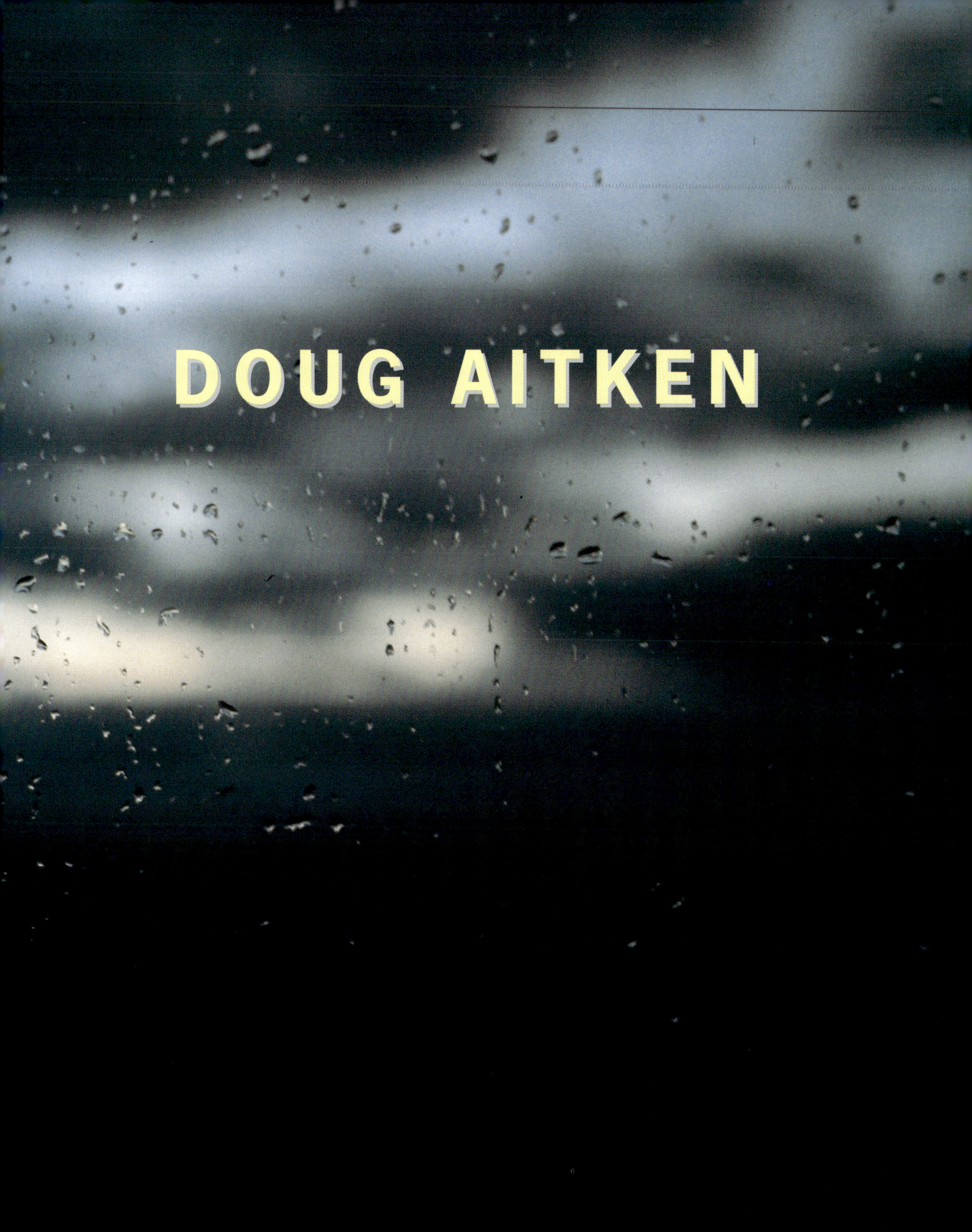

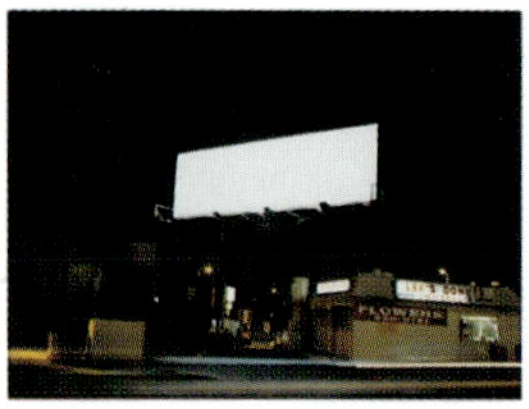

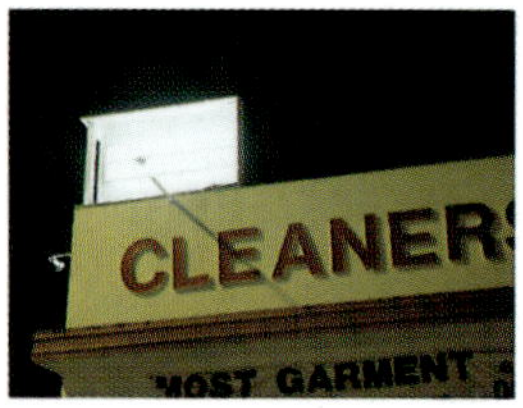

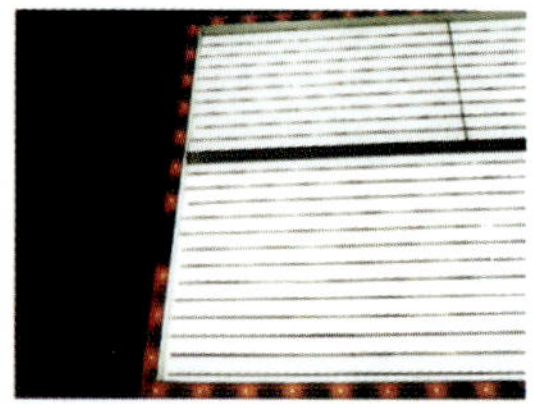

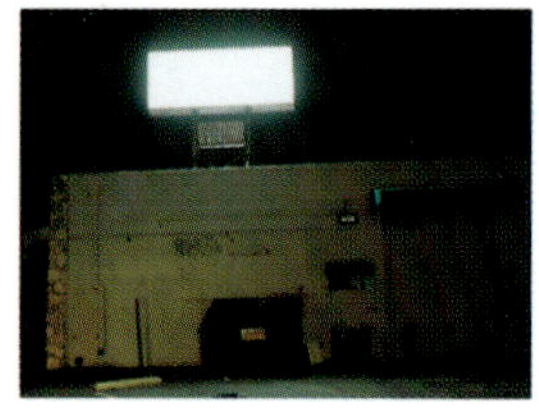

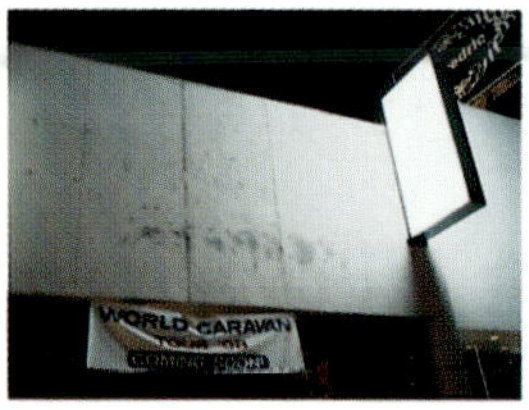

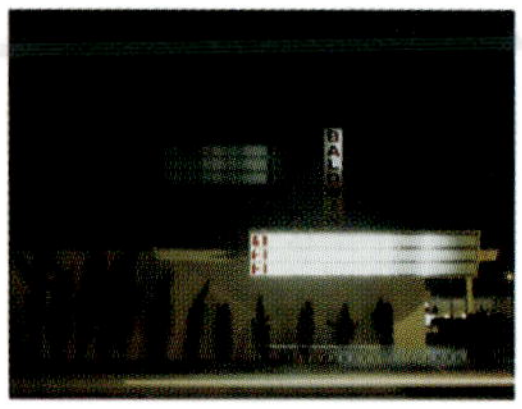

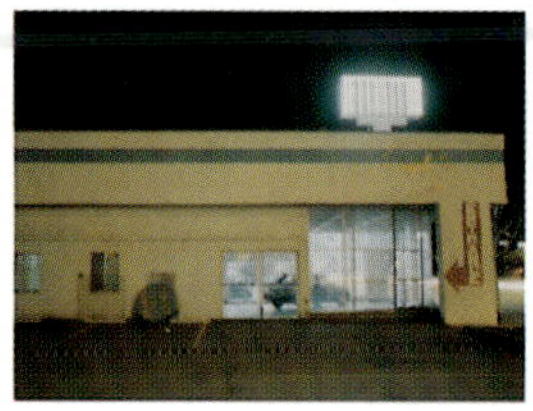

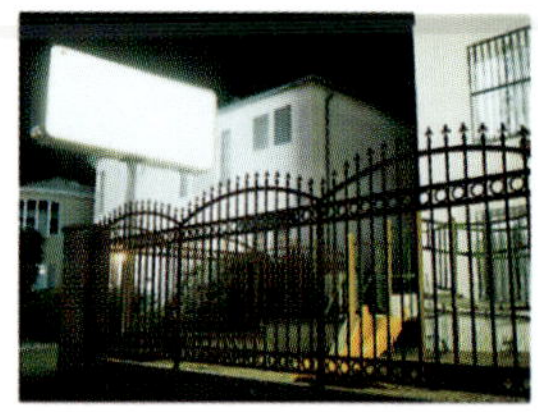

Omega Man

JAMES ROBERTS

Sometimes it's hard to connect with the world; there's just so much going on. Too much wetware flaps about, too many faces silently shout their garbled stories, too much talk fills the air with unwanted fragments of other people's lives. You need a solitary vantage point, an overview. Night is good. You can mediate distance in a car, watching images of the quiet world projected onto the screen of the windows. Street lamps and road markings pulse by in gentle syncopation, regulating your heartbeat, relaxing your breathing. Your journey through space becomes a sequence of two-dimensional vector translations as you follow a road system that feels not so much planned as an evolutionary product of the city itself. You can walk if you wish, and discover a new and more intimate relationship with the burnished concrete of the pavement; the brushed, stamped metal of a public telephone that is suddenly and surprisingly private; the slippery glass, plastics and chrome of storefronts, commercial signage and foyers. All that is enveloped in the calming rays of artificial light is now yours and yours alone.

One's company, two's a crowd. You need to be alone with the world to get in sync with it; to decide whether you want to participate. Alone, you can tune in to the mechanical infrastructure and electronic nervous system of the urban (L.A. for example) and listen to their messages; traverse the landscape (perhaps that of Montserrat) and ponder the meaning of "natural" and the significance of the easy-come-easy-go dwellers whose detritus and flimsy habitations temporarily litter the vista in failed attempts to quantify and commodify it. Solitude and the lens make

JAMES ROBERTS is Senior Editor of *Frieze*, London.

DOUG AITKEN, THE ENTIRE MIRROR, 1998, 8 of a series of 16 c-prints laminated on Plexiglas, 30 x 35" each / DER GANZE SPIEGEL, 8 Bilder aus einer Serie von 16 C-Prints auf Plexiglas, je 11,8 x 13,8 cm.

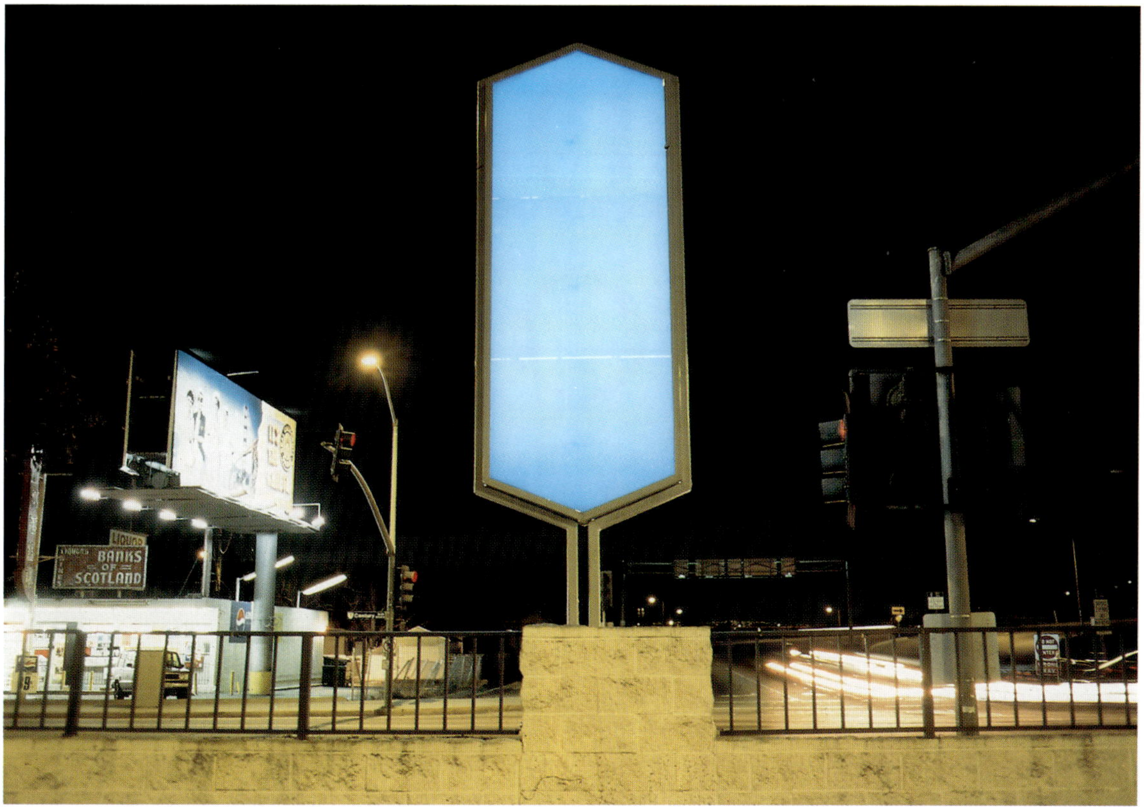

DOUG AITKEN, BEACON, 1999 / LEUCHTFEUER.

you an alien—not in relation to the world, but in relation to other people.

Point the lens at someone else and they become unknowable, their activities incomprehensible. The silhouette of a chain-link perimeter fence or the way the shadows slide off the edge of the pavement are more revealing, and the endless rotation and scanning of a radar dish more alert, more alive than the pellucid face of a young blonde woman who slips from interior to exterior, day to night, in a voyage across the city.

Perhaps it is really all a question of light; the source of illumination. As the retina, film, or CCD array absorbs the world, what it perceives is modulated by the texture of the light and its own perceptual mechanics. Overcast daylight, skylight, fluorescent light, tungsten light—all apply their particular varnish to the world, sealing it or releasing it, concealing it or revealing it to varying degrees. And there are so many ways to see the same thing, even at the same instant: slowed down, sped up, real time or freeze-frame; through the grain of film stock or the differing meshes of analogue or digital video; scanned by a cathode ray, projected by a beam of light through a crystal dot matrix or particles of dye in an Estar film. Each is a different moment of truth, like an old memory or a fresh one; a half-forgotten dream or one you will never forget.

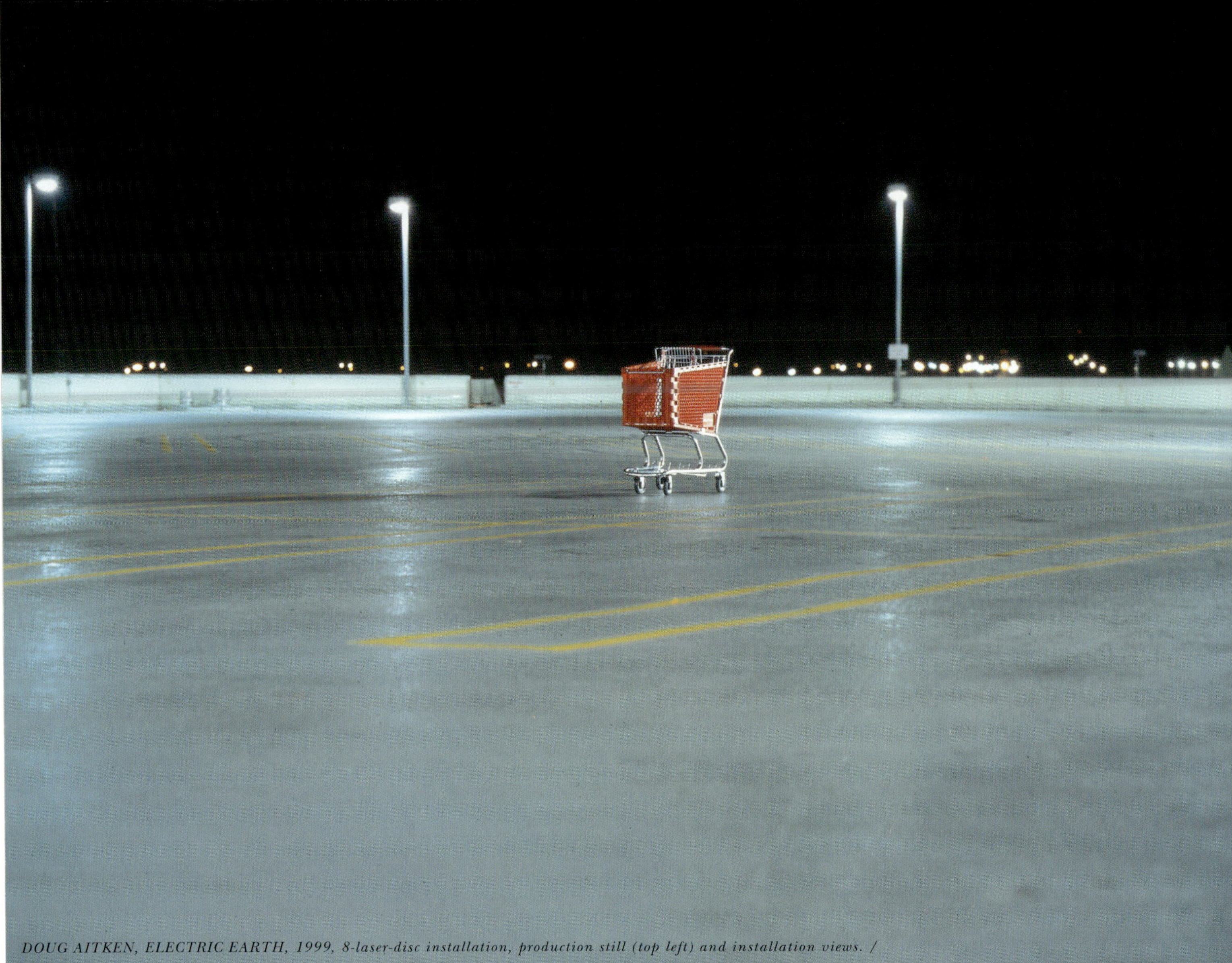

DOUG AITKEN, ELECTRIC EARTH, 1999, 8-laser-disc installation, production still (top left) and installation views. /

ELEKTRISCHE ERDE, Standaufnahme während der Produktion (oben links) und Installationsansichten.

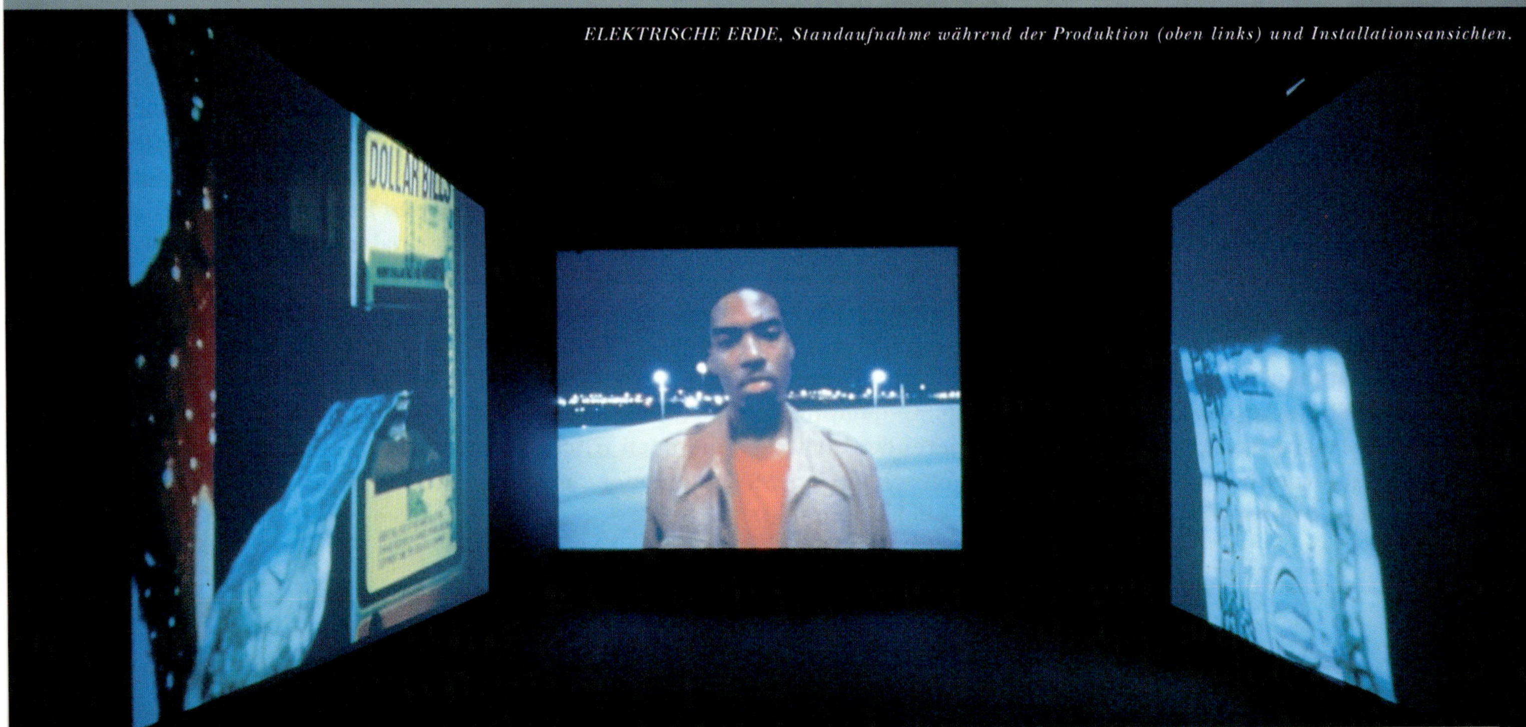

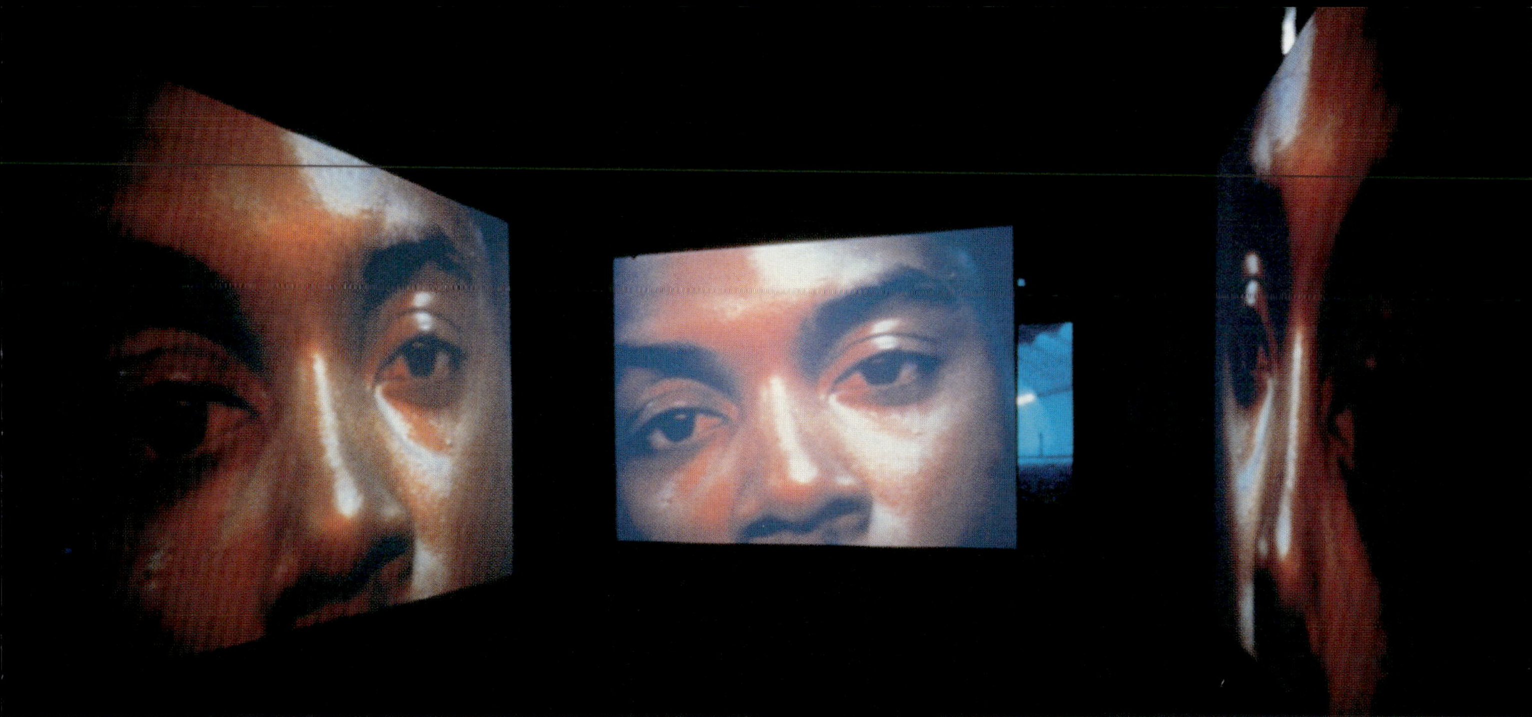

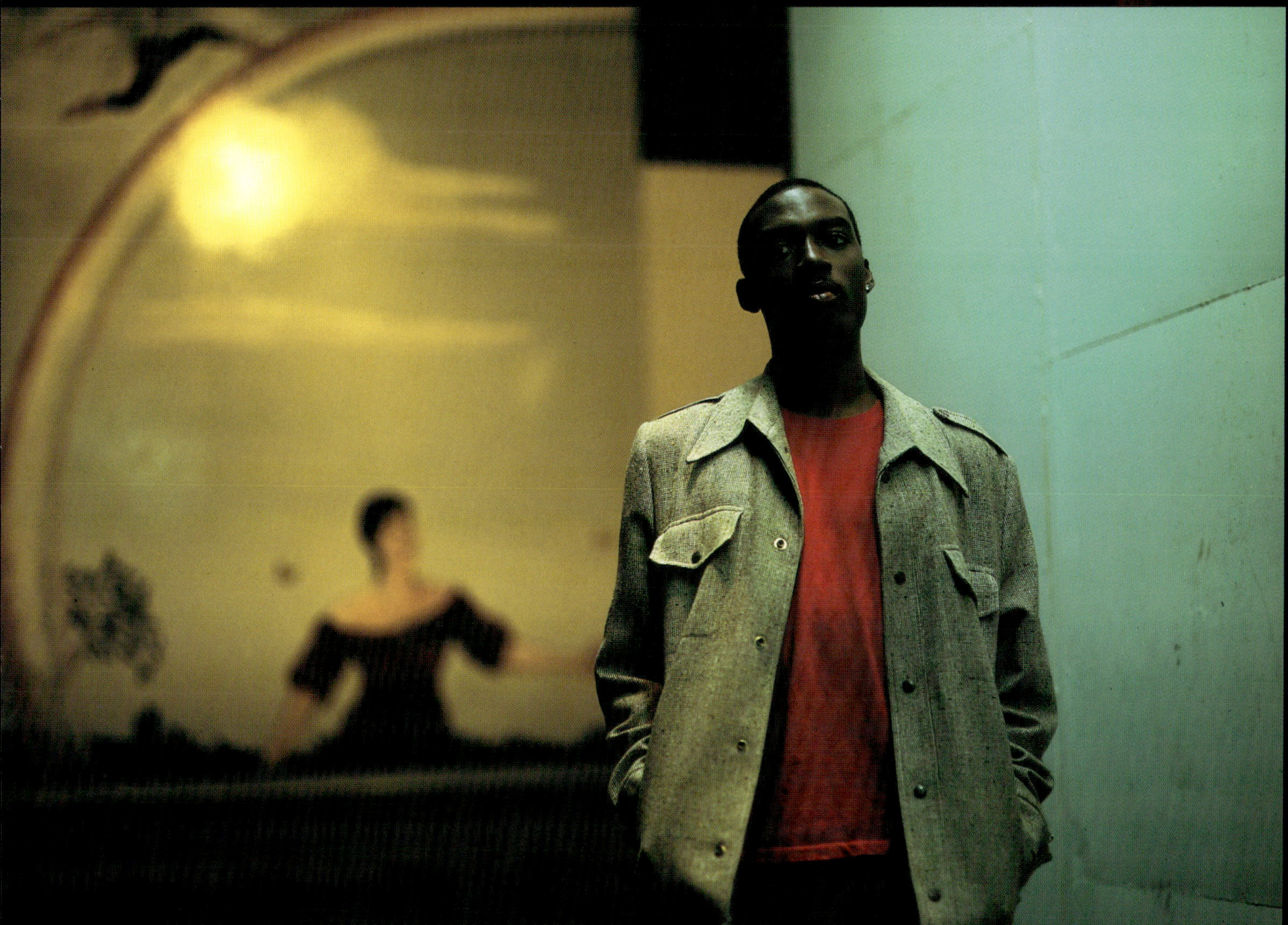

DOUG AITKEN, OVER THE OCEAN, 1999 / ÜBER DEN OZEAN.

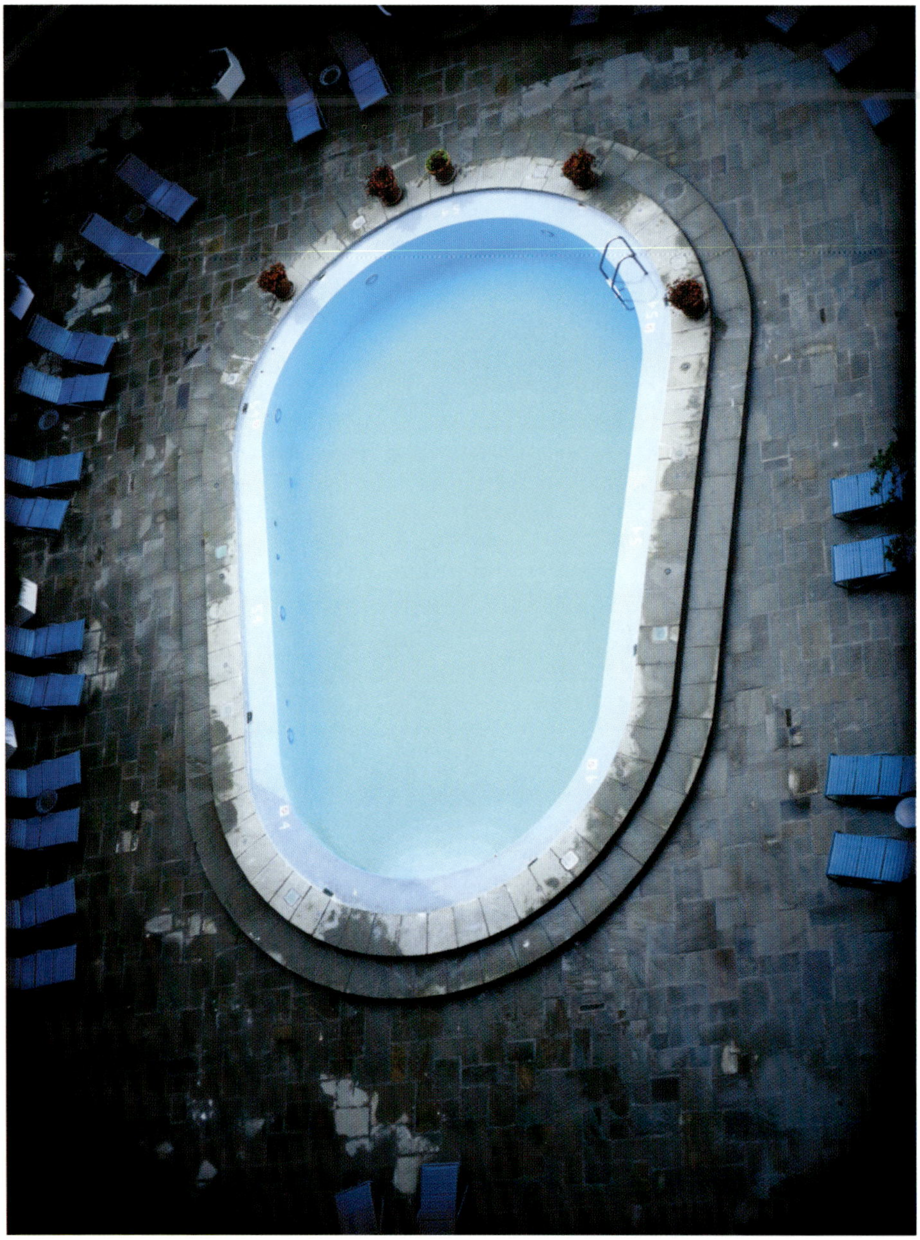

LIQUID TIME

FRANCESCO BONAMI

Godard regards words as images that are in the constant process of birth and death... He certainly follows Cocteau in Pierrot le fou. *In the end isn't our seeing really our feeling the constant "death" in that reality that can only be seen through the camera?*

– Toru Takemitsu, "Conversation on Seeing," in: *Confronting Silence,* Berkeley, 1995.

The one time I swam in the Pacific Ocean was enough for me to realize it was named with a hint of sarcasm. Its calm magmatic surface hides currents that could swallow you like a pill. Doug Aitken was born in one of those Southern California coastal towns where surfing becomes second nature to natives who immerse themselves in the ocean's vastness every morning. When you surf, and I never did, you must stand on top of the wave, and if it breaks you are thrown furiously down into the foam. A couple of years ago, Doug went down in the water, and when he came ashore it was too late. They say that when you are drowning, your life fast-forwards in front of you. Doug Aitken drowned. When his friends got him out, he'd come to the end of his tape. In fact, he may have died for a few long seconds and then come back to life in a kind of hedonistic resurrection. It is very odd to imagine your life ruptured like a jammed video tape, its flow interrupted by a void in which nothing happens. When you wake up, from where do you start? Do you rewind back to the moment life stopped or do you keep going with a few frames missing?

Is death a basic question of editing? When he opened his eyes again Doug knew he'd lost a piece of his footage, but he didn't know where to look for it. And he didn't know what was supposed to have happened in it. You could imagine—coincidental to this particular accident—all of his work as some kind of drowning experience. He fast-forwards and rewinds his thoughts over and over until he gets to the point where the image falls into the right place and the story is told. The viewer, too, is drawn into Aitken's mental process, trapped into his narrative at the very moment it is edited. Aitken's work is like a wave that doesn't pull you in as much as it pushes you under. Because it is never immediately clear what is happening, you have to plunge in and out several times to make sense of it. Aitken creates space that is like a perpetual editing suite in which the viewer must mentally cut and paste until it feels right, or good, or maybe bad.

In BAD ANIMAL (1996) or THESE RESTLESS MINDS (1998), the editing room is set out in a ring. You circle round and round as if on a carousel, watching the

FRANCESCO BONAMI is Senior Curator at the Museum of Contemporary Art, Chicago.

three monitors and tracking the linear progress of the piece, while catching up with it. Linearity is not on Aitken's agenda, but his work is always structured around a kind of emotional continuity. Instead of moving from A to B, you revolve around A as many times as possible before starting to circle B. You circumnavigate a dozen images, as if sailing around an archipelago of small visual and conceptual islands. You encircle the images and the images encircle you. In each work, the filmed landscape assumes the role of a script, while the subject becomes the movement of Aitken's camera.

In an early work, INFLECTION (1992), Aitken approaches the landscape vertically, launching a video camera into the sky with a miniature rocket. We see the confused bird's eye view of a suburban scene caught in rapid ascent and then descent—it's like trying to read a musical score while it is hurtling down from a window. Here, Aitken experiments with picturing the environment through a combination of speed and altitude. In subsequent works, he tilts his mind to the horizontal speed of the ground. This early experiment is a kind of visual haiku, an attempt to tell a short story—that of his origin and bottom to top, top to bottom, penetrating the deepest depth of field with hieroglyphic concision.

In this early work, Aitken grazes the surface of a conflict between deferred time, vertical time, and real time. These relationships will develop into the central concerns of an oeuvre that is about real time extended into a deferred perception: the real time of the author perceived in the deferred time of the viewer. To be inside one of Aitken's installations is to question whether we are experiencing real time and real space. In CATHOUSE (1997), the space is real enough—tactile enough—to create a feeling of claustrophobia. Trapped inside this over-enlarged, carpeted space, the viewer finds his own perverse suburban character mirroring back on him as he watches three people—a woman playing with a glass of water, a boy in his bedroom, and a man (Iggy Pop) swinging on an armchair—in expansive suburban interiors, captured in miniature, window-like monitors set into the wall. All of the subjects of CATHOUSE—both viewers and figures—are locked into a suburban architecture and a strange realm of low

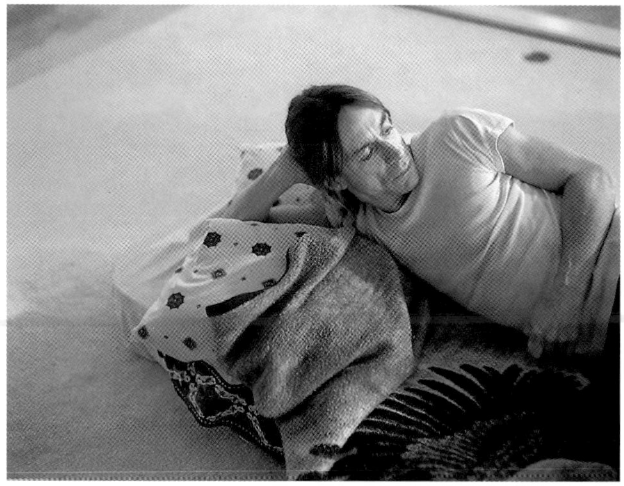

stimulation. Doug Aitken's work is an empirical test of true interactivity and virtuality. As James Cameron, the director of *Titanic*, said, "Film doesn't address what's great about virtual reality, which is interactivity: You move and as you move, the scene changes."[1)] Aitken reaches this point, not by deferring to the viewer's movements, but by shaping his ideas around them, predicting them, and creating a space where the viewer can move, though only in certain ways.

Yet, early on, Aitken allowed the landscape and the viewer to observe each other while avoiding interaction. A good example of this is MONSOON (1995). Filmed in the Guyana jungle where Reverend Jones's followers committed mass suicide in the mid-seventies, the footage describes nothing but waiting for a monsoon to arrive. This contemporary landscape is absorbed by the menacing weather, just as the traumatic historical event has been erased by the excessively fecund landscape. In MONSOON, we see only mounting tension and the latent recollection of fear. The monsoon never arrives. The film ends just before the sky hatches like an egg, just before the final cleansing, like the sect's collective life that ended just before the deception was revealed. Aitken stops short just in front of the truth, leaving hope and despair in tenuous balance. MONSOON is Aitken's first inquiry into the realm of speed.

Speed of light (DIAMOND SEA, 1997), speed of the wind (MONSOON), speed of the human body

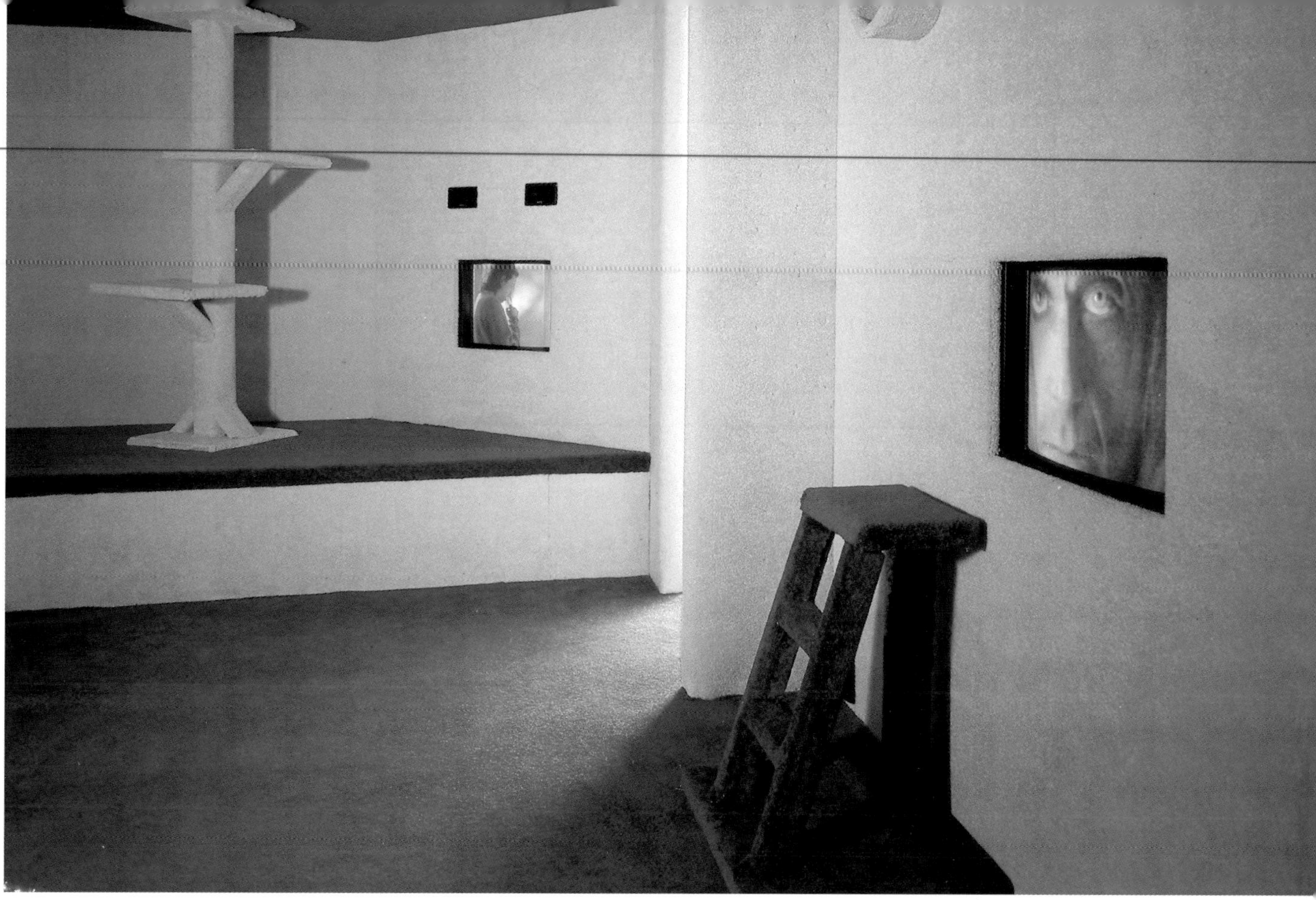

DOUG AITKEN, CATHOUSE, 1997, laser-disc/sound installation, 3 laser-discs and 3 monitors installed in a room of 8 x 24 x 13 feet; installation view (top) and production stills (below and left-hand page) / MIEZENHAUS, 3 Laserdisks und 3 Monitoren in einem Raum von 2,4 x 7,3 x 4 m; Installationsansicht (oben) und Standaufnahmen während der Produktion (unten und links).

(ELECTRIC EARTH, 1999) and of the mind (THESE RESTLESS MINDS), speed of fame (INTO THE SUN, 1999). "Speed Pollution," Paul Virilio says, "reduces the world to nothing,"[2)] and Aitken's work demonstrates a kind of ecological edge that recycles speed into a non-linear, slow-motion story. Perhaps because the artist was born where the rhythm and strength of the waves constantly resounds on the shore, speed attracts him as a tool with which to magnify slowness. Aitken's approach to creating his work reminds me of Craig Breedlove, an unassuming man who breaks land-speed records and sound barriers on the Bonneville Salt Flats of Utah with homemade rockets built in his garage. To build a narrative about speed, or to build a car to overcome speed, requires both

Aitken and Breedlove to dissect the concept of velocity into a series of finely tuned details. Once all the details are clear, they can be condensed into the final tool—the film or the car. The space between Breedlove's vehicle and its broken sound barrier is, for Aitken, the acceleration from concept to narrative, the amount of time that pastes together the first and the last frames of his concepts. Both the artist and the racer challenge and describe speed as a means to celebrate the perfection of stillness. Similarly, in ERASER (1998), Aitken celebrates the speed of a volcanic eruption, which creates the palpable stillness of an island, frozen like a contemporary Herculaneum.

But while Breedlove's smashed records are similar to the cleansing shower of the monsoon that will break the air and the tension, Aitken's works are perpetually suspended in a moment before climax. They are frozen, like his life in those endless seconds on the beach when his brain stopped and death seemed an imminent solution. Though Aitken's ideas do acknowledge destiny and the impossibility of speeding it up. No matter how fast you travel, the day will always last twenty-four hours. But Aitken also believes that in these twenty-four hours, you can pack thousands of movements, thousands of perceptions, or—as in the case of his brief demise—nothing at all. In his most recent production (ELECTRIC EARTH), a young boy rises in the stillness of his bedroom, goes out into the accelerated speed of the surrounding city, and ends up immobile at the mouth of a tunnel that looks like the final void. Nothingness and stillness have their own images, their own virtual time where things exist and don't exist like in *Myst*, the phenomenally successful computer game that is constructed from an abandoned and melancholic virtual reality. Aitken's locations, like the Namibian desert in DIAMOND SEA, or Montserrat Island in ERASER, are poised on the edge of the real. Projecting the viewer into a world where numerous endings are possible, Aitken navigates through unreal places, revealing their different possibilities. The jungle, the desert, or the island are zones where something dramatic may have happened but has since been forgotten. These places are monuments to both slowness and speed: the slowness of the real and the speed of memory. They are the sound barriers that challenge Breedlove and that are, for the rest of us, barriers to an unknown destiny. In these suspended spaces, the violence of the monsoon, the dust of the volcano, and the light of the diamonds propel the landscape toward its own limits. Aitken reads his scripts as fast as he can and records them as slowly as possible. This contradiction produces the energy that generates the final time within the work and the real space for the viewer. The voices of the auctioneers, the vertical flight of the rocket, the winds of Guyana, the refracted light of Namibia—all these culminate in the linear acceleration of Aitken's vision. He places as many people as he can inside his mind, which is transformed into a space following the trail he has laid, encouraging us to think exactly as he does.

1) James Cameron, Interview with Paula Parisi in: *Wired Magazine*, April, 1996.
2) Paul Virilio, Interview with James DerDerian in: *Wired Magazine*, May, 1996.

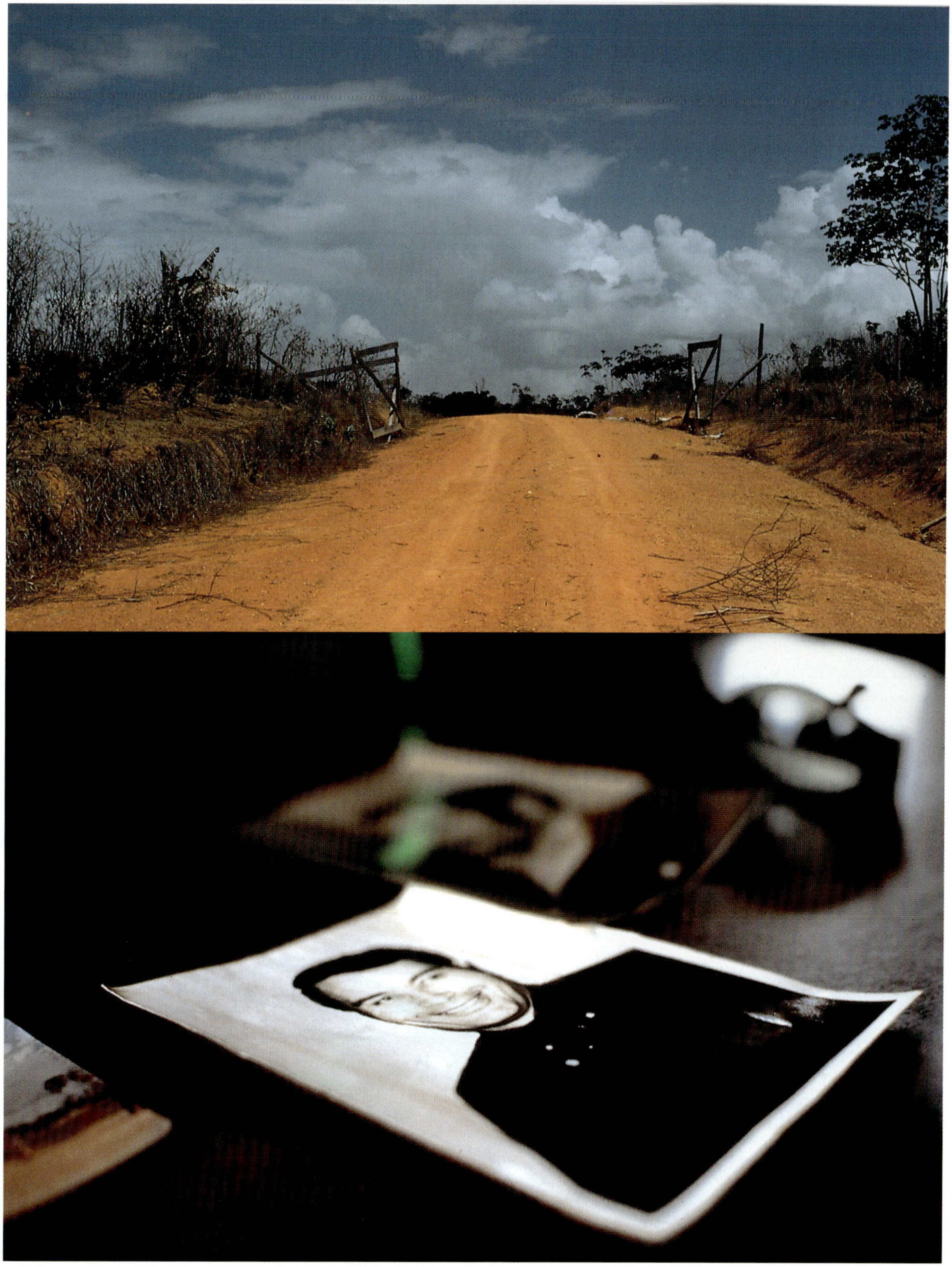

DOUG AITKEN, MONSOON, 1995, video still (top / oben); production still (bottom / unten) / MONSUN.

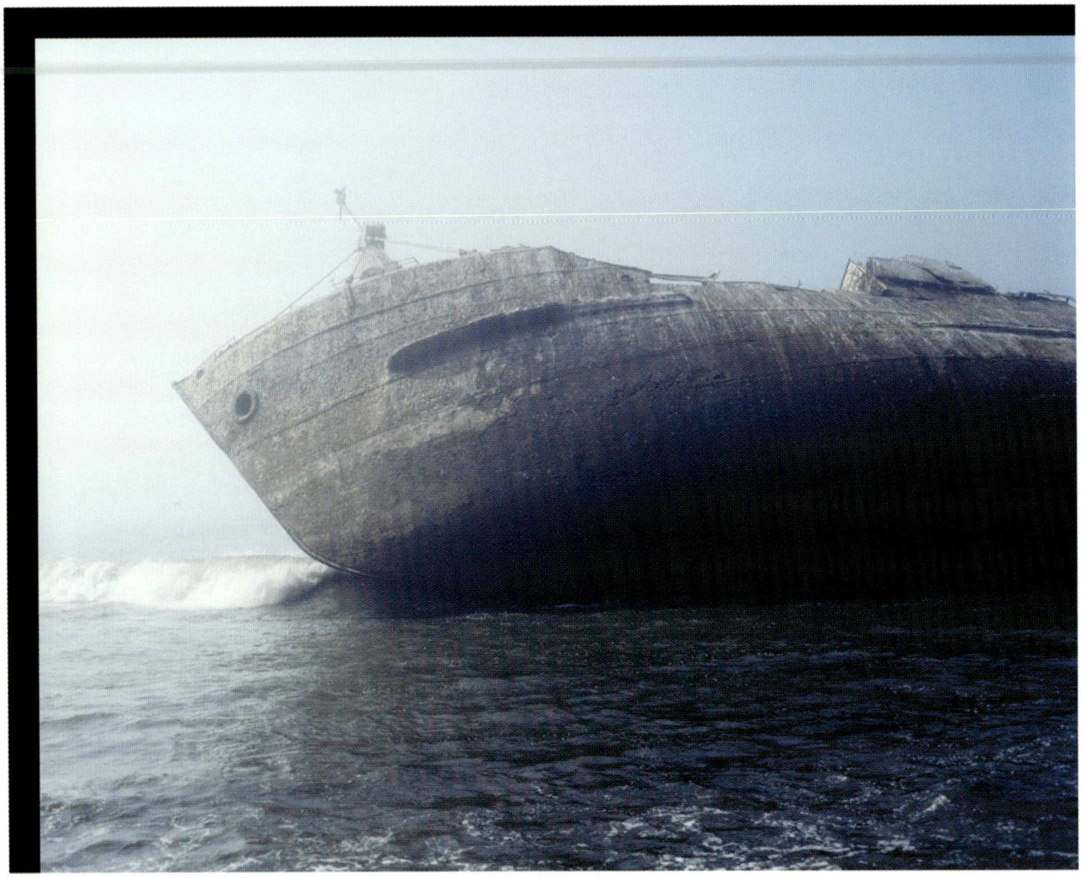

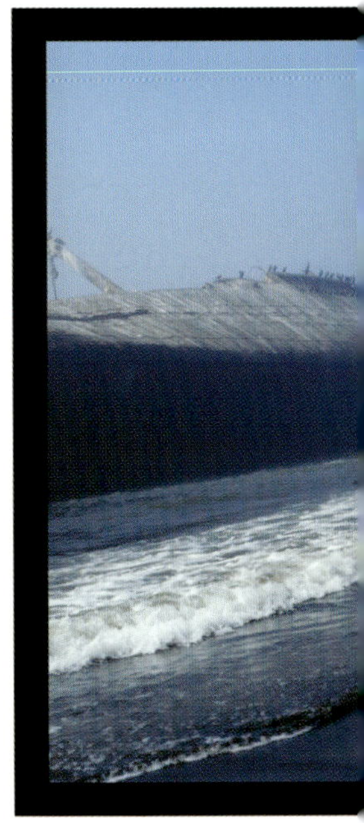

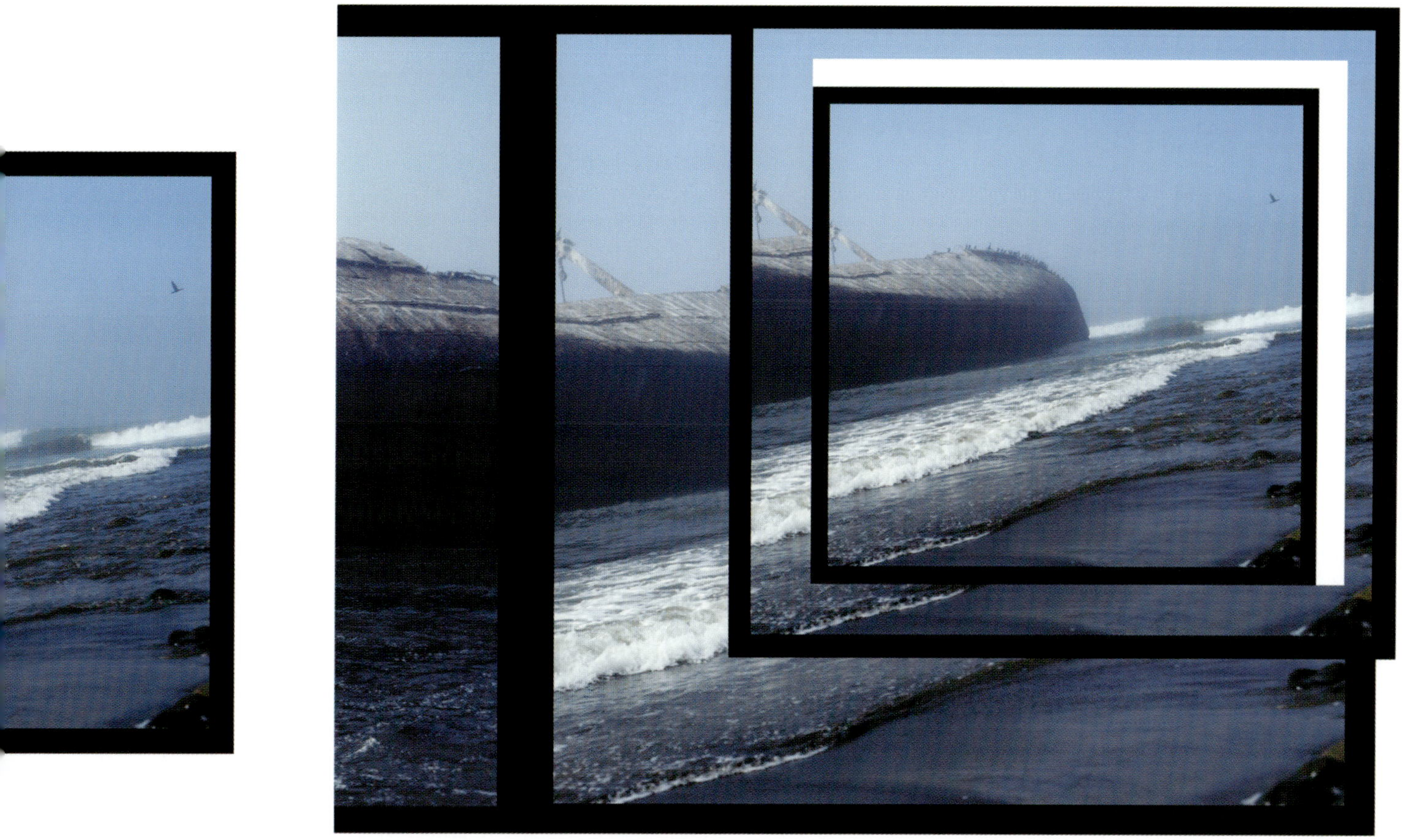

DOUG AITKEN, 2-SECOND SEPARATION, 1999, triptych / 2-SEKUNDEN-AUFSPALTUNG, Triptychon.

FLÜSSIGE ZEIT

FRANCESCO BONAMI

Godard betrachtet Worte als Bilder in einem ständigen Prozess von Geburt und Tod... Sicher erweist er sich in Pierrot le fou als Schüler Cocteaus. Ist unser Sehen nicht am Ende das Erleben des andauernden Todes in jener Realität, die nur durch die Kamera sichtbar wird?

– Toru Takemitsu, «Conversation on Seeing», in: *Confronting Silence,* Berkeley 1995.

Einmal im Pazifik geschwommen und mir war klar, dass man ihn wohl nicht ganz ohne Sarkasmus so getauft hat. Unter seiner ruhigen, zähflüssigen Oberfläche lauern Strömungen, die einen leicht verschlucken können. Aitken stammt aus einer jener südkalifornischen Küstenstädte, wo das Surfen den Bewohnern, die sich jeden Morgen in die Meeresfluten stürzen, zur zweiten Natur geworden ist. Beim Surfen – ich habe es selbst nie ausprobiert – stellt man sich oben auf die Welle und wenn sie bricht, wirbelt sie einen wild im schäumenden Wasser herum. Vor einigen Jahren ging Doug auf diese Art unter und als er ans Ufer gespült wurde, schien es zu spät. Beim Ertrinken sieht man angeblich das eigene Leben wie im Zeitraffer an sich vorbeiziehen. Doug Aitken ist ertrunken. Als seine Freunde ihn aus dem Wasser zogen, war er am Ende seines Bandes angekommen. Vielleicht ist er tatsächlich eine kleine Ewigkeit lang gestorben und dann in einer Art hedonistischer Auferstehung ins Leben zurückgekehrt. Seltsame Vorstellung, dass das Leben einfach anhält wie ein blockiertes Videoband, dass der Lebensfluss unterbrochen wird durch eine Leere, in der nichts geschieht. Wenn man dann wieder aufwacht, wo macht man da weiter? Spult man bis zu dem Augenblick zurück, in dem das Leben anhielt, oder fährt man einfach fort, obwohl man weiss, dass ein paar Bilder fehlen?

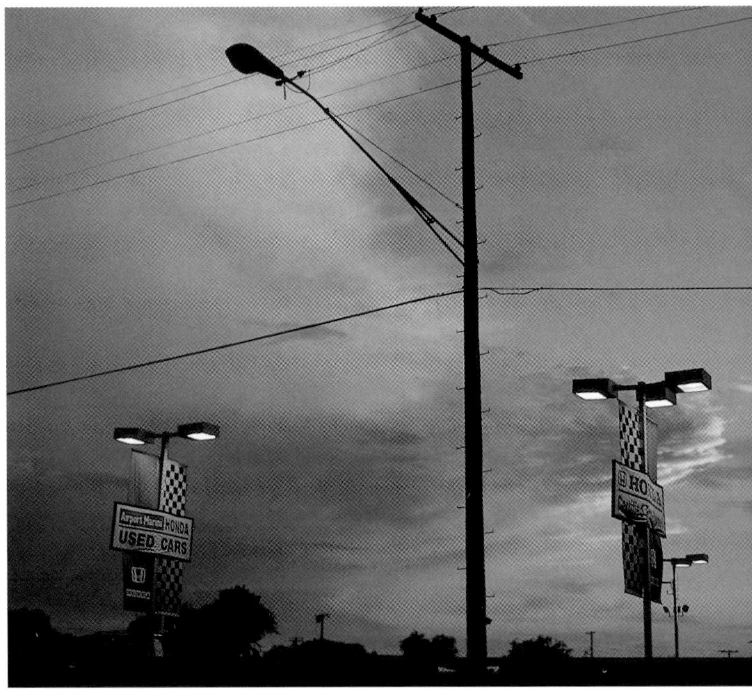

Ist der Tod im Grunde eine Frage der Schnitttechnik? Als Doug die Augen wieder öffnete, wusste er, dass ein Stück aus seinem Film verloren war, hatte aber keine Ahnung, wo er danach suchen sollte. Er konnte sich auch nicht vorstellen, was sich darin

FRANCESCO BONAMI ist Kurator am Museum of Contemporary Art in Chicago.

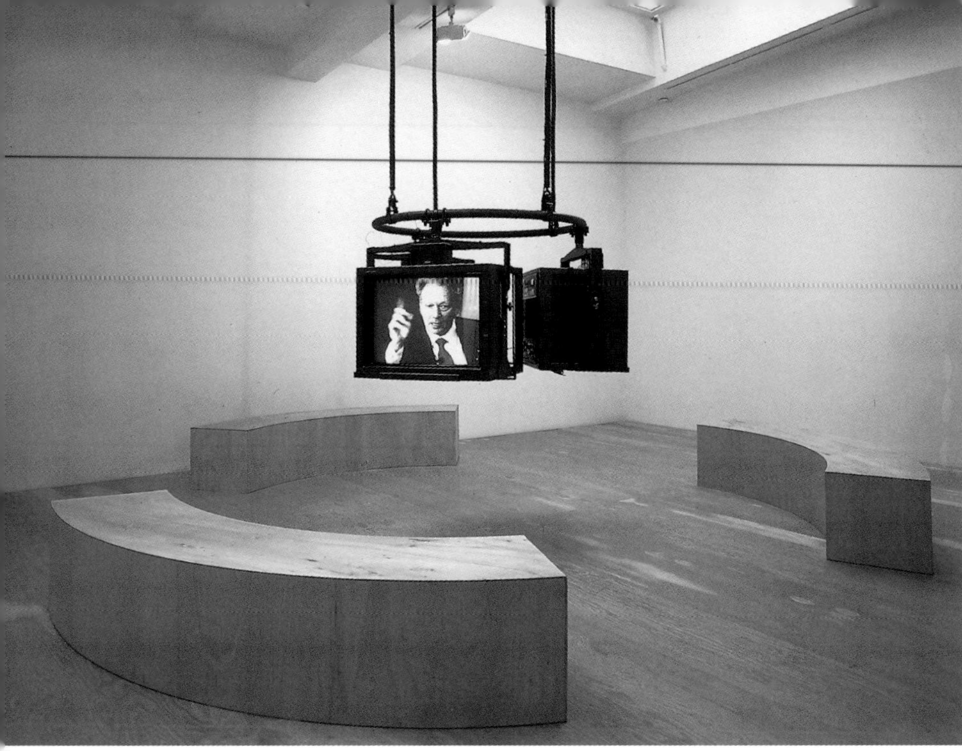

DOUG AITKEN, THESE RESTLESS MINDS, 1998, 3-channel video installation, production still (left-hand page) and installation view / DIESE RUHELOSEN GEISTER, 3-Kanal-Videoinstallation, Standaufnahme während der Produktion (linke Seite) und Installationsansicht.

ereignet haben könnte. Man könnte sich seine ganze Arbeit – passend zu diesem Unfall – als eine Art Ertrinken vorstellen. Er spult seine Gedanken vor und zurück, Mal um Mal, solange bis das Bild an der richtigen Stelle steht und gesagt ist, was zu sagen war. Auch der Betrachter wird in Aitkens Denkprozess hineingezogen und gerät genau im Augenblick ihrer Entstehung in die Fänge seiner Geschichte. Aitkens Werk ist wie eine Welle, die einen weniger fortreisst als nach unten drückt. Denn es wird nie auf den ersten Blick klar, was eigentlich geschieht, man muss mehrmals ein- und auftauchen um sich einen Reim darauf machen zu können. Aitken schafft einen Raum wie eine unendliche Schnittfolge, bei der der Betrachter solange schneidet und seine Gedanken einfügt, bis die Sache stimmt und sich richtig oder gut anfühlt, oder auch nicht.

In BAD ANIMAL (Böses Tier, 1996) oder THESE RESTLESS MINDS (Diese ruhelosen Geister, 1998) ist der Schneideraum ringförmig angelegt. Wie in einem Karussell dreht man sich ständig im Kreis, um die drei Bildschirme zu betrachten und die lineare Entwicklung des Stückes aufzuspüren, bis man ihm folgen kann. Aitken geht es nicht eigentlich um Linearität, dennoch ist seine Arbeit immer in einer gewissen emotionalen Kontinuität konstruiert. Anstatt sich von A nach B zu bewegen, kreist man so oft wie möglich um A, bevor man sich daran macht, B zu umkreisen. So umschifft man ein Dutzend Bilder, als umsegelte man einen Archipel aus lauter kleinen visuellen und konzeptuellen Inseln. Man umkreist die Bilder und wird von ihnen eingekreist. Immer übernimmt die gefilmte Landschaft die Rolle des Drehbuchs, und die Bewegung von Aitkens Kamera ist das eigentliche Thema.

In einer frühen Arbeit (INFLECTION, 1992) nahm Aitken die Landschaft in vertikaler Bewegung auf, indem er mithilfe einer kleinen Rakete eine Videokamera in den Himmel schoss. Wie eine Partitur, die man zu lesen versucht, während sie aus einem Fenster flattert, saust vor unserem Auge die wirbelnde Ansicht einer Vorstadtszene aus der Vogelperspektive in die Höhe und stürzt dann wieder herab. Aitken versucht hier die Umgebung durch eine Kombination von Höhe und Geschwindigkeit abzubilden. In späteren Arbeiten richtet er seinen Blick auf die horizontale Geschwindigkeit des Bodens. Dieses frühe Experiment ist eine Art visuelles Haiku, der Versuch, eine Kurzgeschichte zu erzählen, und zwar die seiner Herkunft, wobei er, von oben nach unten und von unten nach oben, mit hieroglyphenhafter Präzision in die tiefsten Tiefen vordringt.

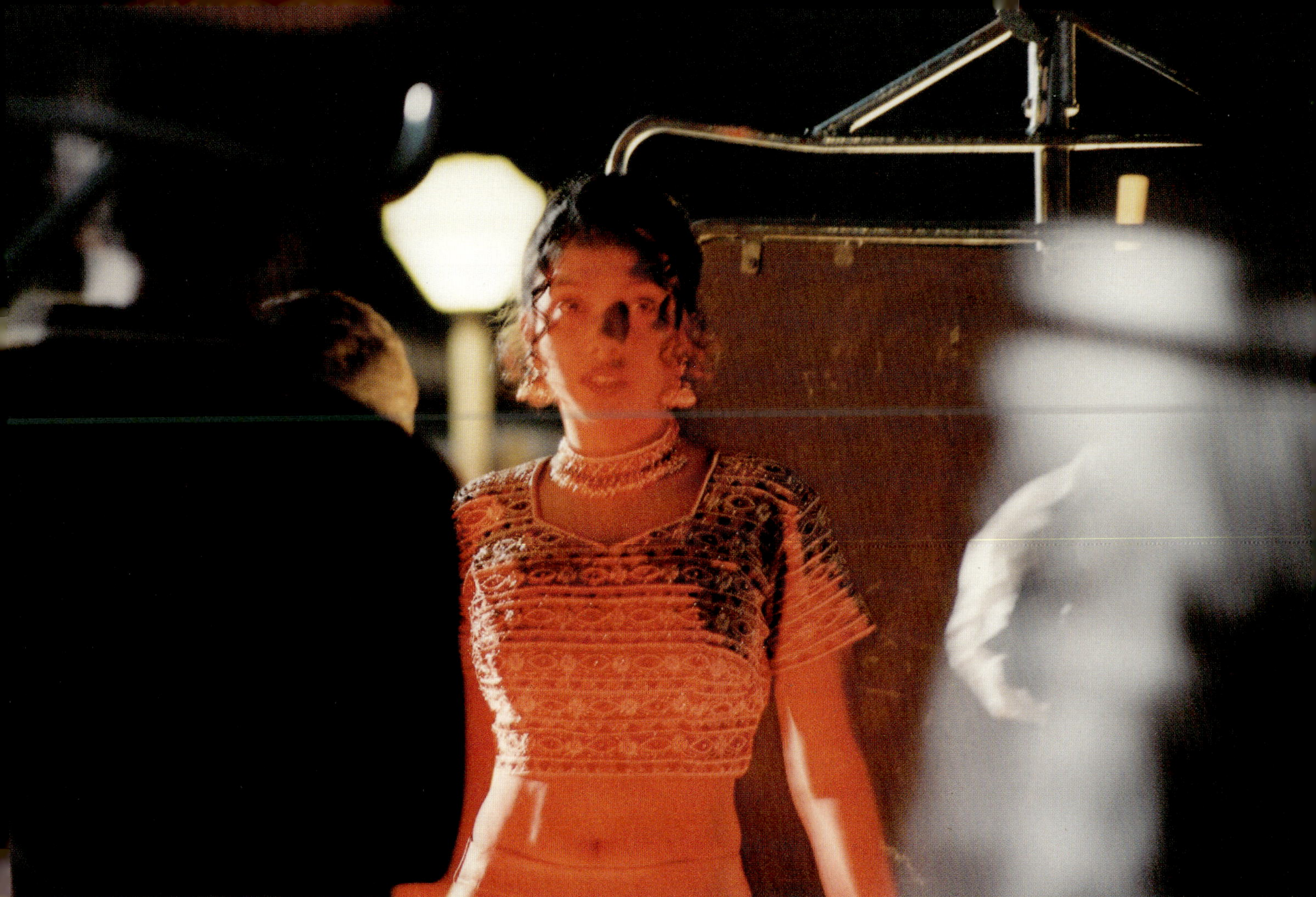

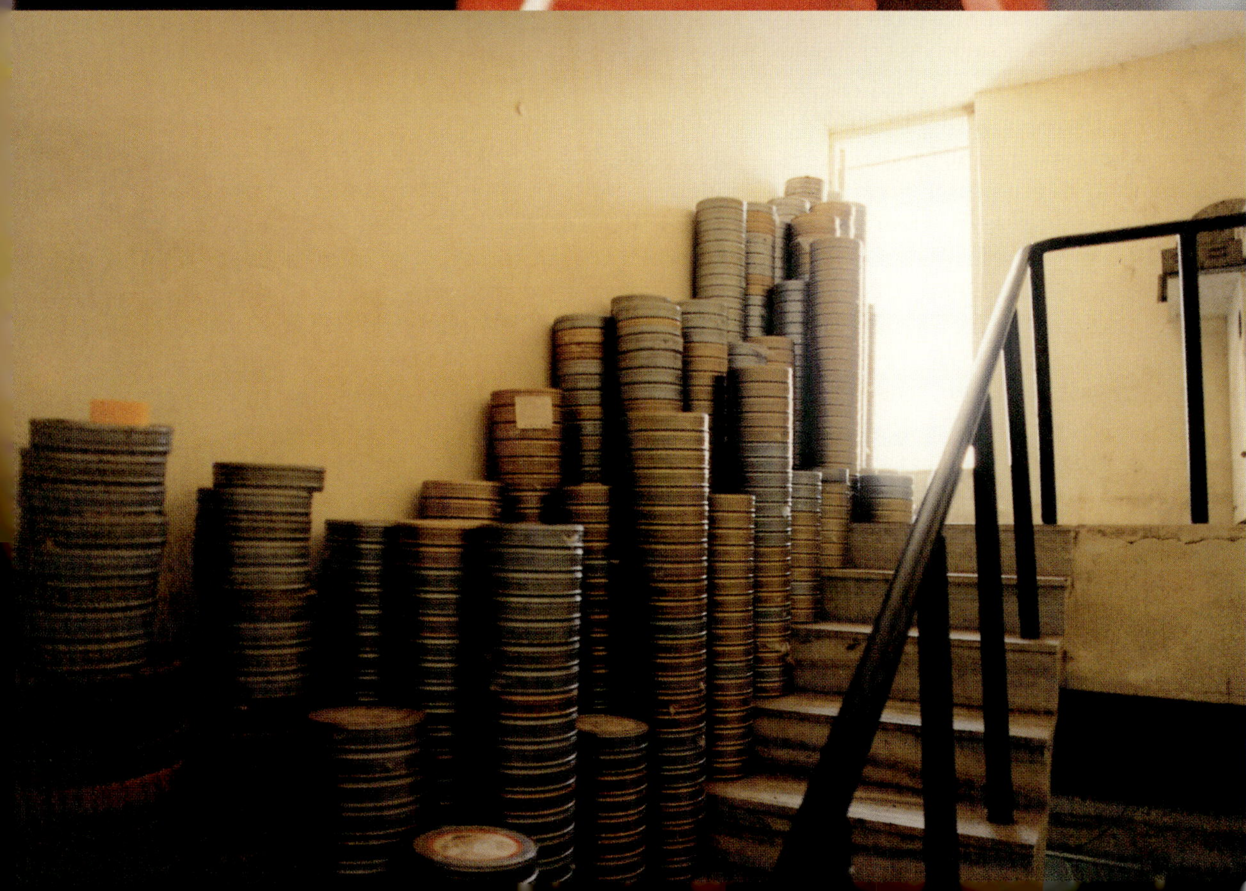

DOUG AITKEN, INTO THE SUN, 1999, 4-laser-disc video installation; production stills (left-hand page) and installation at the Victoria Miro Gallery, London (right-hand page) / IN DIE SONNE, Videoinstallation mit 4 Laserdisks; Standaufnahmen während der Produktion (linke Seite) und Installation (rechte Seite).

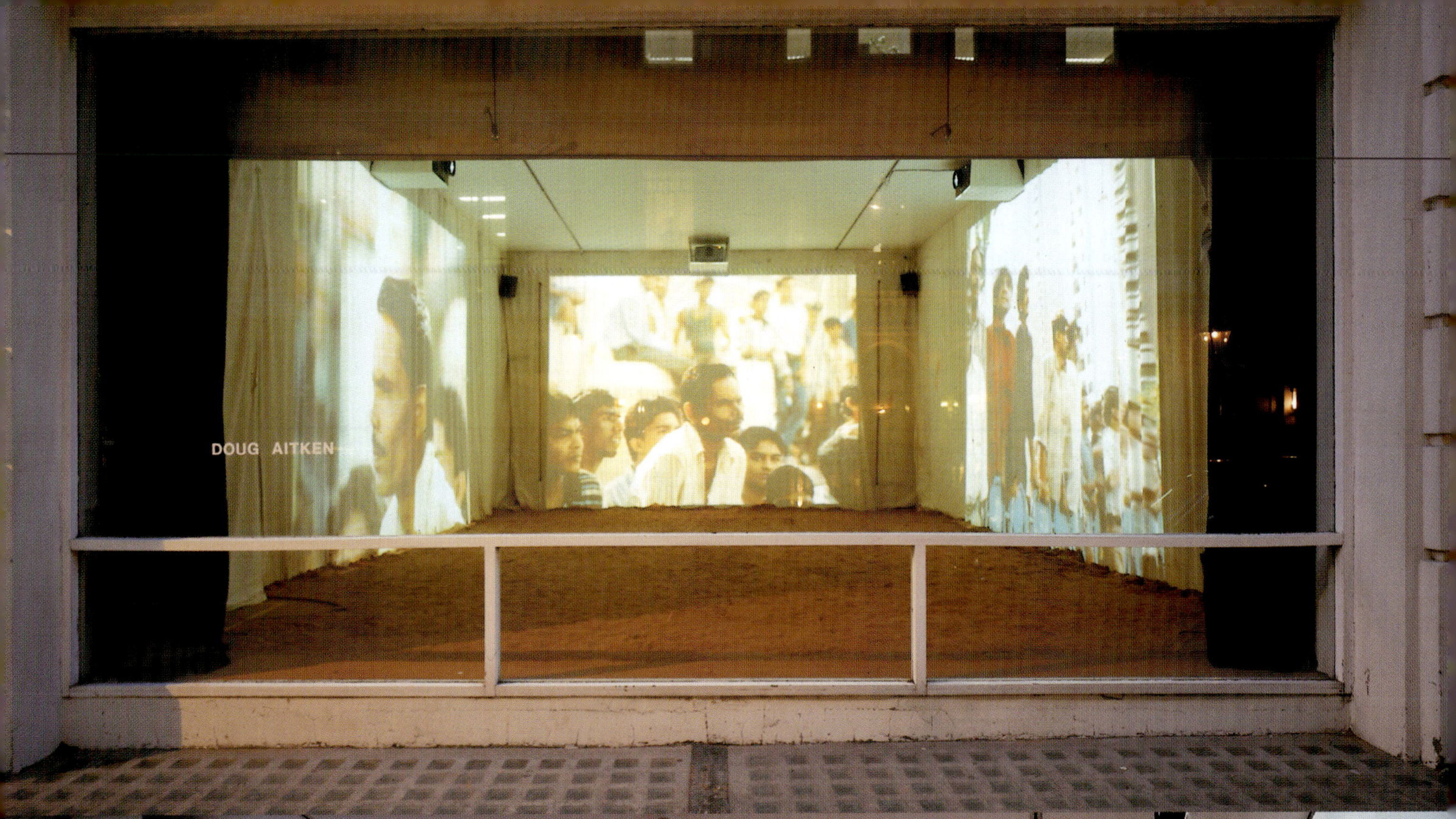
DOUG AITKEN

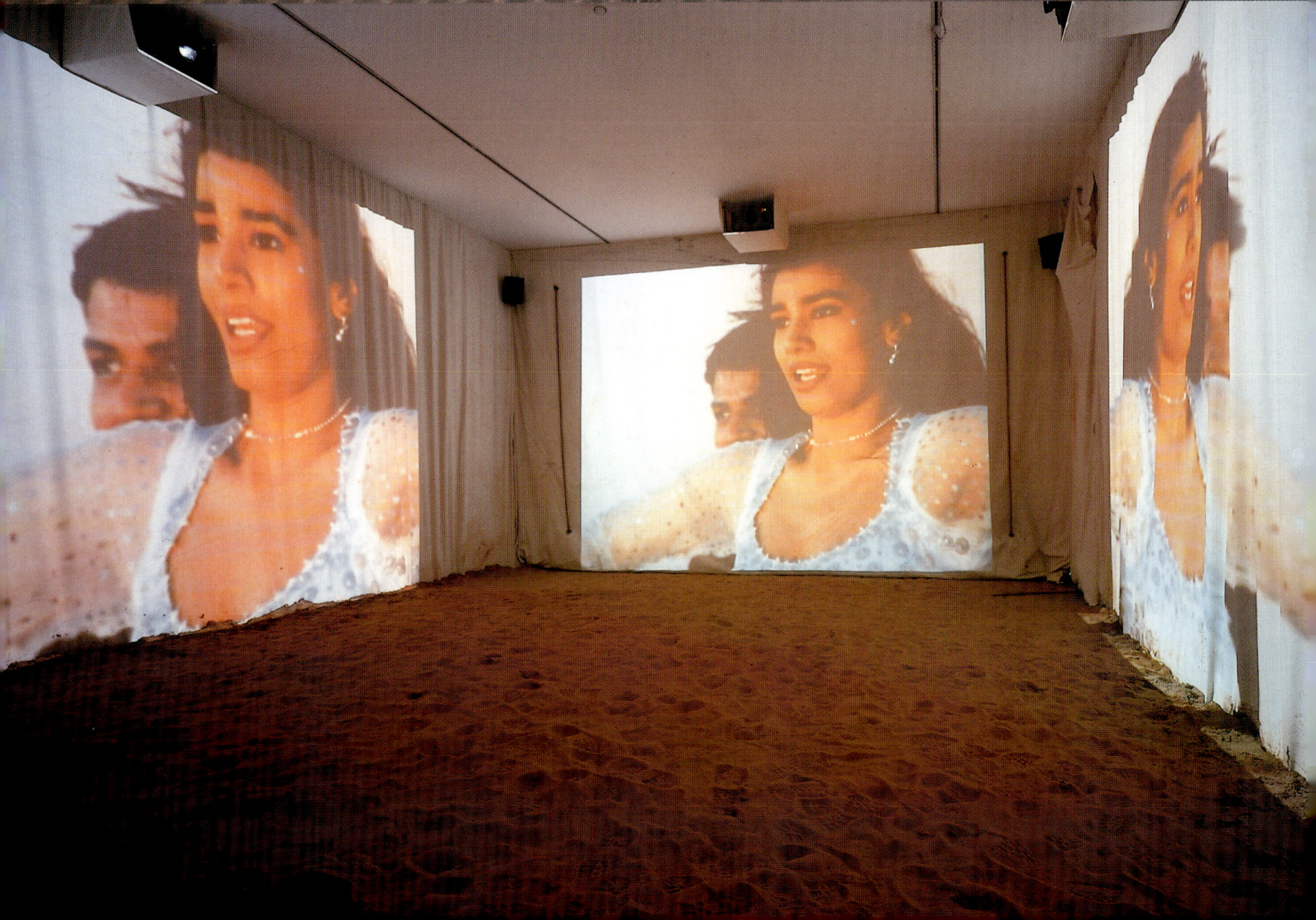

In dieser frühen Arbeit streift Aitken bereits den Konflikt zwischen verzögerter, vertikaler und realer Zeit. Dieser wird später zu einem zentralen Thema seines Werks, das von der Erweiterung der realen Zeit hinein in die – verschobene – Zeit der Wahrnehmung handelt: die reale Zeit des Autors, verlagert in die Zeit des Betrachters. Befindet man sich in einer seiner Installationen, stellt sich automatisch die Frage, ob das, was man gerade erlebt, die reale Zeit und der reale Raum sind. In CATHOUSE (Miezenhaus, 1997) ist der Raum real und greifbar genug, um klaustrophobische Gefühle zu erzeugen. Gefangen in diesem unverhältnismässig vergrösserten und mit Teppichen ausgelegten Raum, erkennt der Besucher seine eigene perverse Vorstadtfigur gleichsam wie im Spiegel, während er drei Menschen beobachtet: eine Frau, die mit einem Glas Wasser spielt, einen Jungen in seinem Schlafzimmer und einen Mann (Iggy Pop), der auf einem Lehnstuhl schaukelt. Sie alle befinden sich in grosszügigen Vorstadt-Interieurs, festgehalten in fensterähnlich in der Wand eingelassenen Kleinbildschirmen. In CATHOUSE sind alle Beteiligten – Betrachter wie Betrachtete – in einer Vorstadtarchitektur und einem seltsam gedämpften Ambiente eingeschlossen. Doug Aitkens Werk ist eine empirische Prüfung von echter Interaktivität und Virtualität. James Cameron, der Regisseur des Films *Titanic*, formulierte es so: «Der Film bringt das, was an der virtuellen Realität so grossartig ist, gar nicht ins Spiel, nämlich die Interaktivität: Man bewegt sich, und durch die Bewegung verändert sich das Bild.»[1] Aitken dagegen tut dies, stellt dabei aber nicht einfach auf die Bewegungen des Betrachters ab, sondern entwickelt seine Ideen um diese Bewegungen herum und nimmt sie vorweg. Dadurch schafft er einen Raum, durch den der Betrachter sich zwar bewegen kann, aber nur auf ganz bestimmte Weise.

Ganz am Anfang konnten sich Landschaft und Betrachter bei Aitken noch begegnen, ohne in eine interaktive Beziehung zu treten. Ein gutes Beispiel dafür ist MONSOON (Monsun, 1995). Der Film wurde im Dschungel von Guyana gedreht, dort wo die Jünger von Reverend Jones Mitte der 70er Jahre Massenselbstmord verübten, und er zeigt nichts als das Warten auf den bevorstehenden Monsun. Die aktuelle Landschaft geht im drohenden Unwetter unter, wie das traumatische historische Ereignis in der üppigen Natur dieser Gegend untergegangen ist. In MONSOON sieht man nichts als steigende Spannung und ein latentes Wiederaufflammen von Angst. Tatsächlich trifft der Monsun niemals ein. Der Film endet, kurz bevor der Himmel platzt wie eine reife Frucht, knapp vor der finalen Reinigung, wie das Leben der Sekte genau vor dem Augenblick endete, in dem die Enttäuschung offenbar geworden wäre. Aitken hält unmittelbar vor dem Moment der Wahrheit inne und belässt Hoffnung und Verzweiflung in spannungsgeladener Balance. MONSOON ist Aitkens erster Schritt zur Erforschung der Geschwindigkeit.

Lichtgeschwindigkeit (DIAMOND SEA / Diamantenmeer, 1997), Windgeschwindigkeit (MONSOON), Geschwindigkeit des menschlichen Körpers (ELECTRIC EARTH / Elektrische Erde, 1999) und des Geistes (THESE RESTLESS MINDS / Diese ruhelosen Geister), Geschwindigkeit des Ruhms (INTO THE SUN / In die Sonne, 1999): «Umweltverschmutzung durch Geschwindigkeit», sagt Paul Virilio, «reduziert die Welt auf ein Nichts.»[2] Aitkens Werk führt eine Art ökologischer Grenze vor, die aus der Geschwindigkeit eine nicht lineare Geschichte in Zeitlupe macht. Vielleicht gerade weil der Künstler an einem Ort aufwuchs, an dem das machtvoll rhythmische Schlagen der Wellen gegen die Küste unablässig zu hören war, wirkt die Geschwindigkeit als Mittel zur Vergrösserung der Langsamkeit so anziehend auf ihn. Aitkens Vorgehen erinnert mich an Craig Breedlove, einen bescheidenen Mann, der in den Bonneville Salt Flats in Utah mit Raketen, die er zu Hause in seiner Garage bastelt, Geschwindigkeitsrekorde erzielt und Schallmauern durchbricht. Um etwas über die Geschwindigkeit zu erzählen oder um ein Auto zu bauen, mit dem man Geschwindigkeitsrekorde fahren kann, müssen beide, Aitken und Breedlove, die Idee der Geschwindigkeit in eine Reihe genau ausgeloteter Details zerlegen. Sobald dann alle Einzelheiten klar sind, lassen sie sich zum fertigen Instrument verdichten – zum Film oder Auto. Dem Abstand zwischen Breedloves Gefährt und der durchbrochenen Schallmauer entspricht bei Aitken die Beschleunigung von der Idee zur Geschichte, der Zeitraum, der Anfang und Ende seiner Vorstellungen zusammenfügt. Sowohl der Künstler wie der

Rennfahrer fordern die Geschwindigkeit heraus und beschreiben sie als ein Mittel, um das Vollkommene der Reglosigkeit feierlich zu unterstreichen. Auf ähnliche Weise feiert Aitken in ERASER (Auslöscher, 1998) die Geschwindigkeit eines Vulkanausbruchs, der die geradezu greifbare Reglosigkeit einer Insel entstehen lässt, erstarrt wie ein zweites Herculaneum.

Doch während Breedloves gebrochene Rekorde eine gewisse Ähnlichkeit mit der reinigenden Wirkung des Monsunregens haben, der die Atmosphäre aufbricht und die Spannung löst, halten Aitkens Werke immer einen Moment vor dem Wendepunkt inne. Sie sind erstarrt, gerade wie sein Leben in jenen endlosen Sekunden am Strand, als sein Gehirn aufhörte zu arbeiten und der Tod als definitive Lösung unmittelbar bevorzustehen schien. Zwar erkennt Aitken das Schicksal durchaus an und sieht ein, dass es sich nicht beschleunigen lässt. Egal wie schnell man reist, der Tag wird immer vierundzwanzig Stunden haben. Aitken glaubt jedoch auch, dass man in diesen Vierundzwanzigstundentag Tausende von Bewegungen packen kann, Tausende von Wahrnehmungen, oder – wie im Falle seines kurzen Aussetzers – gar nichts. In seiner jüngsten Produktion (ELECTRIC EARTH) erhebt sich ein kleiner Junge in der Stille seines Schlafzimmers, geht hinaus in die erhöhte Geschwindigkeit der Stadt und findet sich schliesslich regungslos am Eingang eines Tunnels wieder, der aussieht wie das Tor zur endgültigen Leere. Das Nichts und die Reglosigkeit haben ihre eigenen Bilder, ihre eigene virtuelle Zeit, wo Dinge existieren und nicht existieren, so wie in dem unglaublich erfolgreichen Computerspiel *Myst*, das auf einer verlassen-melancholischen virtuellen Realität aufbaut. Aitkens Schauplätze, etwa die namibische Wüste in DIAMOND SEA oder die Insel Montserrat in ERASER, balancieren an der Grenze des Realen. Der Betrachter wird in eine Welt versetzt, in der verschiedene Ausgänge denkbar sind, während Aitken durch unwirkliche Orte streift und deren unterschiedliche Möglichkeiten aufzeigt. Der Dschungel, die Wüste oder die Insel sind Gegenden, in denen sich etwas Dramatisches ereignet haben könnte, das inzwischen in Vergessenheit geraten ist. Diese Orte sind Monumente der Langsamkeit und der Geschwindigkeit: die Langsamkeit der Realität und die Geschwindigkeit des Erinnerns. Sie sind die Schallmauern, die Breedlove reizen, und für den Rest von uns sind es Schwellen zu einem unbekannten Schicksal. In diesen schwebenden Räumen treibt die Gewalt des Monsuns, der Staub des Vulkans oder das Licht der Diamanten die Landschaft an ihre eigenen Grenzen. Aitken liest seine Drehbücher, so schnell er nur kann, um sie dann so langsam wie möglich umzusetzen. Dieser Widerspruch setzt die Energie frei, welche die endgültige Zeit innerhalb des Werks erzeugt und den realen Raum für den Betrachter schafft. Die Stimmen der Auktionatoren, der Senkrechtflug der Rakete, der Wind in Guyana, das gebrochene Licht Namibias: Sie alle finden ihre Steigerung in der linearen Beschleunigung von Aitkens Vision. Er nimmt so viele Menschen wie möglich in sein Denken auf und dieses wird – vorausgesetzt wir folgen der von ihm gelegten Spur – zu einem Raum, der uns ermutigt genauso zu denken wie der Künstler.

(Übersetzung: Nansen)

DOUG AITKEN, UNTITLED (REARVIEW MIRROR, ABSTRACT), 1966, c-print mounted on Plexiglas, 9 x 13¾" / OHNE TITEL (RÜCKSPIEGEL, ABSTRAKT), C-Print auf Plexiglas, 22,9 x 35 cm.

1) James Cameron, Interview mit Paula Parisi, in: *Wired Magazine*, April 1996.

2) Paul Virilio, Interview mit James DerDerian, in: *Wired Magazine*, Mai 1996.

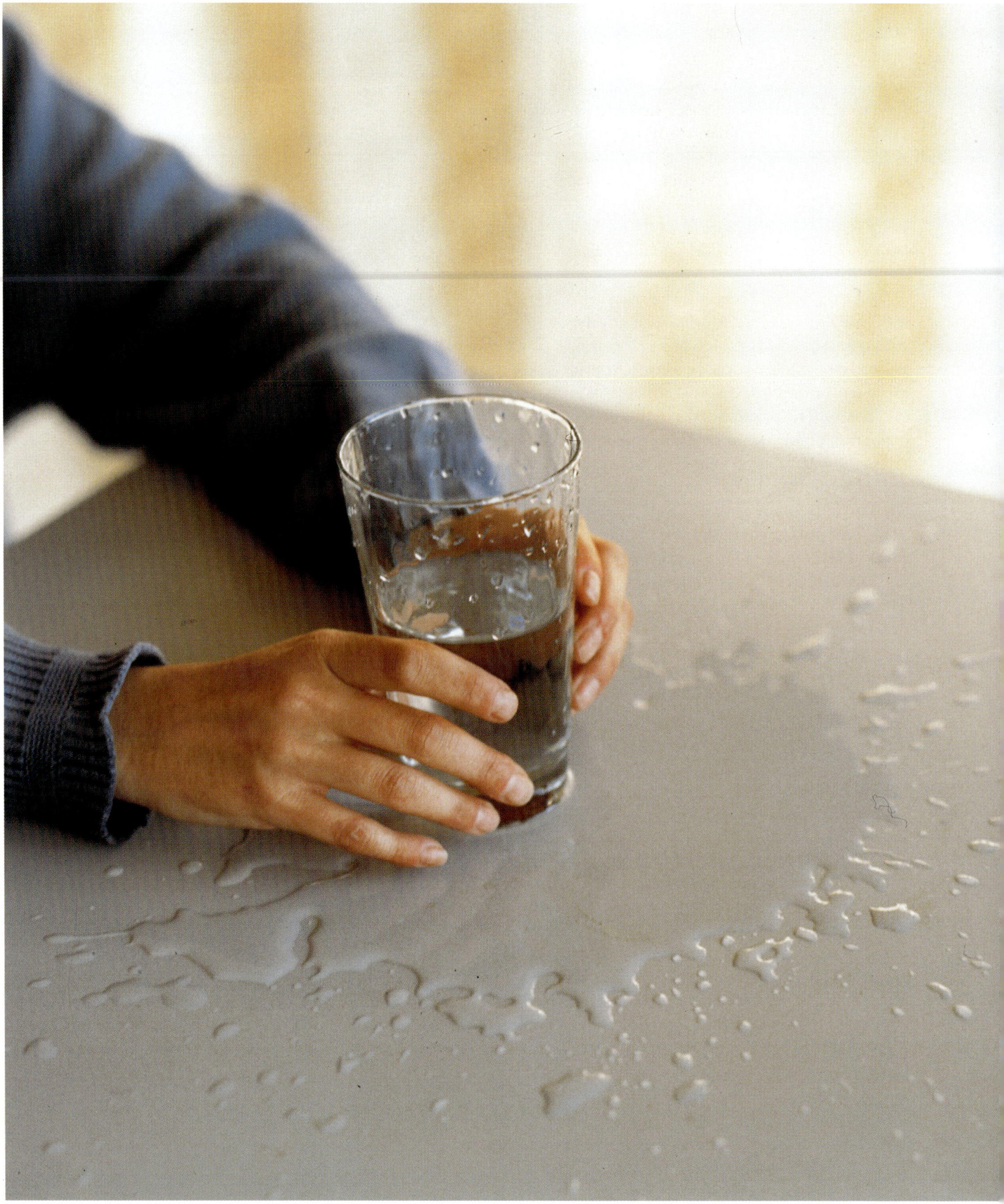

DOUG AITKEN, SEARCHERS, WATER, 1997, c-print laminated on Plexiglas, 16 x 20" / SUCHENDE, WASSER, C-Print auf Plexiglas, 48,3 x 50,8 cm.

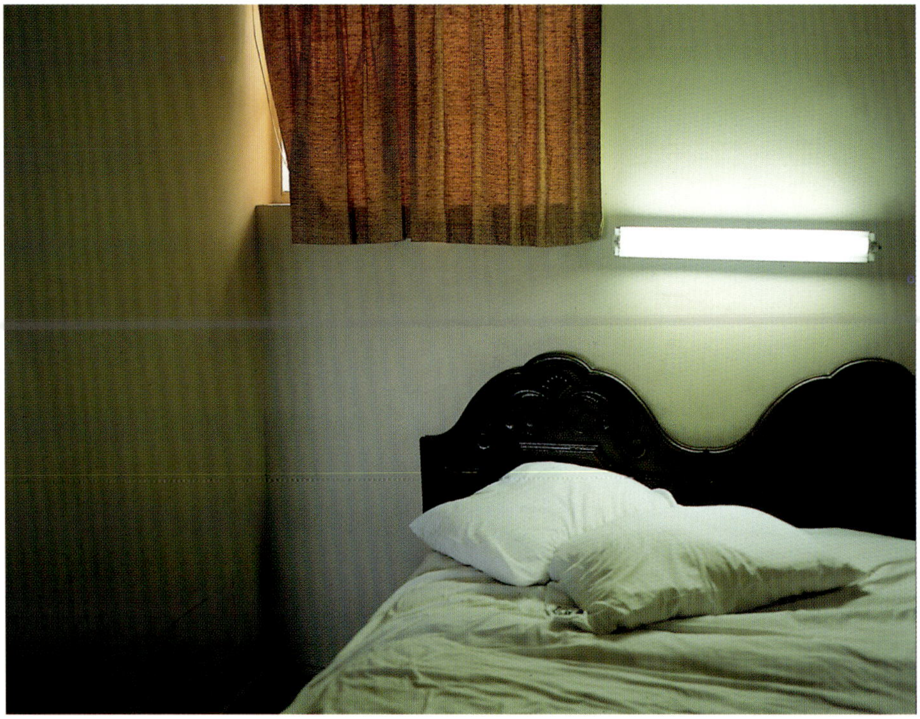

DOUG AITKEN, GREEN SUN, 1999 / GRÜNE SONNE.

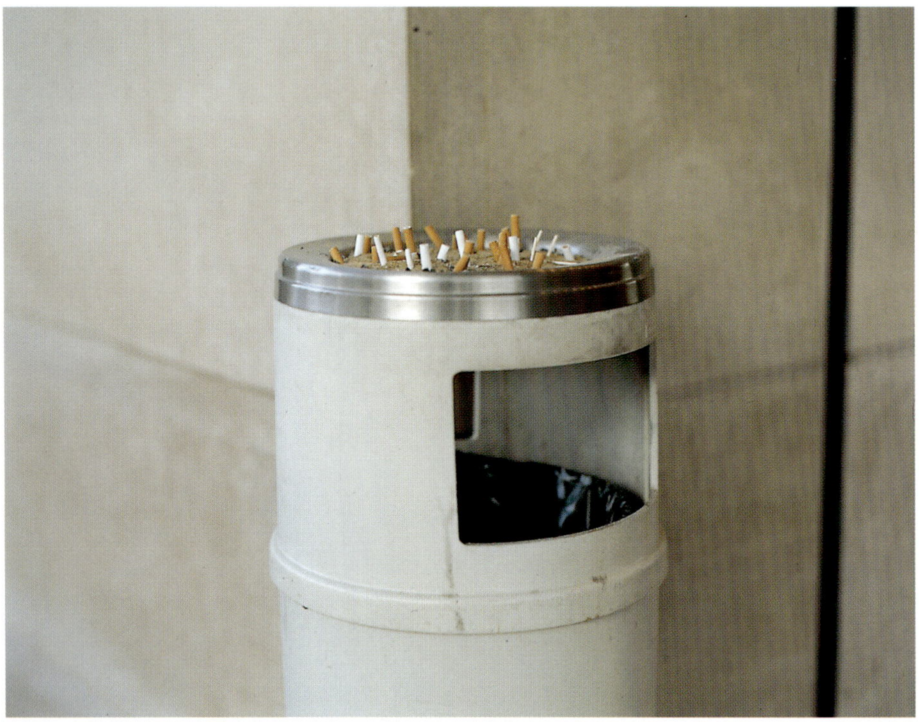

DOUG AITKEN, ISLAND, 1999 / INSEL.

Doug Aitken, ein «Stalker» unseres Fin de Siècle

CHRISTINE VAN ASSCHE

Doug Aitken ist unverkennbar ein Künstler der amerikanischen Westküste. Sein Interesse gilt vor allem der Landschaft, sei es in Guyana, Namibia, Australien oder in der Umgebung von Los Angeles. Er filmt ihre Weite und die sich wandelnden Lichtverhältnisse mit derselben Intensität wie James Turrell. Er verbringt Zeit in dieser Landschaft, analysiert sie und bewegt sich darin wie Robert Smithson. Er beobachtet sie, erforscht sie eingehend, filmt sie aus allen möglichen Blickwinkeln, zu jeder Tages- und Nachtzeit, zu jeder Jahreszeit. Die städtische Landschaft interessiert ihn ebenso sehr wie die Natur.

ELECTRIC EARTH (Elektrische Erde, 1999), die audiovisuelle Installation, die man an der Biennale in Venedig sehen konnte, zeigt einen Mann, der von der Informationsflut und der Ruhelosigkeit seiner Umgebung völlig absorbiert wird. Doug Aitken hat verschiedene Nachtaufnahmen von Los Angeles und der Umgebung des Flughafens gedreht und mit Grossaufnahmen von Händen und Oberkörpern zusammengeschnitten oder mit Bildern des frenetisch tanzenden Mannes selbst. Man hat dabei eine Landschaft vor sich, die jedermann antreffen kann, wenn er durch die Strassen einer amerikanischen Stadt spaziert: Schaufenster von Supermärkten, Neonlicht, Überwachungskameras, Lichtsignale, leere Parkplätze, Tanksäulen, Strassentunnels, Stacheldraht, Verkehrsschilder, Waschsalons, Getränkeautomaten, Radargeräte usw. Wir erleben sozusagen mit, wie Seiten aus einem Katalog voller Bilder und Töne herausgerissen werden, der uns, um mit Walter Benjamin zu sprechen, «winzige Zellen der Realität» vermittelt. Die sehr präzise, schnelle Montage aus Schnitten, Überblendungen, wechselnd scharfen und unscharfen Einstellungen sowie dem Hin und Her zwischen Stadtbildern und Körperfragmenten lässt uns den völlig verkrampften, an Wahnsinn grenzenden Zustand spüren, in dem sich der Mann, den Doug Aitken in der Stadt spazieren führt, befindet. Die komplexe Tonmischung ist perfekt auf Schnitt und Bilder abgestimmt.

Andererseits lässt uns DIAMOND SEA (Diamantenmeer, 1997) – eine Installation mit mehreren Projektionsflächen, die in der namibischen Wüste in Südwestafrika gedreht wurde (und auch in einer linearen Version auf Videoband existiert) – Wüstenlandschaften entdecken, die sich mit Bildern einer

CHRISTINE VAN ASSCHE ist Chefkuratorin am Centre Georges Pompidou in Paris.

DOUG AITKEN, DIAMOND SEA, 1997, color laser-disc, production stills / DIAMANTENMEER, Farblaserdisk, Standaufnahmen.

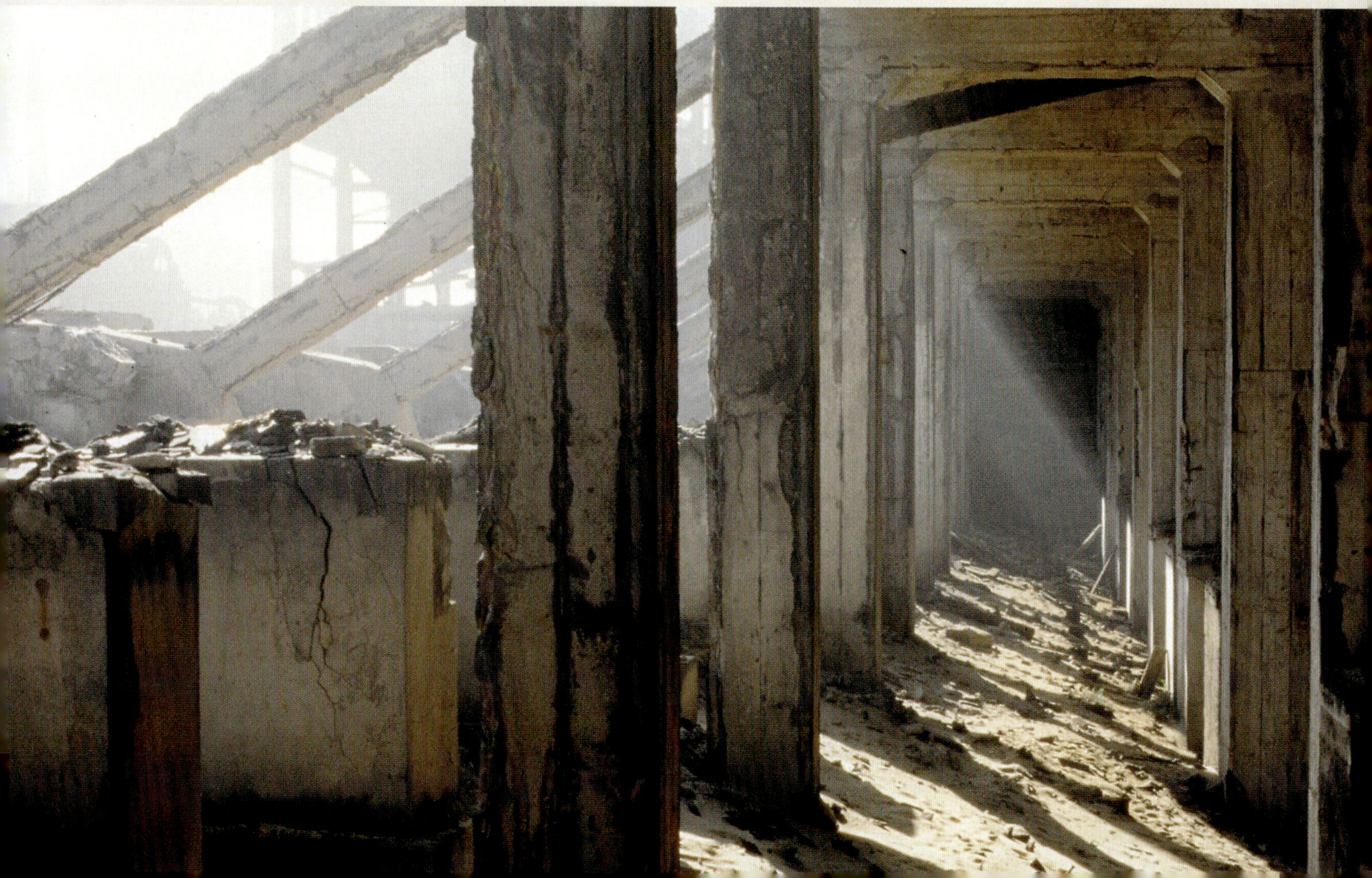

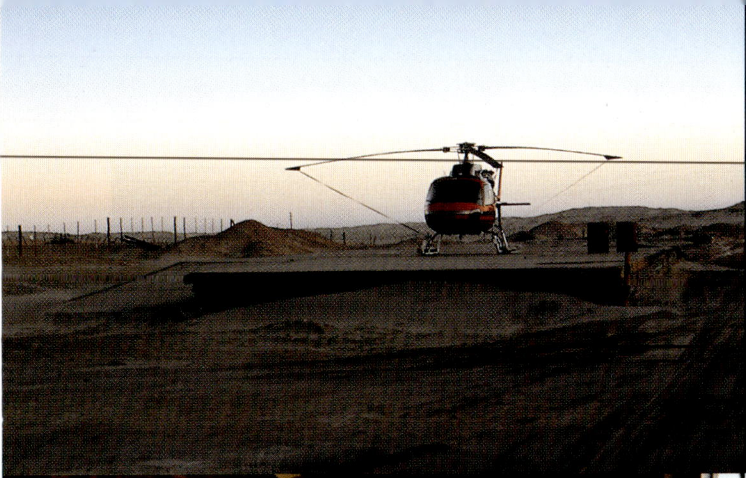
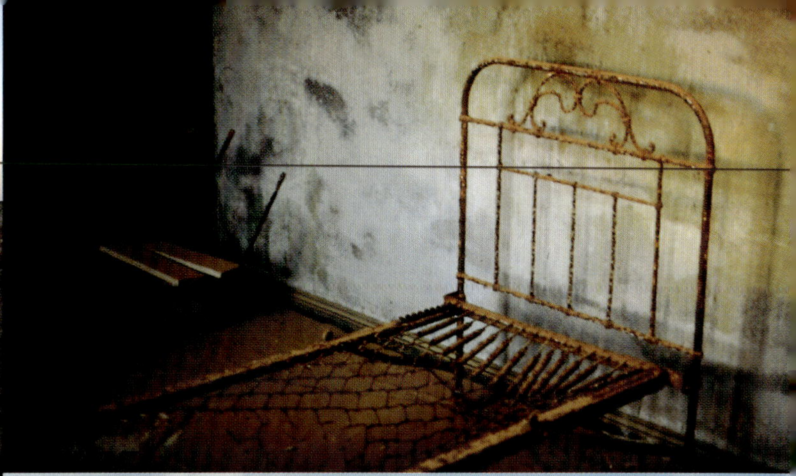
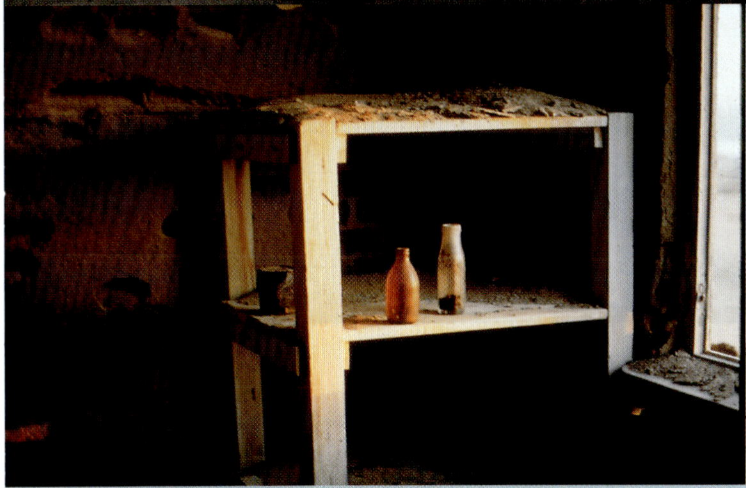
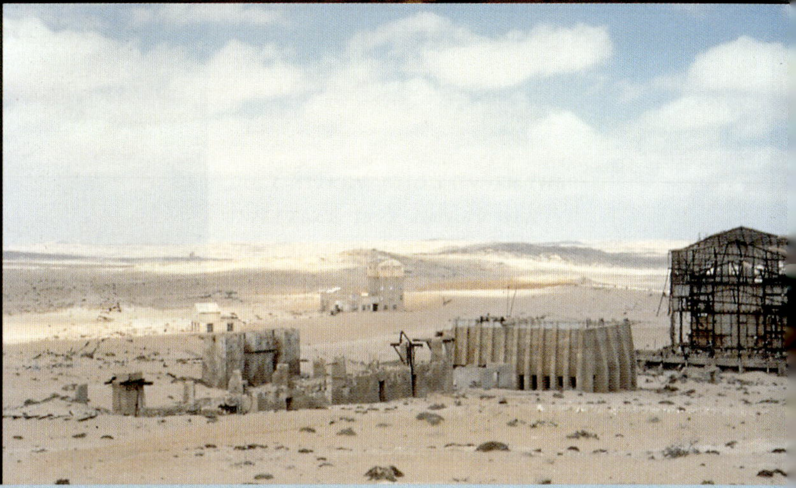
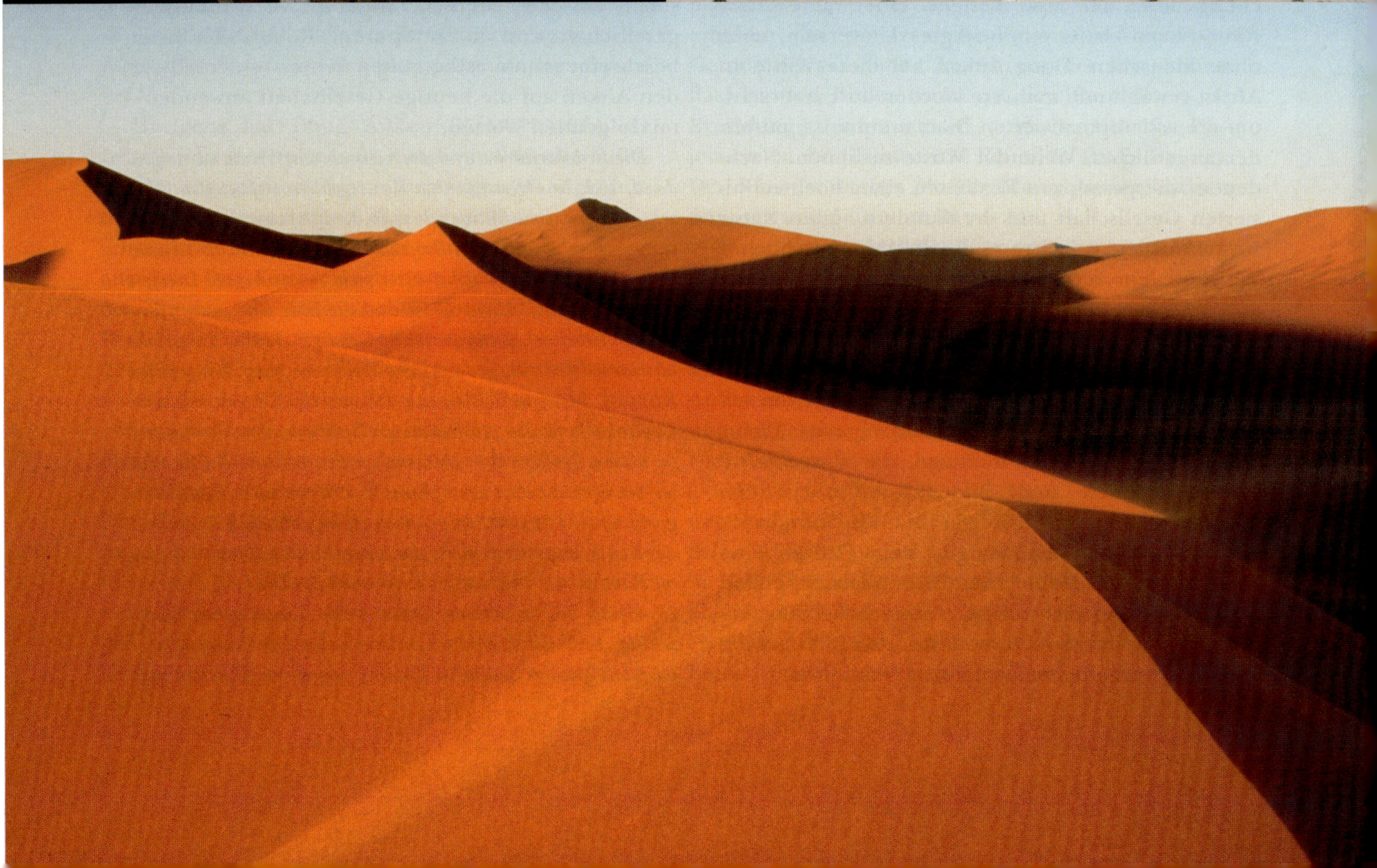

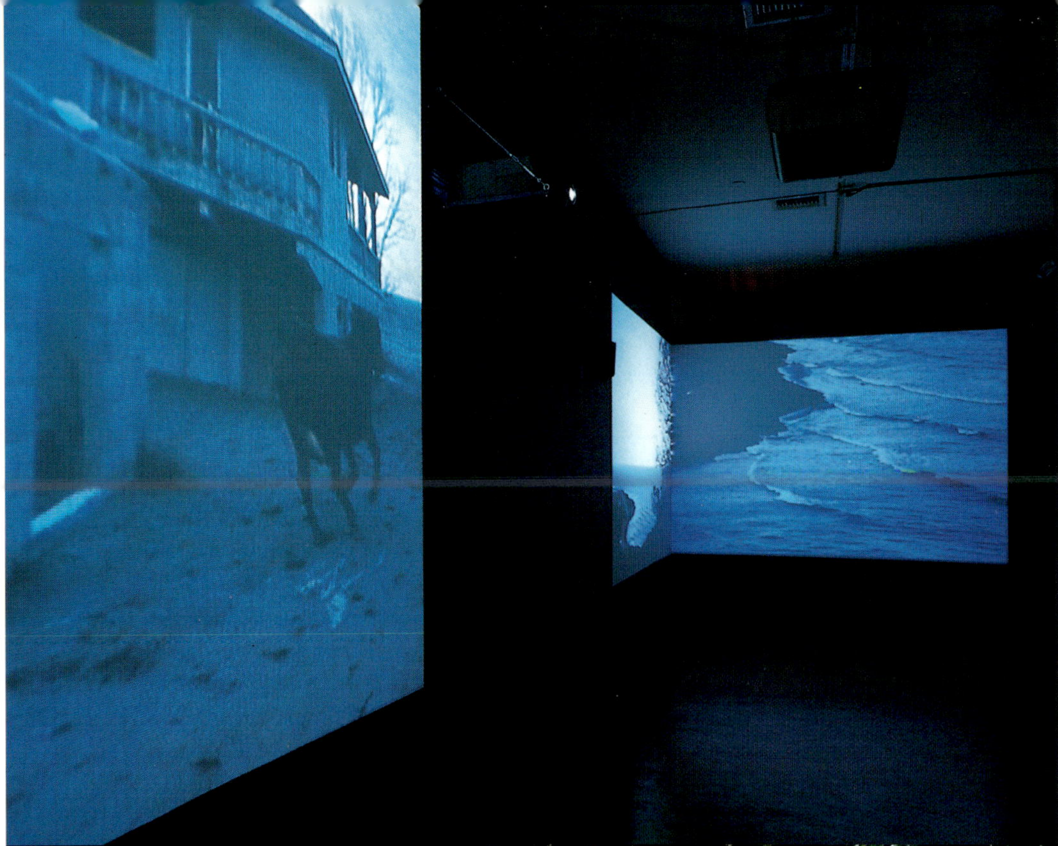

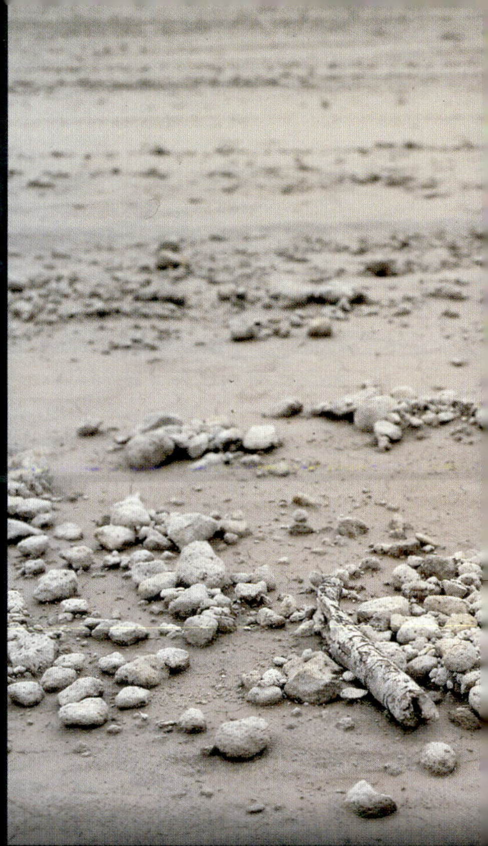

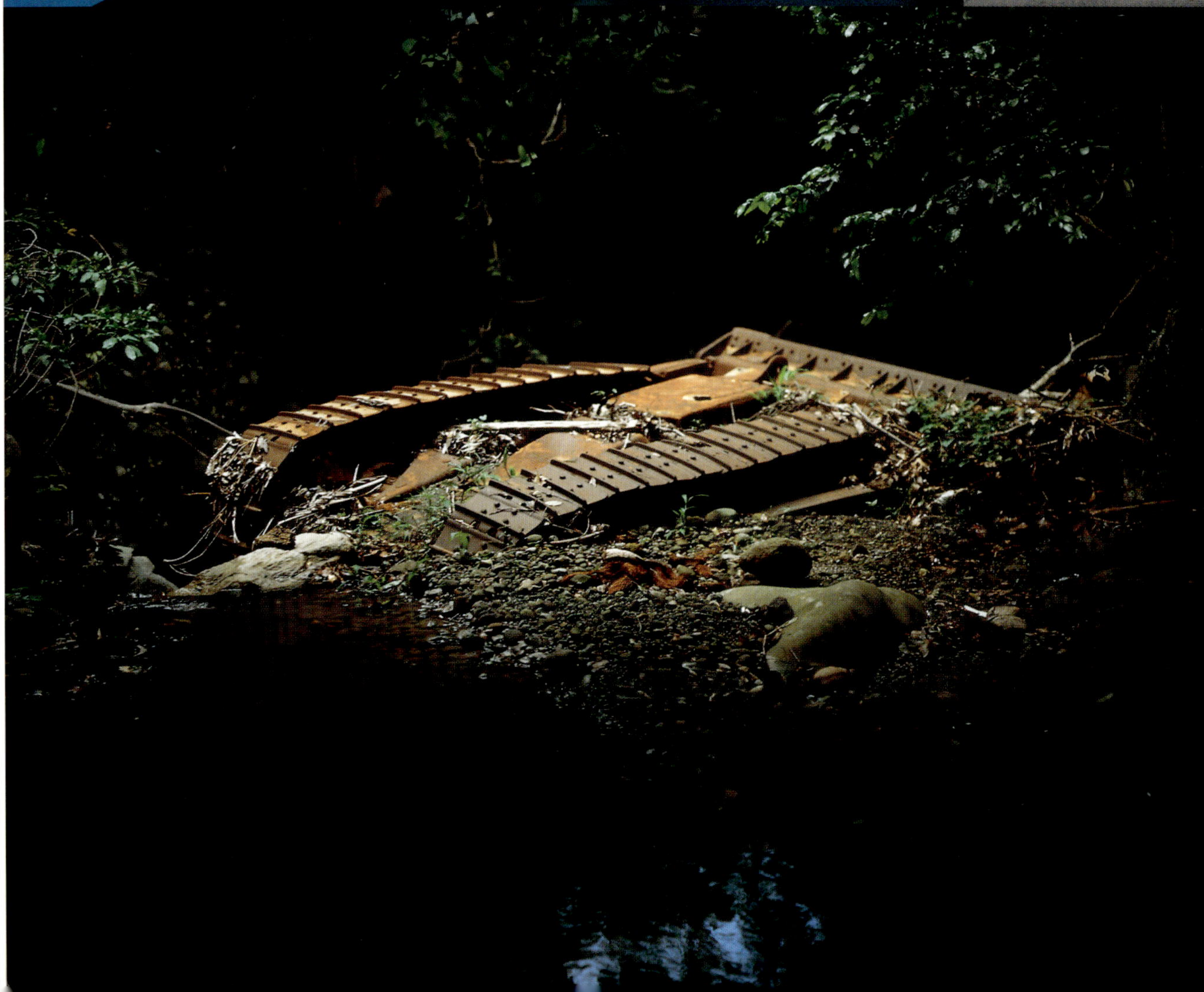

DOUG AITKEN, ERASER, 1998, 7-channel video installation, production stills and installation views at 303 Gallery, New York (top, left-hand page and bottom, right-hand page) / AUSLÖSCHER, 7-Kanal-Videoinstallation, Standaufnahmen und Installationsansichten (links oben und rechts unten).

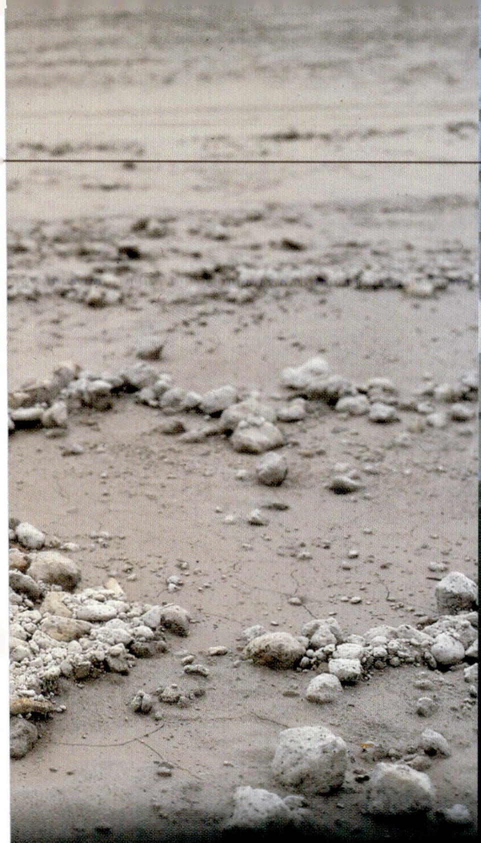

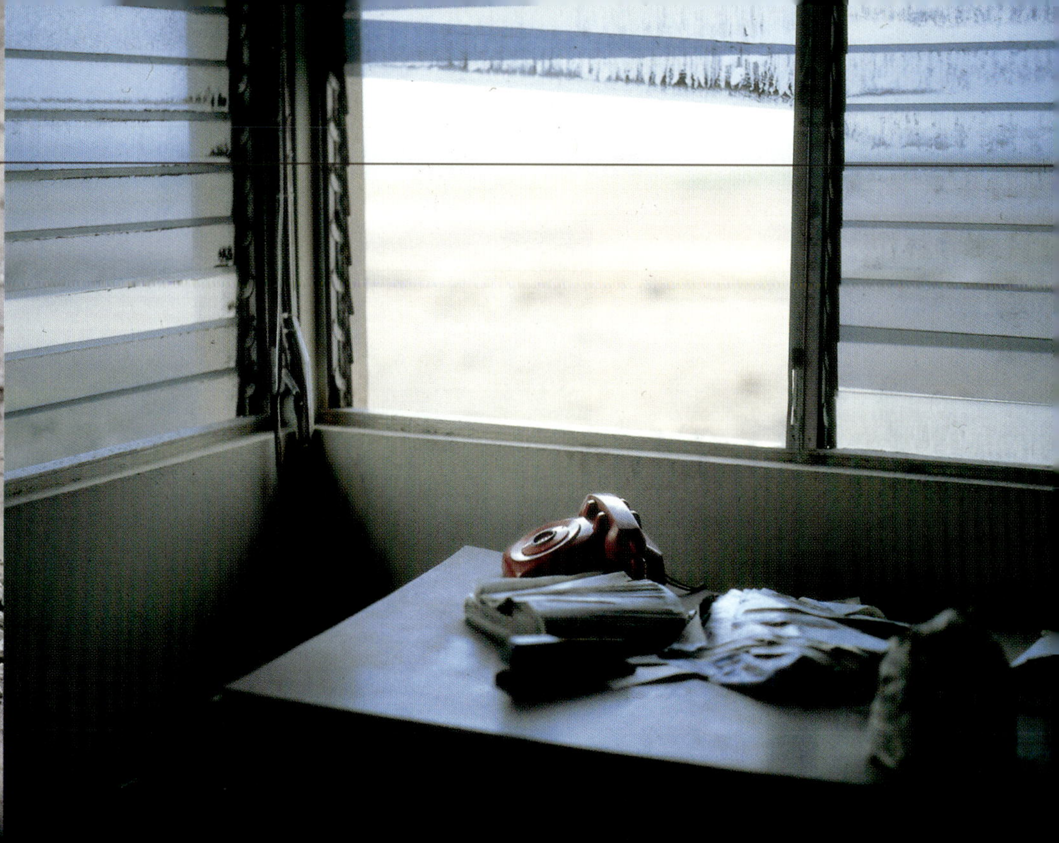

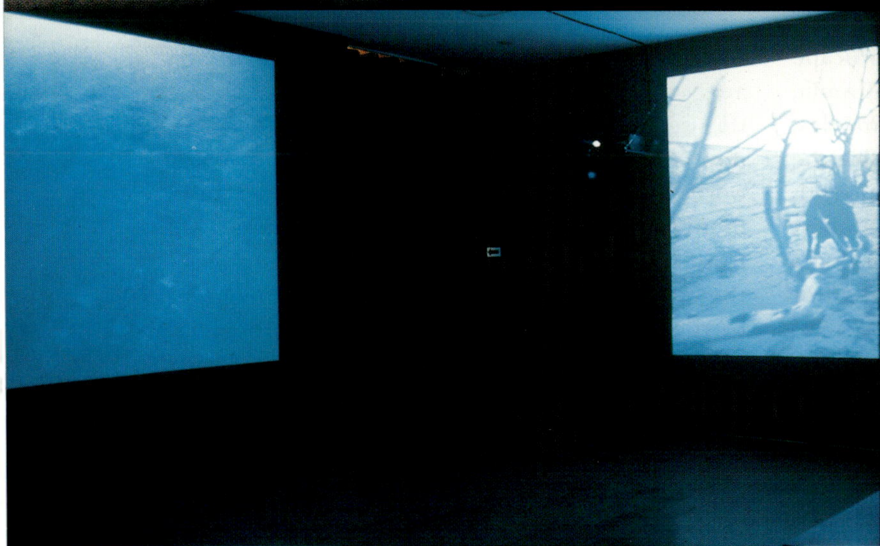

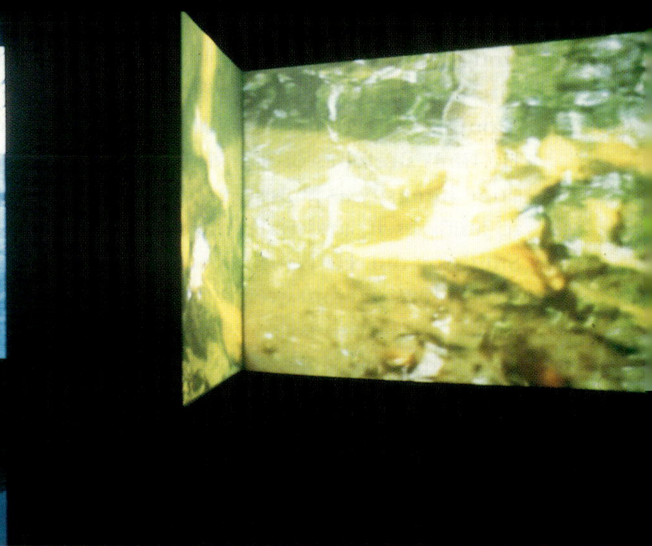

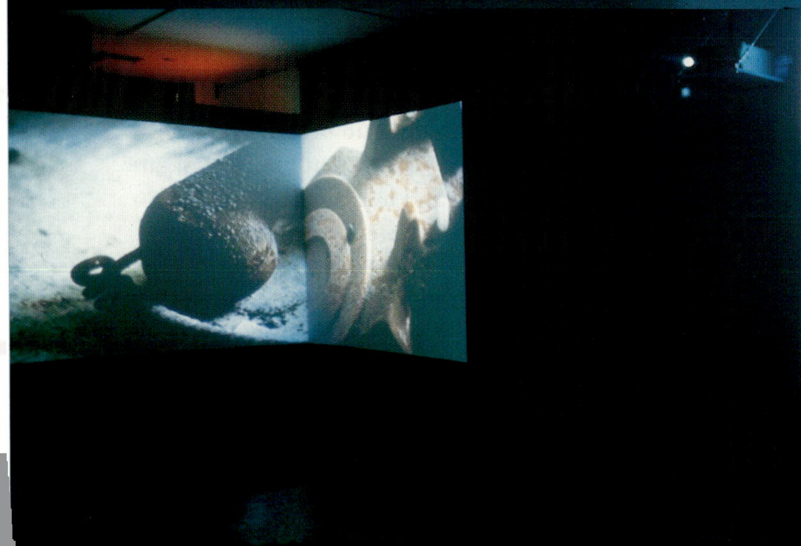

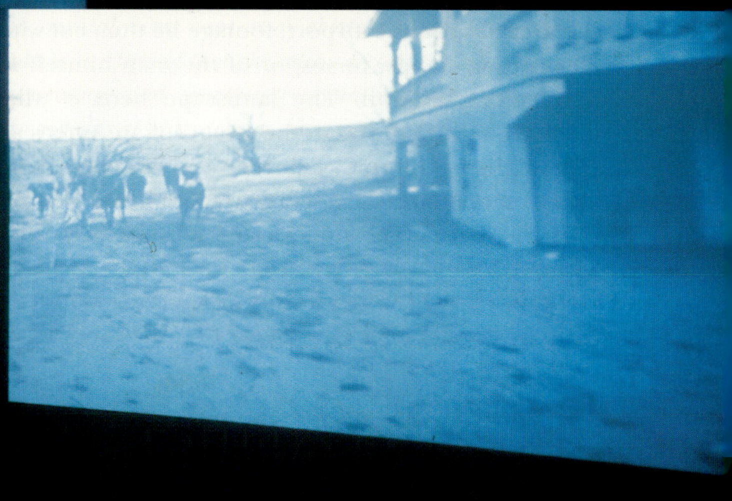

the liberty to create works that pose questions instead of delivering a closed set of information, packaged, condensed and boiled down to a sound bite."[3)]

Aitken's vision of the world leaves little room for man. Only a few traces of human life are noted in DIAMOND SEA and ERASER (1998). The latter work, filmed on the island of Montserrat in the Caribbean, draws us into a wild and hostile landscape where we find agricultural and industrial machinery and abandoned houses under stormy skies. Gradually we are led to discover a post-catastrophic landscape—the remains of the eruption of the island's volcano. Of human life on this island we detect but few signs: a petrified telephone, an interior shot of an empty supermarket, abandoned houses.

Yet ELECTRIC EARTH sets a man dispossessed and disoriented by the acceleration of the world in the center of the industrial landscape of Los Angeles. This character could be from some science fiction film where he plays the last man on earth. The very particular choice of landscape reminds one of the strange plot of land one finds amidst abandoned fields, plant matter, animal remains, and human detritus in Tarkovsky's film *The Stalker.* These landscapes are filmed both as macro- and microcosms, offering us a generous idea of the cosmos while exploring the strata of something concrete. The man who emerges from ELECTRIC EARTH seems to be a "stalker" wandering in an existential void. For Aitken the main character does not play the role of "passenger" or "passer-by"; instead, he is an active figure who does not seem to cross boundaries. That role remains reserved by the artist for the spectator. Furthermore, with Aitken there is no trace of mysticism or any relation to the sublime. We are in the quite real world of today, here at the turn of the century.

In ELECTRIC EARTH, the structure is amply deployed in space, inviting the viewer to discover, from room to room, a progression that proceeds from one wall-sized screen to the next via interstitial scrims. The "stalker" we become moves about, thus activating the narrative both physically and mentally.

Going back in time, we rediscover two earlier videos by Aitken that convey another vision of humanity: HYSTERIA (1998) is a compilation of film clips documenting thirty-five years of collective hysteria experienced during rock concerts. Here, unlike earlier work, the artist shows us the evolution of the mental state of audiences from the first Beatles concert, where they do no more than shout and shriek, to later concerts, where they participate in a great collective movement, as if part of the same body. The evolution depicted in HYSTERIA also draws our attention to those moments at some concerts where spectators are carried away to the point of violence.

There is something rather strange in the way humans are portrayed in hysteric guises in this video about spectators, with regard to Aitken's oeuvre as a whole. The same is true of THESE RESTLESS MINDS (1998), an installation that shows auctioneers alternating on three monitors in an endless litany of words, numbers, and descriptions of their surroundings. These images of superhuman characters are contrasted with seductive shots of banal, everyday surroundings such as garages, trucks, and radar antennas. The result is a view of humanity that tends towards overdose and excess. Man losing control, in the case of HYSTERIA, or tending to excess, in THESE RESTLESS MINDS, are two different aspects of humanity introduced in Aitken's work.

In his vast landscapes, the artist has accustomed us to a human absence marked only by traces left behind. To this vision is added a man dispossessed in a postindustrial "electric" universe. Aitken conceives of man as a nomad who has left his territories behind and fallen prey to "societal" neuroses. We are quite removed from the "post-human" and fragmented vision that we have become accustomed to in the work of his contemporaries. Will the role of "stalker" that Aitken has us, the viewers, playing be that of a passenger in a universe undergoing radical transformation from one century to another?

(Translated from the French by Warren Niesluchowski)

1) Robert Smithson, "A Sedimentation of the Mind: Earth Projects," *The Writings of Robert Smithson*, ed. Nancy Holt (New York: New York University Press, 1979), p. 82.
2) Dan Graham, *Dan Graham* (Santiago de Compostela: Centro Galego de Arte Contemporanea, 1997), pp. 161–162.
3) Francesco Bonami, "Doug Aitken. Making Work without Boundaries," *Flash Art*, May/June, 1998, p. 80.

DOUG AITKEN, PASSENGER, 1998, c-print laminated on Plexiglas, 39 x 48 x ¾" / PASSAGIER, C-Print auf Plexiglas, 99 x 122 x 2 cm.

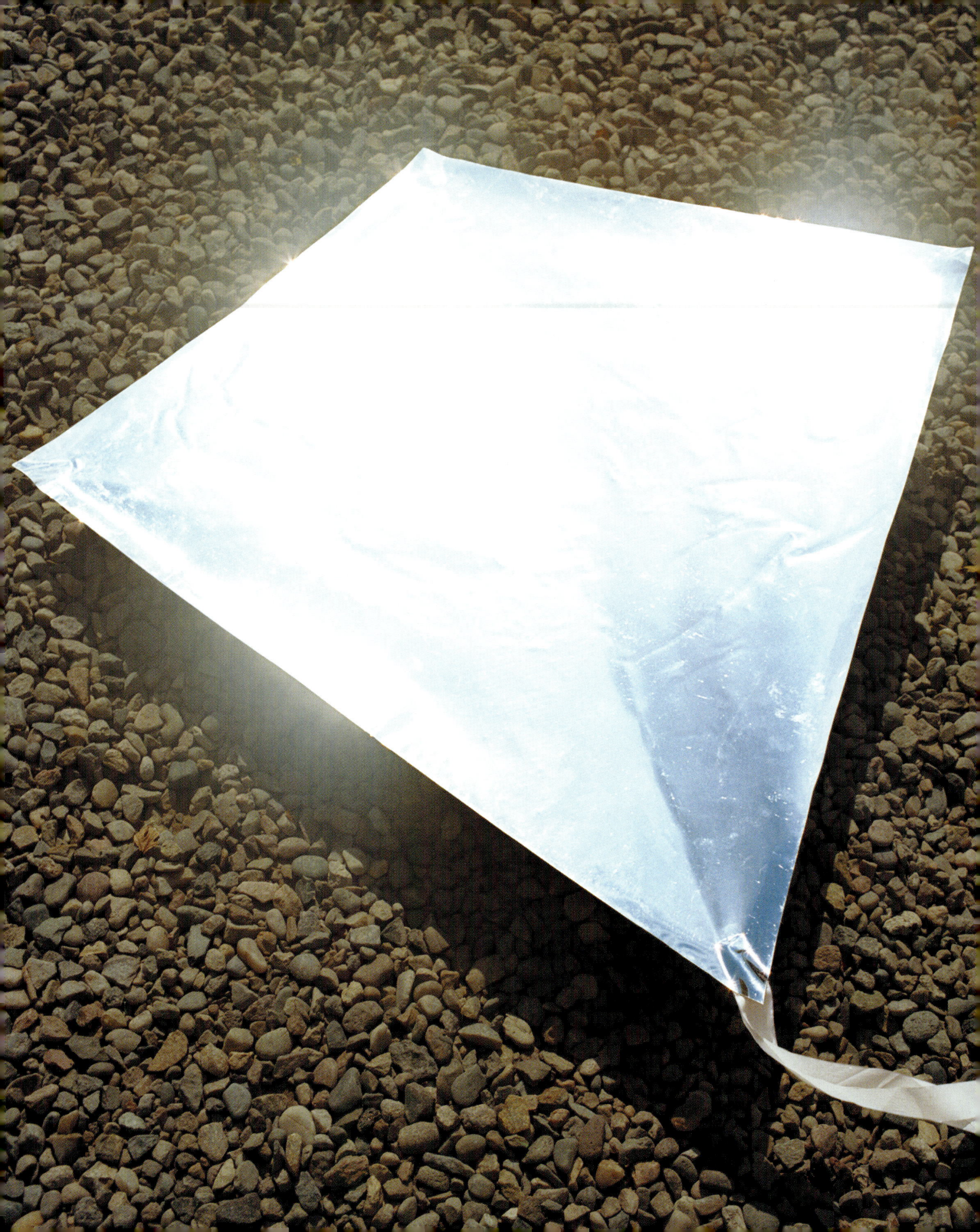

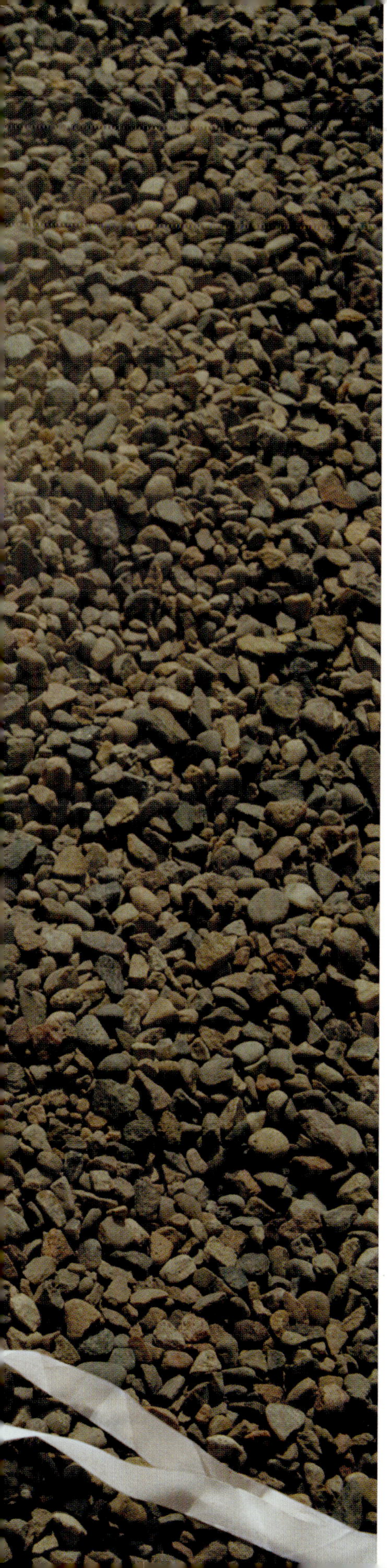

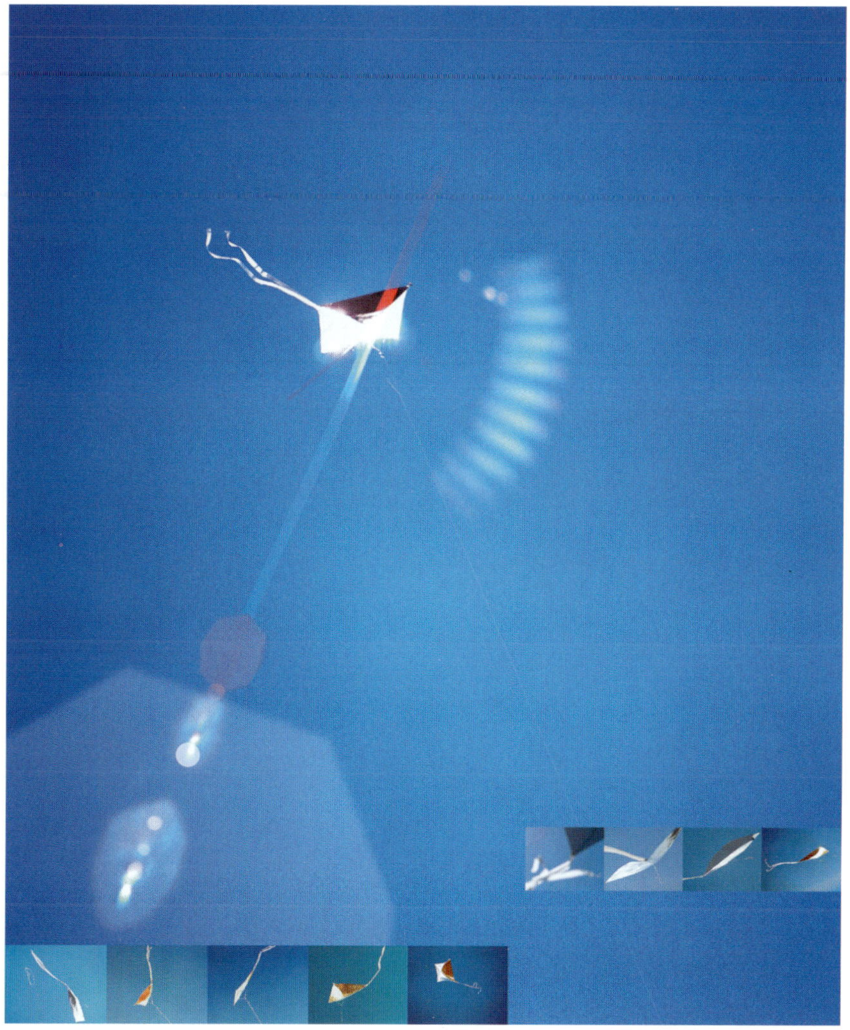

Edition for Parkett DOUG AITKEN

DECREASE THE MASS AND RUN LIKE HELL, 1999

Mirror kite, ca. 34 x 33½", tail 37⅜",
with poster of flying kite, ca. 20 x 15⅝".
Edition of 60, stamped and numbered

DIE MASSE VERKLEINERN UND RENNEN WIE DER TEUFEL, 1999

Spiegeldrachen, ca. 86,5 x 85 cm, Schwanz 95 cm,
Plakat mit fliegendem Drachen, 51 x 39,6 cm.
Auflage: 60, mit Prägestempel und nummeriert

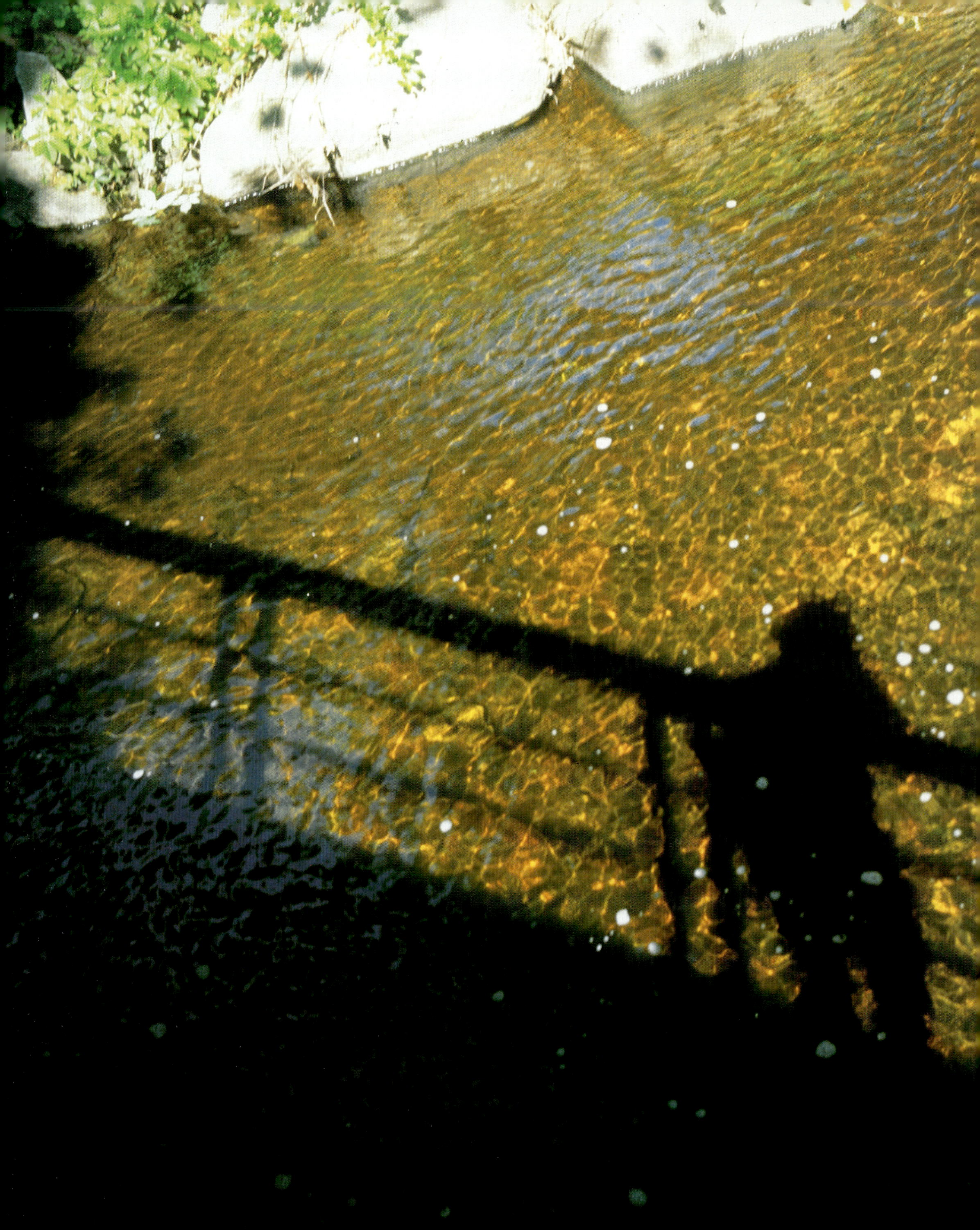

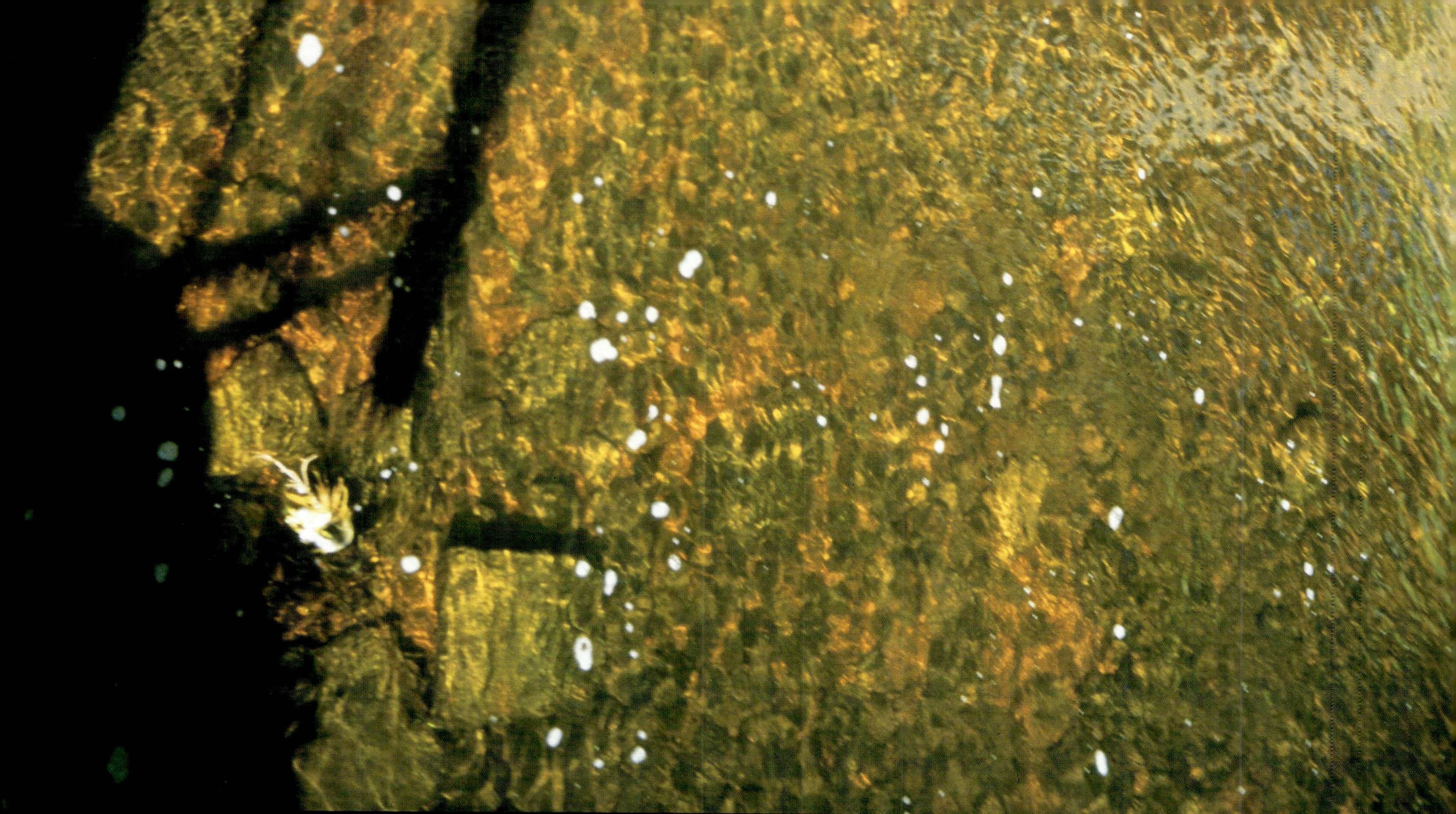

Nan Goldin

ELISABETH LEBOVICI

An den Rändern des Bildes

Ohne jede Diskussion gibt es eine Zeit vor und eine nach Nan Goldin. Ihr Werk, das sich aus Photographien, Tonbildschauen, Büchern und einem Film zusammensetzt und noch längst nicht abgeschlossen ist, hat der Kunst eine Bresche eröffnet, die weit über den Bereich der Photographie hinaus wirksam ist. Eine Bresche, die unwiderruflich ist: Seit die Künstlerin 1981 mit THE BALLAD OF SEXUAL DEPENDENCY (Die Ballade von der sexuellen Abhängigkeit) erstmals an die Öffentlichkeit trat, hat sie nämlich unseren Schönheitsbegriff tatsächlich verändert. Dies gelang ihr dank Bildern, die ohne jedes Vorurteil und jede Wertung auskommen. Indem sie mit einer Schar befreundeter Menschen eine ganze und vollständige Welt erschuf, aus der jedes normative Denken und jeder Bezug auf Normen überhaupt verbannt war. Und schliesslich dadurch, dass sie eine Erzählerin einführte in diese sich unablässig wiederholende Welt, diese «wiedergefundene Zeit»: ihre Zeit, ihre Welt. Ein neuer Schönheitsbegriff? Schon die Romantik und Baudelaire haben natürlich den alten Kanon revidiert und der uralten Anziehungskraft des Hässlichen, Monströsen, des Alters oder des Obszönen ihre eigene Würde verliehen. Aber mit oder vielmehr nach Nan Goldin hat sich nicht der Kanon gewandelt, sondern die Bezugnahme: Die Schönheit ist zu einer Beziehung geworden. Einer Beziehung innerhalb des Bildes, zwischen den photographierten Menschen und der Photographin und damit auch zu den Menschen, die das Bild betrachten werden.

«Nach landläufiger Ansicht ist der Photograph von Natur aus ein Voyeur – der Letzte, den man zu einer Party einladen würde. Doch ich dränge mich nirgends auf: Das ist meine Party. Es ist meine Familie, meine Geschichte», erklärte Nan Goldin.[1] Diese Verteidigung des Persönlichen gegen den Voyeurismus oder des Inneren gegen das Äussere, der Wiederholung gegen das Neue zeigt sich konkret in der Wahl von immer wieder ähnlichen Bildeinstellungen. Man weiss, dass Edward T. Hall, der die «Proxemik», das heisst das menschliche Raumverhalten, erforschte, vier Arten von Raumzonen unterschieden und gemessen hat: erstens die intime Zone (bis 40 cm), wo der Tast- und Geruchssinn die wichtigste Rolle spielen, der Spielraum zwischen Liebenden, Kämpfenden oder zwischen Mutter und Kind; dann der persönliche Bereich (bis 120 cm), das heisst die Umgebung bis auf Armeslänge; ferner der soziale Raum (bis 360 cm), entsprechend etwa der Entfernung im beruflichen Alltag, bei der die Person noch als Ganzes wahrgenommen wird; und schliesslich die öffentliche Zone (über 360 cm). Es ist kein Zufall, dass Nan Goldin im Allgemeinen vor der letzten Stufe Halt macht. Ihre Bilder zeigen nie die Ferne oder

ELISABETH LEBOVICI ist Kunstkritikerin der französischen Zeitung *Libération*.

Page/Seite 62/63: NAN GOLDIN, SELF-PORTRAIT AT GOLDEN RIVER ON BRIDGE, SILVER HILL, 1998 /

Unendlichkeit. Selbst ihre europäischen Landschaftsaufnahmen, das Wasser von Capri (SEA AT CAPRI, ITALY, 1997) oder das Hafenbecken in Venedig (GUIDO AT THE DOCK, VENICE, 1998), enthalten einen Lichtpunkt, der wie ein Scheinwerfer zur Annäherung und Kontaktaufnahme auffordert. Wo Nan Goldin ganz nah an ihre Sujets herangeht, mitunter bis an die Grenze der Halluzination, zeigt sie subjektive Zustände.

Sich im Spiegel betrachten. Im Bett liegen. Allein sein. Zusammen sein. Zum Ausgehen bereit sein. In einer Bar herumhängen. Diskutieren. Schlafen. Weinen. Sich umarmen. Die Handlungen, die Gefühle, die Freuden oder Leiden, die die Bilder zeigen, stehen weder in Zusammenhang mit einer beruflichen Tätigkeit noch mit dem öffentlichen Leben: Da gibt es keine Schule, kein Einkaufszentrum, keinerlei Arbeit; weder Ärzte noch Lehrer. Die Feinde wurden ausgeklammert. Erstaunt stellt man fest, dass die Gesichter, die Blicke – egal ob der Kamera zugewandt oder nicht – und die nackten oder bekleideten Körper auf eine Art gezeigt werden, die keinerlei kulturgeschichtlich vertraute Erinnerungen wachruft. Stellung und Anordnung der Körper knüpfen nicht an die Historienmalerei an, Verweise auf das Kino sind stets sekundär und erfolgen beispielsweise über die Travestie oder Transsexualität. Mit anderen Worten, die Bilder «ähneln» nicht einem künstlerischen Meisterwerk um es wie ein *Tableau vivant* oder ein Stillleben nachzubilden. Dasselbe gilt für die Gegenstände auf den Bildern, denen nichts Symbolisches anhaftet. Tatsächlich wirken sie ebenso vergänglich wie die Personen. Lampe, Bett, Spiegel, Badewanne sind weniger der «Besitz» der Körper, die sie beleuchten oder beherbergen, als dass sie ihnen zum Gebrauch dienen. Ebenso die Orte: Sei es ein Zimmer, eine Bar oder ein Zug – sie sind nicht Eigentum, sondern werden benutzt und abgenutzt. Sie tragen die Spuren der Zeit, sie sind niemals neu, niemals unendlich, nie zeitlos. Die Zeichen der Abnützung verleihen den intimen Situationen einen emotionalen und melancholischen Zug.

Nehmen wir das Porträt von Louise Bourgeois, die Nan Goldin (ebenso wie ihr Haus) für die Zeitschrift *Nest* photographiert hat.[2] (Es sei an dieser Stelle erlaubt, auf die neue Prägnanz von Nan Goldins Aufnahmen älterer Menschen hinzuweisen.) Louise Bourgeois ist eine Persönlichkeit, deren Züge man kennt, unter anderem dank der Photos von Mapplethorpe. Bei Nan Goldin jedoch wird Louise Bourgeois durch die empathische Kraft ihrer Photographien mitgerissen: Das Gesicht, die scharfblickenden, lächelnden Augen scheinen förmlich zur Bildfläche gezogen zu werden, auf die Kamera und auf das Auge des Betrachters zu. Die Art und Weise, wie Nan Goldin die Photographie einsetzt, lässt ihre Figuren, deren Spiegelbilder und die Gegenstände, mit denen sie in Berührung kommen, ganz nahe an der Grenzlinie zum Raum des Betrachters in Erscheinung treten. Nan Goldin markiert nie Distanz, weder eine öffentliche noch eine sittliche. Sie bietet selbst dem Tod die Stirn: Cookie Mueller in ihrem Sarg. Gilles Dusein tot im Spitalbett. Pornographie hätte es darauf abgesehen, dass sie Christus- oder Heiligenfiguren gleichen und uns eine Lektion in Schmerz erteilen. Aber diese leblosen Körper sind frei von Pathos, frei auch von jeglichem morbiden Ästhetizismus und dadurch dem Sichtbaren überantwortet. Der Tod existiert wie das Leben und wird er wie dieses spontan, im Moment, in dem er erlebt wird, festgehalten, entzieht er sich jeder spekulativen Darstellung.

Über ihre neusten Porträtaufnahmen sagt Goldin: «Ja, sie schauen in sich selbst hinein. Ich interessiere mich immer mehr dafür, wie man einem anderen Menschen näher kommen kann, um mit seinen Augen zu sehen und wirklich zu begreifen, was es heisst, ein anderer zu sein. Für mich liegt die eigentliche Frustration darin, dass da eine unüberwindliche Grenze ist.»[3] Dieser Wunsch nach Einfühlung erklärt zweifelsohne ihre Vorliebe für die Kunst Barnett Newmans oder Rothkos: eine *Shining forth*-Malerei, um den Titel eines Gemäldes von Newman aufzunehmen (SHINING FORTH, TO GEORGE, 1961). Eine überwältigende visuelle Erfahrung, die das Gefühl hervorruft, vollkommen konzentriert oder gebannt zu sein angesichts der farbigen Bildfläche, ihrer Brechungen und Übergänge, die sich zu einem einzigen und einzigartigen Erlebnis verdichten.

Ist die Schönheit bei Nan Goldin also eine Beziehung zwischen dem Bild und mir? *I'll Be Your Mirror*, der Titel des in Zusammenarbeit mit der BBC gedrehten Films wie auch des Katalogs zur Retrospektive im Whitney Museum, bringt das Schillernde dieser Beziehung gut zum Ausdruck.[4] Wer wird wessen Spiegel sein? Die Künstlerin jener ihrer Freunde? Umgekehrt? Oder ich? Dieser Dialog zwischen dem «Ich» und dem «Du», diesem «you», dem es im Englischen obliegt, die Distanz festzulegen (das Französische beispielsweise kann ja zwischen Duzen und Siezen wählen), ist auch eine Anregung die Welt politisch zu sehen. Nan Goldin bietet uns diese Welt dar, indem sie uns mit ihr vertraut macht. Dennis Cooper beschreibt diese unmittelbare Identifikation zwischen Nan Goldins und seiner Welt sehr gut: «Manche Bilder sind so banal wie irgendein Schnappschuss, der bei einem festlichen Anlass gemacht wurde. Andere sind dramatisch und schön wie Standbilder des *film noir*. Zusammen erzählen sie eine Geschichte, die nicht nur aus einem einzigen Erzählstrang besteht, sondern ein intimes Geflecht und eine Flut von Körpern und vor allem Gesichtern darstellt, die sich in ihrer Drogen- und Endorphin-Utopie verlieren. Nach neueren Filmen wie *Kids* oder *Trainspotting* ist es schwierig, sich vorzustellen, welche Verwunderung diese so intimen, so behutsamen, so wenig von einer bestimmten Welt gekennzeichneten Ansichten zunächst hervorriefen. (...) Es ist, als ob dank dieser Bilder von Lebensformen, die der meinen so ähnlich sind, mein eigenes chaotisches Verhalten einen Look, einen narrativen Zusammenhang, eine Ästhetik erhielte.»[5] Es gibt eine Realität n a c h Nan Goldin, denn ihre Bilder durchdringen meine Erinnerungen, und mein Gedächtnis ist ein Goldin'sches geworden.

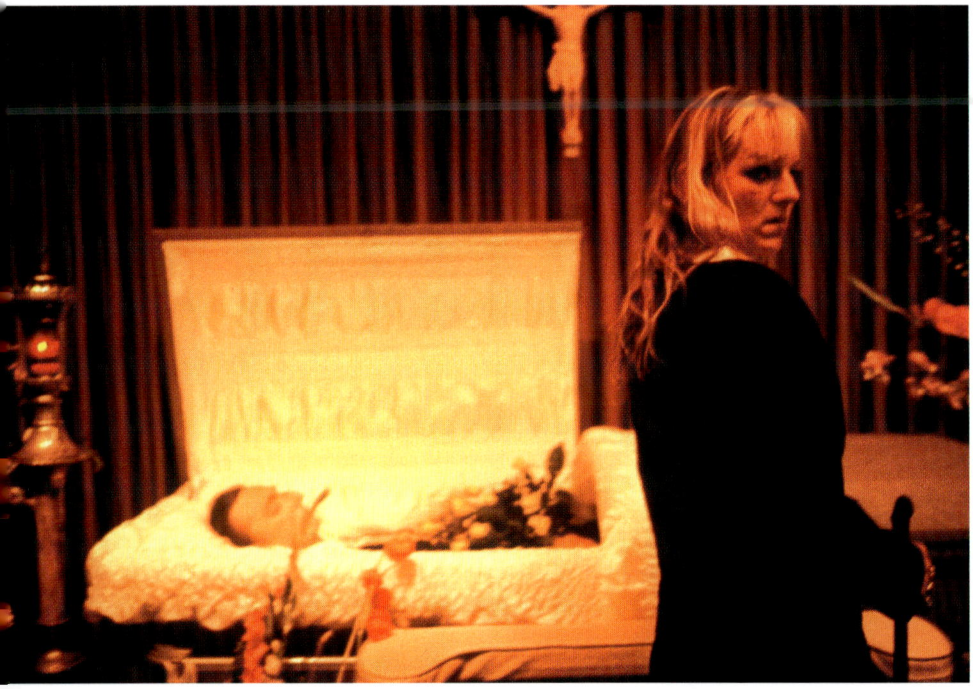

NAN GOLDIN, COOKIE AT VITTORIO'S CASKET, NYC SEPT. 16, 1989 / COOKIE AN VITTORIOS SARG, NEW YORK, 16. SEPT. 1989.

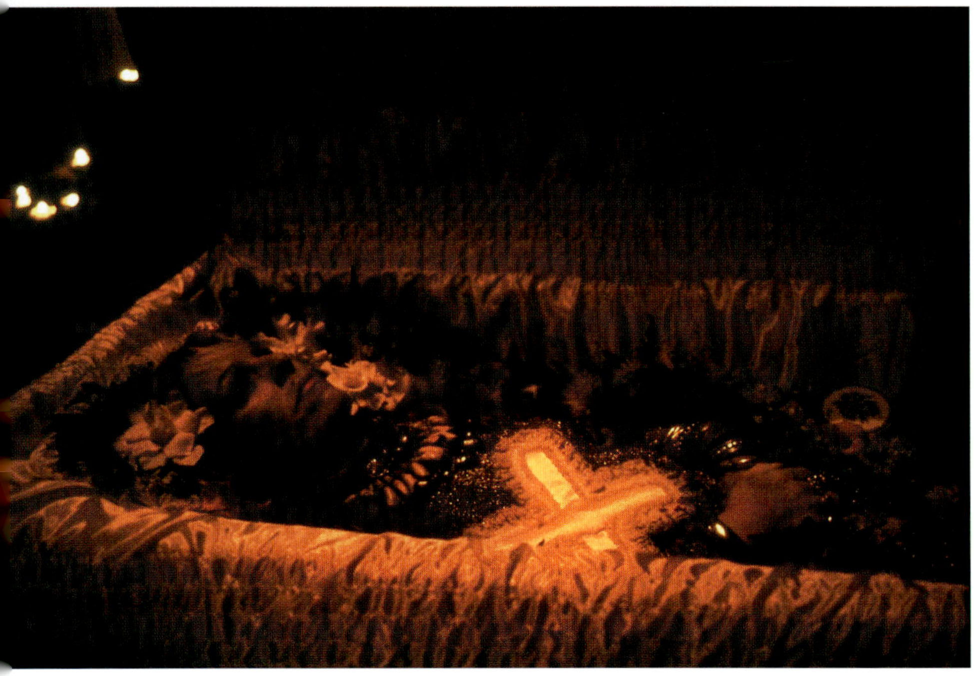

NAN GOLDIN, COOKIE IN HER CASKET, NYC, NOV. 15, 1989 / COOKIE IN IHREM SARG, NEW YORK, 15. NOV. 1989.

Die Intimität jedoch haben andere Photographen, andere Künstler, andere Schriftsteller (Genêt) schon vor ihr entdeckt. Dazu gehört natürlich Robert Frank, gehört Larry Clark mit *Tulsa*, gehören Warhol und Fassbinder. Diese Männer haben die Sicht von innen gewählt, indem sie sich in ihre Bilder hineinversetzten. Einige Frauen, so Lisette Model und Diane Arbus, haben einen freundschaftlichen Blick auf jene Menschen gerichtet, die Foucault als «Anormale» bezeichnet, Männer und Frauen, die ausserhalb der Norm stehen, also bisweilen jeder und jede. Doch während sich die Männer dafür entscheiden können, sich im Innern ihrer Bilder zu positionieren, sind die Frauen seit frühester Kindheit diesem Zwang unterworfen. «Ich kann nicht abstrakt von der Beziehung zwischen einem kleinen Mädchen und seinem Macho-Vater sprechen», sagt Louise Bourgeois und stellt diese Beziehung als Skulptur dar. Basiert die Universalität des Ödipuskomplexes nicht stets auf dem Modell des Knaben, der in die Mutter verliebt ist und zum Nebenbuhler des Vaters wird? Haftet dem Ödipuskomplex beim Mädchen, das sein Objekt wechseln muss, nicht bereits etwas Konstruiertes an? Da sie traditionell im weiblichen Bereich angesiedelt ist, wurde die Intimität lange gering geschätzt, ehe sie zum akzeptierten Bestandteil westlicher Alltagskultur wurde: im Gesundheitswesen wie in Kunst und Literatur; im Fernsehen wie im Strafvollzug. Vielleicht weil jede Auseinandersetzung mit der Intimität damit beginnt, Körper und Gesten konkret wiederzugeben und das einzelne Leben gegenüber der allgemeinen Kultur hervorzuheben; entgegen allen Klischees und Gemeinplätzen, die stets einer anonymen Kultur entspringen, wo ein Schwarzer, eine Lesbe, ein Transsexueller immer die imaginäre Figur des Schwarzen, der Lesbe, des Transsexuellen verkörpert. Um diese Leichtfertigkeit zu unterlaufen, mit der Angehörige einer Minderheit lediglich als Symbole oder Symptome wahrgenommen werden, repräsentieren die Männer, Frauen, Transvestiten und Transsexuellen bei Nan Goldin nichts anderes als ihren Vornamen. Dieser Vorname, mit dem Goldin ihre Sujets benennt, garantiert ihnen ihre unvergleichliche Einzigartigkeit, ohne sich «im Namen des Vaters» und in Bezug auf irgendeine gesellschaftliche Identität aufzudrängen. Die Summe dieser Vornamen und ihre Wiederholung bilden so eine Gemeinschaft, die vom «Du» zusammengehalten wird und ihre Identität – insbesondere jene des Aussenseiters – anders definiert, als die allgemeine Gesellschaftsordnung.

Auf die Frage, ob sie ihre Arbeit als politisch betrachte, antwortete Nan Goldin: «Natürlich. Immer. Es geht darum, was in einer Gesellschaft als privat betrachtet wird öffentlich zu machen. Es geht darum, die wirklichen Lebensgeschichten der Leute zur Sprache zu bringen und nicht bloss Medienversionen, und es geht auch darum, aufzuzeigen, dass im Leben in Sachen Sexualität und Geschlecht alle Möglichkeiten ihre Berechtigung haben und keine Variante weniger legitim ist als eine andere.»[6] Es gilt stets von neuem, ein kollektives Bild zu entwerfen, das gegen das geltende Privileg des Geschlechtsunterschiedes bei der Identitätsbildung jedes Individuums Widerstand leistet, ein Privileg, das einer heterosexistischen Ideologie entspringt. Immer.

Immer: Das Aussergewöhnliche an der Arbeit Nan Goldins ist ihre Abscheu vor der Trauer, die sich in der Weigerung äussert Menschen aufzugeben. Die Einzigartigkeit des autobiographischen Werks von Nan Goldin beruht darauf, dass es durch andere und mit anderen entsteht, in einer unermüdlichen, aber dennoch immer unvorhersehbaren Reorganisation dieser Bilder, die ihr so nahe stehen, dass sie sie nie fallen lässt, und mit denen sie intensive Beziehungen unterhält, indem sie sie immer wieder zu anderen Geschichten zusammenstellt. Hypothese: Arbeitet Nan Goldin vielleicht in der Lücke zwischen Geschichte und Erinnerung, wie Rauschenberg aus der Kluft zwischen Kunst und Leben zu schöpfen versuchte? Eine unwiderrufliche, Schwindel erregende Bresche voller Sehnsucht und Melancholie.

(Übersetzung aus dem Französischen: Irene Aeberli)

1) Auszug aus THE BALLAD OF SEXUAL DEPENDENCY, 1986, zitiert von Vince Aletti, in *Out*, Oktober 1996, S. 94.

2) *Nest*, Nr. 4, Frühjahr 1999.

3) Nan Goldin im Interview mit Scott Rothkopf in der Zeitschrift *The Advocate*, Frühjahr 1999.

4) Das Chanson von Lou Reed geht wie folgt weiter: «I'll be your mirror, reflect what you are in case you don't know… I find it hard to believe you don't know the beauty that you are.»

5) Dennis Cooper, «The Ballad of Nan Goldin», *All Ears: Cultural Criticism, Essays and Obituaries* (New York: Soft Skull Press, 1999).

6) Nan Goldin, interview, «Nobody Symbolizes Anything», *Harvard Gay and Lesbian Review*, vol. IV, No. 3, Sommer 1997, S. 16.

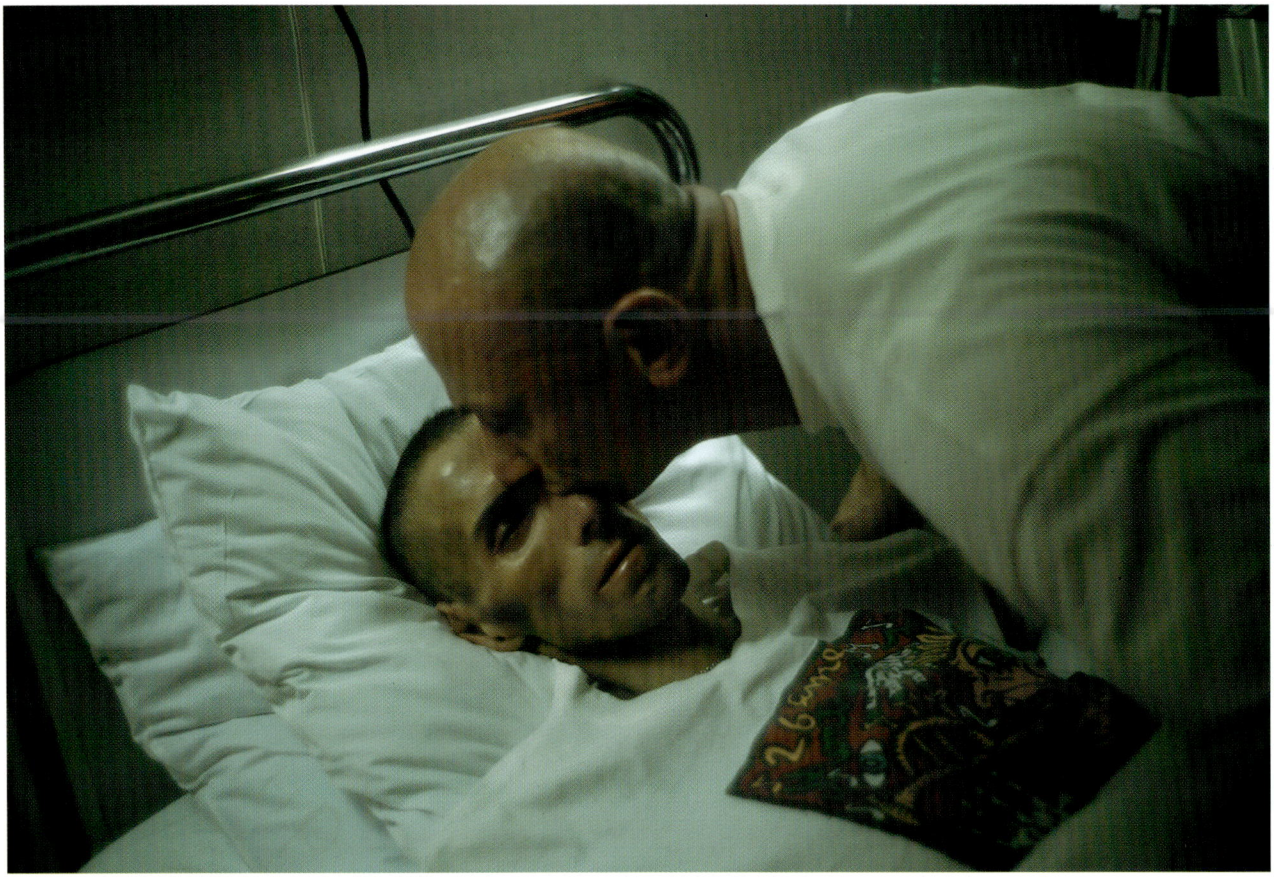

NAN GOLDIN, GOTSCHO KISSING GILLES, PARIS, 1993 / GOTSCHO KÜSST GILLES.

On the Edges of the Image

ELISABETH LEBOVICI

There's no doubt about it—there's a before- and an after-Goldin. Goldin's opus, composed of photographs, slide-shows, books, and a film, a body of work not yet closed, has opened a breach in the fine arts with repercussions far beyond the field of photography. It is an irremediable one: From the artist's first public showing of THE BALLAD OF SEXUAL DEPENDENCY in 1982, she has indeed changed our notion of beauty. She has done this by disseminating images with no preconceptions and no prejudging, making her group of friends, male and female, into a world whole and entire from which normative thinking, even reference to a norm, is banished. And to which, finally, she has added a female narrator of a world continually reiterated, a (Proustian) Time Regained: her world, her time. Is this a new idea of beauty? Of course Romanticism and Baudelaire had obviously changed our canonical notion, by conferring a certain dignity on our long-standing fascination with ugliness, monstrosity, old-age, or impurity. But with Goldin—or rather after her—it is not the canon that has changed, it is our relationship to it. Beauty has become a relationship within the image itself, between the people portrayed and their photographer, and, thereby, also with the people who look at the picture.

"There is a popular notion that the photographer is by nature a voyeur, the last one invited to the party. But I'm not crashing; this is my party. This is my family, my history."[1] This claim of the personal over the voyeuristic, of the interior over the exterior, of reiteration over novelty, is made concrete by a framing that often recurs in her images. Edward T. Hall, in researching "proxemics," that is, the study of how humans use distance, measured and identified four types of distance in particular: first, the intimate, up to sixteen inches, where touch and smell predominate, the space of the loving and maternal distance of struggle; then the domain of the personal, up to four feet, the distance of a handshake; thirdly, social distance, up to twelve feet, that of professional interaction, where the person appears whole; and finally, beyond that, public distance. It is not without significance that Goldin generally stops before reaching the last stage. The spaces circumscribed in her images never describe either the infinite or distances. Even her European landscapes, SEA AT CAPRI, ITALY, 1997 or GUIDO AT THE DOCK, VENICE, 1998, bear within themselves a luminous point, like a beacon calling out for closeness and contact. The states of subjectivity in Goldin's work are achieved by closing in on her subjects, sometimes almost to the point of an addictive hallucination.

Looking in the mirror. Lying in bed. Being alone. Being together. Dressing to go out. Hanging out in a bar. Talking. Sleeping. Crying. Kissing. The actions or feelings, the joys or sorrows, shown in the pictures relate neither to professional activity nor to public life: There's no school, shopping mall, or work, no doctors or teachers. Enemies have been removed. It is striking how the faces and their gazes, whether or not they are looking towards the lens, or the bodies, naked or dressed, evoke so little of our common cultural heritage. The positions and ordering of the bodies are not copied from history painting, and references to cinema are always secondary, mediated, for example, by drag. In other words, the pictures do not "resemble" any artistic masterpiece, as in a *tableau vivant* or a still life. This is also true of the objects included in the pictures; there is nothing at all symbolic about them. They are quite as impermanent as the people portrayed. Lamps, beds, mirrors, tubs: All are not so much the "property" of the bodies they illuminate or shelter but rather something for their use. In the same way, the places, whether a room, a bar, or a train, do not belong, but serve; they are used, never new, never timeless. Signs of use lend the intimacy of the situations an emotional or melancholy mood.

Take the portrait of Louise Bourgeois, along with her house, made by Goldin for *Nest* magazine.[2] Bourgeois is a person whose features, as popularized in photographs by Robert Mapplethorpe, among others, are well known. But Bourgeois is drawn by Goldin into the empathetic force of her photographs; her face and sagacious eyes and smile are brought up to the photographic surface, as it were, towards the lens, and from there to the eye of the viewer. The "manner" in which Goldin uses the camera brings the personages, their reflections, and the objects that touch them flush to the very edge of the border that separates them from the space of the viewer. Goldin never displays any distance, public or chaste. She confronts death: Cookie Mueller in her coffin, Gilles Dusein in the hospital, dead. A pornographic reading would make the people look like Christ or saints, conveying a lesson of pain. But these lifeless bodies are without pathos, without the least hint of morbid aestheticism, and therefore restored to unjudgmental visibility. Death exists just as life does, and when it is spontaneously recorded at the moment it is experienced, it escapes any speculative representation.

ELISABETH LEBOVICI is art critic of the French journal *Libération*.

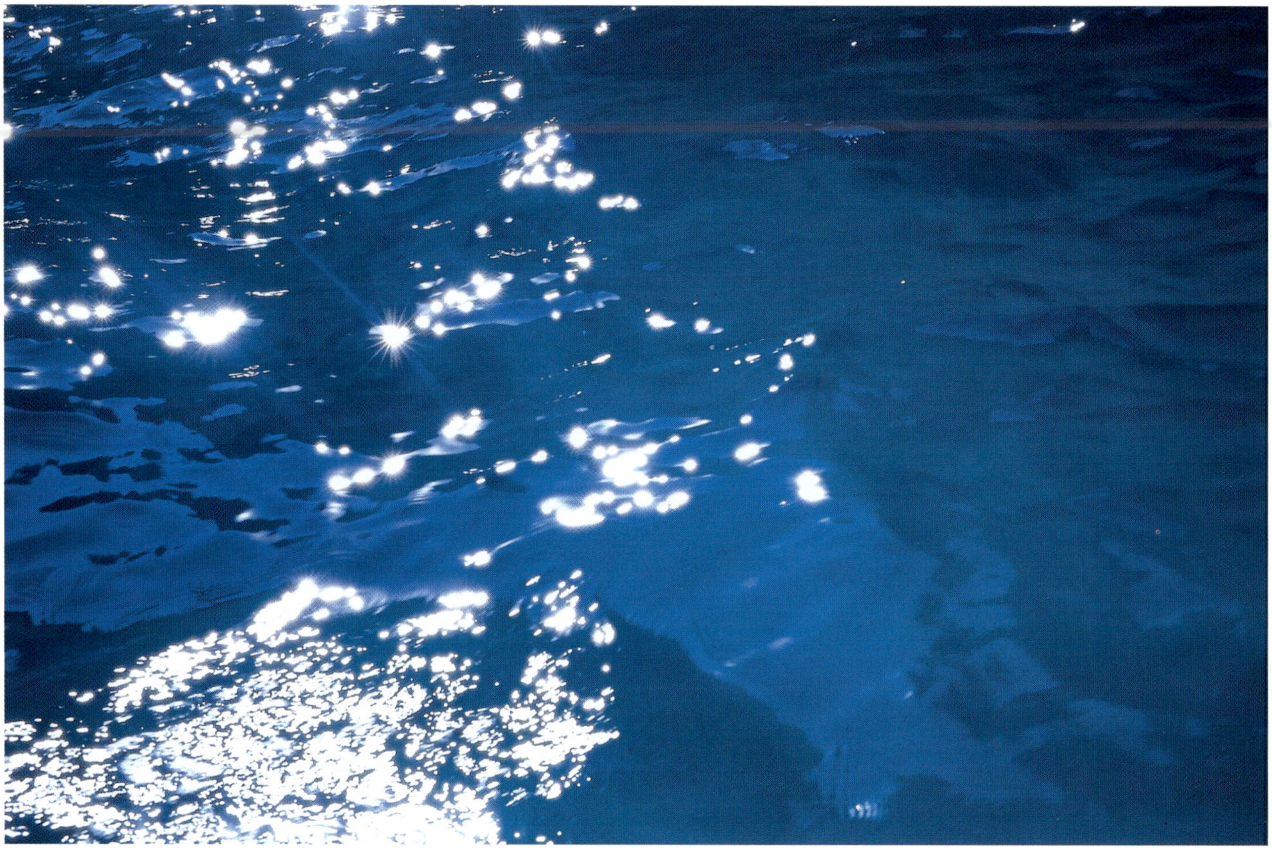

NAN GOLDIN, SEA AT CAPRI, ITALY, 1997 / MEER BEI CAPRI, ITALIEN.

NAN GOLDIN, LOUISE BOURGEOIS, NEW YORK, 1998.

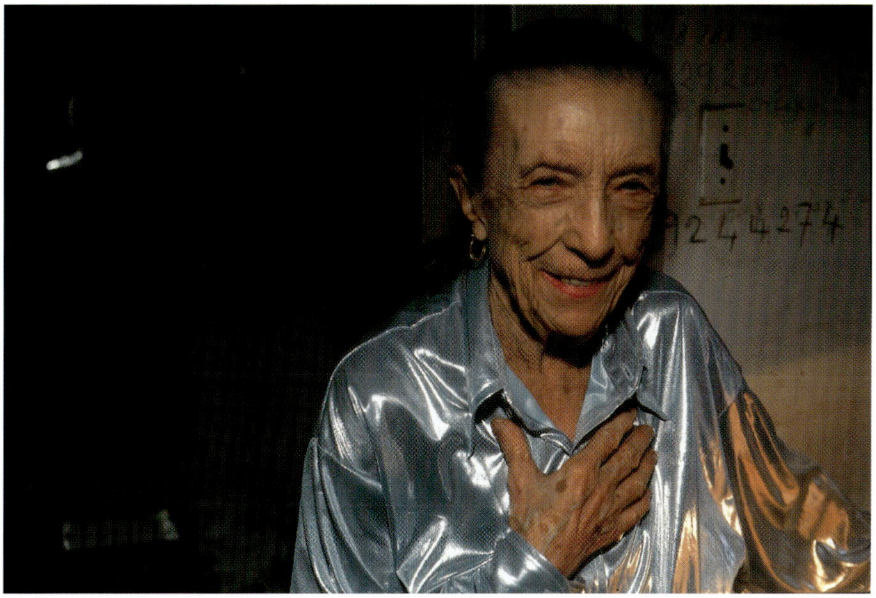

Of the faces she has recently photographed she says, "Yes, they're looking into themselves. I've become really interested in how close you can come to another human being, to see out of their eyes, to really understand what it is to be another person. For me that's the real frustration, the boundary you can never pass."[3] This will to empathy no doubt explains her affinity for the art of Barnett Newman or Mark Rothko, painting "shining forth," to cite the title of a Newman work (SHINING FORTH, TO GEORGE, 1961), a dazzling visual experience that produces the sensation of being entirely and wholly focused or suspended in confrontation with colored surface, its ruptures and passages converging on one unique and singular event.

Thus for Goldin beauty is a relation between the image and the self. *I'll Be Your Mirror*, the title of the film she did for the BBC, and the title of the catalogue for her Whitney retrospective, conveys the ambiguity of the overture.[4] Who will be the mirror of whom? The artist, of her friends? The opposite? Or me? This dialogue between the "I" and "you," the "you" to which English entrusts the task of dealing with distance (the French can choose between the familiar *tu* and the formal *vous*, for example) also provides an impetus to think of the world politically. Goldin offers us this world by making it familiar to us. Dennis Cooper captures this immediate identification between Goldin's world and his: "Some of the images are as ordinary as a snapshot taken on some festive occasion. Others are as dramatic and beautiful as stills from a film noir. Together they tell a story which isn't one, but rather an intimate web and flow of bodies, particularly of faces, lost in their utopia of drugs and endorphins. It is difficult to imagine, after recent films like *Kids* or *Trainspotting*, the surprise one feels at views so intimate, so cautious, and so unstyled, of that world. It was as if, through her pictures of lives so similar to mine, my own fucked-up behavior acquired a look, a narrative coherency, or an aesthetic."[5] There is an after-Nan Goldin, since her images color my memories, and my memory has become a Goldinian one.

The choice of intimacy, however, was made by other photographers, artists, and writers before her, like Genêt. There was, of course, Robert Frank; there was Larry Clark and *Tulsa*; there was Warhol; and there was Fassbinder. Those men made the choice to be in the interior, implicating themselves in their images. A few women, like Lisette Model and Diane Arbus, cast a kind gaze on those whom Michel Foucault called the "abnormal," those outside the norm, who are, at one point or another, each and every one of us. But men can choose to be within their images, while women are compelled from childhood to be within, to be concrete. "I cannot speak in the abstract of the relationship between a little girl and her macho father," says artist Louise Bourgeois. Instead she sculpts it. Is the universality of the Oedipus complex itself not built on the model of the little boy, in love with his mother and a rival to his father? For the girl, obliged to change the object of her love from mother to father, there is already something improvised about the Oedipus complex. Since it has traditionally been associated with the feminine, intimacy was always a devalued concept in Western culture, before becoming established as an irremediable given, in the domain of health as well as in art and literature, on TV as well as in jail. This is perhaps because any work on intimacy begins with making bodies and acts concrete, setting singular lives against the culture, against the clichés and commonplaces that always come from an anonymous culture where a black, a lesbian, or a transsexual always represents the imaginary figure of the Black, the Lesbian, or the Transsexual. To counteract the ease with which members of a minority are merely perceived as symbols or symptoms, the men and women, the transsexuals and transvestites, portrayed in Nan Goldin's pictures represent nothing but their first names. This first name, used by Goldin as the only means of identifying her subjects, endows them with their incomparable singularity without the imposition of the "name of the father" or any other social identity. The sum of these first names and their repetition thus establishes a genuine community, held together by a "you," and with an identity—especially the aspect of being outsiders—that is defined differently from the way society in general defines it.

Asked if she considered her work political, Nan Goldin answered: "Of course. It has a political agenda, it always has. The agenda is about making what is considered private in a society, public. It is about discussing real histories of people's life [sic] rather than media versions of histories and it's about making it clear that all possibilities of gender and sexuality are legitimate in life, and that all possibilities of gender are as valid as any other."[6] One always has to reinvent a collective image that refuses to submit to the privilege accorded to sexual difference in the formation of the identity particular to every individual, a privilege that derives from a heterosexist ideology. Always.

Always: What's so extraordinary about Goldin's work is her disgust with mourning, manifested in her refusal to abandon people. The singularity of her autobiographical work lies in the fact that it is done by others and with others, in a tireless but always unpredictable fashion of reorganizing images so close to her that she can never abandon them, and with which she maintains an intense relationship, each time composing new stories. A hypothesis: Is Goldin striving to work in the space between memory and history, the same way Rauschenberg attempted to work inside the gap between art and life, that irremediable, melancholic, languishing, and vertiginous breach?

(Translated from the French by Warren Niesluchowski)

1) Excerpted from THE BALLAD OF SEXUAL DEPENDENCY, 1986. Cited by Vince Aletti, in *Out*, October 1996, p. 94.
2) *Nest*, no. 4, Spring 1999.
3) Nan Goldin in an interview with Scott Rothkopf, *The Advocate*, Spring 1999.
4) The song, "I'll Be Your Mirror" written by Lou Reed, goes: "I'll be your mirror, reflect what you are, in case you don't know… I find it hard to believe you don't know the beauty that you are."
5) Dennis Cooper, "The Ballad of Nan Goldin," *All Ears: Cultural Criticism, Essays, and Obituaries* (New York: Soft Skull Press, 1999).
6) Nan Goldin interview, "Nobody Symbolizes Anything," *Harvard Gay and Lesbian Review*, Summer 1997, vol. IV, no. 3, p. 16.

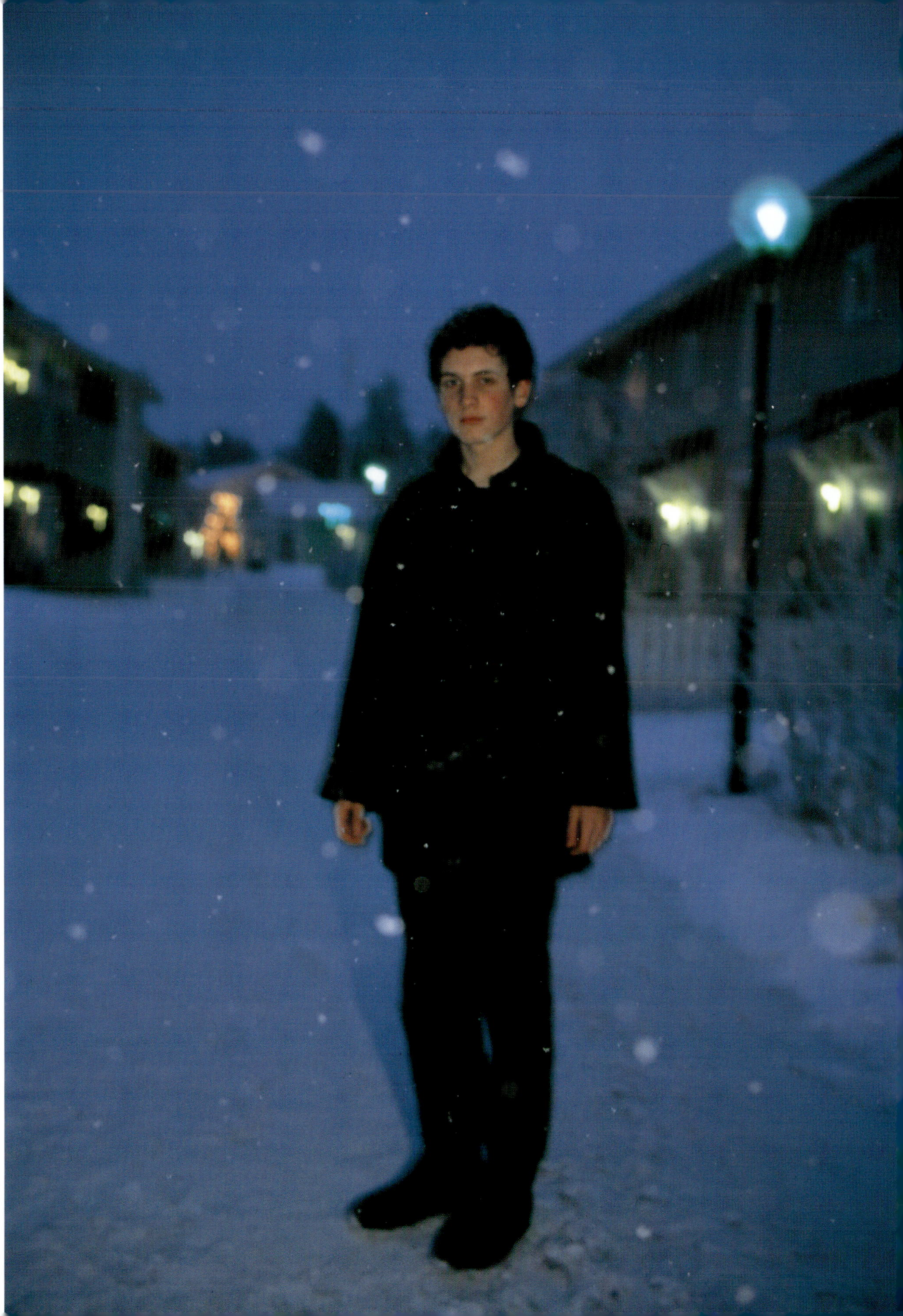

NAN GOLDIN, SIMON IN THE SNOW AT DAWN, CHRISTMAS, UMEÅ, SWEDEN, 1997 / SIMON IM SCHNEE BEI TAGESANBRUCH, WEIHNACHTEN, UMEÅ, SCHWEDEN.

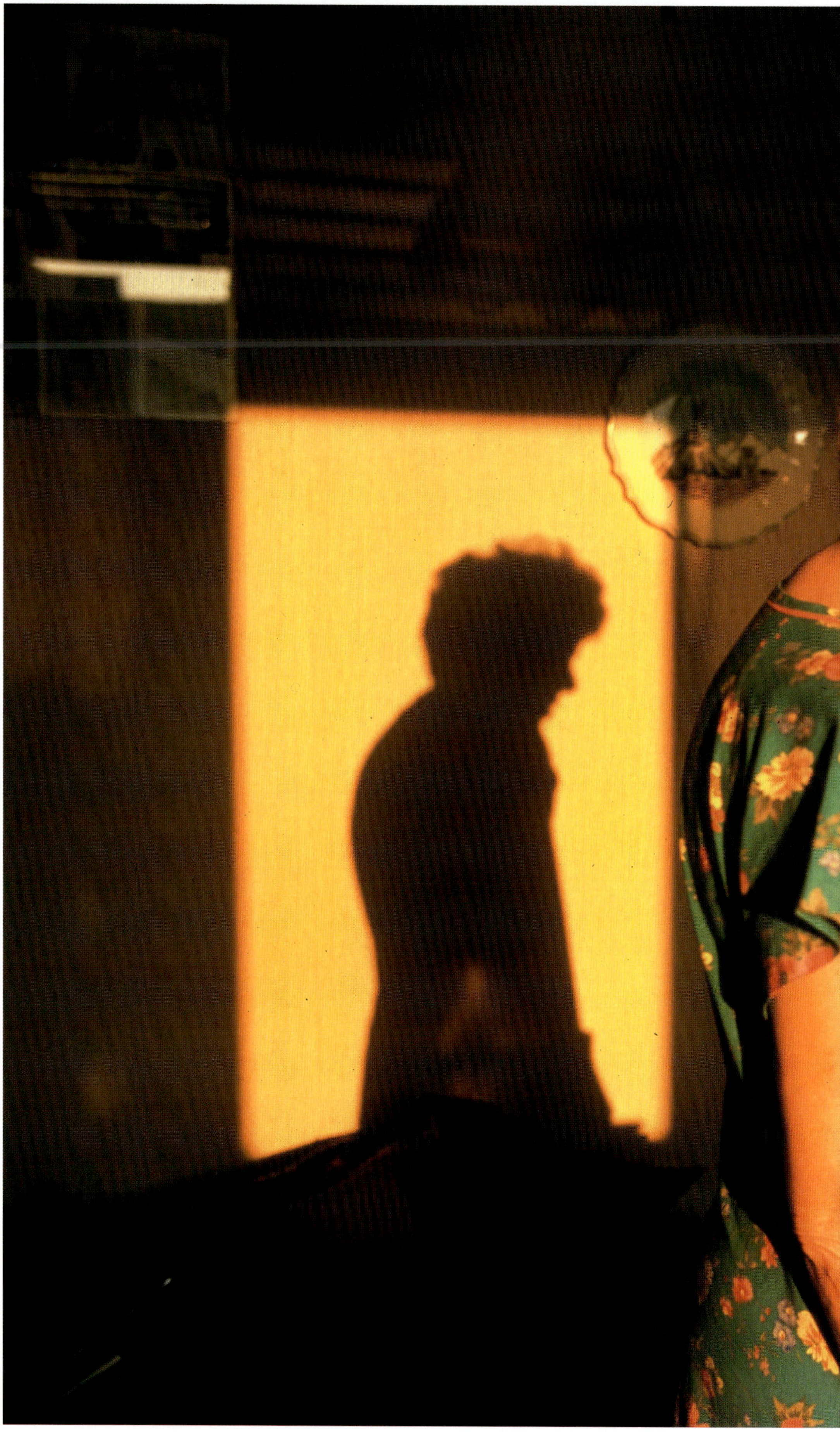

NAN GOLDIN, GUIDO WITH MOTHER AND GRANDMOTHER AND SHADOW, TURIN, 1999 /
GUIDO MIT MUTTER UND GROSSMUTTER UND SCHATTEN, TURIN.

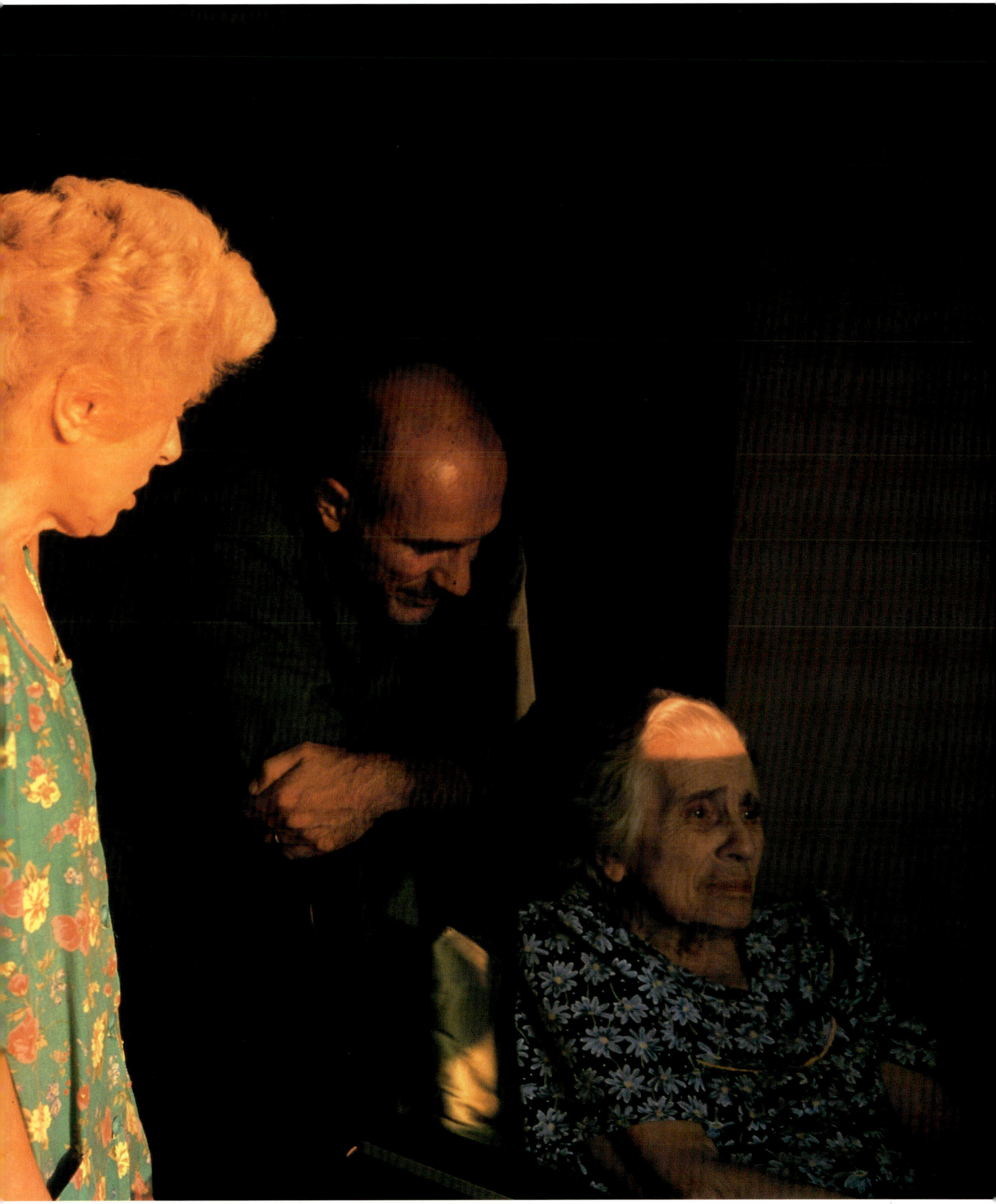

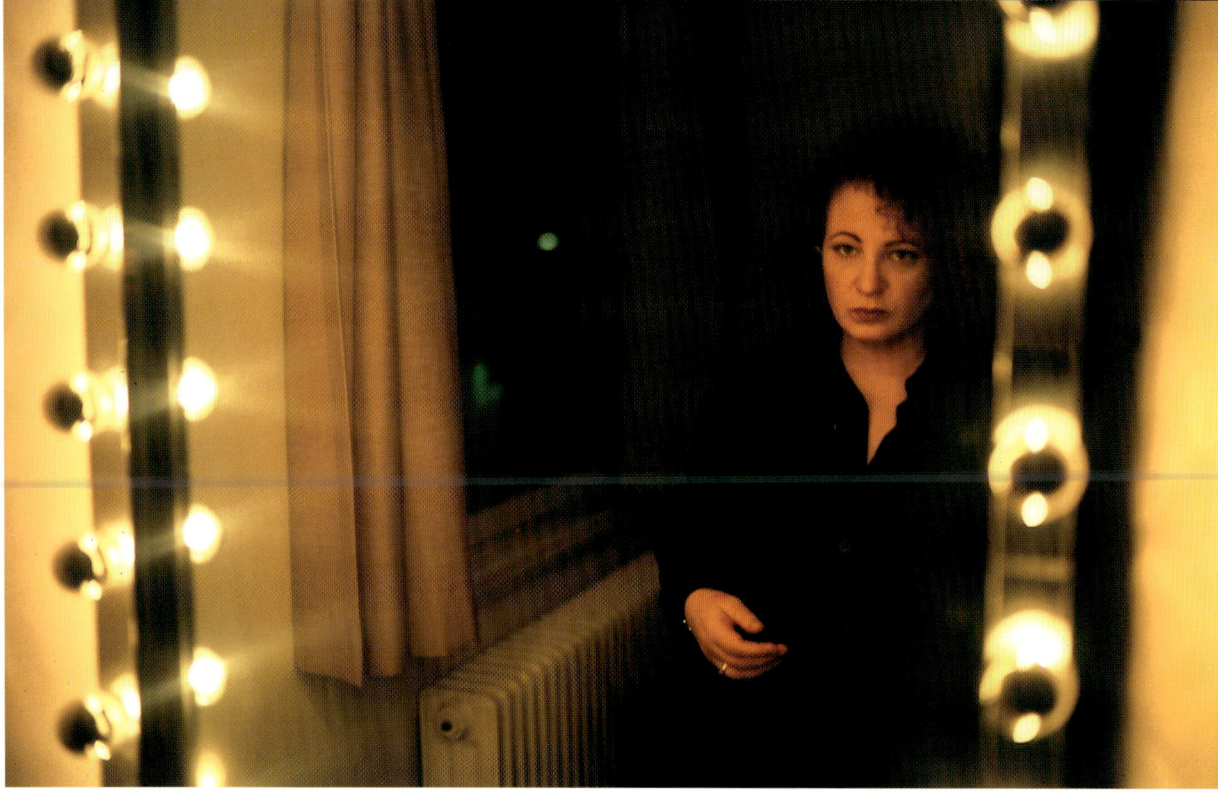

NAN GOLDIN, SELF-PORTRAIT IN HOTEL BAUR AU LAC, ZURICH, 1998 / SELBSTPORTRÄT IM HOTEL BAUR AU LAC, ZÜRICH.

Between Worlds

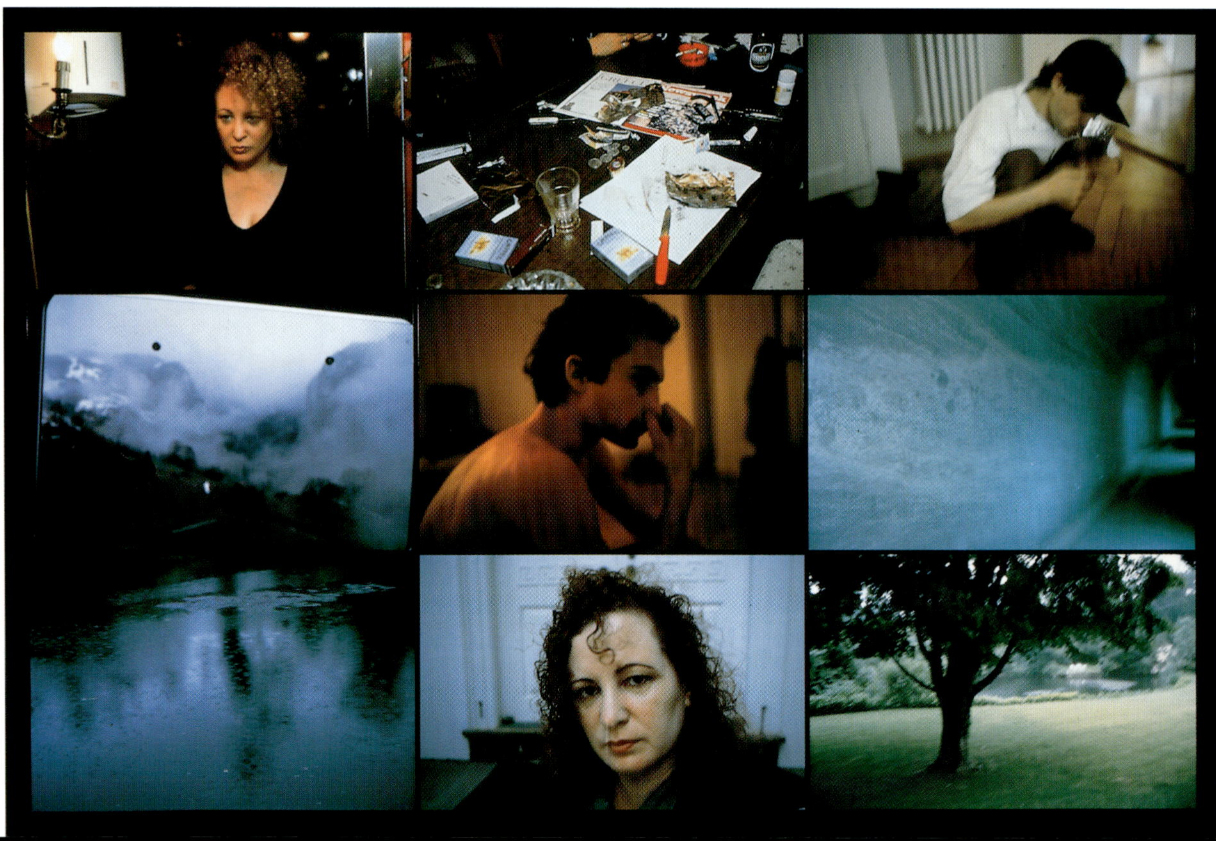

NAN GOLDIN, RELAPSE/DETOX GRID, 1998 / RÜCKFALL/ENTZUG-RASTER.

Nan Goldin's Recent Photographs

ARTHUR C. DANTO

A short while ago, I saw an impromptu exhibition of Nan Goldin's work from the past few years. The photographs, returned from her show at the Houston Museum of Contemporary Art, had just been unpacked and were temporarily lined up against the walls of her New York gallery. As a general rule, Goldin's images will be installed in such a way as to imply narrative or sub-narrative sequences. The fact that these had instead been set down in no particular order somehow prompted me to wonder what I would think of them if I knew nothing about the artist and these were the first things of hers I had seen. How would this imagined new talent stand up against the achievement of Nan Goldin? The main images one remembers from Goldin's 1996 Whitney exhibition tell the story of her life as entwined with the lives of her friends—a powerful story, almost novelistic, with episodes of dangerous love, sexual experimentation, drugs, disease, and death. The story is so compelling that it tends to inflect our response to every subsequent image we see. By pretending that the photographs leaning against the wall were by someone entirely unfamiliar, I thought I might be able to address them on their own terms, eliciting their narrative from their content, without reference to what had come before. It was a way of putting the work in brackets for the sake of an unbiased appreciation.

The artist uses precise descriptive titles, giving names to her subjects and telling us where and when the photograph was taken. Title and image together tell us a great deal. SELF-PORTRAIT IN HOTEL BAUR AU LAC, ZURICH, 1998 shows the artist to be a woman in her early middle years who has chosen to reveal herself as a person of intense introspection. The seriousness of her expression contrasts with the frivolity of the mirror in which we see it. The mirror, framed by light bulbs as in a theatrical dressing room, is not one the woman would have chosen, which the reference to this being a hotel room confirms. In any case, the woman is not scrutinizing her mirrored self so much as contemplating her inner self, leaving us to wonder what she is thinking about. There is a second self-portrait in which the woman shows herself as a shadow, leaning against the railing of a bridge under which a river flows like molten gold. One feels, even without seeing her face, that her expression must be pensive, as it was in the mirror. Rivers are metaphors for life and the flow of time, bridges are metaphors for crossing over from one state of being to another. She is pondering the meaning of her life, and the question of what to do next. What brought her to this hotel in Zurich? What is her story?

One can only conjecture. There is also a montage of nine photographs with the unsettling title RELAPSE/DETOX, 1998. It shows the woman twice, considerably more ravaged than in the self-portraits. These are framed together with some uncertain landscapes, two images of a dark, attractive man, and a table strewn with drug apparatus. One infers that the toxin is heroin, and, this being explicitly a relapse, we know that the woman has been in treatment before. Perhaps the landscapes are seen

ARTHUR C. DANTO is the art critic for *The Nation*, and author of *After the End of Art: Contemporary Art and the Pale of History* (Princeton University Press, 1997).

through the windows of a clinic. Is this the reason, one wonders, why the woman has come to Zurich? Is this what she is thinking about? Is she asking herself why, having succumbed to drugs before, she has, through weakness of will, succumbed again? Does the man in the painful montage explain the woman's predicament? One narrative would be that the woman's need for love trumped her wish to stay free of drugs. What-ever larger narrative is implied by the mirrored self-portrait, the woman ruminating by the river, and the agony of rehabilitation, these images must define its critical moment.

The remaining titles let us in on a great deal more. We read that the photographs were taken in various places—in Lausanne, Florence, Positano, Turin, Berlin, Stockholm, Umeå—as well as in a number of sites in the Northeastern part of the United States. These other sites are less charged with personal meaning, but in the aggregate, they imply that travel is a constant for this woman in the present condition of her life. It is, one must say, an odd itinerary—Swampscott, Massachusetts, Umeå, Pozzoli, Wolfsburg, Winterthur, America, Italy, Switzerland, Sweden, Germany, in whatever order. The woman does not travel for the sake of seeing things—few of the photographs are of sights or marvels, most of them take place in hotel bedrooms, or on hotel terraces, or at tables. They belong more to the genre of snapshots than of postcards. Even the marvelous BREAKFAST IN BED, TORRE DI BELLOSGUARDO, ITALY, 1996 is less a still life than a souvenir of what the woman was served one morning in a markedly upscale inn: flowered porcelain cups and pitchers; crusty rolls, as yet untouched, in one straw basket, fresh fruits in another; one egg in an eggcup. It is a breakfast for two, though only one cup has been used, as if the woman needed her coffee right away, without waiting for her absent partner to join. There are white linen napkins.

In addition to placenames, the titles identify their subjects through first names—David, Sharon, Guido, Pavel, Joey, Simon, David H., Piotr, Kathleen, etc. The woman is on a first name basis with these individuals and, more than this, appears to be on intimate terms with them. David H. is shown showering in one image and sleeping in another. Piotr and Jörg are shown together on a bed, their heads in tender contact. Guido is shown in his bed, Clemens in the bed of the artist herself in the Hotel Carlton Opera in Vienna. David is on her bed in Wolfsburg. Bedroom and bathroom are exclusionary spaces that others are allowed to enter only if related to their occupants like members of a family. One of the earliest of the images shows Ric and Randy embracing (RIC AND RANDY EMBRACING, SALZBURG, 1994). But apart from the seemingly chaste nextness between the two men in PIOTR AND JÖRG ON THE BED, WOLFSBURG, 1997, the subjects are mostly alone except for the invisible photographer, so completely trusted that her presence is not regarded as invasive. Her friends, of course, are not always in or on a bed. Simon, in Umeå, stands in a snowy street in winter darkness, but also buried in the sand at Crane's Beach, in Massachusetts and next to a Ferris wheel at Coney Island. For the most part, the subjects are caught in introspective moments, looking out a window or in a mirror, or simply sitting or standing or lying down. We have no idea of what they do in life—no idea of how the train fare or the hotel bills get paid. Nor do we know if they know one another. There is a strong sense that they are united largely through the artist herself, the fixed center of their eccentric orbits. Descartes describes the mind as a gallery of pictorial representations, and one wonders whether the pictures with which SELF-PORTRAIT IN HOTEL BAUR AU LAC is surrounded are not what also fills the artist's mind. She thinks as much about these friends as she does about herself. But she does not think about what they do or who they are. They sleep, they eat, they wash, they stare, they stand. The children, of course, play. Only in the case of David are we shown a darkroom, identified as his. We know that, like her, he is a photographer. The others are simply individual presences whose relationships to one another are for us to guess at.

Even if one knew nothing about the artist, even if this were her first show, the photographs—which disclose a way of being in the world, an attitude, a set of shared values, a reflective personality—command our interest and respect. The artist is the recorder of a form of life she also lives. Perhaps it is a form of life primarily because she ponders and records it. Perhaps this was true also of the form of life, darker and more dangerous, that we know from Nan Goldin's earlier photographs, where the subjects are engaged in transcending the limits of consciousness and self-identity, are flung together in fierce embrace, displaying their scars or bruises and their young tough bodies. We see the kinds of places they live, with pictures pinned to peeling walls over soiled sheets on worn beds in rooms strewn with garments, papers, telephones, and tape recorders. Doubtless most of what we see would take place whether Goldin was there or not, but it is also true that the world we see through her pictures is a world that exists through those pictures: Her subjects know that they are being observed. So, in a sense she has given their world a unity and a meaning, defining the pictures as art in doing so. They are, Goldin says, "about creating a history by recording a history."[1] That world will always have what philosophers called "objective reality"—it will always, that is, exist in her pictures. In that sense, the world is preserved. But it lacks what those philosophers called "formal reality"—it no longer exists in reality. The persons we see in the new work are, in a sense, homeless, living in impersonal spaces with objects, such as theatrical mirrors or pretty china and stiff linen, in which they have no personal investment. They are, so to speak, between worlds, like the artist herself on her metaphoric bridge. It would be difficult, from the recent work, to derive an idea of the vanished world, before death through AIDS and drug abuse brought it to an end. "A photographer friend used to say to me," Goldin recalls, "well, of course people are going to be interested in your work because look at your subject-matter."[2] This implies that Goldin's art will thrive through prurience. Her photographs show transsexuals primping or on parade, hairy men at the instant of ejaculation, violent lovers poised to batter their partners, couples of every gender on top of one another, everyone living disordered lives in disordered spaces.

This is not the subject matter of the new work. The subjects are subdued, the spaces anonymous; passion itself appears stilled. And the difference shows in the images themselves. Their subjects are often seen in the outdoors rather than in the dark squalor of their former personal habitats. The darkness has lifted from within and without. They are, like Nan Goldin herself in these years, voyagers in quest of a world, the outlines of which neither they nor she has any idea of. Like her, they are on a bridge between two shores. They cannot return from whence they came, but what lies before them has yet to disclose itself. The subject matter of Goldin's new work is a search that is markedly different from the searches for sensation and the intoxication of consciousness that defined the earlier world. It is a search on occasion broken by relapse, as the voyagers return to solutions they know are no longer helpful. It does not surprise me that, in this next stage of their lives, they have acquired some kind of spiritual identity. Somehow, a set of Fatima candles in Portugal, photographed in the same year as RELAPSE/DETOX, seems less a still life than a sign or at least a hope. Human imagination is terribly limited. Whatever Goldin and her friends used to be in their crazy youths, they now fit into a universal pattern of human aspiration. The images in the aggregate could be about any of us, *in mezzo del camin' di nostra vita.*

PIOTR AND JÖRG ON THEIR HOTEL BED, WOLFSBURG, 1997 / PIOTR UND JÖRG AUF IHREM HOTELBETT, WOLFSBURG.

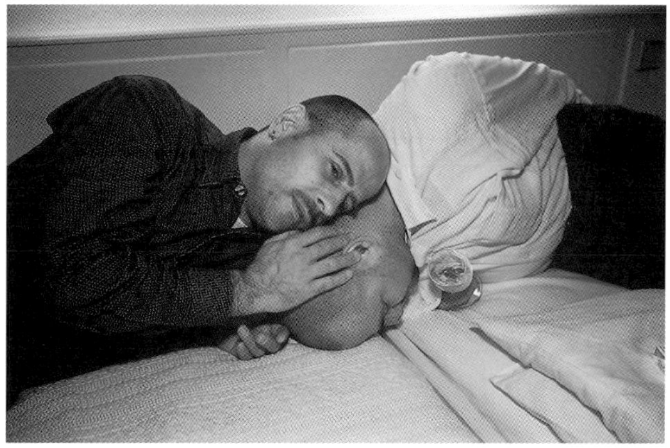

1) "On Acceptance: A Conversation. Nan Goldin Talking with David Armstrong and Walter Keller," in: Nan Goldin, *I'll Be Your Mirror* (Zurich/New York: Scalo, 1996), p. 450.
2) Ibid., p. 447.

Zwischen den Welten

ARTHUR C. DANTO

Vor kurzem sah ich in einer Art improvisierter Ausstellung Nan Goldins Arbeiten der letzten Jahre. Die Photographien waren soeben von ihrer Ausstellung in Houston zurückgekommen und standen nun in einer Reihe gegen die Wand gelehnt in ihrer New Yorker Galerie. In der Regel sind Goldins Bilder jeweils so angeordnet, dass ein narrativer oder subnarrativer Zusammenhang entsteht. Der Umstand, dass die Bilder hier einfach ungeordnet abgestellt worden waren, liess mich phantasieren, was ich wohl von ihnen halten würde, wenn ich nichts von der Künstlerin wüsste und es die ersten Bilder wären, die ich je von ihr gesehen hätte. Wie würde dieses junge Talent meiner Phantasie sich gegenüber der reifen Leistung einer Nan Goldin ausnehmen? Die zentralen Bilder, die uns von Goldins Ausstellung im Whitney Museum 1996 im Gedächtnis geblieben sind, erzählen die Geschichte ihres Lebens als eine mit dem Leben ihrer Freunde verflochtene – eine eindrückliche Geschichte, beinah romanesk, voller gefährlicher Liebschaften, sexueller Experimente, Drogen, Krankheit und Tod. Die Geschichte berührt uns derart, dass sie unsere Reaktion auf jedes weitere Bild, das wir zu sehen bekommen, beeinflusst. Indem ich so tat, als wären die gegen die Wand gelehnten Photographien von jemand völlig unbekanntem, hoffte ich, sie aus sich selbst zu verstehen und ihre Aussage direkt ihrem Inhalt entnehmen zu können, ungeachtet dessen, was vorher war. Es war gleichsam ein Versuch, das Werk in Klammern zu setzen um ihm unvoreingenommen gerecht zu werden.

Die Künstlerin setzt präzise deskriptive Titel, nennt die Namen der photographierten Personen und sagt uns, wann und wo die Aufnahme gemacht wurde. Titel und Bild zusammen erzählen uns einiges. SELF-PORTRAIT IN HOTEL BAUR AU LAC, ZURICH, 1998 (Selbstporträt im Hotel Baur au Lac, Zürich) zeigt die Künstlerin als eine Frau zu Beginn ihrer mittleren Jahre, die sich als intensiv über sich selbst nachdenkender Mensch darstellt. Der ernste Gesichtsausdruck steht im Kontrast zur Frivolität des Spiegels, in dem wir ihn erblicken. Den Spiegel, umrahmt von Glühbirnen wie in einer Theatergarderobe, hätte diese Frau wohl kaum selbst ausgesucht; die Vermutung wird bestätigt durch den Hinweis, dass es sich um ein Hotelzimmer handelt. Wie dem auch sei, die Frau scheint weniger mit ihrem Spiegelbild beschäftigt, als in der Betrachtung ihres inneren Selbst versunken, so dass wir uns fragen, was wohl ihre Gedanken sind. Es gibt ein weiteres Selbstporträt, das die Frau als Schatten zeigt, auf das Geländer einer Brücke gestützt, unter der ein Fluss aus purem Gold zu fliessen scheint. Obwohl man ihr Gesicht nicht sieht, spürt man, dass ihr Ausdruck nachdenklich sein muss, wie zuvor im Spiegel. Flüsse sind Metaphern für das Leben und den Fluss der Zeit, Brücken sind Metaphern für Übergänge von einem Seinszustand in einen anderen. Sie denkt über den

ARTHUR C. DANTO ist Kunstkritiker von *The Nation* und u.a. Autor des Buches *Die Kunst nach dem Ende der Kunst* (Fink, München 1996).

Nan Goldins neue Photographien

NAN GOLDIN, CHLOE IN THE HOSPITAL, NYC, 1999 / CHLOE IM SPITAL, NEW YORK.

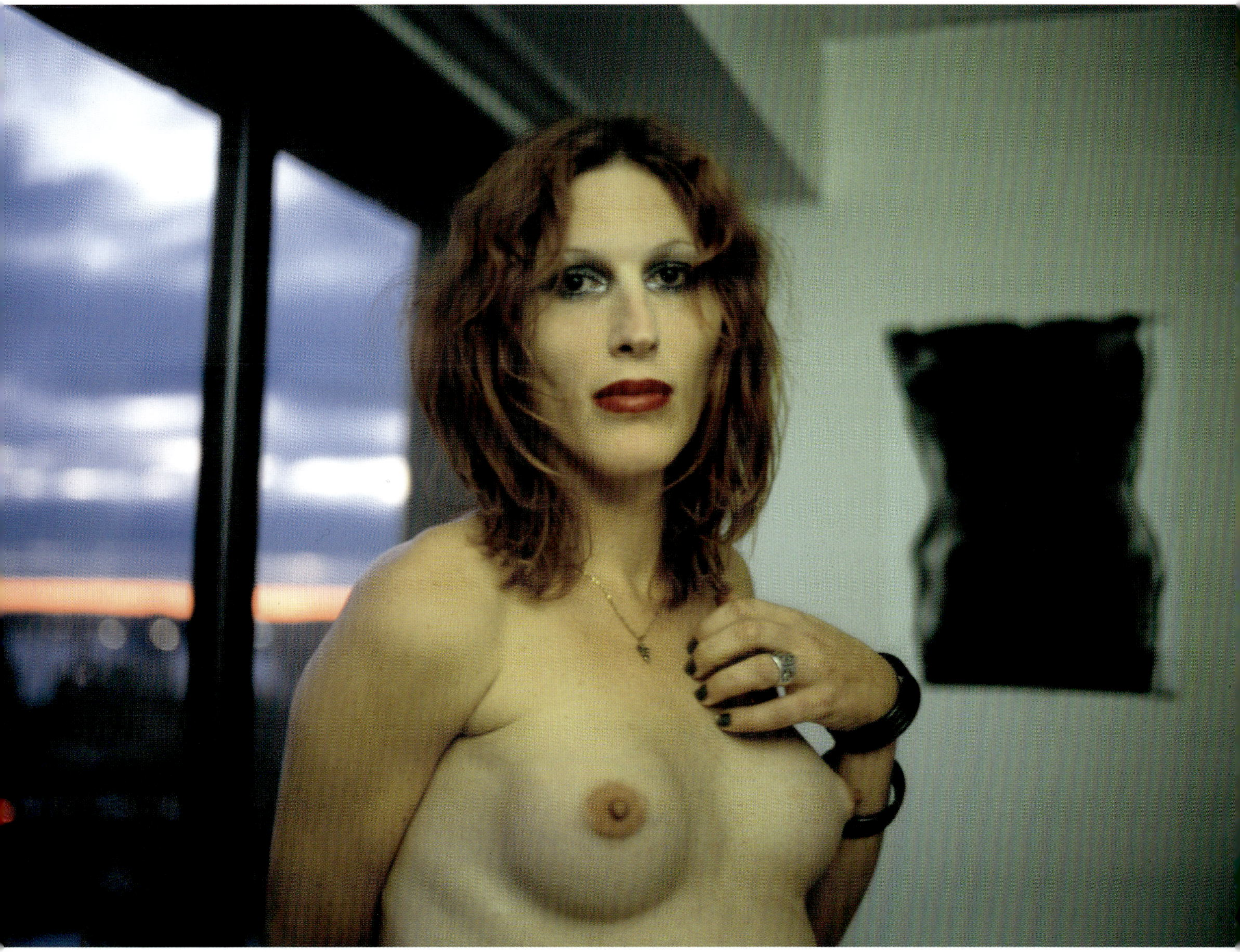

Sinn ihres Lebens nach und fragt sich, was als Nächstes zu tun ist. Was hat sie in dieses Hotel in Zürich geführt? Was ist ihre Geschichte?

Man kann nur Vermutungen anstellen. Da steht auch eine Montage aus neun Photos mit dem beunruhigenden Titel RELAPSE/DETOX (Rückfall/Entzug, 1998). Darauf sieht man die Frau zweimal, und sie sieht um einiges angegriffener aus als in den Selbstporträts. Diese Bilder sind in ein und demselben Rahmen zusammen mit einigen unbestimmbaren Landschaften, zwei Bildern von einem dunklen, attraktiven Mann und einem Tisch mit Drogenutensilien. Es ist anzunehmen, dass es sich um Heroin handelt, und da wir es ausdrücklich mit einem Rückfall zu tun haben, wissen wir, dass die Frau schon früher einen Entzug durchmachte. Vielleicht handelt es sich bei den Landschaften um Ausblicke aus Klinikfenstern. Ist das der Grund, mag man sich fragen, warum die Frau nach Zürich gekommen ist? Ist es dies, worüber sie nachdenkt? Fragt sie sich, warum sie so willensschwach war und wieder rückfällig geworden ist? Ist der Mann in der peinvollen Montage die Erklärung für das Leiden der Frau? Vielleicht war ihr Bedürfnis nach Liebe stärker als der Wille drogenfrei zu bleiben. Welches auch immer der grössere Zusammenhang sein mag, der das Selbstporträt im Spiegel, die Frau am Fluss und den schmerzlichen Entzug miteinander verbindet, diese drei Bilder umreissen sein kritisches Moment.

Die übrigen Titel verraten uns eine ganze Menge mehr. Wir erfahren, dass die Photos an ganz verschiedenen Orten entstanden sind – in Lausanne, Florenz, Positano, Turin, Berlin, Stockholm, Umeå –, aber auch an einigen Orten im Nordosten der Vereinigten Staaten. Letztere sind weniger mit persönlicher Bedeutung aufgeladen, aber zusammen mit den anderen geben sie zu erkennen, dass Reisen zurzeit als fester Bestandteil zum Leben dieser Frau gehört. Dabei fällt auf, dass die Reiseroute ziemlich merkwürdig ist: Swampscott, Massachusetts, Umeå, Pozzoli, Wolfsburg, Winterthur, Amerika, Italien, Schweiz, Schweden, Deutschland, egal in welcher Reihenfolge. Diese Frau reist offenbar nicht, um sich Dinge anzusehen – die wenigsten Photographien zeigen Landschaften oder Sehenswürdigkeiten, die meisten sind in Hotelzimmern, auf Hotelterrassen oder an Tischen aufgenommen worden. Sie sind eher dem Schnappschuss verwandt als der Postkarte. Selbst das wunderbare BREAKFAST IN BED, TORRE DI BELLOSGUARDO, ITALY, 1996 (Frühstück im Bett, Torre di Bellosguardo, Italien) ist weniger ein Stillleben als eine Erinnerung daran, was in diesem wirklich exklusiven Etablissement zum Frühstück serviert wurde: geblümte Porzellantassen und -krüge; in einem Körbchen noch unberührte, knusprige Brötchen, frische Früchte in einem zweiten; ein Ei in einem Eierbecher. Es ist ein Frühstück für zwei, obwohl nur eine Tasse benützt ist, als ob die Frau ihren Kaffee dringend gebraucht hätte, ohne auf ihren abwesenden Partner warten zu können. Und weisse Leinenservietten.

Neben Ortsnamen kommen in den Werktiteln auch Vornamen zur Bezeichnung des jeweiligen Objekts vor: David, Sharon, Guido, Pavel, Joey, Simon, David H., Piotr, Kathleen usw. Die Frau ist mit den abgebildeten Personen so vertraut, dass sie sie beim Vornamen nennt, ja mehr als das, sie scheint mit ihnen wirklich intim befreundet zu sein. David H. sieht man auf einem Bild beim Duschen, auf einem anderen schläft er. Piotr und Jörg sieht man zusammen auf einem Bett, wie sie liebevoll die Köpfe zusammenstecken. Guido sieht man in seinem Bett, Clemens im Bett der Künstlerin im Hotel Carlton Opera in Wien. David ist auf ihrem Bett in Wolfsburg. Schlaf- und Badezimmer sind intime Räume, in die man andere nur eintreten lässt, wenn sie einem so vertraut sind wie Familienmitglieder. Eines der frühesten Bilder zeigt Ric und Randy sich umarmend (RIC AND RANDY EMBRACING, SALZBURG, 1994). Aber abgesehen von der anscheinend keuschen Vertraulichkeit zwischen den beiden Männern in PIOTR AND JÖRG ON THE BED, WOLFSBURG, 1997 (Piotr und Jörg auf dem Bett, Wolfsburg), sind die Personen meistens allein mit der unsichtbaren Photographin, der sie so vollkommen vertrauen, dass ihre Gegenwart nicht als die Intimsphäre verletzend empfunden wird. Natürlich befinden sich ihre Freunde nicht immer im oder auf dem Bett. Simon, in Umeå, begegnen wir in der winterlichen Dämmerung auf einer verschneiten Strasse, aber auch im Sand eingegraben am Strand (Crane's Beach, Massachusetts)

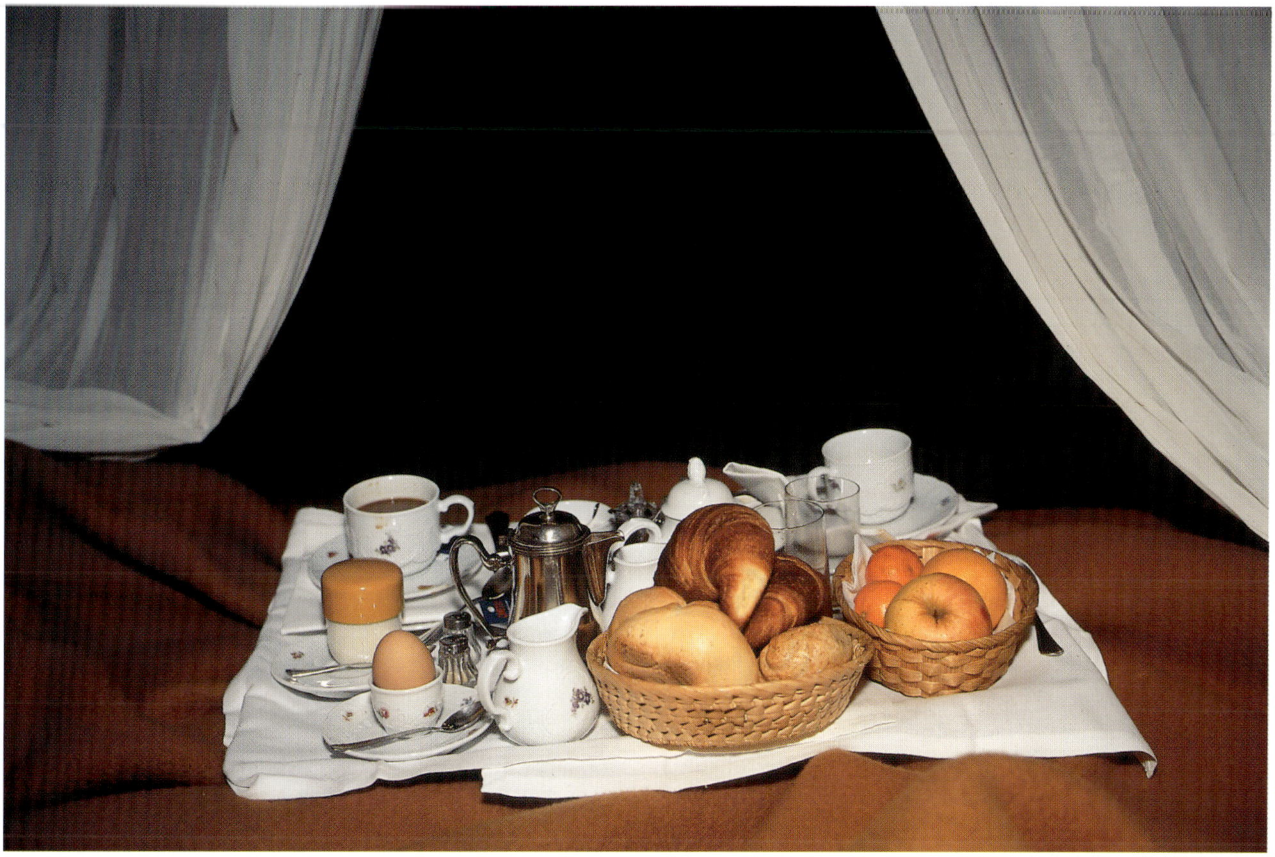

NAN GOLDIN, BREAKFAST IN BED, HOTEL TORRE DI BELLOSGUARDO, ITALY, 1996 / FRÜHSTÜCK IM BETT, HOTEL TORRE DI BELLOSGUARDO, ITALIEN.

oder vor einem Riesenrad auf Coney Island. Meistens sind die Personen in nachdenklichen Momenten festgehalten, sie schauen aus dem Fenster oder in einen Spiegel, oder aber sie sitzen, stehen oder liegen einfach da. Wir haben keine Ahnung, wie sie leben – keine Ahnung, wie sie ihre Fahrkarten oder Hotelrechnungen bezahlen. Wir wissen auch nicht, ob sie einander kennen. Man gewinnt den Eindruck, dass sie hauptsächlich durch die Künstlerin selbst, die den fixen Mittelpunkt ihrer exzentrischen Lebensbahnen bildet, miteinander verbunden sind. Descartes beschreibt den menschlichen Geist als Galerie bildlicher Vorstellungen, und man fragt sich, ob die Bilder, die SELF-PORTRAIT IN HOTEL BAUR AU LAC umgeben, nicht auch Bilder im Kopf der Künstlerin sind. Sie denkt genauso viel über diese Freunde nach wie über sich selbst. Aber sie denkt nicht darüber nach, was sie tun oder wer sie sind. Sie schlafen, sie essen, sie waschen sich, sie schauen, sie stehen. Die Kinder spielen, natürlich. Nur im Fall von David sehen wir auch eine Dunkelkammer, die als die seine bezeichnet wird. Also wissen wir, dass er, wie Goldin, ein Photograph ist. Alle andern sind einfach individuell präsent, und über ihre Beziehungen untereinander können wir nur rätseln.

Selbst wenn man nichts über die Künstlerin wüsste, selbst wenn dies ihre erste Ausstellung wäre, die Photos – die eine Weise des in der Welt Seins enthüllen, eine Haltung, bestimmte gemeinsame Werte, eine nachdenkliche Persönlichkeit – wirken faszinierend und flössen uns Respekt ein. Die Künstlerin hält eine Lebensform fest, die sie selbst auch lebt. Vielleicht wird erst eine Lebensform daraus, weil sie sie reflektiert und festhält. Vielleicht trifft dies auch auf die schwärzere und gefährlichere Lebensform zu, die wir aus Nan Goldins früheren Bildern kennen, in denen es den dargestellten Personen darum geht, die Grenzen des Bewusstseins und ihrer Identität zu sprengen; in denen sie sich heftigen Umarmungen hingeben und ihre Narben, Verletzungen und ihre jugendlich strotzenden Körper zur Schau stellen. Wir sehen, in welcher Art Wohnung sie leben, mit Bildern, die über schmutziger Bettwäsche und zerwühlten Betten an Wände gepinnt sind, von denen die Farbe bröckelt, in Räumen, in denen Kleider, Papiere, Telefonapparate und Kassettenrecorder herumliegen. Sicher würde das meiste von dem, was wir sehen, auch ohne Nan Goldins Anwesenheit stattfinden, aber es ist auch wahr, dass die Welt, die wir durch ihre Bilder wahrnehmen, eine Welt ist, die dank dieser Bilder existiert: Ihre Objekte wissen, dass sie beobachtet werden. So hat Goldin ihrer Welt gewissermassen eine Einheit und eine Bedeutung verschafft und die Bilder dadurch zur Kunst erklärt: Sie sollen «Geschichte schreiben, indem sie Geschichten aufzeichnen».[1] Dieser Welt wird immer eigen sein, was Philosophen einst «objektive Realität» nannten, das heisst, sie wird immer in ihren Bildern existieren. In diesem Sinn ist diese Welt bewahrt. Aber es fehlt ihr, was dieselben Philosophen «formale Realität» nannten, das heisst: In Wirklichkeit gibt es sie nicht mehr. Die Menschen auf den neueren Bildern sind irgendwie heimatlos, sie leben in unpersönlichen Räumen mit Gegenständen wie Theaterspiegeln, edlem Porzellan oder gestärkter Leinenwäsche, mit denen sie persönlich nichts zu schaffen haben. Sie stehen sozusagen zwischen zwei Welten wie die Künstlerin selbst auf ihrer metaphorischen Brücke. Aus den neueren Arbeiten lässt sich kaum eine Vorstellung der verschwundenen Welt vor ihrem Untergang durch Aids und Drogenmissbrauch ableiten. «Ein befreundeter Photograph pflegte mir zu sagen», erinnert sich Goldin: «Natürlich werden sich die Leute für dein Werk interessieren – kein Wunder, bei deinen Sujets.»[2] Das heisst, dass Goldins Kunst ihren Erfolg zum Teil auch einem voyeuristischen Interesse verdankt. Ihre Photographien zeigen Transsexuelle und Transvestiten in der Garderobe oder während der Vorstellung, behaarte Männer beim Ejakulieren, gewalttätige Liebhaber, die zum Schlag gegen ihre Partner ausholen, aufeinander liegende Paare jeglichen Geschlechts; jeder und jede führt ein ungeordnetes Leben in unordentlichen Räumen.

In den neueren Arbeiten ist das Thema ein anderes. Die Menschen sind zurückhaltend, die Räume anonym; die Leidenschaft selbst scheint zur Ruhe gekommen zu sein. Der Unterschied in den Bildern ist offenkundig. Die Personen erscheinen jetzt häufiger im Freien statt wie früher in schmuddligen Räumen. Die innere und äussere Düsternis hat sich gelüftet. Sie sind, wie Nan Goldin in den letzten Jahren auch, zu Reisenden auf der Suche nach einer Welt geworden, von der weder sie noch die Künstlerin wissen, wie sie aussehen wird. Wie Goldin selbst befinden sie sich auf einer Brücke zwischen zwei Ufern. Dahin, woher sie kamen, können sie nicht zurück, und was vor ihnen liegt, wird sich erst zeigen. Das Thema von Goldins neuen Arbeiten ist eine Suche, die etwas ganz anderes ist als jene die frühere Welt bestimmende Suche nach unerhörten Erlebnissen und Bewusstseinsveränderung mittels Drogen. Es ist eine Suche, die gelegentlich von Rückfällen unterbrochen wird, wenn die Reisenden auf Lösungen zurückgreifen, von denen sie bereits wissen, dass es keine sind. Es überrascht mich nicht, dass sie in diesem neuen Stadium ihres Lebens zu einer Art spiritueller Identität gefunden haben. In gewissem Sinn scheinen mir die im selben Jahr wie RELAPSE/DETOX in Portugal photographierten Fatima-Kerzen weniger ein Stillleben zu sein als ein Zeichen oder mindestens ein Schimmer der Hoffnung. Die menschliche Vorstellungskraft ist entsetzlich beschränkt. Was auch immer Goldin und ihre Freunde in ihrer verrückten Jugend waren, heute nehmen sie teil an einem universellen menschlichen Streben. Das Ensemble dieser Bilder könnte jeden von uns meinen, *in mezzo del camin' di nostra vita.*

(Übersetzung: Susanne Schmidt)

1) «Vom Akzeptieren: Ein Gespräch. Nan Goldin unterhält sich mit David Armstrong und Walter Keller», in: Nan Goldin, *I'll Be Your Mirror* (deutsche Ausgabe), Scalo, Zürich/New York 1996, S. 450.

2) Ebenda, S. 447.

LISA LIEBMANN

CHRISTINE FLOATING IN THE SEA, 1999

It occurs to me that Nan Goldin has during the last two decades been a mirror not only to the contemporary people and society she has portrayed with such relentless intimacy, but also to the twenty or so years that enveloped the last turn of the century in art. With this notion in mind, Goldin's eighties correspond roughly to the era of the First World War. Despite significant differences—the combination of war, syphilis, and the devastating flu epidemic of 1918 to1919 carried a statistically far greater toll than that exacted by AIDS during the eighties in the west—the recent decade has in common with that previous period a pervasive and elaborately documented atmosphere of sexual anxiety, as well as the widely felt and expressed shock of a sudden and overwhelming generational loss. Goldin's classic pictures from the eighties—namely THE BALLAD OF SEXUAL DEPENDENCY, her epic, aggregate *lustmord* saga, with its leitmotifs of nightlife and debauchery, violent love and difficult beauty, along with the domestic joys and struggles of a new, young, self-invented and self-proclaimed bohemian class—shares many visual, as well as emotional and societal characteristics with the agonistic urban imagery of work by Egon Schiele, Ernst Ludwig Kirchner, Georg Grosz, and Otto Dix.

As the current decade progressed, this keyed-up and fundamentally expressionistic tone gave way to a more introspective mood. Like Kirchner—who in 1917 and in a state of nervous collapse left Berlin for Switzerland, where he painted Alpine phantasms reminiscent of Kandinsky's animistic nature abstractions from the first decade of the century—Goldin, too, introduced both landscapes and still lifes to what had previously been her densely populated pictorial world. Furthermore, photographs such as BRUCE IN THE SMOKE, SOLFATARA, POZZUOLI, 1995—with its lone, Caspar David Friedrichesque figure—and STEFAN'S LAKE AT MIDDAY, UMEÅ, SWEDEN, 1997—whose near-abstract, near-monochrome evocation of a sublime and tragic emptiness conjures up images out of Christen Kobke and Edvard Munch—likewise suggest a backward progression in art-historical time towards the Symbolist period.

Goldin's is a very northern temperament, in the old-fashioned European sense. Whether in the south of Italy or the north of Sweden, she is on intimate terms with *angst.* Even her earlier pictures, with their often Latin-Catholic inflected interiors and accoutrements—the ambient botanica votives and Spanish-

---

LISA LIEBMANN is a writer and art critic who lives in New York.

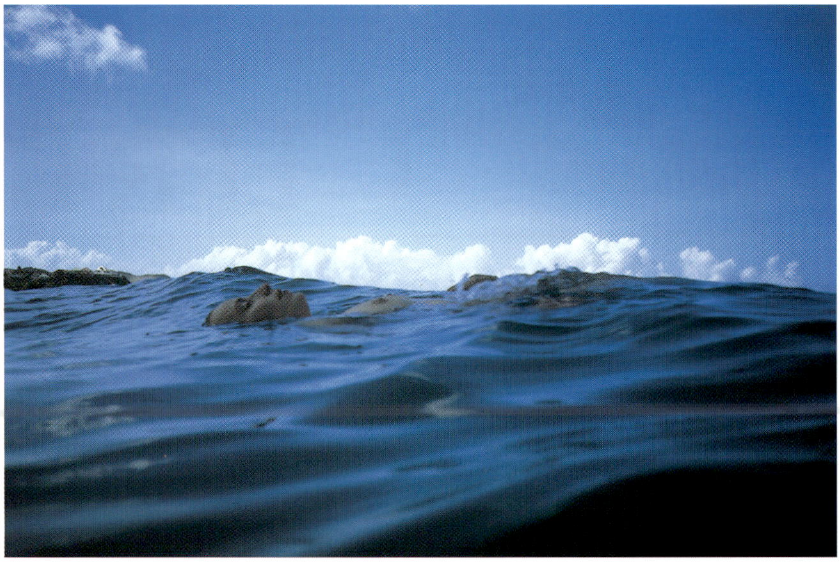

NAN GOLDIN, CHRISTINE FLOATING IN THE SEA, ST. BARTH'S, 1999 / CHRISTINE IM MEER TREIBEND, ST. BARTH'S.

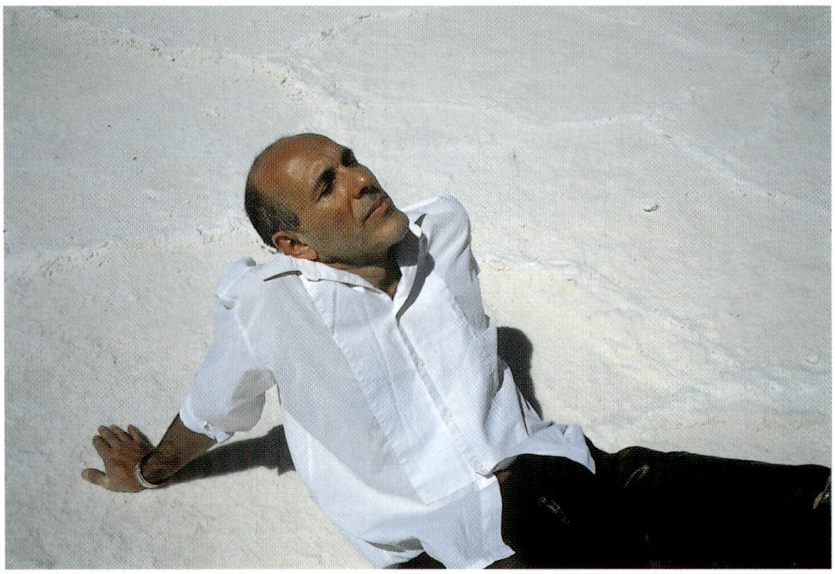

NAN GOLDIN, GUIDO IN THE DESERT, DEATH VALLEY, 1999 / GUIDO IN DER WÜSTE, DEATH VALLEY.

strumpet styles embraced as both inspirational pathos and cheap fashion by many in the downtown demimonde—are somehow more kindred in spirit to Fassbinder, say, or arguably Bergman, than to Fellini or Almodovar. Goldin's great, abiding themes—the *totentanz*, the loss and redemption of the self and of others, empathy vs. scrutiny—have in recent years been cushioned, even at times lightly camouflaged, by success and prosperity. Grand hotel names crop up now in her picture captions, rather than the unnamed rooms, with their unmade beds, that marked her earlier sojourns abroad; and her (always working) vacations are no longer limited to city beaches and her old haunts on the Cape. But a sense of foreboding never fails, however surreptitiously, to impregnate her consciousness and lens. CHRISTINE FLOATING IN THE SEA, ST. BARTH'S, 1999 is a spectacular case in point: This Christine on holiday, serenely floating in deep blue waters—engulfed by a swell that seems also to be carrying her aloft toward some cloud-filled ether—might for all purposes be that mythic daughter of a Danish courtier, drowned and lost forever to the doomed Danish prince; and this Caribbean Sea, which threatens to engulf a tiny, fragile slice of earth as well—a rugged bit of coastline, some austere pitched roofs that look as if they might as easily be at home on the Faro Islands—seems a far cry from a vacationer's paradise.

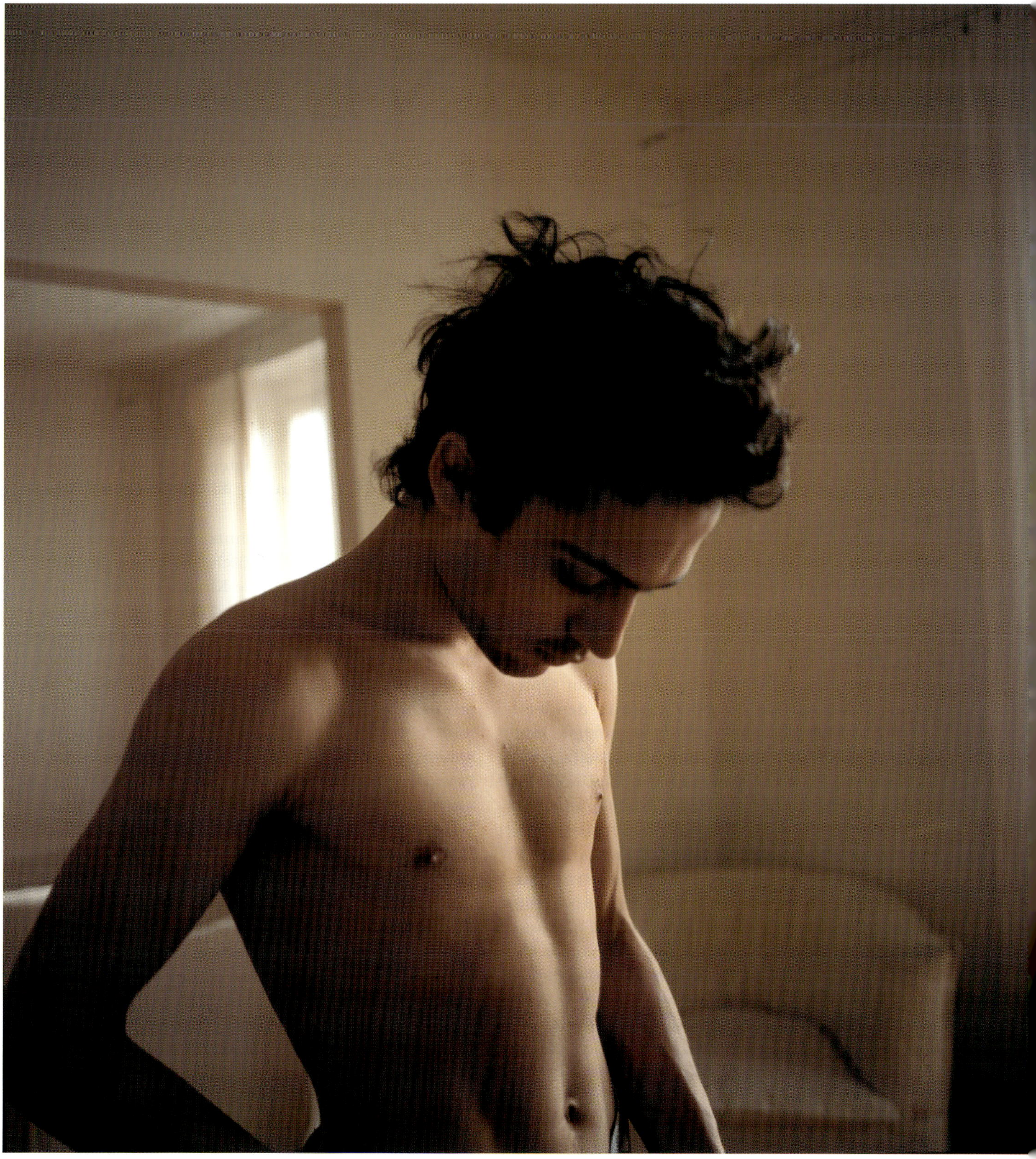

NAN GOLDIN, DAVID H. LOOKING DOWN, ZURICH, SWITZERLAND, 1998 / DAVID H. SCHAUT HINUNTER, ZÜRICH.

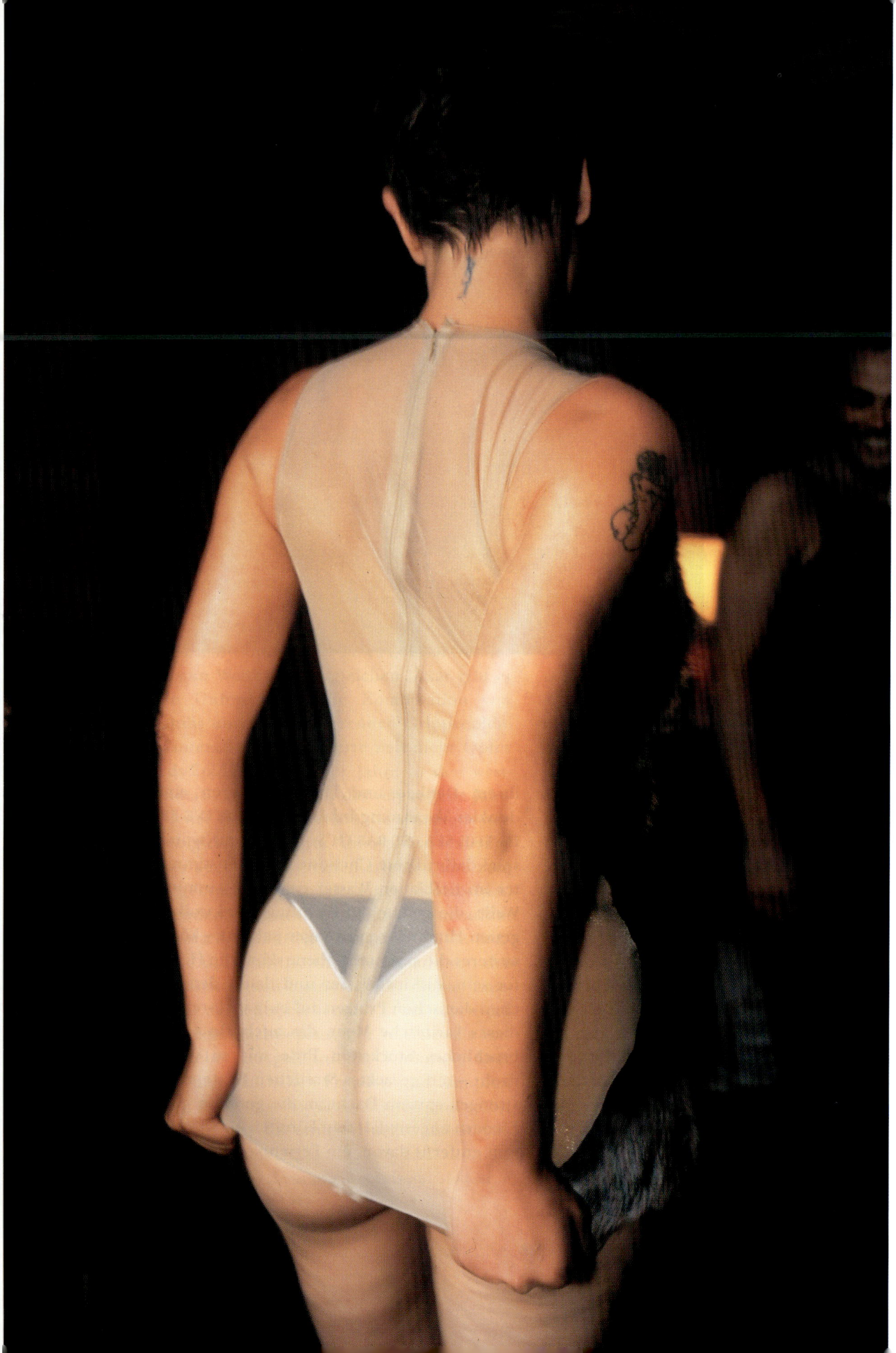

NAN GOLDIN, VALERIE'S BACK, L'HOTEL, PARIS, 1999 / VALERIES RÜCKEN, L'HOTEL, PARIS.

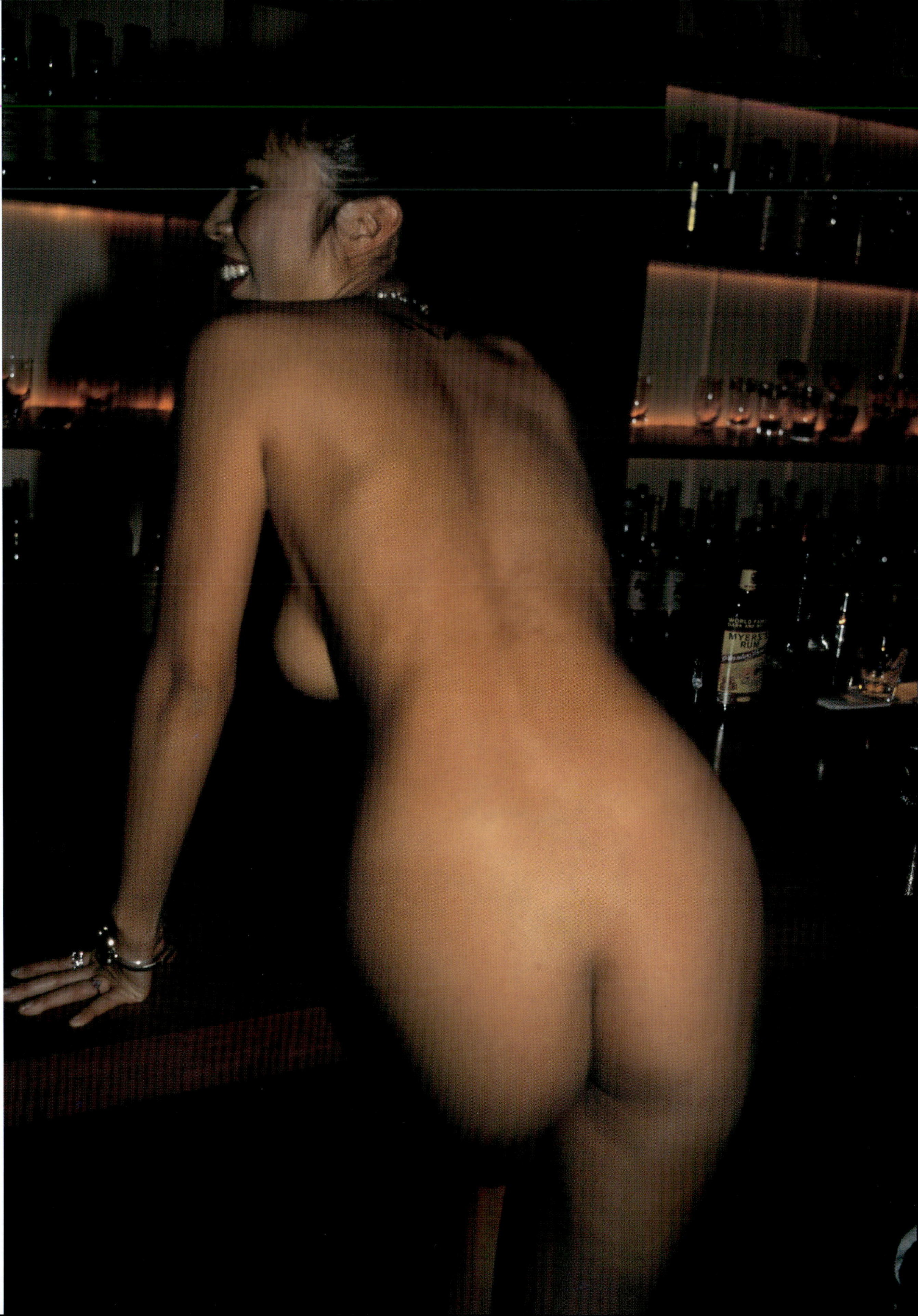

NAN GOLDIN, MASH AT THE BAR, BAR ROUGE, TOKYO, 1998 / MASH AN DER BAR, BAR ROUGE, TOKIO.

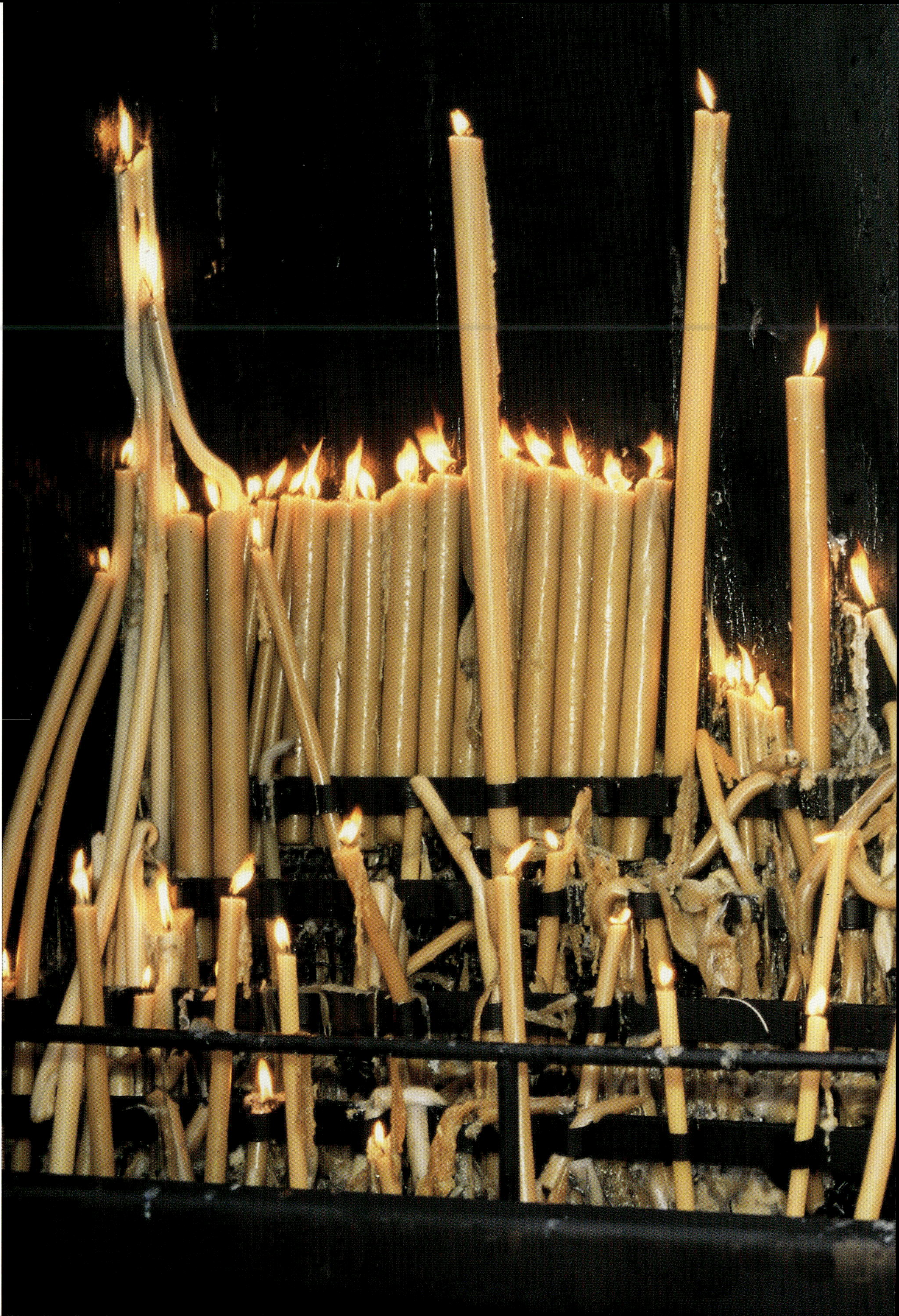

NAN GOLDIN, FATIMA CANDLES, PORTUGAL, 1998 / FATIMA-KERZEN, PORTUGAL.

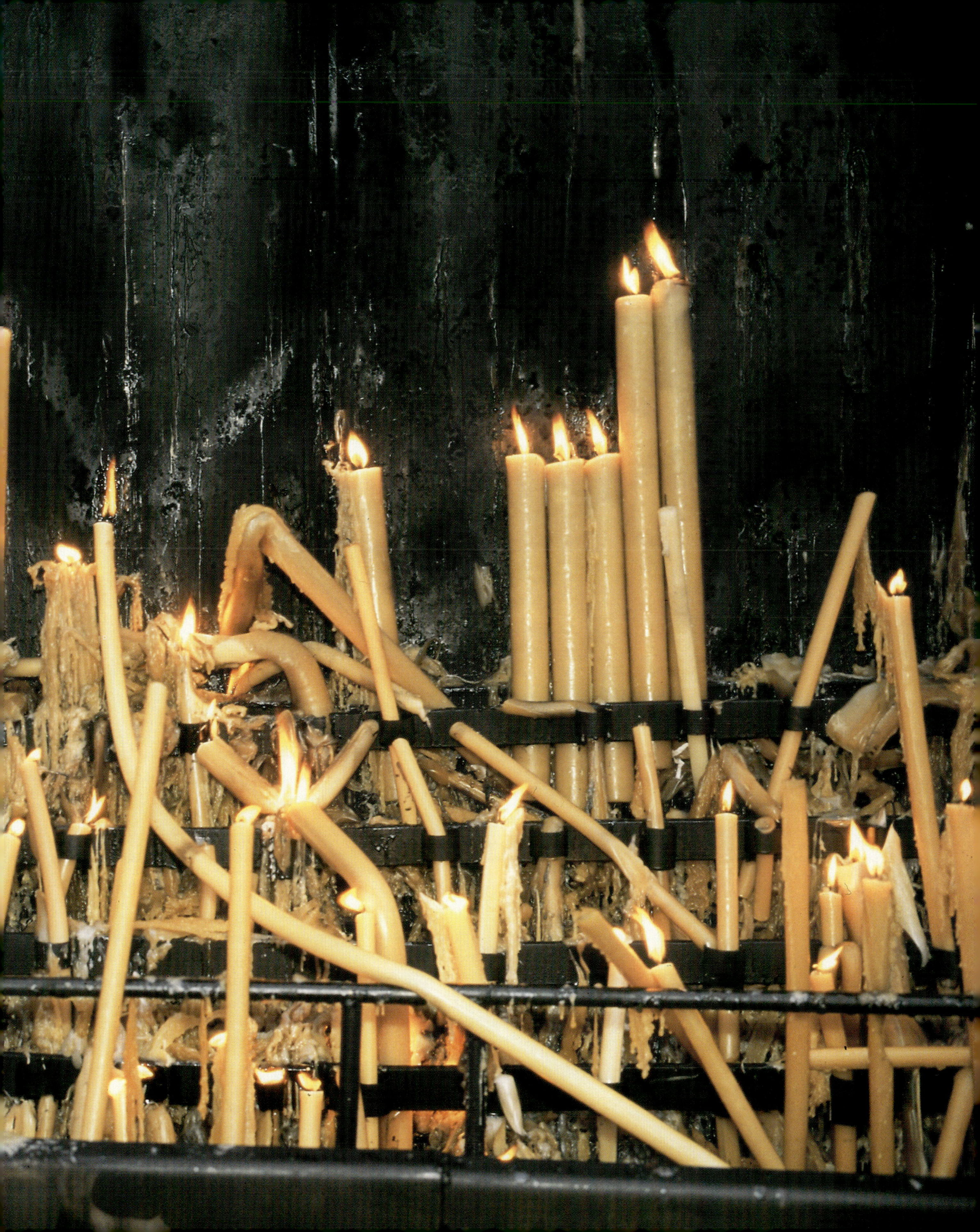

Nan Goldin

The Party's Over

DANA FRIIS-HANSEN

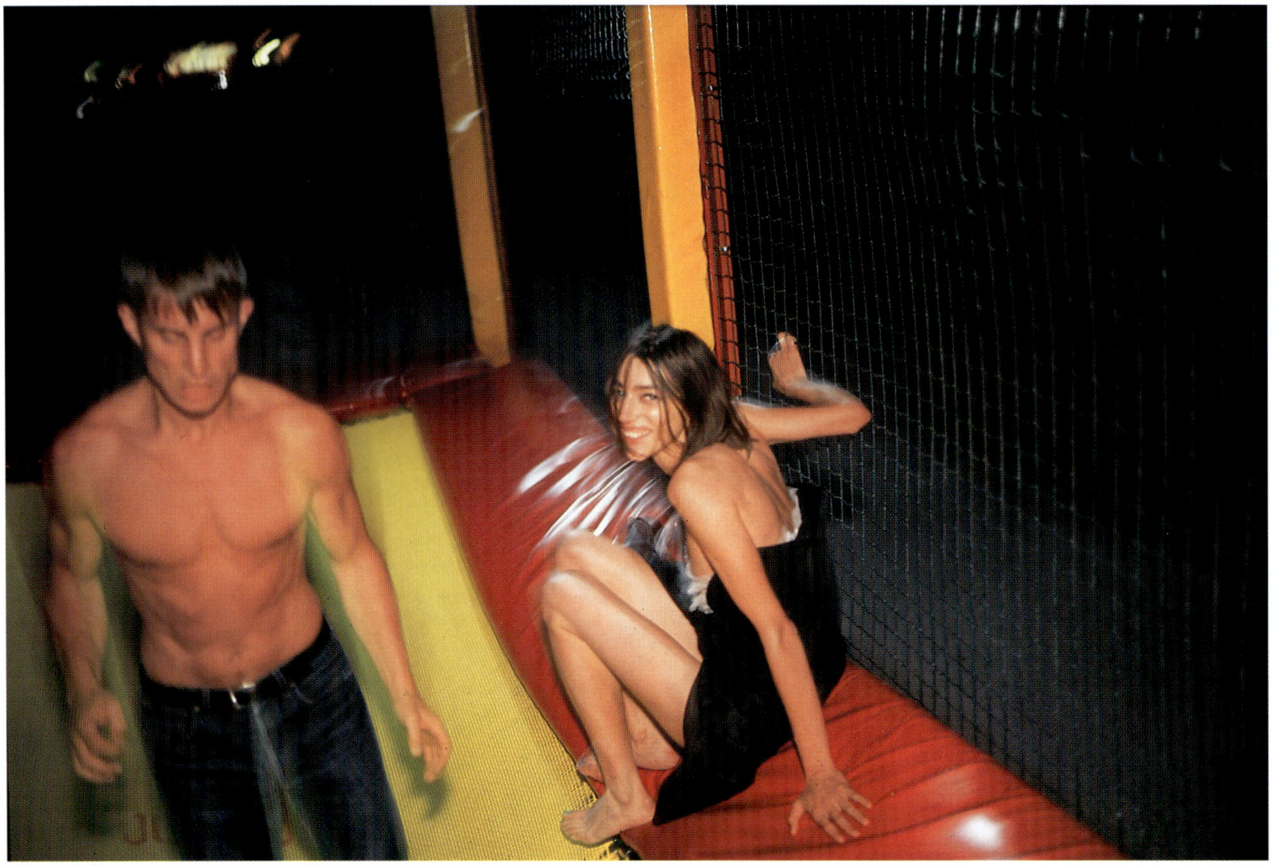

NAN GOLDIN, CLEMENS AND REINE ON THE TRAMPOLINE, PARIS, 1999 / CLEMENS UND REINE AUF DEM TRAMPOLIN, PARIS.

There's no denying that Nan Goldin is a "people person," and that's what makes her a great portraitist. A serious conversation with her is always personal, as Goldin disarms us quickly by opening herself up and by listening to us intensely. All the while we know she's keenly absorbing us, processing what she sees, hears, senses. Considering why her portraits of even near strangers often feel so intimate, she has written, "It has to do with the kind of person I am. I demand a lot, and I do make quick connections that go deep, and I think that carries into my pictures..."[1)]

Throughout the eighties Goldin achieved increasing recognition for her strobe-lit stream of portraits of urban "downtown scenes" at play, now considered to be key documents of that era. But it was with her groundbreaking slide show, THE BALLAD OF SEXUAL DEPENDENCY, first shown in 1982, that Goldin made

DANA FRIIS-HANSEN is Senior Curator of the Contemporary Arts Museum, Houston.

her enduring contribution to photography by "thinking outside the box"—beyond the medium's framed, still, single, silent image. In a series of poetically-sequenced vignettes, Goldin built up thematic "chapters" by scoring an eclectic 45-minute musical soundtrack—from opera to blues to punk and new wave—with 700 slides shown in rapid-fire succession.

Over the years Goldin's photography has best been shown as accumulations of images, where the fragments together become more than the sum of the parts. For example, Goldin's "theme and variation" editing for the slide shows, her portfolios and books on Cookie Mueller and in collaboration with David Armstrong, or the large-scale grids of the early nineties allowed her to tell larger stories about life in these times than she could with one picture. These days Goldin finds a different clarity through powerful single images with enough visual, emotional, and narrative impact to stand on their own. "My recent work isn't as much about people's external behavior and the wildness. It is more about isolating the essential of the other person. It's more about contemplation... But there is still the same degree of passion and intimacy."[2] Goldin has recently been spending time looking at abstract art by artists such as Mark Rothko, Louise Bourgeois, Brice Marden, and Richard Tuttle. This has helped her work to grow more fundamental and less specific.

The roots of this new work are a decade deep and can be found in a series of self-portraits taken when Goldin was hospitalized after bouts of drug use.

I have both literally and physically emerged from darkness and discovered light and have begun to explore these changes visually and metaphorically... The starting point of this new work is a series of psychological self-portraits I began while hospitalized. My community has been deeply impacted by both aids and drug abuse. Survival and recovery have become priorities. This has become a time of healing: physically, emotionally, and spiritually.[3]

Pictures of people still form the core of Goldin's work, but these differ from the earlier New York City scenes of individuals and couples passing through as if on their way to the next party. In the newer portraits, time and place play an expressive role through the quality of light and the atmospheric features of the environments.

Bruce hovers within the steamy smoke at Solfatara, Pozzuoli. Nephew Simon stands patiently in the gently falling snow of a Christmas dawn. Here the people and the atmosphere of the places they inhabit are bonded, the intimate contact is carefully choreographed within Goldin's camera. Pavel lets loose a laugh at twilight on the Italian seacoast. David H. dozes peacefully. Piotr and Jörg embrace. Her father is shaving. Sharon stands naked in the river. The artist's god children playfully perform a belly-dance. One senses less urgency overall—everyone seems more comfortable with time and its passing.

Even when Goldin moves away from the figure, she makes pictures which honor life lived fully. The still life has appeared periodically in Goldin's work, and recent exhibitions have featured several images that also reveal her shifted focus. DAVID'S DARKROOM, NEW HAVEN, 1997 celebrates her friend's accumulation of diverse but personally meaningful images, all squeezed onto precious wall space between two shelves of his studio. Although it marks a morning meal, BREAKFAST IN BED, TORRE DI BELLOSGUARDO, ITALY, 1996 becomes a Caravaggesque memento mori, not only in its foregrounding of suggestive bounty laid out on a rumpled bed, but also in the dark background setting, framed so enticingly by the curtains. Saturated with the spectre of death, FATIMA CANDLES, PORTUGAL, 1998 is at once an homage to Goldin's lost friends and a sign of hope and faith in the spiritual. The camera catches candles in a panoply of suggestive positions from upright and newly lit to stubs long burnt out—many drooping or deformed from the fire. Goldin's recent eye for allegory has become activated everywhere she looks.

Goldin's new work taps into the metaphorical interpretations possible within the natural environment. "I try to break through that glass, that postcard-like one-dimensionality that I used to see when I looked at a landscape, to make a portrait of a place that is imbued with my own emotional reaction."[4] The best landscapes pivot upon how natural light interacts with other atmospheric effects, especially from water in its varied states, becoming characters as significant as the figures themselves. The fog in GUIDO ON THE DOCK, VENICE, 1998 and the shim-

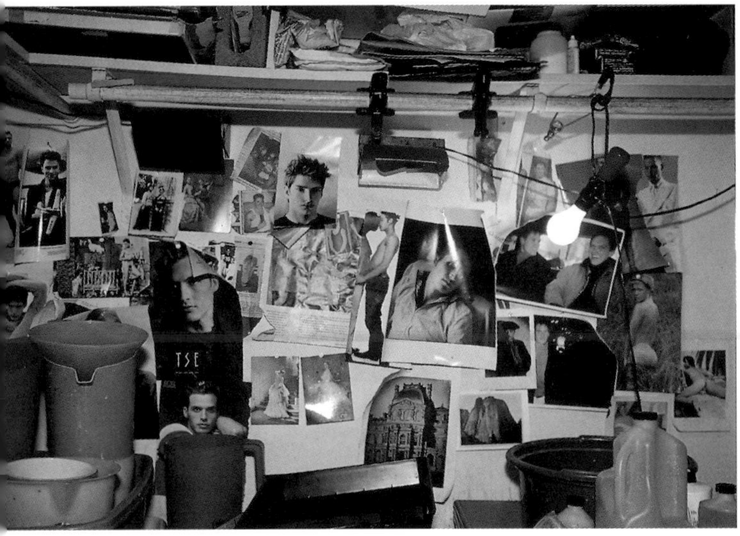

NAN GOLDIN, DAVID'S DARKROOM, NEW HAVEN, 1997 / DAVIDS DUNKELKAMMER, NEW HAVEN.

mering aquamarine reflections of GIGI IN BLUE GROTTO WITH LIGHT, CAPRI, 1997 bring an intensity and emotional pitch that creates an element of drama across the entire image which cannot be delivered solely through the subject at its center. But there is always an intensely personal connection to the place and time, and the photographs are often titled to reveal this. For example, THE SKY ON THE TWILIGHT OF PHILIPPINE'S SUICIDE, WINTERTHUR, 1997 was taken the night a young friend committed suicide just at the age that Goldin's sister had taken her own life, decades before. "I flipped out completely. The sky went crazy," Goldin recalled. "For me this picture is not just an amazing twilight, but has everything to do with loss."[5)]

Goldin continues to make stunning self-portraits, modulating the mood of her image with subtler uses of natural elements. For example, in SELF-PORTRAIT BY THE LAKE, SKOWHEGAN, MAINE, 1996, the window behind the artist mirrors the reflection of a sunset she herself is viewing, wearing an expression that suggests she is lost somewhere between the disappearing sun and her own interior darkness. Another important image, SELF-PORTRAIT AT GOLDEN RIVER ON BRIDGE, SILVER HILL, 1998, brings allegory and autobiography together. This bridge was a site she visited repeatedly on the grounds of a detox clinic she entered after a relapse. The work extends the interaction of water and light that has become so significant in much of Goldin's recent work. Its formal and metaphoric successes begin with its diagonal division of light and dark created by the division between the bridge on which the artist stands with her camera (and thus the viewer's vantage point as well) and the water below, onto which her shadow is projected. In this narrative scene Goldin opens up the poetics of a personal search, harnessing the dialectics of light and dark, object and shadow, solid and liquid, stability and constant change. With the bridge, the shadow, the sparkling reflections, the flowing river and its hard rocky bottom, this picture has become for Goldin, "both a suicide note and a grasping for hope."[6)]

Goldin's photography has changed because she is a different artist now. The staccato slide shows took our breath away with their edgy evidence of individual transgressions and youthful indiscretions, their tragically brutal honesty and their hip music. But the party's over, and by her own photographic accounts, Goldin and her friends are lucky to have survived. Daylight and time away from the city have revealed a different world outside, brushes with tragedy have sent the artist on an inward search, and the losses she has felt within her circle have made her confirm and strengthen bonds with her friends and family.

Goldin's pictures still explore love and loss, the individual and the group, the inside and the outside, but today she relies less on being a "people person" and more on being herself. She takes—and shares—her wider, slightly brighter view of life and makes it into pictures which truly are, as she says, "an essence more enduring than a moment."[7)]

1) Nan Goldin, *Couples and Loneliness* (Tokyo: Korinsha Press, 1998), p. 85.
2) Ibid., p. 95.
3) Goldin, unpublished statement, October 1, 1989.
4) Goldin, in conversation with the author, Houston, June 23, 1999. Taped conversation edited for audio tour to "Nan Goldin: Recent Photographs," Contemporary Arts Museum, Houston, June 25–August 8, 1999.
5) Ibid.
6) Ibid.
7) Goldin, in conversation with the author, New York, April 30, 1999.

Das Fest ist zu Ende

DANA FRIIS-HANSEN

Nan Goldin ist zweifellos jemand, der «von menschlichen Kontakten lebt», und das ist es auch, was sie zu einer grossen Porträtkünstlerin macht. Ein ernstes Gespräch mit ihr ist immer ein persönliches – Goldin entwaffnet uns blitzartig, indem sie sich selbst öffnet und uns sehr gut zuhört. Zur Frage, warum ihre Porträts, selbst solche von ihr beinah fremden Leuten, oft so intim wirken, schrieb sie: «Es hängt damit zusammen, was für ein Mensch ich bin. Ich fordere viel und stelle schnell eine tief gehende Verbindung her, und ich denke, das überträgt sich auf meine Bilder...»[1)]

Im Lauf der 80er Jahre erfuhr Goldin zunehmend Anerkennung für ihre Flut von Blitzlichtporträts der New Yorker Downtown-Szene in Aktion, die heute als Dokumentation jener Zeit par excellence gelten. Es war jedoch ihre bahnbrechende Diaschau THE BALLAD OF SEXUAL DEPENDENCY (Die Ballade von der sexuellen Abhängigkeit), die erstmals 1982 gezeigt wurde, mit der Goldin ihren bleibenden Beitrag zur Photographie leistete, indem sie – jenseits des gerahmten, unbewegten, einzelnen, lautlosen Bildes – «neue Pfade beschritt». Unter Verwendung einer Reihe von poetischen Vignetten und durch das Einspielen eines – von Oper über Blues zu Punk und New Wave – ziemlich bunt zusammengewürfelten, 45-minütigen Soundtracks, baute Goldin thematische Kapitel auf und liess 700 Dias im Schnellfeuertempo aufeinander folgen.

All die Jahre hindurch kamen Goldins Photographien immer am besten zur Geltung, wenn sie in Gruppen gezeigt wurden, wenn das Ensemble der einzelnen Bilder mehr als die Summe der Teile ergab. So erlaubte es beispielsweise die «Thema-und-Variations-Präsentation» von Diaschauen, die Portfolios und Bücher über Cookie Mueller und die Zusammenarbeit mit David Armstrong, aber auch die grossformatigen Raster der frühen 90er Jahre der Künstlerin, längere Geschichten über das Leben in jener Zeit zu erzählen, als das in einem einzelnen Bild möglich gewesen wäre. Heute erreicht Goldin eine ganz andere Klarheit durch starke Einzelbilder, die über genug visuelle, emotionale und narrative Kraft verfügen, um auch allein zu bestehen. «In meinen neueren Arbeiten geht es weniger um das sichtbare Verhalten von Menschen oder das Exzentrische. Es geht mehr um das Herausarbeiten des Wesens einer Person. Das hat etwas eher Kontemplatives... Aber die Leidenschaftlichkeit und Intimität ist deswegen nicht kleiner geworden.»[2)] In jüngster Zeit hat Goldin einige Energie darauf verwendet, sich abstrakte Kunst von Leuten wie Mark Rothko, Louise Bourgeois, Brice Marden oder Richard Tuttle anzusehen. Das hat ihr geholfen in ihrer eigenen Arbeit fundamentaler zu werden, weniger im Spezifischen gefangen zu bleiben.

DANA FRIIS-HANSEN ist Kurator des Contemporary Arts Museum in Houston, Texas.

NAN GOLDIN, GUIDO ON THE DOCK, VENICE, 1998 / GUIDO AUF DEM LANDUNGSSTEG, VENEDIG.

Die Wurzeln dieser neuen Arbeiten gehen ein Jahrzehnt zurück, und zwar auf eine Serie von Selbstporträts, die während eines Klinikaufenthalts nach einer Phase des Drogenkonsums entstanden sind.

Ich bin buchstäblich und physisch aus der Dunkelheit aufgetaucht, habe das Licht entdeckt und begonnen diese Veränderungen visuell und metaphorisch zu erforschen… der Ausgangspunkt dieser neuen Arbeiten ist eine Serie psychologischer Selbstporträts, mit denen ich in der Klinik begonnen habe. Mein Bekanntenkreis hat schwer unter Aids und Drogenmissbrauch gelitten. Das Überleben und Gesundwerden hatte plötzlich erste Priorität. Es wurde eine Zeit der Heilung: körperlich, emotional und geistig.[3)]

Bilder von Menschen stehen nach wie vor im Zentrum von Goldins Arbeit, aber sie unterscheiden sich von den früheren New Yorker Szenen von Individuen und Paaren, die vorüberzogen, als wären sie auf dem Weg zum nächsten rauschenden Fest. In den neueren Porträts spielen Zeit und Ort eine entscheidende Rolle durch ihre Lichtqualität und die atmosphärischen Besonderheiten der jeweiligen Umgebung.

Bruce schwimmt im dampfenden Rauch von Solfatara, Pozzuoli. Neffe Simon steht geduldig im leise fallenden Schnee eines Weihnachtsmorgens. Hier sind die Menschen und die Atmosphäre der Orte, an denen sie sich aufhalten, geerdet, die vertraute Nähe unterliegt der sorgfältigen Choreographie von Goldins Kamera. Pavel lacht laut in der Dämmerung an der italienischen Küste. David H. schläft friedlich. Piotr und Jörg umarmen sich. Ihr Vater rasiert sich. Sharon steht nackt im Fluss. Die Patenkinder der Künstlerin führen verspielt einen Bauchtanz auf. Man fühlt weniger Dringlichkeit als in den früheren Porträts – alle scheinen sich besser zurechtzufinden mit der Zeit und deren Vergänglichkeit.

Auch wenn Goldin sich von der menschlichen Gestalt entfernt, sind ihre Bilder eine Referenz an das voll gelebte Leben. Das Stillleben taucht in

Goldins Werk immer wieder auf, und in neueren Ausstellungen waren mehrere Bilder zu sehen, die ebenfalls Goldins veränderte Sicht auf die Dinge zeigen. DAVID'S DARKROOM, NEW HAVEN, 1997 (Davids Dunkelkammer, New Haven) rückt eine Sammlung unterschiedlichster Bilder ihres Freundes ins beste Licht, Photos, die vor allem persönliche Bedeutung haben und sich alle auf engstem Raum zwischen zwei Gestellen in seinem Studio drängen. Obwohl es nur für ein Frühstück steht, gerät BREAKFAST IN BED, TORRE DI BELLOSGUARDO, ITALY, 1996 (Frühstück im Bett, Torre di Bellosguardo, Italien) zu einem an Caravaggio erinnernden Memento mori, nicht nur was die suggestive Präsentation von Üppigkeit im Vordergrund angeht, sondern auch in der dunklen Hintergrundszenerie, die so beeindruckend eingerahmt wird von den Vorhängen. Voll der Schatten des Todes ist FATIMA CANDLES, PORTUGAL, 1998 (Fatima-Kerzen, Portugal) gleichzeitig eine Hommage an Goldins verstorbene Freunde und ein Zeichen der Hoffnung und des Glaubens ans Spirituelle. Die Kamera fängt Kerzen in einer Fülle suggestiver Zustände und Positionen ein von aufrecht und eben entzündet bis zu längst erloschenen Stummeln, viele davon tropfend und durch die Wärme verkrümmt. Goldins neues Auge fürs Allegorische geht auf, wo immer sie hinschaut.

Goldins neue Arbeiten tippen die möglichen metaphorischen Interpretationen in einer natürlichen Umgebung an. «Ich versuche die Glasscheibe zu durchbrechen, jenes postkartenähnlich Zweidimensionale, das ich zu sehen pflegte, wenn ich eine Landschaft anschaute, und versuche ein Porträt eines Ortes zu machen, das von meiner eigenen Gefühlsreaktion geprägt ist.»[4] Bei den besten Landschaftsbildern geht es um das Zusammenspiel von natürlichem Licht und anderen atmosphärischen Effekten, besonders beim Wasser in seinen verschiedenen Zuständen, die genauso viel Bedeutung und Charakter entwickeln wie menschliche Figuren. Der

NAN GOLDIN, GIGI IN BLUE GROTTO WITH LIGHT, CAPRI, 1997 / GIGI IN BLAUER GROTTE MIT LICHT, CAPRI.

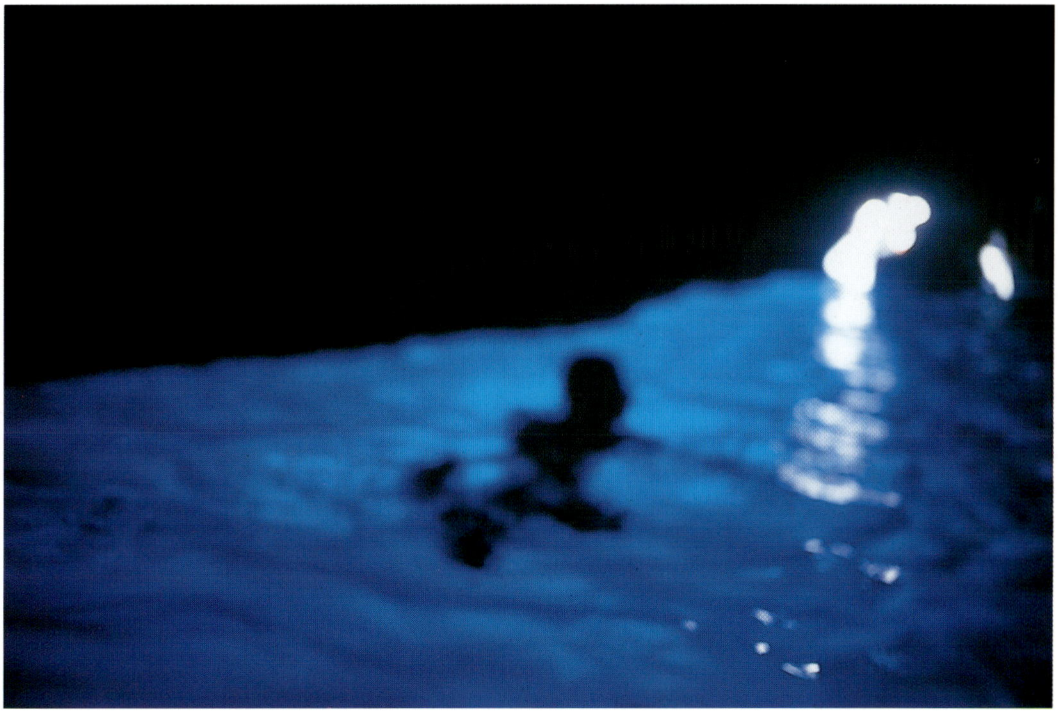

Nebel in GUIDO ON THE DOCK, VENICE, 1998 (Guido auf dem Landungssteg, Venedig) und das schimmernde Aquamarin der Lichtreflexe in GIGI IN BLUE GROTTO WITH LIGHT, CAPRI, 1997 (Gigi in blauer Grotte mit Licht, Capri) bringen eine Intensität und einen Gefühlswert in diese Porträts, die ein dramatisches Element erzeugen, das die im Zentrum des Bildes stehende Person allein nie auszulösen vermöchte. Aber Ort und Zeit jeder Aufnahme sind immer sehr persönlich bestimmt und die Titel sprechen das auch häufig aus. Zum Beispiel entstand THE SKY ON THE TWILIGHT OF PHILIPPINE'S SUICIDE, WINTERTHUR, 1997 (Der Himmel am Abend von Philippines Selbstmord) in der Nacht, als eine junge Freundin Selbstmord verübte, und zwar im selben Alter, wie es Jahrzehnte zuvor Goldins Schwester getan hatte. «Ich rastete völlig aus. Der Himmel spielte verrückt», erinnert sich Goldin. «Für mich zeigt dieses Bild nicht einfach ein faszinierendes Zwielicht, sondern steht schlicht für Verlust.»[5)]

Goldin führt die Reihe ihrer hinreissenden Selbstporträts fort, nur moduliert sie die Stimmung ihrer Selbstbilder jetzt durch raffinierteren Einsatz natürlicher Elemente. Zum Beispiel spiegelt in SELF-PORTRAIT BY THE LAKE, SKOWHEGAN, MAINE, 1996 (Selbstporträt am See, Skowhegan, Maine) das Fenster hinter der Künstlerin den Widerschein des Sonnenuntergangs, den sie selbst mit einem Ausdruck betrachtet, als schwebe sie verloren irgendwo zwischen der untergehenden Sonne und der Dunkelheit in ihrem eigenen Inneren. Ein anderes, wichtiges Bild, SELF-PORTRAIT AT GOLDEN RIVER ON BRIDGE, SILVER HILL, 1998 (Selbstporträt am Golden River auf der Brücke, Silver Hill), verbindet Allegorisches mit Autobiographischem. Die Brücke war ein Ort, den sie oft aufsuchte, sie liegt auf dem Grundstück einer Drogenentzugsklinik, in der sich Goldin nach einem Rückfall aufhielt. Diese Arbeit treibt das Wechselspiel von Wasser und Licht, das in vielen ihrer neuen Arbeiten so wichtig ist, noch weiter. Die formale und metaphorische Abfolge beginnt mit der diagonalen Trennung von Licht und Dunkelheit, die sich aus der Höhe der Brücke ergibt, auf der sich die Künstlerin mit der Kamera (und damit auch das Auge des Betrachters) befindet, und aus dem darunter fliessenden Wasser, auf welches der Schatten der Künstlerin fällt. In dieser sprechenden Szene bringt Goldin poetische Topoi der Identitätssuche ins Spiel, indem sie die Dialektik von Licht und Schatten, Objekt und Schatten, Festem und Flüssigem, Dauer und Veränderung kontrolliert einsetzt. Mit der Brücke, dem Schatten, den funkelnden Lichtreflexen, dem dahinströmenden Fluss und seinem harten, felsigen Grund enthält dieses Bild für Goldin «beides, eine definitive Abschiedsbotschaft und ein hoffnungsvolles Aufatmen».[6)]

Goldins Photographie hat sich verändert, weil sie eine andere Künstlerin geworden ist. Die Stakkato-Diaschauen haben uns den Atem geraubt mit ihren harten Zeugnissen individueller Ausschweifungen und jugendlicher Indiskretionen, ihrer verhängnisvoll brutalen Offenheit und der neusten ausgeflippten Musik. Aber das Fest ist zu Ende, und wie aus Goldins eigenen photographischen Aufzeichnungen zu entnehmen ist, müssen sie und ihre Freunde sich glücklich schätzen überlebt zu haben. Das Tageslicht und etwas «Urlaub» von der Stadt haben sie eine neue Aussenwelt entdecken lassen; tragische Begebenheiten haben die Künstlerin zu einer inneren Suche veranlasst; und die Verluste, die sie in ihrem Kreis erleben musste, festigten die Bande zu Freunden und Familie.

Nan Goldins Bilder erforschen immer noch Liebe und Verlust, Individuum und Gruppe, Inneres und Äusseres, aber heute stützt sie sich weniger auf die Tatsache, dass sie ein kontaktfreudiger Mensch ist, und mehr darauf, sie selbst zu sein. Sie nimmt – und teilt – ihre weiter gefasste, ein bisschen freundlichere Sicht des Lebens und macht Bilder daraus, die wirklich, wie sie selbst sagt, «Wesen sind, die den Moment überdauern».[7)] *(Übersetzung: Susanne Schmidt)*

1) Nan Goldin, *Couples and Loneliness*, Korinsha Press, Tokio 1998, S. 85.
2) Ebenda, S. 95.
3) Goldin, unveröffentlichte Äusserung, 1. Oktober 1989.
4) Goldin im Gespräch mit der Autorin, Houston, 23. Juni 1999. Aufnahme eines Gesprächs für die Audio-Tour zur Ausstellung «Nan Goldin: Recent Photographs» im Contemporary Arts Museum, Houston (25. Juni–8. August 1999).
5) Ebenda.
6) Ebenda.
7) Goldin im Gespräch mit der Autorin, New York, 30. April 1999.

BILDER DER INTIMITÄT

ULMANN-MATTHIAS HAKERT

Insofern Nan Goldins Photographien Geschichten erzählen, tritt der Tod in ihnen auf. Um diese Behauptung aufzustellen, bedarf es nicht einmal der Betrachtungsweise eines Roland Barthes, nach der die vollendete Zukunft des photographischen Moments auf die eigene Sterblichkeit verweist.[1)] In Geschichten von Menschen ist die Begegnung mit dem Tod unvermeidlich. In Goldins Bilderwelt geht es aber nicht um irgendeine *Comédie humaine*, sondern um Nans Welt. Die Leidenschaftlichkeit dieser Bilder folgt nicht blind dem Prinzip der Photographie, für die es nichts gibt, was nicht abzubilden wäre, vielmehr lenkt die Kamera seit Ende der 60er Jahre, als Nan Goldin zu photographieren begann, einen persönlichen Blick auf einen bestimmten Ausschnitt individueller Existenz. Es kommt der Zeitpunkt, zu dem in Nans unmittelbarer Umgebung, in ihrem Freundeskreis, der Tod nicht mehr nur eine allgemein menschliche Gewissheit ist, sondern ein bestimmter. Spätestens ab Mitte der 80er Jahre ist die Realität, die die Photographien der Existenz von Dragqueens und Schwulen oder der Sucht, dem Rausch und der Sexualität verleihen, ohne Aids unvorstellbar. Die Selbstverständlichkeit, mit der manche Photographien nun auch Krankheit und Tote zeigen, ist nicht mehr als ein Beleg für Authentizität – und nicht weniger, denn der Anspruch photographischer Authentizität schockiert.

Der erste Apologet der Daguerreotypie, Dominique François Arago,[2)] und noch ihr späterer Kritiker Charles Baudelaire[3)] sahen in der Technik der Photographie eine objektive Wahrheit triumphieren. Was Arago als Erfolg der Wissenschaft pries, verachtete Baudelaire als Dummheit seines Jahrhunderts, dessen Erbe sich im zwanzigsten Jahrhundert zu einer Folge ungeheurer Katastrophen türmte. Ausgelöst wurde eine Bilderflut des Entsetzens, die allein schon genügen sollte, kein Abbild mehr als verbürgt gelten zu lassen. Tatsächlich wurde die Manipulation der Photographie selbst zum Instrument des Terrors, und der technische Fortschritt der Bildmedien nährte vor allem das Gefühl der Ohnmacht.

«Früher dachte ich, ich könnte verhindern jemanden zu verlieren, wenn ich nur genügend Photos von ihm machte. So stellte ich diese Bilderserie von Cookie aus den 13 Jahren unserer Bekanntschaft zusammen, damit ich sie immer um mich haben könnte. Tatsächlich zeigen sie mir nur, wie viel ich verloren habe.» Der Kommentar Nan Goldins zu ihren eigenen Bildern liest sich wie eine Vignette zum medialen Scherbenhaufen am Ende dieses Jahrhunderts. Wie beim proustschen Erzähler dient die Zeit als Lehrmeister. Wie in *Auf der Suche nach der Verlorenen Zeit* ist der Ausgangspunkt nicht Unwissenheit, sondern Voreingenommenheit, die in der späteren Erfahrung der Wahrheit aufgehoben bleibt. Die Porträts von Cookie, Gilles und anderen Freunden beanspruchen keinerlei Objektivität, sondern sind authentisch in ihrer Parteinahme, dem Verlangen nach Nähe und dem Wunsch, die Dargestellten möchten sich in den Bildern wieder erkennen, als Ausgangspunkt.

1988 kritisierte *ACT UP New York* an einer Ausstellung des Photographen Nicholas Nixon, Aids-Kranke würden als Menschen dargestellt, die man bemitleiden oder fürchten müsse. Das anhaltende Schweigen über Aids hatte umso empfindlicher gegen entwürdigende Bilder des Leidens und Sterbens gemacht, als

ULMANN-MATTHIAS HAKERT ist freier Autor und lebt in Berlin.

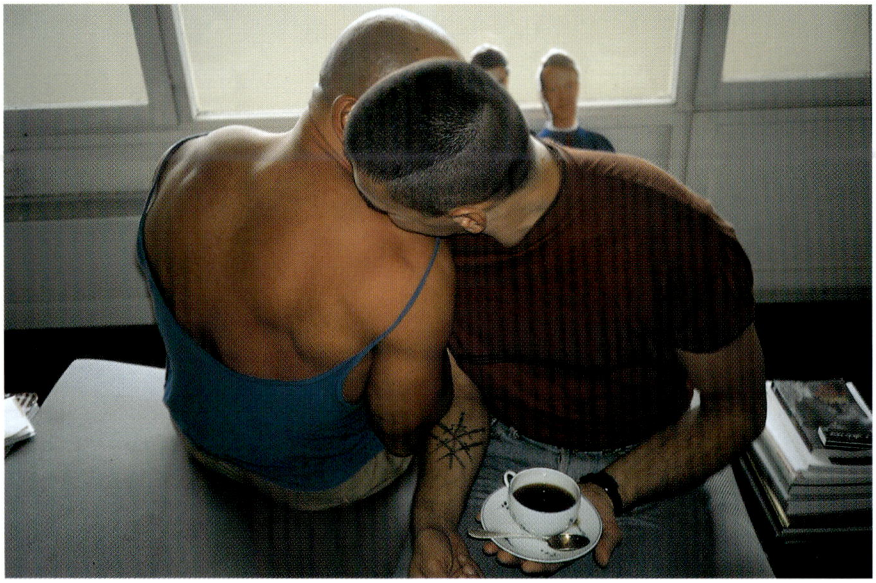

NAN GOLDIN, GILLES AND GOTSCHO EMBRACING, PARIS, 1992 / GILLES UND GOTSCHO KÜSSEN SICH.

es auf der Ächtung der mit HIV/Aids Lebenden beruhte. Goldins im darauf folgenden Jahr entstandenen letzten Porträts von Cookie lassen in ihrer über mehr als ein Jahrzehnt durch die Photographie hergestellten Intimität alles andere als ein vordergründiges Interesse an Krankheit, Schmerz und Tod erkennen. Die Körperlichkeit, in der sich Gilles und Gotscho der Kamera präsentieren, zeigt zärtliche Vertrautheit und Trennung, die sich im Kuss Gotschos für Gilles als unüberwindbar erweist.

Zwangsläufig oder auch beiläufig – je nachdem, ob man auf den Moment der von der Kamera hervorgebrachten Intimität oder auf die Dauer, in der diese Intimität sich entwickelte, blickt – gerieten Goldins Bilder von Mitgliedern ihrer «Familie», die an Aids erkrankten und an dessen Folgen verstarben, zu authentischen Bildern des Lebens mit Aids, weil diese Bilder für den Betrachter als Kommunikation und Identifikation der Photographin mit den Porträtierten erkennbar werden. Es ist die Präsenz Nan Goldins in ihren Bildern, die zuletzt für das Geschehene bürgt, indem sie Einfluss nimmt auf die Selbstinszenierung derjenigen, die sich vor der Kamera exponieren. COOKIES UND VITTORIOS WOHNZIMMER, NYC, WEIHNACHTEN 1989 zeigt nur mehr ein leeres Sofa. Darüber sind Photoporträts von Cookie ins Bild gerückt. Im Glas der Bilder spiegelt sich das Licht der Apparatur, mit der die Photographin arbeitete. Sie selbst ist unsichtbar anwesend wie die Verstorbene.

1) Roland Barthes, *Die helle Kammer*, Suhrkamp, Frankfurt am Main 1989.
2) «Die erste Mitteilung Aragos an die Académie des Sciences, am 7. Januar 1839», in: Wolfgang Baier: *Quellendarstellungen zur Geschichte der Photographie*, Fotokino-Verlag, Halle an der Saale 1964, S. 75 ff.
3) Charles Baudelaire, *Salon de 1859*, in: *Œuvres complètes*, Bd. 2, Bibliothèque de la Pléiade, Gallimard, Paris 1976, S. 614 ff.

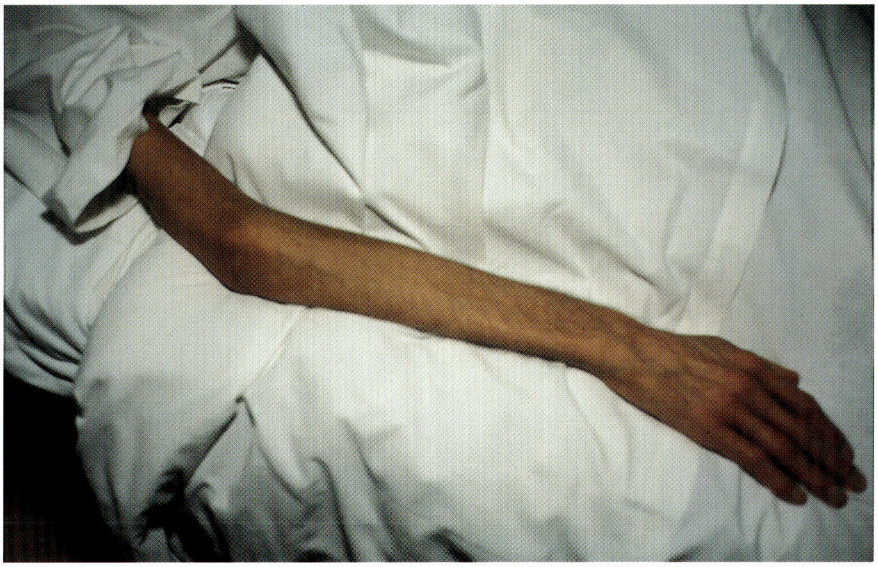

NAN GOLDIN, GILLES' ARM, PARIS, 1993.

IMAGES OF INTIMACY

ULMANN-MATTHIAS HAKERT

Inasmuch as Nan Goldin's photographs tell stories, death always has a say in them. To make this claim, you do not even have to share Roland Barthes's viewpoint that the photographic moment refers to one's own mortality.[1] The encounter with death is inevitable in human experience, but in these photographs we are confronted with Nan's world and not with a generalized *comédie humaine*. The passion of her pictures does not blindly illustrate the principle that there is nothing photography cannot depict, but rather takes a personal look at a specific slice of individual existence. Though Nan Goldin started making photographs in the late sixties, there came a time when in the context of her life among her friends, death was no longer simply a universal certainty but a very specific one. At the latest by the mid-eighties the reality of the existence of drag queens and homo-

ULMANN-MATTHIAS HAKERT is a writer who lives in Berlin.

sexuals, of addiction, intoxication and sexuality, which these photographs convey, would have been inconceivable without AIDS. The self-evidence with which some of her photographs show illness and death is neither more nor less than a proof of authenticity: The claim to photographic authenticity is plain shocking.

Dominique François Arago, the first defender of the daguerreotype,[2] and her later critic Charles Baudelaire[3] saw the technique of photography as the triumph of objective truth. However, what Arago lauded as a great scientific achievement, Baudelaire condemned as the idiocy of his century, whose legacy has led in our century to a series of mushrooming catastrophes. The resulting deluge of horrific images has effectively succeeded in undermining the authenticity of all depiction. Photographic manipulation has itself become an instrument of terror and the technological advances of visual media have merely heightened the feeling of impotence. "I used to think I couldn't lose anyone if I photographed them enough. I put together this series of pictures of Cookie from the thirteen years I knew her in order to keep her with me. In fact, they show me how much I've lost." Nan Goldin's commentary on her own pictures reads like a nutshell description of the technological mess at the end of the twentieth century. Time is the teacher, as it was for Proust's narrator, and as in *Remembrance of Things Past*, the point of departure that is stored in the succeeding experience of truth is not one of ignorance but of partiality. The portraits of Cookie, Gilles, and other friends do not lay claim to objectivity; they are utterly authentic in their subjectivity, in their longing for closeness, and in Goldin's desire for her subjects to be able to recognize themselves in her pictures.

In 1988, ACT UP criticized a New York showing of Nicholas Nixon's photographs for representing AIDS patients as people to be pitied or feared. This persistent refusal to acknowledge AIDS made its victims all the more sensitive to humiliating images of suffering and dying, as they were based on the ostracism of those living with the virus. Goldin's last portraits of Cookie, made the following year with the intimacy of more than a decade of portraiture, show anything but a shallow interest in illness, pain, and death. The way in which Gilles and Gotacho present their bodies to the camera testifies to an ambiguous familiarity and inevitable separation that proves insurmountable in death.

Inevitably or accidentally, depending on whether we mark the moment of intimacy generated by the camera or the time it has taken to develop this intimacy, Goldin's pictures of the members of her family who have contracted and died of AIDS become authentic pictures of life with AIDS: Viewers discover in them the photographer's communication and identification with her subjects. It is Nan Goldin's presence in her pictures that ultimately vouches for their authenticity, inasmuch as she acts upon the way her subjects expose themselves to the camera. COOKIE AND VITTORIO'S LIVING ROOM, NYC, CHRISTMAS, 1989 shows only an empty couch and, above it, photo portraits of Cookie. The photographer's flash equipment is reflected in the glass. She herself is invisibly present like her deceased friend.

(Translation: Catherine Schelbert)

1) Roland Barthes, *Camera lucida* (New York: Hill and Wang, 1981).
2) "Arago's Report for the French Chamber of Deputies on the 3rd July 1938," in: *An Historical and Descriptive Account of the Various Processes of the Daguerreotype and the Diorama,* by Louis J. Daguerre, London, 1839 (New York: Kraus Reprint, 1969), pp. 7–31.
3) Charles Baudelaire, *Salon de 1859,* in: *Œuvres complètes,* vol. 2, Bibliothèque de la Pléiade (Paris: Gallimard, 1976), pp. 614–19.

"Suzanne and Phillipe on the Train, Long Island, 1985"

DEBORAH EISENBERG

By the time one encounters the photograph SUZANNE AND PHILLIPE ON THE TRAIN, LONG ISLAND, 1985, it's likely that one has already seen a number of Goldin's photographs and is familiar with Suzanne, with a gallery of Goldin's friends, and moments in their lives over a period of years—a whole community of photographs. And one will be familiar with the sight, in these pictures, of much being overcome.

Here an atmosphere of fatefulness presses in. We get an immediate impression that the people we're looking at are being conveyed, but it takes a moment (at least it did for me) to understand that the way they're being conveyed is by train, an ordinary train, and not—after having been sorted—by some elaborate mechanical means along a mysterious corridor. The partitions between these people are barriers no more inevitable or insurmountable than the seat backs, we understand after a moment; these are simply people on a train.

But although they're on the train no doubt voluntarily, embattlement and protection are implicit in Suzanne and Phillipe's complicated embrace, their clothing, the bracelet and the potent-looking amulet or adornment Suzanne wears on a delicate chain around her neck, in her expression, vigilant, possibly somewhat defiant, direct, far-seeing. And the people behind Phillipe and Suzanne are blurry and not fully visible, as if they were only provisionally committed to existence, or have been substantially defeated by it. By contrast, Suzanne's astonishing and astonishingly expressive face (or the face which Goldin has enabled us to understand as astonishing and astonishingly expressive) appears as heroically courageous, and Phillipe's sleep as fragile and blessed.

Although conventional and conventionalizing categories of human experience are clearly being probed, mocked, approximated, and exploited by most of the subjects in these photographs, the viewer, on the other hand, is pretty much forced to discard such categories. How—even more, why—would we ever evaluate within this world what is masculine and what is feminine, what is beautiful and what is ugly, what is decent and what is indecent, what constitutes power and what constitutes weakness? Certainly social questions such as these underlie the photographs and also give daily form to our own thrashings through life. But the pictures give us a little relief from these questions, some breathing room, and refresh our feeling of outrage at the triviality and the violence in the way these strictures tend to be so complacently laid down. The mundane appears not only as the enemy of the only sort of experience worth having, but also necessarily as its setting, the matrix from which it, in all its gorgeous plumage, will (if it does) arise.

The most mundane—or mundanifying, if I may—element which Goldin and her gallant subjects appear always to be in battle against is time. Each moment or arc of moments Goldin gives us seems lit-

---

DEBORAH EISENBERG's most recent collection of fiction, *All Around Atlantis*, has been published by Farrar, Straus and Giroux, 1997.

erally captured, a bravura rescue from the rushing erasures of time. Experience and urgent memory triumph in the luscious peculiarity and particularity of the colors, and—despite time's inevitable tendency to domesticate and render things bearable or to reformulate our histories into a semblance of "life"—in the intractability, spontaneity, and piercingness of the images. These are moments of tremendous intensity, and we are allowed an extremely intimate look at them.

Goldin's album-like oeuvre is, of course, an ideal way to express the quality of friendships. And beyond her work there's not too much art that concerns itself deeply and preeminently with friendship; one thinks immediately of *The Magic Flute,* of *Jules et Jim,* but then one is left a bit scratching one's head. After all, friendship is very difficult to represent. Because it moves and changes, it would seem to be best suited to a medium that also moves and changes—the novel, perhaps most obviously. But because friendship is a protean emotional environment, really, rather than a "feeling"—something like the little universe in a terrarium—novelistic friendships often drown in plot or flashier human interactions.

Clearly, SUZANNE AND PHILLIPE ON THE TRAIN—a single image—is a stunning portrait not only of the quality of a particular friendship and a particular moment in it, but also of the quality of friendship itself. And even Goldin's many images of solitary subjects absorbed in inner contemplation, or of "empty" rooms feel to me in part like encapsulations of friendship. Something is always going back and forth between these pictures and you as you look at them, as if the threshold between you were weakening under pressure. Looking at the photographs we recognize along with the photographer the struggle of the subjects to live as they can. And in that act of shared recognition, it feels that our own struggle has been registered as well—the work comes forward to include us.

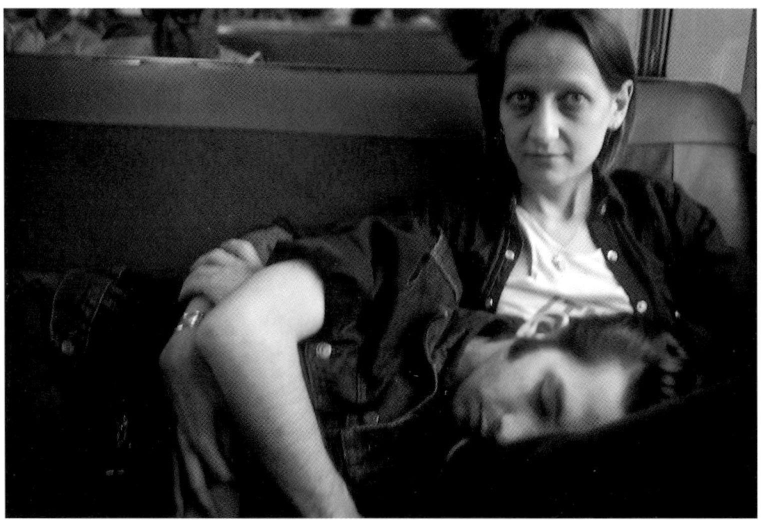

NAN GOLDIN, SUZANNE AND PHILLIPE ON THE TRAIN, LONG ISLAND, 1985 / SUZANNE UND PHILLIPE IM ZUG, LONG ISLAND.

Suzanne und Phillipe im Zug, Long Island, 1985

DEBORAH EISENBERG

Wer auf das Photo SUZANNE UND PHILLIPE IM ZUG, LONG ISLAND, 1985, stösst, wird vorher auch schon andere Bilder von Nan Goldin gesehen haben und vertraut sein mit Suzanne, ja einer ganzen Galerie von Menschen, die der Künstlerin nahe stehen, und einzelnen – über den Zeitraum einiger Jahre verteilten – Momenten aus ihrem Leben. Ein ganzer Clan von Photographien! Auch dass in diesen Bildern viel bewältigt wird, wird einem bekannt vorkommen.

Das Bild, von dem hier die Rede ist, hat etwas Schicksalhaftes. Zwar ist einem sofort klar, dass die Personen, die man sieht, irgendwie befördert werden, doch erkennt man nicht gleich (zumindest ich nicht), dass das Transportmittel ein ganz gewöhnlicher Zug ist, und nicht etwa ein komplizierter mechanischer Apparat, der sie – nachdem sie dafür ausgesondert wurden – einen mysteriösen Korridor entlanggleiten lässt. Auf den zweiten Blick wird deutlich: Die Trennwände zwischen diesen Personen sind Schranken, nicht schwieriger zu umgehen oder zu überwinden als Sitzrücklehnen; es sind schlicht und einfach Menschen im Zug.

Aber auch wenn sie diesen Zug zweifelsohne freiwillig bestiegen haben, drücken Suzannes und Phillipes komplizierte Umarmung, ihre Kleidung, das Armband, das mächtige Amulett oder der Anhänger, den Suzanne an einer dünnen Kette um den Hals trägt, sowie ihr wachsamer, möglicherweise auch etwas herausfordernder, direkter und in die Ferne gerichteter Blick Kampf- und Schutzbereitschaft aus. Die Menschen hinter Phillipe und Suzanne sind verschwommen und halb verdeckt, als ob sie nur eine provisorische Existenz führten oder in ihrer Substanz angegriffen wären. Im Gegensatz dazu wirkt Suzannes erstaunliches und erstaunlich ausdrucksvolles Gesicht (oder das Gesicht, das wir dank Nan Goldin als erstaunlich und erstaunlich ausdrucksvoll wahrnehmen) heroisch entschlossen, während Phillipe leicht und selig zu schlafen scheint.

Obwohl die meisten Personen, die in diesen Photographien auftreten, klischeehafte und klischierende Kategorien menschlicher Erfahrung ausprobieren, verspotten, ausreizen und ausbeuten, ist der Betrachter seinerseits mehr oder weniger gezwungen, solche Kategorien zu verwerfen. Wie, oder vielmehr, warum sollten wir jemals im Rahmen dieser Welt beurteilen, was männlich und was weiblich, was schön und was hässlich, was anständig und was unanständig ist, was Kraft und was Schwäche darstellt? Sicherlich sind gesellschaftliche Fragen wie diese unterschwellig auch in Goldins Photographien vorhanden, so, wie sie auch unseren eigenen Kampf tagtäglich bestimmen. Doch die Bilder lassen uns diese Fragen vorübergehend vergessen, geben uns Raum zum Atmen und liefern unserer Empörung über die banale und gewaltsame Art, mit der diese Zwänge so selbstgerecht institutionalisiert werden, frische Nahrung. Das Profane erscheint nicht nur als Feind jeder lohnenswerten Erfahrung, sondern notgedrungen auch als der Rahmen, die Matrix, aus der sie in ihrer ganzen Pracht (wenn sies denn tut) hervorgeht.

Das profanste – oder, wenn ich es so nennen darf, profanierendste – Element, gegen das Goldin und ihre tapferen Modelle ankämpfen, ist die Zeit. Jeder Augenblick oder jede Folge von Augenblicken, die uns Goldin vermittelt, scheint buchstäblich in einem

DEBORAH EISENBERG ist Schriftstellerin. Zuletzt erschien ihr Band mit Erzählungen, *All Around Atlantis*, bei Farrar, Straus & Giroux, New York 1997.

tollkühnen Akt der rasanten Vernichtung durch die Zeit entrissen. Erfahrung und zwingende Erinnerung triumphieren in der überwältigenden Eigenart und Einzigartigkeit der Farben und in der Hartnäckigkeit, Spontaneität und Eindringlichkeit dieser Bilder, entgegen der unvermeidlichen Tendenz der Zeit, die Dinge zu domestizieren und erträglicher zu machen oder unsere Geschichten so zu formulieren, dass sie den Anschein von «Leben» vermitteln. Es sind Augenblicke von ungeheurer Intensität, die uns in ihrer ganzen Intimität dargeboten werden.

Goldins albumähnliches Werk ist natürlich bestens geeignet das Wesentliche freundschaftlicher Beziehungen auszudrücken. Und neben ihren Arbeiten gibt es wenige Kunstwerke, die sich so eingehend mit Freundschaft auseinander setzen; *Die Zauberflöte* und *Jules et Jim* fallen einem dazu noch ein, aber damit hat es sich dann auch. Das Thema ist schwierig darzustellen. Weil sich Freundschaften ständig im Fluss befinden und verändern, böte sich ein Genre an, das sich ebenfalls ständig verändert – der Roman vielleicht. Da aber Freundschaft eher ein proteisches emotionales Feld ist als ein «Gefühl» – etwas wie ein kleiner Kosmos in einem Terrarium –, geht Freundschaft in Romanen gern in der Handlung oder anderen, spektakuläreren menschlichen Interaktionen unter.

Offensichtlich ist SUZANNE UND PHILLIPE IM ZUG – ein für sich stehendes Einzelbild – nicht nur ein hinreissendes Porträt dieser bestimmten Freundschaft und dieses einen Moments, sondern der Freundschaft überhaupt. Selbst Goldins Bilder von einsamen, in sich versunkenen Menschen oder «leeren» Räumen scheinen mir zum Teil von verpuppten Formen der Freundschaft zu handeln. Zwischen diesen Bildern und uns findet beim Betrachten ein ständiger Austausch statt, als würde die Schwelle zwischen ihnen und uns unter Druck nachgeben. Angesichts dieser Photographien erkennen wir Seite an Seite mit der Photographin den Kampf, den diese Personen führen um ihren Möglichkeiten entsprechend zu leben. Und in diesem gemeinsamen Akt der Erkenntnis fühlen wir uns auch in unserem eigenen Kampf gesehen und verstanden – das Werk kommt auf uns zu und schliesst uns mit ein.

(Übersetzung: Uta Goridis)

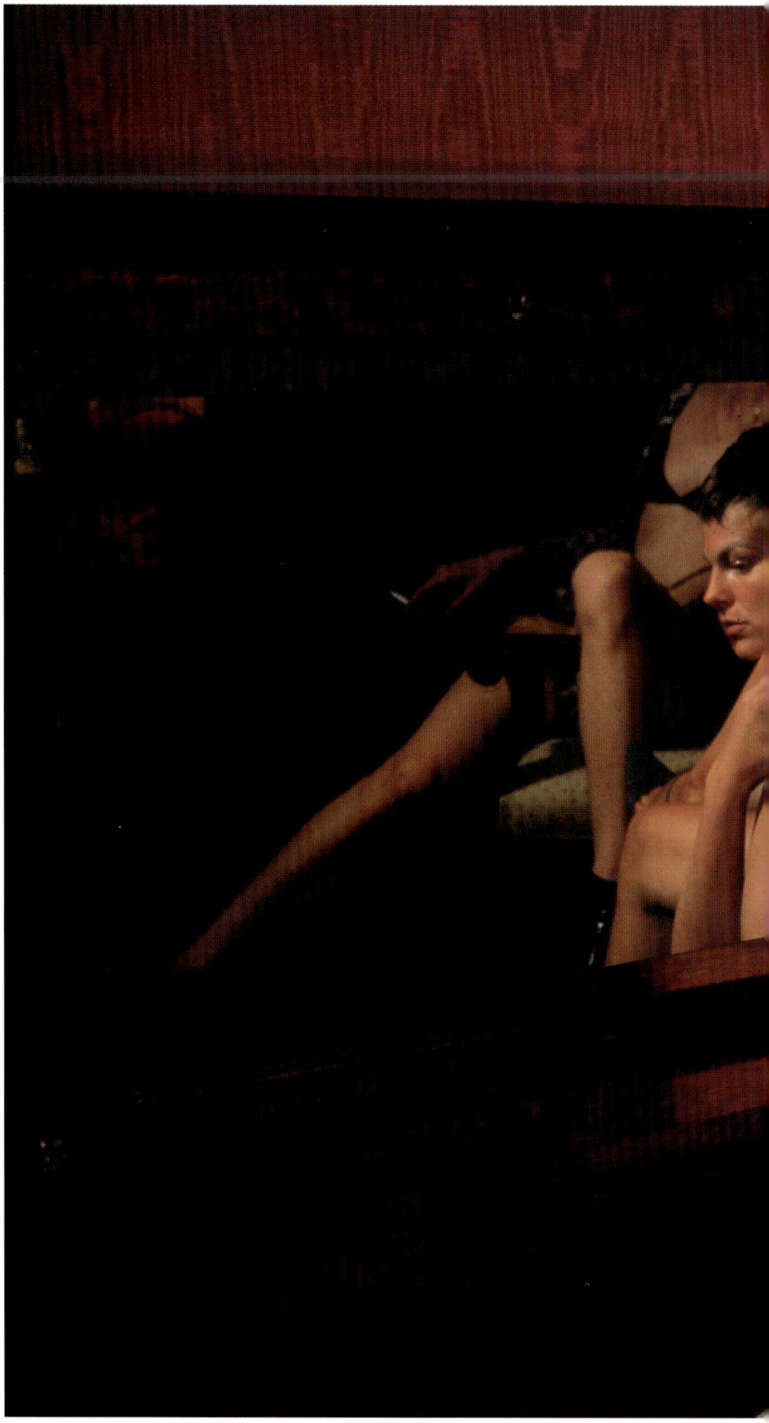

NAN GOLDIN, JOANA AND VALERIE IN THE MIRROR AT THE HOTEL, PARIS, 1999 / JOANA UND VALERIE IM SPIEGEL IHRES HOTELZIMMERS, PARIS.

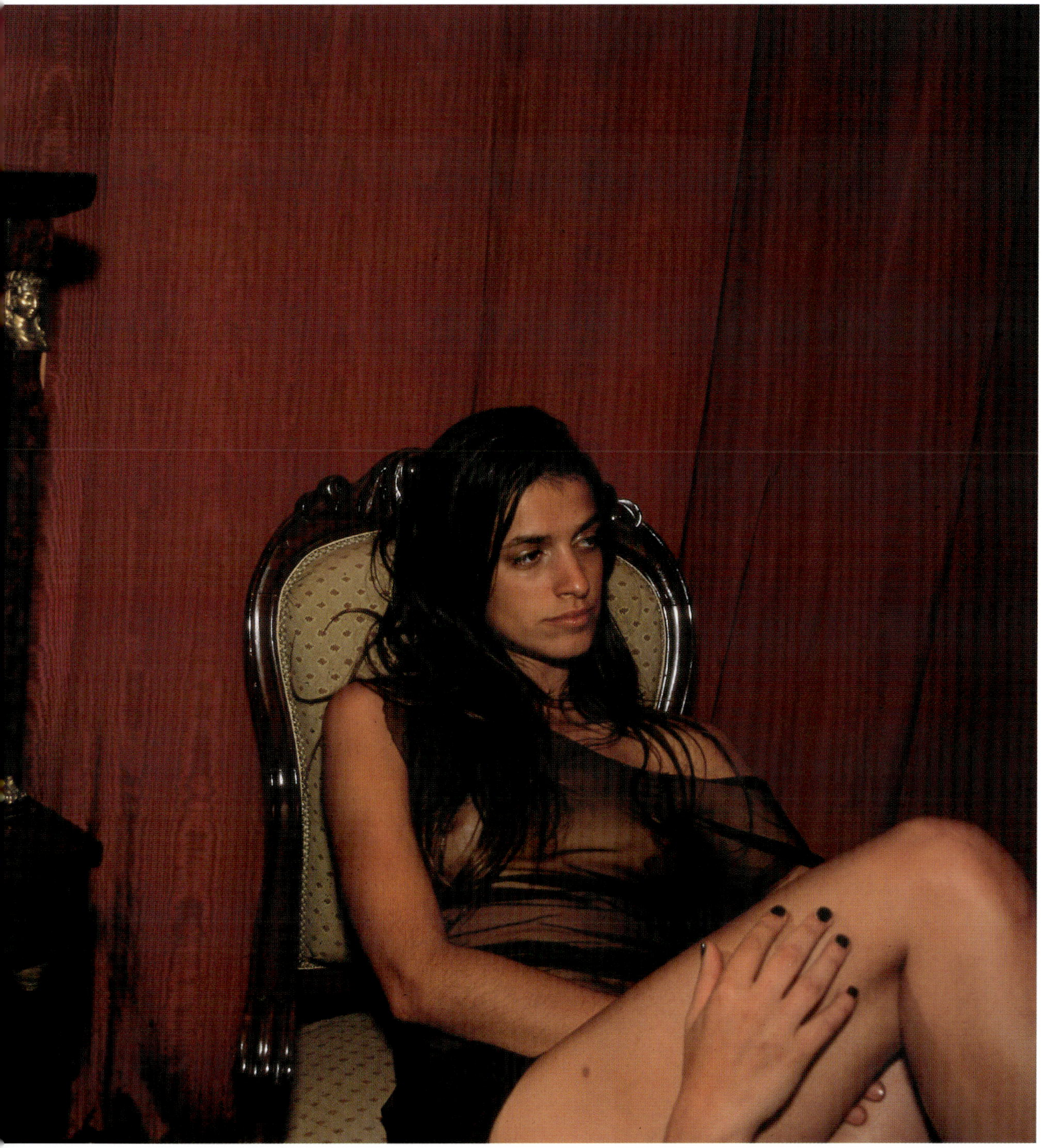

Edition for Parkett **NAN GOLDIN**

LAMBS EARS, 1999 C-print, $15\frac{3}{4}$ x $23\frac{5}{8}$" Edition of 60, signed and numbered

LÄMMEROHREN, 1999 C-Print, 40 x 60 cm Auflage: 60, signiert und nummeriert

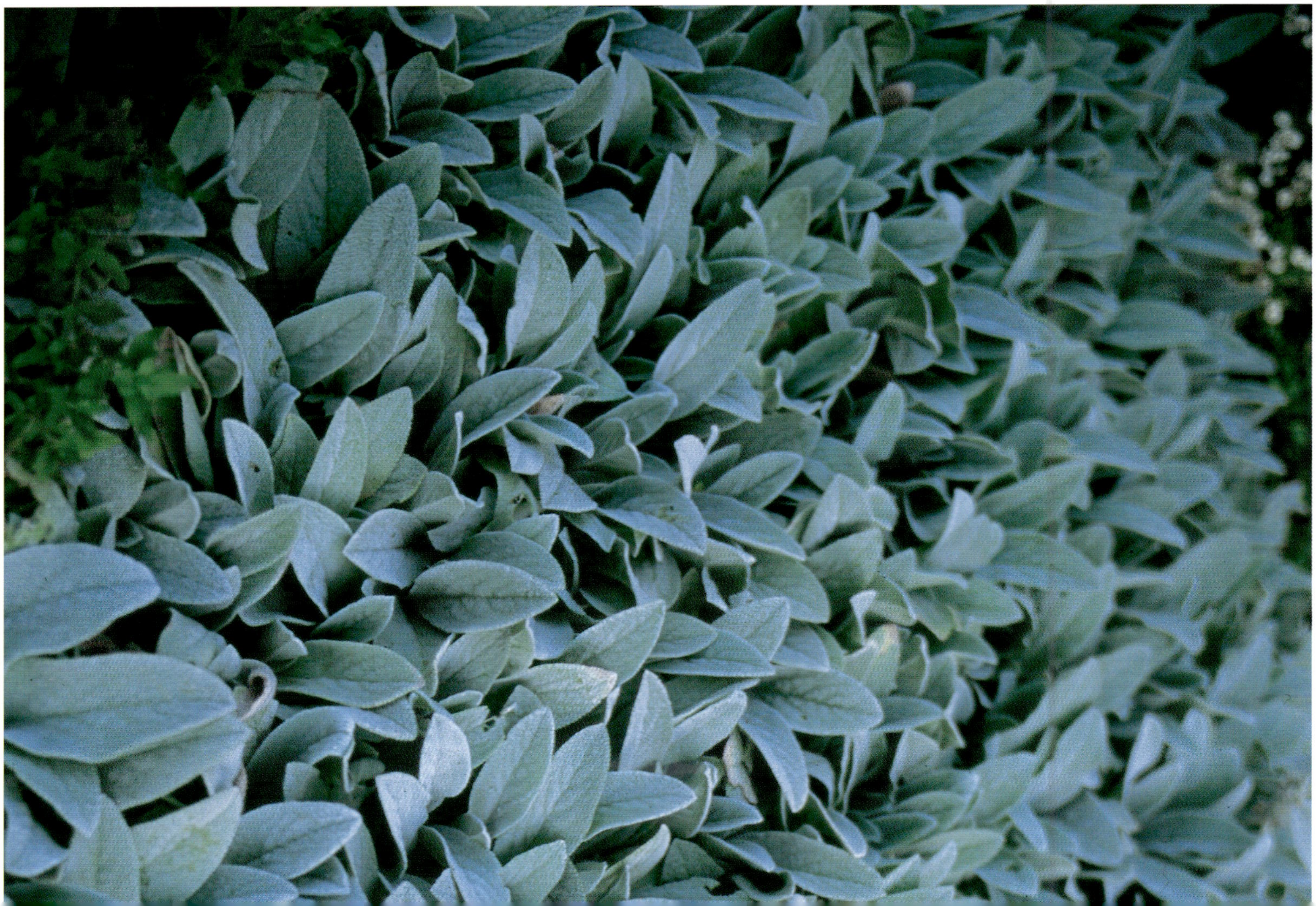

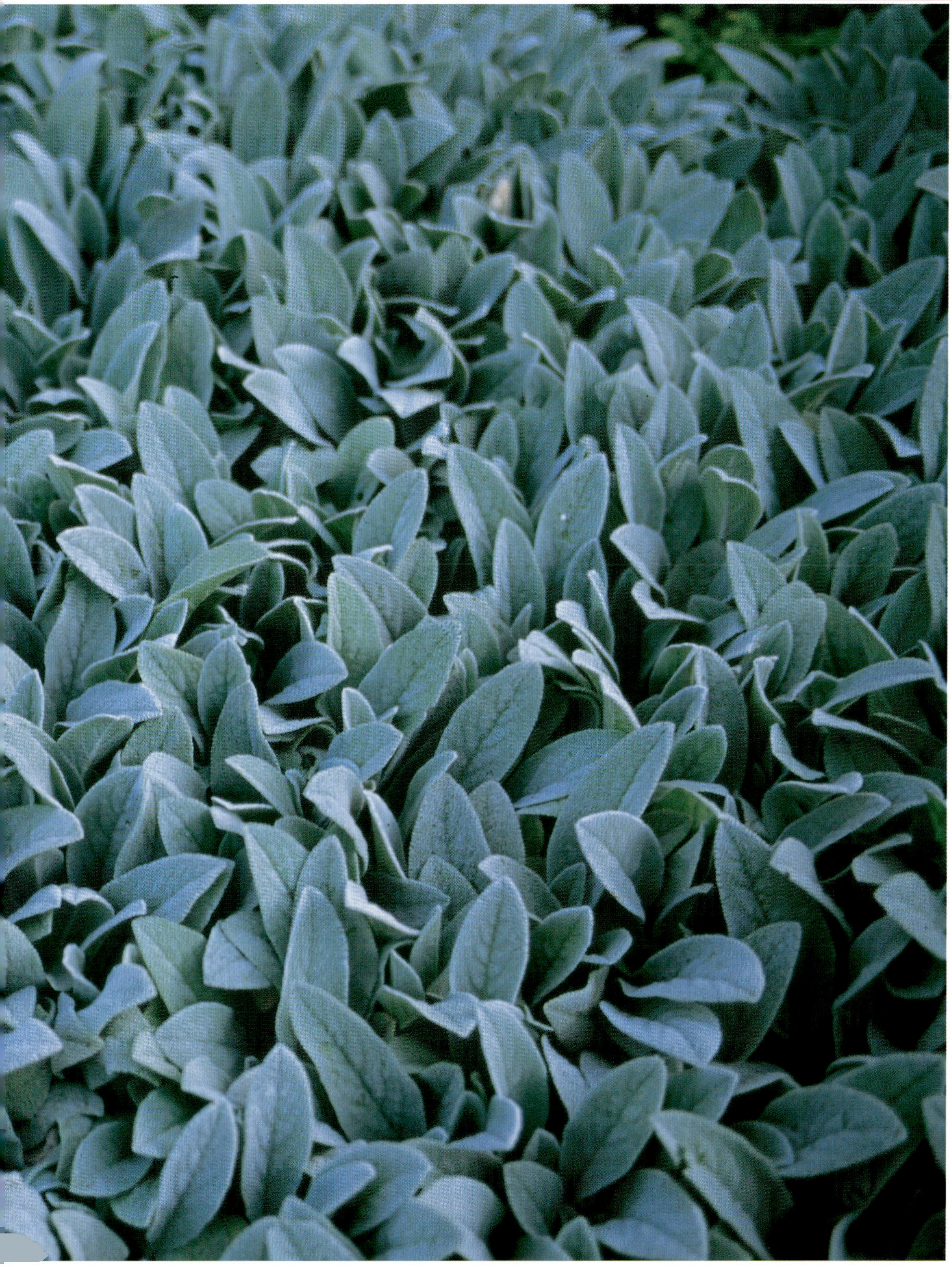

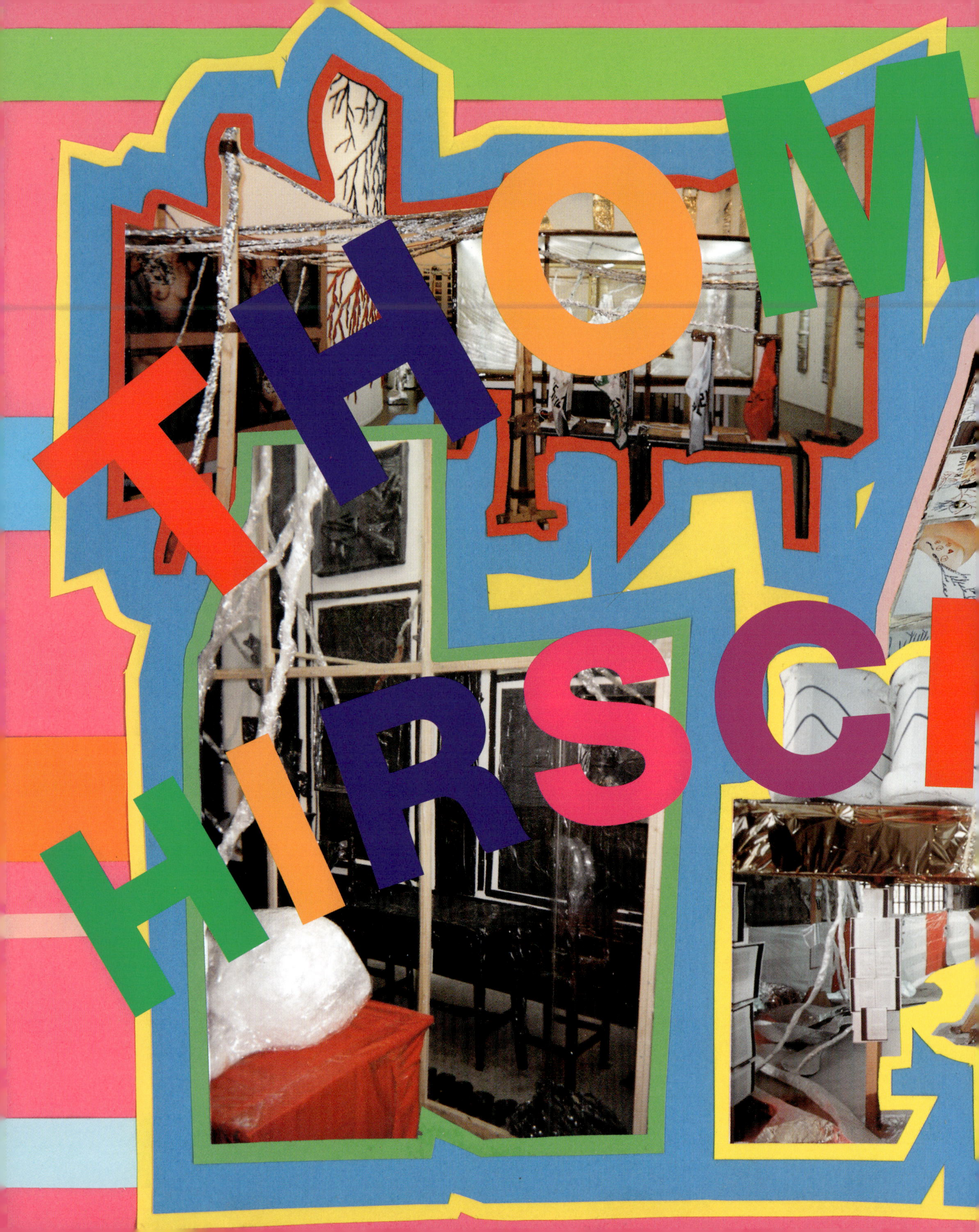
THOM
HIRSC

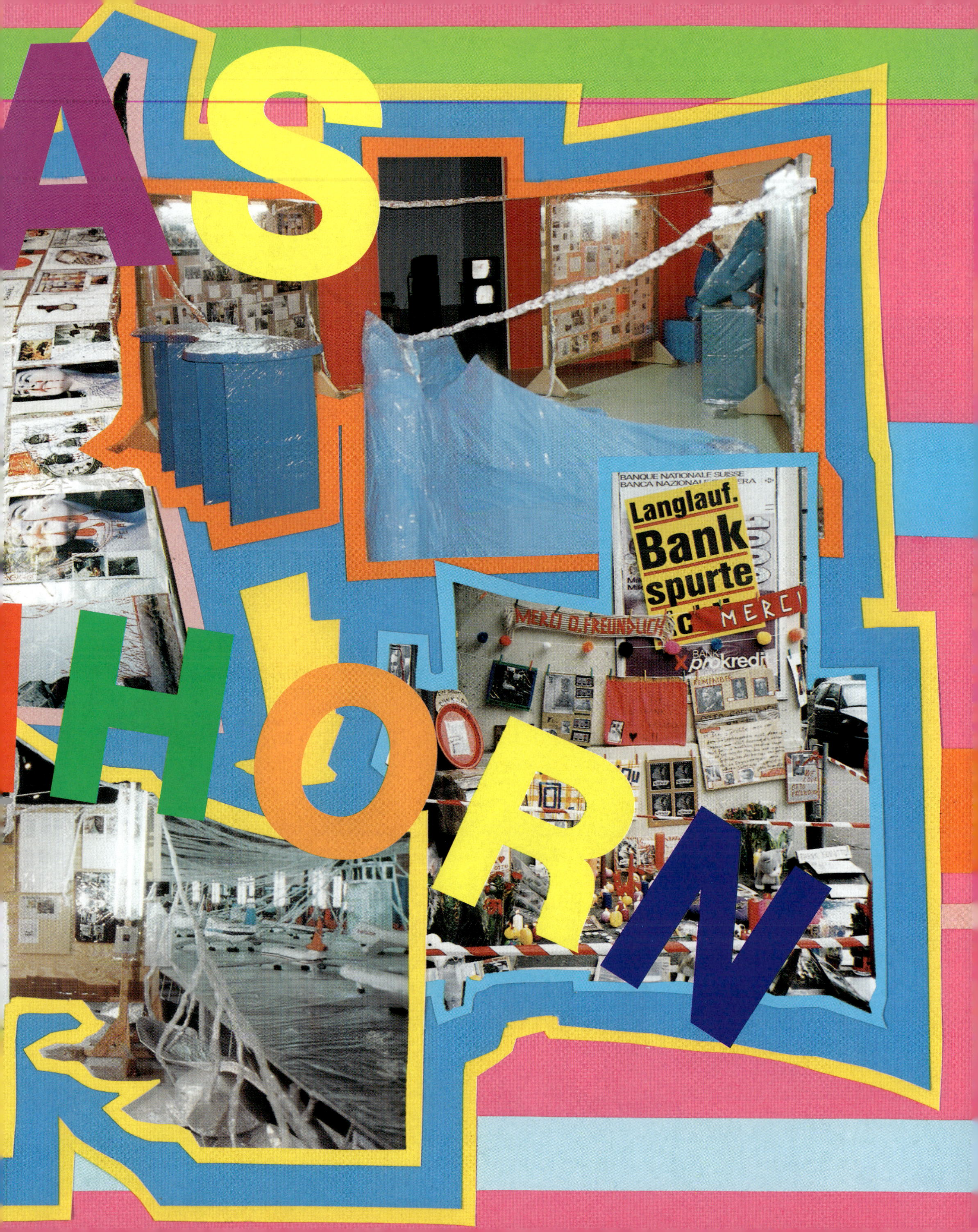
AS
HORN
BANQUE NATIONALE SUISSE
Langlauf.
Bank
spurte
MERCI

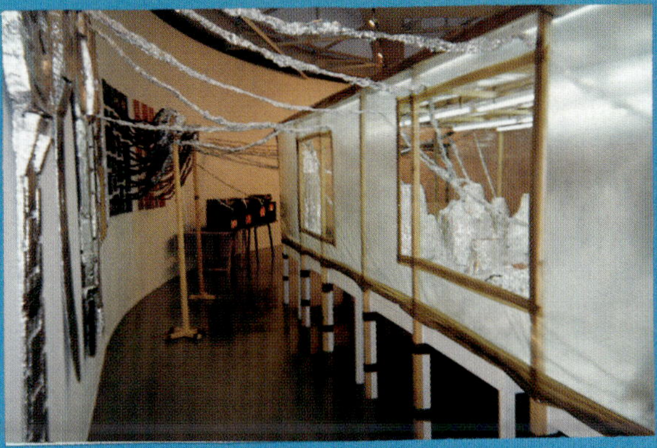

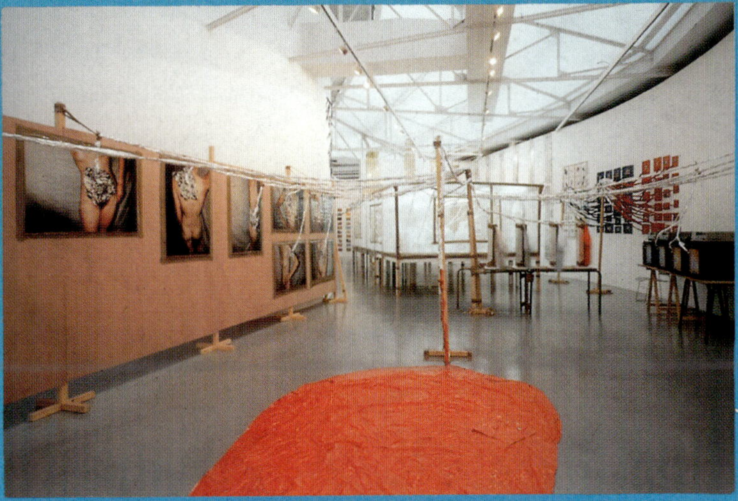

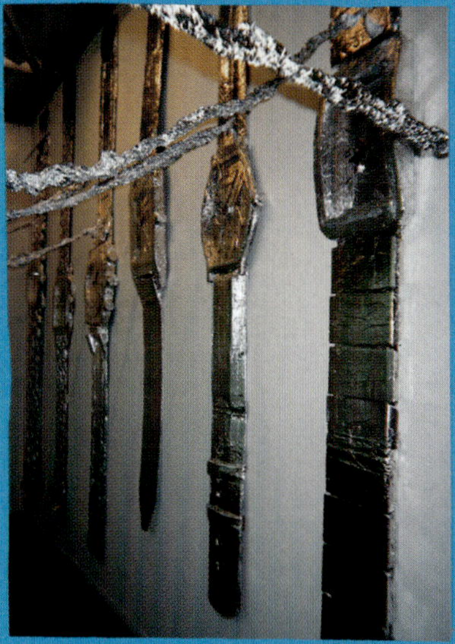

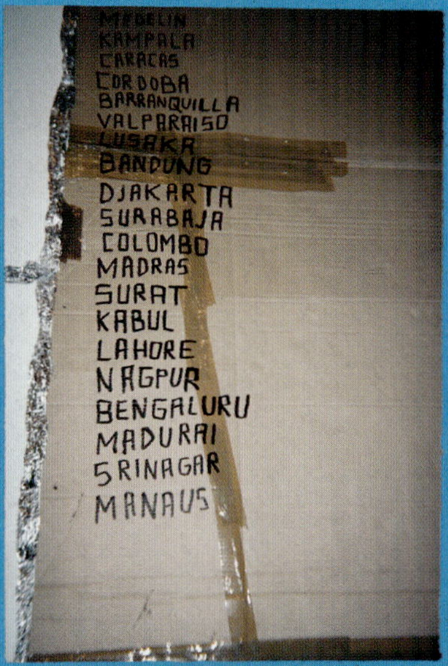

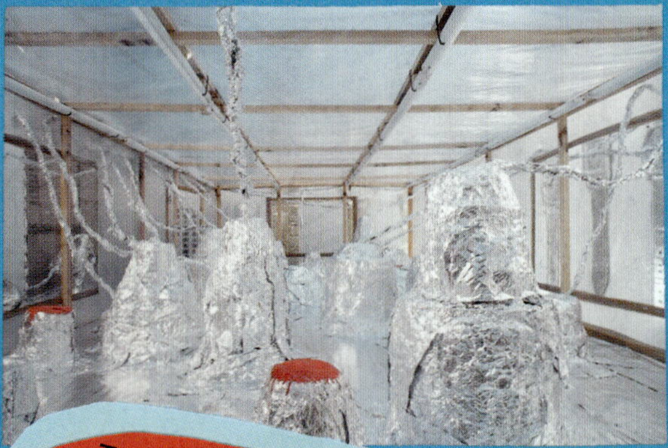

THOMAS HIRSCHHORN, TIME TO GO, 1997, group exhibition / Gruppenausstellung «Delta», Musée d'art moderne de la Ville de Paris, 1997.

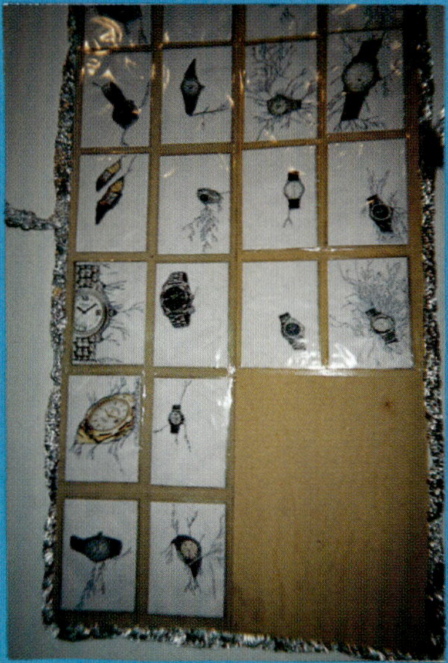

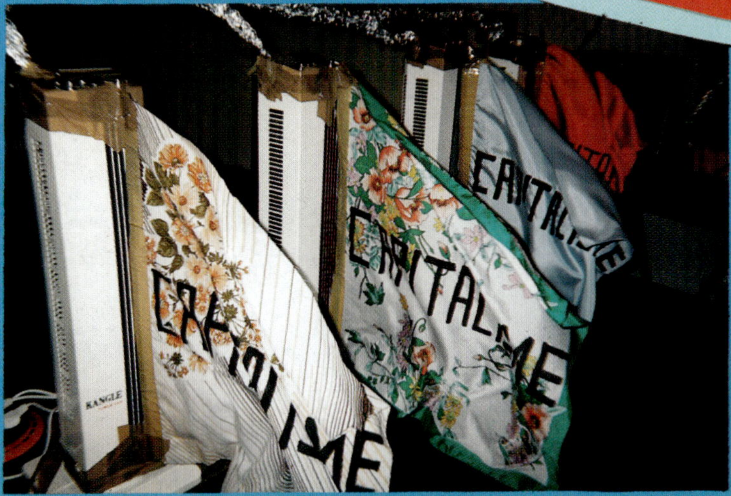

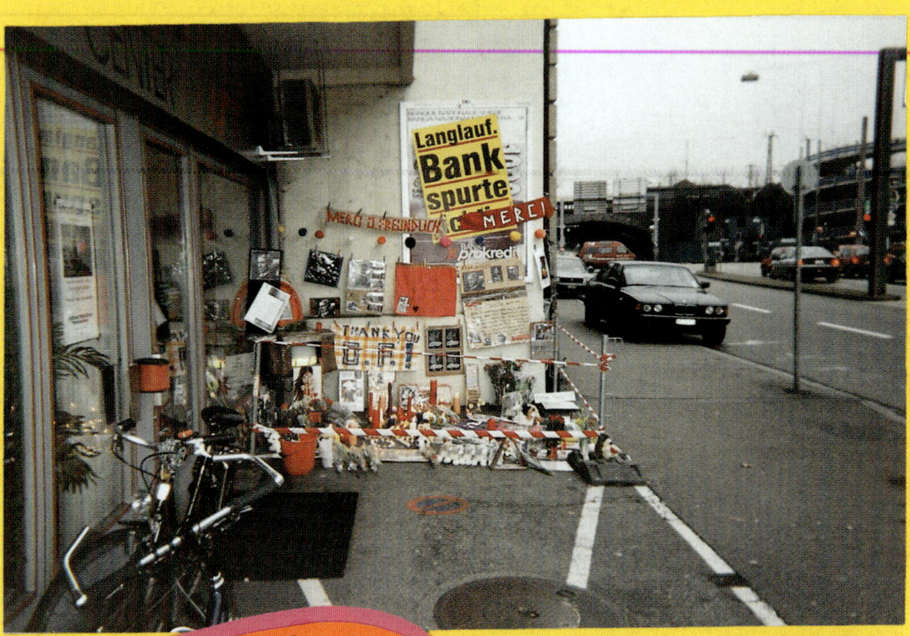

THOMAS HIRSCHHORN, OTTO FREUNDLICH ALTAR, 1998, group exhibition / Gruppen-ausstellung «Non lieux», Kaskadenkondensator, Basel, 1998.

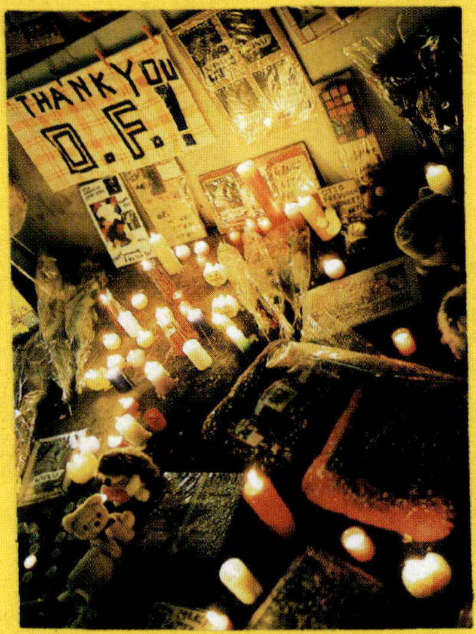

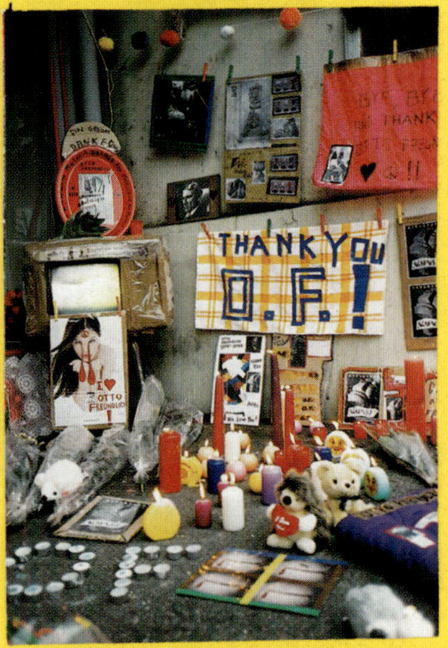

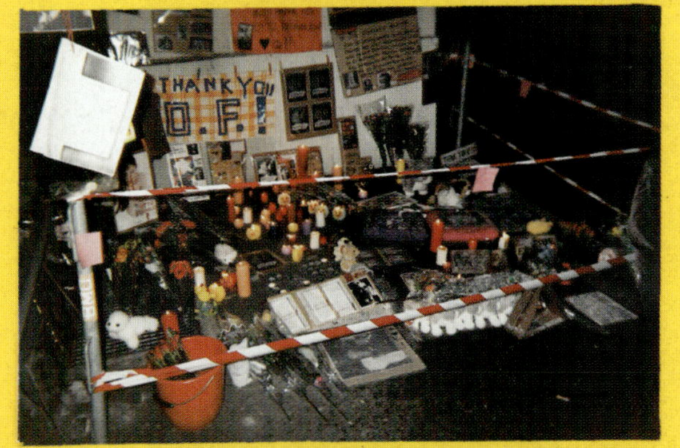

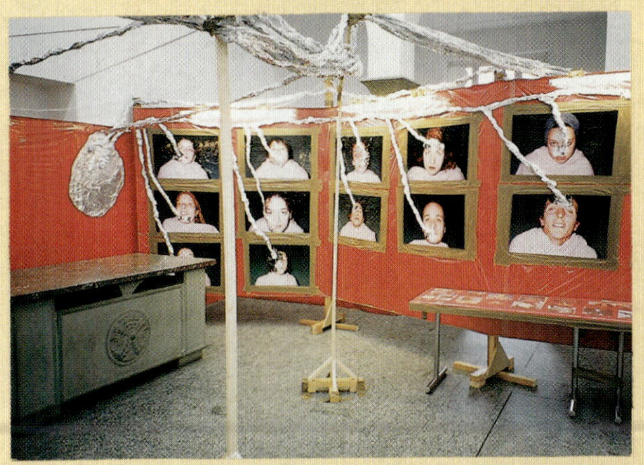

THOMAS HIRSCHHORN,
SWISS ARMY KNIFE, 1998,
Kunsthalle Bern, 1998.

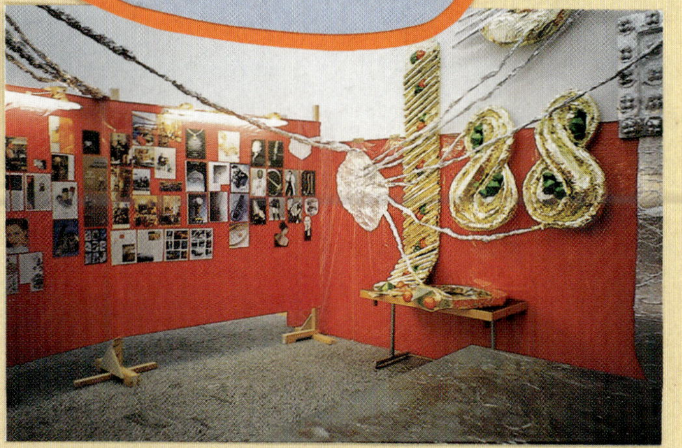

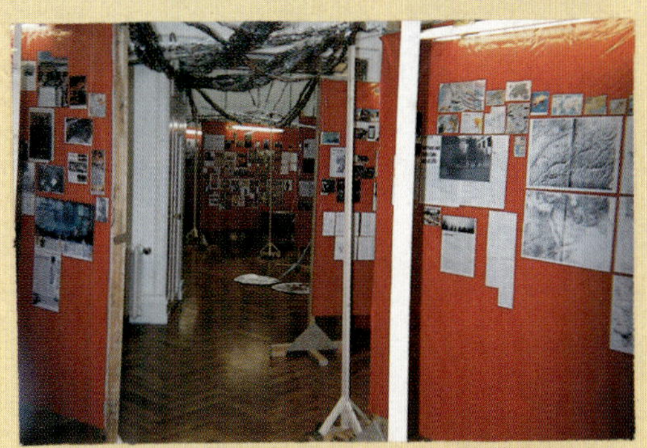

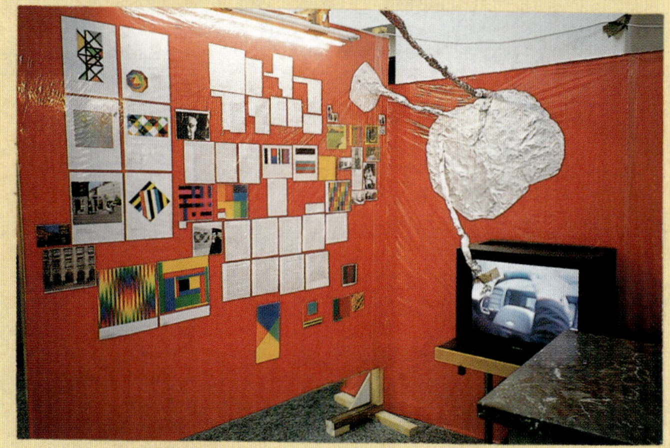

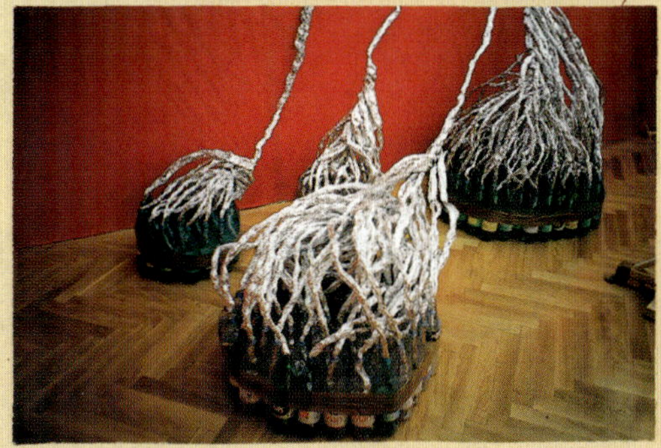

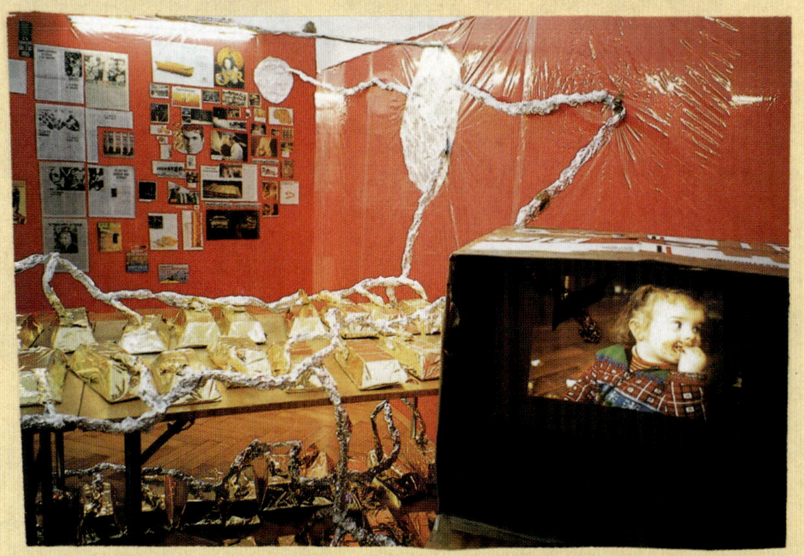

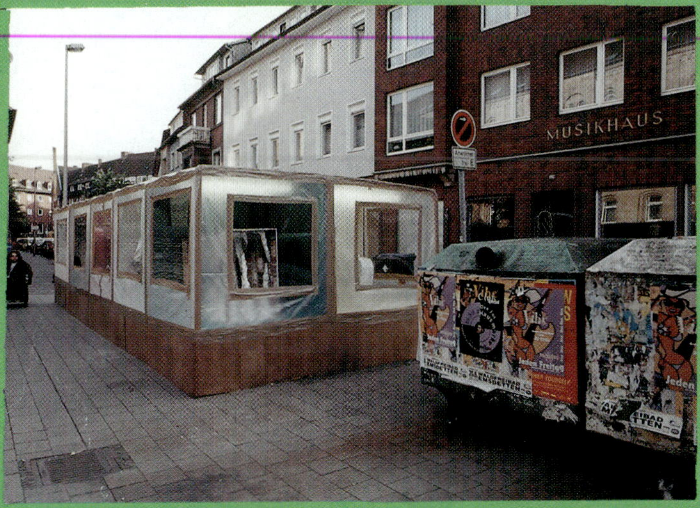

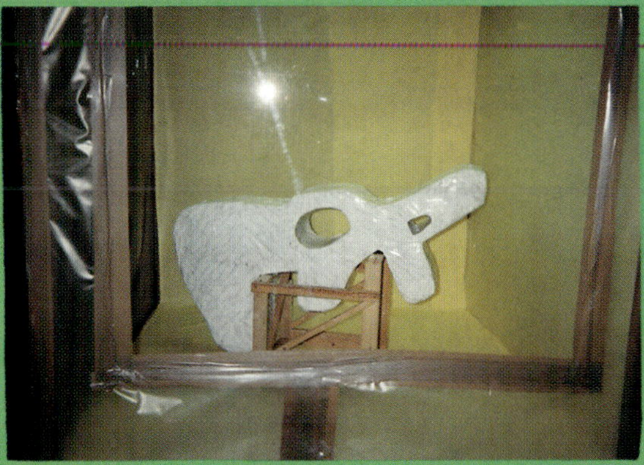

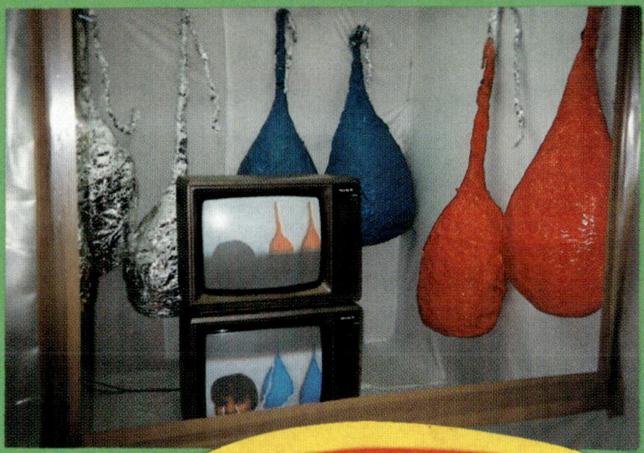

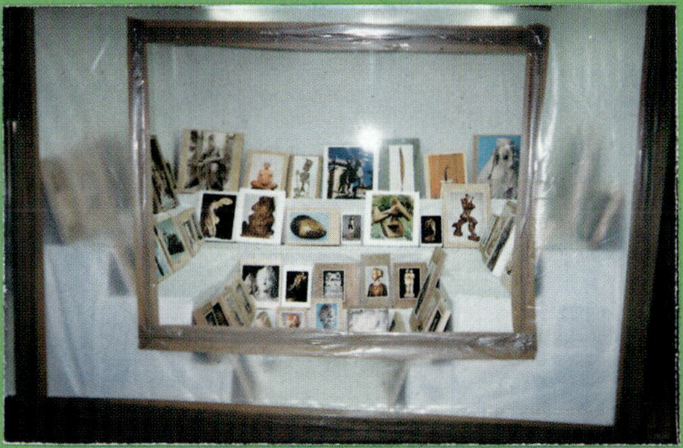

THOMAS HIRSCHHORN, SKULPTUR-SORTIER-STATION, 1997, «Skulptur. Projekte Münster», 1997.

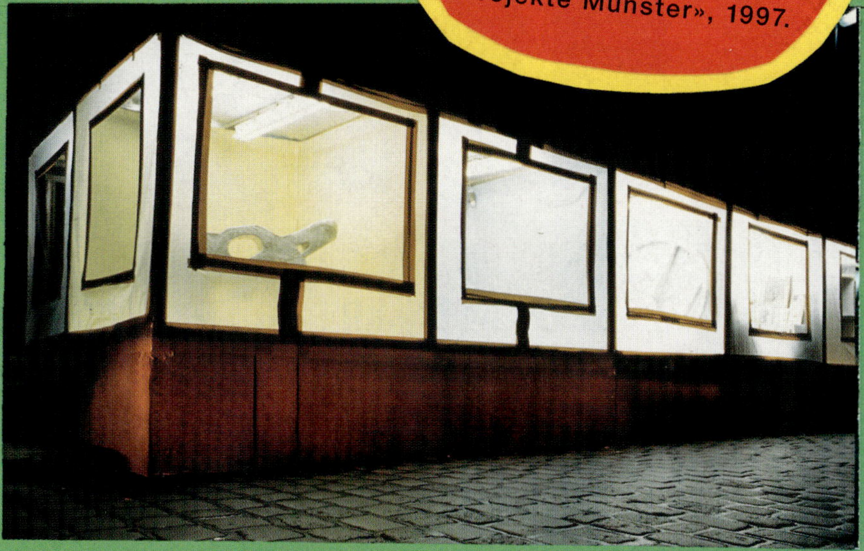

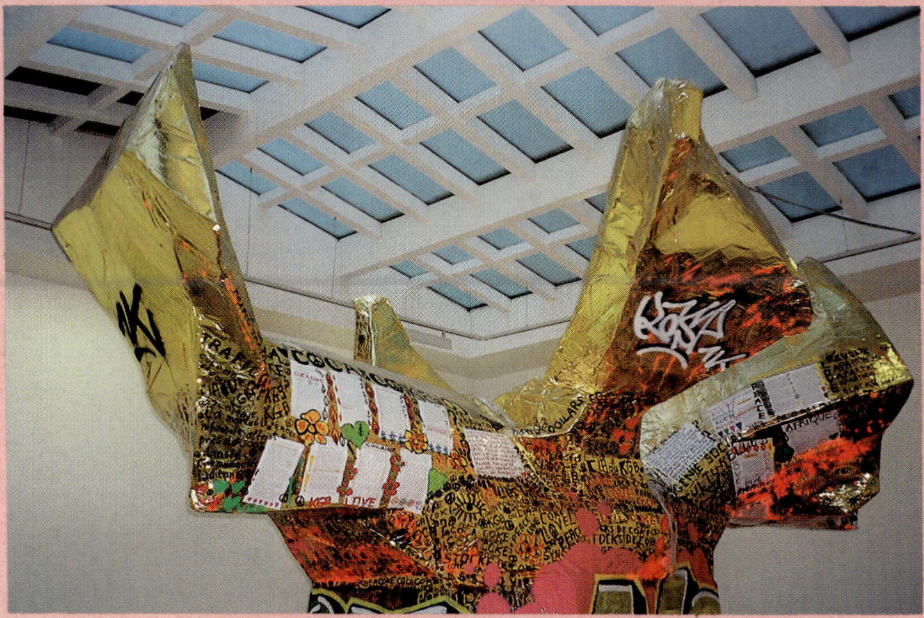

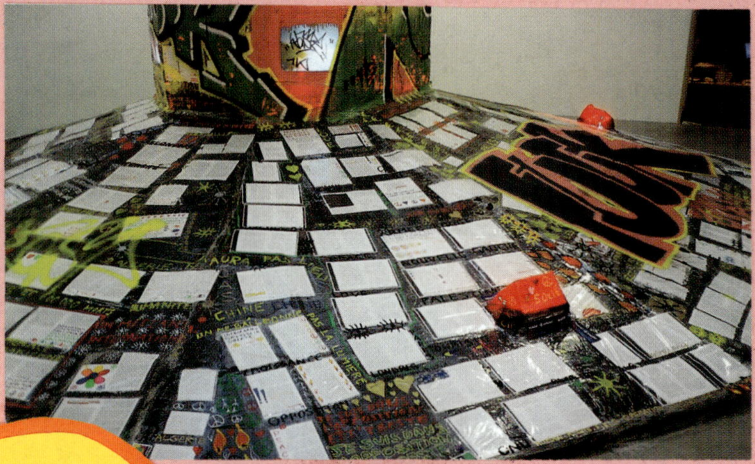

THOMAS HIRSCHHORN, SCULPTURE DIRECT, 1999, Galerie Chantal Crousel, Paris.

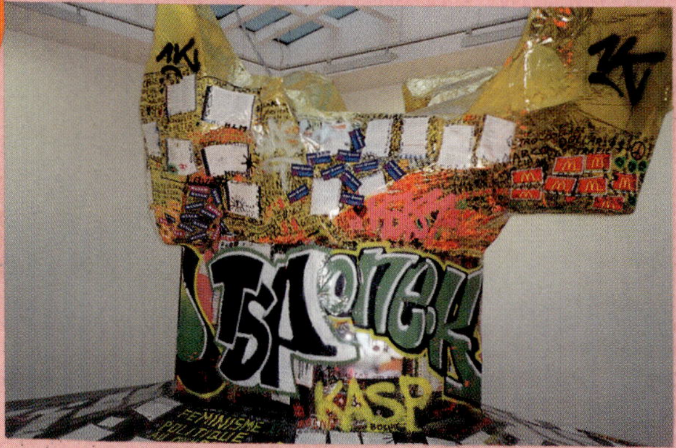

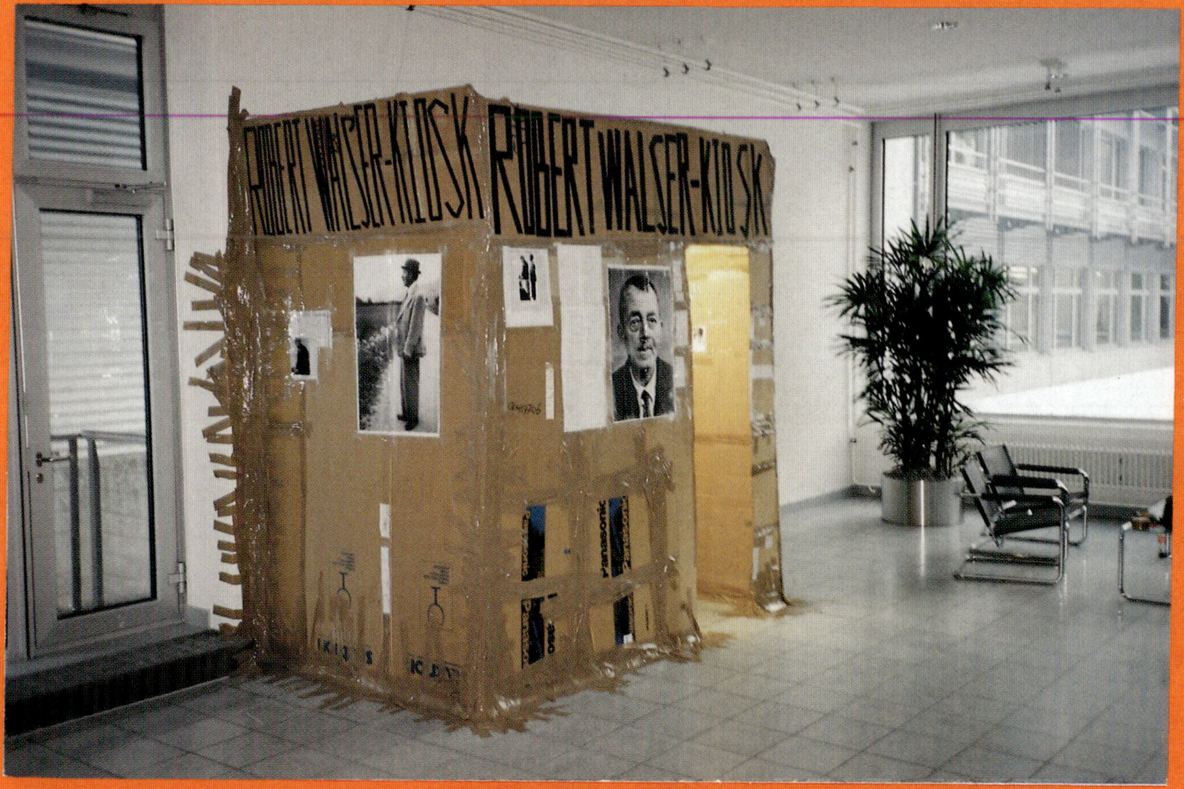

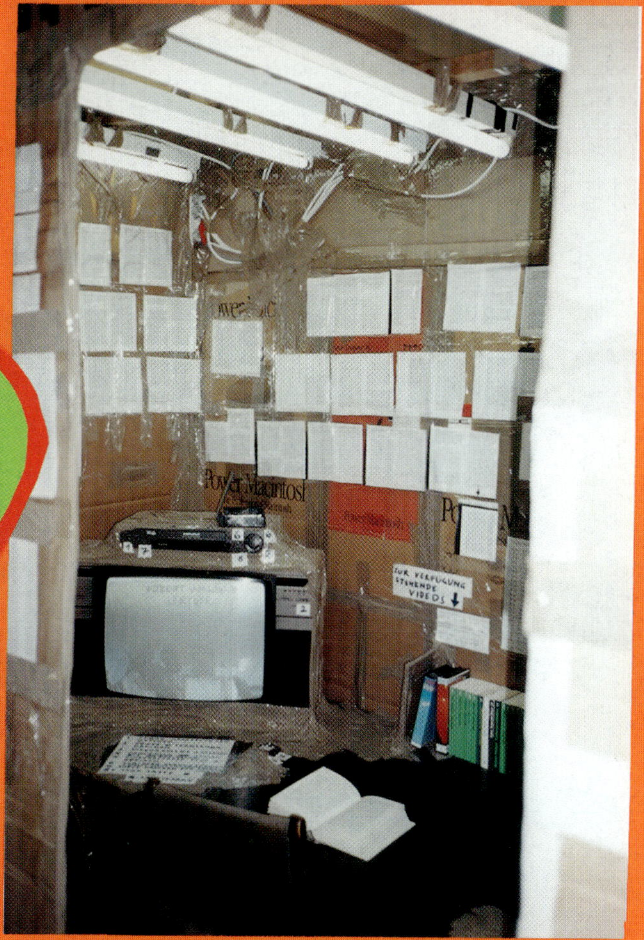

THOMAS HIRSCHHORN,
ROBERT WALSER KIOSK,
NO.1, 1999,
Universität Zürich, 1999.

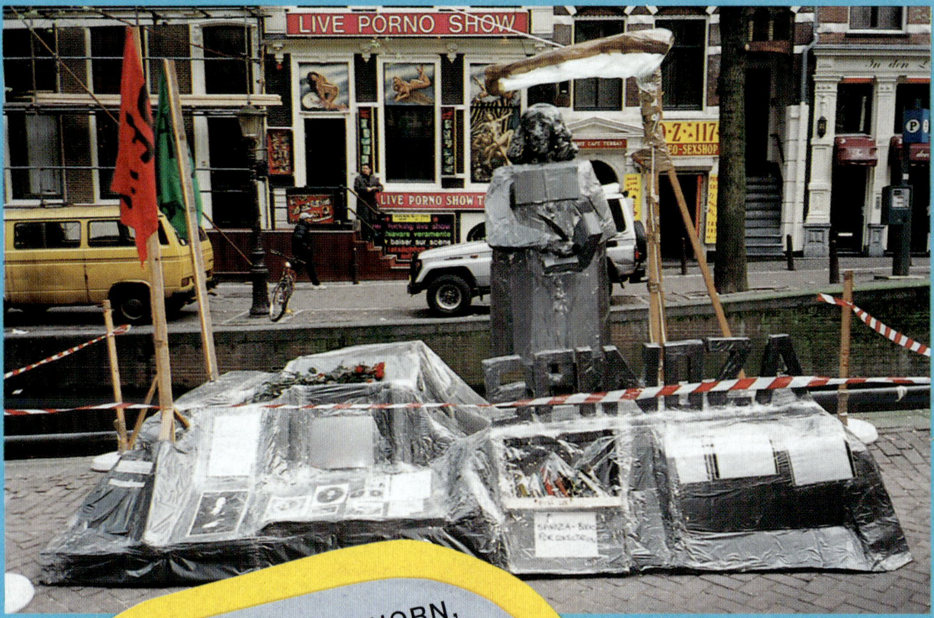

THOMAS HIRSCHHORN, SPINOZA MONUMENT, 1999, group exhibition / Gruppenausstellung «Midnight Walkers, City Sleepers», W 139, Amsterdam, 1999.

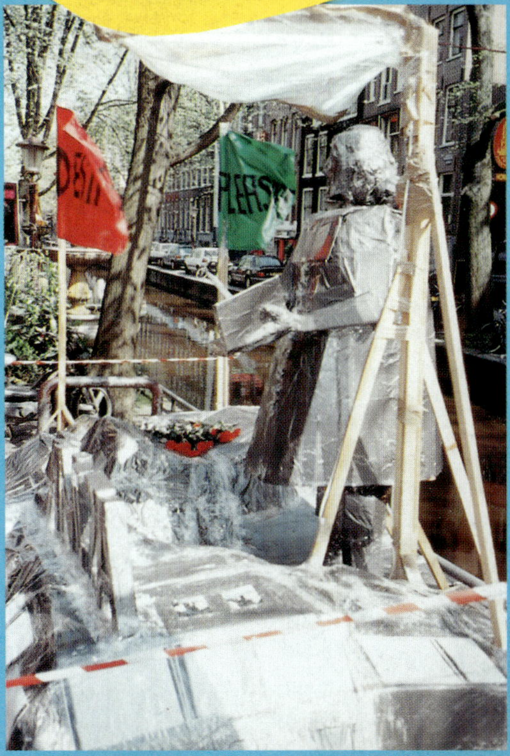

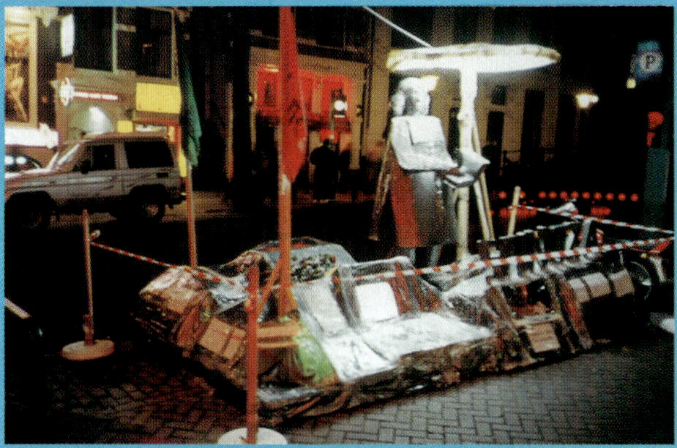

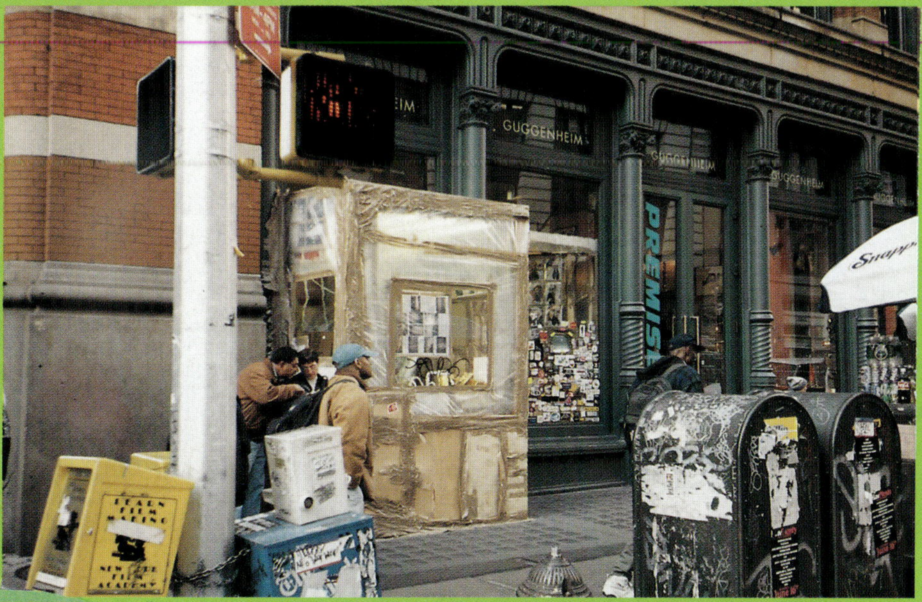

THOMAS HIRSCHHORN, VDP—VERY DERIVED PRODUCTS, 1998, group exhibition / Gruppenausstellung «Premises», Guggenheim Museum Soho, New York, 1998–99.

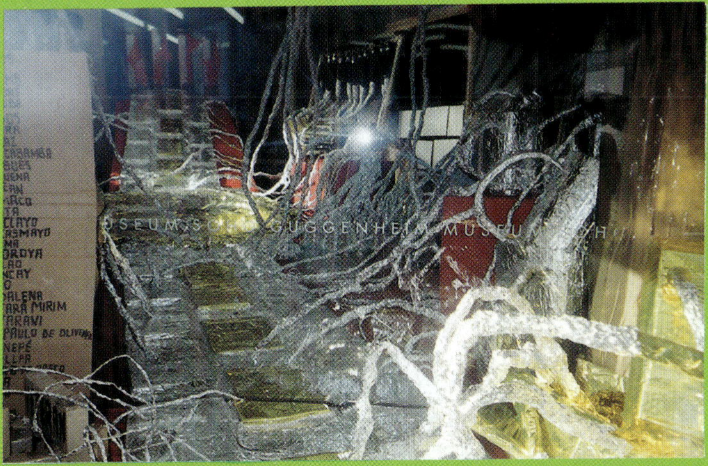

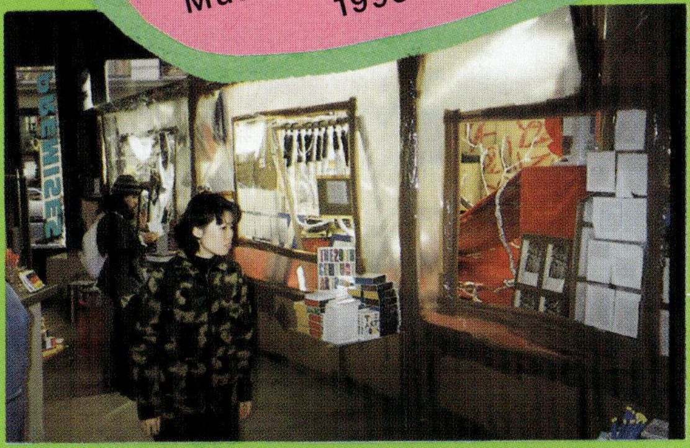

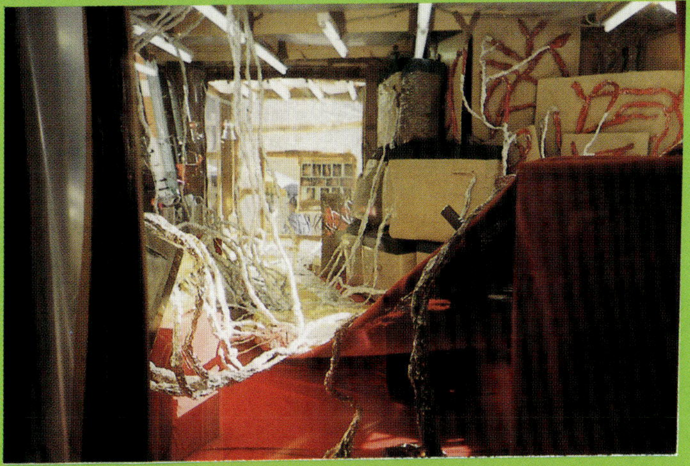

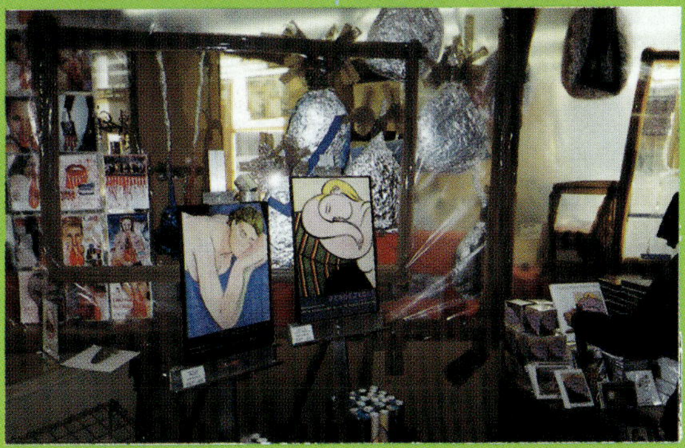

THOMAS HIRSCHHORN,
EIN KUNSTWERK,
EIN PROBLEM, 1998,
Portikus, Frankfurt, 1998;
Kunsthaus Zürich, 1999.

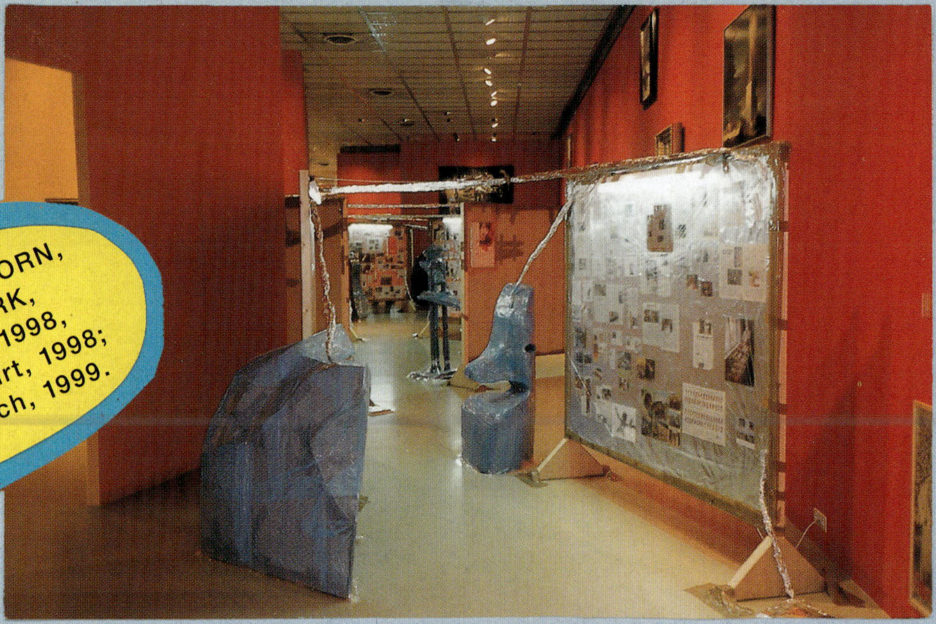

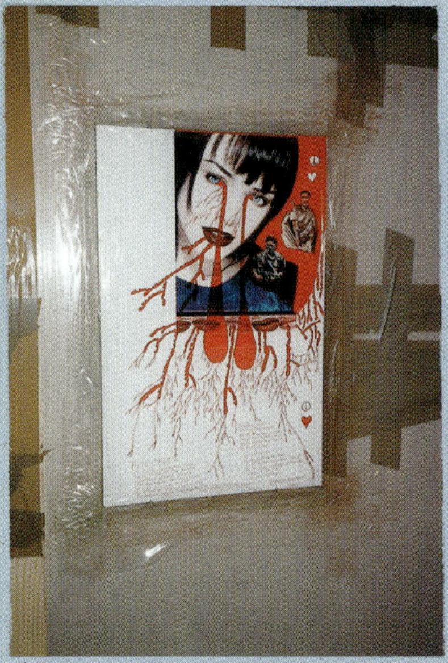

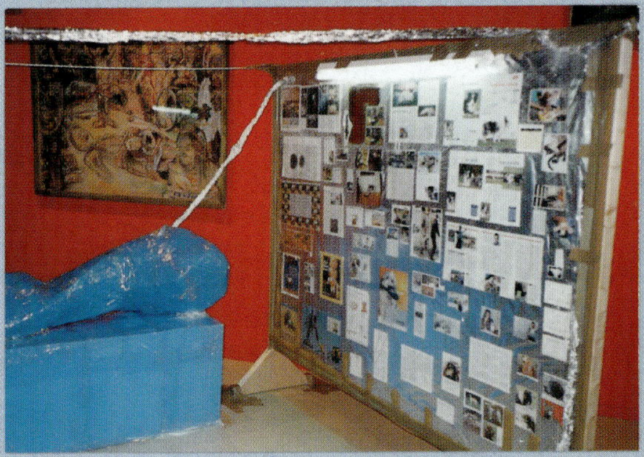

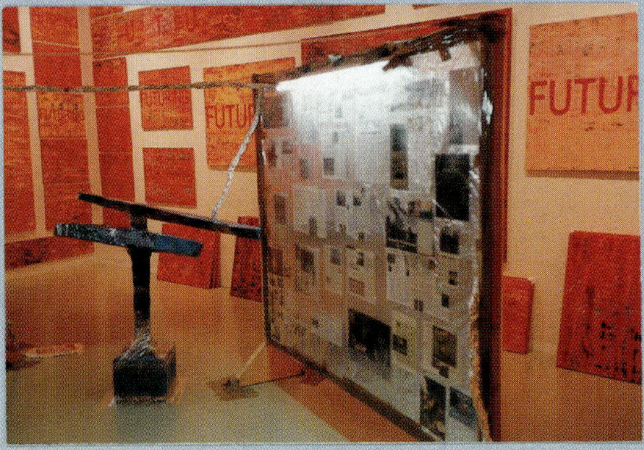

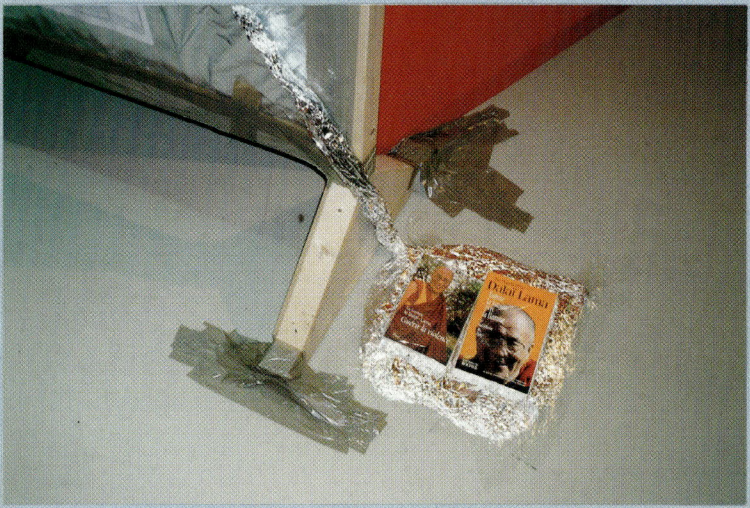

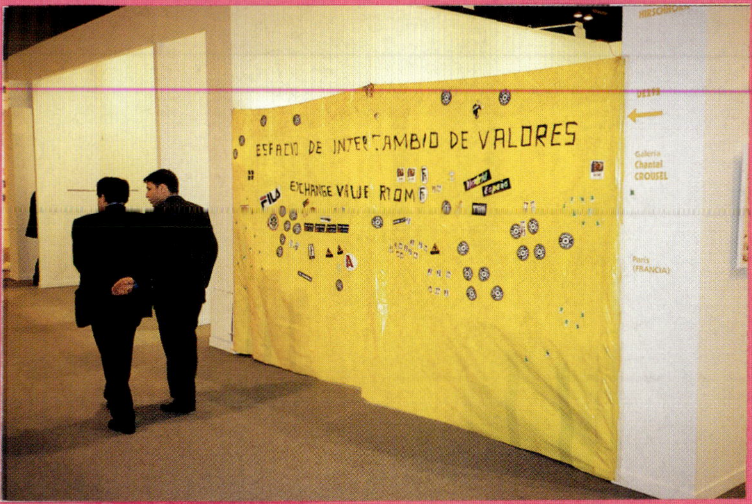

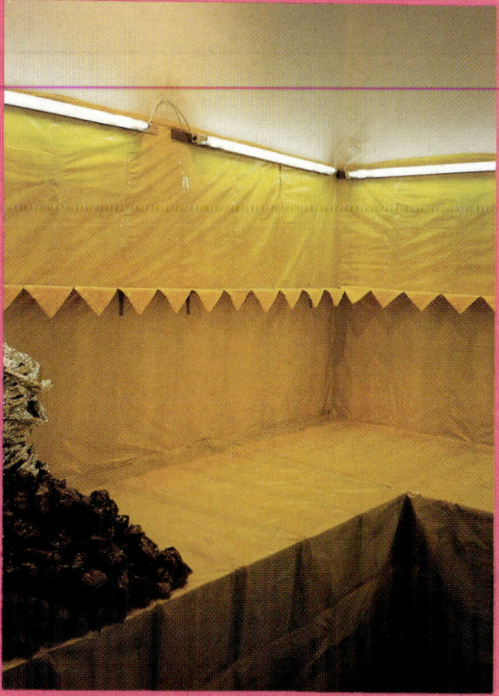

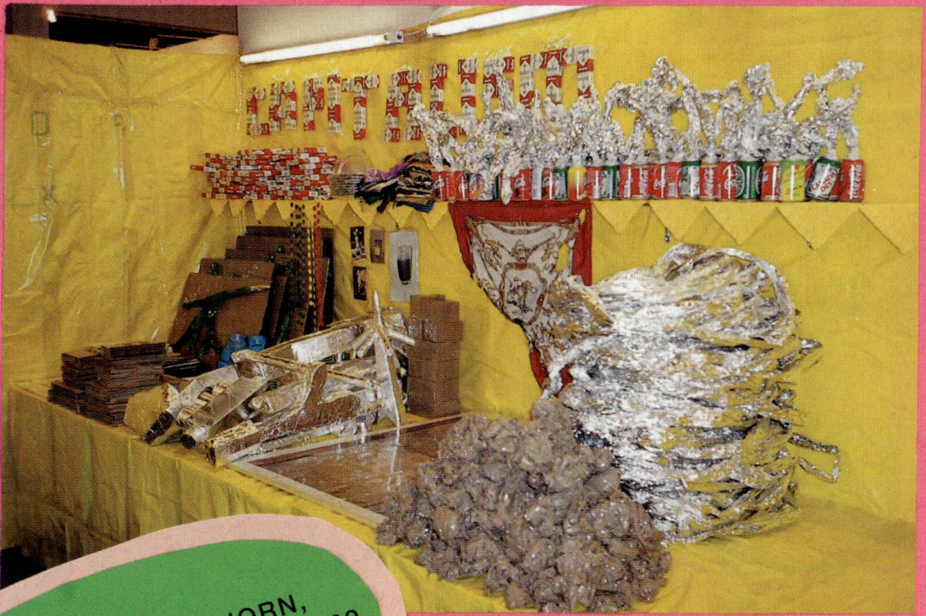

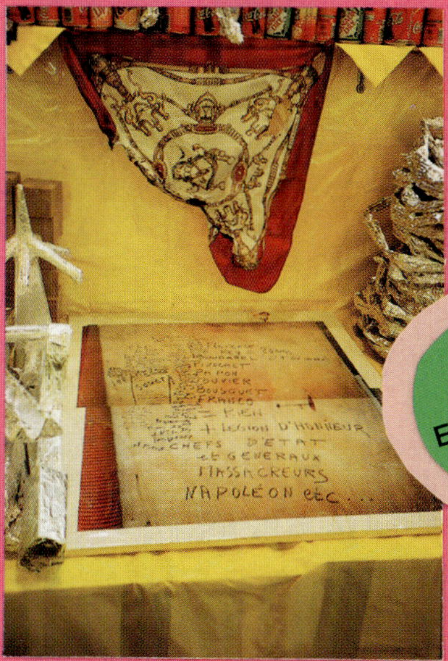

THOMAS HIRSCHHORN,
EXCHANGE VALUE ROOM, 1999,
ARCO, Madrid, 1999.

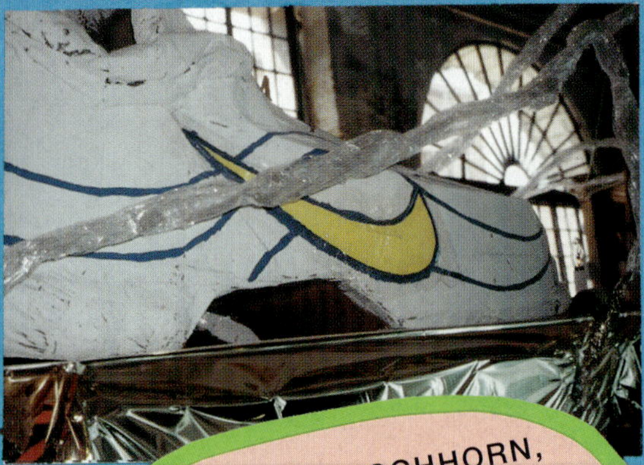

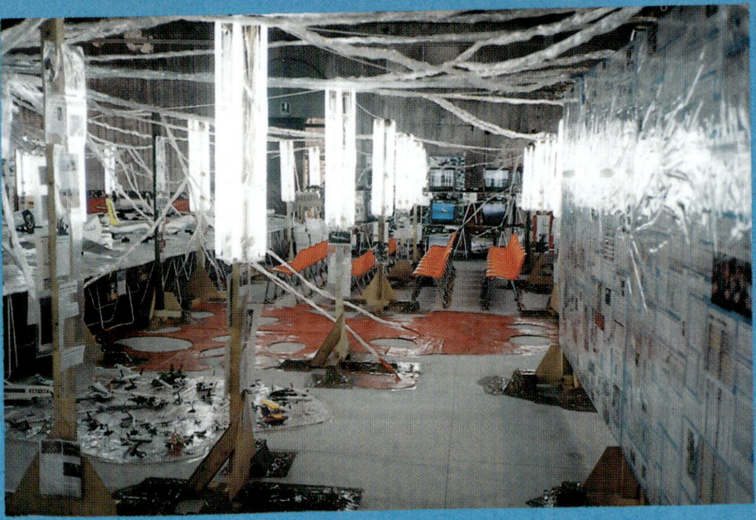

THOMAS HIRSCHHORN, FLUGPLATZ WELT / WORLD AIRPORT, 1999, Biennale Venedig / Venice Biennale, 1999.

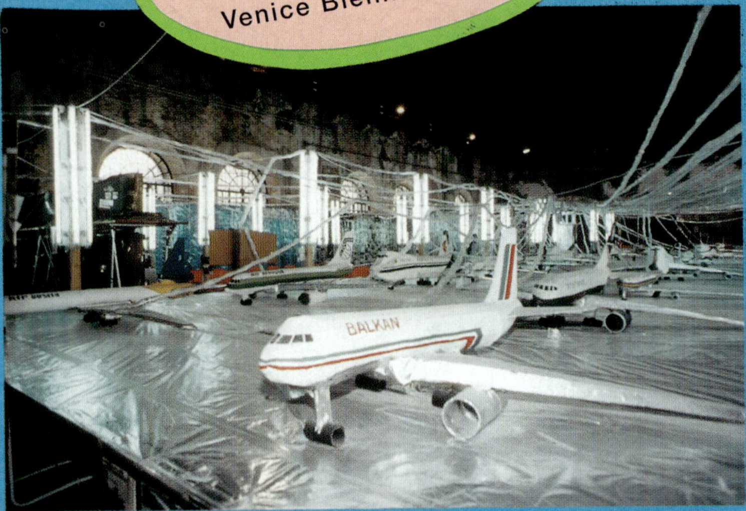

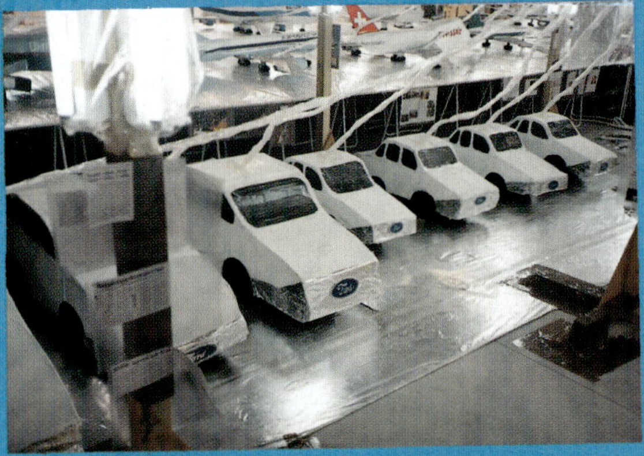

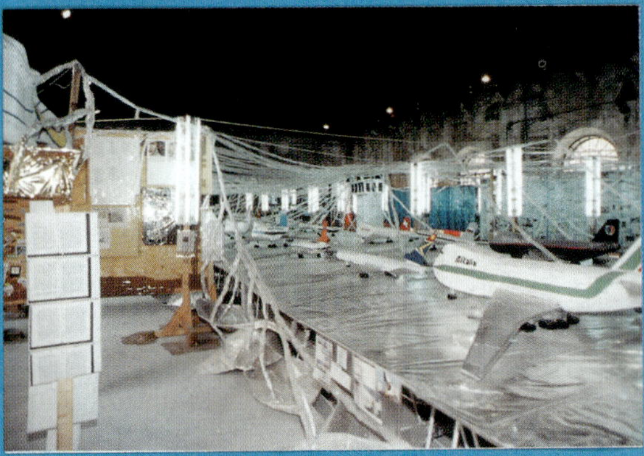

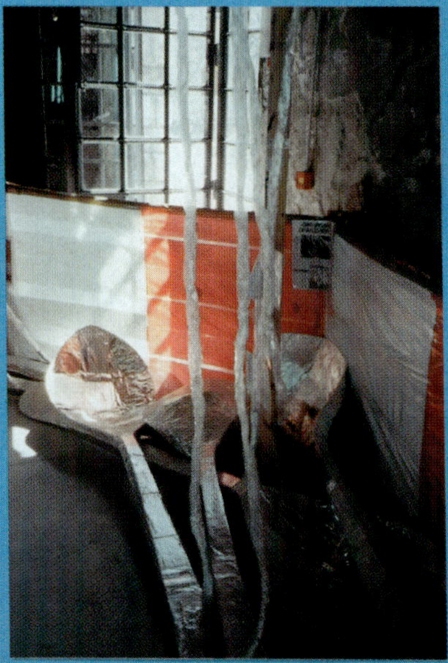

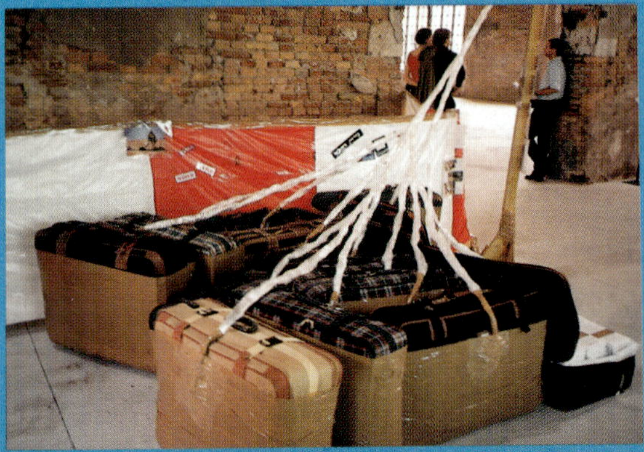

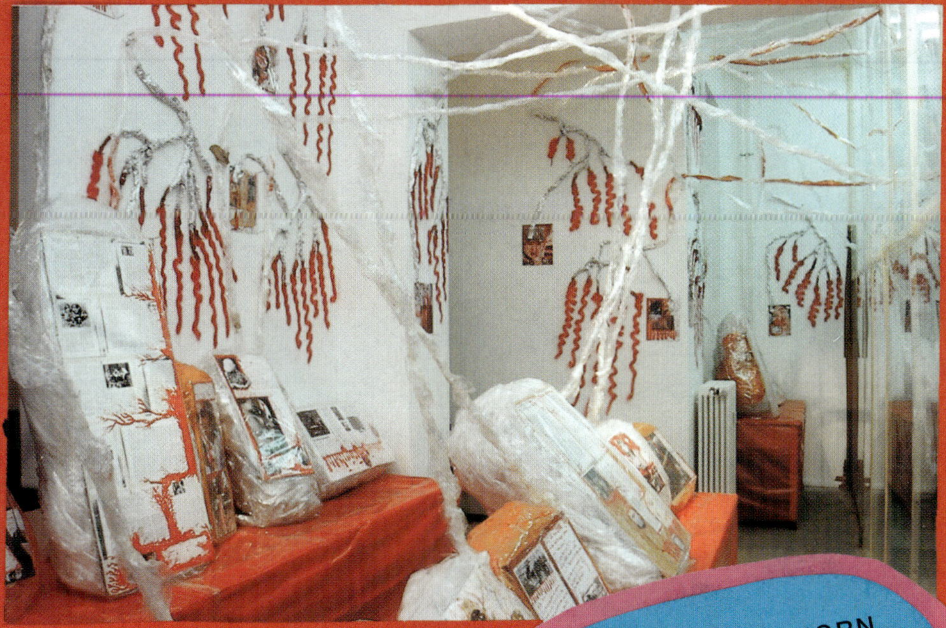

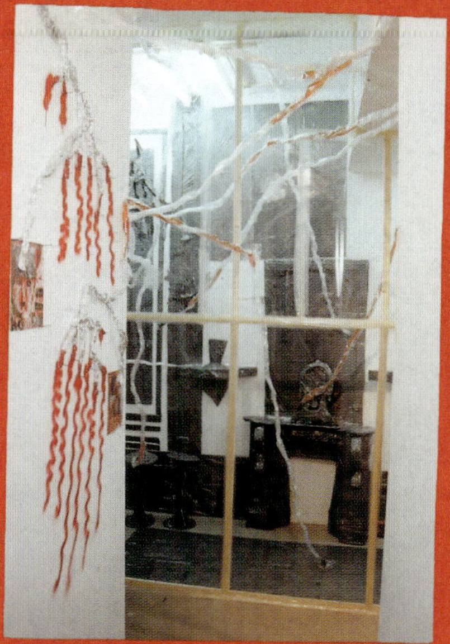

THOMAS HIRSCHHORN, BERNSTEINZIMMER, 1999, Galerie Arndt & Partner, Berlin, 1999.

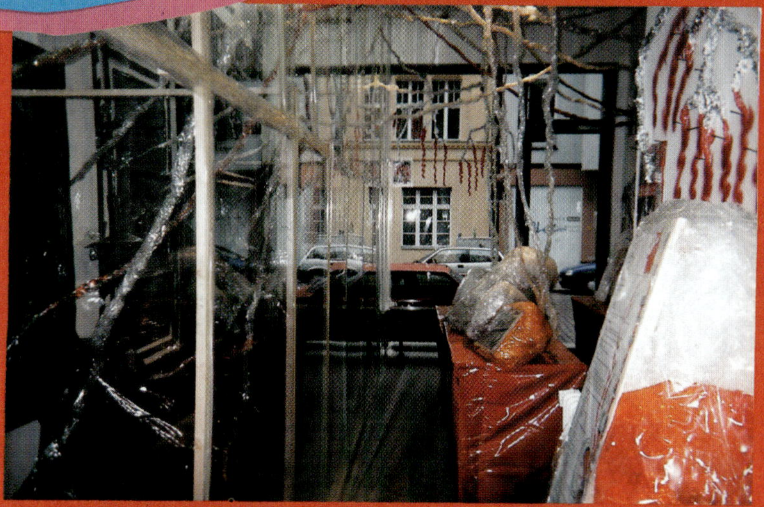

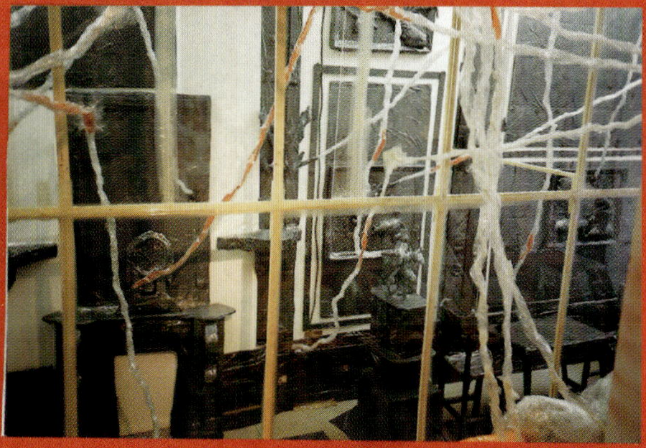

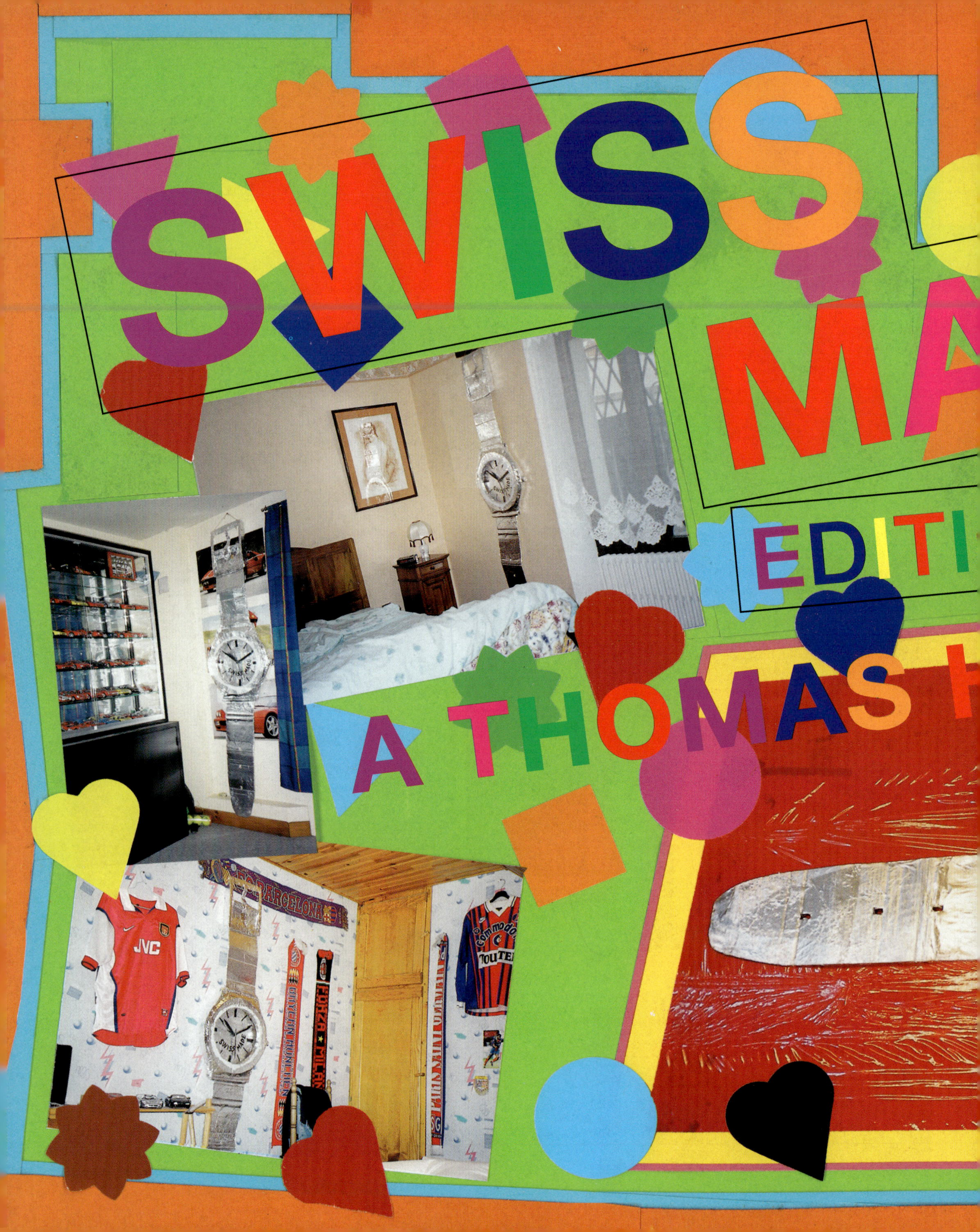
SWISS
MA
EDITI
A THOMAS H

EDITION FOR PARKETT

THOMAS HIRSCHHORN, SWISS MADE, 1999

Karton, Aluminiumfolie, Filz, Holz, Plastik, Klarsichtfolie, in 3 Teile zerlegbar, insgesamt 220 x 50 x 8 cm. Auflage: 50, signiert und nummeriert.

Cardboard, aluminum, foil, felt, wood, plastic, transparent foil, in three pieces, overall size ca. $86\frac{5}{8}$ x $19\frac{11}{16}$ x $3\frac{1}{8}$". Edition of 50, signed and numbered.

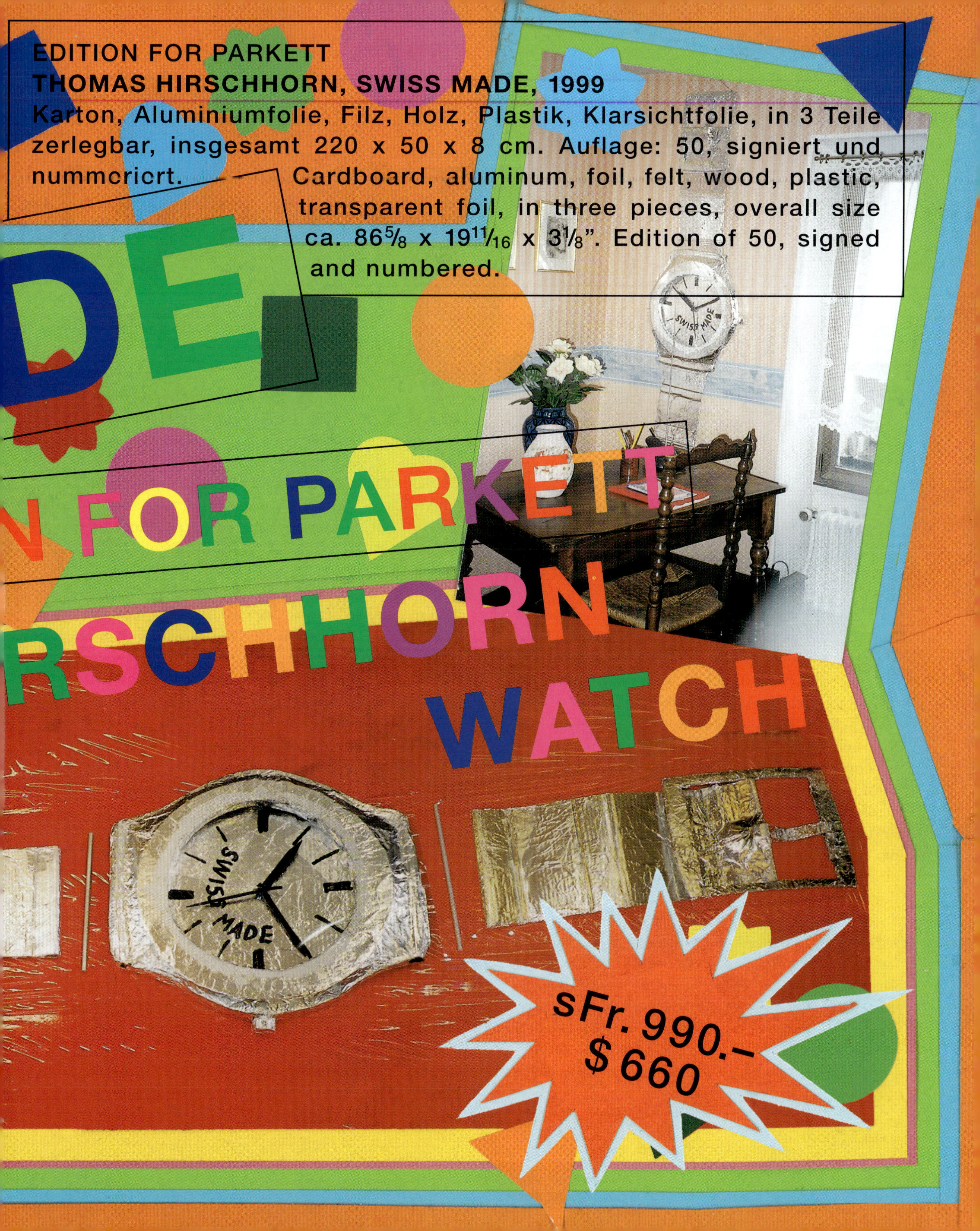

Thomas Hirsch

ROBERT FLECK

Am Anfang stand eine Ausstellung im Pariser Jeu de Paume. Catherine David arbeitete damals noch am Museum und hatte zwei jüngere Künstler, deren Namen in Paris weitgehend unbekannt waren, zu ihrer jeweils ersten Einzelausstellung in einem französischen Museum eingeladen. Einer der beiden Künstler, die sich umständehalber in einem Raum zusammengezwängt fanden, hiess Thomas Hirschhorn. Seine Ausstellung war höchst eigenartig. Ausgeschnittene Flächen, halb Bilder, halb Skulpturen, waren geometrisch, aber in verschiedenen Höhen der Wand entlang aufgehängt und zum Teil mit einem Stoff in rosaroter Farbe unterlegt, einem ähnlichen Ton, wie ihn Museen für klassische Kunst als Wandfarbe verwenden. Dazu gab es auf Hüfthöhe, derselben Wand entlang, einen weiss überzogenen Tisch, auf dem ähnliche Flächenfragmente lagen, nebeneinander gereiht, aber doch irgendwie ungeordnet. Diese flächigen Fragmente hatten unterschiedliche Oberflächen, die bisweilen anziehend und luxuriös wirkten, sich aus der Nähe aber als Billigmaterial entpuppten. Einige waren mit Alufolie überzogen, andere mit Cellophan umwickelt. Manche wiesen Plastikoberflächen auf wie Küchenmöbel oder schicke, postmoderne Skulpturen.

Thomas Hirschhorns Ausstellung im Jeu de Paume Anfang 1994 bedeutete eine verwunderliche Begegnung. Auf die Frage, wer dieser junge, bisher in Paris unbekannte Künstler sei, sagte ein Pressebetreuer: «Ein junger Künstler, der in Paris arbeitet.» Ein neuer französischer Künstler also? Das Bild war nicht so falsch. Diese Interpretation ist anhand des Werks von Thomas Hirschhorn auch heute durchaus möglich, wenn man das geistige Universum ausser Betracht lässt, aus dem diese Arbeit fliesst. Innerhalb der französischen Kunst gibt es seit den 60er Jahren eine «dekonstruktivistische» Tradition, die aus der strukturalistischen, analytischen oder postmodernen Zergliederung des bürgerlichen Begriffs von Malerei, Skulptur und Tafelbild neue Bedeutungsgehalte der bildenden Kunst zu gewinnen sucht. Dieser Tradition gehört zum einen die Bewegung «Support-Surface» an, die in den späten 60er und den 70er Jahren ideologisch interessant war, aber plastisch in der Entwicklung stecken blieb und ausserhalb Frankreichs kaum eine Rolle spielt. Aber auch französische Künstler von Weltdimension wie Christian Boltanski und Daniel Buren sind von diesem

ROBERT FLECK, geboren in Wien, derzeit Direktor des internationalen Post-Graduate-Programms an der Ecole régionale des Beaux-arts in Nantes, Frankreich, ist Kurator für bildende Kunst der neuen Biennale von Turin (April/Mai 2000) und Co-Kurator der Ausstellung «Surfing the Millennium» in der Kunsthalle Wien (Oktober 2000–März 2001). Er schreibt an einer Geschichte der Mühl-Kommune (Verlag Walther König, Köln).

horn

«Dekonstruktivismus» der Malerei und Skulptur geprägt, den zugleich Philosophen wie Gilles Deleuze und Jacques Derrida in ihrem angestammten Bereich des Denkens betrieben.

Endlich ein französischer Künstler, der diese Tradition beherzt aufgreift und mit ihr unabhängig umgeht? Man konnte die erste Museumsausstellung von Thomas Hirschhorn in Paris dahingehend deuten. Tatsächlich spielt zwar nicht der Stil, aber das Gedankengut und das formale Repertoire dieser französischen Tradition der Dekonstruktion eine bedeutende Rolle im plastischen Universum von Thomas Hirschhorn. Ein französischer Künstler, so zeigte die Ausstellung, konnte sich hinter dem Namen Thomas Hirschhorn nicht verbergen. Niemand aus der jüngeren Generation hatte bis dahin in Paris diese weitgehend negativ erlebte Tradition der letzten dreissig Jahre aufgegriffen. Jedenfalls deutete die Ausstellung auf eine überraschende Unabhängigkeit von den cartesianischen Regeln der französischen Kunst hin. Hirschhorns Ausstellung im Jeu de Paume Anfang 1994 stellte viele Fragen, auf die erst die Arbeiten der letzten Jahre eine Antwort gaben.

Im darauf folgenden Jahr fand in Bordeaux die Ausstellung «Shopping» statt. Das CAPC-Museum suchte sein Image in der Stadt aufzubessern. Jérôme Sans als Gastkurator lud internationale Künstler ein, Installationen für Luxusläden zu konzipieren. Hirschhorn wählte dazu den obszönsten Ort, nämlich eine Bankfiliale. Sein Beitrag war mit Abstand das beste Werk der Ausstellung. Hirschhorn konstruierte einen hausähnlichen Verschlag aus durchsichtigen Plastikplanen, der sich von weitem als Baustellenschutz für Arbeiten an der Bankfiliale ausnahm. Aus der Nähe betrachtet, war der Boden im transparenten Häuschen mit Schildern aus Pappe und Holz belegt, deren Aufschriften auf Obdachlose und andere Geschädigte der Zweidrittelgesellschaft hinwiesen, als ob ihnen das Haus nachts als Unterschlupf und tagsüber als Lager für verschiedene Schilder diene, die zum Betteln notwendig sind. Formal handelte es sich um eine zwingende Skulptur, die auch unabhängig vom Kontext der Ausstellung im urbanen Zusammenhang existierte und die anonymen ästhetischen Praktiken von Arbeitslosen aufgriff, um einen lockereren, unabhängigen Anklang an Minimal Art herzustellen. Im Inneren des Häuschens aus Plastikfolien war ein ähnliches Experiment mit Flächenfragmenten zu sehen wie in der Ausstellung im Jeu de Paume, nur liess sich der Malerei-Charakter dieser Anhäufung hier erst auf den zweiten Blick aus den scheinbar eindeutigen Botschaften erschliessen, die auf die beiläufig ausgeschnittenen Schilder geschrieben waren (etwa: «Ich habe Hunger und ersuche Sie um zehn Francs»).

Spätestens mit dieser Arbeit wurde deutlich, dass es sich bei Hirschhorn um einen Künstler mit einem höchst individuellen Ansatz und einem aussergewöhnlich sicheren Formgefühl handelt. Die späteren Arbeiten, für die «Skulptur. Projekte Münster», 1996, danach im Portikus, zuletzt an der Biennale in Venedig 1999, weisen durchwegs Eigenschaften auf, die sich schon in den zitierten Werken in Paris und Bordeaux finden. In erster Linie ist Thomas Hirschhorn ein Künstler, der sich durch die Verwendung von Zwischenformen freiarbeitet. Jedes Werk bedeutet eine gewagte Vermischung von hoch künstlerischen Formen und Materialien einerseits und anonymen, minder bewerteten Ausdrucksmitteln andererseits. Der ästhetische Druck der verschiedenen Traditionen zeitgenössischer Kunst wird dabei wie in einem Dampfkessel abgelassen. Man mag bei vielen Arbeiten Hirschhorns, zuletzt in Venedig, an das Haus des Facteur Cheval denken. Doch naiv ist dieser Künstler keineswegs. Ähnlich wie Buster Keaton im Stummfilm geht Thomas Hirschhorn von einer radikal antiillusionistischen Position aus. Ein sehr bewusster und reflektierter Künstler bedient sich hier naiver, anscheinend amateurhafter Mittel sowie «unmöglicher

Materialien» wie Plastikplanen und Tesa-Film, um neue Ausdrucksbereiche im historischen Kontext der zeitgenössischen Kunst aufzuspannen. Viele seiner Werke sind eine Parodie auf die politisch korrekte Sozialkunst der letzten Jahre, mit der es ihm gelingt, belastete Traditionen der Moderne – wie die geometrische Abstraktion, zu der er eine natürliche Neigung verspürt, und die Minimal Art – mit Leichtigkeit zu erfüllen und locker aufzugreifen. Am ehesten ist diese Kunst ästhetischer Zwischenstadien mit Franz West zu vergleichen, der auf seine Art das schwerfällige Erbe des Wiener Aktionismus in eine persönliche Arbeit mit dem Skulpturbegriff umkehrt.

In zweiter Hinsicht arbeitet Thomas Hirschhorn in seinen Skulpturen und malereiähnlichen Arbeiten an einem präzisen Vokabular, das sich ständig weiter entwickelt ohne zum ideologisch definierten Formenkanon zu gerinnen. Hirschhorn spielt den französischen Dekonstruktivismus gegen die abstrakte Geometrik schweizerischer Herkunft aus, die ihm sichtlich näher liegt, während er die französische philosophische und plastische Tradition offensichtlich genauestens kennt, wie schon früher die zahlreichen Künstler-Immigranten in Paris: Brancusi, Giacometti oder Hartung. Gegen beides setzt er die Art Brut-Haltung eines Louis Soutter, die bei ihm omnipräsent ist und ihm leicht von der Hand geht. Er gleicht sie aber wiederum durch die Eleganz und das dekorative Gefühl aus, das selbst der französischen Art Brut eines Gaston Chaissac eignet.

Dies soll nicht bedeuten, Thomas Hirschhorn kümmere sich besonders um Traditionen. Zwar ist der Künstler historisch sehr bewusst, doch die Spannung seiner Arbeiten stammt aus dem Verhältnis von ausserkünstlerischer Spontaneität und der Reflexion über die heutige soziale und ästhetische Position des Künstlers. Im Gegensatz zur neokonzeptuellen Ästhetik der politisch korrekten Kunst der letzten Jahre, zu soziologischen Darstellungsformen oder interaktivem Design, mischt Hirschhorn – nicht unähnlich den Post-Impressionisten vor hundert Jahren – die verschiedensten Register durcheinander um in einer ästhetisch ermüdeten, ausgelaugten Situation wieder ein neues expressives Potential zu erarbeiten. In gewisser Hinsicht steht dieser Arbeitsweise das Werk von Dieter Roth Pate. Hirschhorn nimmt dabei den Objekt- und Skulpturbegriff der Postmoderne der 80er Jahre als Ausgangspunkt um durch verschiedene antikulturelle Praktiken frischen Wind an diesem Paradigma zu erzeugen.

Der dritte Aspekt des Werks von Thomas Hirschhorn hat weder mit dem subkulturellen Inhalt (im Sinne von Pasolini) zu tun noch mit der formalen Stringenz der Arbeiten. Kaum ein anderer jüngerer Künstler der letzten Jahre hat das Denken so ernst genommen, im Sinne der zitierten französischen Tradition, wonach jedes Denken notwendigerweise ein «Denken des Aussen» (Maurice Blanchot) bezeichnet. Alle Arbeiten von Thomas Hirschhorn bewegen sich an der Grenze von Kunst und Nichtkunst, von Innen und Aussen, Normalität und Wahnsinn. Das ist bei weitem die interessanteste Dimension seiner Arbeit. Die Installationen von Hirschhorn handeln von Kommunikation, stellen aber zugleich jegliche Kommunikabilität in Frage. Man spürt, dass es sich nicht um eine formale Fragestellung handelt, sondern um eine existenzielle Dimension. Ähnlich wie bei Bruce Nauman – ohne damit einen Vergleich anstellen zu wollen – handelt jede Aussage nahezu unabhängig von der Form in erster Linie von der Unmöglichkeit des Sprechens. Dieses grundlegende Motiv liegt allen Arbeiten von Thomas Hirschhorn zu Grunde. Es verleiht ihnen auch jene Sicherheit und Selbstverständlichkeit sowohl was die ausserkünstlerischen Bezüge wie was die formalen Überlegungen im Rahmen der neueren Geschichte von Malerei und Skulptur betrifft. Jede Ausstellung von Thomas Hirschhorn handelt von der Schwierigkeit, in gleich welcher Sprache zu sprechen, und bediene sie sich eines bildnerischen Vokabulars. Da dieser Inhalt jenseits ästhetischer Dimensionen liegt, ist Hirschhorns Arbeit so evident.

Erst letzthin, anlässlich der Biennale von Venedig, haben wir zum Beispiel durch Zufall festgestellt, dass die Muttersprache sowohl von Thomas Hirschhorn als auch von mir Deutsch ist. Allerdings hat jeder von uns im Deutschen einen derart ausgeprägten Akzent, dass wir einander kaum verstehen. Also sprechen wir lieber schlecht französisch miteinander. Auch das hat eng mit Thomas Hirschhorns Arbeit zu tun.

Thomas Hirschhorn

ROBERT FLECK

It began with an exhibition at Jeu de Paume in Paris. Catherine David was working there at the time and had invited two young artists, relatively unknown in Paris, to mount their first solo exhibitions in a French museum. The two artists were crowded together in the same room due to a shortage of space; one of them was named Thomas Hirschhorn. His exhibition looked odd—to put it mildly. He had mounted cutouts, half picture, half sculpture, on the wall in a geometric pattern but at different heights, some of them against a background of pink fabric resembling the wallpaper in museums of classical art. In addition there was a white-topped table running the length of the wall at hip height, with similar cutouts on it, placed next to each other but somehow still jumbled. These flat fragments had a variety of surface structures, some looking highly attractive and luxurious but of cheap manufacture on closer inspection. Some had a layer of tin foil, others were wrapped in cellophane. Still others were plastic coated like kitchen furniture or chic postmodern sculptures.

Thomas Hirschhorn's exhibition at Jeu de Paume in early 1994 proved to be an astonishing encounter. On inquiring about this young artist, unknown in Paris, I was told that he was "a young artist who works in Paris." Ah, a new French artist? The idea was not that far-fetched. This interpretation could still apply to Thomas Hirschhorn's work today, apart from the mental universe that inspires it. Since the sixties French art has been informed by a tradition which has tried to construct new meanings by "deconstructing" the bourgeois concepts of painting and sculpture in structural, analytical or postmodern terms. This tradition is reflected on the one hand by the "Support Surface" movement, which made an ideological impact in the sixties and seventies but ceased to mature in plastic terms and barely made a ripple outside of France. On the other hand, French artists of international renown, like Christian Boltanski or Daniel Buren, were also influenced by the "deconstructivism" of painting and sculpture, pursued at the time by philosophers like Gilles Deleuze and Jacques Derrida in their own field of endeavor.

Have we here at long last a French artist who heartily embraces this tradition and gives it an independently creative twist? Thomas Hirschhorn's first museum show in Paris could certainly have been given such a reading. Not the style but the thinking and the formal repertory of French deconstructivism certainly do play a significant role in Hirschhorn's plastic universe. However, the exhibition demonstrated that a French artist could not be hidden behind the name of Thomas Hirschhorn. None of the younger generation in Paris had ever addressed the largely negative experience of this thirty-year tradition. Moreover, the exhibition signaled a surprising independence from the Cartesian rules of French art. Hirschhorn's exhibition at Jeu de Paume in early 1994 posed a number of questions that have only been answered in his works of the past few years.

ROBERT FLECK, director of the international post-graduate program at the Academy of Art in Nantes, France, is curator for the visual arts at the new Torino Biennale (April/May 2000) and co-curator of "Surfing the Millennium" at the Vienna Kunsthalle (October 2000 to March 2001).

Thomas Hirschhorn,

PHILIPPE VERGNE

Dear Thomas,

A few days ago I was reading a text by Professor Reiner Speck devoted to James Lee Byars's THE PERFECT TEAR (1984). He describes the phenomenon of tears not as a weakness, but as a normal physiological reaction, as natural, no doubt, as laughing and smiling. "The tears secreted daily and unnoticed by others protect the eye against drying out; they also wash out foreign particles. Only strong irritation, triggered, for example, by emotion or lesions, causes increased secretion or a flow of tears."[1)]

A strong irritation: Now that I think of it, this is the effect produced by your work, its strength and its power. Thomas, your work annoys me. It annoys me in the sense that it resists, in the sense that from the very first time I saw it, in the Jeu de Paume in Paris in 1994, to FLUGPLATZ WELT/WORLD AIRPORT this summer at the Venice Biennale, its development has never ceased to disturb and bother me. This includes the most recent announcement, which I received just a few days ago, on which there is a reproduction of the flame of the Statue of Liberty that stands on the Pont de l'Alma in Paris, and which has now become a shrine to the memory of Princess Diana. Artists and their commentators go on and on analyzing the possibilities of the Monument, after the War, before the new century. There is no end questioning what the waning century may and should commemorate. Diana? Popular beliefs as construed by the media? The extreme inconceivability of a monument to freedom? Or just of what remains of it? And here you're no help. You set a trap for us, putting before us something in the end we only want to (or are only able to) disregard—kitsch, the taste of the Diana cult. I know you don't like the word, but in this piece, this postcard, there is a form of irony. I don't have to wait for your response to say I don't think irony is one of your weapons. I think this 'petty' taste, which I distinguish from 'bad' taste, is of concern and interest to you. It's irritating that you should linger over something that with distance can only make us smile, for that story, Diana and the Paparazzi, is of no interest; we are way above that sort of thing. That story is for others, those who read newspapers that we don't... In doing so, Thomas, in becoming attached to an accumulation of signs that approximate juvenile feelings, you embarrass us. You embarrass us because that information is too simple, too dumb, too "popular" or populist, too direct. But that simplicity, which is irritating, which from time to time irritates me, is your strength. That simplicity, like the tears we find in your installations, is something we do not notice but which prevents us from becoming dry.

Let's go back to irritation. Some time ago, I was asked the following question: "If you were to ask Thomas Hirschhorn a question, what would it be?" *Taking the recent history of sculpture into consideration, into which space would you wish your work to be inscribed?* This answer met with little success. But the answer was in itself an attempt not to ask the expected question, that of the political nature of your work, its transgressive dimension. The answer derived from a perhaps simplistic will to situate your work in the domain not of practical politics, but of sculptural practice. Why? On the one hand, so as not to try and fit the term political into any recipe; on the other, to try and better understand what you mean when you say, "I think one should not make political art; one should make art politically. But in any case you can't just declare this."[2)] And finally because even now, I cannot dissociate your work from a formally precise investigation that seems to proceed as much virally as programmatically, and which over the years has developed a specific vocabulary. Whether you like it or not, there is now a Thomas Hirschhorn style,

---

PHILIPPE VERGNE is a curator of visual arts at the Walker Art Center.

You Are So Annoying

which you yourself have been led to verbally identify under the name of "display" or "layout," thus distancing yourself from the verbal facility of the term "installation." This desire to refuse the fact of the matter is also annoying.

I would like to distinguish two elements in your work: on the one hand, the vocabulary, and on the other, its more general syntax. On the whole, one could reduce it to a pragmatic or economic mode: doing things with the means available. Going back to my own experience of your work, this vocabulary was already in place in the exhibition at the Jeu de Paume in 1994: boards, pieces of cardboard, sawhorses, pictures found in newspapers and magazines collaged onto cardboard, your handwriting in ballpoint pen, plastic sheeting, large rolls of Scotchtape, and harsh, clinical fluorescent lighting. Then later, unstaged video images shown in real time, candles, plastic flowers, reproductions of artworks, plywood paneling, Xeroxes, garbage cans, and sheets of aluminum foil.

These "poor" and "dirty" elements without qualities are all handworked. With you, Thomas, there are few if any readymades. You even insist on the importance of this notion of "work," as if to make artistic activity into something more normal, even banal. Art, making art, is your daily activity; as you say, it's your capital. Might this be an attempt to create a direct link between production as traditionally defined in the economic world, and artistic production? Could it thus be a direct response to Joseph Beuys, whom you admire, and his attempts to redefine capital?[3] Elsewhere, in an interview with Alison Gingeras, you spoke of Beuys: "For me Beuys liberates the term 'sculpture' from aesthetic volumes. He is able to give back to the word 'sculpture' its potential. He removes it from a practice based in so-called noble materials. This first point is very important to my practice."[4]

Let us go back to this practice. You have made luxury symbols (Mercedes, Chanel, Volkswagen) out of somewhat pathetic aluminum foil, putting them on display in vitrines made out of cardboard or plastic. You glue advertisements onto old cartons, you bring together images different by nature, different images on one surface: fashion and instruments of torture, Chanel and military parades, BMW and massacres, Nike and Kosovo, neo-Nazis and the Louvre. Around the images, there is always a question or a summons in ballpoint: Loser? Winner? Help me understand these images; I think they're beautiful. I want to forget! I want to resist! Is it art? Thank you very much! I still don't get it! In this cardboard sign series, which you entitle LES PLAINTIFS, LES BÊTES, LES POLITIQUES (The Plaintive, The Dumb, The Politicals), you pummel us with these questions, which of course we do not want to ask ourselves, and to which no one will give you an answer. Or if you get one, it will no doubt be to tell you that the connections you make are juvenile, and your questions naive, contradictory, or even demagogical... And from your side you respond that today the best way to fight back is with stupidity.[5] There, too, you annoy me! What stupidity are you talking about? That of your images and their simplicity, or the stupidity of the writing that invades the cardboard signs? Is it mine? Or theirs? Or that of Rolex? You see, you're doing it again; you undo any interpretation. You throw questions at us, but of course, you don't answer. That would be too easy. And in one sense, that's why LES PLAINTIFS, LES BÊTES, LES POLITIQUES takes on such importance in your work. In my eyes it is a matrix for what you put forth. To draw a parallel with another artist, Gerhard Richter, it is your ATLAS, a kind of program. You ask questions, but don't expect any answers. You do not defend anything.

Let's go back to sculpture.

You invade the spaces of the vocabulary, material, questions, and images available to you. Interior or exterior, you saturate the world with your questions. You adopt the principle, "more is more, less is less"; you make it into your syntax, dismissing our modernist dogma with a wave of your hand... You seem not to believe in it, or if you do, it's not essential. You look for what is essential, and put art and the world on the scales. When one realizes that more than half the century has attempted to reconcile art and life with the dream of changing the world, your questioning becomes irritating.

With ONE ARTWORK, ONE PROBLEM (1998) at the Portikus in Frankfurt, you seem to suggest that modernity and art do not measure up. In the space, you set up twenty panels of the kind used during elections, each with press clippings, photographs, and reflective surfaces (to reflect). Each panel sets forth a current issue: Palestine, Northern Ireland, unemployment, the Gulf War, nuclear power, Kosovo, fisheries, drugs, animal rights... Since the exhibition space was not large enough to accommodate the world's problems, you added two additional galleries of transparent plastic sheeting: The world can see the art, and art can see the world. Each problem is linked to another one with a ribbon of wrinkled aluminum foil. Along the same principle, each problem is linked to a "modern-style" abstract sculpture roughly executed in cardboard and blue plastic. Fragile and rickety, the sculptures could be used to illustrate Robert Filliou's equivalence principle, *Bien fait, mal fait, pas fait* (Well done, poorly done, undone). The spatial arrangement prevents easy movement through the work; one has to try and go around the problems without jostling the sculpture. The center of the space is inaccessible, and any overall view of the whole is impossible. There is too much text for us to read everything, no matter how willing we are. It's stifling, and I prefer looking at the sculpture.

The same principle is at work in FLUGPLATZ WELT/WORLD AIRPORT in Venice. The same rough-and-ready materials are used to construct in the center of an immense hall a scaled down model of an international "global" airport, circled by the world and its problems in the form of texts and images, too much text to read entirely, too much to really activate. Yet there is not enough space for the comfort of a middle or central position. You seem to be telling us that the center is not livable. Likewise, you invade the corners and no "global" view is possible. It's annoying. The very form of your sculpture makes the material and the information of which it is composed illegible, or at the very least makes reading it troublesome. You're of no help; you play at super-communication, but stage the loss of meaning. The cumulative quality of your sculpture casts us back into our unbearable condition and our fortunate inability to circumscribe the world within some truth or morality.

There is an anecdote in Kafka's notebooks that illustrates the human inability to find a space. "A group of train travelers had an accident in a tunnel, at a place from which one could no longer see the light from the entrance. As for the exit, it seemed so tiny that you would continually spot it, then immediately lose it from view. In between, one was never sure whether it was the beginning or the end of the tunnel."[6)]

Thomas, your airport is the tunnel, and this is irritating because it indicates an impossibility, perhaps that of Beuys's social sculpture. In the catalogue *Zeitgeist*, Beuys describes and stresses the importance of his work HIRSCHDENKMAL FÜR GEORGE MACIUNAS (1982) in the following way: "Monuments to the stag are accumulators in which human beings and all other spirits meet to work together (...) at ordering the world into Proper Form."[7)] It is this proper form which seems to me beyond reach when I experience your work, unless that proper form is the flame in homage to Diana. Thomas, help me; I don't understand that sculpture. I want to resist it; I find it beautiful.

(Translated from the French by Warren Niesluchowski)

1) Reiner Speck, "The Perfect Tear," in: *James Lee Byars, The Epitaph of Con.Art Is Which Questions Have Disappeared?*, ed. by Carl Haenlein, ex. cat. (Hannover: Kestner Gesellschaft, 1999), p. 213.
2) Thomas Hirschhorn, "Lettre à Thierry," in: *Auflage*, ex. cat. (Kunstmuseum Luzern; Centre d'Art Contemporain, Fribourg; Künstlerhaus Bethanien, Berlin, 1995–96), p. 16.
3) Thomas Hirschhorn, "J'aime Joseph Beuys" (I love Joseph Beuys), ibid., p. 31.
4) Thomas Hirschhorn, interview with Alison Gingeras, in: *Thomas Hirschhorn*, ex. cat. (London: Chisenhale Gallery, 1998).
5) Ibid.
6) Franz Kafka, quoted in Giorgio Agamben, *L'Homme sans contenu* (Paris: Editions Circé, 1996).
7) *Zeitgeist*, ed. by C. M. Joachimides/N. Rosenthal, ex. cat. (Berlin: Kunstbuch Berlin & Albert Hentrich Verlag, 1982), p. 82.

PHILIPPE VERGNE

Thomas Hirschhorn, du gehst mir auf die Nerven!

Lieber Thomas

Vor ein paar Tagen las ich einen Text von Reiner Speck über den Künstler James Lee Byars und sein Werk THE PERFECT TEAR (1984). Er beschreibt darin das Phänomen der Tränen, wobei er diese nicht als Zeichen der Schwäche darstellt, sondern als natürliche physische Reaktion, nicht minder natürlich als Lachen oder Lächeln: «Die täglich – für das Gegenüber unbemerkt – sezernierten Tränen schützen das Auge vor Austrocknung und schwemmen kleine Fremdkörper aus. Nur bei stärkeren Reizen – ausgelöst durch Emotion oder Läsion – kommt es zu vermehrter Sekretion, zum Tränenfluss.»[1)]

PHILIPPE VERGNE ist Kurator des Walker Art Center in Minneapolis, USA.

Eine starke Irritation: Das ist, wenn ich es mir überlege, genau die Wirkung, die deine Arbeit auslöst. Es ist ihre Qualität, ihre Stärke. Thomas, deine Arbeit geht mir auf die Nerven! Sie nervt, weil sie sich widersetzt, weil das, was du schaffst – von der ersten Ausstellung deiner Werke, die ich 1994 in der Galerie Nationale du Jeu de Paume in Paris gesehen habe, bis zu FLUGPLATZ WELT/WORLD AIRPORT an der diesjährigen Biennale in Venedig –, mich permanent «stört». Das gilt auch für deine vor ein paar Tagen bei mir eingetroffene letzte Einladungskarte, auf der die Flamme der Freiheitsstatue abgebildet ist, die am Pont de l'Alma in Paris steht und nun zu einer Gedenkstätte für Diana geworden ist. Die Künstler und Kunstkritiker werden nicht müde, die

Möglichkeiten des Denkmals in der Nachkriegszeit, kurz vor der Jahrtausendwende, zu erörtern. Sie werden nicht müde sich zu fragen, was denn das zu Ende gehende Jahrhundert in feierlicher Erinnerung behalten darf oder soll. Diana? Die von den Medien konstruierte Volksmeinung? Das in den letzten Zügen liegende Freiheitsdenkmal? Oder einfach was davon noch übrig ist? Und du bist uns dabei keine Hilfe; du lockst uns in die Falle, indem du uns das vor Augen führst, was man eigentlich nur ignorieren will und kann: den Kitsch, den Geschmack des Dianakultes. Ich weiss, dass du das Wort nicht magst, aber steckt in diesem Werk, in dieser Ansichtskarte nicht vielleicht auch eine Form von Ironie? Ich warte deine Antwort gar nicht ab und sage gleich, dass ich nicht der Meinung bin, Ironie sei eine deiner Waffen. Ich glaube, dass dich dieser «kleine Geschmack», den ich vom «schlechten Geschmack» unterscheiden möchte, interessiert und berührt. Es ist irritierend, dass du dich mit dem abgibst, wofür wir nur ein distanziertes Lächeln übrig haben, denn diese Geschichte von Diana und den Paparazzi interessiert uns nicht, bewegen wir uns doch in viel höheren Gefilden. Diese Geschichte ist für die anderen, für Leute, die jene Zeitungen lesen, die wir nicht lesen... Indem du das tust, Thomas, indem du es dir zur Aufgabe machst, alle Attribute einer pubertären Gemütsbewegung zusammenzutragen, berührst du uns peinlich. Du bringst uns in Verlegenheit, weil die Information, die du uns lieferst, zu simpel, zu dumm, zu populistisch oder populär und zu direkt ist. Aber diese Simplizität, die irritiert, auch mich immer wieder irritiert, ist deine Stärke. Und sie hat wohl eine tränenähnliche Funktion in deiner Installation: etwas, was nicht auffällt, aber verhindert, dass wir austrocknen und spröde werden.

Kommen wir auf die Irritation zurück. Vor einiger Zeit wurde ich gefragt: Wenn Sie Thomas Hirschhorn eine Frage stellen müssten, welche wäre das? Meine Antwort: *In welchem Gebiet ist dein Schaffen vor dem Hintergrund der neueren Geschichte der Plastik anzusiedeln?* Diese Antwort fand wenig Anklang, obwohl ich eigentlich nur versucht hatte, nicht die erwartete Frage zu stellen, nämlich jene nach dem politischen Charakter deiner Arbeit und ihrer subversiven Dimension. Sie war Ausdruck meines möglicherweise zu sehr vereinfachenden Wunsches, deine Arbeit nicht im Umfeld einer politischen, sondern einer skulpturalen Praxis anzusiedeln. Warum? Einerseits, um der unüberlegten und inflationären Verwendung des Begriffs «politisch» entgegenzuwirken, andrerseits, weil ich besser verstehen möchte, was du mit deiner Aussage meinst: «Ich denke, es geht nicht darum, politische Kunst zu machen, sondern Kunst auf politische Weise zu machen, und das deklariert man doch nicht.»[2)] Schliesslich auch, weil deine Arbeit für mich immer untrennbar mit einer präzisen formalen Recherche verbunden ist, die sich auf ebenso virale wie programmatische Weise zu entwickeln scheint und im Laufe der Jahre ein eigenes Vokabular hervorgebracht hat. Ob du es willst oder nicht, es gibt jetzt einen Thomas-Hirschhorn-Stil, der dir im Übrigen auch die Bezeichnung «Display» oder «Layout» für deine Arbeiten abverlangt hat, um deine Vorbehalte gegenüber der sprachlichen Banalität des Wortes «Installation» zum Ausdruck zu bringen. Auch diese Weigerung, einen bestehenden Sachverhalt zu akzeptieren, ist ein Ärgernis.

Ich möchte zwei Elemente deiner Arbeit herausstreichen: einerseits das Vokabular und andrerseits die Syntax. Beide scheinen ganz pragmatisch, ökonomisch darauf ausgerichtet zu sein, mit den verfügbaren Mitteln auszukommen.

Wie ich persönlich erfahren konnte, ist dieses Vokabular schon seit der Ausstellung im Jeu de Paume 1994 im Gebrauch. Bretter, Stücke braunen Kartons, Holzböcke, Bilder aus Zeitungen und Zeitschriften, gefunden und auf Karton geklebt, deine Schrift mit Bic-Kugelschreiber, Plastikfolien, breite Klebebandrollen, brutales, klinisches Neonlicht; später dann Videobilder ohne Regie, in Echtzeit, Kerzen, Plastikblumen, Reproduktionen von Kunstwerken, Sperrholzplatten, photokopierte Texte, Kehrichtsäcke, zerknüllte Alufolie.

Diese «armen», «schmutzigen», qualitätslosen Elemente sind alle von Hand bearbeitet. Es gibt bei dir, Thomas, keine Ready-mades oder nur sehr wenige. Und du bestehst ausdrücklich auf dem Begriff Arbeit. Als ob du das künstlerische Schaffen banalisieren, normalisieren wolltest. Die Kunst, das Kunstmachen ist deine Arbeit und, wie du sagst, dein Kapital. Ist das vielleicht dein Versuch, eine direkte

Verbindung herzustellen zwischen traditionell wirtschaftlich verstandener Produktion und künstlerischer Produktion? Und ist es vielleicht auch eine Antwort auf den von dir bewunderten Joseph Beuys und seine Versuche das Kapital neu zu definieren?[3)]

Gegenüber Alison Gingeras hast du dich über die Bedeutung, die Beuys für dich hat, wie folgt geäussert: «Für mich befreit Beuys den Begriff der Skulptur von ästhetischem Ballast. Er schafft es, dem Wort ‹Skulptur› seine Kraft zurückzugeben. Er trennt es von einer auf sogenannte edle Materialien fixierten Praxis. Dieser Punkt ist für meine Arbeit sehr wichtig.»[4)]

Kommen wir auf deine Praxis zurück. Du bildest luxuriöse Markenzeichen (Mercedes, Chanel, Volkswagen) mit etwas schäbiger Alufolie nach und stellst sie in Vitrinen aus Karton und Plastik zur Schau. Du klebst Reklamebilder auf alte Kartons und stellst Bilder und Botschaften unterschiedlichster Art auf demselben Untergrund einander gegenüber: Mode und Folterungen, Chanel und Militärparade, BMW und Massaker, Nike und Kosovo, Neonazis und Meisterwerke aus dem Louvre. Und rund um die Bilder schreibst du mit Kugelschreiber Fragen hin, appellierst an das Publikum: «Loser? Winner? Helfen Sie mir, diese Bilder zu verstehen, ich finde sie schön. Ich will vergessen! Ich will mich widersetzen! Ist das Kunst? Vielen Dank! Ich verstehe nichts mehr!» In dieser Serie von Kartons mit dem Titel LES PLAINTIFS, LES BÊTES, LES POLITIQUES (Die Klagenden, die Dummen, die Politischen) setzt du uns mit diesen Fragen zu, die sich niemand stellen will, auf die dir auch niemand antworten wird, oder falls doch, dann höchstens um dir zu sagen, dass deine Vergleiche pubertär sind, deine Fragen naiv, widersprüchlich, ja demagogisch... Und du antwortest deinerseits, dass die beste Kampfmethode heutzutage die Dummheit sei.[5)] Da nervst du mich schon wieder! Von welcher Dummheit sprichst du denn? Von jener deiner Bilder, ihrer Simplizität, der Dummheit des Geschreibsels, das sich über deine Kartons ergiesst? Von meiner Dummheit? Von ihrer? Jener von Rolex? Siehst du, du fängst schon wieder an und vereitelst jede Interpretation. Du bombardierst uns mit Fragen und lieferst selbst natürlich keine Antworten. Das wäre zu einfach. Und in gewisser Weise nimmt LES PLAINTIFS, LES BÊTES, LES POLITIQUES deshalb in deiner Arbeit einen wichtigen Platz ein. Es ist in meinen Augen die Matrix dessen, was du inszenierst. Es ist, um eine Parallele zu einem anderen Künstler, Gerhard Richter, zu ziehen, sozusagen dein ATLAS, eine Art Programm. Du stellst Fragen ohne eine Antwort abzuwarten, du willst nichts verteidigen...

Doch zurück zur Skulptur.

Mit diesem Vokabular, diesen Materialien, diesen Fragen und diesen Bildern überflutest du die Räume, die dir zur Verfügung stehen. Egal ob in Innen- oder Aussenräumen, du überschwemmst die Welt mit deinen Fragen. Du gehst nach dem Prinzip *more is more, less is less* vor, das du zu deiner Syntax gemacht hast, und fegst unsere modernistischen Dogmen vom Tisch... Du scheinst nicht an sie zu glauben, oder falls doch, ist das nicht wesentlich. Du suchst etwas, was wesentlich wäre, und legst Kunst und Welt auf eine Waage. Angesichts der Tatsache, dass man gerade über ein halbes Jahrhundert lang versucht hat, Kunst und Leben mit dem Traum, die Welt zu verändern, in Einklang zu bringen, werden deine Fragereien zum Ärgernis.

In der 1998 im Portikus in Frankfurt gezeigten Arbeit EIN KUNSTWERK, EIN PROBLEM scheinst du uns weismachen zu wollen, dass die Moderne, die Kunst den gestellten Anforderungen nicht gewachsen ist. Du hast im Ausstellungsraum zwanzig Plakatwände aufgestellt, wie sie für Wahlplakate verwendet werden. Auf jeder Plakatfläche sieht man Zeitungsausschnitte, Photos, spiegelnde Flächen (zur Reflexion?). Jede Plakatfläche nimmt ein aktuelles Problem auf: Palästina, Nordirland, Arbeitslosigkeit, Golfkrieg, Atomkraft, Fettleibigkeit, Kosovo, Fischerei, Drogen, Tierschutz... Da der Ausstellungsraum nicht gross genug ist, um die Probleme der Welt aufzunehmen, hast du ihn mit zwei Galerien aus transparentem Kunststoff gegen aussen erweitert: So kann die Welt die Kunst sehen, und die Kunst kann die Welt sehen. Jedes Problem ist durch ein Band aus zerknitterter Alufolie mit einem anderen Problem verknüpft. Jedes Problem ist nach demselben Prinzip mit einer abstrakten «modernen» Skulptur verbunden, die grob aus Karton und blauem Kunststoff gefertigt ist. Diese Gebilde sind wacklig, fragil und könnten den

Grundsatz *bien fait, mal fait, pas fait* (gut gemacht, schlecht gemacht, nicht gemacht) von Robert Filliou illustrieren. Die Anordnung im Raum erschwert ein freies Zirkulieren. Es gilt, sich um die Plakate herumzubewegen, ohne an die Skulpturen zu stossen; die Mitte des Raums ist unzugänglich, ein Gesamtüberblick nicht möglich. Es hat so viele Texte, dass man sie beim besten Willen nicht alle lesen kann, das ist erdrückend, ich betrachte lieber die Skulpturen.

Dasselbe Prinzip wird in Venedig bei FLUGPLATZ WELT/WORLD AIRPORT befolgt. Wiederum kommen dieselben behelfsmässigen Materialien zum Einsatz, mit denen in der Mitte eines riesigen Saales das verkleinerte Modell eines internationalen, «globalen» Flughafens gebaut wurde, umlagert von der Welt und ihren Problemen in Form von Texten und Bildern, zu zahlreichen Texten, als dass man sie alle lesen, alle verstehen, wirklich aktiv teilnehmen könnte. Und es ist zu wenig Platz, um sich bequem von der Mitte aus umzusehen. Das Zentrum ist unzugänglich, scheinst du uns mitzuteilen. Auf dieselbe Art bemächtigst du dich der Ecken, so dass kein Gesamtüberblick möglich ist. Das nervt. Die Form deiner Skulptur macht das Material, die Informationen, aus denen sie sich zusammensetzt, unlesbar oder erschwert das Lesen zumindest erheblich. Du hilfst uns nicht. Du führst die Hyperkommunikation vor und inszenierst den Verlust der Orientierung. Die vielen Anhäufungen in deiner Plastik führen uns unsere unerträgliche Situation vor Augen und unsere glückliche Unfähigkeit, die Welt im Rahmen einer Wahrheit, einer Moral zu erfassen.

In Kafkas Oktavheften gibt es eine Passage, die diese Unfähigkeit des Menschen, seinen «Raum» wiederzufinden, illustriert: «Wir sind, mit dem irdisch befleckten Auge gesehn, in der Situation von Eisenbahnreisenden, die in einem langen Tunnel verunglückt sind, und zwar an einer Stelle, wo man das Licht des Anfangs nicht mehr sieht, das Licht des Endes aber nur so winzig, dass der Blick es immerfort suchen muss und immerfort verliert, wobei Anfang und Ende nicht einmal sicher sind.»[6)]

Thomas, dein Flughafen ist dieser Tunnel, und er irritiert, da er eine Unmöglichkeit aufzeigt. Vielleicht jene von Beuys' sozialer Skulptur. Beuys beschreibt und unterstreicht die Bedeutung seines Werks HIRSCHDENKMAL FÜR GEORGE MACIUNAS (1982) wie folgt: «Die Hirschdenkmäler sind Akkumulationsmaschinen, an denen Menschen und alle anderen Geister sich treffen, um gemeinsam zu arbeiten und dabei die entscheidenden Gesichtspunkte zu besprechen, die nötig sind (...) die Weltlage in die richtige Form zu bringen.»[7)] Es ist diese «richtige Form», die mir unerreichbar scheint, wenn ich mich mit deiner Arbeit auseinander setze, es sei denn, diese richtige Form bestehe in der Flamme zu Ehren Dianas. Thomas, hilf mir, ich verstehe diese Skulptur nicht, ich will mich ihr widersetzen, und ich finde sie schön.

(Übersetzung aus dem Französischen: Irene Aeberli)

1) Reiner Speck, «The Perfect Tear», in: Carl Haenlein (Hrsg.), *James Lee Byars, The Epitaph of Con.Art Is Which Questions Have Disappeared?*, Ausstellungskatalog der Kestner Gesellschaft, Hannover 1999, S. 106.

2) Thomas Hirschhorn, «Lettre à Thierry», in: *Auflage*, Ausstellungskatalog, Kunstmuseum Luzern; Centre d'Art Contemporain, Fribourg; Künstlerhaus Bethanien, Berlin 1995–1996, S. 16.

3) Thomas Hirschhorn, «J'aime Joseph Beuys», ebenda, S. 31.

4) Gespräch zwischen Alison Gingeras und Thomas Hirschhorn, in: *Thomas Hirschhorn*, Ausstellungskatalog, Chisenhale Gallery, London 1998.

5) Ebenda.

6) Franz Kafka, Das dritte Oktavheft, in: *Hochzeitsvorbereitungen auf dem Lande und andere Prosa aus dem Nachlass*, S. Fischer Verlag, Frankfurt 1980, S. 54.

7) Joseph Beuys, in: C. M. Joachimides, N. Rosenthal (Hrsg.), *Zeitgeist*, Ausstellungskatalog, Kunstbuch Berlin & Albert Hentrich Verlag, Berlin 1982, S. 82.

Vernunft im Widerstreit

KRIEG DER DIFFÉRANCE II

MARCUS STEINWEG

Die Wirklichkeit unserer Zeit, die Tatsächlichkeit und Notwendigkeit unserer Gegenwart heisst, die Grenze als solche gegenwärtig werden zu lassen, heisst in gewisser Weise, die Bedeutung bis an ihre Grenze zu treiben.
Jean-Luc Nancy[1)]

Was mich am meisten interessiert, sagt ein Freund, was mich in Atem hält oder in Lust, hat mit dieser Grenze zu tun, die wie ein Schnitt in meine Träume reisst. Was davon wäre erzählbar und wieviel davon beträfe die Philosophie?

Mit welchen Worten den Horizont ermessen, das Spielfeld möglicher E n t s c h e i d u n g e n, der, wie man sagt, einheitsversprechenden subjektiven Funktionen des Verstandes, der Urteilskraft oder der Vernunft? Den Möglichkeitsraum also von Urteilen der theoretischen und der praktischen, der ästhetischen, der – vernunftkritischen Vernunft. Einer a l l g e m e i n e n Vernunft, zu deren Wirklichkeit das gefährliche Spiel mit dem eigenen Unvermögen gehört, mit dem Begehren von Unmöglichem, mit dem latenten Selbstverlust im Selbst. Mit dem, was, wenn es Spielraum hat, einen infektiösen Schmerz freizusetzen imstande ist; und einen dem Ökosystem der r e i n e n Urteilskraft ursprünglich innewohnenden virtuellen Widerstand aktiviert, der die Logik der f r e i e n Entscheidung irreversibel erschüttert und kompromittiert.

Dem Akt der Wahl also, der Entscheidung, ist ein gewisses Vertrauen eingeschrieben, eine schwer vermeidbare Hoffnung noch der hoffnungslosesten Urteilsnahme, in ein s o l c h e s Aussen zu treten, das als dieser vage, inkommensurable Raum der Selbstvermittlung, der Verständigung, der Kommunikation, eine bestimmte Kompatibilität, eine Sinn stiftende Verwandtschaft aufweist zu diesem S e l b s t - i n n e n r a u m, in dem Bedeutung vermeintlich erst entsteht. Dieses Vertrauen wäre nicht einfach Beispiel eines naiven Dualismus, einer einfachen Innen-Aussen-Dialektik. Es wäre schon Unterbrechung jeder Form von Dialektik, Vertrauen auf den irreduziblen Wahnsinn von Vernunft. Darauf, dass sie im Aussen – und dieses Aussen ist es, das den Raum der Verrücktheit, einer zuletzt internen Drift bezeichnet – W i e d e r e r k e n n u n g findet und Aufnahme, wie durch einen besten, ewig fremd gebliebenen Freund. Eine Aufnahme, die zuletzt Selbstaufnahme bedeutet an den Kreuzungspunkten dieser komplizierten Horizontverschachtelung, die die Trennlinie zwischen Innen und Aussen, Vernunft und Wahnsinn (dem, was man in direkter Entgegenstellung so

MARCUS STEINWEG ist Schriftsteller und lebt in Köln. Anlässlich der Teilnahme Thomas Hirschhorns an der Biennale in Venedig 1999 erschien sein Text «Krieg der Différance I».

nennt) zu einem Ort der Erfahrung von Unentscheidbarkeit macht.

Was man Wahnsinn nennen kann und Verlust von Bedeutung, wäre eine Hauptachse des so entworfenen Diagramms. Jede Koordinate erfährt Bestimmung im notwendigen Bezug auf die mögliche Unmöglichkeit von Sinn. Die Erfahrung von Nicht-Sinn ist Erfahrung im Allgemeinen, akut und unaufhebbar inhärent. Der Nicht-Sinn – das, was Berechnung, Strategie, Gesetze und Regeln unterbricht, eine gewisse Idee also von Horizontalität zum Einsturz bringt, was diese Fassung übersteigt, transhorizontale Ekstasis erfordert – wäre der andere Horizontwert einer veränderten Vorstellung von Horizontalität.[2] Eines Horizontverständnisses, das dem Diktat einer Endabsicht der menschlichen Vernunft[3] das um irreduzible Aporieerfahrung erweiterte Hoffnungsmodell einer guten Absicht ohne Ende anzuschliessen weiss. Das Gute an dieser Absicht wäre gerade dies, dass sie masslos ist in ihrem Drang und jeden Abschluss des Entscheidungsspiels in seiner Vorläufigkeit durchquert. Ihr einen zuletzt quasireligiösen, mindestens, so sagt man wohl, realpolitisch naiven Infinitismus vorzuwerfen, trifft sie kaum.[4] Diese Durchquerung ist zugleich zögerlich und dezisiv.

Ein Unmöglichkeits-Horizont ... um nicht zu vergessen, um unvergessen zu machen – für mehr als diesen einen Augenblick einer Kreuzung der Erfahrung von Unmittelbarkeit mit dieser ins Reale erweiterten Unmittelbarkeit –, was die Idee der Funktion an die Nicht-Funktionalität von Ideen bindet. Dass die konkrete Handlung, dort, an den Schnittstellen gerade der horizontalen Vorstellung ihres geregelten, antizipierten, erfolgsversprochenen Verlaufs, der glücklichen Linie, an die Tatsächlichkeit der Drift, der Orientierungslosigkeit und Ohnmacht gekoppelt ist. An ein Unbestimmtheitsmoment, auf welches die Idee nicht erst adäquater Selbstvermittlung notwendig rückbezogen sein muss, aber schon die Idee der Idee, die Ordnung der Rückkehr und die Logik des Begriffs. Was die Überlegung in den Anfangsgrund der westlichen Denkgeschichte weist, der dann ein Abgrund heissen muss oder ein fortwährender Krieg. Ein Unmöglichkeits-Horizont ... auch um in Erinnerung zu rufen, dass diese allgemeine Vernunft eine gewisse inkommensurable Mitwisserschaft, eine Begleiterschaft erfährt, indem sie weiss. Ein Selbst-Gewusstsein vor allem, durch dieses, wovon sie nichts wissen will (wovon sie nicht wissen will, dass es sie weiss), dessen Vorkommen sie deshalb leugnet, was sie wie ein Gespenst von sich stösst, wie etwas, das in seiner Ungreifbarkeit so masslos bedrückt, eine unglückliche Kindheit, ein Hässliches, das man am besten eilig vergisst.

Ahnungen oder Erinnerungen, derer sie sich unter Berufung auf ihre Prinzipien der Klarheit und Distinktion verstärkt seit Descartes entledigen zu können glaubt; dass sie es ist, wenn sie so häufig auch vorgibt von diesem Phantom nichts zu wissen, die gewusst wird oder geliebt bis in den dauerhaften Verlust ihrer geschichtsbildenden Autorität. Die Vernunft, das ist das, wovon ein gewisser Wahnsinn, der Wahnsinn, der sie selber ist, nicht lassen kann; Zielpunkt einer in nächtigsten Strebungen artikulierten Lust. Dieser Tendenz ins Leere, in die Weite der unvermessbaren Nacht, in der das Wasser der Herkunft sich mit dem Wasser dieser grossen Welle, die man Zukunft nennt, mit dem, was kommt oder im Kommen ist, mit den Strömen des immer singulären Begehrens, den hyperbolischen Hoffnungen und Selbstversprechungen, den Partikularhorizonten der Bioteleologien der auch blinden, halb bewusstlosen Maschinen, die wir sind, verbunden hat zu einer dunklen dichten Masse ohne Licht. Von dieser Nacht unendlich zu erzählen, von dort her, wo das Ende des Tages mit dem anderen Ende des anderen Tages unentscheidbar zusammenzufallen scheint, wäre Merkmal jedes Denkens, das dem Wahnsinn der Vernunft auch seine Wahrheit anerkennt.

1) Jean-Luc Nancy, *Das Vergessen der Philosophie*, übers. von Horst Brühmann, Passagen-Verlag, Wien 1987, S. 83.

2) Das Verhältnis von Horizont und Entscheidung behandelt Jacques Derrida, in: ders., *Gesetzeskraft. Der «mystische Grund der Autorität»*, übers. von Alexander García Düttmann, Suhrkamp, Frankfurt am Main 1991, u. a. S. 53ff.

3) Immanuel Kant, *Kritik der reinen Vernunft*, hrsg. von Raymund Schmidt, Felix Meiner, Hamburg 1990, B 697ff.

4) «Freiheit», sagt Hermann Lübbe, «gewinnt die Theorie gerade dadurch, dass sie der Logik des Politischen nicht bedingungslos gehorcht.» In: *Theorie und Entscheidung. Studien zum Primat der praktischen Vernunft*, Rombach, Freiburg 1971, S. 11.

Reason in Conflict THE WAR OF DIFFÉRANCE II

MARCUS STEINWEG

The reality of our time, the factuality and the necessity of our present day, entails activating an awareness of the limit as such: pushing meaning to its limit, as it were. Jean-Luc Nancy[1)]

What interests me most, says a friend, what I find exciting or pleasurable is related to this limit, which cuts through my dreams like a slice. But how much of this can be narrated and how much is relevant to philosophy?

With what words can we measure the field of possible d e c i s i o n s, the horizon of the subjective functions of intellect, judgment, or reason that supposedly hold a promise of unity? That is, the potential field of judgments made by theoretical, practical, aesthetic reason, and by reason critical of reason. Included in the reality of a g e n e r a l reason is the dangerous game with its own inadequacy, with the desire for the impossible, with the latent loss of the self in the self. With that which is capable of unleashing contagious pain if given the leeway, and thereby activates a virtual resistance originally inherent in the ecosystem of p u r e reason, which irreversibly unsettles and compromises the logic of f r e e decision.

Inscribed therefore within the act of choice, of decision, is a certain trust, an almost unavoidable hope, a commitment to the most hopeless act of judgment, thereby stepping into s u c h an exterior, which is a vague, incommensurable space of self-mediation, of communication that shows a certain compatibility, a meaningful kinship with the i n t e r i o r s p a c e o f t h e s e l f, which is supposed to be the source of meaning. This trust is not simply an example of naïve dualism, of a simple dialectics of inside and outside. It would in fact subvert any kind of dialectical faith in the irreducible madness of reason. Faith in the fact that it finds r e c o g n i t i o n in the outside—and this outside is what denotes the

MARCUS STEINWEG is a writer living in Cologne. His essay "The War of Différance I" was published on the occasion of Thomas Hirschhorn's contribution to the Venice Biennale, 1999.

space of madness, of an ultimately internal drift—and acceptance, as if by a best and eternally alien friend. Acceptance that ultimately signifies self-acceptance at the point where complex, interlocked horizons intersect, which turns the dividing line between inside and outside, between reason and madness (as it is called in cases of direct antithesis) into a place marked by the experience of nondecision.

What one can call madness and loss of meaning would be a principle axis of the resulting diagram. Each coordinate is necessarily defined in reference to the possible impossibility of meaning. The experience of nonmeaning is experience per se, acute and inescapably inherent. Nonmeaning, which obstructs calculation, strategy, laws, and rules and thus causes a certain notion of horizontality to collapse, which transcends this version and requires transhorizontal ecstasy, would be the other horizon of an altered notion of horizontality.[2] A notion that unites the dictate of an ultimate intention of human reason[3] with a model of hope, expanded by irreducible aporia, in a good intention without end. The good thing about this intention would be precisely that it is immoderate and would frustrate any conclusion of the decision-making game in its provisionality. To accuse it of an infinitism that is ultimately quasi-religious or at best naïve in terms of realpolitik is irrelevant, to say the least.[4] This frustration is both hesitant and decisive at once.

A horizon of impossibility ... in order not to forget, in order to make unforgotten—for more than this one moment of intersection of the experience of immediacy with this immediacy expanded into reality—is that which binds the idea of function to the nonfunctionality of ideas. In order not to forget that the concrete act at the interface of the horizontal idea, this regulated, anticipatory, promising course, of the happy line, is coupled with the factuality of drift, disorientation, and impotence. With an element of indeterminacy, to which the idea of not merely adequate self-mediation must necessarily recur but also the idea of the idea, the order of recurrence, and the logic of the concept. This directs our reflection towards the first foundations of the history of Western thought, which must then be called an abyss or constant warfare. A horizon of impossibility ... partly a reminder as well that this general reason entails a certain incommensurable shared knowledge, a complicity, in that it knows. A self-knowing above all through that which it does not want to know anything about (does not want to know that it knows), therefore denying its existence, driving it away like a ghost, like something infinitely oppressive in its impalpability, an unhappy childhood, something ugly that is best quickly forgotten.

A belief in the ability of reason to rid itself of intimations or memories—all the more so since Descartes—by recurring to principles of clarity and distinctness: Although it often pretends to know nothing of this phantom, it is what is known or loved even to the lasting loss of its historical influence and authority. Reason, that is what a certain madness, the madness that it is itself, cannot leave alone; the target of a desire articulated in the darkest nocturnal strivings. This tendency towards the void, towards the wide expanses of immeasurable night, in which the water of origin has combined with the water of that great wave we call Future, with that which is to come or is coming, with the streams of ever singular desire, of hyperbolic hopes and self-promises, the particular horizons of bioteleologies even of the blind, half-unconscious machines that we are, into a dark, dense mass without light. To speak without end of this night, from the point where the end of the day seems to merge indistinguishably into the other end of another day, would be a feature of all thinking that acknowledges that the madness of reason also has its truth.

(Translation: Gino Fittucci)

1) Jean-Luc Nancy, *L'Oublie de la philosophie* (Paris: Ed. Galilée, 1986). The quotation here is translated from the German (*Das Vergessen der Philosophie,* transl. from the French by Horst Brühmann, Vienna: Passagen-Verlag, 1997), p. 83.

2) On the relationship of horizon and decision see: Jacques Derrida, *Force de loi: Le "Fondement mystique de l'autorité"* (Paris: Ed. Galilée, 1994).

3) Immanuel Kant, *Critique of Pure Reason,* transl. by Werner S. Pluhar (Indianapolis: Hackett, 1996), B 697 ff.

4) According to Hermann Lübbe, "The theory acquires freedom precisely by not unconditionally obeying the logic of the political." In: *Theorie und Entscheidung. Studien zum Primat der praktischen Vernunft* (Freiburg: Rombach, 1971), p. 11.

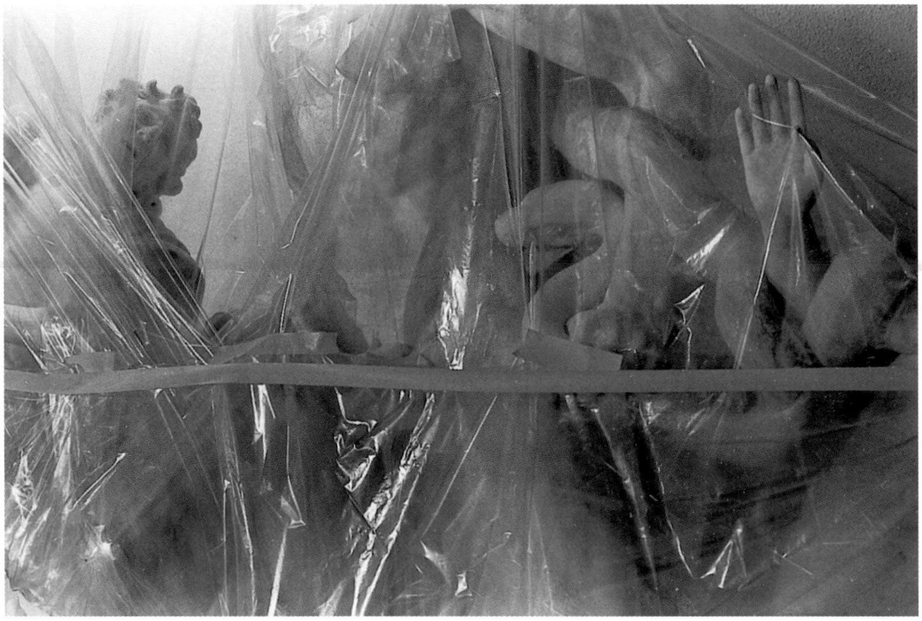

LOUISE LAWLER, STORAGE, 1984, black-and-white photograph, 15 1/4 x 23" / LAGER, Schwarzweissphoto, 38,7 x 58,4 cm.

LOUISE LAWLER, THREE, 1984, black-and-white photograph, 15 1/4 x 23" / DREI, Schwarzweissphoto, 38,7 x 58,4 cm.

ANDREA KROKSNES

Louise Lawler:

Zwei schwere Goldrahmen, Rücken an Rücken, nur durch eine Stellwand getrennt, geben ihre Gemälde nicht preis. Die barocken Gegenstände müssen sich im «white cube» der Galerie verlaufen haben, deren einziges Ornament ihre Thermostate sind. Diese Inszenierung des Rahmens – einer sonst unbeachteten, peripheren Erscheinung – als konstituierendes, zentrales Element ist typisch für Lawlers Bildkompositionen: das autonome Kunstobjekt als Mythos, der nur durch ein schützendes Umfeld gespeist und aufrechterhalten wird. Louise Lawlers Photographien von Kunstwerken und ihren Kontexten wurden oft als scharfe Institutionskritik und Neuauflage Duchamp'scher Endspielstrategien interpretiert. Eine genauere Bildanalyse der einzelnen Arbeiten schien nicht nur überflüssig zu sein, sondern auch im Widerspruch zu ihrer Absage an Originalität und Autonomie des einzelnen Kunstwerks zu stehen. Lawlers Liebe zum Detail und die fast malerischen Kompositionen ihrer Photographien wurden meist geflissentlich übersehen oder aber irritiert wahrgenommen und wegen ihrer Nähe zur abstrakten Malerei der klassischen Moderne (von Malewitsch bis Color Field) kritisiert.

Eine ihrer Photographien zeigt zur einen Hälfte Jasper Johns' WHITE FLAG, zur anderen die grob gerippte Stellwand des Auktionshauses Christie's. Fifty-fifty Kunst und Business sozusagen, wobei sich das monochrome WHITE FLAG PAINTING und die

ANDREA KROKSNES schreibt zurzeit an einer Dissertation über Louise Lawler. Sie lebt in Hamburg.

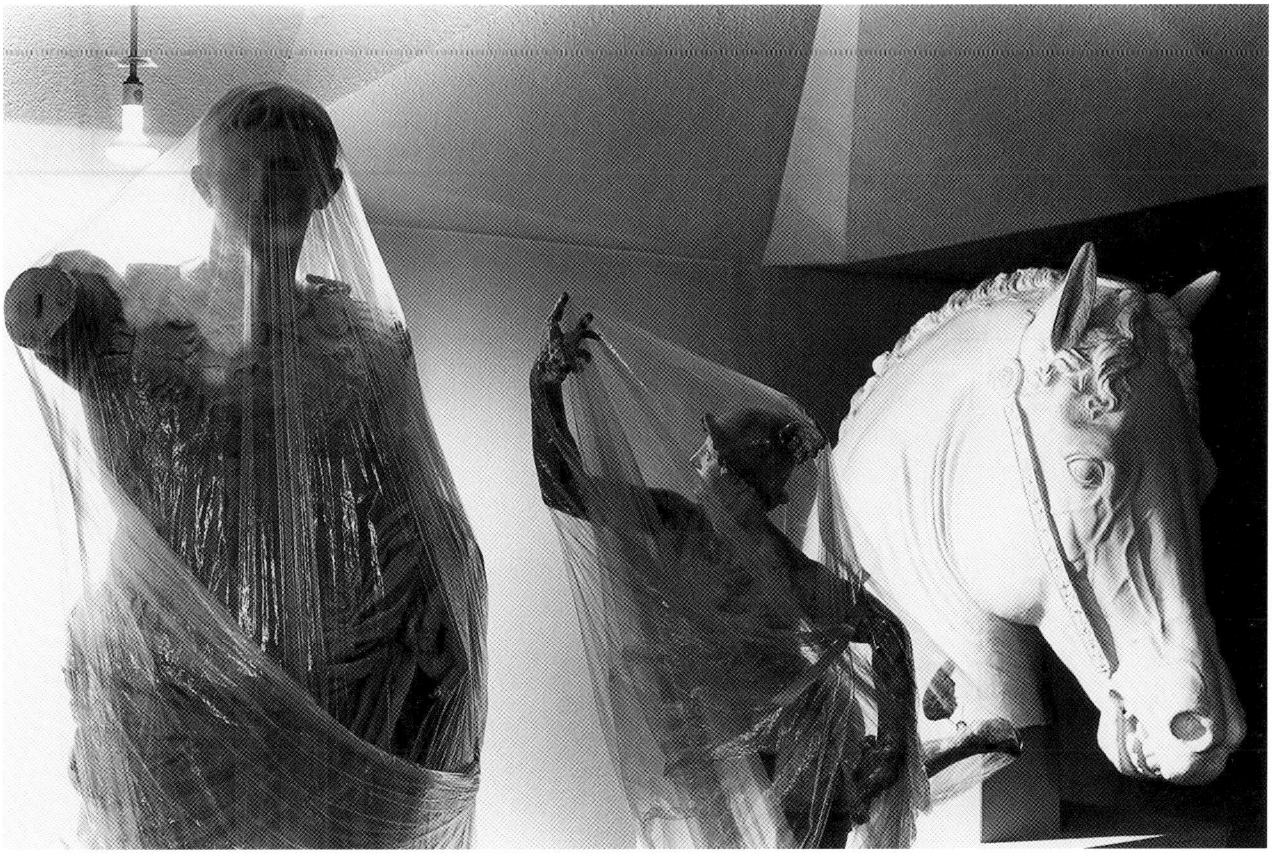

Geister der Moderne

rauh geprägte Stellwand ästhetisch nicht beeinträchtigen, sondern eher harmonisch ergänzen. Als Bildunterschrift liefert Lawler einen Text, der schlicht die Namen der Vorstandsdirektoren des Auktionshauses aufzählt. Lawlers Arbeiten dokumentieren eindrucksvoll den Verlust der Aura von Kunst, die nun – von ihrem Kultwert befreit – als Warenfetisch auf dem Markt zirkuliert. Gleichzeitig versucht sie jedoch ein Stückchen dieser Aura – wenn auch nur in unserer Erinnerung – wieder wachzurufen. Ähnlich wie bei Walter Benjamin, der als einer der ersten die Kunst im Zeitalter ihrer technischen Reproduzierbarkeit unter die Lupe nahm, ist Lawlers Verhältnis zum Verlust des Kultwertes von Kunst nicht ganz eindeutig. Einer ihrer Kristallbriefbeschwerer zeigt die mit Computern ausgestattete Rezeptionstheke einer Galerie, daneben an der Wand, dicht an dicht, die kleinformatigen Zeichnungen Allan McCollums. Keine gleicht der nächsten genau. Und doch können sie sich als Einzelwerke nicht behaupten. McCollums Arbeiten sind endlose, rein mechanische Variationen eines Prototyps. «She made no attempt to rescue art from ritual» (Sie machte keinen Versuch die Kunst vor dem Ritual zu retten), behauptet der Text, den Lawler dieser Arbeit gegenüberstellt. Aber die darunter abgebildeten Ja/Nein-Kästchen zum Ankreuzen verleihen dem vermeintlich persönlichen Statement die harmlose Neutralität eines Fragebogens.

Louise Lawlers Kunstwerke entstehen in einer Welt der Massenmedien, in der uns der unaufhörliche Fluss von Bildern in einem Strudel der Simulation gefangen hält. Walter Benjamins optimistische Vision der befreiten Bilder hat sich in diesem Szenario verflüchtigt. Für Lawlers Arbeiten ist die Gesellschaft des Spektakels, die Zeichenzirkulation und die damit zusammenhängende Osmose zwischen kultureller und ökonomischer Sphäre eine selbstverständliche Grundvoraussetzung. Trotzdem schleicht sich wie bei Benjamin immer wieder eine gewisse Melancholie ein, wenn sie ein längst unzeitgemässes Theaterarchiv oder einen verstaubten Museumskeller photographiert, in dem sich klassische griechische Statuen zwischen Kisten und Ventilatoren auszuruhen scheinen. Lawler scheint angetrieben von einer unvollendeten Trauerarbeit um das längst begrabene Versprechen des autonomen Kunstobjekts der Moderne.

In der bereits erwähnten Paperweight-Arbeit wird dies besonders deutlich. Allan McCollum erteilt mit seinen unendlichen Serien von Replikationen dem autonomen Kunstwerk eine Absage. Die Geste der Rebellion, die das autonome Kunstobjekt durch eine Ästhetik der Verweigerung ausdrückte, zerplatzt bei McCollum wie eine Seifenblase. McCollums Arbeiten führen vor, wie jegliches transgressive Potential erstickt, sobald das Kunstwerk in den Warenverkehr eintritt. Wenn Lawler nun Allan McCollums «Degree-zero»-Kunst noch einmal photographiert, und das wiederum Kunst nennt, passiert etwas Inte-

LOUISE LAWLER, FOUR BETWEEN TWO DOORS, 1993/98, cibachrome, 24 x 30⅝" / VIER ZWISCHEN ZWEI TÜREN, Cibachrome, 61 x 77,8 cm.

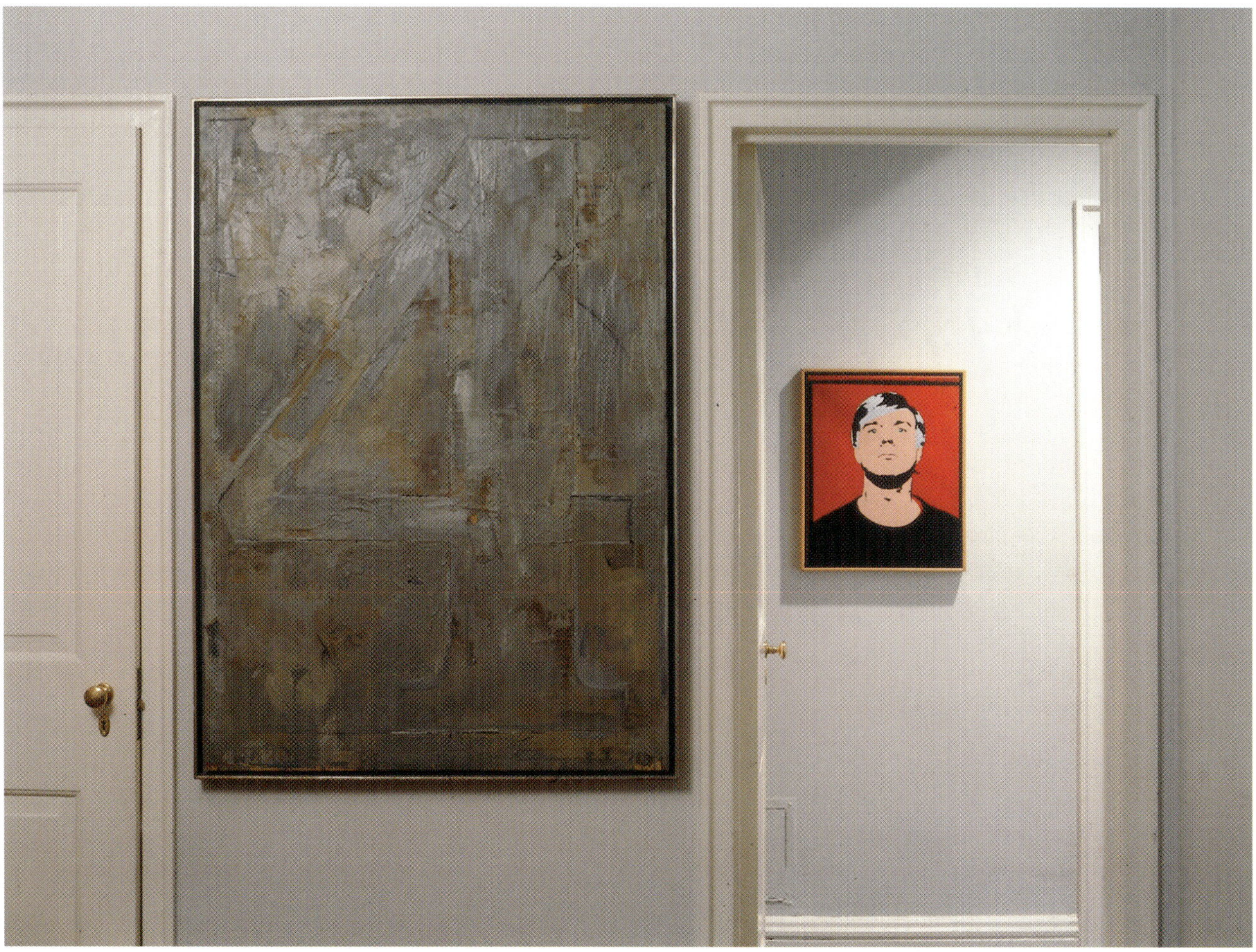

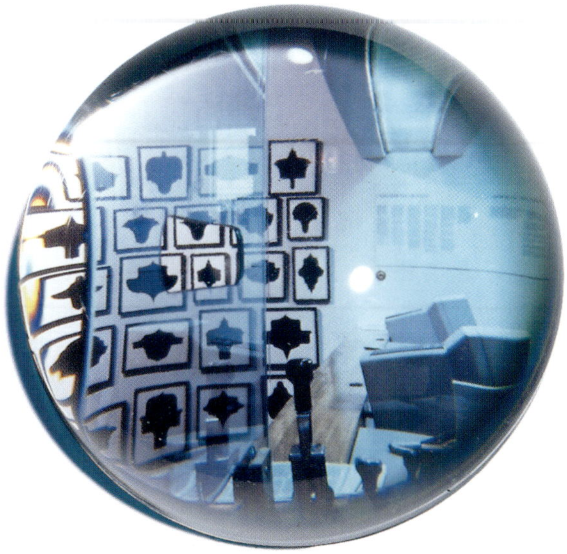

LOUISE LAWLER, UNTITLED (COLLECTION OF 60 DRAWINGS), 1992–93, cibachrome, crystal, felt, 2" high, 3½" in diameter / OHNE TITEL (SAMMLUNG VON 60 ZEICHNUNGEN), Cibachrome, Kristallglas, Filz, 5 cm hoch, 8,9 cm Durchmesser.

ressantes: Das bereits tote Kunstobjekt wird durch die photographische Verdoppelung noch einmal getötet. Dieser Doppelmord resultiert paradoxerweise in einer Wiederbelebung des Objekts. Während McCollums Arbeiten die Kunst vom Ritual befreien, kann man Lawler Glauben schenken, wenn sie – als Frage getarnt – behauptet: «She made no attempt to rescue art from ritual.» Denn ihre Arbeiten, die sich explizit mit den Schauplätzen der Kunstwelt auseinandersetzen, sind fast die einzigen Objekte an diesen Orten, die sich in ihrer natürlichen Umgebung befinden; also nicht dekontextualisierte Fetischobjekte, sondern Arbeiten, die gerade im musealen Ausstellungskontext ihre Vitalität entfalten.

Die Wahl des Mediums Photographie fasst diese Dialektik in Lawlers Arbeiten noch einmal zusammen. Kracauer fand in der Photographie eine Dialektik von Darstellung und Erinnerung, die zwischen Ausstellungswert und historischer Gegenstandserfahrung angesiedelt ist: Die Photographie versuche die Erinnerung an den Tod zu bannen, gleichzeitig sei aber das Dargestellte bereits nicht mehr gegenwärtig. Mit Hilfe der photographischen Reproduktion manifestiert Lawler das Verschwinden des materiellen Objekts und seiner geschichtlichen Eingebundenheit. Die glänzenden Spiegelungen, von denen Lawler so fasziniert ist und die sie in ihren Photos immer wieder einfängt, sind immaterielle Überreste der verlorenen Objektwelt der Moderne. Einst waren diese Kunstwerke konkret und als ganzheitliche Objekte im Raum des Betrachters zu erfahren. In Lawlers Photographien huschen nur noch die amputierten und körperlosen Geister dieser Kunstwerke an uns vorbei. Andrerseits tauchen in Lawlers Werk immer wieder Materialien, Texturen und Töne auf, die räumlich und körperlich-sinnlich erfahrbar sind und vom Betrachter in Beziehung gesetzt werden müssen, so dass die flache Ahistorizität ihrer Photographien relativiert und Formen historischer Erinnerung freigesetzt werden.

Lawlers Briefbeschwerer etwa verlangen eine unmittelbare räumlich-zeitliche Gegenstandserfahrung des einzelnen Objekts. Um die Photographie unter der gläsernen Halbkugel erkennen zu können, muss der Betrachter mit der Nase ganz dicht an das Objekt heran. Dabei wird der öffentliche Raum der Galerie völlig ausgeblendet und der Betrachter versinkt in einer Miniaturwelt der wunderlichsten Dinge. Der monadische Standpunkt des Betrachters und sein Rückzug aus der Welt rufen das Verfahren der Camera obscura wach. Jonathan Crary analysierte prägnant, wie diese seit dem ausgehenden fünfzehnten Jahrhundert die Beziehung zwischen Betrachter und Welt definierte und ein neues Verständnis von Subjektivität ankündigte. Einerseits beschwört Lawler mit ihren Briefbeschwerern die Objektwelt des Museums in der Erinnerung des Betrachters herauf. Andrerseits wird vermieden auf den klassischen modernen Dualismus von Betrachter und Welt, Subjekt und Objekt zurückzugreifen. Es werden vielmehr auch hier – ganz nach postmoderner Manier – die Kategorien durchlässig, wenn das vermeintliche Subjekt des Betrachtens sich in die magische Kugel vertieft und nun für andere Anwesende zum Objekt ihres Blickes wird. Die Kontrolle und Autonomie des betrachtenden Subjekts wird in Lawlers Arbeiten immer wieder unterlaufen, wenn der Betrachter oder die Betrachterin im Sog des allgegenwärtigen Spektakels verloren geht. Die Briefbeschwerer veranschaulichen diese Ambivalenz noch einmal: Auf der einen Seite verkörpern sie oder erinnern zumindest an klassische Objekte ästhetischer Kontemplation, die im Museum ausgestellt und aufbewahrt werden; auf der anderen Seite bietet Lawler die gleichen Briefbeschwerer auch im Museumsshop als Souvenirs zum Kauf an. Obwohl Museen das Kunstobjekt dem Markt entziehen, hat das fetischisierte Museumsobjekt viel mit der entfremdeten Warenwelt gemein. Selbst das Museum kann nicht den Warencharakter des modernen Objektes verleugnen. Der Prozess der Fetischisierung des Kunstwerkes, in dem Lebendiges durch Totes ersetzt wird, kann verglichen werden mit der Warenlogik des kapitalistischen Marktes. Die Glaskuppel der Briefbeschwerer verwandelt die Bilderwelt darunter in versteinerte Andenken. Die gleiche Glaskuppel macht die Arbeiten jedoch auch zum marktgängigen Souvenirartikel. Lawler betont hier die Kontinuität zwischen Museum und Markt, denn die musealen Konservierungsmethoden verwandeln jedes Kunstwerk in ein Objekt der Neugierde und des Luxus und verhelfen ihm so zu seinem Debüt auf dem Warenmarkt.

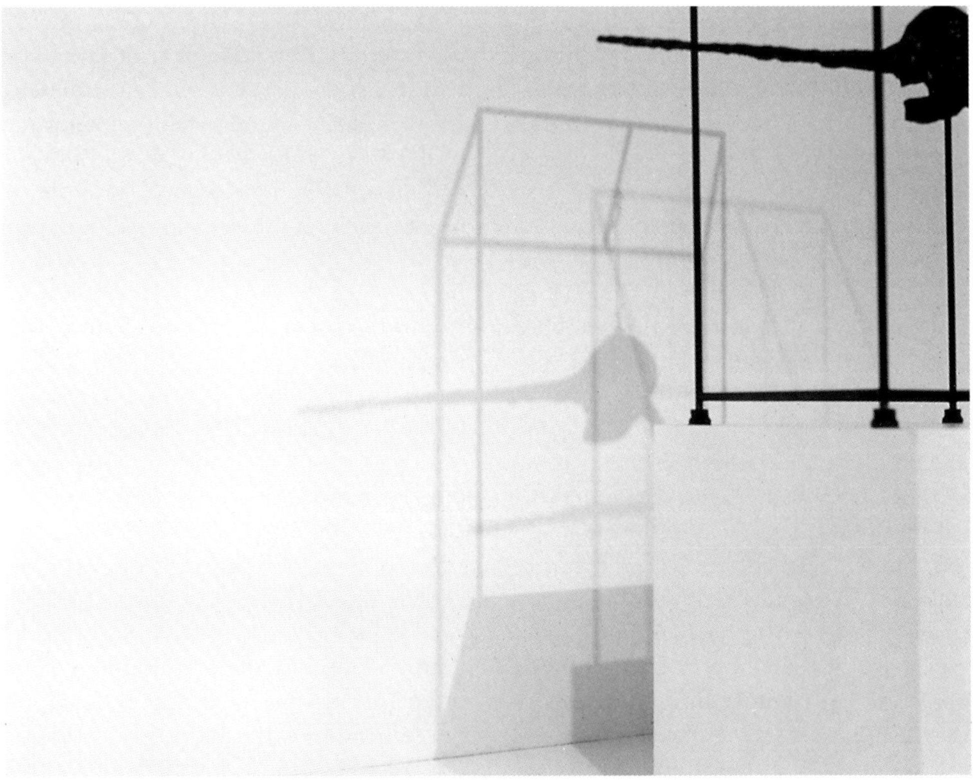

LOUISE LAWLER, FEDERAL OFFENSE, 1997/99, cibachrome, 40 x 49½ / STAATSBELEIDIGUNG, Cibachrome, 101,6 x 125,7 cm.

Die musealen Konservierungsvorrichtungen – Vitrinen, Glas und Schaukästen – sind ein wiederkehrendes Motiv in Lawlers Werk. Eine ihrer Photographien zeigt die Plastik einer Ballerina von Degas zusammen mit kleineren Tanz- und Körperstudien auf verschieden grossen Sockeln, beschützt von einem gläsernen Schaukasten. Die breite schwarze Metallumrandung lässt den Glaskubus wie einen Käfig und die erstarrten Tänzerinnen wie turnende Äffchen im Zoo erscheinen. Der Text, den Lawler als Begleitung zu diesem Bild gewählt hat, ist eine Anekdote: «Im folgenden Jahr blieb ihr gläserner ‹Käfig› während der ersten zwei Wochen der Ausstellung leer. Als sie endlich ausgestellt wurde, verglich sie ein Kritiker mit einem ‹abgetriebenen Fötus›, den man, wäre er nur etwas kleiner, ‹versucht wäre in einem Glas in Alkohol einzulegen›.» Lawler beschreibt in Photographie und Text den Alptraum einer Institution, die Kunstwerke beschützen will, indem sie ihnen das Leben nimmt. Die Vitrinen und anderen Glasbehälter des Museums sind Ausdruck einer Reaktion auf die immer flüchtiger werdende visuelle Erfahrung in der modernen Welt. Das museale «Einmachen» von Objekten muss als Versuch eines Aufhaltens oder Einfrierens der immer kinetischer werdenden Wahrnehmung der Welt verstanden werden. Der kontemplative Betrachter wird in diesem Szenario selbst zu einem Fossil aus längst vergangenen Tagen. Sogar im Museum war der kontemplative Betrachter von Anfang an ein Mythos, denn seine Erfahrungen im Museum waren ähnlich schnelllebig wie das Flanieren durch Geschäftspassagen, Bahnhöfe oder botanische Gärten. Weder hier noch dort kann sich der Betrachter auf das einzelne Objekt einlassen, das sich bruchstückhaft neben, vor und hinter anderen Objekten und Bildern präsentiert. In Lawlers Photographie der Degas'schen Tänzerin sehen wir rechts und links des zentral postierten Schaukastens einen Ausschnitt der bevölkerten Museumsgalerie. Der Betrachter ist auch hier kein in Kontemplation Versunkener, sondern ein verwischter Schatten. Er ist in der bewegten Menge kaum noch als Einzelner identifizierbar. Mit Hilfe einer langen Belichtungszeit führt Lawler die Anachronistik des Museums vor, das mit ausgefeilten Konservierungs- und Präsentationsmethoden den Besucher zum besinnlichen Betrachten bringen will, wo dessen Sehgewohnheiten längst andere sind. Eine zweite Photographie zeigt dieselbe Ballerina von Degas im New Yorker Metropolitan Museum, aber diesmal ohne Publikum. Auch hier wird uns, die wir nun die Betrachterrolle einnehmen, der Zugang zum Objekt erschwert. Hinter dem Schaukasten, der nur die Ballerina enthält, ist eine zweite Vitrine aufgebaut, die kleinere Skulpturen auf verschiedenen Höhen zur Schau stellt. Die gläsernen Schaukästen selbst sind auf dieser Photographie fast unsichtbar, so dass der Eindruck entsteht, die verschiedenen, teilweise ungelenk verdrehten Körper bewegten sich schwerelos im Raum – mal von oben, mal von unten gesehen. Unerwartete Blickwinkel, Ausschnitte und Reihungen, die die Körper niemals ganz, sondern immer fragmentiert abbilden, begegnen uns bereits im Werk von Degas. Lawler führt mit ihren Photographien diese Dezentralisierung des Blicks konsequent weiter. Oft gibt es zwei oder drei Variationen eines Themas: Mal ist nur der Ausschnitt leicht verschoben, mal der Blickwinkel ein anderer. Mal in Farbe und mal in Schwarzweiss kombiniert sie ihre Photographien mit Textfragmenten zu ständig sich wandelnden Arrangements. Das Medium Photographie dient ihr dazu, die multiplen Zugangsmöglichkeiten und Subjektpositionen des Betrachters auszuloten. Die Objekte auf Lawlers Bildern sind niemals im Zentrum ihrer Kompositionen oder als ganze abgebildet, sondern sind bruchstückhafte Erinnerungen an ein unversehrtes Objekt und intaktes Subjekt. Lawler hat den Glauben an das moderne Kunstwerk und sein Subjekt verloren, trauert aber gleichzeitig um das uneingelöste Versprechen eines autonomen, in radikaler Opposition zur Gesellschaft stehenden Kunstwerks. Mit der Betonung des Bruchs und des Fragments knüpft Lawler an avantgardistische Praktiken wie Collage und Montage an. Diese Bezugnahme ist aber nicht nur als melancholische Erinnerungsarbeit zu verstehen. Lawlers Arbeit birgt in sich vielmehr die Hoffnung, dem Erstickungstod im Museum zu trotzen. Indem sie die Orte der Kunst zu ihrem natürlichen Umfeld wählt, verweigert sie sich der Dekontextualisierungsdynamik dieser Institutionen. Ja, sie benötigt den musealen Kontext und Sinnzusammenhang um ihr transgressives Potential entfalten zu können.

ANDREA KROKSNES

Louise Lawler:

Two weighty gold frames, back to back on a partition, do not reveal their paintings. It seems as if the baroque objects have accidentally strayed into the "white cube" of the gallery, decorated only by its thermostats. This display of the frame—ordinarily a discounted, peripheral item—as constituent and central is typical of Lawler's compositions: The autonomous art object is a myth, nurtured and sustained only by its protective environs.

Louise Lawler's photographs of artworks and their context have frequently been interpreted as a pointed institutional critique and a re-edition of Duchamp's endgame strategies. A closer analysis of her individual pieces not only seems superfluous but also contradicts her disavowal of the original and autonomous work of art. As a rule, Lawler's love of detail and the almost painterly composition of her photographs has been assiduously ignored. Or if it has been perceived, it has been criticized for its closeness to the abstract painting of classical modernism—from Malevich to color field painting.

One of Lawler's photographs shows half of Jasper Johns's WHITE FLAG on one side and the rough, unfinished shelves at Christie's on the other. Art and business, half-and-half so to speak, while the monochrome WHITE FLAG painting and the shelves are not at aesthetic odds with each other but, in fact, harmoniously complementary. For the caption of the piece, Lawler merely lists the names of the board of directors at Christie's. Her works impressively convey the loss of the aura in art, which, freed of its cult value, can now circulate on the market as a commodity fetish. At the same time, however, she tries to evoke a bit of that old aura, even if only in our memories. Like Walter Benjamin, who was one of the first to examine art in the age of reproducibility, Lawler's concern with the loss of the cult value of art is not entirely unambiguous. One of her crystal paperweights shows the reception desk of a gallery with its bank of computers cheek by jowl with a wall full of Allan McCollum's small format drawings. None of McCollum's drawings are exactly alike, and yet they can't be taken as originals either; they are endless, purely mechanical variations of a prototype. The caption Lawler opposes to this piece claims that "she made no attempt to rescue art from ritual." But the little yes-or-no boxes to be ticked off underneath the caption lend to this seemingly personal statement the innocent neutrality of a questionnaire.

Louise Lawler's art comes out of a world of mass media, in which an endless flood of images is caught up in a maelstrom of simulation. Walter Benjamin's optimism about images being liberated through the media has evaporated in the mist of this scenario. The society of the spectacle—the circulation of signs and the attendant osmosis between cultural and economic spheres—has become the self-evident premise of Lawler's work. Nonetheless, in her case as in Benjamin's, a certain melancholy always creeps into her pictures of long outmoded theater archives or the dusty cellars of a museum where classical Greek statues have come to rest between boxes and ventilators. Lawler's work seems to be driven by the unfinished task of mourning modernism's long buried promise of the autonomous art object.

This is especially apparent in the above-mentioned paperweight. Allan McCollum has written off the autonomous work of art with his infinite series of replications. The gesture of rebellion expressed in

ANDREA KROKSNES is currently writing a dissertation on Louise Lawler. She lives in Hamburg.

Specters of Modernism

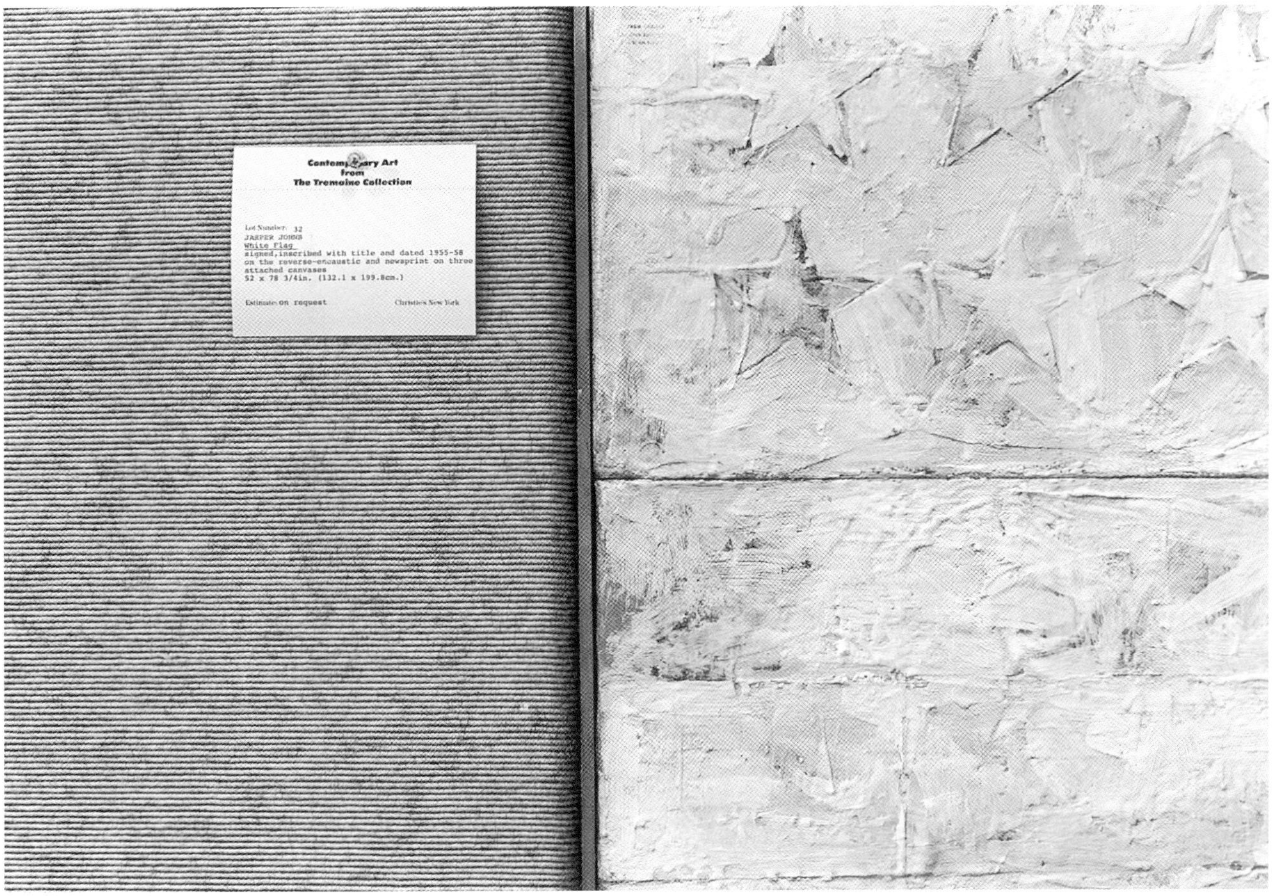

LOUISE LAWLER, BOARD OF DIRECTORS, 1989, black-and-white photograph, 16 x 22¼" / VERWALTUNGSRAT, Schwarzweissphoto, 40,6 x 56,5 cm.

the autonomous artwork's aesthetics of refusal has burst like a soap bubble in McCollum's work. All transgressive potential is manifestly smothered when the work of art moves into the commercial market. And when Lawler rephotographs McCollum's "degree zero" art and calls it art again, something interesting happens: Photographic duplication kills an art object that is already dead. This double murder paradoxically resuscitates the object. While McCollum's works liberate art from ritual, Lawler makes a credible claim that is camouflaged as a question: "She made no attempt to rescue art from ritual." In fact, works that explicitly address art world venues are practically the only objects in these places that could be said to be located in their natural habitat—in other words, that are not decontextualized fetishes but rather works that depend on the museum context to unfold their full potential.

This dialectic is further distilled in Lawler's art through her choice of the medium of photography. Siegfried Kracauer saw in photography a dialectics of representation and remembrance that lies between exhibition value and historical experience. Photography seeks to ban the memory of death, but at the same time, the referent is no longer present. With the help of photographic reproduction, Lawler makes manifest the disappearance of the physical object and its historical embeddedness. The shiny reflections that fascinate Lawler and that she captures in her photographs are the immaterial remains of the lost object world of modernism. These art objects used to be concrete items that viewers were able to experience as whole objects in space. In Lawler's photographs, we are left only with their

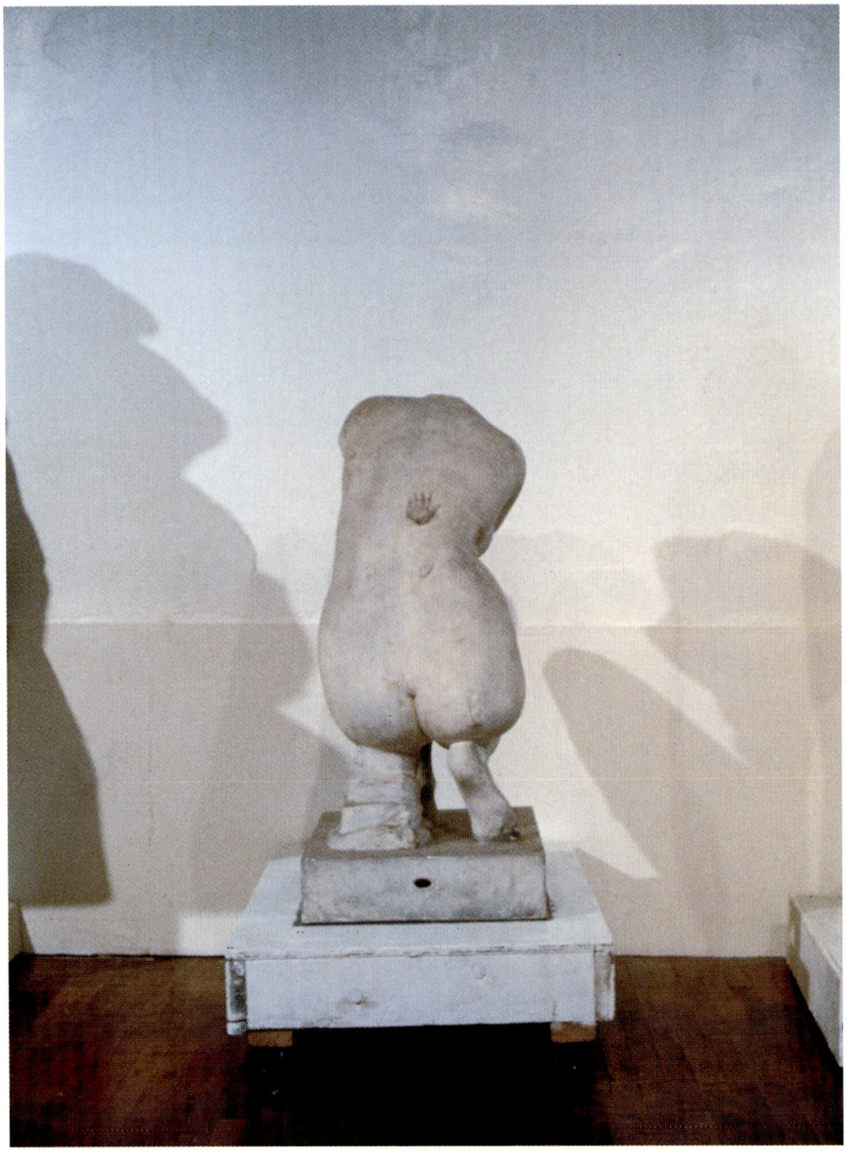

LOUISE LAWLER, HAND ON HER BACK, 1997, cibachrome, $60^{1}/_{2}$ x $43^{1}/_{2}$" / HAND AUF IHREM RÜCKEN, Cibachrome, 153,7 x 110,5 cm.

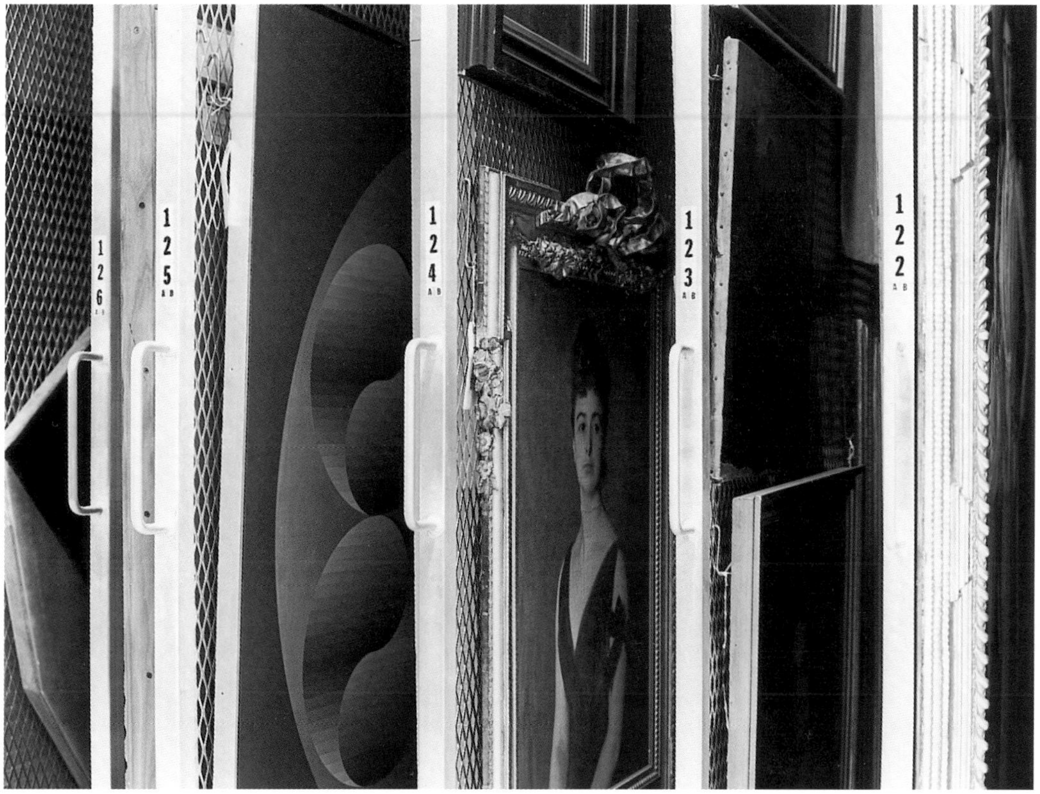

LOUISE LAWLER, SARGENT, 1990, black-and-white photograph,
29¼ x 33" / Schwarzweissphoto, 74,3 x 83,8 cm.

amputated and disembodied ghosts. On the other hand, materials, textures, and tones that can be physically and sensually experienced keep cropping up in Lawler's work. These must be put into a context by the viewer so that the flat ahistoricism of her photographs can be relativized and the forms of historical remembrance released.

Lawler's paperweights, for example, necessitate the experience of each object in time and space. In order to be able to read the photograph under the glass dome, the viewer must almost press his/her nose against the object. The space of the gallery is thereby completely blocked out and the viewer immersed in a wondrous miniature world. The viewer's monadic standpoint and withdrawal from the world recalls the method of the camera obscura. Jonathan Crary presents a striking analysis of how the camera obscura has defined relations between viewer and world since the end of the fifteenth century, ultimately ushering in a new understanding of subjectivity. Lawler's paperweights evoke memories of the object world of the museum without returning to classical modernism's dualism of viewer and world, subject and object. Instead, in perfect postmodern fashion, categories become pervious when the supposed subject of the viewing, absorbed in the magic sphere, becomes the object at which other visitors gaze. Lawler undermines the control and autonomy of the viewing subjects who are drawn into the vortex of the omnipresent spectacle. The paperweights underscore this ambivalence: On the one hand, they embody—or are at least reminiscent of—the classical objects of aesthetic contemplation that are traditionally displayed and preserved in museums. On the other, Lawler offers the same paperweights for sale as souvenirs in the museum shop. Not even museums can persist in denying the commodification of the modern art object; although museums take art off the market, the fetishized museum object still has a great deal in common with the alienated commodified world outside. The process of making a fetish of artworks, of replacing life with death, can be compared to the logic of the capitalist market. The glass dome of the paperweight converts the images it protects into petrified keepsakes. But that same glass dome also transforms the works into marketable souvenirs. Lawler illustrates the continuity between museum and market by demonstrating how museum methods of conservation turn every work of art into an object of curiosity and a luxury item, ultimately enhancing its market value.

The equipment of conservation—vitrines, glazing, display cases—is a recurring motif in Lawler's work. One of her photographs shows the sculpture of a Degas ballerina with other small studies in dance and anatomy on different sized bases inside a glass display case. The wide black metal frame turns the glass cube into a cage and makes the dancers look like monkeys at a zoo frozen in acrobatic action. The caption of this piece is an anecdote: "The following year her glass 'cage' remained empty for the first two weeks of the exhibition. When finally exposed she was likened by one critic to an 'expelled fetus' which if smaller '...one would be tempted to pickle in a jar of alcohol.'" Lawler's photograph and text exemplify the institutional nightmare of killing a work by attempting to preserve it. The vitrines and other glass containers of the museum are indicative of a reaction to our increasingly fleeting visual experience of the world. The "preserves" that museums make must be understood as an attempt to arrest or freeze an increasingly kinetic perception of the world. In this scenario, the contemplative viewers themselves become fossils of long bygone days. In fact, the contemplative viewer has always been a myth, even in the museum, because the act of viewing is as short-lived as strolling through a shopping mall, a railroad station, or botanical gardens. The single object presented piecemeal next to, in front of, or behind other objects and images cannot be studied in peace. In Lawler's photograph of Degas's ballerina, we see a section of the crowded museum gallery to the left and right of the centered display case. Here, too, the people are not viewers in absorbed contemplation, but fuzzy shadows. It is almost impossible to identify single viewers in the moving crowd. Through her use of long exposure times, Lawler reveals the anachronism of devising elaborate methods of conservation and presentation to encourage a meditative approach among viewers long accustomed to a different kind of visual behavior.

A second photograph shows Degas's ballerina at New York's Metropolitan Museum of Art, but this time without any viewers. Once again we, who now slip into the role of viewer, are not offered easy access to the object. Behind the display case, which contains only the dancer, is a second display case containing several smaller sculptures placed at different heights. The two glass cases can barely be seen in this photograph, creating the impression that the various and at times contorted bodies are suspended in space, to be viewed from above or below. Unexpected vantage points, cropping and sequencing, bodies never seen in their entirety—these devices are all familiar from the work of Degas himself. Lawler follows this decentralization of the gaze to its logical conclusion. Often we have two or three versions of an image: She may vary its cropping or angle of vision, she may use color or black-and-white film, and she presents her photographs with fragments of text in constantly changing combinations. Lawler uses the medium of photography to explore multiple means of accessing and positioning the subject. The objects in her pictures are never in the center of her compositions and never pictured in their entirety; they are always fragmented memories of an intact object and subject. Lawler has lost faith in the modern work of art and its subject, but she still mourns the unfulfilled promise of the autonomous artwork that stands in radical opposition to society. By emphasizing the break and the fragment, she links into avant-garde practices such as the aesthetics of collage and montage. But this back reference is not simply a matter of melancholy recollection. Rather, Lawler's work is sustained by the wish to escape death by asphyxiation in the museum. By choosing the sites of art as her natural habitat, she refuses to be caught up in the dynamics of decontextualization in these institutions. On the contrary, the transgressive potential of her oeuvre can flourish only in the context of the museum and the meanings it purveys.

(Translation: Catherine Schelbert)

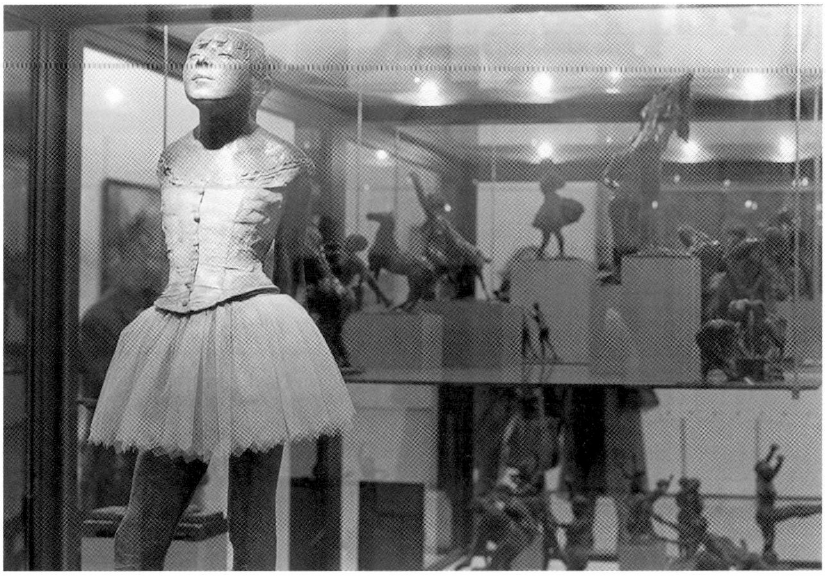

LOUISE LAWLER, GLASS CAGE, 1991/93, two black-and-white photos with text on mat, 28 x 32" and 28 x 25" / GLASKÄFIG, zwei Schwarzweissphotos mit Text unter dem Bild, 71,1 x 81,3 cm und 71,1 x 63,5 cm.

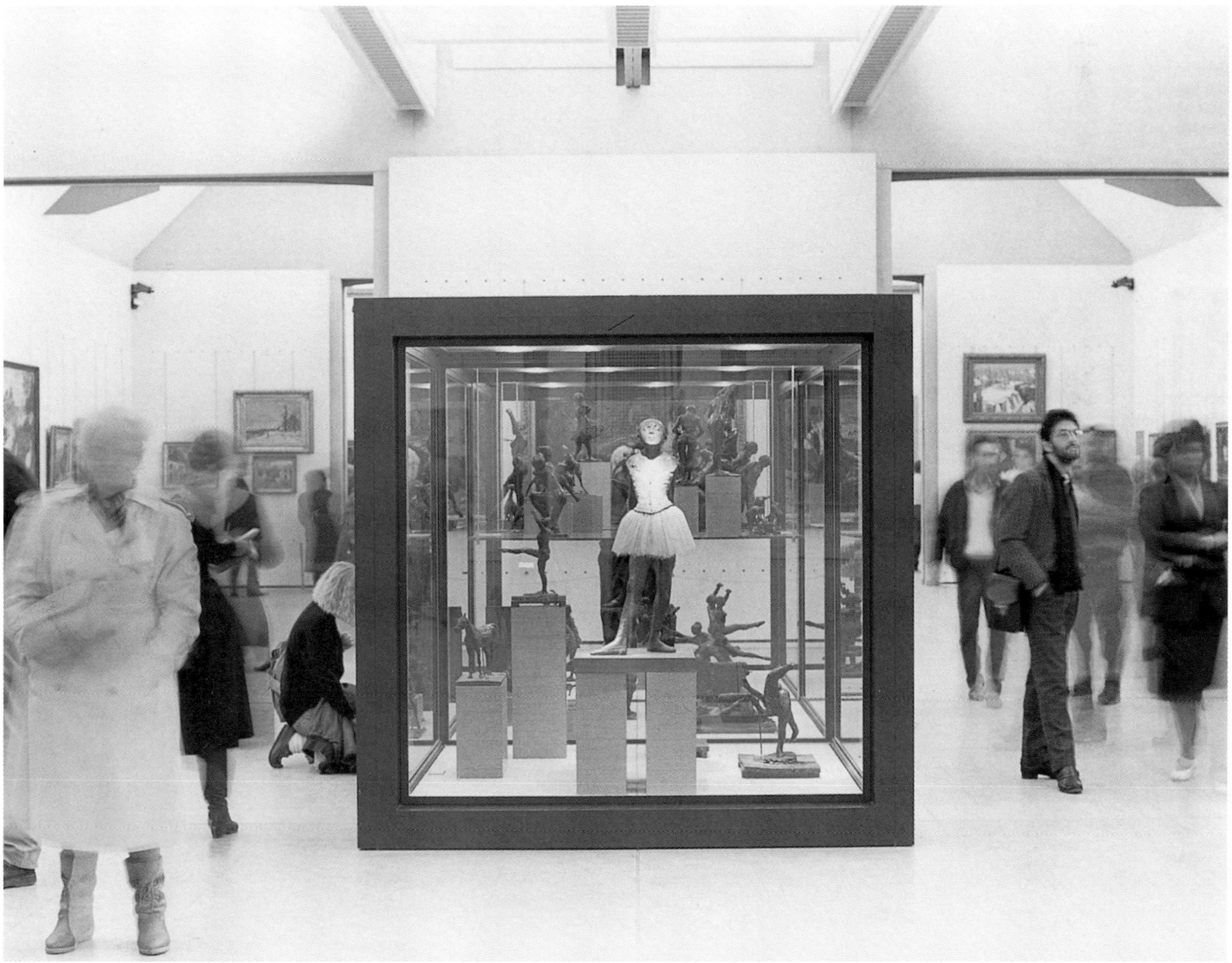

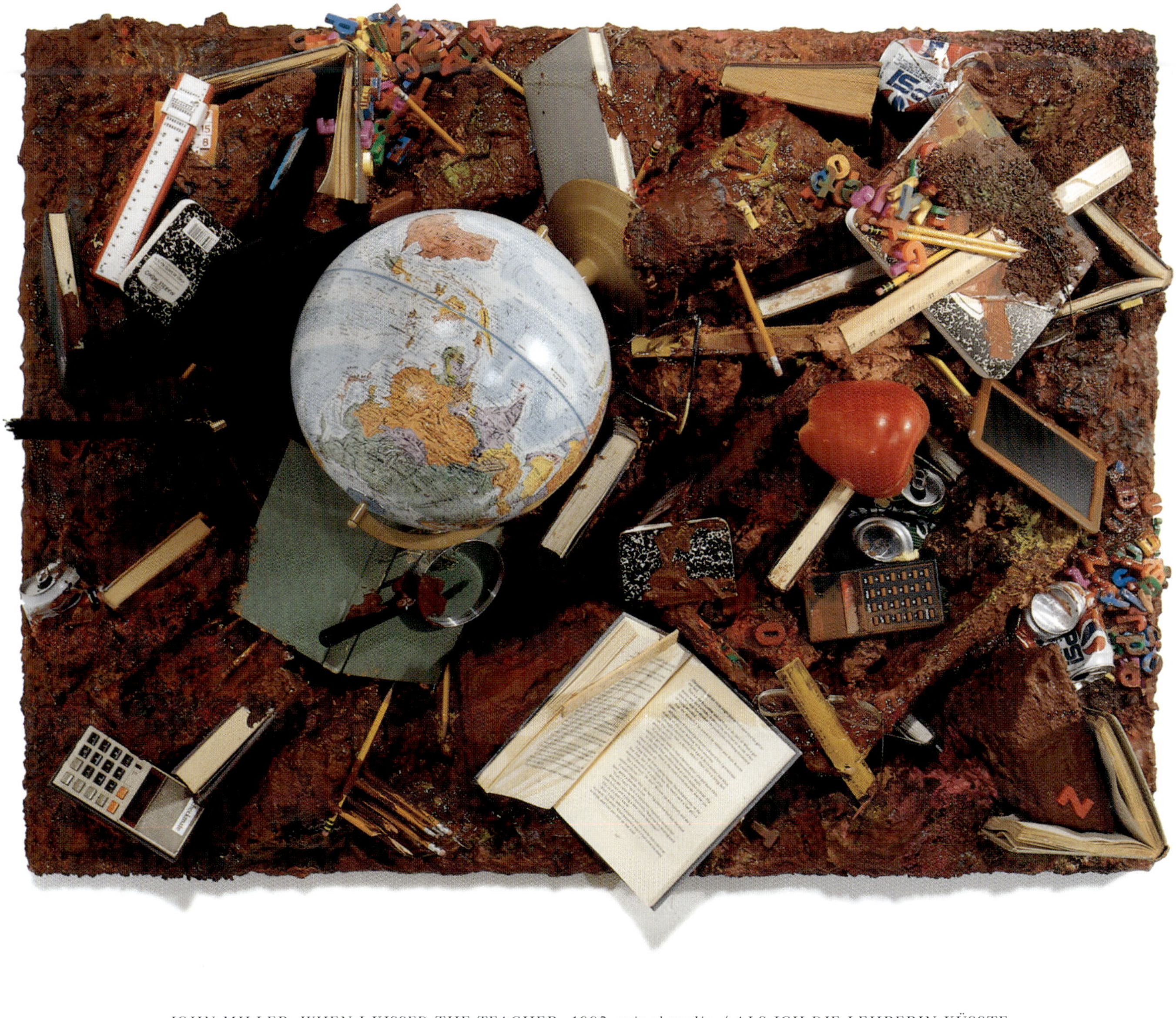

JOHN MILLER, WHEN I KISSED THE TEACHER, 1993, mixed media / ALS ICH DIE LEHRERIN KÜSSTE.

JOHN MILLER, THE DARK AGES, 1996, mixed media, 4 x 2½ x 2½" / DAS MITTELALTER, 10,2 x 6,4 x 6,4 cm.

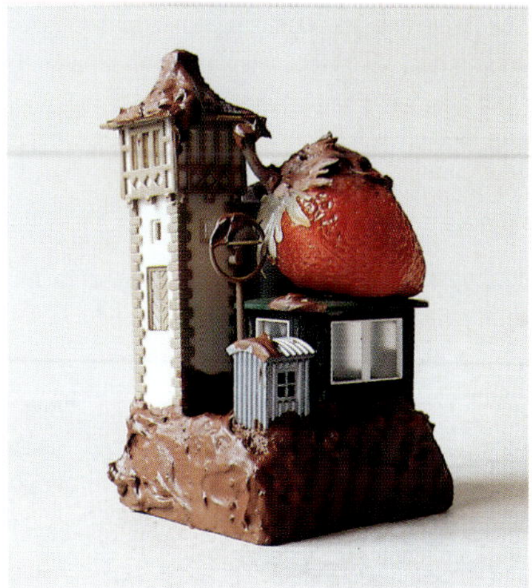

John Miller

LIONEL BOVIER

Among such contemporaries as Mike Kelley and Jim Shaw, but also Tony Oursler and Stephen Prina (all of whom studied at the California Institute for the Arts and, as it is often pointed out, under the aegis of John Baldessari), John Miller embodies a singular position: He articulates the synthesis of an ideologically committed critique of representation with a postconceptual shift towards the "real."[1] Using completely stereotyped genres (figurative painting, travel photography, landscape painting, and so on), Miller (like Sherrie Levine or Richard Prince) has, since the end of the seventies, challenged the function of the author and the concomitant loss of "aura" for the artwork. Yet this critique is only a means of revealing the repressed aspect of the ideological aggregates of day-to-day late-capitalist Western culture.

Miller's close attention to the hidden agendas of representation (especially sexual and social ones) informs his approach to artistic practice both as a writer and as an artist. He asserts for instance, in an early text on Allan McCollum's work ("What You Don't See Is What You Get"), that "if the convulsions of appropriation art have taught us anything, it is historical dialectics: Each cultural artifact can be rewritten indefinitely and, therefore, is always open to contest."[2]

Miller suggests that, according to the psychoanalytical subtext of the SURROGATES, "if the picture is the phallus," then with the notion of "surrogate," the artist "... has cast a depreciating gaze on the phallocentric bias of representation."[3] Likewise, Miller explains that in Kelley's work, it "becomes apparent how the postmodern recapitulation of various representational modes (including modernist abstraction) is driven by feminist inquiry."[4] Thus, he not only

LIONEL BOVIER is a freelance writer and curator, who teaches theory of design at the Ecole cantonale d'art of Lausanne. Together with Yves Aupetitallot, he has recently organized the first retrospective of John Miller's work at Le Magasin in Grenoble. This exhibition is on view at the Kunstverein Hamburg in December 1999.

acknowledges the preeminence of feminist deconstruction in this rewriting process, but also links the SURROGATES with the idea that patriarchy is not necessarily a universal, pan-historical structure. As Miller recalls, in a recent interview:[5)]

This approach was part of a broad tendency running through art criticism at the time. Andrea Fraser later wrote a more extensive Lacanian analysis of McCollum's work and I also wrote a short text that suggested reframing Douglas Crimp's "Picture Theory" in more explicitly feminist terms.[6)] The SURROGATES offered themselves up as blank slates, inviting any number of potential readings.

Produced in this specific critical and theoretical context, Miller's first group of brown, "faux" abstract paintings culminated in a small sculpture. As the artist describes, in this phallus/fecal column made from plaster and painted with brown acrylic paint (UNTITLED, 1985), "some various Freudian and Lacanian notions converge: that in the infantile mind, feces appear as a detachable phallus; that the phallus is an impostor and must remain veiled; that upright posture, because it is a signifying posture, is also an 'imposture,' that these meanings are rhetorical, not literal."

In general, the brown paint obviously invites a psychoanalytic reading: As Nancy Spector has put it "... (it embodies) a convergence of both the Freudian and the Marxist understandings of the fetish as a substitute for some fundamental (sexual or economic) lack."[7)] John Miller also called it "... an allegory of Neo-Expressionism: the impasto connoting excrement which in turn connotes money."[8)] The brown paint thus functions both as a sign indexing a theoretical and political reading of the art production and a comment on the artistic context of his own production. Moreover, the works deploy this shit-like paint as a weapon of resistance to aesthetic appropriation. That is the tactical value of their "abjection." Miller notes:

When I first started the brown impasto work, "abjection" was not yet a key term in art criticism. (...) When I first showed my brown, abstract paintings with the brown phallus, people only talked about deconstruction. The body and transgression never came up. The vocabulary for that wasn't yet available. And I don't mean to suggest that either "body" or "transgression" offer a correct meaning and that deconstruction is wrong. But that suggests how certain readings are more viable than others at different times.

Even if one could argue that these works still resist aesthetic appropriation, one has to admit that they have been legitimized within the art world by the development of theories connecting art to the unmasking of the repressed, and particularly through the importance of the "abject" as a characterization of the strategies at play in the works of artists such as Robert Gober, Mike Kelley, Cindy Sherman, or Kiki Smith. It is this modification in the context of reception that Miller qualifies as the "contingency of an artistic strategy." And that is why he uses such a wide range of methods, beginning series such as the "Middle of the Day" photographs and the TV game show paintings soon after the "institutional acceptance" of the brown works. Then, one cannot avoid noticing that all these works raise questions about value: How do we decide what something is worth? How does that translate into the value of something else? How do we decide, then, how to use our time?

Miller once criticized the disenchanted idealism of Baudrillard's "simulacrum" by saying that the "art world is a place as good as any to begin to take action,"[9)] thus maintaining the necessity of a radical critique of culture within culture. The constant shifting throughout his work might be an effective way to maintain the potential of this critique. At the same time, Miller has never engaged in an instrumentalized version of art. Nor does he fail to recognize that it is "never a question of building a bridge between art and other discourses, like politics or science, because that would already presume an autonomy of art. If anything, it would be an additive process: this plus that plus ..."[10)] The problem of value is never evoked in relation to art alone but because it concerns society in its entirety.

In Miller's work, the question of attributing a (symbolic) value to things, of translating this quality into another system of value, and of producing such "things" is connected to another axis: time. In a series of paintings from the eighties, he decided to start and finish one work within the same day. In the "Middle of the Day" series, he takes photographs between noon and two p.m., a time that is considered bad both from a photographer's point of view (because of lighting conditions) and devoid of events from a social perspective (because of the division between labor time, leisure time, and resting time). In the game show paintings, he freezes a specific moment within the narrative of the show by taking a picture (first a photo, then a painting) of it. He then reveals the social functions of these rituals and underlines their main ideological aspects. Through all these changes of artistic strategies at play, a permanent interrogation is attached to the temporal dimensions (classically considered as less "artistic" than spatial ones) in order to reassess the fabrication of value as a constructed time-frame within the political economy of Western society. He explains:

When people say, "Time is money," of course, that's oppressive. It's axiomatic to the wage/labor equation. Money signifies value. Or, a better way of putting it is that money mobilizes value through exchange. All that's predicated on rationalizing and standardizing time as an abstraction and as a constant. Without this understanding of time, you can't have wages. I'm concerned with what money fails to represent and with the kinds of experience that cannot be rationalized that way. I'm not even sure that what I have characterized as "a rationalization" is that at all; it may be only a presumption of rationality. Nor do I claim that my work ever gets outside of this structure, but it does, at least, make it seem less automatic—or, maybe, more automatic. Time really can never be separated from space (that's part of the way it's abstracted) but, by focusing on the time/value nexus, I try to construe artworks more sociologically than formally. Traditionally, an artwork is supposed to exemplify a transcendent value, a sublime value or, at least, what is best about culture. Often, this coincides with an unreflected appeal to timelessness or universality.

Miller's recently constructed game show set entitled THE LUGUBRIOUS GAME (1999) represents one way of assembling these different signifying elements. Viewers see only the arena for the game—an apparatus that includes furniture and architectural elements, as well as a pile of dirt, newspapers, dildos, and money—not the show itself.

The (...) game show allows for the symbolic circulation of goods within a family that is not a family; it creates a surrogate family out of an arbitrary set of contestants, the

JOHN MILLER, GLAD HAND, 1998 / FROHE HAND.

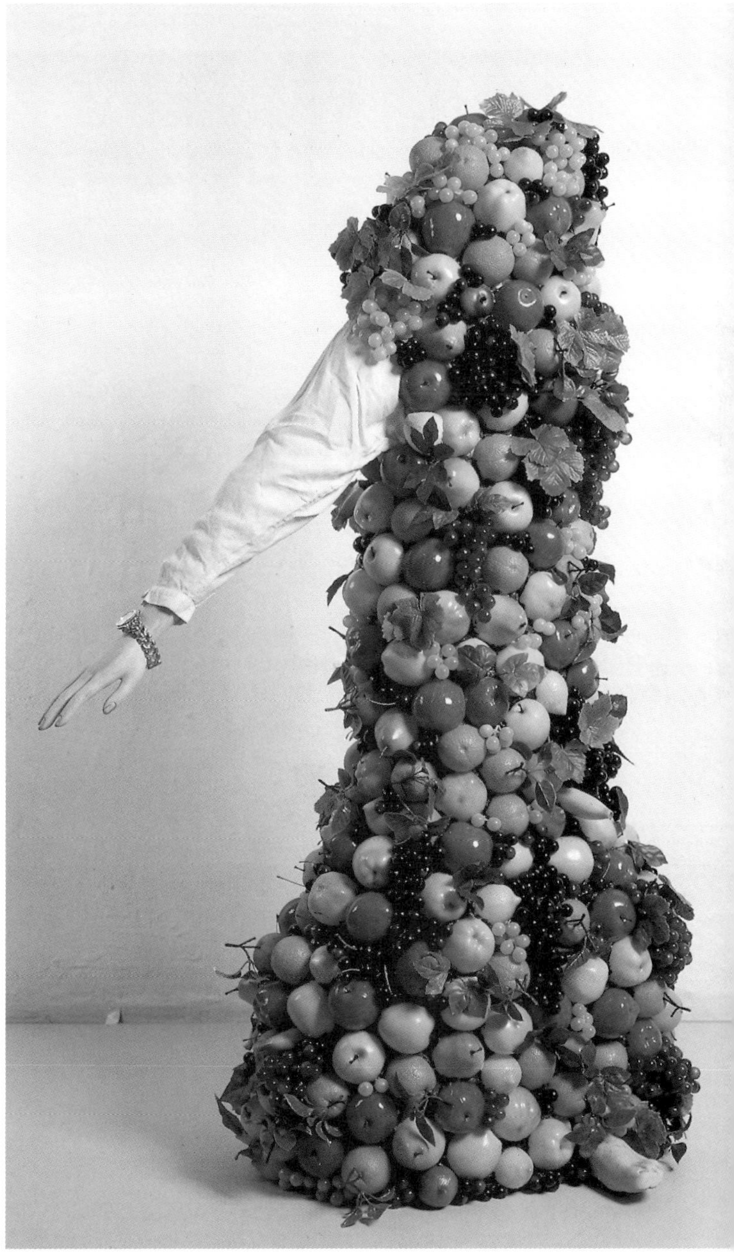

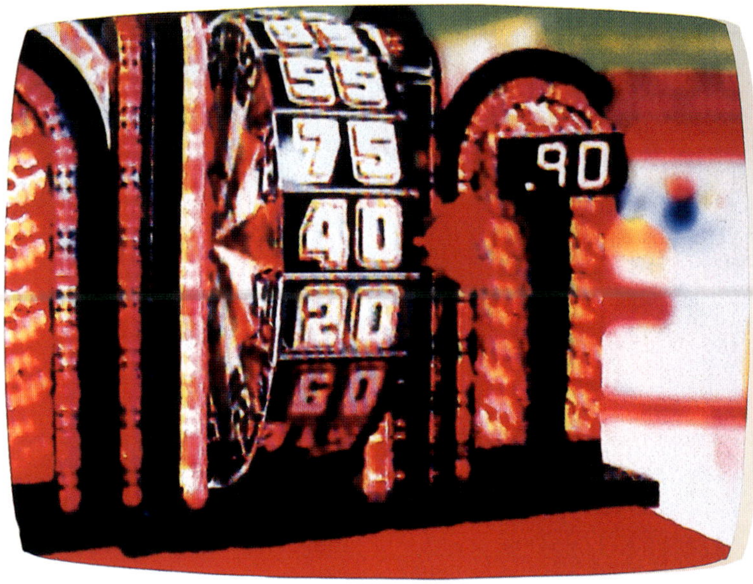

JOHN MILLER, WELCOME TO MY WORLD, 1999, acrylic on canvas with sound, 50 x 70" / WILLKOMMEN IN MEINER WELT, Acryl auf Leinwand mit Sound, 127 x 178 cm.

studio audience and the (vicarious) broadcast audiences. It is nominally about normative acquisition and accumulation, but it functions instead as a kind of potlatch of not only the material goods, but also emotions … Driving this spectacle is the animism of the commodity fetish, the irrational core of an otherwise overdetermined political economy. The rules of the games tear accumulation loose from its habitual moorings in the wage/labor equation and deliver it up to chance.[11)]

The set thus combines the shit references of the brown impasto works with issues developed in the game show paintings. It conflates the audience of art with that of the TV studios. Moreover, the problematics of time and value are implicated in the game itself. And, by focusing on such ritualized media events, one can therefore wonder if Miller is not finding here a key metaphor for the systemic function of the artwork.

1) In the sense that theoreticians such as Hal Foster have characterized it lately.
2) John Miller, "What You Don't See Is What You Get: Allan McCollum's Surrogates, Perpetual Photos and Perfect Vehicles," in *Artscribe*, no. 61, January/February 1987, pp. 32–36.
3) Ibid.
4) John Miller, "The Mortification of the Sign. Mike Kelley's Felt Banners," *Mike Kelley*, ex. cat. (Chicago: The Renaissance Society, 1988), pp. 16–23.
5) All quotations not specified are from an interview conducted by the author during the preparation of the exhibition and published in the first issue of *MAG* (Grenoble: Centre National d'Art Contemporain, 1999).
6) The artist refers here to his essay "Suture and Picture Theory," in: *Suture—Phantasmen der Vollkommenheit (Fantasies of Totality)*, ed. by P. Adams and S. Eiblmayr (Salzburg: Salzburger Kunstverein 1995), pp. 25–31.
7) Nancy Spector, "More Shitty Art," in: *John Miller. Economies parallèles/Parallel Economies*, ex. cat. (Grenoble: Le Magasin, Centre National d'Art Contemporain, 1999), pp. 31–32.
8) John Miller, "The Commodity as a Country Music Theme," in: *Journal*, vol. 5, no. 41 (Los Angeles: LAICA, Spring 1985), pp. 26–30.
9) John Miller, "Baudrillard and His Discontents," *Artscribe*, no. 63, May 1987, pp. 49–51.
10) Carsten Höller in *Artforum* (vol. XXXVII, no. 7, March 1999), quoted by John Miller in the discussion mentioned above (note 5).
11) John Miller, "Playing the Game," in: *John Miller. Economies parallèles/Parallel Economies*, op. cit., pp. 26–28.

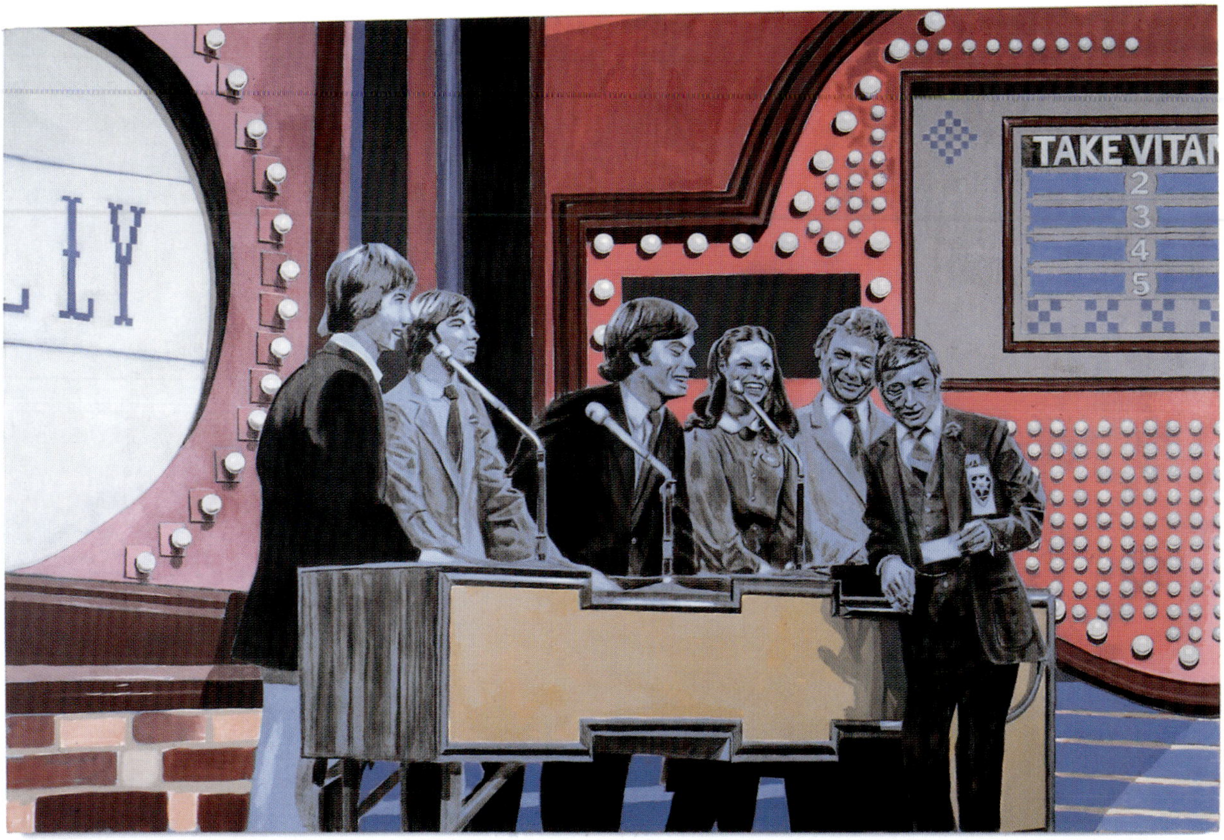

JOHN MILLER, FAMILY FEUD, 1995, acrylic on canvas, 54 x 80" /
FAMILIENFEHDE, Acryl auf Leinwand, 137,2 x 203,2 cm.

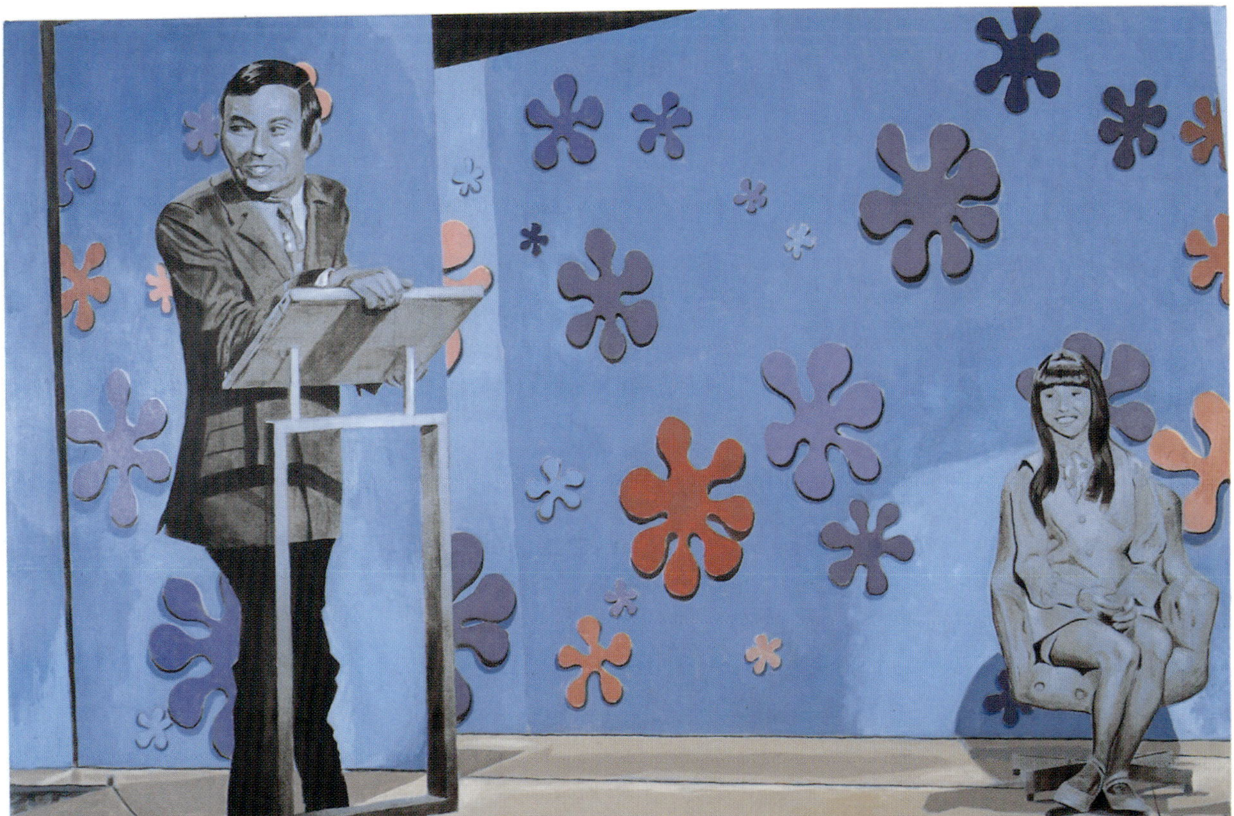

JOHN MILLER, THE DATING GAME, 1995, acrylic on canvas, 54 x 80" /
DAS RENDEZ-VOUS-SPIEL, Acryl auf Leinwand, 137,2 x 203,2 cm.

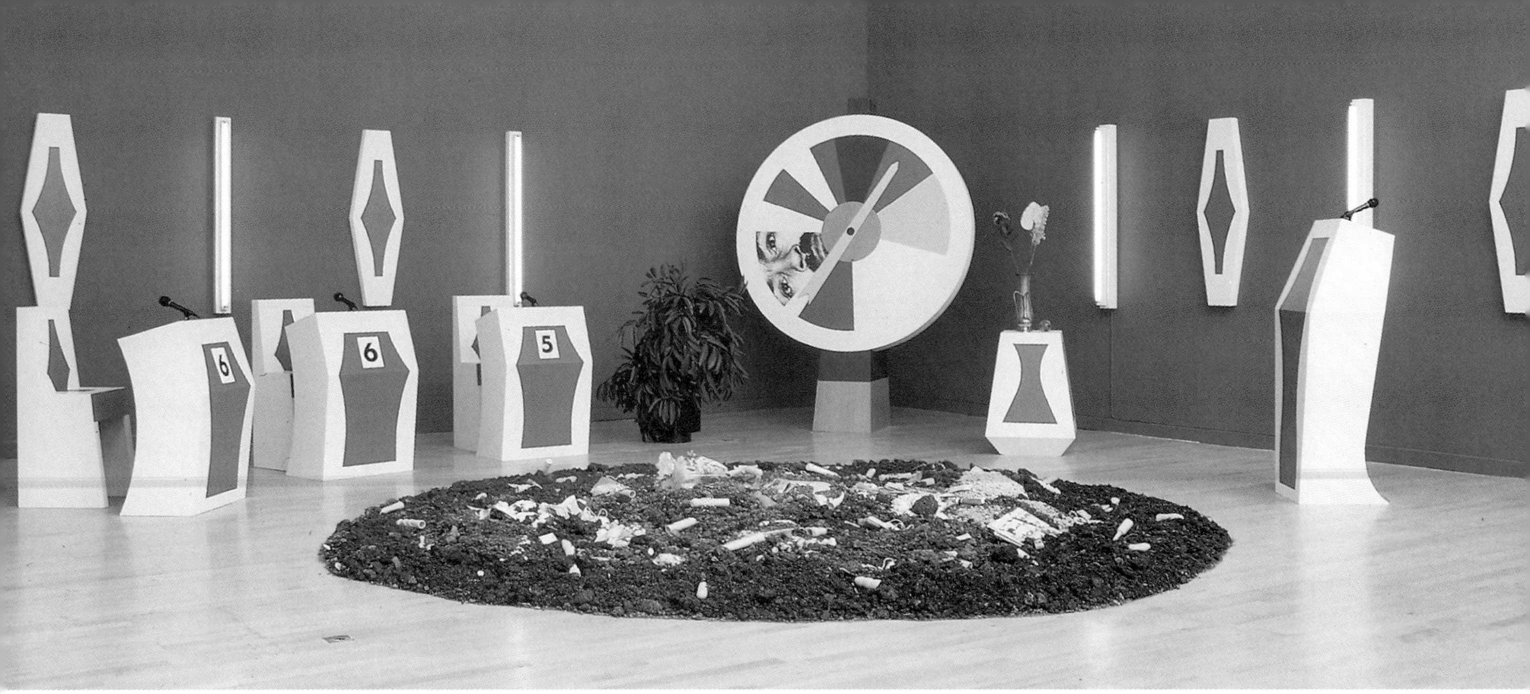

John Miller

LIONEL BOVIER

Unter zeitgenössischen Künstlern wie Mike Kelley und Jim Shaw, aber auch Tony Oursler und Stephen Prina (die alle am California Institute for the Arts studiert haben, und zwar, wie gern hervorgehoben wird, unter der Ägide von John Baldessari), nimmt John Miller eine besondere Stellung ein: Er schafft die Synthese einer ideologisch engagierten Darstellungskritik und der postkonzeptuellen Hinwendung zum «Realen».[1] Unter Verwendung völlig stereotyper Genres (figurative Malerei, Reisephotographie, Landschaftsmalerei usw.) hat Miller seit Ende der 70er Jahre (wie Sherrie Levine oder Richard Prince) die Funktion des Autors und demzufolge auch die Aura des Kunstwerks in Frage gestellt. Diese Kritik ist jedoch nur ein Mittel um den verdrängten Aspekt der ideologischen Bestandteile unserer spätkapitalistischen westlichen Alltagskultur aufzuzeigen.

Millers aufmerksame Beobachtung der verborgenen Implikationen bildlicher Darstellung (insbesondere sexueller und sozialer Art) prägt seine Auffassung der künstlerischen Tätigkeit sowohl als Schriftsteller wie als bildender Künstler. So versichert er zum Beispiel in einem frühen Text zum Werk von Allan McCollum («What You Don't See Is What You Get»/«Was man nicht sieht, ist was man bekommt»): «Wenn uns die Verrenkungen der Appropriationskunst etwas gelehrt haben, so ist es historische Dialektik: Jedes kulturelle Kunstprodukt

LIONEL BOVIER ist freier Autor und Kurator. Er lehrt an der Ecole cantonale d'art in Lausanne. Gemeinsam mit Yves Aupetitallot organisierte er die erste John-Miller-Retrospektive im Le Magasin in Grenoble, die im Dezember 1999 auch im Kunstverein Hamburg zu sehen ist.

kann unbeschränkt neu formuliert werden und bleibt deshalb immer dem Wettbewerb ausgesetzt.»[2]

Dem psychoanalytischen Subtext der SURROGATES (Surrogate) zufolge, meint Miller: «Wenn das Bild der Phallus ist», so wirft der Künstler mit dem Ausdruck «Surrogat» einen «abschätzigen Blick auf die phallozentrische Tendenz bildlicher Darstellung überhaupt.»[3] Weiter erklärt Miller, dass in Kelleys Werk sichtbar werde, «wie das postmoderne Wiederaufgreifen verschiedener bestehender Darstellungsmodi (einschliesslich der modernen Abstraktion) von feministischen Fragestellungen angeregt sei».[4] Damit anerkennt er nicht nur die herausragende Bedeutung der feministischen Dekonstruktion für diesen Neuformulierungsprozess, sondern bringt die SURROGATES auch mit dem Gedanken in Verbindung, dass das Patriarchat nicht notwendig eine universelle, panhistorische Ordnung sein muss. In einem kürzlich gegebenen Interview erinnert sich Miller[5]:

Diese Haltung entsprach einer in der Kunstkritik jener Zeit verbreiteten Tendenz. Kurz darauf lieferte Andrea Fraser eine ausführlichere Lacan'sche Analyse zu McCollums Arbeit und ich verfasste ebenfalls einen kurzen Text, in dem ich vorschlug, Douglas Crimps «Bildtheorie» unter klar feministischen Gesichtspunkten neu zu durchleuchten.[6] Die SURROGATES boten sich als unbeschriebene Blätter an und luden zu allen möglichen Lesarten ein.

Entstanden in diesem besonderen kritischen und theoretischen Kontext, gipfelte Millers erste Gruppe brauner «falscher» abstrakter Bilder in einer kleinen Skulptur. Wie der Künstler selbst beschreibt, fallen in dieser mit brauner Acrylfarbe bemalten, phallisch-fäkalen Säule aus Gips «verschiedene Freud'sche und Lacan'sche Begriffe zusammen, nämlich: dass der Stuhlgang in der kindlichen Vorstellung als abtrennbarer Phallus erscheint; dass der Phallus etwas Ungehöriges ist und verhüllt werden muss; dass die aufrechte Stellung, weil es eine bedeutungsgeladene Stellung ist, ebenfalls etwas «Ungehöriges» an sich hat und dass diese Bedeutungen metaphorisch und nicht wörtlich zu verstehen sind».

Im Allgemeinen lädt die braune Farbe offensichtlich zu einer psychoanalytischen Deutung ein. Nancy Spector hat es so formuliert: «... (sie verkörpert) das Zusammenfallen freudianischer und marxistischer Interpretationen des Fetischs als Ersatz für einen grundlegenden (sexuellen bzw. ökonomischen) Mangel.»[7] John Miller nannte das auch «... eine Allegorie des Neo-Expressionismus: Impasto-Malerei, die an Scheisse erinnert, die wiederum mit Geld in Verbindung gebracht wird».[8] Die braune Farbe hat bei Miller also gleichzeitig die Funktion eines Zeichens, das auf eine theoretische und politische Interpretation der Kunstproduktion verweist, und eines Kommentars zum künstlerischen Kontext seiner eigenen Produktion. Darüber hinaus ist die an Scheisse erinnernde Farbe auch eine wirksame Abwehr gegen eine rein ästhetische Rezeption. Das ist der taktische Wert des «Abscheus». Miller hält fest:

Als ich mit den braunen Impasto-Arbeiten begann, war «Abscheu» noch kein Terminus der Kunstkritik. (...) Und als ich meine braunen, abstrakten Bilder mit dem braunen Phallus zum ersten Mal zeigte, sprachen die Leute nur von Dekonstruktion. Körper oder Grenzüberschreitung war kein Thema. Das Vokabular dafür war noch nicht vorhanden. Damit will ich nicht sagen, dass «Körper» und «Grenzüberschreitung» die richtige Bedeutung vermitteln und Dekonstruktion falsch ist. Aber es zeigt, wie gewisse Interpretationen zu bestimmten Zeiten näher liegen als andere.

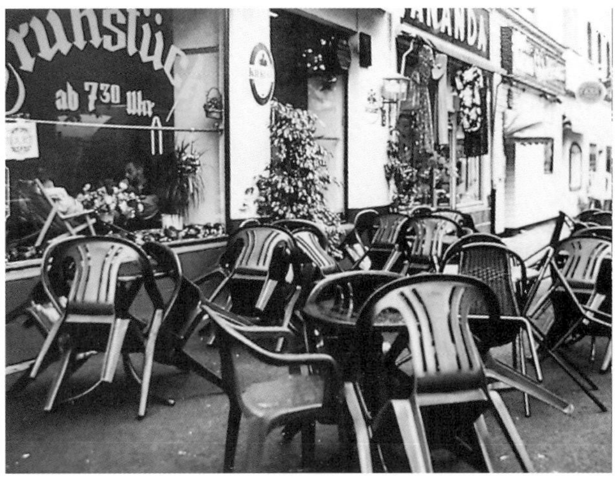

JOHN MILLER, UNTITLED, MAY 20, 1994 / OHNE TITEL.

Selbst wenn man behaupten wollte, dass diese Arbeiten sich einer ästhetischen Rezeption nach wie vor entziehen, muss man doch zugeben, dass sie innerhalb des Kunstbetriebs ihre Legitimation gefunden haben dank der Entwicklung von Theorien, die die Kunst mit der Enthüllung des Verdrängten in Verbindung brachten, und besonders durch die Bedeutung des «Abscheulichen» als strategisches Merkmal in Werken von Künstlern wie Robert Gober, Mike Kelley, Cindy Sherman oder Kiki Smith. Es ist diese Veränderung im Kontext der Rezeption, die Miller als das «Kontingente jeder künstlerischen Strategie» bezeichnet. Deshalb arbeitet er mit einer derart breiten Methodenpalette und beginnt – kurz nachdem seinen braunen Arbeiten «institutionelle Akzeptanz» zuteil wurde – Serien wie die *Middle-of-the-Day*-Photographien oder die *TV-Game-Show*-Bilder. Ferner kann man nicht darüber hinwegsehen, dass all diese Arbeiten Wertfragen aufwerfen: Wie bestimmen wir, wie viel etwas wert ist? Wie überträgt sich das auf den Wert von etwas anderem? Wie entscheiden wir schliesslich, wie wir unsere Zeit nutzen wollen?

Miller kritisierte einmal den entzauberten Idealismus von Baudrillards «Simulacrum», indem er sagte, dass die «Kunstwelt ein Ort so gut wie jeder andere sei, um aktiv zu werden»,[9] und beharrte damit auf der Notwendigkeit einer radikalen Kulturkritik innerhalb der Kultur selbst. Die fortwährenden Veränderungen in seinem Werk mögen ein wirksames Mittel sein, um das Potenzial dieser Kritik lebendig zu erhalten. Gleichzeitig hat sich Miller nie auf eine Instrumentalisierung der Kunst eingelassen, noch hat er je übersehen, dass es «nie um den Brückenbau zwischen Kunst und anderen Diskursen, etwa Politik oder Wissenschaft, gehen kann, weil das schon die Autonomie der Kunst voraussetzen würde. Wenn überhaupt, wäre es ein additiver Prozess: dies, plus das, plus …»[10] Die Wertfrage wird nie allein im Hinblick auf die Kunst gestellt, sondern weil sie die Gesellschaft als Ganzes angeht.

In Millers Werk ist die Frage des den Dingen einen (symbolischen) Wert Zuschreibens, der Übertragung dieser Qualität in ein anderes Wertsystem und der Produktion solcher Dinge mit einer anderen Achse verknüpft, und zwar mit jener der Zeit.

JOHN MILLER, THE MIDDLE OF THE DAY SERIES, 1994–1997: 5-2-96, c-print, 10 x 8" / DIE TAGESMITTE-SERIE: 2. 5. 96, C-Print, 25,4 x 20,3 cm.

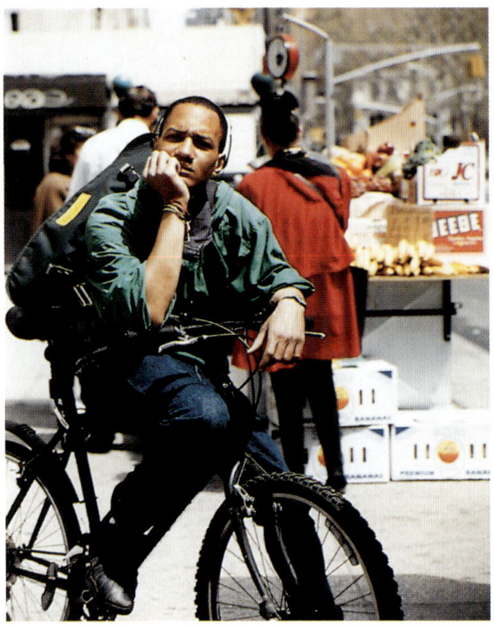

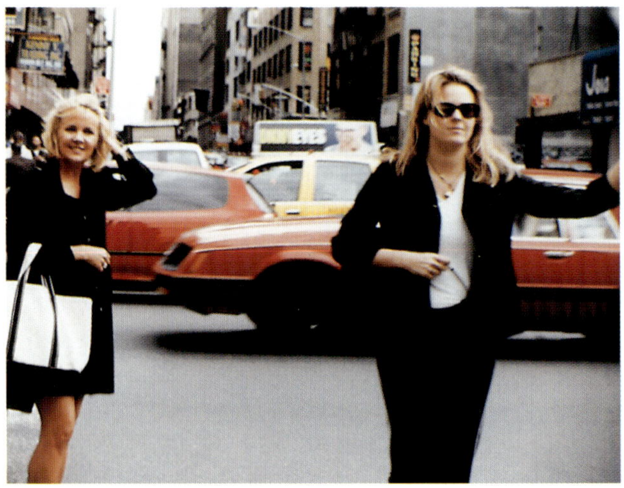

JOHN MILLER, THE MIDDLE OF THE DAY SERIES, 1994–1997: 4-25-96, c-print, 8 x 10" / DIE TAGESMITTE-SERIE: 25. 4. 96, C-Print, 20,3 x 25,4 cm.

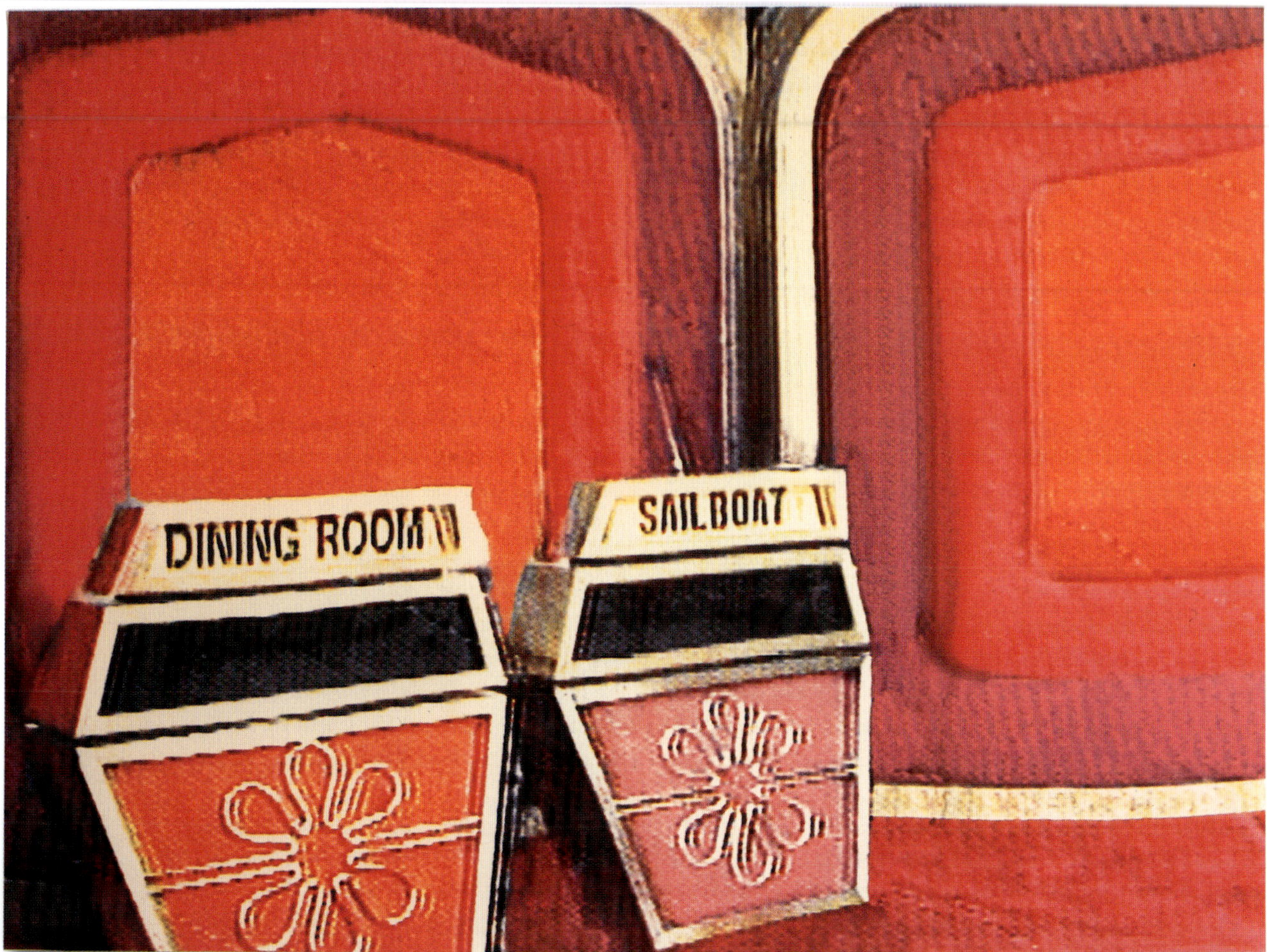

JOHN MILLER, OBJECT PART, 1998, acrylic on canvas, 55¼ x 78¾" / OBJEKTTEIL, Acryl auf Leinwand, 140 x 200 cm.

Für eine Serie von Bildern aus den 80er Jahren hatte er beschlossen, jedes Werk innerhalb eines Tages zu beginnen und fertig zu stellen. Für die *Middle-of-the-Day*-Serie photographiert er zwischen Mittag und zwei Uhr nachmittags, einer Zeit also, die einerseits aus photographischen Gründen (wegen der Lichtbedingungen) ungünstig ist und andrerseits gesellschaftlich betrachtet (wegen der Unterteilung in Arbeitszeit, Freizeit und Ruhezeit) eher ereignisarm ist. In den *Game-Show*-Bildern hält er in seinem Bild (zunächst photographisch, später als gemaltes Bild) einen bestimmten Augenblick im Ablauf der Show fest. Darauf enthüllt er die gesellschaftliche Funktion dieser Rituale und streicht ihre wichtigsten ideologischen Aspekte hervor. Durch all diese wechselnden künstlerischen Strategien werden die zeitlichen Dimensionen (die traditionell als weniger «künstlerisch» gelten als die räumlichen) unablässig hinterfragt, um die Produktion von Wert als konstruierten Zeitrahmen innerhalb der politischen Ökonomie der westlichen Gesellschaft einsehbar zu machen. Er sagt dazu:

Wenn die Leute sagen, «Zeit ist Geld», so ist das natürlich deprimierend. Es entspricht der Gleichsetzung von Lohn und Arbeit. Geld bedeutet Wert. Oder um es besser zu sagen, Geld mobilisiert Werte durch Austausch. All das beruht auf einer Rationalisierung und Standardisierung der Zeit als einer abstrakten Konstanten. Ohne dieses Verständnis von Zeit gäbe es keine Löhne. Mich interessiert, was Geld alles nicht repräsentieren kann und welche Erfahrungen sich nicht auf diese Weise rationalisieren lassen. Ich bin nicht einmal sicher, ob das, was ich als «Rationalisierung» beschrieben habe, überhaupt eine solche ist; es könnte auch nur eine angenommene Rationalität sein. Ich behaupte auch nicht, dass meine Arbeit sich je ausserhalb dieser Strukturen bewegt, aber wenigstens lässt sie sie weniger automatisch erscheinen – oder vielleicht auch noch automatischer. Die Zeit lässt sich nie wirklich vom Raum trennen (das ist ein Teil des Abstraktionsprozesses), aber indem ich vermehrt auf die Zeit-Wert-Verbindung schaue, versuche ich Kunstwerke eher soziologisch als formal zu entwickeln. Traditionell gilt ein Kunstwerk als exemplarische Darstellung eines transzendenten Wertes, eines erhabenen Wertes oder immerhin des besten Teils einer Kultur. Oft geht dies mit einem unreflektierten Rückgriff auf Zeitlosigkeit oder Universalität einher.

Millers kürzlich entstandene *Game-Show*-Werkgruppe THE LUGUBRIOUS GAME (Das trostlose Spiel, 1999) stellt eine Möglichkeit der Kombination dieser verschiedenen bedeutungstragenden Elemente dar. Die Betrachter sehen nur den Schauplatz des Spiels, eine Kulisse mit Möbeln und architektonischen Elementen nebst einem Dreckhaufen, Zeitungen, Dildos und Geld, aber nicht das Spiel selbst.

Die (...) Game-Show sorgt für die symbolische Zirkulation von Gütern innerhalb einer Familie, die keine ist; sie schafft eine Ersatzfamilie bestehend aus einer beliebigen Gruppe von Mitstreiterinnen und Mitstreitern, dem Publikum im Studio oder dem (ersatzweise) eingeblendeten Publikum. Offiziell geht es um das gewöhnliche Erwerben und Anhäufen von Gütern, aber tatsächlich funktioniert das Ganze als eine Art Ritual der Verteilung von Gastgeschenken, bei dem es nicht nur um materielle Güter, sondern auch um Emotionen geht ... Angetrieben wird dieses Spektakel von einem animistischen Tanz um das Goldene Kalb, dem irrationalen Kern einer sonst überdeterminierten politischen Ökonomie. Die Spielregeln lösen die Güterakkumulation aus ihrer üblichen Verankerung in der Lohn-Arbeit-Gleichung und überlassen sie dem Zufall.[11)]

Die Werkgruppe vereint die Verweise auf Scheisse in den braunen Impasto-Arbeiten mit Themen, die sich in den *Game-Show*-Bildern entwickelten. Sie bringt das Kunstpublikum mit dem Publikum der Fernsehstudios in Verbindung. Zudem ist die Problematik von Zeit und Wert schon im Spiel selbst enthalten. Und man mag sich fragen, ob Miller, wenn er derart ritualisierte Medienereignisse aufs Korn nimmt, dabei nicht auf eine zentrale Metapher für die systemische Funktion des Kunstwerks stösst.

(Übersetzung: Wilma Parker)

1) In dem Sinn, wie es Theoretiker wie Hal Foster kürzlich beschrieben haben.
2) John Miller, «What You Don't See Is What You Get: Allan McCollum's Surrogates, Perpetual Photos and Perfect Vehicles», *Artscribe*, Nr. 6, Januar/Februar 1987, S. 32–36.
3) Ebenda.
4) John Miller, «The Mortification of the Sign. Mike Kelley's Felt Banners», in: *Mike Kelley*, Ausstellungskatalog, The Renaissance Society, Chicago 1988, S. 16–23.
5) Sofern nichts anderes erwähnt ist, stammen alle Zitate aus einem Gespräch des Autors mit dem Künstler, erstmals publiziert in der ersten Ausgabe von *MAG*, Centre National d'Art Contemporain, Grenoble 1999.
6) Der Künstler bezieht sich hier auf seinen Essay «Suture and Picture Theory», in: *Suture – Phantasmen der Vollkommenheit*, hrsg. von P. Adams und S. Eiblmayr, Salzburger Kunstverein, Salzburg 1995, S. 25–31.
7) Nancy Spector, «More Shitty Art», in: *John Miller. Economies parallèles/Parallel Economies*, Ausstellungskatalog, Le Magasin, Centre National d'Art Contemporain, Grenoble 1999, S. 31–32.
8) John Miller, «The Commodity as a Country Music Theme», *Journal*, Vol. 5, Nr. 41, Frühjahr 1985, ICA Los Angeles, S. 26–30.
9) John Miller, «Baudrillard and His Discontents», *Artscribe*, Nr. 63, Mai 1987, S. 49–51.
10) Carsten Höller in einer neueren Ausgabe von *Artforum*, zitiert von John Miller (im oben erwähnten Gespräch, vgl. Anm. 5).
11) John Miller, «Playing the Game», in: *John Miller. Economies Parallèles / Parallel Economies*, op. cit., S. 26–28.

FERNANDO MELANI und das Behausungsspiel

RUDOLF SCHMITZ

«Auch die Kunst ist nicht mehr als eine Wolke von Teilchen in einer bestimmten Ordnung, deren Interpretation, wie alles andere heute, nicht leicht fällt in einer Welt, die in einem Meer der Quantität, Komplexität, Komplementarität, der ‹Unsicherheit› (...) zu versinken droht.» Es ist ziemlich offensichtlich, dass das Werk eines Künstlers, der in dieser Weise über die Kunst spricht, schwerer zu hüten ist als ein Sack Flöhe. Als Fernando Melani 1985 im Alter von 78 Jahren starb, hinterliess er der toskanischen Gemeinde Pistoia sein Atelierhaus samt allen darin befindlichen Werken, damit sie es der Öffentlichkeit zugänglich hielte. Tatsächlich unterscheidet es sich von allen Künstlerhäusern, die man kennt. Denn das zweistöckige Reihenhaus am Corso Gramsci zeigt keinerlei biographische Referenz, bewahrt keine Gegenstände des persönlichen Bedarfs oder Geschmacks, sondern überrascht durch das strikte Auslöschen der persönlichen Spur. Das – unter anderem – ist die prägnante Erfahrung, die man in Melanis Atelierhaus machen kann: dass eine erweiterte künstlerische Anschauung in der Abstraktion von sich selbst, im Ausschalten falscher Subjektivität beruht.

Melani hat ein Leben strenger Gewohnheit geführt – immer derselbe blaue Arbeitsanzug, derselbe gelbe Schal, dasselbe Restaurant, dieselbe Bar, dieselben Wege in der Stadt – um das Alltägliche möglichst auszuschalten und sich störungsfrei den «Erfahrungen» der Kunst zu widmen. Diese Atmosphäre von Konzentration teilt sich in seinem Haus heute noch mit. Es ist geprägt von einer asketischen Verdrängung des Persönlichen, die man allerdings bald als Vermächtnis einer äusserst entschiedenen, radikalen Persönlichkeit empfindet. Die Werke, mit denen Wände, Decken, Fussböden, Türen überhäuft sind, scheinen nicht diesen einzigen, sondern zahlreiche Urheber zu haben, so heterogen sind sie und im besten Sinn stillos. Bisweilen ist kaum zu entscheiden, ob etwas lediglich Materialhäufung oder schon «Werk» ist – Übergänge sind fliessend. Hat jener Plastiksack, gefüllt mit abgebrannten Streichhölzern, bereits Kunststatus, oder ist er einfach nur der Speicher eines tausendfach wiederholten Vorgangs und damit Dokumentation der verrinnenden Lebenszeit eines passionierten Rauchers? Auch die in Rechteckform geschnittenen Aluminium- und Kupferbleche, befestigt an einer Ateliertür, scheinen sich noch, wie diverse Pendelinstrumente und primitive Maschinchen, im aktiven Zustand der Versuchsanordnung zu befinden.

Der Besuch der «Casa Melani» ist jedoch kein Akt der Nostalgie, wie man leicht vermuten könnte. Gerade heute, wo biographische Existenz und künstlerischer Ausdruck sich unwiderruflich entkoppeln, wo die neuen Medien der Kunst Ortlosigkeit und Virtualität suggerieren, muss die Empfehlung eines «Künstlerhauses» als Symptom rück-

---

RUDOLF SCHMITZ ist Kritiker und Journalist und lebt in Frankfurt am Main.

wärts gewandter Ordnungssuche erscheinen. Die «Casa Melani» allerdings passt in kein Stereotyp. Sie lässt sich vielmehr als Erinnerung an die Zukunft verstehen, weil sie auf spezielle Art das Behausungsspiel zur Anschauung bringt, auf das die Kunst zweifellos immer angewiesen sein wird. Dieses Künstlerhaus deckt das «System Kunst» innerhalb und mit den Mitteln der Kunst auf. Der weit gespannte und letztlich einem intellektuellen Impuls entspringende Horizont des Fernando Melani käme ohne den festen Rahmen dieses Hauses, also ohne diese durch räumliche Wahrnehmung gestützte Sphäre gar nicht zum Vorschein. Es darf bezweifelt werden, ob Melanis Werk ausserhalb des Ambientes seines Hauses überhaupt «ausstellbar» wäre. Dieser Gesichtspunkt ist entscheidend, will man den Status seiner künstlerischen Aktivität beurteilen. Was sonst üblicherweise die Exegeten tun, nämlich das «System» und die Problemstellungen eines Künstlers rekonstruieren, hat hier – in unnachahmlicher Autonomie – die Form raumzeitlicher Agglomeration und Durchdringung angenommen. Sogar die Perspektive einer möglichen Entropie zeichnet sich ab. Dieser das Werk charakterisierende «Naturalismus» hat unmittelbar mit Melanis Prämissen zu tun.

Seine 1945 einsetzende künstlerische Aktivität fand ihren Massstab in der avancierten naturwissenschaftlichen Forschung. Für Melani, zeit seines Lebens Mitglied der kommunistischen Partei, lieferte das Weltbild der Quantenphysik die Begründung, warum es nur noch abstrakte Kunst geben könne. Entsprechend sah er den Künstler als Element eines Energiefeldes aus bewegten Materieteilchen, der noch einmal, wie schon in der klassischen Moderne, die unbegrenzte Freiheit des Materials erforschen kann. Melani verstand sich als Medium, das sich in die Energieprozesse des Materiekosmos möglichst störungsfrei, aber katalysatorisch einklinken sollte. Das Zauberwort, das der Künstler-Forscher schliesslich entdeckte, um sein Weltverhältnis und seine Kunstauffassung zu begründen, hiess «Vibration». Es meinte die Kraftfelder, die Materialien um sich verbreiten, ihre Teilhabe an einer grossen kosmischen Schwingung, ihre Mobilität im Zustand scheinbarer Ruhe.

Melanis Künstlerhaus vermittelt die ebenso befremdende wie faszinierende Erfahrung, dass hier ein Künstler seine Aktivitäten in der Nähe zur experimentellen Naturwissenschaft entwickelte und geradezu behavioristisch vorging. Von diesem «exzentrischen» Standpunkt aus fand er für bestimmte Erscheinungsformen der Kunst – etwa die Monochromie – entscheidend andere Begründungen und Ausprägungen. Melani entdeckte die kompositorischen und gattungsüberschreitenden Freiheiten der abstrakten Kunst mittels eines verschärften Naturalismus, indem er beispielsweise verschieden geformte Holzstücke in Primärfarben bemalte und lose aneinander fügte. Seine «Bilder» und «Zeichnungen» wirken quer stehend zur üblichen Blickrichtung, als seien Kategorien wie Linie, Kontur, Form, Gestalt durch tiefer dringende Akupunktur ersetzt worden, als sei eine bestimmte Gestaltungslogik in der Mitte durchschnitten und biete sich stattdessen im Profil dar. Oft gewinnt man den Eindruck, Melani habe bestimmte Materialien einfach miteinander reagieren lassen, sich mittels einer erstaunlichen Mikro-Aufmerksamkeit in die Geheimnisse der Materie versetzt und dabei den künstlerischen Eingriff in Richtung «Zero» minimiert.

Als er zu Beginn der 60er Jahre die Eigenschaften von Draht, Metallen und Legierungen untersuchte, fand er zahlreiche Wege, die Auflösung der Schwerkraft zu suggerieren: in der schwebenden Dreidimensionalität der «kleinen Wolken», «kleinen Theater» und «Spinnennetze». Es gibt bei Melani, der von den Marktmechanismen des Kunstbetriebs weitgehend unberührt blieb, nicht jenen verhängnisvollen Mechanismus, irgendwann die experimentale Phase zu beenden, um nur noch ästhetisch verfeinerte Kristallisationen derselben Problemstellung zu bieten. 1977 nahm Melani teil an einer Ausstellung, die sich der «Arte non Arte» widmete, also der Fragestellung, welche Praktiken das kunstinhärente Wissen befördern oder dazu führen können, dass etwas schliesslich als Kunst gilt.

Die letzten fünf Jahre seines Lebens verbrachte Melani damit, nicht nur in seinem Haus zu arbeiten, sondern dort häufig seine Freunde zu empfangen, mit ihnen zu diskutieren und sie an seinen Experimenten teilhaben zu lassen. In einem der Räume, nahe den Buchregalen, sind noch heute mehrere Wäscheleinen gespannt, auf denen monochrome, mit grüner, gelber, roter, schwarzer, weisser Ölfarbe getränkte Lappen hängen. Diese antigravitätische Luftnummer zeugt – sozusagen – in exemplarischer Weise von Melanis lebenslanger Leidenschaft, eine bestimmte universale Auffassung von Kunst in trockene Tücher zu bringen. Weshalb eben auch die Tücher zur Kunst gehören. Und die Wäscheleinen. Von den Wäscheklammern ganz zu schweigen.

Alle Bilder zu Fernando Melani stammen aus «Fernando Melani: la casa-studio, le esperienze, gli scritti dal 1945 al 1985», Bruno Corà (Hrsg.), Electa, Milano 1990.

All images of Melani and his work are from "Fernando Melani: la casa-studio, le esperienze, gli scritti dal 1945 al 1985," ed. by Bruno Corà (Milano: Electa, 1990).

Fernando Melani in seinem Atelier in der Casa Melani /
The artist in his studio at the Casa Melani.

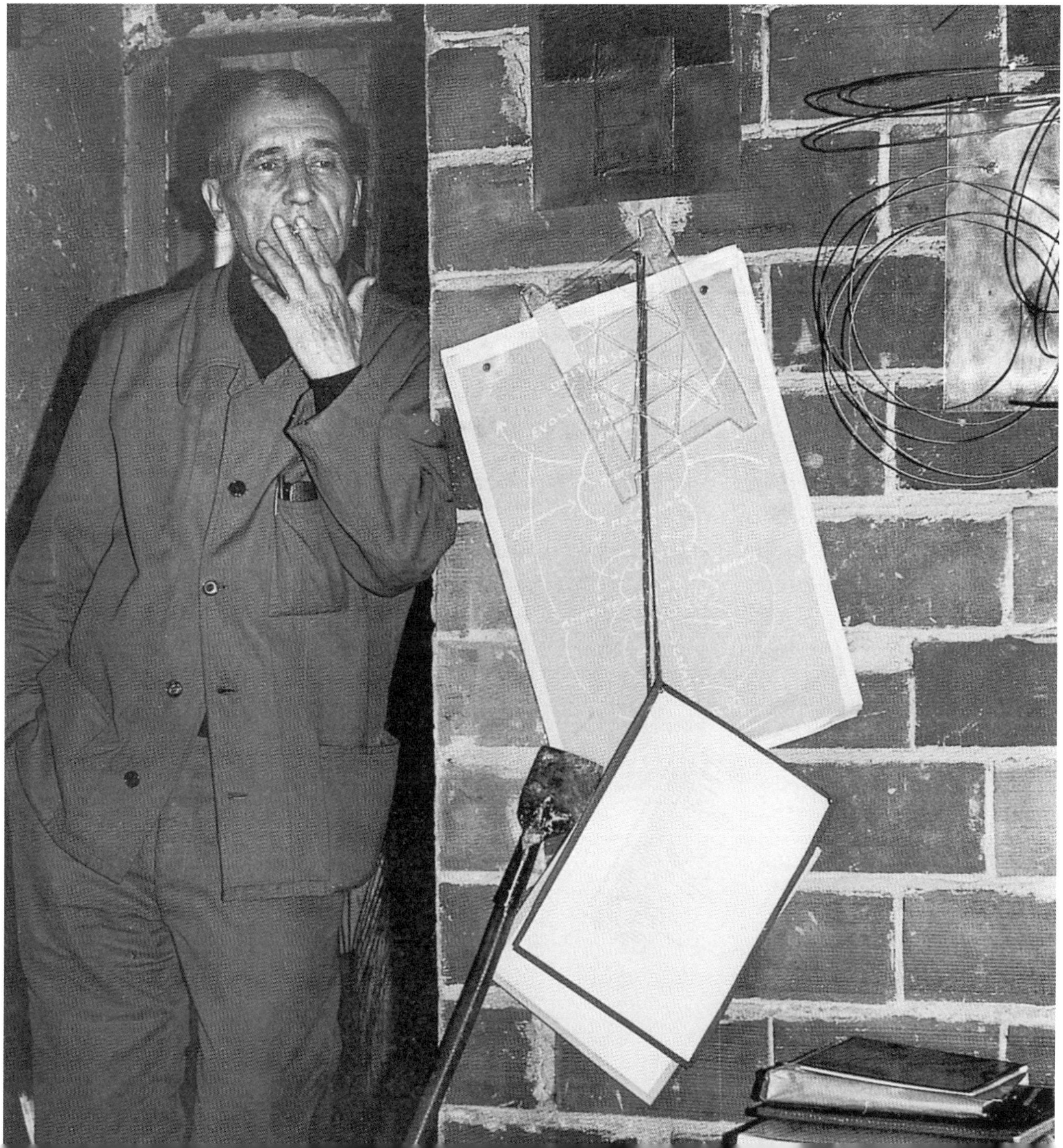

FERNANDO MELANI: Art and Habitat

RUDOLF SCHMITZ

"Art, too, is nothing more than a cloud of particles fixed in a certain way whose interpretation, like everything else today, isn't easy in this world immersed in a sea of quantity, of complexity, of complementarity, of 'uncertainty' (...)." Obviously the work produced by an artist who talks about art in these terms is likely to be rather elusive, to say the least. When Fernando Melani died in 1985 at the age of 78, he left his live-in studio plus its entire contents to the parish of Pistoia in Tuscany, so that the public would always have access to his work. And it is different from other artist's houses as we know them. The two-storey, terraced house in Corso Gramsci provides no biographical details, there are no carefully preserved personal items used or chosen by the artist; instead the visitor is taken aback to find that there is a complete absence of personal touches. That in itself is one of the salient experiences to be had from a visit to Melani's studio: the realization that an extended concept of looking at art depends on abstraction from the self, on the deactivation of false subjectivity.

Melani lived a strictly regulated life—always the same blue work-suit, the same yellow scarf, the same restaurant, the same bar, the same route into the town—in order to exclude as much as possible of the everyday and to devote himself, with a minimum of interference, to the "experiences" of art. This atmosphere of concentration is still palpable in the house, which is marked by an ascetic suppression of all things personal, and yet soon one registers this very quality as the legacy left to us by an extremely decisive, radical personality. It hardly seems possible that the works—completely obscuring walls, ceilings, floors, and doors—originated from one person, surely there must have been numerous artists at work here—for the works themselves are so heterogeneous and, in the best sense, style-less. At times it is hard to decide whether something is just a heap of materials or a "work"—there are no clear-cut transitions. That plastic bag, filled with used matches—does it merit the status of a work of art, or is it just recording an action repeated a thousand times, documenting the lifespan of an obsessive smoker? And the pieces of aluminum and copper, cut into rectangles and fixed to the studio door, still seem—like the various pendulum-devices and primitive little machines—to be actively involved in some experiment.

Nevertheless, a visit to the "Casa Melani" has nothing to do with nostalgia, as one might easily expect. Particularly nowadays, with biography and artistic expression irrevocably uncoupling, and with the new art-media evoking placelessness and virtuality, the idea of recommending a visit to an "artist's house" must appear like a symptom of some retrograde desire for order. But the "Casa Melani" does not fit any stereotype. It is more like a memory of the future, because it renders visible, in a quite particular way, the question of "habitat" that art will doubtlessly always be affected by. This artist's house reveals a certain "art system" within and by means of art. We would never be able to distinguish the wide-reaching (ultimately intellectually-based) horizons of Fernando Melani's art without the fixed framework of this house, in other words, without that particular sphere supported by our own spatial perception. One could be forgiven for wondering whether Melani's work would be at all "exhibitable" without the ambience of this house. This is a crucial point, if one wants to assess the status of his artistic activities. Usually those interpreting a body of work try to reconstruct the artist's "system" and problematics; but here—with inimitable autonomy—the work itself has replaced this procedure with an agglomeration of interpenetrating space and time. There is even a hint of possible entropy here. This "naturalism"—in itself characteristic of Melani's output—is directly linked to the underlying precepts of his thinking.

RUDOLF SCHMITZ is a freelance critic and journalist who lives in Frankfurt am Main, Germany.

FERNANDO MELANI, IL SACCO DI FIAMMIFERI SPENTI / SACK VOLL GEBRAUCHTER STREICHHÖLZER (undatiert) / BAG OF USED MATCHES (no date).

FERNANDO MELANI, Werk ohne Titel (Inv. No. 270), verschiedene Drahtsorten und Metallteile, 96 x 120 x17 cm / untitled piece, several kinds of wire and metal parts, $37^{3}/_{4}$ x $47^{1}/_{4}$ x $6^{11}/_{16}$".

Das Atelier im zweiten Stock: Wand gegenüber der Tür / The second-floor studio: wall facing the door.

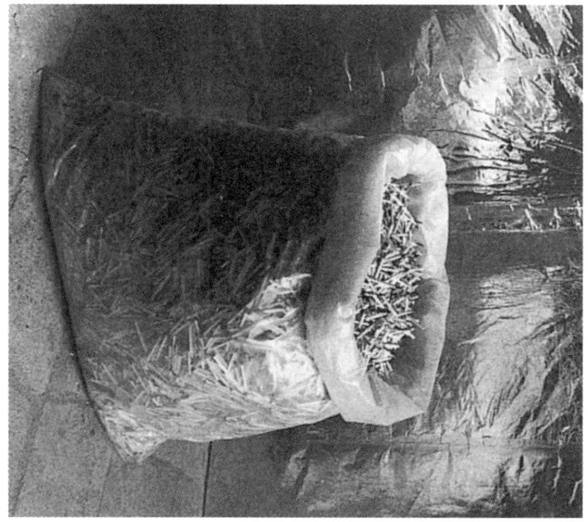

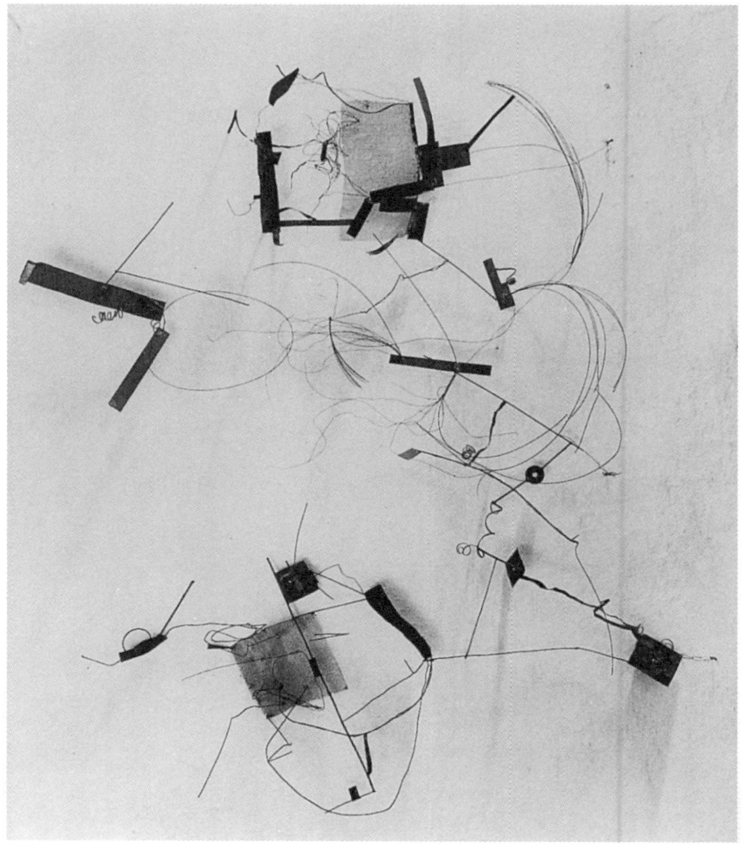

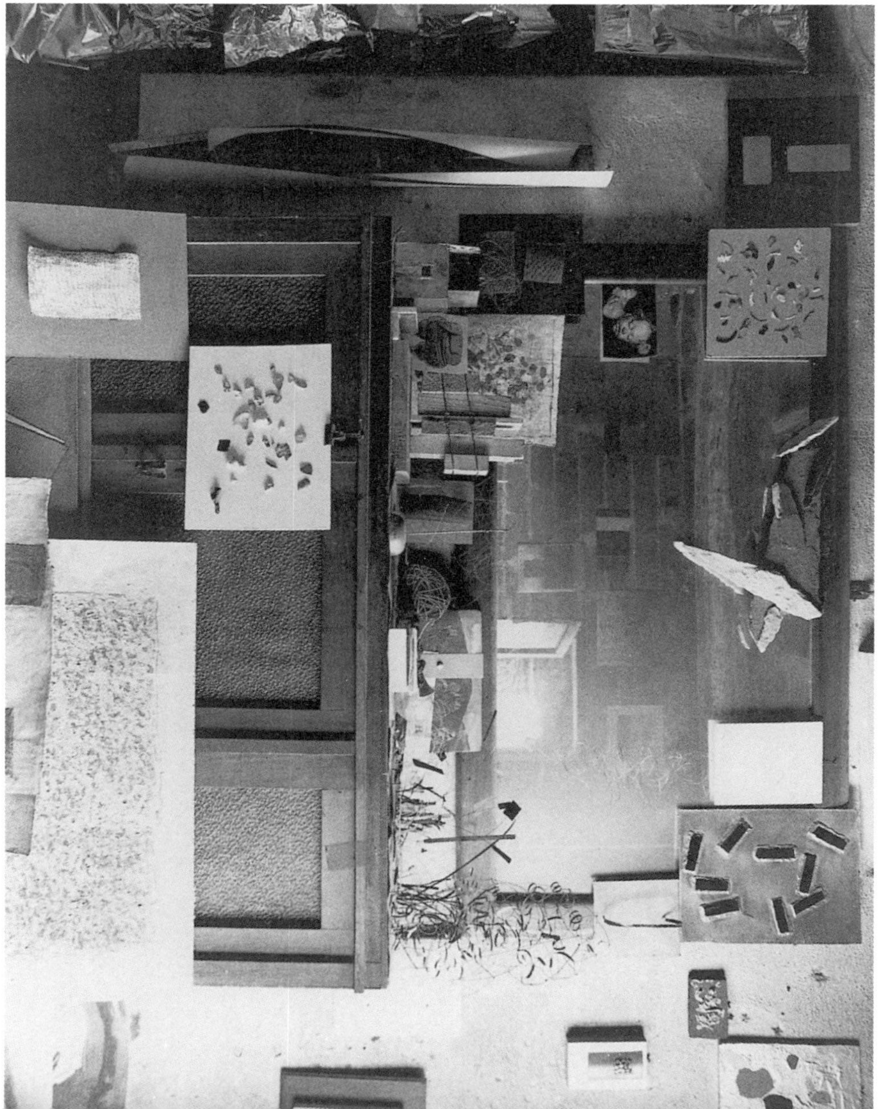

His artistic work, starting in 1945, took advanced scientific research as its yardstick. For Melani, a life-long member of the Communist Party, quantum physics was the reason why now there could only be abstract art. Accordingly he saw the artist as an element in an energy field of mobile particles of matter, who can re-explore—as in Classical Modernism—the unlimited freedom of the material. Melani saw himself as a medium whose role was to lock into the energy-processes of the physical cosmos, with minimal disruption and yet with catalytic effect. The magic word that this research-artist came to in the end—which he used to describe his relationship with the world and his concept of art—was "vibration." This referred to the force-fields that proliferate materials around themselves, and to their part in a grand, cosmic oscillation, their mobility in a state of apparent rest.

Melani's artist's house conveys the unnerving yet fascinating impression that here an artist was pursuing his activities in close proximity to experimental science, and indeed proceeding in a positively behaviorist manner. From this "eccentric" starting point he evolved very different grounds for and manifestations of certain visual aspects of art—such as monochromaticism. Melani discovered the compositional, multi-genre freedoms of abstract art via his own heightened naturalism—for instance painting variously formed pieces of wood in primary colors and loosely linking these together. His "pictures" and "drawings" seem not to be seen from the usual angle, as though categories like line, contour, form, and shape had been replaced by more penetrative acupuncture, as though the logic of a particular form had been cut through in the middle and that form was now seen in profile instead. One frequently has the feeling that Melani simply lets certain materials react to and with each other, and that he has—by virtue of his astounding micro-alertness—found a way right into the secrets of physical matter, and has thereby minimized the artistic intervention, almost bringing it down to "zero."

In the early sixties, when he was exploring the qualities of wire, metals, and alloys, he found numerous ways to suggest the abolition of gravity, as in the floating three-dimensionality of his "little clouds," "little theatres" and "spiders' webs." Melani's work—for he himself remained largely untouched by the machinations of the art market—has no fateful mechanism that at some point shuts down the experimental phase, leaving only aesthetically refined crystallizations of the original problematics. In 1977 Melani took part in an exhibition dedicated to "Arte non Arte," that is to say, looking at the question as to which practices promote that knowledge shared only by artists and which practices can lead to something being more widely regarded as art.

During the last five years of his life, Melani not only worked in his live-in studio, but often received his friends there, engaged in discussion with them, and had them take part in his experiments. Even today, near the bookshelves in one of the rooms, there are still a number of washing lines with monochrome rags hanging from them. The rags have been steeped in green, yellow, red, black or white oil paint, and the whole has the effect of an anti-gravitational air-piece that in itself seems to exemplify Melani's undying ambition to hold aloft his own particular universal concept of art. Which is why the rags are art. And the washing line. Not to mention the pegs.

(Translation: Fiona Elliott)

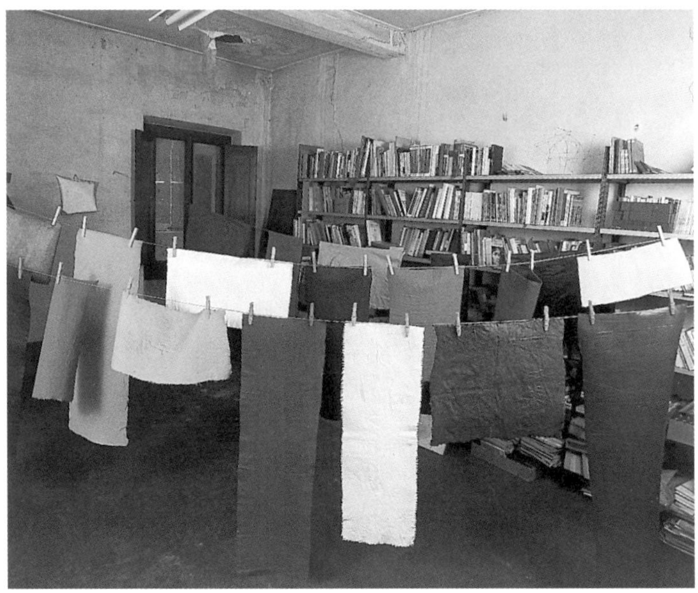

Raum in der Casa Melani / Room at the Casa Melani.

CUMULUS

Aus Europa

IN JEDER AUSGABE VON PARKETT PEILT EINE CUMULUS-WOLKE AUS AMERIKA UND EINE AUS EUROPA DIE INTERESSIERTEN KUNSTFREUNDE AN. SIE TRÄGT PERSÖNLICHE RÜCKBLICKE, BEURTEILUNGEN UND DENKWÜRDIGE BEGEGNUNGEN MIT SICH – ALS JEWEILS GANZ EIGENE DARSTELLUNG EINER BERUFSMÄSSIGEN AUSEINANDERSETZUNG.

IN DIESEM HEFT ÄUSSERN SICH HANS ULRICH OBRIST, FREIER KURATOR UND PUBLIZIST AUS ZÜRICH, ZURZEIT IN PARIS LEBEND, UND CONNIE BUTLER, CO-KURATORIN AM MUSEUM OF CONTEMPORARY ART (MOCA), LOS ANGELES.

Retrace Your Steps: Remember Tomorrow

Eine Ausstellung im Sir John Soane's Museum

Auf mich wirkten im Soane's Museum immer die Beziehungen, die Zwischenräume besonders anregend und inspirierend, die Bezüge, die sich zwischen den verschiedenen Inhalten und Objekten entwickeln, und die aussergewöhnlichen Anblicke, die sich ganz zufällig ergeben, und plötzlich sieht man sein eigenes Spiegelbild. Es ist ein unglaublich reichhaltiger, anregender Ort, und kein Besuch gleicht dem nächsten oder vorhergehenden.

– Cerith Wyn Evans im Gespräch mit Margret Richardson und Hans Ulrich Obrist, London 1999

Leute fragen oftmals, wenn sie durch den Haupteingang das Museum betreten: Welchen Weg sollen wir gehen?
Die Antwort ist: Nun, man kann hier beginnen oder dort, das steht jedermann frei.

– Margret Richardson im Gespräch mit Cerith Wyn Evans und Hans Ulrich Obrist, London 1999

HANS ULRICH OBRIST

Da ist ein Ort, den muss man einfach gesehen haben.

Anlässlich eines Treffens im Musée d'Art Moderne de la Ville de Paris 1995 erzählt mir Cerith Wyn Evans viel von Sir John Soane, was wenige Wochen später einen ersten gemeinsamen Besuch des gleichnamigen Museums auslöst. Cerith und ich beginnen uns regelmässig im Museum zu treffen. Nach und nach entsteht dabei eine imaginäre Ausstellung, die sich im Verlaufe der nächsten zwei Jahre im Dialog mit Margret Richardson, der Direktorin des Museums, konkretisiert.

Sichtbar/Unsichtbar

Zahlreich sind die posthumen Museen und Gedenkstätten, die ausschliesslich einem einzigen Künstler, Architekten, Autor gewidmet sind, wo versucht wird, Arbeitsbedingungen oder Lebenssituationen festzuhalten bzw. artifiziell zu rekonstituieren. Viel seltener sind Museen, die wie das Sir John Soane's Museum von Künstlern zu Lebzeiten als Gesamtkunstwerke konzipiert werden und als solche erhalten bleiben. 1833, vier Jahre vor seinem Tod, hat Soane sein Haus zum Museum deklariert und sich durch parlamentarischen Beschluss vom Staat ratifizieren lassen, dass dieses auch nach seinem Tode erhalten bliebe. Die Soane'schen Sammlungen umfassen vier Kategorien: antike Fragmente, Malerei von Canaletto via Hogarth bis Turner, Architekturzeichnungen (etwa Zeichnungen von Piranesi) sowie Soanes eigene Werke in Form von Architekturmodellen und Zeichnungen.

Obwohl das Sir John Soane's Museum regelmässige Öffnungszeiten hat und alljährlich über 90 000 Besucherinnen und Besucher zählt, ist es ein Ort, der vor allem durch persönliches Weitersagen bekannt ist. Das Paradoxon des wohl gehüteten, aber zugleich sehr öffentlichen Geheimnisses sowie die permanente Gratwanderung zwischen Sichtbarkeit und Unsichtbarkeit bilden den Ausgangspunkt der geplanten Ausstellung.

Cerith Wyn Evans hinterfragt die Trennung von öffentlichem und privatem Raum im Museum, wobei sein eigentlicher Eingriff im Raum fast nicht sichtbar sein wird. Die Arbeit rutscht in den vorhandenen Kontext, verschmilzt mit diesem und wahrt trotzdem Möglichkeiten des Ausdrucks. Vertrautes erscheint in einer anderen Perspektive als Nichtvertrautes.

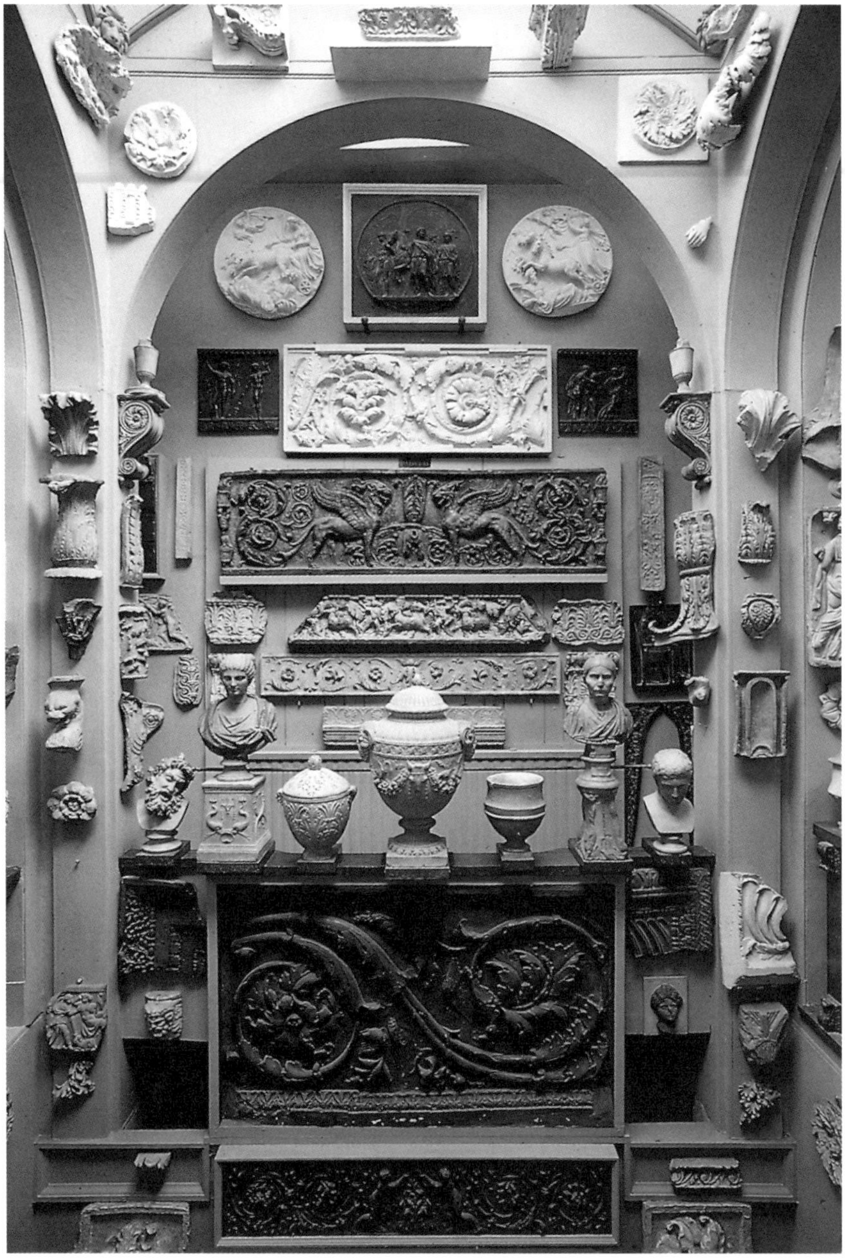

Sir John Soane's Museum, London, Dome, north wall, June 1999 / Dom, Nordwand. (PHOTO: GEREMY BUTLER)

Lincoln Inn Fields – Fournier Street

Dadurch, dass das Museum den Massstab eines Wohnhauses hat, gewinnen die Besucherinnen und Besucher ein anderes Verhältnis zu den Exponaten als in einer monumentalen Museumsarchitektur. Die von Adorno beklagte Trennung der Museen von der Welt der gelebten Erfahrung wird überwunden.

Ganz in diesem Sinne posieren Gilbert & George einen Nachmittag lang im Soane's Museum und trinken Tee aus Soanes Teetassen. Das dabei entstehende Photo wird gerahmt auf Soanes Esszimmertisch ausgestellt, gleich neben einem Photo, das Gilbert & George in ihrem eigenen Haus in der Fournier Street in East London zeigt. Gilbert & George und Soane verbindet die Art und Weise, wie sie in ihrem organisch wachsenden und sich stetig verdichtenden Haus auf der Suche nach der unendlichen Komplexität des Lebens sind, wie in ihren Sammlungen Dinge aus der Gegenwart neben Dingen aus der Vergangenheit stehen.

GILBERT & GEORGE spend an afternoon in the museum, drinking tea out of Soane's cups / posieren im Museum und trinken Tee aus Soanes Tassen.

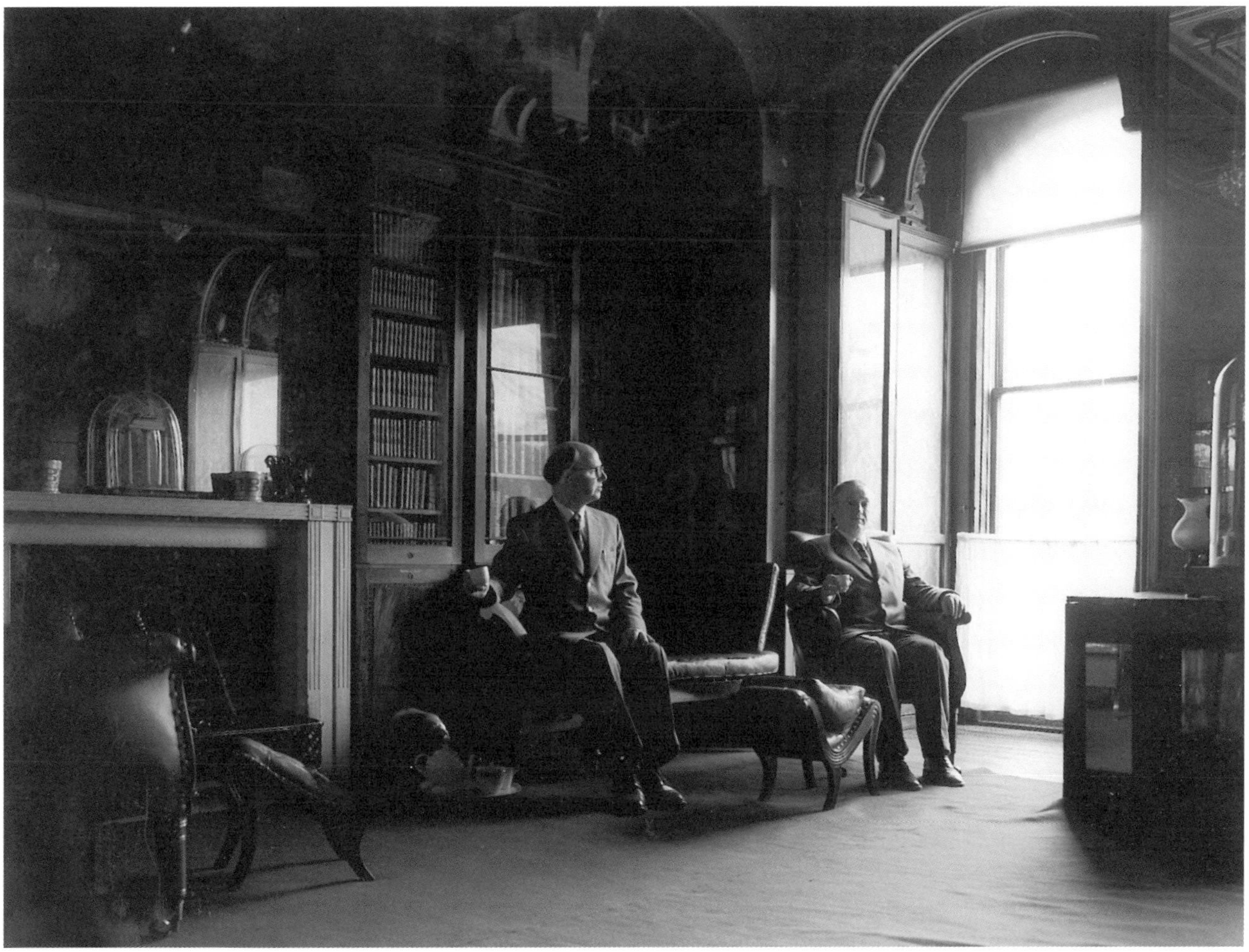

The Picture Room/Der Bilderraum

Aber wissen wir genau, wo der Raum abbricht, wo er sich biegt, wo er sich trennt und wo er sich wieder verbindet?

– Georges Perec über sein Buch *Träume von Räumen*

Die räumliche Verinnerlichung des Soane's Museum erinnert uns an Heinrich Kürz, den jungen (fiktiven) Maler in Georges Perecs *Ein Kunstkabinett (Un Cabinet d'Amateur)*, der den Bierbrauer und Sammler Hermann Raffke mit über 100 Bildern aus seinem Sammlungskabinett gemalt hat. Perec spricht von einer «Schwindel erregenden Spiritualität der Ewigen Wiederkunft», von einem «komplexen Spiel mit dem Echten und Falschen» sowie vom «magischen Charme immer kleinerer Wiederholungen». Die Perec'sche Komplexität der Raum- und Bildverschachtelungen führt uns in den Bilderraum von Sir John Soane's Museum. Für die Dauer der geplanten Gegenwartsausstellung wird als neue Hauptattraktion des Picture Room ein hier erstmals ausgestelltes, neues Gemälde von Richard Hamilton zu sehen sein. Dieses erschliesst sich den Besucherinnen und Besuchern erst, wenn die beweglichen Wände des Bilderraumes geöffnet werden. Der Vorteil dieser flexiblen, vielschichtigen Hängung, wie sie zu Soanes Zeiten auch in vielen Galerien üblich war, ist nebst der Raumökonomie auch die Tatsache, dass man die Bilder aus verschiedenen Winkeln betrachten kann.

Soanes Licht

Wir rühmen uns des Lichts; wenn wir aber unklugerweise in die Sonne sehen, so wirft sie uns in Dunkelheit... Das Licht... ward uns nicht gegeben, um es beständig anzustarren, sondern um weiter Dinge zu entdecken, die von unserer Erkenntnis entfernter sind.

– John Milton [1)]

Soane hat seine Effekte weniger durch Ornamente oder ornamentale Reduktion erreicht, sondern durch Raum, Farbe und Licht. Gerade die Frage des Lichtes hat in der Soane-Rezeption erst in den letzten Jahren an Wichtigkeit gewonnen, so zum Beispiel im einflussreichen Text von Arata Isozaki, der in Asien einen wahren Soane-Boom ausgelöst hat. Das Museum eröffnet verschiedene von Soane konstruierte Lichtzustände, die sich überlagern und vermischen. Der Besucher begegnet direktem, indirektem, reflektivem, gebrochenem, gestreutem oder refraktivem Licht (Dank an Georges Perec, den Meister der Listen). Licht spielt auch in der Auseinandersetzung der Künstlerinnen und Künstler mit dem Museum eine wichtige Rolle.

Richard Hamiltons Auseinandersetzung mit den vielschichtigen Lichtzuständen im Soane's Museum manifestiert sich in seinem Photo für das Plakat der Ausstellung, wo der Blick verschiedene Glas- und Spiegelschichten durchdringt: Ungleiche strukturelle Elemente werden im Soane'schen Labyrinth der verschachtelten Bedeutung aufs Unerwartetste kombiniert, wobei sich – ähnlich wie in Piranesis *Carceri* mit ihren ins Unendliche gespiegelten Treppenhäusern – Verbindungen in alle Richtungen eröffnen. Hamiltons Photo zeigt uns die von Soane angelegte, partizipatorische Dimension des *Pars pro toto*, sodass, im Gegensatz zu Besuchen in Kuriositätenkabinetten, inmitten des unglaublichen Overloads überraschenderweise keine sensorische Passivität entsteht. Dies verdanken wir der Nichtabgeschlossenheit der architektonischen Fragmente sowie der nicht vorgegebenen Richtung des Museumsbesuchs, welche die Möglichkeiten der Ergänzung und der Fortsetzung eröffnen. Anish Kapoor plant den dynamischen Stillstand: Eine Tischskulptur mit gelbem Spiegel erweist sich bei genauerem Hinsehen als extrem schnell rotierendes Honigrezeptakel. Koo Jeong-a baut an einem kleinen, kompakten, klaren, spiegelnden Raum, der sich mehr und mehr verdichtet.

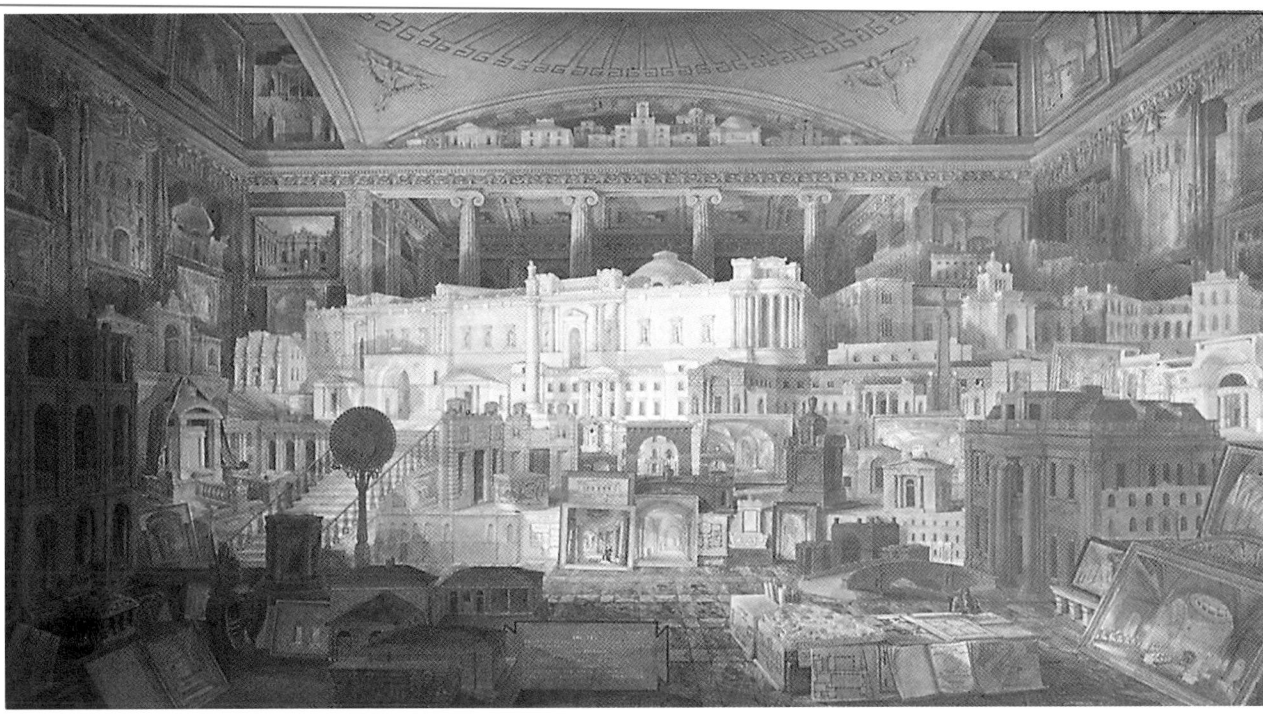

Sir John Soane's Museum, The Picture Room, "Buildings designed from 1780 to 1815" / Der Bilderraum, «Von 1780 bis 1815 entworfene Gebäude».

Unerwartete Perspektiven

Bruce Mau plant eine Projektion auf das existierende Display und wird dieses damit um weitere konnektive Möglichkeiten bereichern. Sein Mississippi-Museum sowie ein von ihm und Frank Gehry geplantes Coca-Cola-Museum sind beide von Soane beeinflusst. Für die Ausstellung wird Mau eine Installation entwickeln, die Soanes Praxis weiterführt, Hierarchien zwischen wichtigen und unwichtigen Exponaten fliessend zu halten und bedeutungsvolle Objekte neben wertlosen Fundstücken zu zeigen. Maus Arbeit projiziert Soane in die Gegenwart des Internet. Die Exponate werden dadurch verstärkt als ein materielles Netzwerk erfahren. Einen genauso unerwarteten Blick auf Soane wirft Lucius Burckhardt, der das Soane's Museum seit den frühen 60er Jahren besucht. Burckhardts Projekt für die Ausstellung handelt von den wenig bekannten *Garden Follies* des Sir John Soane. Burckhardt beginnt mit der Frage, wie es dazu kam, «dass Sir John Soane ein recht bescheidenes Büchlein über Gartenhäuschen produzierte», und zeigt uns, dass Gartenhäuschen aufwiesen, «was der Architektur nicht erlaubt war: Sie waren chinesisch, ägyptisch, gotisch und natürlich auch klassisch.» Rem Koolhaas zeigt seinen Wettbewerbsentwurf für ein neues Museum Moderner Kunst in Rom. Er verwendet das Soane's Museum als Museum im Museum; neben dem Whitney- und dem Guggenheim-Museum wird das Soane's Museum zu einer Möglichkeit, einer Wahrheit, die von unzähligen anderen Wahrheiten umgeben ist, die es im komplexen Museum der Gegenwart zu verschränken gilt. Im Rahmen des von Koolhaas umrissenen «Katalogs von Museumsbedingungen» steht das Soane's Museum für Zartheit beziehungsweise Empfindlichkeit (Delicacy).

In progress

Weitere Projekte von Katharina Fritsch, Tom Gidley, Douglas Gordon, Joseph Grigely, Jacques Herzog & Pierre de Meuron, Isaac Julien, Christina Mackie, Steve Mc Queen, Cedric Price, Liisa Roberts, Rosemarie Trockel, Richard Wentworth, Yung Ho Cheong, The Museum of Jurassic Technology, nanomuseum, nvisible Museum sind zurzeit im Entstehen.

Alle teilnehmenden Künstlerinnen und Künstler gestalten jeweils eine Postkarte, die am Eingang des Museums inmitten der offiziellen Ansichtskarten des Museums verkauft wird. Auf Labels wird verzichtet – die heute im Museum vorhandenen Labels wurden erst nach dem Tod Soanes in viktorianischer Zeit angebracht, zu seinen Lebzeiten lag stattdessen jeweils eine Textbeschreibung der einzelnen Exponate auf dem Esszimmertisch. Ein von Cerith Wyn Evans gestaltetes Faltblatt mit Plan wird die Ausstellung auf anderem Wege erschliessen: Ohne angehalten zu sein, didaktischen Paneelen oder Tonguides zu folgen, zeichnet jeder Besucher seinen eigenen Parcours. Richard Hamilton macht das Plakat zur Ausstellung, der Ausstellungstitel von Douglas Gordon tritt in unterschiedlichen Formen in Erscheinung. Cedric Price hält einen Vortrag in der Küche des Museums.

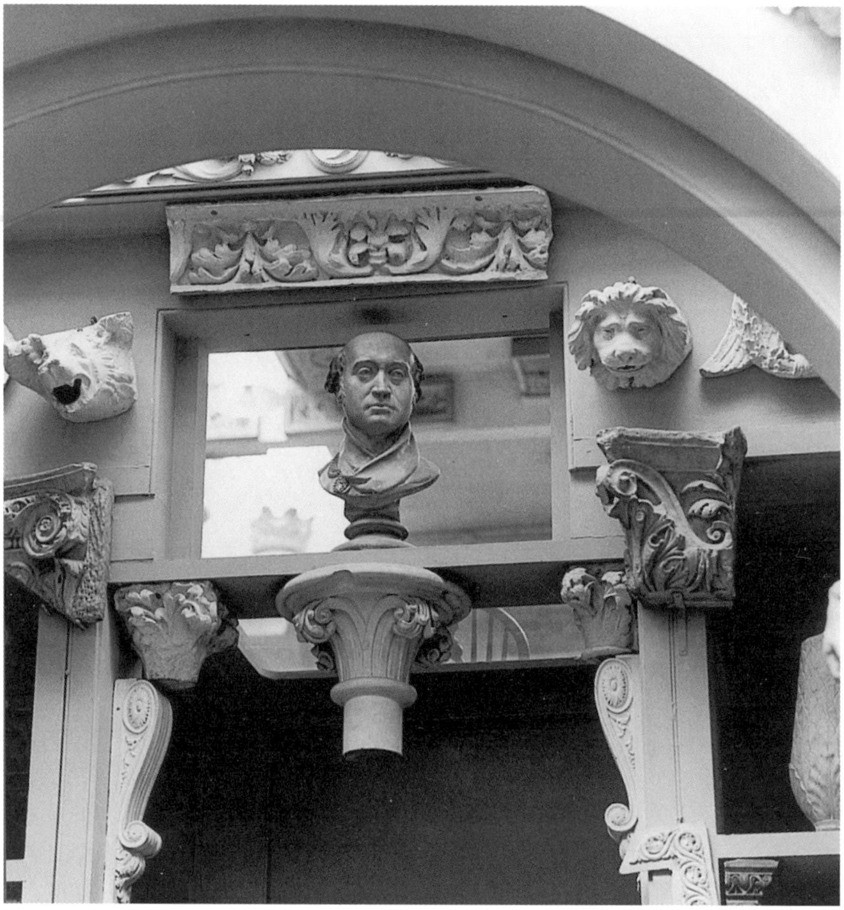

RICHARD HAMILTON, THE SOANE MUSEUM, 1999, photograph, work in progress for exhibition poster / Photo für das Ausstellungsplakat.

Daten

Die Ausstellung dauert vom Dezember 1999 bis März 2000. Für 2001 ist ein Ausstellungsprojekt von Peter Fleissig über das «nvisible Museum»[2] geplant, ein innovatives Museum der 90er Jahre, das seine Sammlung an Freunde und Bekannte ausleiht. Im Gegensatz zum Sir John Soane's Museum, wo alle Exponate an einem Ort versammelt sind, ist das «nvisible Museum» ein Netzwerk, ein nomadisches Museum der Zwischenräume.

1) John Milton, *Aeropagitica*, übers. v. Wilhelm Bernhardi, in: *John Milton und der Ursprung des neuzeitlichen Liberalismus, Studienausgabe der politischen Hauptschriften John Miltons*, E.W. Tielsch (Hrsg.), Gerstenberg Verlag, Hildesheim 1980, S. 112.
2) Vgl. dazu Peter Fleissig, «Lèche-Vitrine», in: *Parkett*, No. 35, 1993, S. 108.

Retrace Your Steps: Remember Tomorrow

An Exhibition in Sir John Soane's Museum

I was always very stimulated and inspired by the relationships, the interstices in the Soane's Museum, the conversations that are happening between various narratives, various objects and these extraordinary vistas that you come upon by accident and then you catch a reflection of yourself. It is an incredibly complex, stimulating place and no one visit is ever the same as the next visit.

– Cerith Wyn Evans in conversation with Margret Richardson and Hans Ulrich Obrist, London, 1999

People often wonder which way to go when they come into the main entrance of the museum.
The answer is, well, you can go there or you can go there, it's a choice.

– Margret Richardson in conversation with Cerith Wyn Evans and Hans Ulrich Obrist, London, 1999

HANS-ULRICH OBRIST

There Is a Place You Must Know.

At a meeting at the Musée d'Art Moderne de la Ville de Paris in 1995, Cerith Wyn Evans told me a lot about Sir John Soane, which inspired me to make my first visit to the museum of the same name. Cerith and I began to meet regularly in the museum. After a while the idea of an imaginary exhibition began to take shape and, in the course of the following two years, it crystallized in conversation with Margret Richardson, the director of the museum.

Visible/Invisible

Numerous are the posthumous museums and memorials devoted exclusively to one artist, architect, or author, and designed to preserve or artificially reconstruct the namesake's original working or living conditions. Much rarer are the museums conceived by artists in their lifetimes as a gesamtkunstwerk and preserved as such. The Sir John Soane's Museum is a case in point. In 1833, four years before he died, Soane established his house as a museum and negotiated an Act of Parliament to ensure its preservation after his death. His holdings fall into four categories: antique fragments, paintings from Canaletto to Hogarth and Turner, architectural drawings (such as Piranesi's), and Soane's own work in the form of architectural models and drawings.

Although the Sir John Soane's Museum has regular opening hours and attracts some 90 000 visitors a year, it has acquired a reputation primarily by word of mouth. The paradox of a well-guarded and yet public secret as well as the permanent pull between visibility and invisibility are the considerations that motivate the coming exhibition.

Cerith Wyn Evans questions the distinction between public and private space in a museum, whereby his intervention in the room will be almost invisible. The work slides into the existing context, blends into it, and yet still retains possibilities of expression.

Seen in a different perspective, the familiar becomes unfamiliar.

Lincoln Inn Fields—Fournier Street

Since the museum has the dimensions of a home, visitors do not have the same relationship to the works on display as they would in monumental museum architecture. The gulf between the museum and the world of living experience, criticized by Adorno, has been bridged.

Gilbert & George will spend an afternoon in the museum, drinking tea out of Soane's cups. The resulting photograph will be framed and placed on Soane's dining room table next to the photograph of Gilbert & George in their own house on Fournier Street in East London. Gilbert & George show a kinship with Soane in the way they investigate the infinite complexity of life in their organically growing and steadily more compact home, where things accumulated from the present and from the past are allowed to coexist side by side.

The Picture Room

But do we know exactly where the room stops, where it bends, where it separates and where it joins up again?

– Georges Perec about *Espèces d'espaces*

The use of space in the Soane Museum reminds us of Heinrich Kuerz, the young (fictional) painter in Georges Perec's *Un Cabinet d'Amateur*, who painted the beer brewer and collector Hermann Raffke over 100 times with over 100 pictures from his collection. Perec speaks of the "staggering spirituality of the eternal second coming," of a "complex game of authenticity and fraudulence," and of the "magic charm of smaller and smaller repetitions." The complexity of Perec's convoluted rooms and images takes us into the Picture Room of the Sir John Soane's Museum. For the duration of the planned contemporary exhibition, there will be a new main attraction in the Picture Room, a painting by Richard Hamilton, to be premiered here. Visitors can see the painting only when the partitioning walls of the Picture Room are open. This flexible mode of hanging, a common device used by many galleries in Soane's day as well, not only has the advantage of saving space, it also allows the viewing of paintings from different angles.

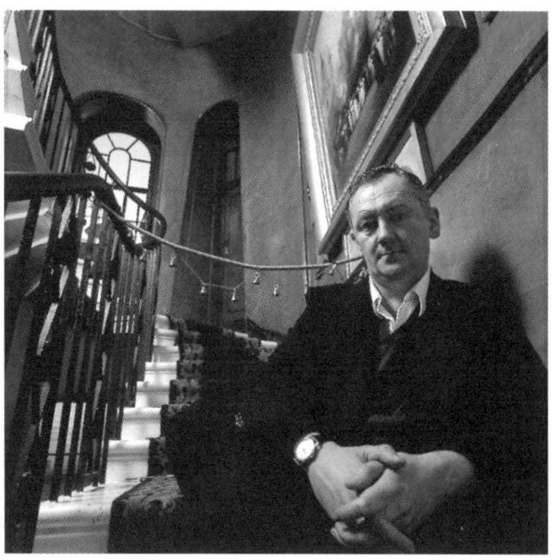

"Retrace Your Steps: Remember Tomorrow," Sir John Soane's Museum, London, 10 December 1999 – 25 March 2000.
Participating artist Cerith Wyn Evans.
Participating artist Isaac Julien.

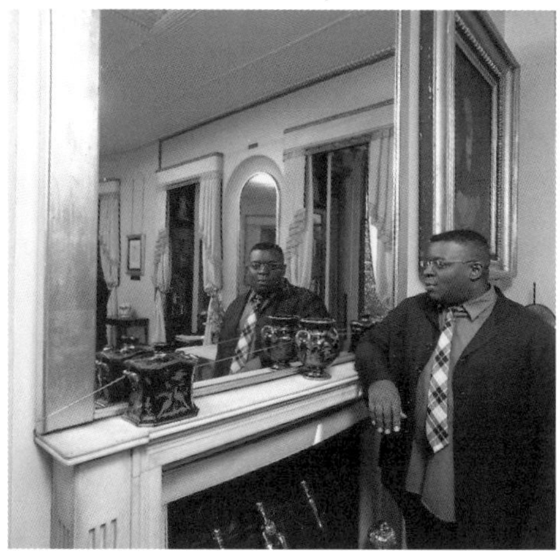

Soane's Light

We boast our light; but if we look not wisely on the Sun itself, it smites us into darkness... The light which we have gained, was given us, not to be ever staring on, but by it to discover onward things more remote from our knowledge. – John Milton[1)]

Soane achieved his effects not through ornamentation or ornamental reduction but through space, color, and light. Scholarship on Soane has just recently begun to recognize the importance of light in the architect's work, for instance, in Arata Isozaki's essay, which has unleashed a veritable Soane boom in Asia. The museum reveals various superimposed and merging states of light, constructed by Soane. Visitors encounter direct, indirect, reflected, broken, dispersed, or refracted light (I bow to master list-maker Georges Perec). Light also plays an important role for artists in their dealings with the museum.

Richard Hamilton's response to the complexity of the lighting in the Soane's museum is manifest in his poster for the exhibition, in which the gaze penetrates several layers of glass and mirrors. Disparate structural elements come together in startlingly unexpected combinations in the Soane labyrinth of convoluted meanings, with links opening up in all directions like the staircases mirrored into infinity in Piranesi's *Carceri.* Hamilton's photo shows us the participatory dimension of *pars pro toto* in Soane's approach so that surprisingly, no sensory passivity results despite the incredible overload—in contrast to a curio museum. This derives from the fact that the architectural fragments are not closed off, that the direction of the visitor's tour is not predetermined, and that there is room for possible additions and continuations. Anish Kapoor has planned a dynamic standstill: A table sculpture with a yellow mirror proves on closer inspection to be a container of honey revolving at extremely high speed. Koo Jeong-a is at work on a small, compact, clear, reflecting room that is becoming more and more compressed.

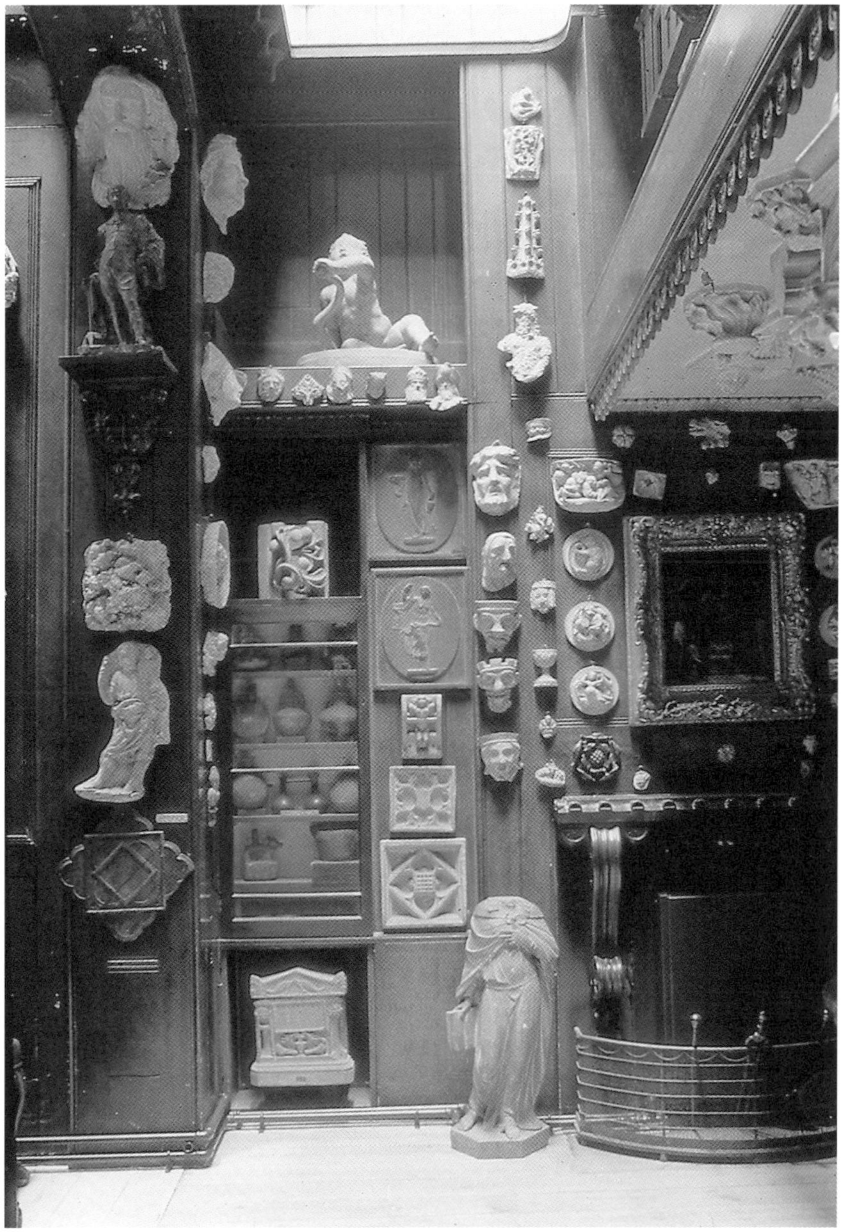

Sir John Soane's Museum, "Monk's Parlour" / Mönchs-Sprechzimmer.

Unanticipated Perspectives

Bruce Mau plans to project images onto the existing display, thereby enhancing the associative potential. His Mississippi Museum and the Coca-Cola Museum (with Frank Gehry) are both influenced by Soane. Mau is devising a project for the exhibition that will extend Soane's practice of ignoring the hierarchy of important and unimportant exhibits by showing significant objects next to worthless found items. Mau's work catapults Soane into today's Internet. The exhibits will be imbedded in a material network. Lucius Burckhardt, a regular visitor of the Soane's Museum since the sixties, has come up with an equally unexpected twist. His project deals with Sir John Soane's little known *Garden Follies* and why the architect chose to "produce such a modest little volume on garden houses." According to Sir John Soane, garden houses—Chinese, Egyptian, Gothic, and, of course, Classical in style—gave free rein to what was otherwise architecturally condemned. Rem Koolhaas will present his competition model for a new Museum of Modern Art in Rome. He uses the Soane's Museum as a museum in a museum. Along with the Whitney and the Guggenheim Museums, the Sir John Soane's Museum becomes one possibility, one truth among the myriad truths that must be comprised in a such complex undertaking as a museum of contemporary art. Within the framework of Koolhaas's "Catalogue of Museum Specifications," the Soane's Museum stands for delicacy.

In Progress

Projects by Katharina Fritsch, Tom Gidley, Douglas Gordon, Joseph Grigely, Jacques Herzog/Pierre de Meuron, Isaac Julien, Christina Mackie, Steve McQueen, Cedric Price, Liisa Roberts, Rosemarie Trockel, Richard Wentworth, Yung Ho Cheong, The Museum of Jurassic Technology, nanomuseum, nvisible Museum. All participating artists will create a postcard that will be on sale at the entrance to the museum along with the regular postcards.

The works on view in the exhibition will not be labeled since labels were later appended to Soane's collection in the Victorian Age. In Soane's day, a description of the items was lying on the dining room table. Visitors will have a fold-out designed by Cerith Wyn Evans with a plan of the exhibition. They will not be advised to follow didactic panels or recorded guides but will choose their own paths through the exhibition. Richard Hamilton will design the poster. The title by Douglas Gordon will appear in many different forms. Cedric Price will give a lecture in the kitchen of the museum.

Dates

The exhibition will be open from December 1999 to March 2000. For the year 2001 an exhibition project of Peter Fleissig on the nvisible Museum[2] is planned: an innovative museum of the nineties that involves lending his collection to friends and acquaintances. In contrast to Sir John Soane's Museum, where all the art is in one place, the nvisible Museum is a network, a nomadic museum of interstices.

(Translation: Catherine Schelbert)

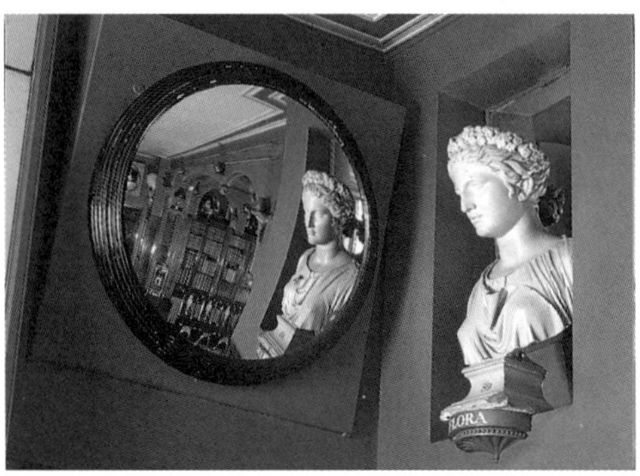

Sir John Soane's Museum, Dining Room, detail / Detail im Speisezimmer.

1) John Milton, *Areopagitica*, 1644, in: Malcolm W. Wallace, ed., *Milton's Prose, A Selection* (London: Oxford University Press, 1963), pp. 311–12.
2) See also Peter Fleissig, "Lèche-Vitrine," in: *Parkett*, no. 35, 1993, p. 102.

CUMULUS

From America

IN EVERY EDITION OF PARKETT, TWO CUMULUS CLOUDS, ONE FROM AMERICA, THE OTHER FROM EUROPE, FLOAT OUT TO AN INTERESTED PUBLIC. THEY CONVEY INDIVIDUAL OPINIONS, ASSESSMENTS, AND MEMORABLE ENCOUNTERS—AS ENTIRELY PERSONAL PRESENTATIONS OF PROFESSIONAL ISSUES.

OUR CONTRIBUTORS TO THIS ISSUE ARE CONNIE BUTLER, ASSOCIATE CURATOR AT THE MUSEUM OF CONTEMPORARY ART, LOS ANGELES, AND HANS ULRICH OBRIST, A WRITER AND FREELANCE CURATOR FROM ZURICH WHO CURRENTLY LIVES IN PARIS.

West of Everything

CONNIE BUTLER

Michael Parekowhai gets a little wistful when describing his monumental sculpture THE INDEFINITE ARTICLE (1990). Parekowhai, a self-described Maori Charles Ray, indulges in the agility of the ready-made text with his highly fabricated riffs on the cultural signs of his native New Zealand. The sculpture spells out the pronoun sentence "I AM HE" in giant white letters, which loom overhead as they form a kind of two-and-a-half-meter-high thicket across the floor. In New Zealand the "I AM" is well known to be from Colin McCahon, the near mythic painter revered as the greatest artist in the modern history of the country. McCahon, who died in 1987, persists as the shadow under which all artists work and whose most interesting resuscitation is coming from a generation of emerging artists who choose to rework or simply go around the legend.

Parekowhai, who added the "HE" to the legendary "I AM" remembers that McCahon likened the experience of his moody paintings to a walk in the landscape. "He" is also Maori for "wrong" and the three-word phrase interestingly consists of letters contained in the artist's first name. Wrong place, wrong time, wrong artist—this is the identity that Parekowhai embraces and lovingly mucks around in. He has fashioned an identity that is both friendly "native" and sardonic, a cultural critique displayed in his show-stealing TEN GUITARS (1999) made for Artspace in Auckland and part of the recent "Asia Pacific Triennial" in Brisbane. Charming his audience like a regular-guy Sinatra with a song, the most common expression in modern Maori culture, he remixes Engelbert Humperdinck's folksy "Ten Guitars."

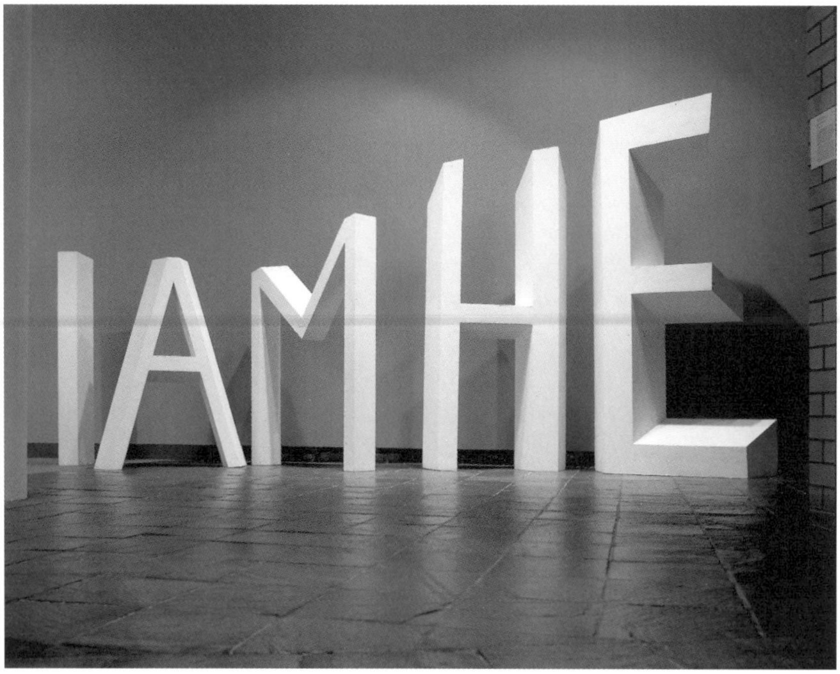

MICHAEL PAREKOWHAI, THE INDEFINITE ARTICLE, 1990, oil paint on wood, installation at the Waikato Museum of Art and History, Hamilton, New Zealand / DER UNBESTIMMTE ARTIKEL, Ölfarbe auf Holz. (PHOTO: DAVID COOK)

Abstract light-box works, which frame the guitars, stand in for the ribs of the *marae*, the Maori meeting house, a common and mythic place.

In Maori, the indigenous language of New Zealand, the word "maori" means ordinary, regular, everyday. What is interesting to me is that there is nothing at all ordinary about being a young Maori artist, working in a society made officially bi-cultural in 1990, doing Colin McCahon via Duchamp in the insular New Zealand art world, and having aspirations well beyond the identity trap which has already garnered him a good degree of visibility in the international art world. Parekowhai has staked out a wide and hybrid territory in which his work functions beyond the local and yet is deeply committed to it. The work is poignant, gorgeously fabricated, a bit cocky, and is located in an exotic and, in western terms, exoticizing cultural position. This is what makes it provocative.

The lure of Parekowhai's local is endlessly fascinating on a number of levels, not the least of which is the precarious moment of the New Zealand art world which, I'm suggesting, might be roughly compared to that of Los Angeles. One native artist expressed a fear of becoming Australia—fractured by the mainstream, Euro-American art world's fickle interest and internationalized by feverish, biennial induced art-tourism. With recent exhibitions such as "Headlands" (1992) curated by Auckland's Artspace curator Robert Leonard and shipped to Australia, "Toi, Toi, Toi" (1999) organized by René Block for the Museum Fridericianum in Kassel and the Auckland Art Gallery, and "The World Over" (1996) organized by the Stedelijk Museum and the City Gallery in Wellington, the complexity and richness of what is actually going on in the country situated geographically the farthest from Europe is beginning to be understood and theorized by the international art audience and curatorial machine. And yet, there is no question that the most compelling practice here is idiosyncratic and regional. Emerging artists wonder how their work will travel and I catch myself wondering if traveling will wreck it.

Outside of Europe and the United States—that is, west of the "no there, there" that is here—Los Angeles is subsumed into Euro-America, a demonized specter of economic and cultural colonialism. Living and working in Los Angeles in all its cultural diversity, political volatility and promise (bicultural models seems light years away) offers the daily challenge of problematizing this monolithic view of North America. Somewhere between the proliferation of sophomoric McDonalds critique art and the endless abstracting of L.A. modernism lies an infinitely more dispersed and agitated identity. At the recent Asia Pacific Triennial the four North American participants of approximately seven hundred in attendance all work in the western border regions of the United States, specifically Los Angeles and Texas (as well as one native Australian/New Yorker sent by *Artforum*). Perhaps this is to be expected given the Pacific orientation of the exhibition and conference. What is striking from this vantage, sitting as we do on the rim of the Pacific in the middle of the coast of the Americas, is that looking west (instead of east to Europe via New York as the Los Angeles art world absolutely still does) might enact a global/local identity that is Los Angeles now—a productive curatorial accounting of this distinctly non-European, in fact Asian and Latin American city.

The particular provincialism of Los Angeles (as opposed, say, to New York) offers the dizzying situation of being liberated from a rich art history we only recently learned to care about, and being enamored of our burgeoning internationalism. It's not uncommon, for example, to encounter young painters who don't know Lee Mullican, the recently deceased California painter whose astoundingly beautiful works embody the rich and under-theorized territory of Native American culture's relationship to modernism. In the forties and early fifties, with fellow painters Gordon Onslow Ford and Wolfgang Paalen, Mullican's style and zeitgeist, called "dynatonic," combined homegrown mysticism and an abstract language drawing on sources like the Navajo sand paintings.

LEE MULLICAN, MINERAL PENS, ca. 1948, ink and watercolor on paper, $14\frac{1}{2}$ x $11\frac{1}{2}$" / MINERALSTIFTE, Tusche und Wasserfarbe auf Papier, 36,8 x 29,2 cm. (PHOTO: GRANT SELWYN FINE ART, BEVERLY HILLS)

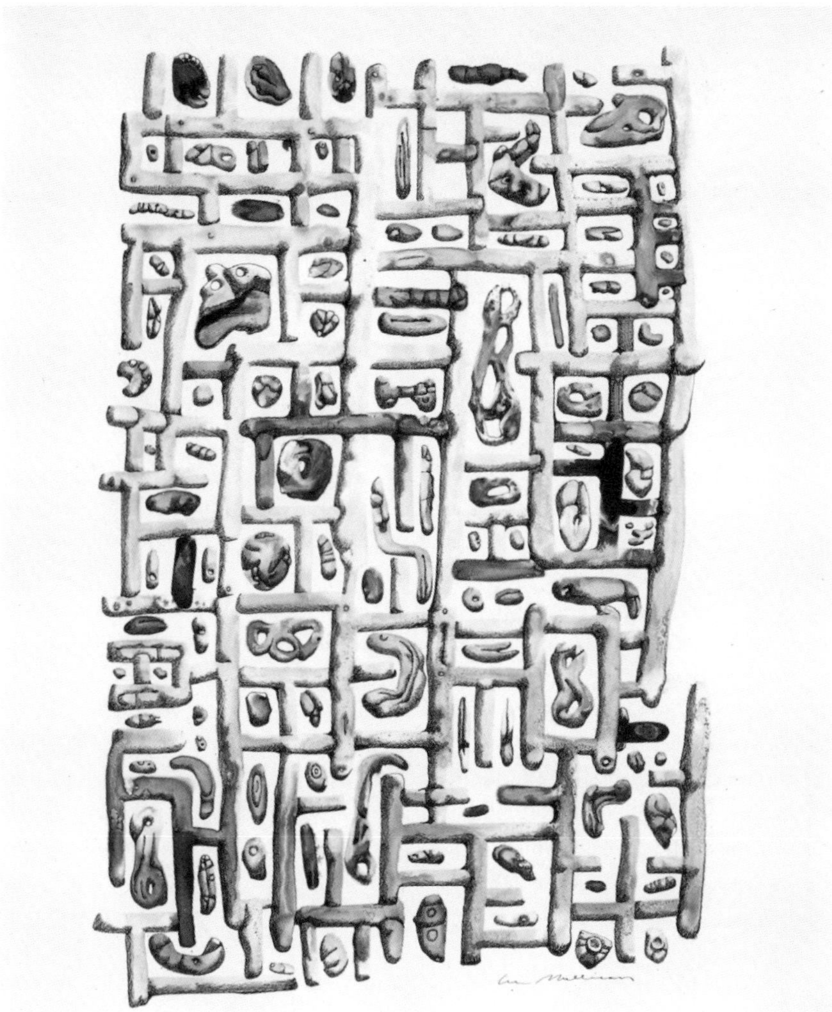

The programmatic "internationalism" of West Coast museums committed to late-twentieth-century art is absolutely European based, despite current and proactive forays into Latin America. The cultural diversity and Pacific Rim geography of this city are addressed only in essentializing, multiculturalist terms. Perhaps this was appropriate for the last decade, but post-riot Los Angeles demands a more sophisticated, post-colonial response. One simultaneously internalizes the local and global imperatives when working here, a situation analogous perhaps to curatorial practice in any one of the centers of art production that are not the economic center that is still undeniably New York. Speaking on a panel about international exhibitions organized by the MAK Center/ Schindler House, Los Angeles, in 1998, Okwui Enwezor (pre-documenta) remarked on the invisibility of black artists or artists of Latin or Asian descent in the major galleries. Armed with E-mail and cellular phones, international visitors to Los Angeles engage in a kind of curatorial sampling, wanting to see the same eight artists forgetting that everything in Los Angeles is miles apart and hours by car. During the nineties the focus on Los Angeles has reached a fever pitch. The zenith began in 1992, with the smash-hit exhibition "Helter Skelter: L.A. Art in the 1990s," organized by Museum of Contemporary Art curator Paul Schimmel, which explored the noirish tendencies in Los Angeles art-making. Now repackaged in hyperbolic exhibitions all over Europe, these artists are part of the first generation to reap the economic benefit of the L.A. mania. The Louisiana Museum's "Sunshine and Noir," organized in 1996, provided a culminating cumulus from America, originating in Europe, mistakenly shipped and ending its tour in Los Angeles. Somehow these shows with their loopy, freeway-sign-design aesthetic and quippish, news magazine titles should never come home. Most revealing is the fact that many self-identified Chicano or Latino artists who participated in the "Helter Skelter" exhibition were omitted from European versions of the show. The practices of artists like Victor Estrada or Manuel Ocampo are often read through the work of Mike Kelley or Paul McCarthy among whose own influences are the largely white, middle class histories of performance and feminism in Los Angeles—both of which have yet to be written and curated.

The hype and myth-making about art and artists in Los Angeles nevertheless reached their most shrill hysteria with the recent spate of articles on the local art schools: *The New York Times Magazine* breathlessly followed *Artforum*'s astounding blunder published last spring. In an effort to dispense with L.A., New York scrambled to catch up with *Spin* magazine's MTV-style profile of the UCLA kids. Each young artist was featured in color bearing a tool, only to exaggerate the ongoing debate (which no one here is actually engaged in) about Art Center being the school that thinks and doesn't make, and UCLA being the school that ... you get the idea. The oversimplifications multiply: A focus on biography and historical revisionism marginalizes essential histories. The Feminist Art Program at Cal Arts, the Pomona College Art Gallery and University of California, Irvine art gallery all contributed to recognizing the early histories of environmental and conceptual art. The opening lines of *The New York Times Magazine* article gives a hint of this "Access Hollywood"-style journalism:

Chris Burden began his career with a literal bang. His SHOOTING PIECE required a friend to fire a bullet into his left arm from a distance of 15 feet. Perhaps that's why, when we recently met at the University of California at Los Angeles, I found it hard to imagine him patiently sitting through faculty meetings. Time does strange things. You wait long enough and even the most outrageous rebels end up grading papers and sharing career tips with students... It was a shining afternoon, and the air was fragrant with the scent of eucalyptus trees... [1]

And so the mythology goes exponentially on. Does anyone mean to suggest it would have been better if Chris Burden had reached an untimely demise in his own student performance work than go on and build a studio in Topanga Canyon and teach young artists to do the same?

I have considered making a case for rethinking the L.A. exotic. Could the fiction and the daily, always-mediated truth of the "other" coast somehow be regularized? To recall New Zealand for a moment, the slippage between *Wallpaper* magazine's Auckland, the *pakeha* girls (white chicks) with bell bottoms and maori feathers in their hair, and Michael Parekowhai's bi-culturalism is compelling territory. Parekowhai's exotic/de-exoticized regular guy persona repositions him just out of reach of the colonizing gaze of his audience. Like a number of his urban Maori artist colleagues, he performs his identity and complicates our participation in his staged community. He welcomes us into the bifurcated terrain of his high-tech *marae* and makes us comfortable.

Back in Los Angeles, post-City of Quartz artists working within the legacy of Ed Ruscha's *Sunset Strip* series engage the topography on their own terms. The golden landscape trope, the haze through which the coast is understood has been repositioned in terms of the glaring, banal reality in the city that, seismically speaking, has no right to exist. In 1972, Los Angeles based artist Bill Leavitt made an installation called CALIFORNIA PATIO which was shown at the Pomona College Gallery. He described the banal environment with a potted, grocery store tree and a cheap sliding glass door as evoking a common yet mythic place.[2] Leavitt works in a studio nestled in the trees on the East Side of the Silverlake reservoir. It's a mixed use neighborhood with the highest concentration of modernist domestic architecture anywhere in the United States, alongside casual shacks and lower income bungalows which cling to the hills above the *China Town*-era reservoir. The serene landscapes, which occupy him now, are composite narratives made by conflating cinematic views of the city experienced at night. They are intimate and vaguely reverential. Leavitt reinvests the nightscape with the disjunctive texture of this romantic local where the modernist houses are serviced by the Hispanic population that lives next

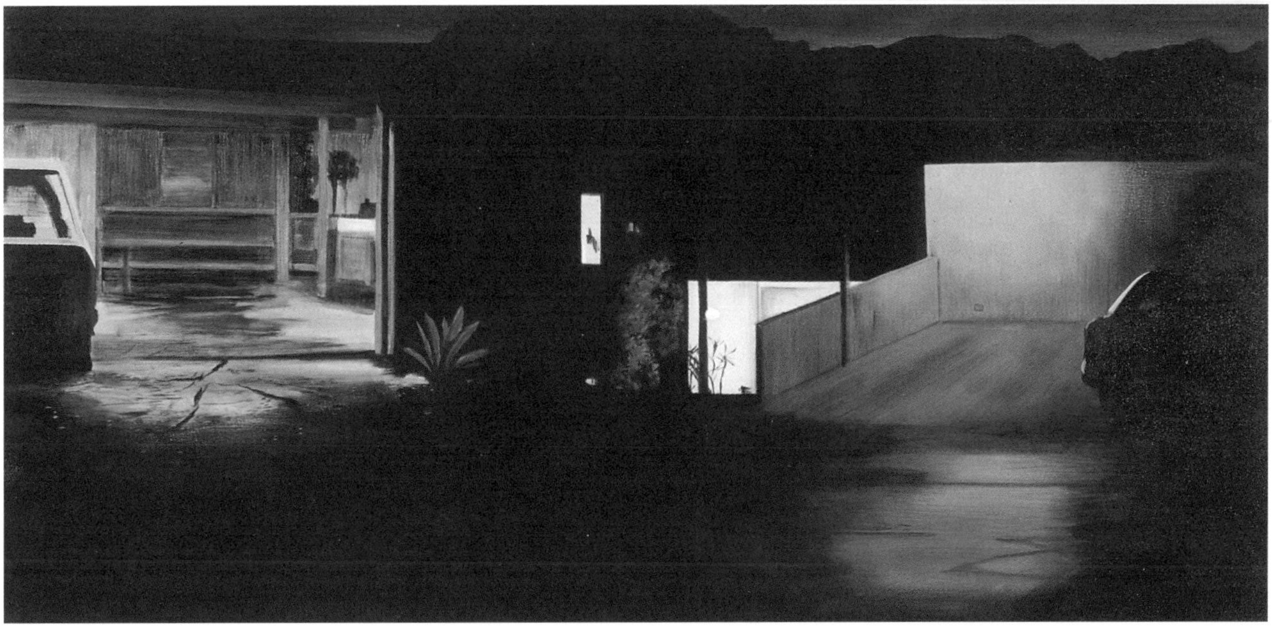

WILLIAM LEAVITT, SILVERLAKE GARAGE AND CARPORT, 1999, oil on canvas, 30 x 60" / SILVERLAKE-GARAGE UND EINSTELLPLATZ, Öl auf Leinwand, 76,2 x 152,4 cm. (PHOTO: MARGO LEAVIN GALLERY, LOS ANGELES)

door to the south of Sunset or the north in Glendale. Beck lives down the street and, on a clear winter day, you can see the San Bernardino mountain range that backs into Las Vegas and Arizona, more or less.

Extending the tradition of the new topographic photographers, whose cool, paired down images focused a reductive, minimalist eye on the exurban west, artists such as Catherine Opie, Miles Coolidge, Christina Fernandez, Jose Alvaro Percides, and others navigate the terrain of mini-malls and prop 187. The Mike Davis imaginary, hyper-catastrophic terrain is remapped by reading through the lived everyday. This is, of course, what Quentin Tarantino has done so brilliantly in his films by recasting Jim Thompson's city noir as the harshly lit, hideously strip-malled city that is experienced at the infuriatingly nowhere speed of 30 miles per hour. Opie, Coolidge, Fernandez, and Percides re-politicize roadside architecture by foregrounding the socio-political which always simmers close to the surface. Opie's multi-cultured mini-malls, Coolidge's serene panoramas of the central valley where migrant workers fuel the economy, and Fernandez's beautiful sweatshop portraits each function as social documents. Percides makes arranged photographs of children playing in the yard at the mostly Hispanic school where he teaches in southeastern Los Angeles. The kids play on the inside of the jungle gym, explore the underneath of their desks and fill in the asphalt cracks of their urban playground. These simple interventions occupy the liminal space between here and there.

Two of the most interesting L.A.-based practices navigating the socially inscribed landscape are the collaborative Center for Land Use Interpretation (C.L.U.I.) and Adobe L.A. C.L.U.I. is a collective of artists, geographers, and interested folk who make Smithsonesque field studies, off site/non-site exhibitions, field trips, and other projects that co-exist comfortably as activism and art making. Calling themselves a "research organization dedicated to improving the collective understanding of the human/land dialectic," they work to recover histories of the dystopic west. Recent exhibitions include photographs of the earthworks in their present, entropic state and the postcards of Merle Porter which form a travelogue of the West Coast.

West of Everything.[3] The rim of the Pacific. On the edge of a vast and generative space. That's where we are, right? I've been thinking about those turn-of-the-century landscapes representing the westward expansion of the frontier which was defined by the 1890 census as the margin of settlement with a density of two or more people per square mile and was declared closed the same year.[4] Now L.A. has a population bigger than all of New Zealand. I remember flying home for the holidays—New York/L.A. There's a point after the Mississippi River where it gets really flat and the land is arranged in mesmerizing patterns of overlapping discs. Circular irrigation. And the light changes too. Or is it the memory of the glistening, harsh white light and shimmering space harnessed by Light and Space artists Robert Irwin, Maria Nordman, and James Turrell working in the lineage of a constructed, European revisioning of the west—the golden, painted light of the chosen land?[5]

I'm fascinated by the notion of the edge one hundred years ago. The middle of the continent delineated as the Mississippi River by the Chicago World's Columbian Exposition in 1893. Indigenous tribes of the south pacific imported for "exhibition" to the northern brink of the western frontier. Yesterday's expositions are today's expo artists traversing the globe and responding to a prescribed nomadism.[6] I'm obsessed by the role of girl architect Mary Jane Colter who, from 1905 to 1939, designed tourist outposts for recreation expansionist Fred Harvey. Appropriating Native American motifs, she adorned the interiors of lodges and rest stops from Kansas City to the end of the line at L.A.'s Union Station. "3000 Miles of Hospitality" was the company's motto. The representation of the west is best understood moving through its landscape: from California's Central Valley to the sprawling urban suburbs of Holy Land, Lakewood, California. Here is where Chris Burden drives his jeep to Topanga Canyon and the eucalyptus trees rustle on the campus of UCLA, where artists take their students on field trips to see earthworks.

Many of the thoughts in this text are drawn from a paper given by the author as part of the "Curating Now" conference organized by the Govett-Brewster Art Gallery, New Plymouth, New Zealand, September 1999.

1) Deborah Solomon, "How to Succeed In Art," *The New York Times Magazine*, June 27, 1999.
2) From "Narrative Statement," artist's statement in conjunction with exhibition at Margo Leavin Gallery, July/August, 1999.
3) Turner, Frederick Jackson, "Significance of the Frontier," *Selected Essays of Frederick Jackson Turner: Frontier and Section*, (Englewood Cliffs, New Jersey: Prentice-Hall, 1961), p. 38.
4) Tompkins, Jane, *West of Everything: The Inner Life of Westerns* (New York: Oxford University Press, 1992).
5) I thank Francis Pound for a recent conversation on the same phenomenon in nineteenth century New Zealand landscape and topographic painting, as well as my New Zealand colleges Jim and Mary Barr, Greg Burke, Wyston Curnow, Giovanni Intra, Robert Leonard, and others for providing an introduction to their landscape.
6) At the Asia Pacific Triennial conference, Manila-based writer and independent curator Marion Pastor Roces explored the notion of "expo art," an idea which has also been invoked by Peter Schjeldahl in conjunction with the recent Venice Biennale.

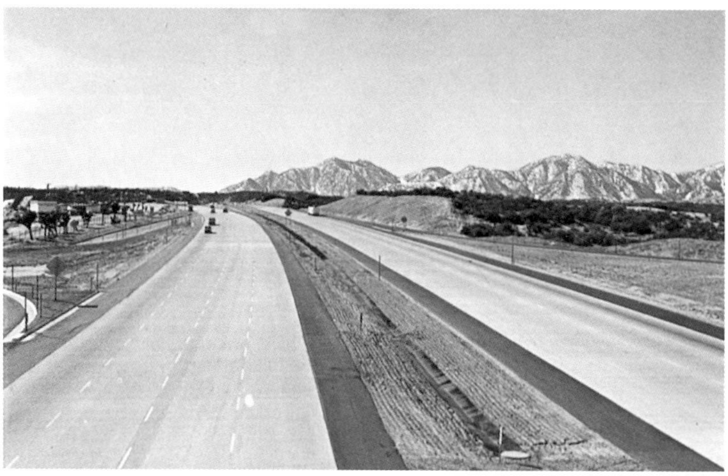

MERLE PORTER, SUMMIT—CAJON PASS, 1985, one of thousands of Porter's unique postcards / CAJON-PASSHÖHE, eine der vielen tausend Postkarten Porters.

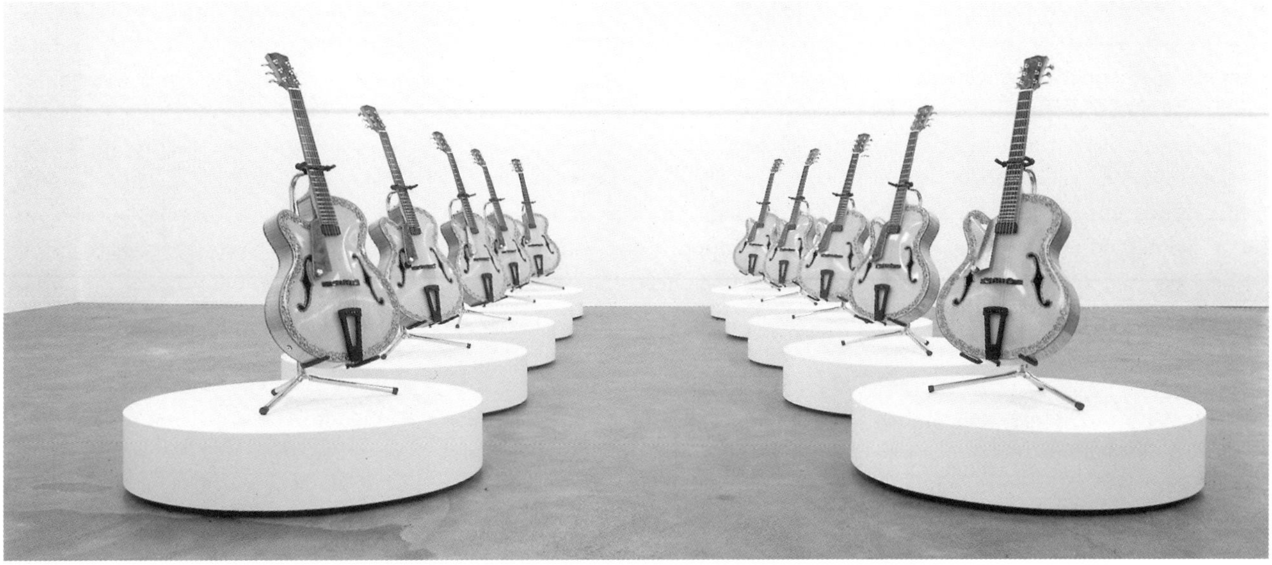

MICHAEL PAREKOWHAI, TEN GUITARS, 1999 / ZEHN GITARREN. (PHOTO: JENNIFER FRENCH)

Westlich von ungefähr allem

CONNIE BUTLER

Michael Parekowhai wird etwas wehmütig, wenn er seine monumentale Skulptur THE INDEFINITE ARTICLE (Der unbestimmte Artikel, 1990) beschreibt. Parekowhai, wie er selbst sagt, ein Maori-Pendant zu Charles Ray, schöpft die Beweglichkeit von Readymade-Texten genüsslich aus in seinen raffinierten Improvisationen über kulturelle Chiffren seiner Heimat Neuseeland. Die Skulptur buchstabiert den Satz «I AM HE» (Ich bin er) in grossen weissen Lettern, die einen bedrohlich überragen und eine undurchdringliche zweieinhalb Meter hohe Schranke bilden. In Neuseeland weiss man, dass das I AM von Colin McCahon stammt, dem beinahe legendären Künstler, der als grösster einheimischer Maler der Moderne verehrt wird. McCahon starb 1987, aber nach wie vor arbeiten alle neuseeländischen Künstler in seinem Schatten. Eine viel versprechende Revitalisierung erfährt er jedoch gerade durch eine Generation junger Künstler, die beschlossen hat, die Legende entweder zu überarbeiten oder einfach zu umgehen.

Parekowhai, der das «HE» zum legendären «I AM» hinzufügte, erinnert sich, dass McCahon die Erfahrung seiner schwermütigen Bilder mit einem Spaziergang im Freien verglich. «He» heisst in Maori auch «falsch» und alle drei Wörter zusammen enthalten fünf Buchstaben aus dem Vornamen des Künstlers. Falscher Ort, falsche Zeit, falscher Künstler – das ist die Identität, die Parekowhai überstreift und mit der er liebevoll herumwerkelt. Er hat sich eine Identität entworfen, die ebenso freundlich «heimatlich» wie sarkastisch ist, kulturkritisch auch, wie er in seiner Show-Parodie TEN GUITARS (1999) vorführt, die für Artspace in Auckland entstand und auch an der letzten Asiatisch-Pazifischen Triennale in Brisbane gezeigt wurde. Er schmeichelt seinem Publikum wie ein waschechter Sinatra mit einem Lied, der alltäglichsten Ausdrucksform in der modernen Maori-Kultur, und mischt den Engelbert-Humperdinck-Folksong «Ten Guitars» neu auf. Abstrakte Leuchtkörper, die die Gitarren einfassen, stehen dabei für die Rippen des *Marae*, des Maori-Gemeinschaftshauses, zugleich ein gemeinschaftlicher und mythischer Ort.

In Maori, der Eingeborenensprache Neuseelands, bedeutet das Wort «maori» gewöhnlich, normal, alltäglich. Was mich interessiert, ist, dass es alles andere als gewöhnlich und alltäglich ist, ein junger Maori-Künstler zu sein, der in einer seit 1990 offiziell bikulturellen Gesellschaft arbeitet, Colin McCahon in der Kunstszene der neuseeländischen Inseln via Duchamp angeht und Ziele anstrebt weit jenseits der Identitätsfalle, die ihm bereits zu einem beträchtlichen Bekanntheitsgrad in der internationalen Kunstwelt verholfen hat. Parekowhai hat ein weites hybrides Gebiet abgesteckt, in dem seine Arbeit jenseits alles Lokalen funktioniert und dennoch tief darin verwurzelt ist. Seine Werke sind treffsicher, wunderbar gearbeitet, etwas eitel und in einer exotischen oder, westlich gesprochen, exotisierenden kulturellen Ecke angesiedelt. Das macht sie zur Provokation.

Die Anziehungskraft von Parekowhais Ort ist unendlich und hat zahlreiche Aspekte. Nicht der geringste ist der heikle Moment, in dem sich die Kunstwelt Neuseelands befindet, die, denke ich, mit der von Los Angeles vergleichbar ist. Ein einheimischer Künstler gab seiner Angst Ausdruck «australisiert» zu werden – verheizt für das flüchtige Interesse der euro-amerikanischen Mainstream-Kunstwelt und internationalisiert durch den fieberhaften Kunsttourismus im Gefolge der Biennale. In neueren Ausstellungen – so «Headlands» (1992 von Aucklands «Artspace»-Kurator Robert Leonard), die auch in Australien gezeigt wurde, oder «Toi, Toi, Toi» (1999 von René Block für das Museum Fridericianum in Kassel und die Auckland Art Gallery organisiert) und «The World Over» (1996 vom Stedelijk Museum und der City Gallery in Wellington auf die Beine gestellt) – beginnt das internationale Kunstpublikum und die Ausstellungsmaschinerie den komplexen Reichtum dessen, was wirklich in diesem am weitesten von Europa entfernten Land vor sich geht, allmählich zu begreifen und theoretisch zu erfassen. Dennoch besteht kein Zweifel darüber, dass die überzeugendste Kunst hier ihre Wurzeln im Ureigenen und Regionalen hat. Junge Künstler fragen sich, wie ihre Arbeit reisen wird, und ich ertappe mich bei der Frage, ob das Reisen sie nicht ruinieren wird.

Ausserhalb Europas und der Vereinigten Staaten – das heisst, westlich des «kein dort, dort», das hier ist – zählt man Los Angeles zu Euro-Amerika, ein dämonisiertes Gespenst des ökonomischen und kulturellen Kolonialismus. Das Leben und Arbeiten in Los Angeles mit all seiner kulturellen Vielfalt, seinen politischen Unfassbarkeiten und Versprechungen (bi-kulturelle Modelle scheinen Lichtjahre entfernt) fordert täglich dazu heraus, diese monolithische Sicht Nordamerikas in Frage zu stellen. Irgendwo zwischen der Überproduktion unausgegorener Kritikerkunst à la McDonalds und der endlosen Abstraktion des L.A.-Modernismus liegt eine unendlich disparatere und bewegtere Identität. An der jüngsten Asiatisch-Pazifischen Triennale kamen alle vier zugelassenen Nordamerikaner (von insgesamt rund siebenhundert Bewerbern) aus dem äussersten Westen der Vereinigten Staaten, insbesondere aus Los Angeles und Texas. Vielleicht dachte man, damit sei der pazifischen Ausrichtung von Ausstellung und Konferenz Genüge getan. Was aus diesem Blickwinkel auffällt, da wir nun mal in der Mitte der Küste beider Amerikas am Rand des Pazifiks sitzen: Der Blick nach Westen (statt nach Osten, nach Europa via New York, wie ihn die Kunstszene von Los Angeles nach wie vor und ausschliesslich pflegt) entspräche der global-lokalen Identität des heutigen Los Angeles wohl viel eher und bedeutete endlich ein produktives, kuratorisches Rechenschaft Ablegen dieser eindeutig nicht-europäischen, sondern tatsächlich asiatischen und lateinamerikanischen Stadt.

Der besondere Provinzialismus von Los Angeles (etwa im Gegensatz zu New York) bietet den Schwindel erregenden Eindruck, von einer reichen Geschichte der Kunst befreit zu sein, die wir erst in jüngster Zeit schätzen gelernt haben, und ganz im Banne des blühenden Internationalismus zu stehen. So ist es zum Beispiel nicht ungewöhnlich, jungen Malern zu begegnen, die noch nie von Lee Mullican gehört haben, dem kürzlich verstorbenen Maler aus Kalifornien, dessen ergreifend schöne Arbeiten das ergiebige und theoretisch wenig erforschte Gebiet des Verhältnisses zwischen ursprünglicher amerikanischer Kultur und Moderne ausloten. In den 40er und frühen 50er Jahren vereinte Mullicans Stil (zusammen mit Malerkollegen wie Gordon Onslow Ford und Wolfgang Paalen) im sogenannt «dynatonischen» Zeitgeist den heimischen Mystizismus mit einer abstrakten Sprache, die auf Quellen wie die Sandbilder der Navajo zurückging.

Der programmatische «Internationalismus» der Westküstenmuseen, die sich der Kunst des zwanzigsten Jahrhunderts widmen, ist absolut europäisch ausgerichtet, trotz der zurzeit stattfindenden, allfälliger Kritik vorbeugenden Vorstösse nach Lateinamerika. Die kulturelle Vielfalt dieser Stadt und ihre geographische Randlage am Pazifik werden nur im Rahmen eines theoretisierenden Multikulturalismus angesprochen. Das mochte im letzten Jahrzehnt noch angemessen sein, aber das Los Angeles nach den Rassenkrawallen verlangt eine differenziertere, postkolonialistische Antwort. Wenn man hier arbeitet, verinnerlicht man die lokalen und globalen Imperative gleichermassen, was vielleicht analog für die Ausstellungsarbeit in jeder Kunstmetropole gilt, die nicht zugleich wirtschaftliches Zentrum ist, und das ist nach wie vor und unleugbar New York. An einer Podiumsdiskussion über internationale Ausstellungen (organisiert vom MAK Center im Schindler House, Los Angeles, 1998) liess sich Okwui Enwezor (noch bevor er zum Leiter der kommenden «Documenta» ernannt wurde) über die Unsichtbarkeit der schwarzen Künstler sowie der Künstler lateinamerikanischer oder asiatischer Abstammung in den bedeutenden Galerien aus. Bewaffnet mit E-Mail und Handy steigern sich internationale Besucher von Los Angeles in eine Art kuratorischen Sammeleifer und wollen immer dieselben acht Künstler sehen, wobei sie gern verges-

ADOBE L.A., LA POSADA: DIVINE INTERVENTIONS ON THE L.A. BORDER OR THE ARCHITECTURE OF MIRACLES, 1996, collective project */ DAS GASTHAUS: GÖTTLICHE INTERVENTION AN DER GRENZE VON L.A. ODER DIE ARCHITEKTUR DER WUNDER,* Kollektivprojekt.

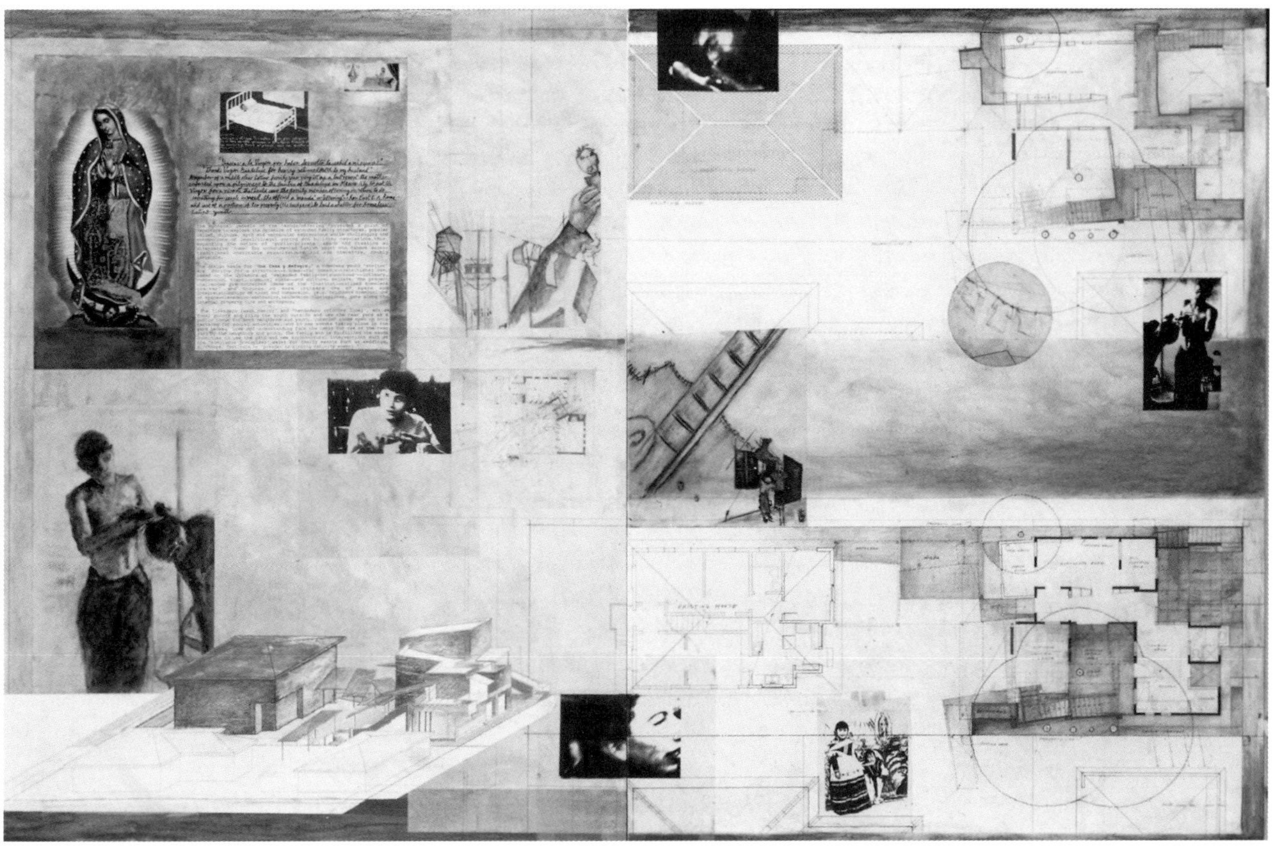

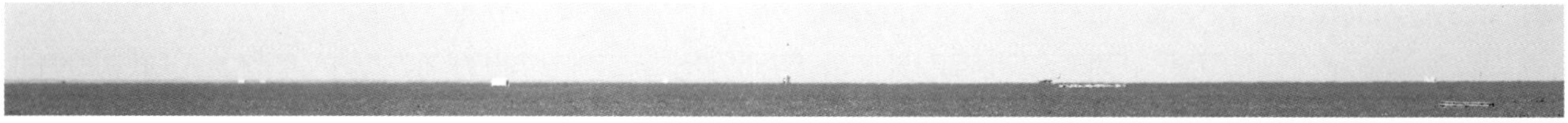

MILES COOLIDGE, NEAR TULARE LAKE, 1998, color photograph mounted on galvanized steel over magnetic strip, 10 ¾ x 133" / AM TULARE-SEE, Farbphotographie auf verzinktem Stahl mit Magnetstreifen, 27,3 x 337,8 cm. (PHOTO: ACME, LOS ANGELES)

sen, dass alles in Los Angeles meilenweit und mehrere Autostunden voneinander entfernt ist. Während der 90er Jahre erreichte das Interesse für Los Angeles seinen Siedepunkt. Der Höhenflug begann 1992 mit dem Paukenschlag der Ausstellung «Helter Skelter: L.A. Art in the 1990s» (organisiert vom Kurator des Museum of Contemporary Art, Paul Schimmel), die die schwarzen Züge, die sogenannten «Noir»-Tendenzen im Kunstschaffen von L.A. unter die Lupe nahm. Neu verpackt und in etwas übertriebener Form in ganz Europa herumgereicht, gehören diese Künstler nun zur ersten Generation, die ökonomisch von der L.A.-Mania profitiert. Die Ausstellung «Sunshine and Noir» des Louisiana Museum, 1996, stellte den absoluten Höhepunkt eines «Cumulus aus Amerika» dar, der seinen Ursprung in Europa hatte, versehentlich über den Atlantik verschifft wurde und schliesslich in Los Angeles landete. Irgendwie trafen diese Ausstellungen mit ihrer verschlungenen, nach allen Seiten offenen *Sign-Design*-Ästhetik und den witzigen, schlagzeilenartigen Zeitschriften-Titeln nie wirklich ins Schwarze. Bezeichnend ist die Tatsache, dass viele sich ihrer Herkunft bewusste, aus Mexiko oder Lateinamerika stammende Künstler, die an der «Helter Skelter»-Ausstellung noch teilgenommen hatten, von den europäischen Versionen derselben ausgeschlossen blieben. Die Arbeiten von Leuten wie Victor Estrada oder Manuel Ocampo werden oft anhand von Werken Mike Kelleys oder Paul McCarthys interpretiert, deren Einflüsse man wiederum in den mehrheitlich weissen mittelständischen Traditionen der Performance und des Feminismus in Los Angeles findet – die beide ebenfalls noch ihrer Dokumentation und Ausstellung harren.

Das Geschrei und die Legendenbildung um Kunst und Künstler in Los Angeles erreichten ihre extremste Hysterie mit der jüngsten Artikelflut über die lokalen Kunstschulen: Das *New York Times Magazine* konnte gar nicht schnell genug den atemberaubenden Bockmist aufgreifen, den *Artforum* im letzten Frühjahr publiziert hatte. Im Bemühen mit L.A. kurzen Prozess zu machen beeilte sich New York das Porträt der UCLA-Kids, das die Zeitschrift *Spin* im üblichen MTV-Stil gezeichnet hatte, noch zu überbieten. Jeder der jungen Künstler wurde in Farbe und mit seinem Werkzeug in der Hand abgebildet, nur um die laufende Debatte (an der hier eigentlich niemand beteiligt ist) noch mehr anzuheizen, dass das Art Center die Schule sei, die denke und nichts tue, und UCLA (University of California, L.A.) die Schule, die ... Sie merken, worauf es hinausläuft. Eine Multiplikation allzu simpler Vereinfachungen: Der Blick auf die Biographie und ein historischer Revisionismus verdrängen die eigentlichen historischen Entwicklungen. Das Feministische Kunstprogramm von Cal Arts, die Pomona College Art Gallery und die Irvine Art Gallery der University of California trugen alle zum Erkennen der frühen Entwicklungen von Environment- und Konzeptkunst bei. Die Anfangszeilen des Artikels im *New York Times Magazine* mögen einen Eindruck von diesem «Auf dem Sprung nach Hollywood»-Journalismus vermitteln:

Chris Burden begann seine Karriere buchstäblich mit einem Knall. Für sein SHOOTING PIECE musste ihm ein Freund aus einer Distanz von viereinhalb Metern eine Kugel in den linken Arm schiessen. Vielleicht deshalb fand ich es, als ich ihn kürzlich an der University of California traf, so schwer, mir vorzustellen, dass er geduldig in Fakultätssitzungen ausharrte. Die Zeit vollbringt merkwürdige Dinge. Man muss nur lange genug warten und selbst die wildesten Rebellen verteilen schliesslich Noten für Aufsätze und geben ihren Studenten Karrieretipps ... Es war ein strahlender Nachmittag und in der Luft lag der Duft von Eukalyptus ...[1)]

Und so wächst der Mythos in einer exponentiellen Kurve ins Unendliche. Will etwa jemand andeuten, es wäre besser gewesen, Chris Burden hätte während seiner Performance-Arbeit als Student einen frühzeitigen Tod erlitten, statt hinzugehen und sich sein eigenes Studio im Topanga Canyon zu bauen und nun angehende Künstler zu lehren dasselbe zu tun?

Ich habe schon daran gedacht, für eine Neueinschätzung der L.A.-Exotik zu pladieren. Liessen sich Fiktion und Alltag, jedes immer schon eine vermittelte Wahrheit der anderen Seite, irgendwie in eine Ordnung bringen? Denken wir einen Moment an Neuseeland zurück: Die Spannweite zwischen dem Auckland der Zeitschrift *Wallpaper*, den *Pakeha*-Girls (weisse Mädchen) mit ihren Schellenröckchen und Maori-Federn im Haar und Michael Parekowhais Bi-Kulturalität umspannt ein eindrückliches Gebiet. Parekowhais exotische und zugleich entexotisierte Figur des «anständigen Kerls» positioniert ihn gerade knapp ausserhalb der Reichweite des kolonisierenden Blicks seines Publikums. Wie einige seiner Maori-Künstlerkollegen aus der Stadt führt er seine Identität vor und macht damit unsere Teilnahme an seiner Bühnengemeinschaft etwas komplizierter. Er heisst uns willkommen auf dem zwiespältigen Terrain seines Hightech-*Marae* und lässt es uns gut gehen.

Drüben in Los Angeles behandeln die Post-*City-of-Quartz*-Künstler[2], die noch unter dem Einfluss von Ed Ruschas *Sunset-Strip*-Bildern arbeiten, die Topographie nach eigenen Regeln. Der Tropus der idealen Landschaft, der goldene Schleier, durch den man diese Küste zu sehen pflegte, macht allmählich der augenfälligen, banalen Realität des Lebens in dieser Stadt Platz, die seismologisch betrachtet gar nicht existieren dürfte. 1972 schuf der in Los Angeles arbeitende Künstler Bill Leavitt eine Installation namens CALIFORNIA PATIO (Kalifornien-Innenhof), die in der Pomona College Gallery gezeigt wurde. Er gab die banale Umgebung durch den eingetopften Baum eines Gemüseladens und eine billige Glasschiebetür wieder, so dass man sich an einen alltäglichen und dennoch mythischen Ort erinnert fühlte.[3] Leavitt arbeitet in einem Studio, das zwischen Bäumen eingebettet auf der Ostseite des Silverlake-Reservoirs liegt. Es ist eine Gegend, die auf unterschiedlichste Weise genutzt wird und die mit der grössten Dichte moderner Wohnarchitektur in den Vereinigten Staaten aufwarten kann, dicht neben bescheidenen Schuppen und einfachen Bungalows, die oberhalb des alten Reservoirs aus der *Chinatown*-Ära am Hang kleben. Die heiteren Landschaften, die ihn heute beschäftigen, sind zusammengesetzte «Geschichten»; sie entstehen in einem Verdichtungsprozess aus gefilmten nächtlichen Stadtansichten. Sie wirken intim und leicht ehrfürchtig. Leavitt verleiht der Nachtlandschaft wiederum die zwiespältige Wirkung dieser romantischen Gegend, wo moderne Villen von einer spanisch sprechenden Bevölkerung sauber gehalten werden, die selbst südlich des Sunset Boulevard oder weiter nördlich in Glendale wohnt. Beck wohnt etwas weiter die Strasse runter und an einem klaren Wintertag kann man den San-Bernardino-Hügelzug sehen, hinter dem Las Vegas und Arizona liegen, mehr oder weniger.

Künstlerinnen und Künstler wie Catherine Opie, Miles Coolidge, Christina Fernandez, Jose Alvaro Percides und andere haben die Tradition der neuen Landschaftsphotographie, deren kühle, knappe Bilder einen reduktiv minimalistischen Blick auf den Westen ausserhalb der städtischen Zentren werfen, erweitert und beackern den Boden der kleinen Einkaufszentren

CHRISTINA FERNANDEZ, TT&T FASHIONS, 1996,
color print, 30 x 40"/ Farbprint, 76,2 x 101,6 cm.

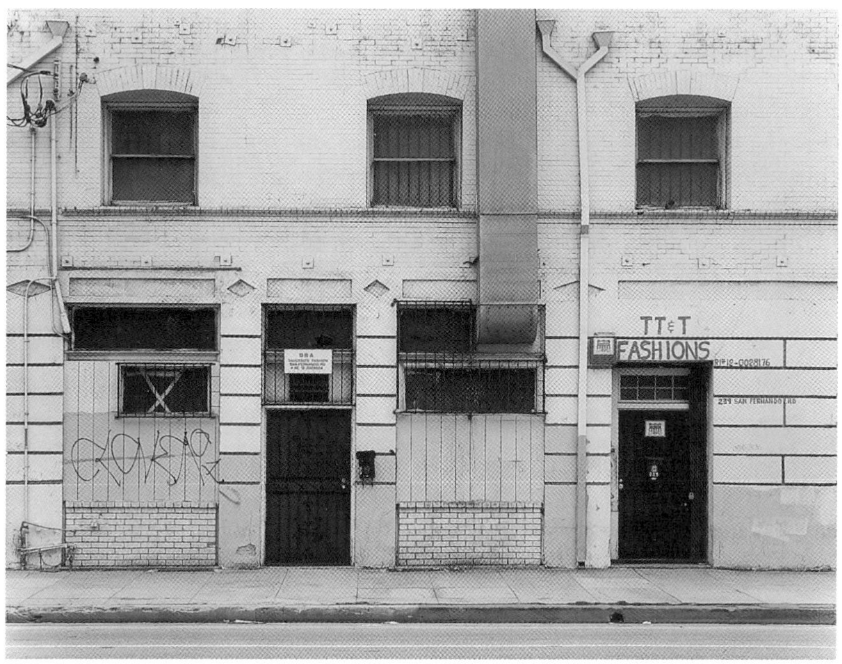

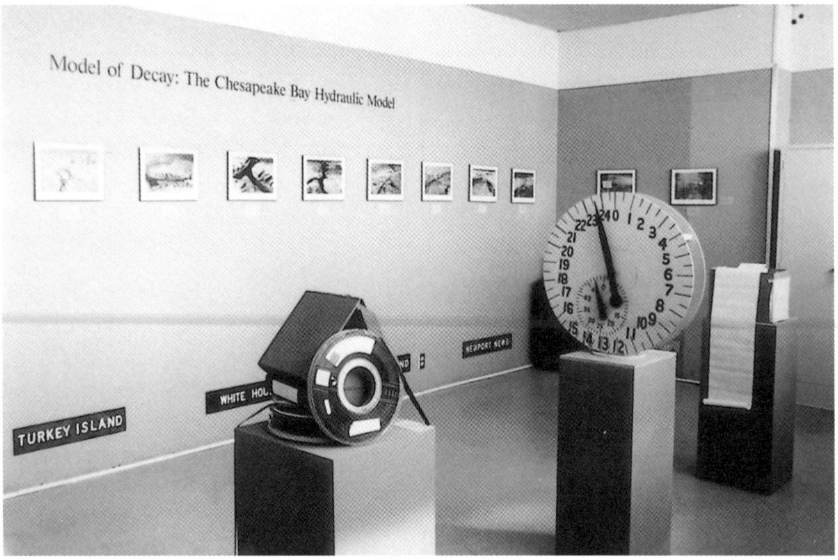

"Model of Decay": Chesapeake Bay Hydraulic Model, installation view at CLUI, Los Angeles, 1998 / «Zerfallsmodell»: Chesapeake-Bay-Pumpenmodell, Ausstellung im CLUI, Los Angeles.

und der gesetzlichen Verordnung 187 (Massnahmen gegen illegale Einwanderer). Mike Davis' Bild des imaginären Superkatastrophengebiets erfährt im Licht des gelebten Alltags eine Korrektur. Und das ist natürlich genau, was Quentin Tarantino in seinen Filmen so grossartig vorführt, wenn er Jim Thompsons düstere Verbrecherstadt als grell beleuchtete, endlose Einkaufsmeile reinszeniert, die im irrwitzigen Nulltempo von 30 Meilen pro Stunde abgefahren werden muss. Opie, Coolidge, Fernandez und Percides repolitisieren die Architektur entlang dieser Strassen, indem sie sozialpolitische Aspekte in den Vordergrund rücken, die überall unmittelbar unter der Oberfläche brodeln. Opies multikulturelle Mini-Einkaufszentren, Coolidges heitere Panoramen des Central Valley, dessen Wirtschaft von Gastarbeitern in Schwung gehalten wird, sowie Fernandez' wunderbare Porträts von schlecht bezahlten Fabrikarbeitern sind allesamt gesellschaftliche Dokumente. Percides macht gestellte Photos von spielenden Kindern auf dem Schulhof der vorwiegend von Einwanderern besuchten Schule im Südwesten von Los Angeles, in der er unterrichtet. Die Kinder spielen zwischen den Kletterstangen, untersuchen die Unterseite ihrer Pulte und füllen die Spalten im Asphalt ihres urbanen Spielplatzes auf. Diese einfachen Interventionen bewegen sich auf der Schwelle zwischen hier und dort.

Zwei der interessantesten Versuche im Umgang mit der gesellschaftlich geprägten Landschaft in L.A. sind das Center for Land Use Interpretation (CLUI) und Adobe L.A. CLUI ist ein Kollektiv von Künstlern, Geographen und anderen interessierten Leuten, die Feldstudien in der Art von Smithson, Off-site- und Non-site-Ausstellungen, Feldforschungsreisen und andere Projekte durchführen, die problemlos als gesellschaftliches Engagement oder Kunst akzeptiert werden, und damit ihr Auskommen finden. Sie bezeichnen sich selbst als «wissenschaftliche Organisation zur Verbesserung des kollektiven Verständnisses der dialektischen Beziehung zwischen Mensch und Landschaft» und versuchen Geschichten eines dystopischen Westens auszugraben. Neuere Ausstellungen zeigen Photographien der *Earthworks* in ihrem gegenwärtigen entropischen Zustand sowie die Postkarten von Merle Porter, die einen einzigen grossartigen Reisebericht von der Westküste abgeben.

Westlich von allem.[4] Am Ufer des Pazifik. Am Rand eines ungeheuren und fruchtbaren Raumes. Da befinden wir uns, nicht? Ich habe über jene Landschaftsbilder der Jahrhundertwende nachgedacht, die die Erweiterung der Grenze nach Westen darstellen, welche in der Volkszählung von 1890 mit einer Siedlungsdichte von zwei oder mehr Leuten pro Quadratmeile begründet und im selben Jahr als abgeschlossen erklärt wurde.[5] Heute ist die Bevölkerungszahl von Los Angeles grösser als jene von ganz Neuseeland. Ich erinnere mich an einen Flug nach Hause über die Feiertage, New York–Los Angeles. Da kommt ein Punkt nach dem Überfliegen des Mississippi, wo es wirklich flach wird und das Land als faszinierendes Muster sich überschneidender Scheiben erscheint. Kreisförmig angelegte Bewässerungsanlagen. Auch das Licht wechselt. Oder ist es nur die Erinnerung an das gleissende, grellweisse Licht und den schimmernden Raum in der Hand von Licht- und Raumkünstlern wie Robert Irwin, Maria Nordman und James Turrell, die in der direkten Nachfolge einer konstruierten, europäischen Neuinterpretation des Westens arbeiten: das goldene, malerische Licht des auserwählten Landes?[6)]

Ich finde interessant, was vor hundert Jahren als Randzone galt: Während der Kolumbien-Ausstellung im Rahmen der Weltausstellung von Chicago 1893 schien sie noch entlang des Mississippi in der Mitte des Kontinents zu verlaufen. Eingeborenenstämme aus dem südlichen Pazifik wurden zu Ausstellungszwecken zum nördlichsten Zipfel der Westgrenze gebracht. Den Ausstellungen von gestern entsprechen die ausstellenden Künstler von heute, die auf dem Globus herumreisen und gezwungenermassen ein Nomadenleben führen.[7)] Mich fasziniert auch die Rolle, die die junge Architektin Mary Jane Colter spielte, die von 1905 bis 1939 für Fred Harvey, den Inhaber einer aufstrebenden Imbisskette, Touristenlokale entwarf. Unter Verwendung indianischer Motive dekorierte sie die Innenräume von Rasthäusern und Autorestaurants von Kansas City bis ans Ende der Kette bei der Los Angeles Union Station. «3000 Meilen Gastfreundschaft», lautete das Motto der Firma. Die Darstellung des Westens versteht man am besten, wenn man sich durch seine Landschaft bewegt: vom Central Valley bis zu den endlosen Vororten von Holy Land, Lakewood, Kalifornien. Das ist der Ort, wo Chris Burden seinen Jeep zum Topanga Canyon lenkt und wo die Eukalyptusbäume auf dem Campus der University of California, L.A. rauschen, wo Künstler ihre Schüler auf Feldforschungstrips mitnehmen und ihnen die *Earthworks* zeigen.

(Übersetzung: Wilma Parker)

Die Gedanken in diesem Text stammen zum grossen Teil aus einem Beitrag der Autorin zur Konferenz «Curating Now» im September 1999, organisiert von der Govett-Brewster Art Gallery in Plymouth, Neuseeland.

1) Deborah Solomon, «How to Succeed in Art», *The New York Times Magazine*, 27. Juni 1999.
2) *City of Quartz: Excavating the Future of Los Angeles* lautet der Titel einer Studie von Mike Davis (Vintage Books, New York 1992; Verso, London 1990). Demselben Buch ist auch der Ausstellungstitel «Sunshine & Noir» entliehen.
3) Aussage des Künstlers anlässlich einer Ausstellung in der Margo Leavin Gallery, Los Angeles, im Juli/August 1999.
4) Frederick Jackson Turner, «Significance of the Frontier», *Selected Essays of Frederick Jackson Turner: Frontier and Section*, Prentice-Hall, Englewood Cliffs, New Jersey, 1961, S. 38.
5) Jane Tompkins, *West of Everything: The Inner Life of Westerns*, Oxford University Press, New York 1992.
6) An dieser Stelle möchte ich Francis Pound danken für das kürzlich geführte Gespräch über dasselbe Phänomen in Neuseelands Landschaftsmalerei des neunzehnten Jahrhunderts sowie meinen neuseeländischen Kollegen Jim und Mary Barr, Greg Burke, Wyston Curnow, Giovanni Intra, Robert Leonard u.a. dafür, dass sie mich mit ihrer Landschaft vertraut gemacht haben.
7) An der Konferenz zur Asiatisch-Pazifischen Triennale durchleuchtete Marion Pastor Roces, freischaffende Autorin und Kuratorin aus Manila, den Begriff der Ausstellungskunst, den auch Peter Schjeldahl im Zusammenhang mit der jüngsten Biennale in Venedig ins Spiel brachte.

MARY E. J. COLTER, WATCHTOWER, ca. 1932, commercial photo signed by Mary E. J. Colter / WACHTTURM, signiertes Reklamephoto. (PHOTO: FRED HARVEY CO./GRAND CANYON NATIONAL PARK MUSEUM)

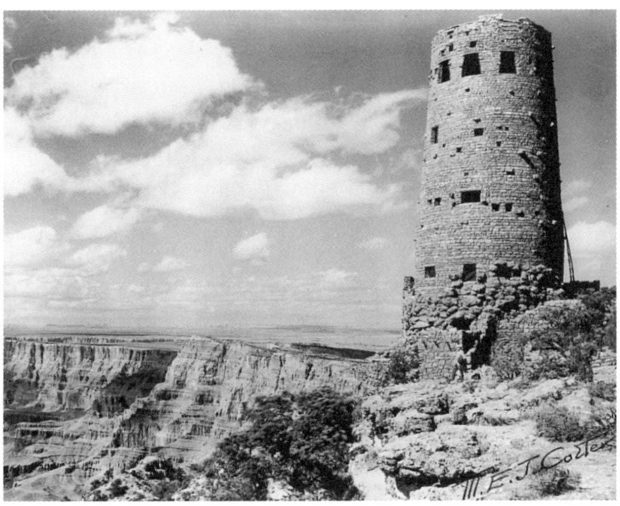

MARY E. J. COLTER, LOOKOUT STUDIO FRONT ENTRANCE, ca. 1915 / AUSSICHTSRAUM, VORDEREINGANG. (PHOTO: FRED HARVEY CO./GRAND CANYON NATIONAL PARK MUSEUM)

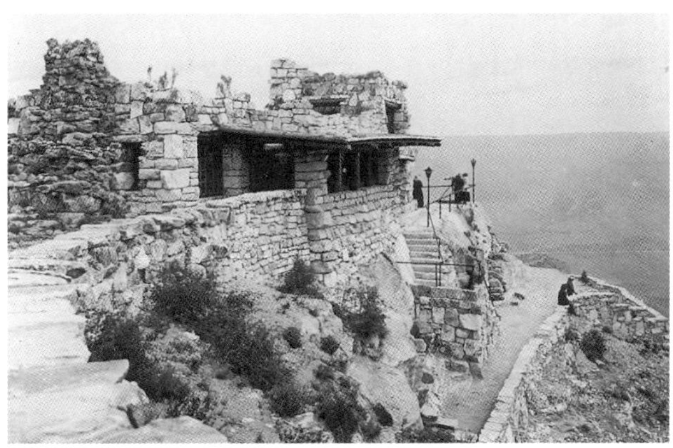

JURI STEINER

BALKON

Fouiller entre les mots

In einer Zeit, in der die Kommunikation nicht mehr ohne «Tele» auskommt und an Firmen wie diAx, Orange oder Swisscom verpachtet ist, spuken Annelise Costes Nachrichten durch den SMS-Briefkasten meines Handys: Es sind kryptische Kühlschrankbotschaften, die Annelise an die binären Pinboards ihrer Bekannten heftet. Der digitale Briefumschlag auf dem Display blinkt, über die «Menu»-Taste ruft man sie ab.

Und wie ihre Nachrichten spukt Annelise selbst durch Zürichs Kunstzirkel. Das erste Mal traf ich sie Anfang 1998 in der Bibliothek des Kunsthauses, leidlich aufgeschmissen, ein Greenhorn aus Marseille, ohne Wissen um die Benutzungsbestimmungen der schweizerischen Institution. Sie sprach nicht viel, ausschliesslich Französisch, leise mit leichter Rebellen-Attitüde hinter burschikoser Tristesse: Annelise, Gaststudentin an der Hochschule für Gestaltung und Kunst, Zürich.

Das Erste, was sie mir zeigte, waren zwei ungeschnittene Videos. Bei beiden handelte es sich um Poetisierungen des Alltags. Zum einen inszenierte Annelise ein Wettrennen zwischen zwei Tramhaltestellen mit den Linien 13 beziehungsweise 4. Das andere Tape dokumentierte den Versuch, die permanent unterkühlte Temperatur Zürichs qua Sympathie zu steigern.

Das Tram-Piece war amüsant: Die Linie 4 gab der jungen Sprinterin keine Chance und fuhr mit voller Kraft davon. Die intrigierte Chauffeuse dachte wohl, dass es sich bei der neben dem Tramzug herhastenden Annelise um einen ausgeflippten Junkie handle. Die Linie 13 wurde von einem Gentleman chauffiert, der Annelise höflich siegen liess.

Das Temperatur-Video wurde unter dem grossen Thermometer an der Tramhaltestelle Bahnhofquai gedreht. Freundinnen und Freunde fanden sich bei der grossen rot leuchtenden LCD-Anzeige ein um allein kraft ihrer guten Vibes die Grade klettern zu lassen – was erstaunlicherweise gelang.

Die Videos gehören zur Zeit des Aktionismus von 1998. Inzwischen hat Annelise eine Einzelausstellung in Zürichs Kleinem Helmhaus hinter sich, jener städtischen Institution, die vor ein paar Jahren in die Schlagzeilen kam, als der Stadtpräsident höchstpersönlich Ellen Cantors Porno-Kunst zensierte.

War der soziale Impact von Annelises Videos noch auf kondensierte Momente konzentriert, so gestaltete sie ihre Ausstellung vom vergangenen Frühling zum Dauer-Happening. Schlafen, essen, zeichnen – alles vor Ort. An die weissen Wände heftete sie Blatt um Blatt ihre Messages mit ziemlich eindeutigem Tagebuchcharakter.

Liebe und Hass geben die Parameter, auch Einsamkeit; dazwischen stehen zeichnerische Ausflüge, die die rohe Kalligraphie verlassen, ab und an ein Vögelchen und immer wiederkehrend eine aus vollen Rohren urinierende Metamaschine: «Bizarreries, férocité, monstruosité», steht dazu auf einem Blatt. Kunsthistorische Referenzpunkte sind Kippenbergers Hotelzeichnungen und Grigelys Notizblock: Wie Kalifilter und Dufterfrischer läutern diese Grössen Annelises Poesie. Pissoirpoesie?

Der flüchtige Gedanke wird flüchtig niedergeschrieben, falsche Syntax durchgestrichen. Der knappe Hass, die kleine Sehnsucht erhält als Text griffige Wichtigkeit, bleibt standhaft im Raum und raunzt Unartiges in die Runde, Unartiges und Aufrichtiges, das sich nicht an das anonyme Lustobjekt irgendwo da draussen wendet, sondern wohl an einen konkreten oder zumindest angedachten Sparringpartner für den Vollkontakt. Daniele Buetti oder Thomas Hirschhorn sind kontrollierte Akademiker im Vergleich zu Annelise Coste, die, wenn sie von Leidenschaft und Lust schreibt, zur Inkorporation ihrer Botschaft wird, eine Anaïs Nin der kurzen Liebes- und Abschiedsbriefe. Auch wenn sich in ihren Arbeiten, die sie Dessins nennt, radebrechende Typographie und Kalligraphie als Kunst und Literatur vereinen, so liefert Annelise keine Erosmatrix Greenawayschen Zuschnitts. Annelise «fouille entre les mots», wie sie sagt, sie stöbert wie eine belletristische Partisanin zwischen den Worten, um auf das zu stossen, was die Orange-Sektenanhänger uns im warmluftigen, kalifornischen Steppensand vorgaukeln: qualitativ intensivierte Kommunikation gegen Platitüden.

JURI STEINER ist Kritiker und Ausstellungsmacher und lebt in Zürich.

Fouiller entre les mots

JURI STEINER

In an age in which communication can no longer do without "tele" and has been leased to such companies as diAx, Orange, or Swisscom, news from Annelise Coste haunts my mobile phone's SMS mailbox. She puts cryptic fridge messages on her friends' binary pin boards. The digital envelope blinks on the display and you push the menu button to call them up.

And like her messages, Annelise herself haunts Zurich's art circle. I met her for the first time in early 1998 where she was adrift at the Kunsthaus library, a greenhorn from Marseilles, ignorant of the Swiss institution's user regulations. She did not talk much, and only French, softly, with a touch of the rebel behind her boyish tristessa: Annelise, visiting student at the Zurich School of Art and Design.

The first thing she showed me were two uncut videos of poeticized daily life. In one of them she stages a race between two stops with the streetcar lines 13 and 4. The other video attempts to enlist sympathy in the enhancement of Zurich's permanently subnormal temperatures.

The streetcar piece was amusing: The number 4 line, accelerating full speed ahead, didn't give the young sprinter half a chance. The intrigued driver probably wrote off the woman racing alongside her vehicle as some crazed junky. In contrast, the gentleman driver of the number 13 line graciously permitted Annelise to win.

The temperature video was filmed under the large thermometer at the Bahnhofquai streetcar stop. Friends stationed themselves next to the big red lettering of the LCD display hoping that their good vibes would make the temperature rise—which they did, to everyone's surprise.

The videos belong to the period of actionism in 1998. Annelise has since been given a solo exhibition at the Kleines Helmhaus in Zurich, the municipal institution that made headlines a few years back when the city's mayor took it upon himself to personally censor Ellen Cantor's porno art.

While the social impact of Annelise's videos focused on a single, condensed incident, she designed her exhibition last spring as a nonstop happening. Sleeping, eating, drawing—all on site. In the end the white walls were covered with sheet after sheet of unmistakably diary-like messages.

Love and hate defined the parameters, and loneliness too, with bursts of drawing in between that abandoned the coarse calligraphy and showed the occasional little bird and a constantly recurring meta-machine urinating out of full tubes. Next to it a piece of paper read *bizarreries, férocité, monstruosité.* Art historical points of reference are Kippenberger's hotel drawings and Grigely's notebook, like water filters and air fresheners purifying Annelise's poetry. Pissoir poesy?

The fleeting thought fleetingly noted down, faulty syntax crossed out. Lean hatred and petty longing acquire gripping importance as text, stand firmly in space, and eject wayward complaints, wayward candor that does not address some anonymous, detached object of desire, but rather a concrete or at least specifically envisioned sparring partner for total contact. Daniele Buetti and Thomas Hirschhorn are controlled academics in comparison to Annelise Coste, who turns into her own message incarnate when she writes about passion and pleasure, an Anaïs Nin of brief love letters and briefer good-byes. Even though mangled typography and calligraphy are united as art and literature in her works, which she calls *dessins*, Annelise does not deliver an Eros matrix of Greenaway ilk. Annelise *fouille entre les mots*, as she puts it herself; she ransacks words like a belletristic partisan, digging up something akin to what Orange sectarians flaunt in the breezy warmth of Californian sands: qualitatively intensified communication versus platitudes.

(Translation: Catherine Schelbert)

JURI STEINER is a critic and curator who lives in Zurich.

MUCH i LOVE YOU

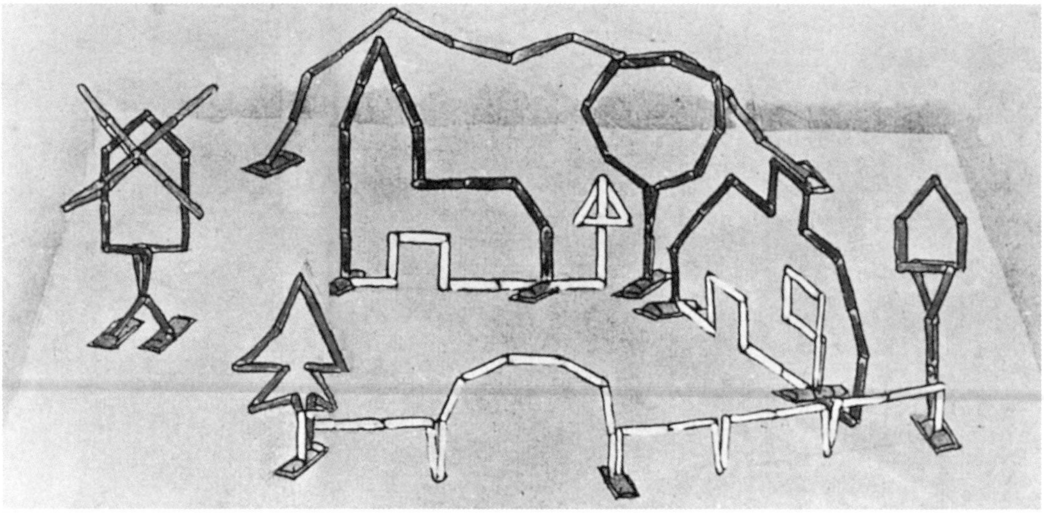

DAS ZOLLSTOCKSPIEL, 1928 / THE YARDSTICK GAME.
Morgenstern, Polke, Slominski: Dieses Spiel hat Tradition / A game with tradition.

(BILD: M. BAUER, CH. MORGENSTERNS LEBEN & WERK)

Garderobe

'gär-ˌdrōb

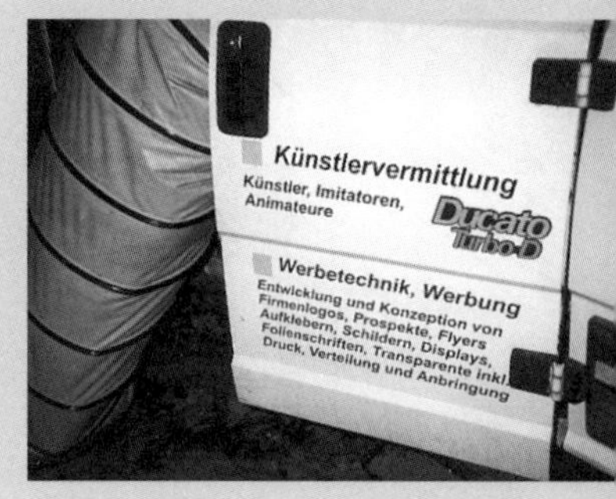

(PHOTO: FLAVIA VOG

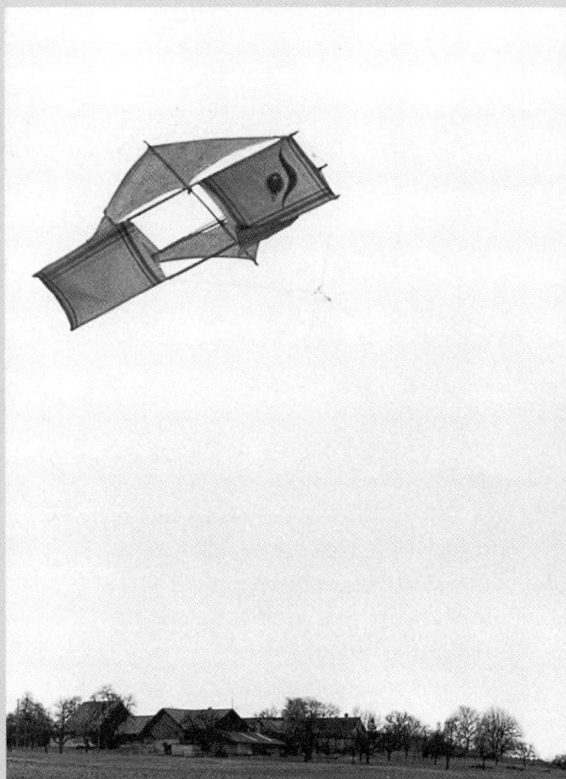

ANA LAPTROP, NONREFLECTING KITE OVER BETTWIL, 1973

Stipendium / Bourse 2000 Centre genevois de gravure contemporain

Zur Förderung von zeitgenössischen Druckgraphik- und Multiple-Editionen vergibt da Centre genevois de gravure contemporaine für das Jahr 2000 ein Stipendium von F 6000.– an Künstlerinnen und Künstler aus der Schweiz oder dem Ausland, die ein en sprechendes Projekt einreichen. Das Stipendium wird in Partnerschaft mit der UBS Genf, vergeben.
Eingabeschluss ist Mittwoch, der 1. März 2000. Anmeldeformulare sind auf Anfrage e hältlich. Weitere Auskünfte und Unterlagen erhalten Sie bei Julien Babel, Centre gen vois de gravure contemporaine, Montag bis Freitag, 14 bis 17 Uhr (vom 23. Dezember b 10. Januar geschlossen).

Dans le but d'encourager l'édition et de promouvoir l'art imprimé (gravure, sérigraphi offset, ...) et le multiple (livre d'artiste, livre-objet, objet, ...) dans la création artistiqu contemporaine, le Centre genevois de gravure contemporaine décernera pour l'anné 2000 une bourse d'un montant de 6000 Sfr., destinée à des artistes suisses ou étrange qui présenteront un projet dans le but de produire une édition.
Cette bourse 2000 est attribuée avec le partenariat de l'UBS SA, Genève.
Le règlement et les formulaires d'inscription sont disponibles sur simple demande. L inscriptions seront définitivement closes le mercredi 1er mars 2000. Pour toute précisio ou renseignement complémentaire, veuillez vous adresser à Julien Babel, du lundi au ve dredi, de 14.00 à 18.00 (Le Centre reste fermé du 23 décembre 1999 au 10 janvier 2000.)

Centre genevois de gravure contemporaine, 17 route de Malagnou, CH-1208 Genèv
Tel.: 022-735 12 60; Fax: 022-735 28 97

Anzeigenbedingungen: Kauf eines Abonnements bzw. eines Geschenkabonnements be Platzierung eines Inserates. / Advertising rates: Order of one (gift) subscription per ad

PARKETT

ARTISTS' EDITIONS FOR PARKETT SUBSCRIBERS

57

The PARKETT Series is created in collaboration with artists, who contribute an original work available exclusively to the subscribers in the form of a signed limited SPECIAL EDITION. The available works are also reproduced in each PARKETT issue.

Each SPECIAL EDITION is available by order from any one of our offices in New York or Zurich. Just fill in the details below and send this card to the office nearest you. Once your order has been processed, you will be issued with an invoice and your personal edition number. Upon receipt of payment, you will receive the SPECIAL EDITION. (Please note that supply is subject to availability. PARKETT does not assume responsibility for any delays in production of SPECIAL EDITIONS. Postage is not included.)

☐ As a subscriber to PARKETT, I would like to order the following Special Edition(s), signed and numbered by the artist.

PARKETT No.	ARTIST	NAME:
PARKETT No.	ARTIST	ADDRESS:
PARKETT No.	ARTIST	CITY:
PARKETT No.	ARTIST	STATE/ZIP:
PARKETT No.	ARTIST	COUNTRY:
PARKETT No.	ARTIST	PHONE:

☐ I have indicated my way of payment on the reverse side of this form.

Send this form to the PARKETT office nearest you:

PARKETT PUBLISHERS 155 AV. OF THE AMERICAS NEW YORK, NY 10013 PHONE (212) 673-2660 FAX (212) 271-0704

PARKETT VERLAG QUELLENSTRASSE 27 CH-8031 ZÜRICH TELEFON +41-1-271 81 40 FAX +41-1-272 43 01

PARKETT VERLAG TANNENWALDALLEE 17 D-61348 BAD HOMBURG FAX 06172-937 444 www.parkettart.com

PARKETT

KÜNSTLEREDITIONEN FÜR PARKETT-ABONNENTEN

57

Die PARKETT-Buchreihe entsteht in Zusammenarbeit mit Künstlern, die eigens für die Abonnenten einen Originalbeitrag in Form einer limitierten und signierten EDITION gestalten. Diese Editionen sind auch in der Zeitschrift abgebildet und können mit dieser Bestellkarte in jedem unserer Büros in Zürich, Frankfurt oder New York bestellt werden. Sie erhalten dann Ihre persönliche Editionsnummer und eine Rechnung. Sobald wir Ihre Zahlung erhalten haben, schicken wir Ihnen Ihre Edition(en). (Lieferung nur solange vorrätig. PARKETT übernimmt keine Verantwortung für allfällige Verzögerungen bei der Herstellung der Vorzugsausgaben. Versandkosten zuzüglich.)

☐ Ich bin PARKETT-Abonnent(in) und bestelle folgende EDITION(EN), numeriert und vom Künstler signiert:

PARKETT Nr.	KÜNSTLER/IN	NAME:
PARKETT Nr.	KÜNSTLER/IN	STRASSE:
PARKETT Nr.	KÜNSTLER/IN	PLZ/STADT:
PARKETT Nr.	KÜNSTLER/IN	LAND:
PARKETT Nr.	KÜNSTLER/IN	TEL.:

☐ Meine Zahlungsweise habe ich auf der Rückseite angegeben.

Senden Sie die Bestellkarte an das PARKETT-Büro in Ihrer Nähe:

PARKETT VERLAG QUELLENSTRASSE 27 CH-8031 ZÜRICH TELEFON +41-1-271 81 40 FAX +41-1-272 43 01

PARKETT VERLAG TANNENWALDALLEE 17 D-61348 BAD HOMBURG FAX 06172-937 444 www.parkettart.com

PARKETT PUBLISHERS 155 AV. OF THE AMERICAS NEW YORK, NY 10013 PHONE (212) 673-2660 FAX (212) 271-0704

PARKETT

SUBSCRIBE, COMPLETE OR SEND A GIFT SUBSCRIPTION TO THE BEST BOOK SERIES ON CONTEMPORARY ARTISTS

57

I subscribe to the PARKETT series, starting with issue no. ______

- ☐ for 1 year (3 issues) at US$ 80 (USA/Canada), SFr. 118.– (Europe), SFr. 140.– (Rest of the world).
- ☐ for 2 years (6 issues) at US$ 145 (USA/Canada), SFr. 215.– (Europe), SFr. 265.– (Rest of the world).
- ☐ for 1 year (3 issues) at a 20% student discount (US$ 65 for USA/Canada, SFr. 95.– for Europe). A copy of my student ID is enclosed.

Send a gift subscription in my name, starting with issue no. ______

- ☐ for 1 year (3 issues) at US$ 80 (USA/Canada), SFr. 118.– (Europe), SFr. 140.– (Rest of the world).
- ☐ for 2 years (6 issues) at US$ 145 (USA/Canada), SFr. 215.– (Europe), SFr. 265.– (Rest of the world).

A gift card in my name will be sent to the recipient.

Postage included. All prices subject to change.

☐ I wish to complete my PARKETT collection and order the following issue no(s):

____

at SFr. 43.– each (up to no 43: SFr. 30.–; no. 44–48: SFr. 39.–), postage not included. Within the USA & Canada $ 32 (up to no. 43: $ 19.50; no. 44–48: $ 29), add postage: $ 5 (USA), $ 10 (Canada). (Sold out: No. 1–10, 13, 16, 19, 27, 29–31, 35)

☐ I wish to order the catalog raisonné of all PARKETT Artists' Editions from 1984–98 (60 pages, 120 color ill., published for the show at the Ludwig Museum, Cologne), for SFr. 15.– (USA: $ 12), excl. postage.

☐ I wish to order ________ copies of the new set of 101 postcards featuring PARKETT Artists' Editions for SFr. 48.– (USA: $ 32) per set, excl. postage.

NAME: ______________________________

ADDRESS: ______________________________

CITY: ______________________________

STATE/ZIP: ______________________________

COUNTRY: ______________________________

TEL.: ______________ FAX: ______________

GIFT RECIPIENT: ______________________________

ADDRESS: ______________________________

CITY: ______________________________

STATE/ZIP: ______________________________

COUNTRY: ______________________________

☐ Charge my Visa Card ☐ Mastercard ☐ AMEX

Card No. ________________ Expiration date ________

☐ Payment enclosed (US check or money order) ☐ Bill me

DATE ______________________________

SIGNATURE ______________________________

Send this form to the PARKETT office nearest you:

PARKETT PUBLISHERS 155 AV. OF THE AMERICAS NEW YORK, NY 10013 PHONE (212) 673-2660 FAX (212) 271-0704

PARKETT VERLAG QUELLENSTRASSE 27 CH-8031 ZÜRICH TELEFON +41-1-271 81 40 FAX +41-1-272 43 01

PARKETT VERLAG TANNENWALDALLEE 17 D-61348 BAD HOMBURG FAX 06172-937 444 www.parkettart.com

PARKETT

ABONNIEREN, VERVOLLSTÄNDIGEN ODER VERSCHENKEN SIE DIE UMFASSENDSTE BUCHREIHE ÜBER GEGENWARTSKÜNSTLER

57

Ich abonniere die PARKETT-Reihe ab Nr. ______

- ☐ für 1 Jahr (3 Ausgaben) zu: DM 130.– (BRD), SFr. 108.– (Schweiz), SFr. 118.– (übriges Europa).
- ☐ für 2 Jahre (6 Ausgaben) zu: DM 238.– (BRD), SFr. 190.– (Schweiz), SFr. 215.– (übriges Europa).
- ☐ für 1 Jahr (3 Ausgaben) mit 20% Studentenermässigung (BRD: DM 104.–/Schweiz: SFr. 87.–/Europa: SFr. 95.–). Eine Kopie meines Studentenausweises lege ich bei.

Ich verschenke ein PARKETT-Abonnement ab Nr. ______

- ☐ für 1 Jahr (3 Ausgaben) zu: DM 130.– (BRD), SFr. 108.– (Schweiz), SFr. 118.– (übriges Europa).
- ☐ für 2 Jahre (6 Ausgaben) zu: DM 238.– (BRD), SFr. 190.– (Schweiz), SFr. 215.– (übriges Europa).

Das Geschenk-Abo mit einer Geschenkkarte wird in meinem Namen versandt.

Preise einschliesslich Versandkosten. Preisänderungen vorbehalten.

☐ Ich möchte meine PARKETT-Sammlung vervollständigen und bestelle die folgende(n) noch erhältliche(n) Ausgabe(n) Nr. ______________ zu je DM 49.–/SFr. 43.– (bis Nr. 43: DM 35.–/SFr. 30.–; Nr. 44–48: DM 45.–/SFr. 39.–, zzgl. Versandkosten (vergriffen: Nr. 1–10, 13, 16, 19, 27, 29–31, 35)

☐ Ich bestelle das Werkverzeichnis der PARKETT-Künstlereditionen von 1984–98 (60 S., 120 Farbabb., erschienen zur Ausstellung im Museum Ludwig, Köln) für DM 18.–/SFr. 15.– zzgl. Versandkosten.

☐ Ich bestelle ________ Ex. des neuen Postkarten-Sets mit 101 PARKETT-Künstlereditionen zum Preis von DM 55.–/SFr. 48.– pro Set, zzgl. Versandkosten.

NAME: ______________________________

STRASSE: ______________________________

PLZ/STADT: ______________________________

LAND: ______________________________

TEL.: ______________ FAX: ______________

BESCHENKTE(R): ______________________________

STRASSE: ______________________________

PLZ/STADT: ______________________________

LAND: ______________________________

☐ Ich zahle mit Visa ☐ Eurocard/Mastercard ☐ AMEX

Karten Nr. ________________ Gültig bis ________

☐ Mein Scheck über SFr./DM ______________ liegt bei.

☐ Bitte senden Sie mir eine Rechnung.

DATUM ______________________________

UNTERSCHRIFT ______________________________

Senden Sie die Bestellkarte an das PARKETT-Büro in Ihrer Nähe:

PARKETT VERLAG QUELLENSTRASSE 27 CH-8031 ZÜRICH TELEFON +41-1-271 81 40 FAX +41-1-272 43 01

PARKETT VERLAG TANNENWALDALLEE 17 D-61348 BAD HOMBURG FAX 06172-937 444 www.parkettart.com

PARKETT PUBLISHERS 155 AV. OF THE AMERICAS NEW YORK, NY 10013 PHONE (212) 673-2660 FAX (212) 271-0704

COMPLETE YOUR PARKETT LIBRARY
VERVOLLSTÄNDIGEN SIE IHRE PARKETT-BIBLIOTHEK

OUT OF PRINT / VERGRIFFEN: **NO. 1** ENZO CUCCHI, **2** SIGMAR POLKE, **3** MARTIN DISLER, **4** MERET OPPENHEIM, **5** ERIC FISCHL, **6** JANNIS KOUNELLIS, **7** BRICE MARDEN, **8** MARKUS RAETZ, **9** FRANCESCO CLEMENTE, **10** BRUCE NAUMAN, **12** ANDY WARHOL, **13** REBECCA HORN, **16** ROBERT WILSON, **17** FISCHLI/WEISS, **19** JEFF KOONS, MARTIN KIPPENBERGER, **22** CHRISTIAN BOLTANSKI, JEFF WALL, **25** KATHARINA FRITSCH, **26** GÜNTHER FÖRG, PHILIP TAAFFE, JAMES TURRELL, **27** LOUISE BOURGEOIS, ROBERT GOBER, **29** CINDY SHERMAN, JOHN BALDESSARI, **30** SIGMAR POLKE, **31** DAVID HAMMONS, MIKE KELLEY, **35** GERHARD RICHTER, **38** ROSS BLECKNER, MARLENE DUMAS

For out-of-print issues you can register your name and address with Parkett and you will be notified, if your issue(s) become(s) available on the secondary market / Für vergriffene Bände nimmt der Verlag gerne Ihren Suchauftrag entgegen und macht Ihnen bei allfälliger Verfügbarkeit im Handel ein Angebot.

COLLABORATIONS

ELLSWORTH KELLY
VANESSA BEECROFT
JORGE PARDO
KELLEIN, FER, MAURER, RIMANELLI
BRYSON, TAZZI, SEWARD, AVGIKOS
FERGUSON, VÉGH, VAN WINKEL
FRANGENBERG, BUSH
GREG HILTY: **CERITH WYN EVANS**
THOMAS Y. LEVIN: **CHRISTIAN MARCLAY**
LYNNE COOKE: **DIANA THATER**
LES INFOS: DIANE LEWIS
CUMULUS: ADRIAN DANNATT, PETR NEDOMA

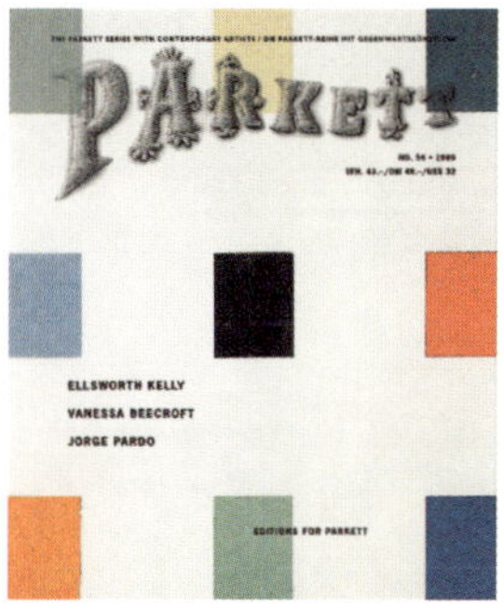

No. 56 - ISBN 3-907582-06-3

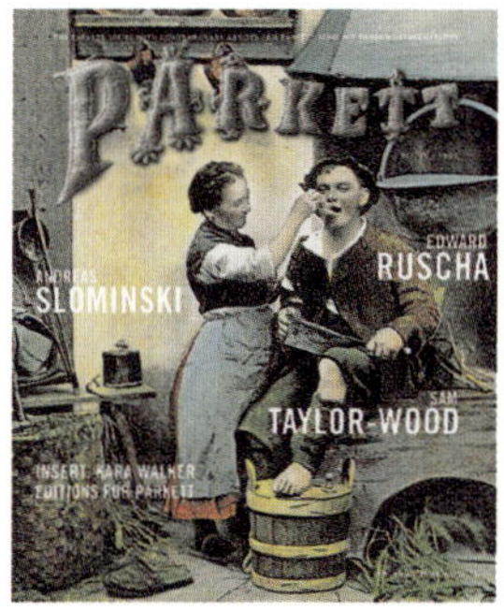

No. 55 - ISBN 3-907582-05-5

EDWARD RUSCHA
ANDREAS SLOMINSKI
SAM TAYLOR-WOOD
PERRONE, HIGGIE, SINGERMAN, SCHENKER
SCANLAN, SPECTOR, FREY, HEYNEN
GROYS/FUNCKE/HOFFMANN, BRONFEN
BONAMI, LAJER-BURCHARTH
INSERT: **KARA WALKER**
BORIS GROYS: **PAVEL PEPPERSTEIN**
RUDOLF SCHMITZ: **ALEXANDER KLUGE**
BEATRIX RUF: **EIJA-LIISA AHTILA**
CUMULUS: MICHELLE NICOL, SUELY ROLNIK

RONI HORN
MARIKO MORI
BEAT STREULI
SCHORR, GUNNARSSON, GOROVOY, LEWIS
SPECTOR, BRYSON, NAKAZAWA, NICHOLS
GOODEVE, STALS, DANTO, AMANO, SMITH
INSERT: **MATTHEW RITCHIE**
VINCENT KATZ: **ALEX KATZ**
HORST BREDEKAMP: **STEPHAN VON HUENE**
PAUL D. MILLER: **SHIRIN NESHAT**
LES INFOS:
OKWUI ENWEZOR & WILLIAM KENTRIDGE
CUMULUS: VALÉRIA PICCOLI, MARIA LIND

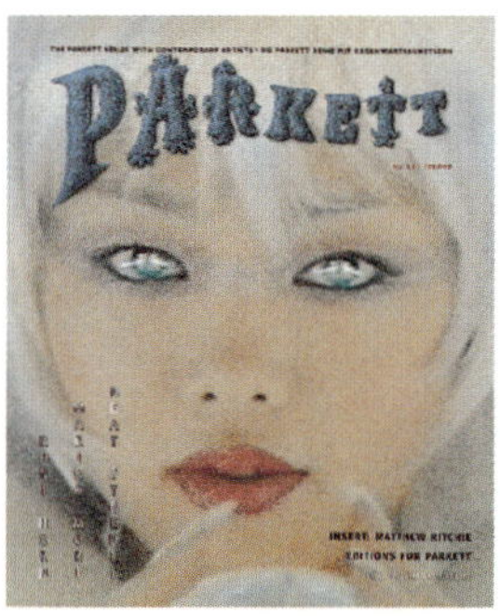

No. 54 - ISBN 3-907582-04-7

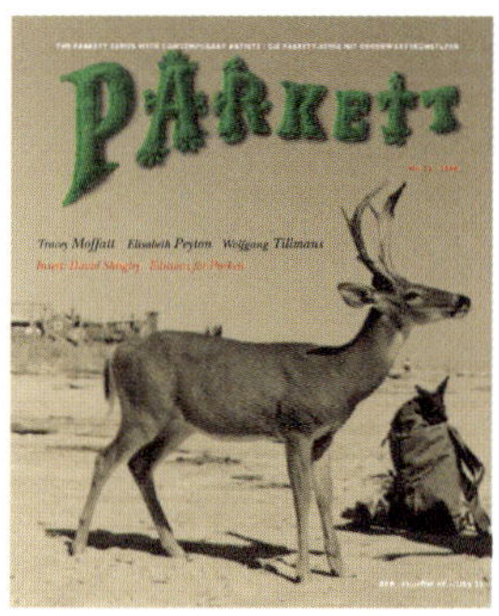

No. 53 - ISBN 3-907582-03-9

TRACEY MOFFATT
ELIZABETH PEYTON
WOLFGANG TILLMANS
MARTIN, LAJER-BURCHARTH, RIMANELLI
PILGRIM, URSPRUNG, LIEBMANN, MATSUI
WAKEFIELD, BUDNEY, NESBITT, ZIEGLER
INSERT: **DAVID SHRIGLEY**
CATHERINE BERNARD: **JOHAN GRIMONPREZ**
BERNARD MARCADÉ: **ROBERT GOBER**
LES INFOS DE L'ENFER: VALERIA LIEBERMANN
CUMULUS: BLESSING, AUPETITALLOT
BALKON: STEINER/MAGNAGUAGNO

KAREN KILIMNIK
MALCOLM MORLEY
UGO RONDINONE
SCHORR, BÜRGI, JUNCOSA, MORLEY,
ENSZTEJN, BONAMI, VERWOERT, HOPTMAN,
INSERT: **THOMAS BAYRLE**
ED WHITE: **JEAN MICHEL OTHONIEL**
NEVILLE WAKEFIELD: **RICHARD SERRA**
GILDA WILLIAMS: **GILLIAN WEARING**
ROBERT GRESKOVIC: **MERCE CUNNINGHAM**
CUMULUS: WALKER, KURZMEYER
BALKON: CECILIA VICUÑA

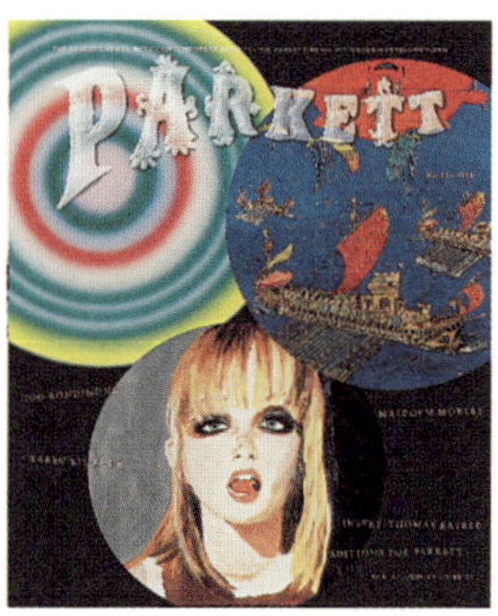

No. 52 - ISBN 3-907582-02-0

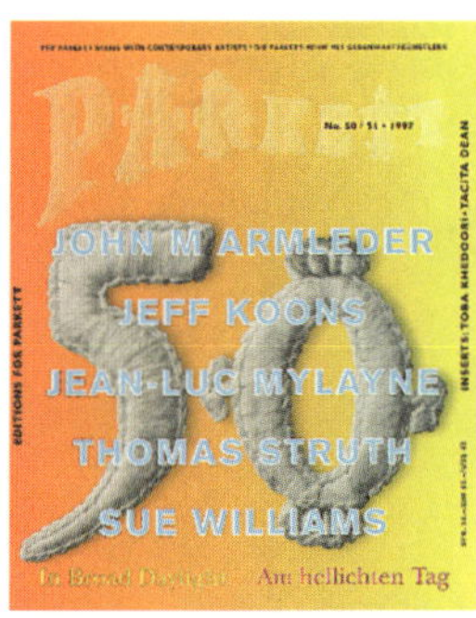

50/51 - ISBN 3-907582-00-4

JOHN M ARMLEDER, JEFF KOONS
JEAN-LUC MYLAYNE
THOMAS STRUTH, SUE WILLIAMS
DI PIETRANTONIO, BOVIER, MUNIZ,
SEWARD, LOERS, NICHOLS GOODEVE,
COOKE, DION, ARNAUDET, MYLAYNE,
CURIGER, LINGWOOD, OKUTSU, BRYSON,
SCHJELDAHL, NESBIT, DANNATT, CAMHI
INSERTS: **TOBA KHEDOORI, TACITA DEAN**
ONFRAY: **HYACINTHE RIGAUD,** NICOL: **SAM SAMORE**
MURPHY, VAN DER WALLE, STEINER,
KURT W. FORSTER: **FRANK GEHRY**
CUMULUS: COLEMAN, BIRNBAUM

LAURIE ANDERSON
DOUGLAS GORDON
JEFF WALL
FLOOD, BEZZOLA, FERGUSON
GILLICK/GORDON, BRYSON, PONTBRIAND
SCHORR, ANDERSON, BURCKHARDT, BUDNEY
INSERT: **SILVIA BÄCHLI**
COLIN DE LAND: **JOHN WATERS**
ROBERT STORR: **SEYDOU KEITA**
DANIELA SALVIONI: **CLEGG & GUTTMANN**
CUMULUS: KITTELMANN, MEYER

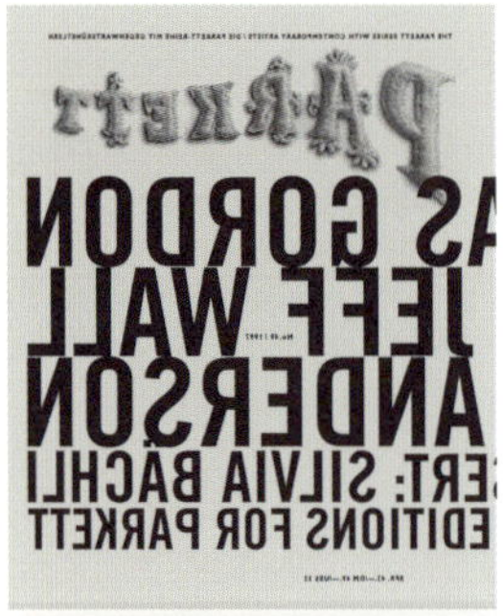

No. 49 - ISBN 3-907509-99-4

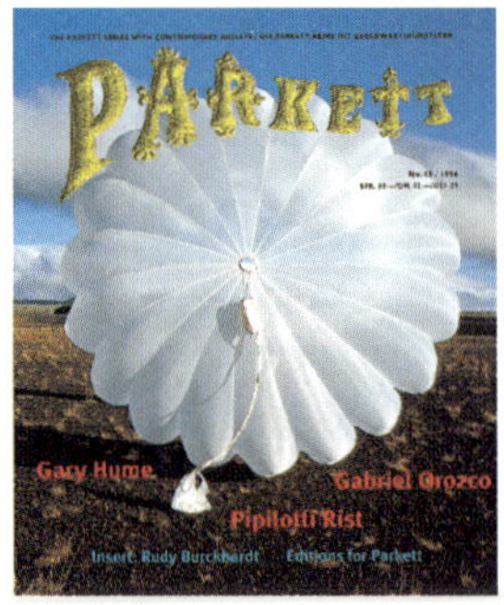

No. 48 - ISBN 3-907509-98-6

GARY HUME
GABRIEL OROZCO
PIPILOTTI RIST
BOVIER, MUIR, FOGLE, BONAMI
DE ZEGHER, SPECTOR, URSPRUNG
BABIAS, COLOMBO, ANDERSON
INSERT: **RUDY BURCKHARDT**
VINCENT KATZ: **RUDY BURCKHARDT**
VAN DER WALLE: **CHARLES LONG & STEREOLAB**
FAYE HIRSCH: **BRUCE CONNER**
CHRISTOPH DOSWALD: **IAN ANÜLL**
CUMULUS: LEGGAT, SCHNEIDER

TONY OURSLER
RAYMOND PETTIBON
THOMAS SCHÜTTE
COOKE, RICHARD, NERI,
LEWIS, GROYS, ALS, RUGOFF,
GOODEVE, SEARLE, MARI, REUST,
WAKEFIELD, LOOCK, JANUS
INSERT: **ZOE LEONARD & CHERYL DUNYE**
JURI STEINER: **EMMA KUNZ**
MAX WECHSLER: **CHRISTOPH RÜTIMANN**
SUSAN MORGAN: **DIANE ARBUS**
CUMULUS: PRINCENTHAL, BOVIER/CHERIX

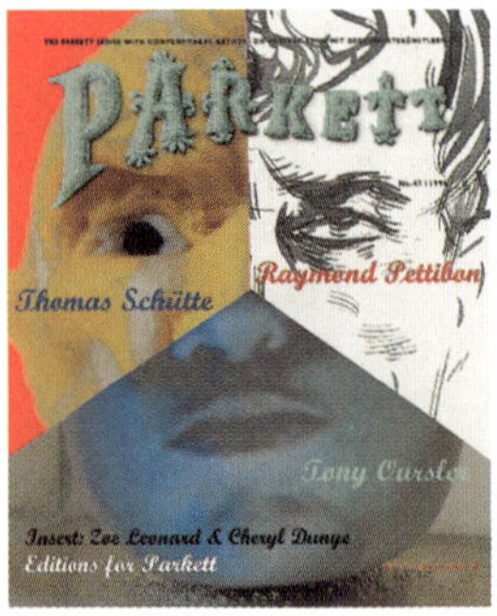

No. 47 - ISBN 3-907509-97-8

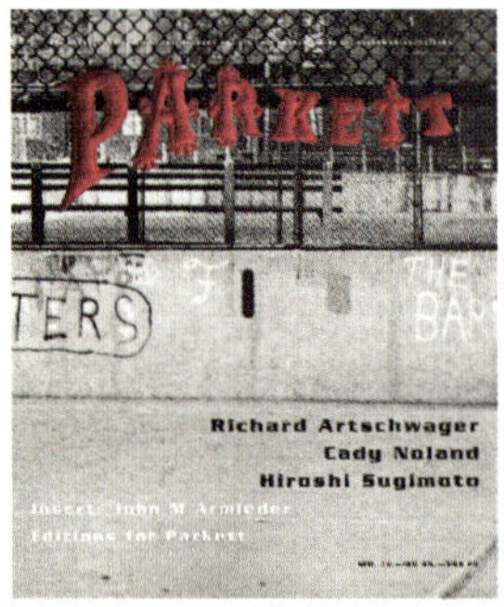

No. 46 - ISBN 3-907509-96-X

RICHARD ARTSCHWAGER
CADY NOLAND
HIROSHI SUGIMOTO
DEITCHER, SCHAFFNER, FORSTER, MUNIZ
ARMSTRONG, RELYEA, BOGDAN, GOODEVE
NICKAS, BRYSON, RUGOFF, DENSON
INSERT: **JOHN M ARMLEDER**
ROLAND WÄSPE: **ERWIN WURM**
DANIEL BIRNBAUM: **ÖYVIND FAHLSTRÖM**
LES INFOS DU PARADIS: ROBERT FLECK
CUMULUS: MILLER, VETTESE
BALKON: MARTIN HELLER

MATTHEW BARNEY
SARAH LUCAS
ROMAN SIGNER
BRYSON, ONFRAY, SEWARD, GOODEVE,
SALTZ, VAN ADRICHEM, SCHORR, FREEDMAN,
JOUANNAIS, BITTERLI, DOSWALD,
VIEWING, WECHSLER, DELAND
INSERT: **ELLIOTT PUCKETTE**
HEIDI GILPIN: **WILLIAM FORSYTHE**
ROBYN McKENZIE: **GEOFF LOWE**
MICHAEL TARANTINO: **CHANTAL AKERMAN**
CUMULUS: McEVILLEY, WAKEFIELD

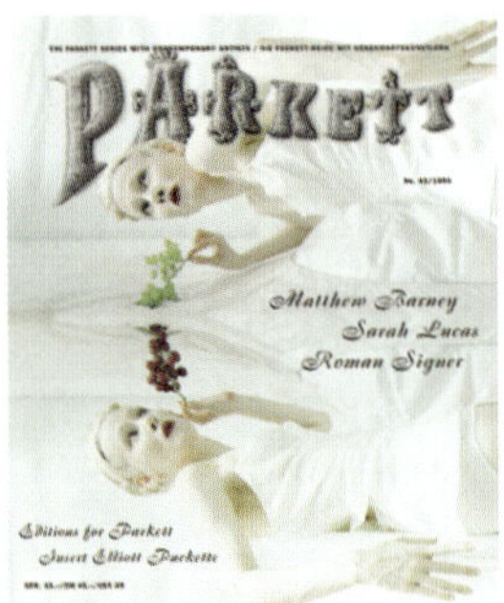

No. 45 - ISBN 3-907509-95-1

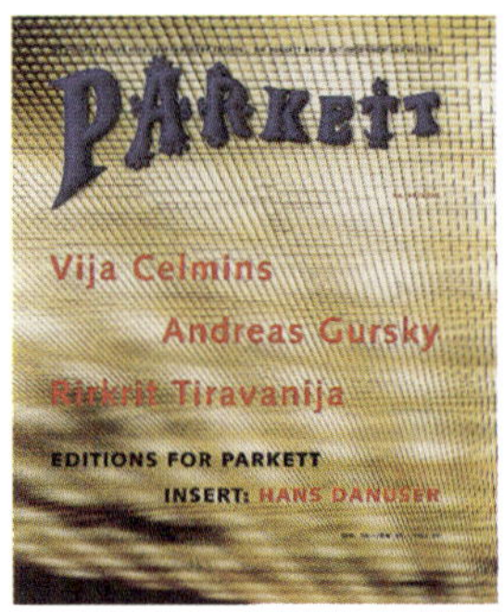

No. 44 - ISBN 3-907509-94-3

VIJA CELMINS
ANDREAS GURSKY
RIRKRIT TIRAVANIJA
PRINCENTHAL, LEWIS, SILVERTHORNE
SHIFF, CRIQUI, BURCKHARDT, WAKEFIELD
SCHORR, MELO, GILLICK, FLOOD, STEINER
INSERT: **HANS DANUSER**
LES INFOS: LIAM GILLICK & DOUGLAS GORDO
LYNNE COOKE, DAVID DEITCHER
DANIEL KURJAKOVIC: **MARIE JOSÉ BURKI**
NAN GOLDIN: **PETER HUJAR**
NOEMI SMOLIK: **ANDREAS SLOMINSKI**
JASON SIMON: **MARK DION**
LUK LAMBRECHT: **MARK LUYTEN**

JUAN MUÑOZ
SUSAN ROTHENBERG
LYNNE COOKE, ALEXANDRE MELO
JAMES LINGWOOD, GAVIN BRYARS
ROBERT CREELEY, INGRID SCHAFFNER
JEAN-CHRISTOPHE AMMANN
MARK STEVENS, JOAN SIMON
INSERT: **ROBERT SMITHSON**
NEVILLE WAKEFIELD
MICHELLE NICOL: **CARSTEN HÖLLER**
HANS-ULRICH OBRIST: **FABRICE HYBERT**

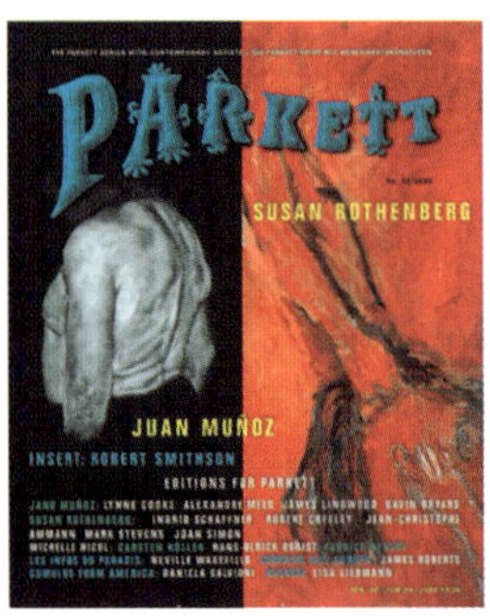

No. 43 - ISBN 3-907509-93-5

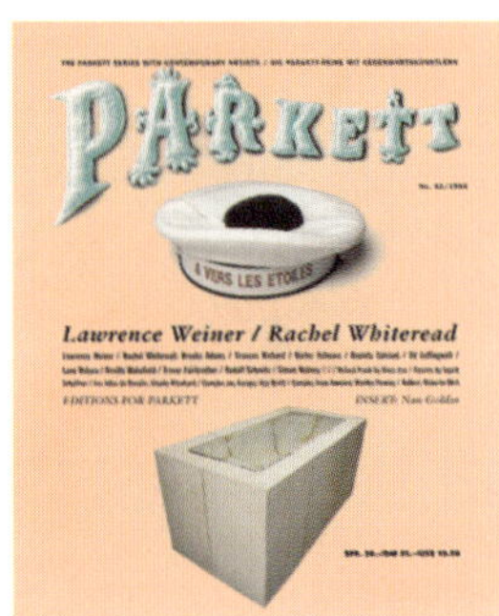

No. 42 - ISBN 3-907509-92-7

LAWRENCE WEINER
RACHEL WHITEREAD
BROOKS ADAMS, FRANCES RICHARD
DIETER SCHWARZ, DANIELA SALVIONI
ED LEFFINGWELL, LANE RELYEA
NEVILLE WAKEFIELD, RUDOLF SCHMITZ
TREVOR FAIRBROTHER, SIMON WATNEY
INSERT: **NAN GOLDIN**
VINCE LEO: **ROBERT FRANK**
CLAUDE RITSCHARD: **MARKUS RAETZ**

FRANCESCO CLEMENTE
GÜNTHER FÖRG
PETER FISCHLI / DAVID WEISS
DAMIEN HIRST
JENNY HOLZER
REBECCA HORN
SIGMAR POLKE
HOLLAND COTTER, BORIS GROYS
MAX WECHSLER, DAVID RIMANELLI
JOAN SIMON, GORDON BURN
GILBERT LASCAULT, WERNER SPIES
BICE CURIGER, JEFF PERRONE
G. ROGER DENSON, VIK MUNIZ
DAVE HICKEY

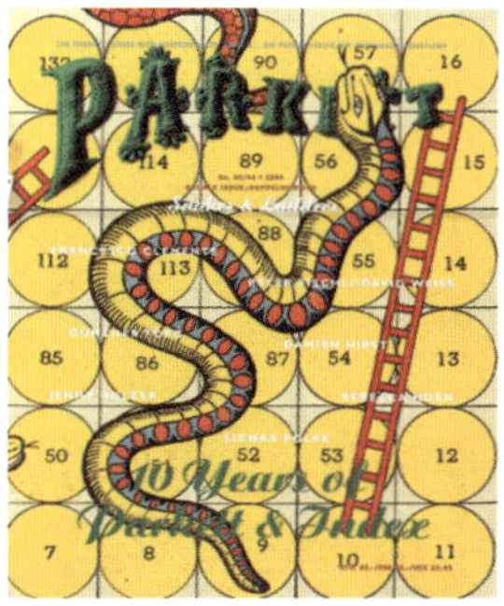

40/41 - ISBN 3-907509-90-0

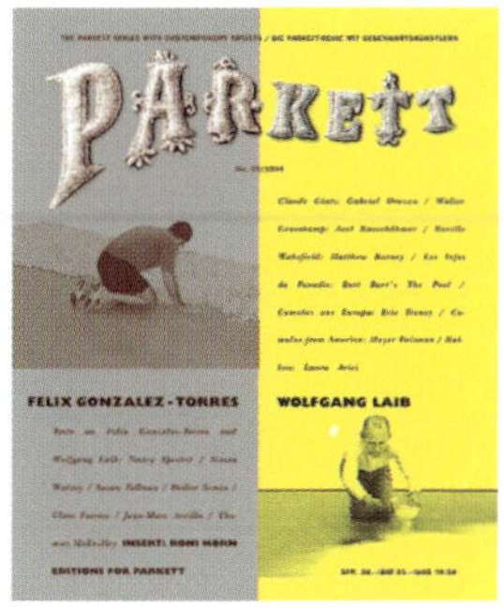

No. 39 - ISBN 3-907509-89-7

FELIX GONZALEZ-TORRES
WOLFGANG LAIB
NANCY SPECTOR, SIMON WATNEY,
SUSAN TALLMAN, DIDIER SEMIN,
CLARE FARROW, JEAN-MARC AVRILLA,
THOMAS McEVILLEY
CLAUDE GINTZ: **GABRIEL OROZCO**
WALTER GRASSKAMP: **AXEL KASSEBÖHMER**
NEVILLE WAKEFIELD: **MATTHEW BARNEY**
INSERT: **RONI HORN**
LES INFOS DU PARADIS: **BURT BARR**
CUMULUS: **MEYER VAISMAN**

CHARLES RAY
FRANZ WEST
KLAUS KERTESS, CHRISTOPHER KNIGHT
PETER SCHJELDAHL, ROBERT STORR
JAN AVGIKOS, AXEL HUBER
MARTIN PRINZHORN, ELISABETH
SCHLEBRÜGGE, HARALD SZEEMANN,
DENYS ZACHAROPOULOS
INSERT: **PIPILOTTI RIST**
JEAN BAUDRILLARD
HANS RUDOLF REUST: **LUC TUYMANS**
PARKETT INQUIRY:
CHERCHEZ LA FEMME PEINTRE!

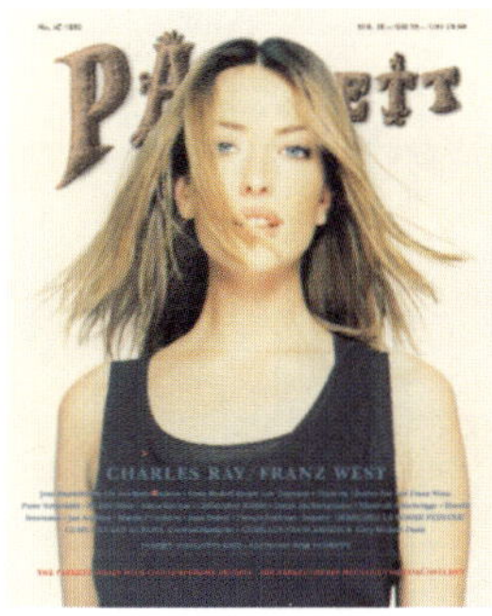

No. 37 - ISBN 3-907509-87-0

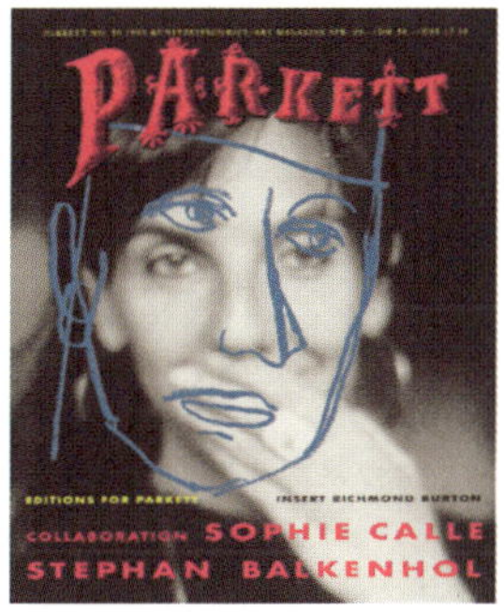

No. 36 - ISBN 3-907509-86-2

STEPHAN BALKENHOL
SOPHIE CALLE
NEAL BENEZRA, VIK MUNIZ, MAX KATZ
JEAN-CHRISTOPHE AMMANN
LUC SANTE, JOSEPH GRIGELY
PATRICK FREY, ROBERT BECK
INSERT: **RICHMOND BURTON**
URSULA PANHANS-BÜHLER: **EVA HESSE**
DOUGLAS BLAU: **JON KESSLER**
KIRBY GOOKIN: **LIZ LARNER**
LÁSZLÓ FÖLDÉNYI:
RUDOLF SCHWARZKOGLER

ILYA KABAKOV
RICHARD PRINCE
BORIS GROYS, ROBERT STORR
JAN THORN-PRIKKER
CLAUDIA JOLLES, EDMUND WHITE
SUSAN TALLMAN, DANIELA
SALVIONI, KATHY ACKER
INSERT: **TATSUO MIYAJIMA**
GUDRUN INBODEN: **ASTA GRÖTING**
LYNNE COOKE: **GARY HILL**
PATRICK McGRATH: **STEPHEN ELLIS**

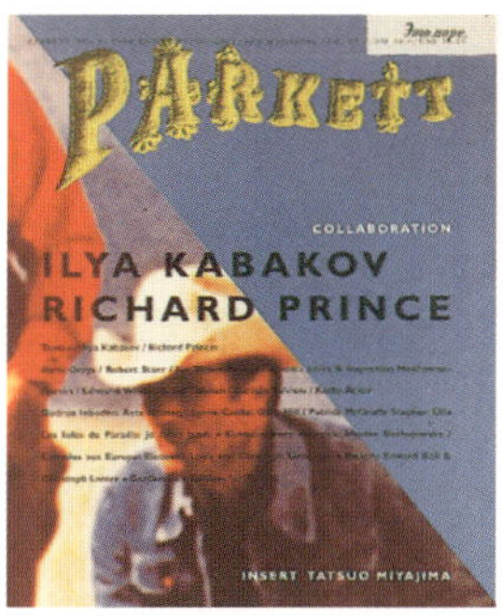

No. 34 - ISBN 3-907509-84-6

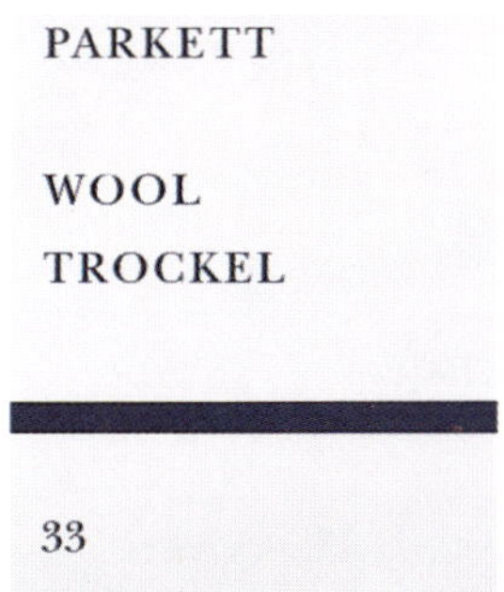

No. 33 - ISBN 3-907509-83-3

ROSEMARIE TROCKEL
CHRISTOPHER WOOL
VERONIQUE BACCHETTA,
BARRETT WATTEN,
ANNE WAGNER, JIM LEWIS,
GREIL MARCUS, JEFF PERRONE,
DIEDRICH DIEDERICHSEN
INSERT: **ADRIAN SCHIESS**
MARINA WARNER: **PENIS PLENTY**
G. ROGER DENSON:
DENNIS OPPENHEIM
CAMIEL VAN WINKEL

IMI KNOEBEL
SHERRIE LEVINE
RUDOLF BUMILLER
RAINER CRONE/DAVID MOOS
LISA LIEBMANN, DANIELA SALVIONI
ERICH FRANZ, HOWARD SINGERMANN
INSERT: **DAMIEN HIRST**
SHEENA WAGSTAFF: **VIJA CELMINS**
JIM LEWIS: **LARRY CLARK**
LIAM GILLICK: **BETHAN HUWS**
THOMAS KELLEIN: **WALTER DE MARIA**

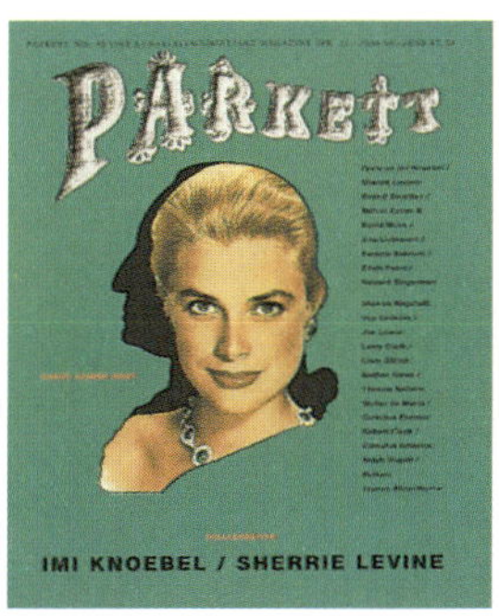

No. 32 - ISBN 3-907509-82-X

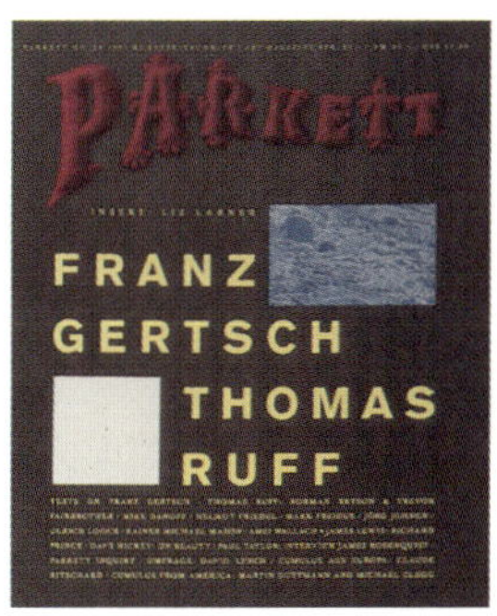

No. 28 - ISBN 3-907509-78-1

FRANZ GERTSCH
THOMAS RUFF
HELMUT FRIEDEL, ULRICH LOOCK
I. MICHAEL DANOFF, AMEI WALLACH
RAINER MICHAEL MASON
MARC FREIDUS, JÖRG JOHNEN
TREVOR FAIRBROTHER/NORMAN BRYSON
INSERT: **LIZ LARNER**
JAMES LEWIS: **RICHARD PRINCE**
DAVID HICKEY:
THE INVISIBLE DRAGON/
DER UNSICHTBARE DRACHEN
PAUL TAYLOR: **JAMES ROSENQUIST**

ALIGHIERO E BOETTI
JEAN-CHRISTOPHE AMMANN
GIOVAN BATTISTA SALERNO
RAINER CRONE & DAVID MOOS
FRIEDEMANN MALSCH
JEAN-PIERRE BORDAZ
ALAIN CUEFF
INSERT: **CINDY SHERMAN**
SHEENA WAGSTAFF:
SOPHIE CALLE
HERBERT LACHMEYER/
BRIGITTE FELDERER: **FRANZ WEST**
JUTTA KOETHER: **MIKE KELLEY**

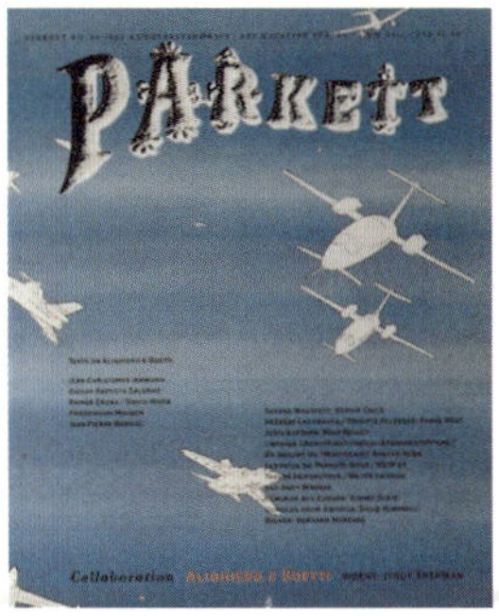

No. 24 - ISBN 3-907509-74-9

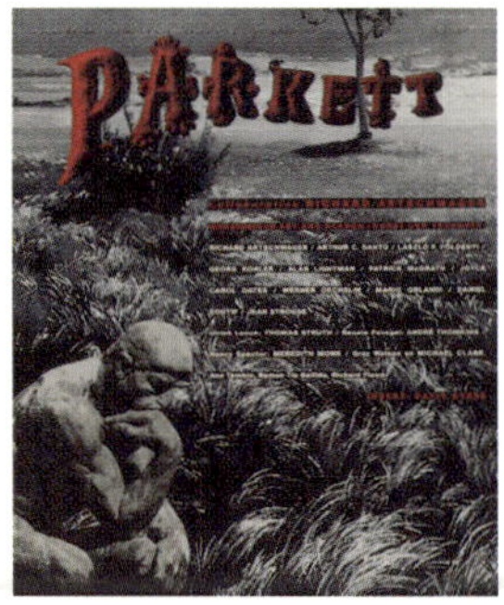

No. 23 - ISBN 3-907509-73-0

RICHARD ARTSCHWAGER
ARTHUR C. DANTO, GEORG KOHLER,
MARIO A. ORLANDO, JOYCE
CAROL OATES, WERNER OECHSLIN,
ALAN LIGHTMAN, PATRICK
McGRATH, DANIEL SOUTIF,
LASZLO F. FÖLDENYI, JEAN STROUSE
INSERT: **DAVID BYRNE**
RENATE PUVOGEL: **ANDRÉ THOMKINS**
ULRICH LOOCK: **THOMAS STRUTH**
NANCY SPECTOR: **MEREDITH MONK**

ALEX KATZ
JOHN RUSSELL, BROOKS ADAMS,
DAVID RIMANELLI, FRANCESCO
CLEMENTE, MICHAEL KRÜGER,
RICHARD FLOOD, PATRICK FREY,
CARL STIGLIANO, BICE CURIGER,
GLENN O'BRIEN
INSERT: **WILLIAM WEGMAN**
LISA LIEBMAN: **ROBERT GOBER**
JACQUELINE BURCKHARDT:
GIULIO ROMANO

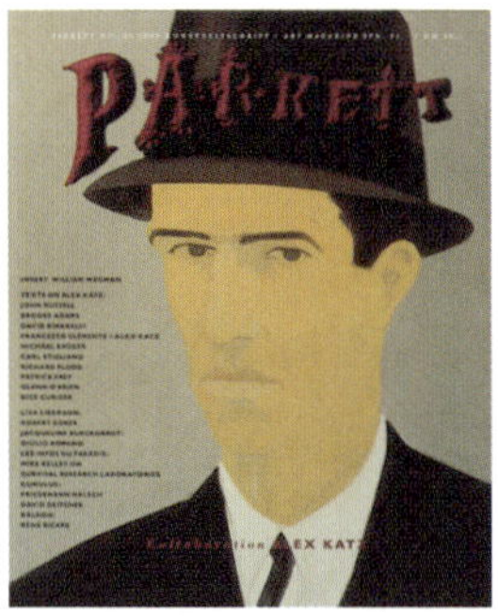

No. 21 - ISBN 3-907509-71-4

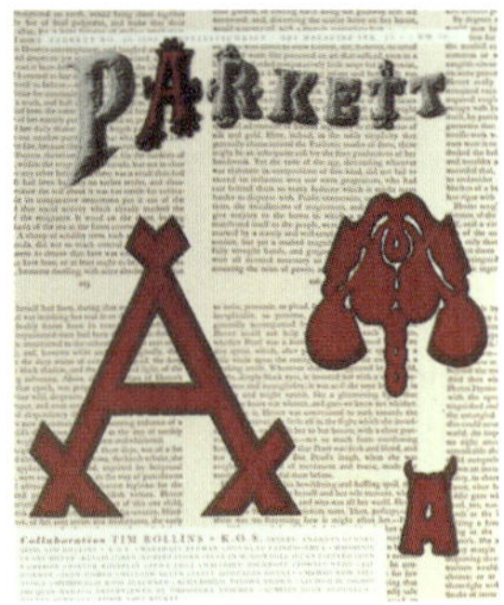

No. 20 - ISBN 3-907509-70-6

TIM ROLLINS + K.O.S.
MARSHALL BERMAN
TREVOR FAIRBROTHER
STATEMENTS, DIALOGUE 5
INSERT: **ANDREAS GURSKY**
MICHAEL NASH: **BILL VIOLA**
STEPHEN ELLIS: **ROSS BLECKNER**
KLAUS KERTESS: **TRISHA BROWN**

EDWARD RUSCHA
DAVE HICKEY, DENNIS HOPPER
ALAIN CUEFF, JOHN MILLER
CHRISTOPHER KNIGHT
INSERT: **BOYD WEBB**
JAN THORN-PRIKKER: **WOLS**
LYNNE COOKE: **TONY CRAGG**
BROOKE ADAMS: **JULIAN SCHNABEL**
DER KÜNSTLER ALS EXEM-
PLARISCH LEIDENDER?
EINE UMFRAGE / THE ARTIST AS A
MODEL SUFFERER? AN INQUIRY

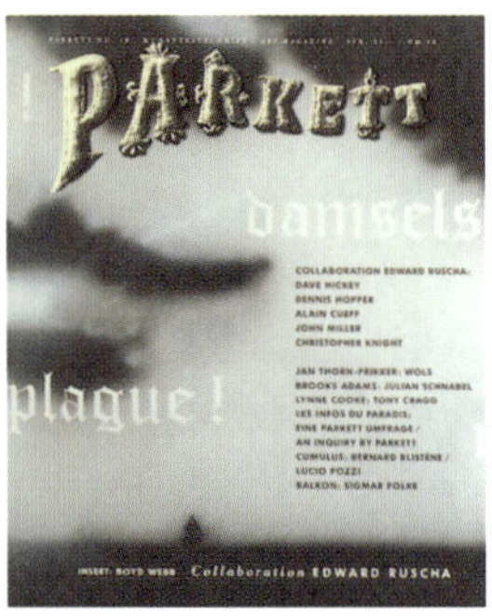

No. 18 - ISBN 3-907509-68-4

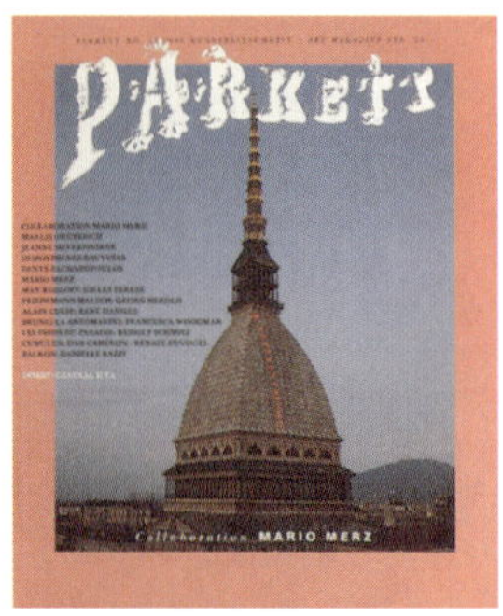

No. 15 - ISBN 3-907509-65-X

MARIO MERZ
MARLIS GRÜTERICH, JEANNE
SILVERTHORNE, DEMOSTHENES
DAVVETAS, HARALD SZEEMANN,
DENYS ZACHAROPOULOS
INSERT: **GENERAL IDEA**
MAX KOZLOFF: **GILLES PERESS**
FRIEDEMANN MALSCH:
GEORG HEROLD
BRUNELLA ANTOMARINI:
FRANCESCA WOODMAN

GILBERT & GEORGE
DUNCAN FALLOWELL, MARIO
CODOGNATO, JEREMY COOPER,
DEMOSTHENES DAVVETAS,
WOLF JAHN
INSERT: **ROSEMARIE TROCKEL**
ROBERT STORR: **NANCY SPERO**
HAIM STEINBACH: **MANIFESTO**
JÖRG ZUTTER: **THOMAS HUBER**

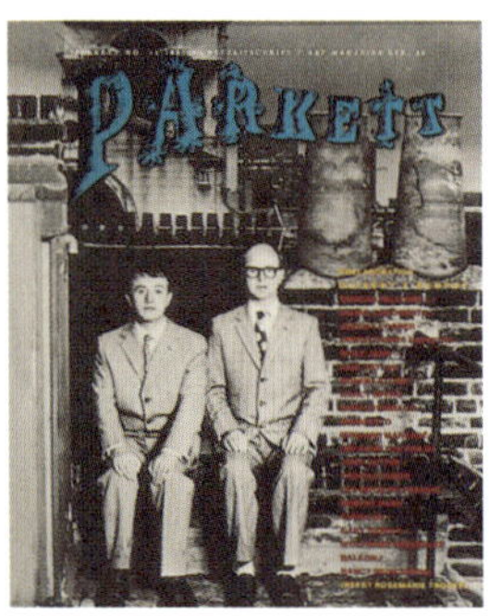

No. 14 - ISBN 3-907509-64-1

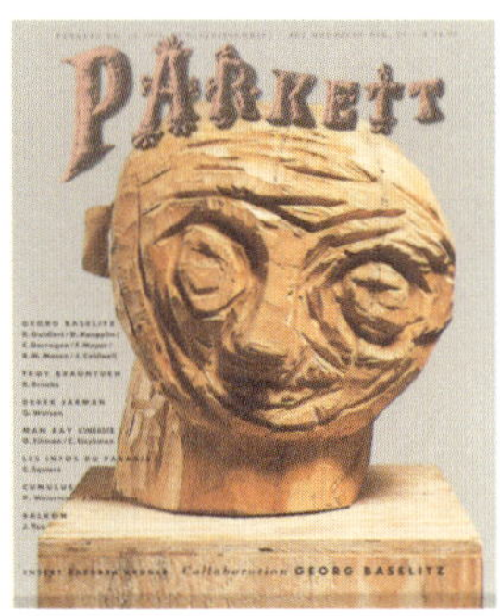

No. 11 - ISBN 3-907509-61-7

GEORG BASELITZ
REMO GUIDIERI, DIETER
KOEPPLIN, ERIC DARRAGON,
RAINER MICHAEL MASON, FRANZ
MEYER, JOHN CALDWELL
INSERT: **BARBARA KRUGER**
GRAY WATSON: **DEREK JARMAN**
CAROL SQUIERS:
PHOTO OPPORTUNITY
ROSETTA BROOKS:
TROY BRAUNTUCH

PARKETT

ARTISTS' MONOGRAPHS & EDITIONS / KÜNSTLERMONOGRAPHIEN & EDITIONEN,

FOR AVAILABILITY SEE NEXT PAGE / LIEFERBARKEIT SIEHE FOLGENDE SEITE

Doug Aitken, vol. 57
Laurie Anderson, vol. 49
John Armleder, vol. 50/51
Richard Artschwager, vol. 23, vol. 46
John Baldessari, vol. 29
Stephan Balkenhol, vol. 36
Matthew Barney, vol. 45
Georg Baselitz, vol. 11
Vanessa Beecroft, vol. 56
Ross Bleckner, vol. 38
Alighiero e Boetti, vol. 24
Christian Boltanski, vol. 22
Louise Bourgeois, vol. 27
Sophie Calle, vol. 36
Vija Celmins, vol. 44
Francesco Clemente, vol. 9 & 40/41
Enzo Cucchi, vol. 1
Martin Disler, vol. 3
Marlene Dumas, vol. 38
Eric Fischl, vol. 5
Peter Fischli/David Weiss, vol.17, 40/41
Günther Förg, vol. 26 & 40/41
Katharina Fritsch, vol. 25
Franz Gertsch, vol. 28
Gilbert & George, vol. 14
Robert Gober, vol. 27
Nan Goldin, vol. 57
Felix Gonzalez-Torres, vol. 39
Douglas Gordon, vol. 49
Andreas Gursky, vol. 44
David Hammons, vol. 31
Thomas Hirschhorn, vol. 57
Damien Hirst, vol. 40/41
Jenny Holzer, vol. 40/41
Rebecca Horn, vol. 13 & 40/41
Roni Horn, vol. 54
Gary Hume, vol. 48
Ilya Kabakov, vol. 34
Alex Katz, vol. 21
Mike Kelley, vol. 31
Ellsworth Kelly, vol. 56
Karen Kilimnik, vol. 52
Martin Kippenberger, vol. 19
Imi Knoebel, vol. 32
Jeff Koons, vol. 19, 50/51
Jannis Kounellis, vol. 6
Wolfgang Laib, vol. 39
Sherrie Levine, vol. 32
Sarah Lucas, vol. 45
Brice Marden, vol. 7
Mario Merz, vol. 15
Tracey Moffatt, vol. 53
Mariko Mori, vol. 54
Malcolm Morley, vol. 52
Juan Muñoz, vol. 43
Jean-Luc Mylayne, vol. 50/51
Cady Noland, vol. 46
Bruce Nauman, vol. 10
Meret Oppenheim, vol. 4
Gabriel Orozco, vol. 48
Tony Oursler, vol. 47
Jorge Pardo, vol. 56
Raymond Pettibon, vol. 47
Elizabeth Peyton, vol. 53
Sigmar Polke, vol. 2, 30 & 40/41
Richard Prince, vol. 34
Markus Raetz, vol. 8
Charles Ray, vol. 37
Gerhard Richter, vol. 35
Pipilotti Rist, vol. 48
Tim Rollins & K.O.S., vol. 20
Ugo Rondinone, vol. 52
Susan Rothenberg, vol. 43
Thomas Ruff, vol. 28
Edward Ruscha, vol. 18 & 55
Thomas Schütte, vol. 47
Cindy Sherman, vol. 29
Roman Signer, vol. 45
Andreas Slominski, vol. 55
Beat Streuli, vol. 54
Thomas Struth, vol. 50/51
Hiroshi Sugimoto, vol. 46
Philip Taaffe, vol. 26
Sam Taylor-Wood, vol. 55
Wolfgang Tillmans, vol. 53
Rirkrit Tiravanija, vol. 44
Rosemarie Trockel, vol. 33
James Turrell, vol. 25
Jeff Wall, vol. 22 & 49
Andy Warhol, vol. 12
Lawrence Weiner, vol. 42
Franz West, vol. 37
Rachel Whiteread, vol. 42
Sue Williams, vol 50/51
Robert Wilson, vol. 16
Christopher Wool, vol. 33

vol.	Collaboration		
57	Doug Aitken	m	e
	Nan Goldin	m	e
	Thomas Hirschhorn	m	e
56	Vanessa Beecroft	m	e
	Ellsworth Kelly	m	e
	Jorge Pardo	m	e
55	Edward Ruscha	m	e
	Andreas Slominski	m	e
	Sam Taylor-Wood	m	
54	Roni Horn	m	e
	Mariko Mori	m	
	Beat Streuli	m	e
53	Tracey Moffatt	m	e
	Elizabeth Peyton	m	
	Wolfgang Tillmans	m	
52	Karen Kilimnik	m	e
	Malcolm Morley	m	e
	Ugo Rondinone	m	e
50/51	John Armleder	m	e
	Jeff Koons	m	e
	Jean-Luc Mylayne	m	e
	Thomas Struth	m	
	Sue Williams	m	e
49	Laurie Anderson	m	e
	Douglas Gordon	m	
	Jeff Wall	m	
48	Gary Hume	m	
	Gabriel Orozco	m	
	Pipilotti Rist	m	
47	Tony Oursler	m	
	Raymond Pettibon	m	
	Thomas Schütte	m	e
46	Richard Artschwager	m	
	Cady Noland	m	e
	Hiroshi Sugimoto	m	
45	Matthew Barney	m	
	Sarah Lucas	m	e
	Roman Signer	m	e
44	Vija Celmins	m	
	Andreas Gursky	m	
	Rirkrit Tiravanija	m	e
43	Juan Muñoz	m	e
	Susan Rothenberg	m	e
42	Lawrence Weiner	m	e
	Rachel Whiteread	m	
40/41	Francesco Clemente	m	e
	Peter Fischli/David Weiss	m	
	Günther Förg	m	
	Damien Hirst	m	
	Jenny Holzer	m	
	Rebecca Horn	m	
	Sigmar Polke	m	e
39	Felix Gonzalez-Torres	m	

vol.	Collaboration		
	Wolfgang Laib	m	e
38	Ross Bleckner	m	
	Marlene Dumas	m	
37	Charles Ray	m	
	Franz West	m	e
36	Stephan Balkenhol	m	e
36	Sophie Calle	m	e
35	Gerhard Richter		
34	Ilya Kabakov	m	
	Richard Prince	m	e
33	Rosemarie Trockel	m	e
	Christopher Wool	m	
32	Imi Knoebel		
	Sherrie Levine		
31	David Hammons		
	Mike Kelley		
30	Sigmar Polke		
29	John Baldessari		
	Cindy Sherman		
28	Franz Gertsch	m	e
	Thomas Ruff	m	e
27	Louise Bourgeois		
	Robert Gober		
26	Günther Förg	m	
	Philip Taaffe	m	
25	Katharina Fritsch	m	e
	James Turrell	m	e
24	Alighiero e Boetti	m	e
23	Richard Artschwager	m	
22	Christian Boltanski	m	
	Jeff Wall	m	
21	Alex Katz	m	e
20	Tim Rollins + K.O.S.	m	
19	Martin Kippenberger		
	Jeff Koons		
18	Ed Ruscha	m	
17	Peter Fischli/David Weiss		
16	Robert Wilson		
15	Mario Merz	m	
14	Gilbert & George	m	
13	Rebecca Horn		
12	Andy Warhol		
11	Georg Baselitz	m	
10	Bruce Nauman		
9	Francesco Clemente		
8	Markus Raetz		
7	Brice Marden		
6	Jannis Kounellis		
5	Eric Fischl		
4	Meret Oppenheim		
3	Martin Disler		
2	Sigmar Polke		
1	Enzo Cucchi		

m = available monograph / erhältliche Monographie, e = available edition / erhältliche Edition
Delivery subject to availability at time of order / Lieferung solange Vorrat

Each volume of PARKETT is created in collaboration with artists, who contribute an original work specially made for the readers of PARKETT. The works are available in a signed and numbered Special Edition. Prices are subject to change. Postage is not included.

EDITIONS FOR PARKETT

Jeder PARKETT-Band entsteht in Collaboration mit Künstlern, die eigens für die Leser von PARKETT Originalbeiträge gestalten. Diese Vorzugsausgaben sind als nummerierte und signierte Editionen erhältlich. Preisänderungen vorbehalten. Versandkosten und MwSt. (Schweiz) nicht inbegriffen.

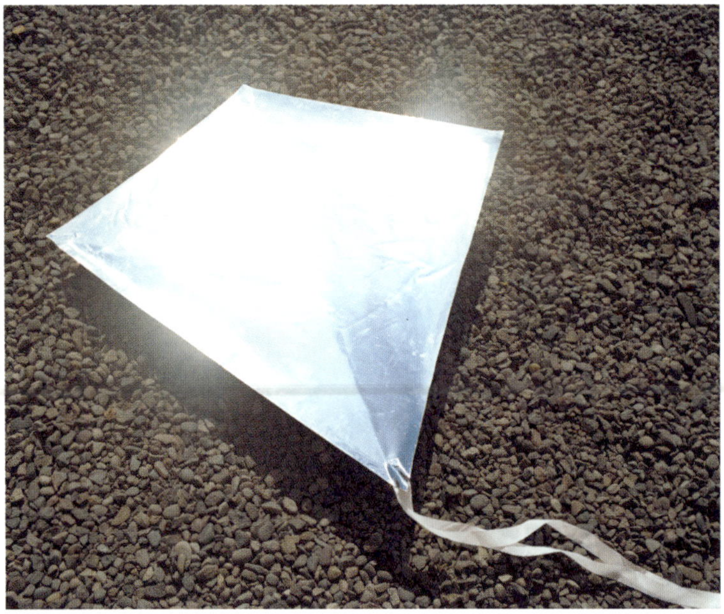

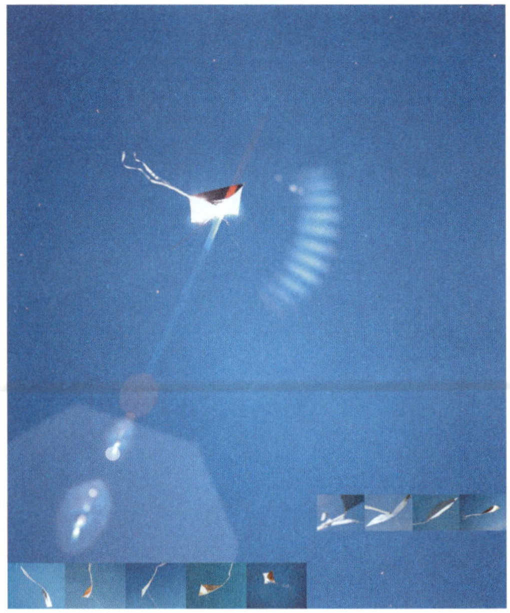

PARKETT 57

DOUG AITKEN

DECREASE THE MASS AND RUN LIKE HELL, 1999

Mirror kite, ca. 34 x 33½", tail 37⅜",
with poster of flying kite, ca. 20 x 15⅝".
Edition of 60, stamped and numbered. **$ 660 / € 620**

DIE MASSE VERKLEINERN UND RENNEN WIE DER TEUFEL, 1999

Spiegeldrachen, ca. 86,5 x 85 cm, Schwanz 95 cm,
und Plakat mit fliegendem Drachen, 51 x 39,6 cm.
Auflage: 60, mit Prägestempel und nummeriert, **sFr. 990.–**

Feather the light and cast a spell: This kite preys on reflection.

Lichthungriger Luftflitzer hängt seinen Reflexionen nach.

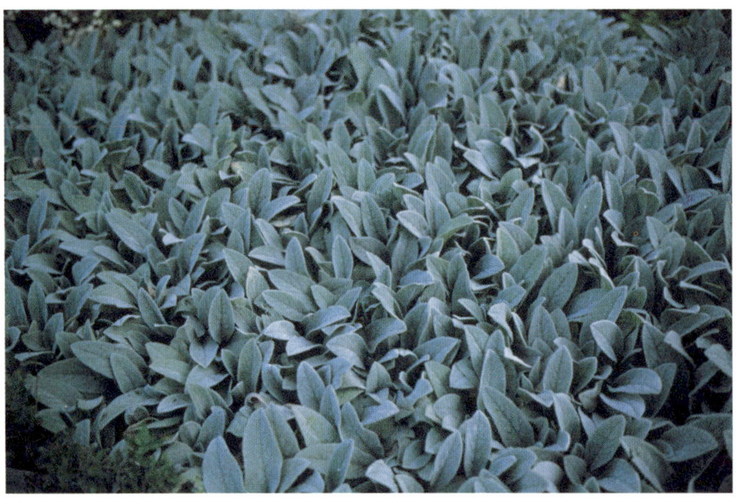

L'heure bleu: A moment of silence immerses us in the sensual fragrance of whispering sage.

L'heure bleu: Ein Salbeifeld spitzt die Ohren.

PARKETT 57

NAN GOLDIN

LAMBS EARS, 1999

C-print, 15¾ x 23⅝"
Edition of 60, signed and numbered, **$900 / € 880**

LÄMMEROHREN, 1999

C-Print, 40 x 60 cm
Auflage: 60, signiert und nummeriert, **sFr. 1400.–**

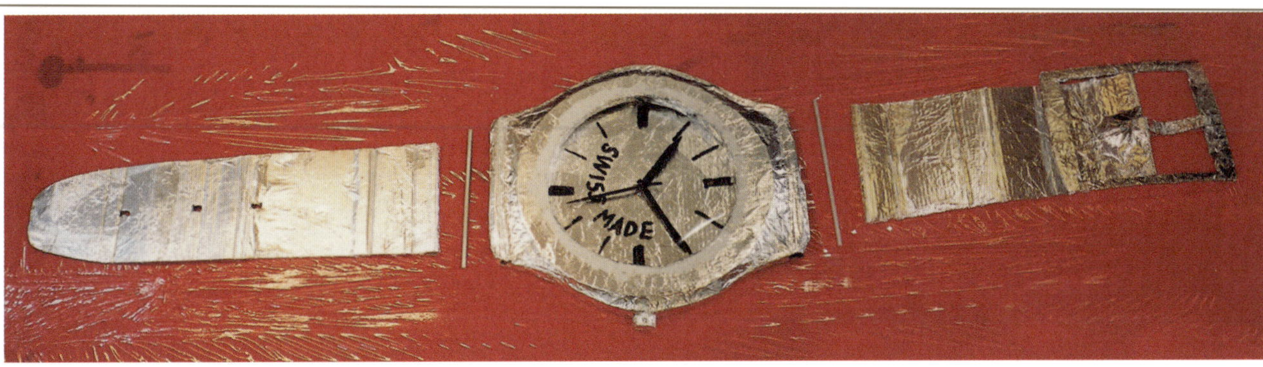

Die definitive Überuhr: überspannt, überzogen, überbordend, überzwerch.

The ultimate watch: a glittering lesson in mastering the millennium by exploding the fiction of time.

PARKETT 57

THOMAS HIRSCHHORN

SWISS MADE, 1999

Karton, Aluminiumfolie, Filz, Holz, Plastik, Klarsichtfolie, in 3 Teile zerlegbar, insgesamt 220 x 50 x 8 cm. Auflage: 50, signiert und nummeriert, **sFr. 990.–**

Cardboard, aluminum foil, felt, wood, plastic, transparent foil, in three pieces, overall size ca. 86⅝ x 19¹¹⁄₁₆ x 3⅛". Edition of 50, signed and numbered, **$ 660 / € 620**

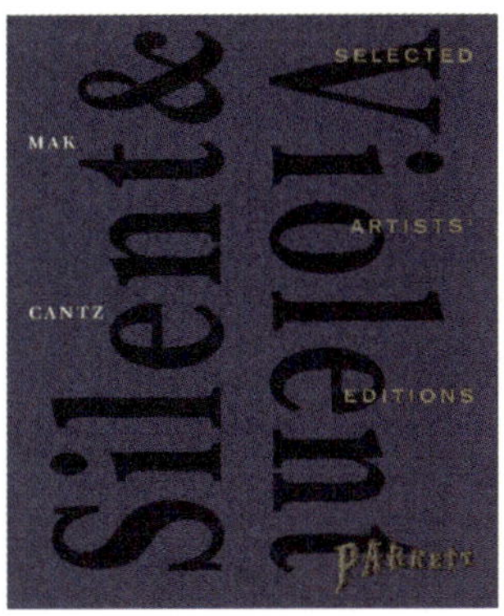

SILENT & VIOLENT

CATALOG RAISONNÉ OF ALL PARKETT ARTISTS' EDITIONS
from No. 1–44, 183 pages, 144 in color
text by Susan Tallmann, short biographies of all artists

WERKVERZEICHNIS ALLER PARKETT-KÜNSTLER-EDITIONEN
von Nr. 1–44, 183 Seiten, davon 144 in Farbe
Text von Susan Tallmann, Kurzbiographien der Künstler

sFr. 49.– / $ 39 / € 30

ISBN 3-89322-796-3 (engl.), ISBN 3-89322-787-3 (dt.)

NEW PARKETT-POSTCARD SET
featuring 105 artists' editions made for Parkett

DAS NEUE PARKETT-POSTKARTEN-SET
mit 105 Editionen, die von Künstlern für Parkett geschaffen wurden.

sFr. 48.– / $ 32 / € 30

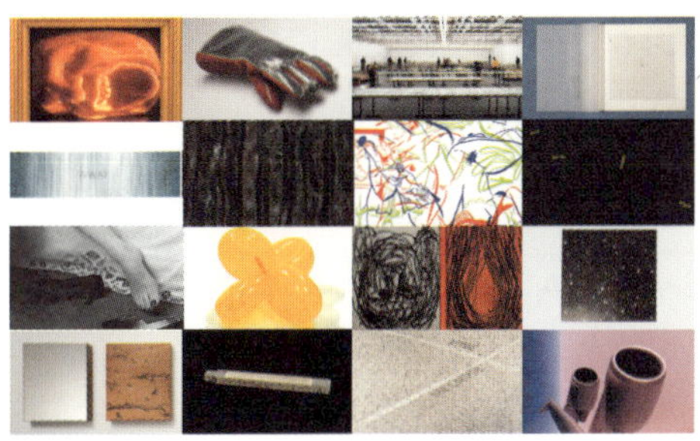

E X H I B I T I O N S

ZÜRICH

Gallery	Address	Exhibition	Dates
ACP VIVIANE EHRLI	Klingenstrasse 42, 8005 Zürich, Tel. 01 463 63 53	NEUERÖFFNUNG	**MÄRZ–APRIL 2000**
THOMAS AMMANN FINE ART	Restelbergstrasse 97, 8044 Zürich, Tel. 01 360 51 60	ACCROCHAGE	
ARS FUTURA	Bleicherweg 45, 8002 Zürich, Tel. 01 201 88 10	LOTHAR HEMPEL	**14.1.–26.2.2000**
BOB VON ORSOUW	Limmatstrasse 270, 8005 Zürich, Tel. 01 273 11 00	ALBRECHT SCHNIDER	**27.11.99–22.1.2000**
		PHILIP AKKERMAN	**29.1.–26.2.2000**
MAI 36 GALERIE	Rämistrasse 37, 8001 Zürich, Tel. 01 261 68 80	LAWRENCE WEINER	**27.11.99–15.1.2000**
		THE ARMORY SHOW 2000	**25.2.–28.2.2000**
MARK MÜLLER	Gessnerallee 36, 8001 Zürich, Tel. 01 211 81 55	JOACHIM BANDAU – Aquarelle Guest-Room: ULRICH KOCHINKE – Zeichnungen	**8.1.–18.2.2000**
		MARKUS WEGGENMANN Malerei Guest-Room: Surprise 2	**26.2.–7.4.2000**
		RETO BOLLER – Malerei Guest-Room: Surprise 3	**15.4.–27.5.2000**
SEMINA RERUM IRÈNE PREISWERK	Cäcilienstrasse 3, 8032 Zürich, Tel. 01 251 26 39	MIREILLE GROS	**BIS 22.1.2000**
		OLIVER GODOW	**29.1.–11.3.2000**
		CÉCILE WICK	**18.3.–29.4.2000**
ANNEMARIE VERNA	Neptunstrasse 45, 8032 Zürich, Tel. 01 262 38 20	DAN FLAVIN (1933–1996), untitled 1969	**BIS 5.2.2000**
		FRED SANDBACK	**10.2.–25.3.2000**
		RICHARD TUTTLE	**30.3.–20.5.2000**

EXHIBITIONS

GALERIE SCHEDLER	Josefstrasse 53 8005 Zürich Tel. 01 440 61 20	UWE WITTWER	**BIS 29.1.2000**
		HANS WITSCHI	**11.2.–18.3.2000**
		Eliane Rutishauser, Christoph Schneeberger, Stephanie Schneider/P77: Margaret Morgan	**24.3.–29.4.2000**
		high five (beauty and sports)	**5.5.–5.6.2000**

JAMILEH WEBER	Waldmannstrasse 6 8001 Zürich Tel. 01 252 10 66	25 JAHRE GALERIE JAMILEH WEBER	**BIS 29.1.2000**

BERN

GALERIE FRIEDRICH	Lorrainestrasse 19 3013 Bern Tel. 031 331 33 30	STEFAN GRITSCH	**BIS 21.1.2000**
		ANA AXPE	**28.1.–3.3.2000**
		DOMINIQUE LÄMMLI	**10.3.–19.4.2000**

GENÈVE

DANIEL VARENNE	8, rue Toepffer 1206 Genève Tel. 022 789 16 75	PAINTINGS AND DRAWINGS 19TH AND 20TH CENTURY	

ST. GALLEN

WILMA LOCK	Schmiedgasse 15 9001 St. Gallen Tel. 071 222 62 52	MARK FRANCIS-BERNARD FRIZE IMI KNOEBEL, BEAT ZODERER,	**BIS 15.1.2000**
		FRANZ ERHARD WALTHER (Wortbilder) ERWIN WURM (Fotos)	**18.1.–11.3.2000**
		KELLY WOOD	**21.3.–7.5.2000**

ZUG

KUNSTHAUS ZUG	Dorfstrasse 27 6300 Zug Tel. 041 725 33 44	Projekt Sammlung (4) RICHARD TUTTLE Replace the Abstract Picture Plane (1996–1999) und ein Foto-Essay von Guido Baselgia	**BIS 13.2.2000**

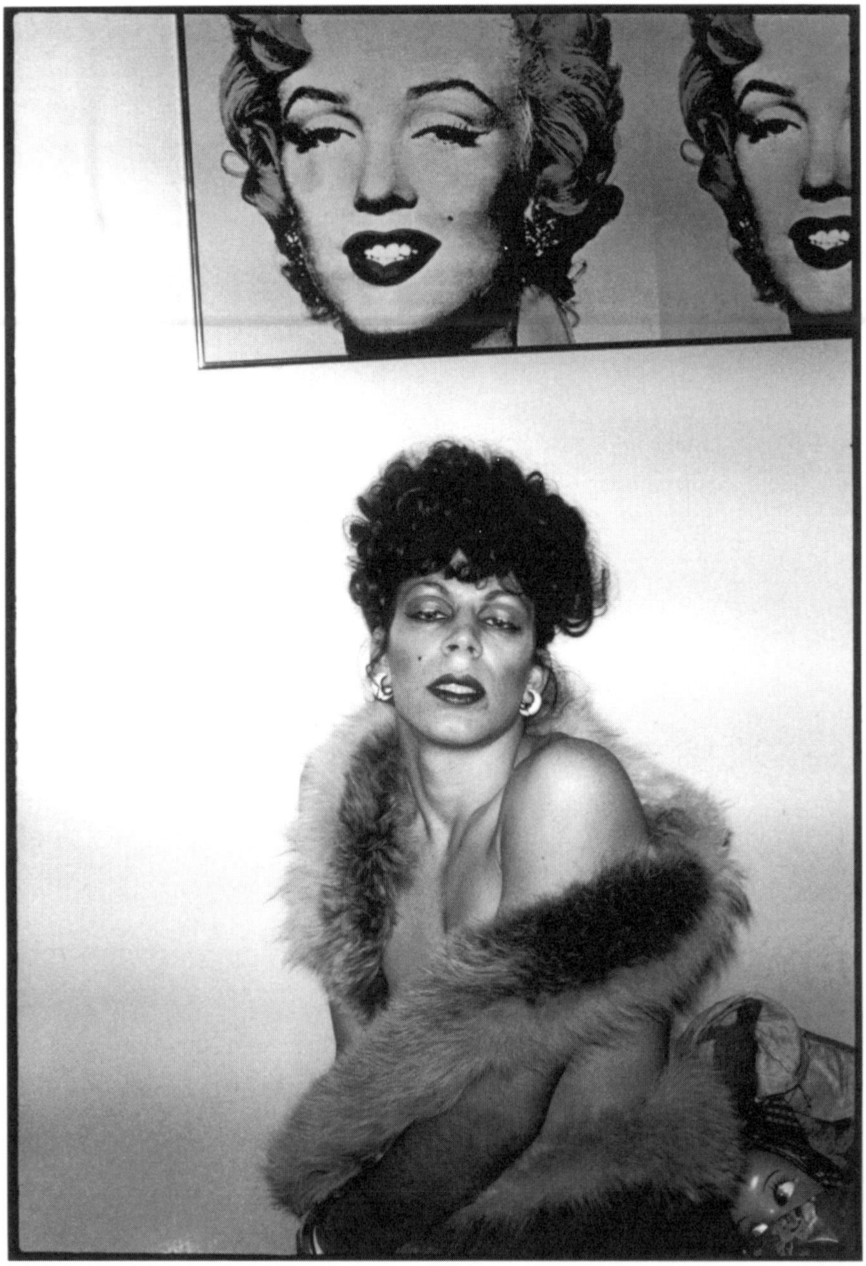

Ivy with Marilyn, Boston 1973 gelatin silver print 20 x 16 inches

Nan Goldin is represented by
Matthew Marks Gallery

523 W24th Street New York
212 243 0200 fax 212 243 0047
gallery@mmarks.com
www.artnet.com/mmarks.html

DOUG AITKEN

3 0 3 GALLERY
525W. 22ND ST. - NEW YORK
TEL: +1 212 255 11 21

VICTORIA MIRO GALLERY
21 CORK STREET - LONDON
TEL: +44 171 734 50 82

HAUSER & WIRTH & PRESENHUBER
LIMMATSTRASSE 270 - ZURICH
TEL: +41 1 446 80 60

DECEMBER

THOMAS STRUTH

JANUARY – FEBRUARY

JAMES COLEMAN

FEBRUARY – MARCH

TACITA DEAN

MAURIZIO CATTELAN

MARIAN GOODMAN GALLERY

24 WEST 57TH STREET NEW YORK, NY 10019 TEL 212 977-7160

FAX 212 581-5187 GOODMAN@MARIANGOODMAN.COM

Arndt & Partner

Sophie Calle
Peter Friedl

Thomas Hirschhorn

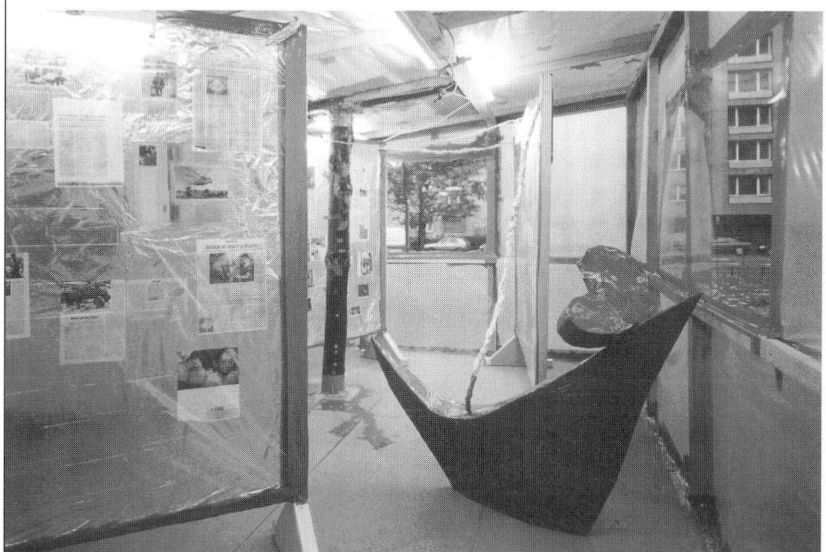

Thomas Hirschhorn, „Ein Kunstwerk, Ein Problem", Ausstellungsansicht, Portikus, Frankfurt a/M, 1998

Fabrice Hybert
Via Lewandowsky
Bjarne Melgaard
Max Mohr
Nedko Solakov
Hiroshi Sugito
Mathilde ter Heijne
Susan Turcot

Arndt & Partner
Auguststraße 35
D-10119 Berlin

Telefon +49 (30) 280 81 23
Fax +49 (30) 283 37 38
Email arndt@arndt-partner.de
http://www.arndt-partner.de

MONA HATOUM

FABRICE GYGI

THOMAS HIRSCHHORN

JOCHEN GERZ

WOLFGANG LAIB

ANTHONY CRAGG

ABIGAIL LANE

MOSHE NINIO

SOPHIE CALLE

GABRIEL OROZCO

NOBUYOSHI ARAKI

SIGMAR POLKE

JAVIER PÉREZ

DARREN ALMOND

THOMAS RUFF

ABSALON

YOON JA & PAUL DEVAUTOUR

RIRKRIT TIRAVANIJA

JOSÉ MARÍA SICILIA

JANA STERBAK

SLEEPING WATERS

DARREN ALMOND / FABRICE GYGI / RACHEL HARRISON / MOSHE NINIO
NOVEMBER - DECEMBER 1999

VIDEO COLLECTION A.S.S.N.

(Ars Sine Scientia Nihil)

N°1 : CORALY SUARD-HIRSCHHORN
INTERVIEW THOMAS HIRSCHHORN / JEAN-CHARLES MASSÉRA

GALERIE CHANTAL CROUSEL / 40 RUE QUINCAMPOIX / F - 75004 PARIS

T. 01 42 77 38 87   F. 01 42 77 59 00   GALERIE.CHANTAL.CROUSEL@WANADOO.FR   WWW.CROUSEL.COM

15. JANUAR BIS 12. MÄRZ 2000

JASON RHOADES

GALERIE HAUSER & WIRTH

Limmatstrasse 270, 8005 Zürich / Tel: +41 1 446 80 50, Fax: +41 1 446 80 55 / e-mail: info@ghw.ch
Öffnungszeiten: Di bis Fr 12 bis 18 Uhr, Sa 11 bis 16 Uhr

15. JANUAR BIS 12. MÄRZ 2000

KAREN KILIMNIK

GALERIE HAUSER & WIRTH & PRESENHUBER

Limmatstrasse 270, 8005 Zürich / Tel: +41 1 446 80 60, Fax: +41 1 446 80 65 / e-mail: info@ghwp.ch
Öffnungszeiten: Di bis Fr 12 bis 18 Uhr, Sa 11 bis 16 Uhr

2000

IMI KNOEBEL

ARMORY SHOW

GÜNTHER FÖRG

WINSTON ROETH

ART BASEL

MARY HEILMANN

JEAN-MARC BUSTAMANTE

PALOMA VARGA-WEISZ

HELMUT DORNER

vera munro

GALERIE VERA MUNRO

HEILWIGSTRASSE 64

20249 HAMBURG

TELEFON 040 - 47 47 46

TELEFAX 040 - 47 25 50

MAI 36 GALERIE

VITO ACCONCI
FRANZ ACKERMANN
IAN ANÜLL
JOHN BALDESSARI
STEPHAN BALKENHOL
TROY BRAUNTUCH
ANKE DOBERAUER
PIA FRIES
ANDREAS GURSKY
LES LEVINE
RITA MCBRIDE
HARALD F. MÜLLER
MATT MULLICAN
MANFRED PERNICE
CHRISTOPH RÜTIMANN
THOMAS RUFF
JÖRG SASSE
PAUL THEK
LAWRENCE WEINER
RÉMY ZAUGG

LAWRENCE WEINER

November 27, 1999 – January 15, 2000

The Armory Show 2000

New York, February 25 – 28, 2000

Rämistrasse 37, CH-8001 Zürich, Tel. 01 261 68 80, Fax 261 68 81 *spring 2000*

February

Seth Kaufman/John Morris

April

Jim Hodges

ANTHONY MEIER FINE ARTS
3007 Jackson Street San Francisco, CA 94115 (415) 351-1400

Jean-Marc Bustamante

Inédits

Tableaux 1978–1982

13 JANUARY – 26 FEBRUARY 2000

Didier Vermeiren

2 MARCH – 2 APRIL 2000

Patrick Vanden Eynde

6 APRIL – 6 MAY 2000

Richard Artschwager

11 MAY – 10 JUNE 2000

ART FAIRS

TEFAF Maastricht

18 – 26 MARCH 2000

ART Brussels

31 MARCH – 4 APRIL 2000

Xavier Hufkens

Sint-Jorisstraat 6–8 rue Saint-Georges

Brussel 1050 Bruxelles

TEL. 32 (0)2 646 63 30 – FAX 32 (0)2 646 93 42

info@xavierhufkens.com
http://www.artnet.com/xhufkens.html

Open Tuesday to Saturday, noon to 6 pm

Sadie Coles HQ

winter/spring

Jim Lambie	december
Ugo Rondinone	january
Sarah Lucas	february
Elizabeth Peyton	march
John Currin	may

35 Heddon Street London W1R 7LL UK www.sadiecoles.com
Tel +44 (0) 20 7434 2227, Fax +44 (0) 20 7434 2228

GALLERIA MASSIMO MININI

MICHELANGELO PISTOLETTO SALVO
MARCO MAZZUCCONI SOL LEWITT
MAURIZIO CATTELAN J.G. DOKOUPIL
ALIGHIERO E BOETTI PETER HALLEY
MARCO BAGNOLI ROBERT BARRY
ETTORE SPALLETTI DANIEL BUREN
LUCIANO FABRO HAMISH FULTON
PIERO GILARDI EVA MARISALDI
DAN GRAHAM BERTRAND LAVIER
MARIO AIRO' MATTHEW MC. CASLIN
LUIGI ONTANI IAN HAMILTON FINLAY
GIULIO PAOLINI DIDIER VERMEIREN
CARLA ACCARDI ANDRE CADERE
STEFANO ARIENTI ANISH KAPOOR
ALBERTO GARUTTI BERNAR VENET
ALESSANDRA TESI GER VAN ELK
VANESSA BEECROFT JAN FABRE
GERWALD ROCKENSCHAUB SERSE

Via L. Apollonio 68 - 25128 Brescia (I)
phone +39.030.381950 - fax +39.030.392446
E-Mail galleriaminini@numerica.it

karyn lovegrove gallery

Simon Periton
January 8–February 5

Candida Höfer
February 12–March 11

Polly Apfelbaum
March 18–April 22

Ricky Swallow
April 29–May 27

Karyn Lovegrove Gallery
6150 Wilshire Boulevard #8
Los Angeles CA 90048 USA
Telephone: 323 525 1755
Facsimile: 323 525 1245
Email: lovegrovek@aol.com
www.karynlovegrovegallery.com

GALERIA ■ HELGA DE ALVEAR

DR. FOURQUET 12, 28012 MADRID. TEL:(34) 91 468 05 06 FAX:(34) 91 467 51 34
E-MAIL:dealvear@aleph-arts.org http://aleph-arts.org/dealvear

December 1, 1999 - January 22, 2000

KARIN SANDER

ESTUDIO ▲ **HELGA DE ALVEAR**

"RAGTIME"

ANTONI ABAD
PEP AGUT
HELENA ALMEIDA
NÚRIA CANAL
DANIEL CANOGAR
HANNAH COLLINS
JOHN COPLANS
DOUGLAS GORDON
BRUCE NAUMAN
ANTONI TÀPIES

GALERIE LELONG ZÜRICH

«PARS PRO TOTO»

ARCHITECTURAL PHOTOGRAPHY

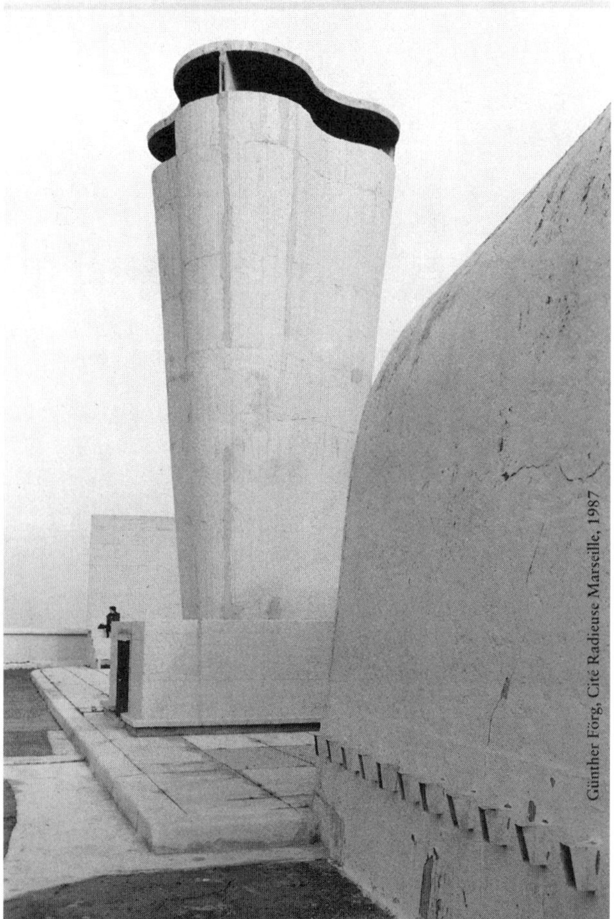

Günther Förg, Cité Radieuse Marseille, 1987

27 NOVEMBER 1999 (OPEN WEEKEND) – 15 JANUARY 2000

GALERIE LELONG ZÜRICH
UTOQUAI 31 • CH-8008 ZÜRICH
TEL.(+41-)1-251 11 20 • FAX 262 52 85
Opening Hours: Tu–Fr 11am–6pm • Sa 11am–4pm

John M Armleder
Sylvie Fleury
Gaylen Gerber
Peter Z. Herzog
Thomas Hirschhorn
Jean-Luc Manz
Thom Merrick
Olivier Mosset
Gerwald Rockenschaub
Muntean/Rosenblum
Adrian Schiess

Galerie Susanna Kulli
Davidstrasse 40
CH-9000 St. Gallen
Tel. 071 223 59 58
Fax 071 223 59 35
susanna.kulli@avtive.ch
Offen:
Di bis Fr 14–18, Sa 10–17

14. JANUAR – 4. MÄRZ 2000

Albert OEHLEN

Martin KIPPENBERGER

10. MÄRZ – 29. MAI 2000

GALERIE GISELA CAPITAIN

AACHENER STR. 5 D-50674 KÖLN TEL 0221-25 66 76 FAX 25 65 93

10 December 1999 to 31 January 2000

Thomas Hirschhorn

galerie erna hécey 25 bvd du Prince Henri L-1724 Luxembourg t: + 352 24 11 74 f: + 352 24 15 89
e-mail: galerie.erna.hecey@online.lu gallery hours: tue - fri 2 - 7 pm, sa 11am - 5 pm

L.A. Galerie – Lothar Albrecht

Domstrasse 6, D-60311 Frankfurt, Telefon: (49) 69 - 28 86 87, Fax: (49) 69 - 28 09 12

Representing:

HIROSHI SUNAIRI July – Aug. 2000
OLIVER BOBERG
BERNARD FAUCON
ROBERT F. HAMMERSTIEL Jan. – Feb. 2000
JOHN HILLIARD
TRACEY MOFFATT May – June 2000
LUKAS EINSELE
JOAN FONTCUBERTA
NAOAYA HATAKEYAMA
EDGAR LISSEL
KEN LUM Sept. – Oct. 2000
MABEL PALACIN
LOIS RENNER March – April 2000
JAVIER VALLHONRAT

ART FAIRS:

ART BASEL
ART COLOGNE
ART FORUM BERLIN
ART FRANKFURT
THE ARMORY SHOW, NY

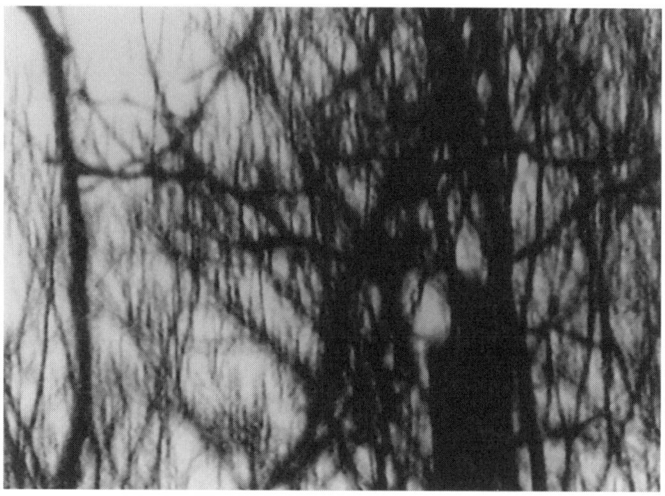

enclosed no.1, digital b/w photograph, 84 x 112 cm

NAN HOOVER FOTOARBEITEN UND ZEICHNUNGEN (ZUR AUSSTELLUNG ERSCHEINT EIN KATALOG) **27.11.-15.1.2000**

FLASH 99 AN EXHIBITION OF YOUNG EMERGING ARTISTS IN COLLABORATION WITH INTERNATIONAL GALLERIES **22.02.-03.3.2000**

GALERIE PATRIK FRÖHLICH
GALERIE PATRIK FRÖHLICH
Mittwoch bis Freitag Samstag

DIENERSTRASSE 21, 8004 ZÜRICH, FON+FAX: 01 242 89 00, email:patrikfroehlich@access.ch, www.artnet.com/pfroehlich.html

GALERIE MEERT RIHOUX

SYLVIE EYBERG — January 2000

ENRICO CASTELLANI — Feb.–March 2000

RICHARD TUTTLE — April–May 2000

RUE DU CANAL 13
1000 BRUSSELS
VAARTSTRAAT 13
1000 BRUSSEL
FAX 02/219.37.21
TEL 02/219.14.22

Schedler
Aktiengesellschaft

Galerie Schedler
Josefstrasse 53
CH 8005 Zürich
T +41 1 440 61 20
F +41 1 440 61 21
zurich@schedler.ch

Tuesday to Friday 12 - 6 p.m.
Saturday 11 a.m. - 4 p.m.

Galerie und Edition Schedler
Dorfstrasse 56
CH 8532 Warth
T +41 52 747 19 46
F +41 52 747 19 48
warth@schedler.ch

Saturday 2 - 5 p.m.
Sunday 11 a.m. - 5 p.m. and by appointment

www.schedler.ch
Member of
Association of Swiss Galleries AGS

Galerie Schedler Zurich

Uwe Wittwer
until 29 January 2000
(Publication available)

Hans Witschi
11 February to 18 March

Eliane Rutishauser, Christoph Schneeberger, Stephanie Schneider / P77: Margaret Morgan
24 March to 29 April

high five (beauty and sports)
5 May to 5 June

Representing:
Jean Crotti, Jan Czerwinski, Allen Frame, Max Grüter, Dieter Hall, Christoph Hänsli, Attila Richard Lukacs, Andrea Muheim, Richard Müller, Hironori Murai, Walter Pfeiffer, Eliane Rutishauser, Monika Rutishauser, Stefan Saner, Gary Schneider, Christoph Schneeberger, Pierre Sutter, Christoph Wachter, Rodney White, Alfred Wirz, Hans Witschi, Uwe Wittwer

Attend the leading international conference of more than 4,000 artists, art historians, and visual arts professionals. Over 120 scholarly sessions, the largest job placement service of its kind, annual trade and book exhibit, plus many special events.

The 88th Annual Conference of the *College Art Association*

February 23 to 26, 2000 in New York City at the New York Hilton and Towers

Log on to our web site at www.collegeart.org

CAA

ART YEAR

THE INTERNATIONAL EXHIBITION GUIDE

2000

Artyear is published by

hopefulmonster editore via Santa Chiara 30 10122 Torino Italy
0039.011.4367197 fx 0039.011.4369025 e-mail hopmonst@tin.it

Alquié Anselmo Appel Arienti Bagnoli Baj Barzagli Beecroft Bernstein Bertoni Beuys Bianchi Blanchard Boetti Borrelli Burri Ceroli Chia Chiari Clemente Consagra Corneli Corsini Costa Clegg & Guttmann Cucchi De Maria Dibbets Fabro Ferrara Fontana Gastini Gilardi Gorgoni Graetz Grünfeld Guidieri Hofstadter **hopefulmonster** Icaro Isgrò Katz Kirkeby Kossuth Kounellis Lewitt Lionni Livsic Mainolfi Manzoni Maraniello Marc Mauri Merz Messina Mochetti Mondino Münch Nannucci Nicolaus Nunzio Oldenburg Ontani Paladino Paolini Pascali Pellizza Penone Pichler Pirri Pistoletto Plessi Poirier Pomodoro Quarzo Rossino Rotella Rückriem Ruiz Mignone Salvadori Sartelli Scarpitta Schnabel Serres Shine Staccioli Studio Azzurro Tilson Trotta Uncini Vedova Voltolini Wastijn & Deschuymer Wood Woodman Zorio

gallery bob van orsouw limmatstrasse 270 8005 zurich
phone +41-1-273 11 00 fax +41-1-273 11 02

november 27 until january 22, 2000 **albrecht schnider**

january 29 until february 26, 2000 **philip akkerman**

the armory show new york, february 25 until 28, 2000

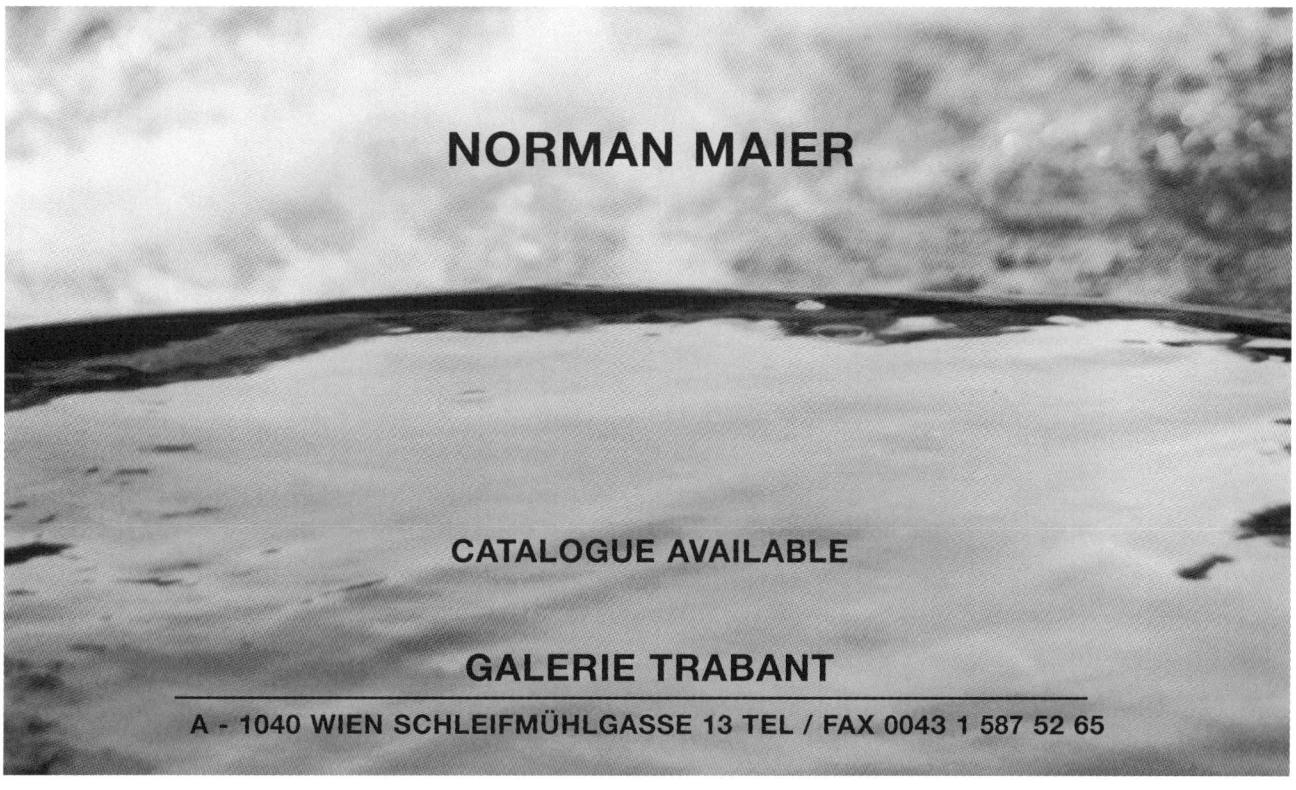

STUDIO
ARTE
ECHTVERGOLDUNGEN
MODERNE
EINRAHMUNGEN
Studio Arte Flückiger & Fischbach AG
Stauffacherquai 46, 8004 Zürich
Telefon 01-241 86 71
Telefax 01-241 35 85

MODERNE EINRAHMUNGEN

WIR HABEN ALLE RAHMEN FÜR DIE AUSSTELLUNGEN DER PARKETT - EDITIONEN IM CENTRE D'ART CONTEMPORAIN, GENF, IM MUSEUM LUDWIG, KÖLN, IM LOUISIANA MUSEUM, DÄNEMARK, UND IM HILL SIDE FORUM, TOKYO, HERGESTELLT.

ZU UNSEREN KUNDEN ZÄHLEN:

KUNSTSAMMLER, MUSEEN, GALERIEN, INDUSTRIE UND PRIVATE.

Kunsttransporte in alle Erdteile

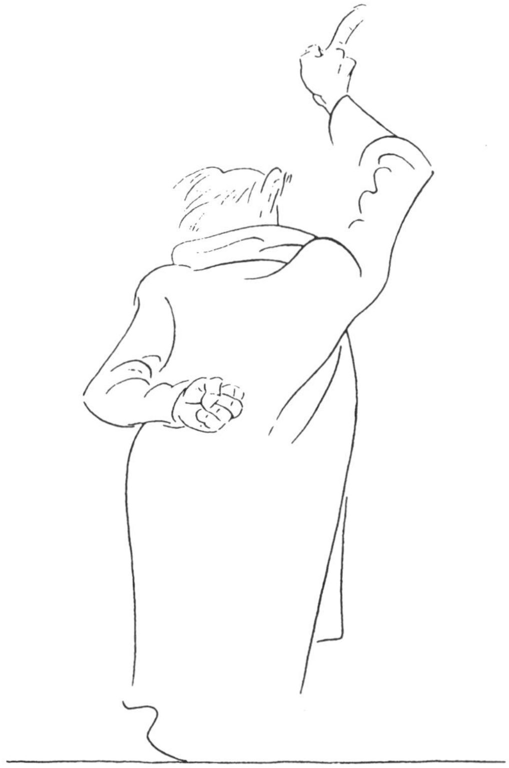

«In den Kunsttransporten, wer nicht das Beste hat,
hat nichts» *(frei nach Olaf Gulbransson)*

MÖBEL-TRANSPORT AG

für sorgfältige Transporte

Gaswerkareal
8010 Zürich
Tel. 01 733 51 11
Fax 01 730 88 80

Genuastrasse 14
4142 Münchenstein-Basel
Tel. 061 331 88 55
Fax 061 331 80 47

E-Mail: moebel@moebel-transport-ag.com
http://www.moebel-transport-ag.com

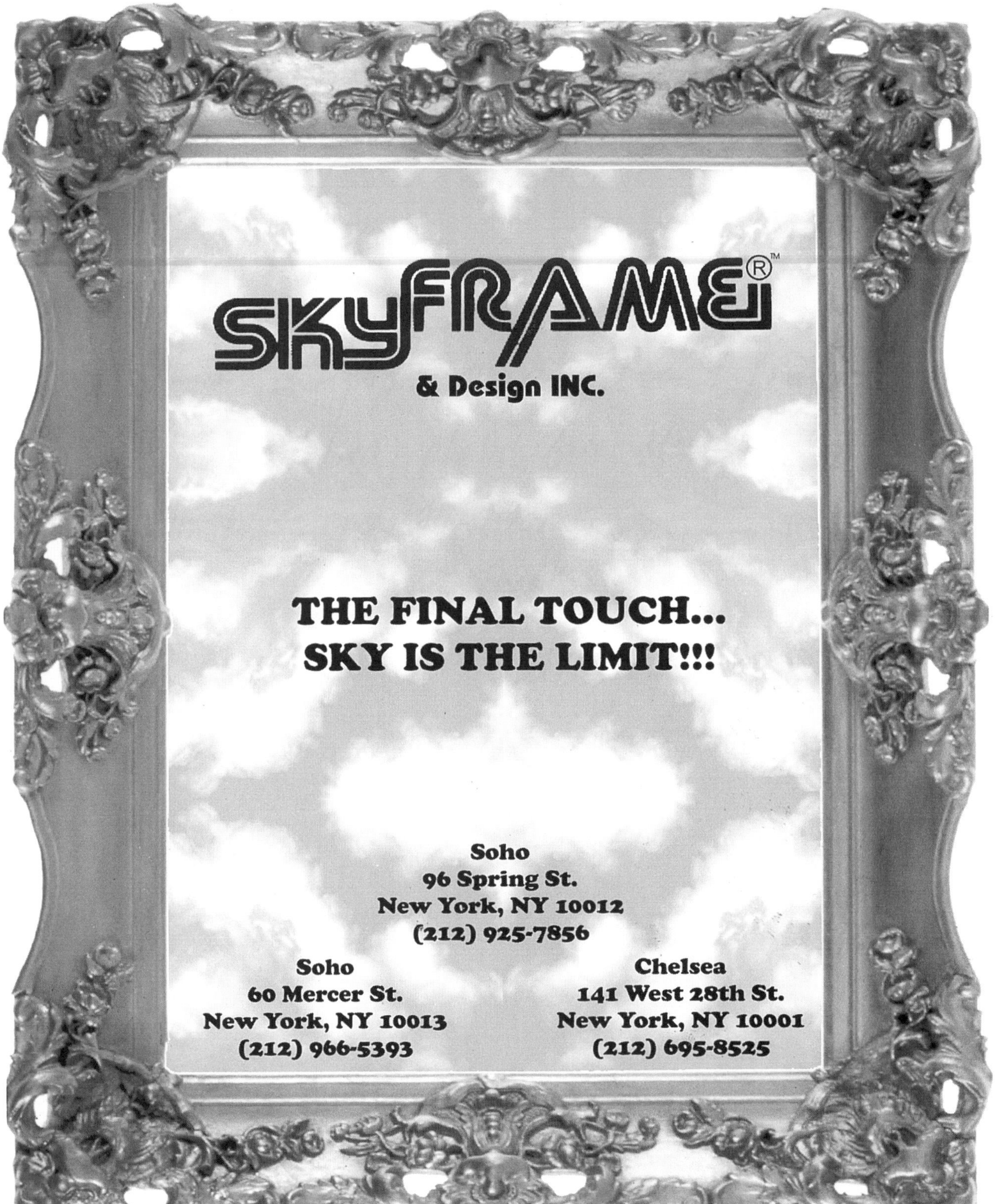
SKYFRAME
& Design INC.
THE FINAL TOUCH...
SKY IS THE LIMIT!!!
Soho
96 Spring St.
New York, NY 10012
(212) 925-7856
Soho
60 Mercer St.
New York, NY 10013
(212) 966-5393
Chelsea
141 West 28th St.
New York, NY 10001
(212) 695-8525

Zürichsee
Druckereien AG

[METZGER REHNER BRICCOLA]

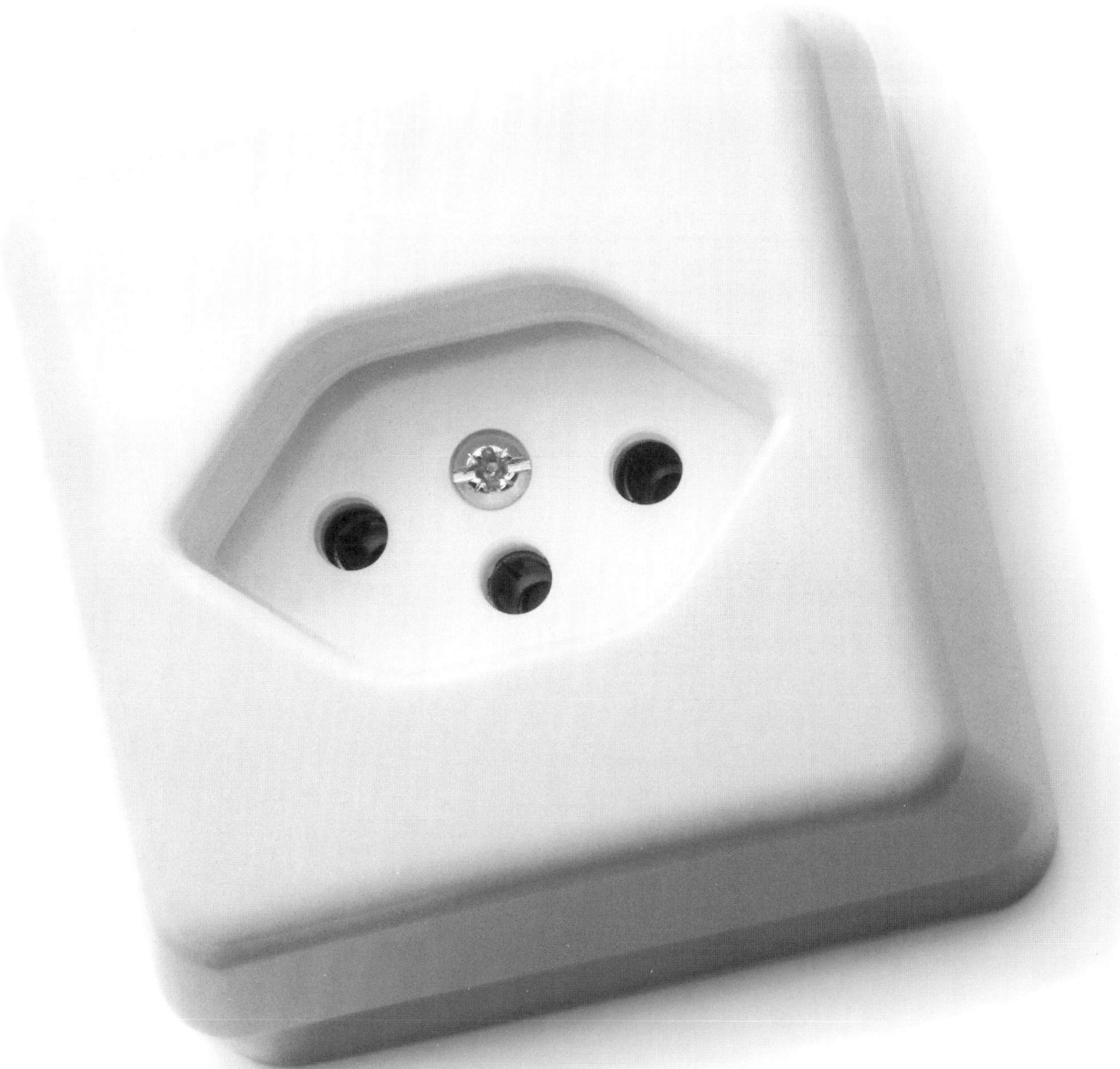

Kontaktfreudig: Zürichsee Druckereien AG • Seestrasse 86 • Postfach • 8712 Stäfa • Tel. 01 928 53 03 • Fax 01 928 53 10 • Internet www.zsd.ch

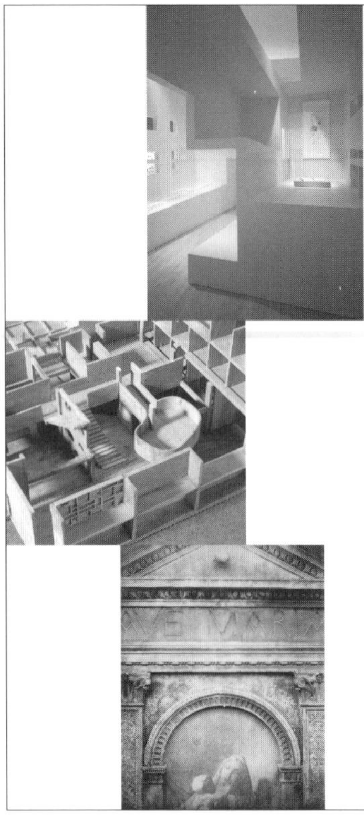

10

En chantier: The Collections of the CCA, 1989–1999

From 24 November 1999 to 30 April 2000

CCA

To celebrate the CCA's 10th anniversary, this exhibition features more than 350 prints, drawings, photographs, rare books, manuscripts, toys, and models dating from the 15th century to today.
Publication available at the CCA Bookstore and by mail.

Canadian Centre for Architecture
1920, rue Baile, Montréal, Québec, Canada. 514 939.7026 or www.cca.qc.ca

Presented by
Investors Group

Photo: © CCA, Montréal. © FLC/SODRAC (Montréal).

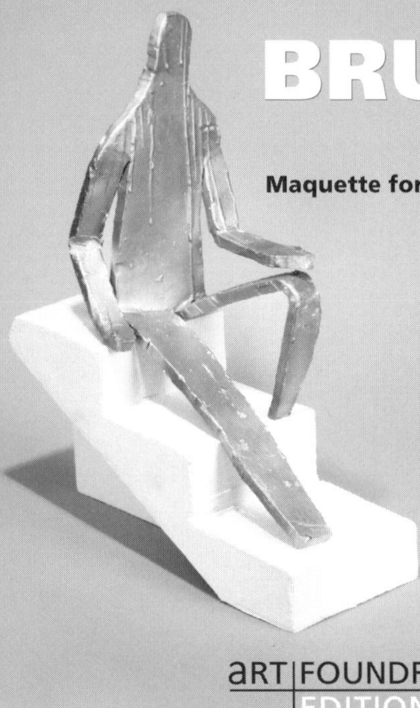

BRUCE NAUMAN

Maquette for 5 Foot 8 Inch Figure, 1998

Cast Bronze and Plaster
19 x 5.75 x 14.5 inches, 48.3 x 14.6 x 36.8 cm
An Art Foundry Edition of 15

Represented by

Konrad Fischer Gallery *Düsseldorf*
Sperone Westwater Gallery *New York*
Donald Young Gallery *Chicago*

art|FOUNDRY EDITIONS

505 471.7184 fax 505 471.6426 artfoundry.net

PO Box 8107 Santa Fe New Mexico 87504 USA

MUSEUM MODERNER KUNST STIFTUNG LUDWIG WIEN

MMK SL W

50 Jahre Kunst aus Mitteleuropa 1949-1999

Aspekte/ Positionen

18. 12. 1999 – 27. 2. 2000

Miró-Klee-Tanguy

18. 3. – 14. 5. 2000

Lois Weinberger

10. 3. – 24. 4. 2000

Palais Liechtenstein
Fürstengasse 1 · 1090 Wien

20er Haus
Arsenalstraße 1 · 1030 Wien

Mehr Informationen über diese Ausstellungen finden Sie im Internet!

Internet: http://www.MMKSLW.or.at/MMKSLW/
E-mail: museum@MMKSLW.or.at

2000

15. Januar – 12. März **PIERRE HUYGHE**

25. März – 21. Mai **SHARON LOCKHART**

7. Juni – 13. August **SARAH MORRIS**

26. August – 22. Oktober **MANFRED PERNICE**

4. November – 31. Dezember **RICHARD PHILLIPS**

KUNSTHALLE ZÜRICH

Limmatstrasse 270 CH-8005 Zürich Tel (01) 272 15 15 Fax (01) 272 18 88 e-mail: kunsthallezh@access.ch

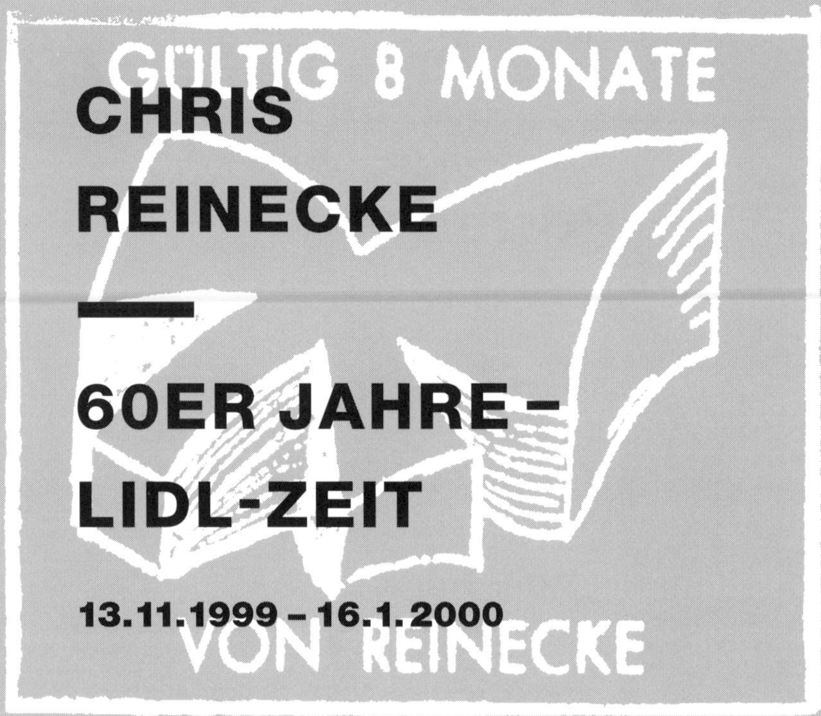

CHRIS REINECKE

—

60ER JAHRE – LIDL-ZEIT

13.11.1999 – 16.1.2000

Kunstmuseum Düsseldorf
Ehrenhof 5 · 40479 Düsseldorf

Tel. +49 (0) 221. 89 92 460
Fax +49 (0) 221. 89 29 173

Öffnungszeiten:
dienstags – sonntags 11 – 18 Uhr
während der Chardin-Ausstellung
freitags bis 21 Uhr, Heiligabend
und Sylvester geschlossen,
1. und 2. Weihnachtstag geöffnet

Begleitend zur Ausstellung erscheint im Verlag der Buchhandlung Walther König das Buch »Chris Reinecke, 60er Jahre – Lidl-Zeit«, hrsg. von Barbara John, Susanne Rennert und Stephan von Wiese.

Adam Fuss — 20.11.1999 - 16.1.2000
Less of a Test than Earth

Daido Moriyama — 29.1. - 26.3.2000
Stray Dog

Wendy Ewald — 8.4. - 4.6.2000

FOTOMUSEUM
WINTERTHUR

Grüzenstrasse 44
CH-8400 Winterthur
Tel: 052/233 60 86
www.fotomuseum.ch

Di – Fr 12 – 18 Uhr
Sa/So 11 – 17 Uhr

29. Januar bis 26. März 2000
Stefan Banz

8. April bis 4. Juni 2000
Mike Kelley

17. Juni bis 13. August 2000
Maurizio Cattelan

migros museum, Limmatstrasse 270, CH-8005 Zürich, Tel. +41 1 277 20 50, Fax +41 1 277 62 86
Opening hours are thuesday to friday 12 to 6 PM, saturday and sunday 11 to 5 PM
visit us at www.migrosmuseum.ch

«migros museum»
Museum für Gegenwartskunst Zürich
THE REAL THING

The Jan van Eyck Akademie is an international post graduate centre for fine art, design and theory. Each department develops its own programme directed towards the individual needs of participants. Critical research, joint seminars and workshops, and a programme of public events encourage the dialogue between the departments. Special reserach areas include Transcultural studies and Design and media.

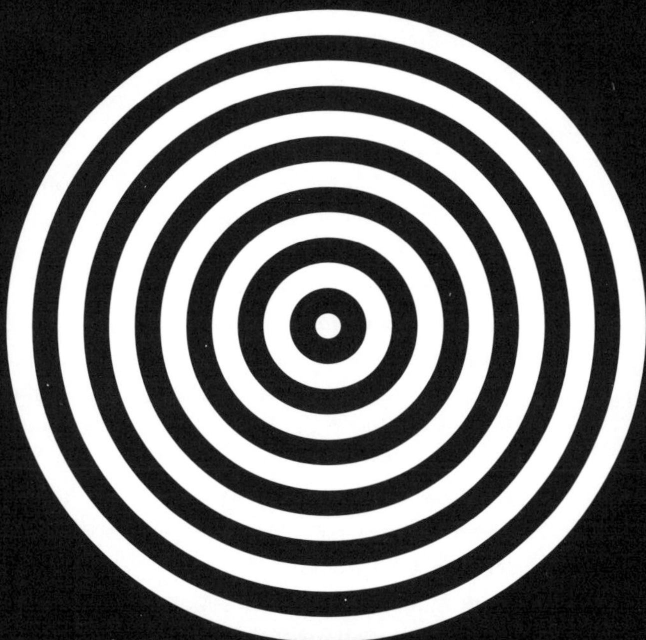

Jan van Eyck Akademie

Fine art
Design
Theory

If you are interested, please write, call, or e-mail for further information, an application form and our 2000 brochure to:
Academieplein 1, 6211 KM
Maastricht, Netherlands
telephone +31.43.350.3737
fax +31.43.350.3799
e-mail info@janvaneyck.nl

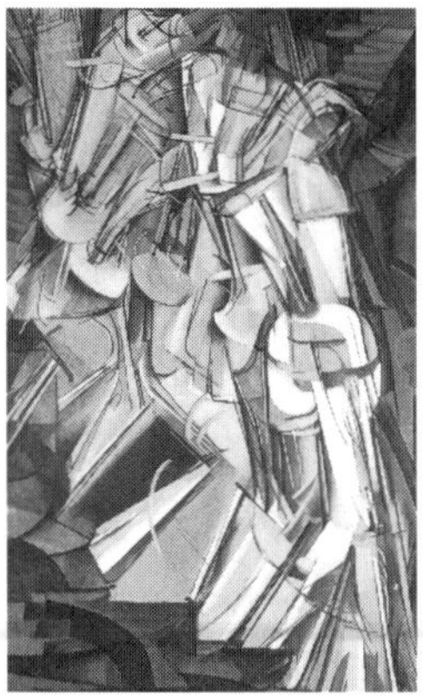

The Armory Show 2000

The New North Pavilion
11th Avenue & 39th Street New York City

Friday, February 25, 2000, 12-8PM
Saturday, February 26, 2000, 12-8PM
Sunday, February 27, 2000, 12-8PM
Monday, February 28, 2000, 12-6PM

Opening Night Benefit for Dia Center for the Arts
Thursday, February 24, 2000, 6.30-9.30PM

THE INTERNATIONAL FAIR OF NEW ART TEL 212-777-3338

ACME. Los Angeles
Brooke Alexander NY
Alexander and Bonin NY
Mitchell Algus Gallery NY
American Fine Arts, Co. NY
Andréhn-Schiptjenko Stockholm
Angles Gallery Santa Monica
Art: Concept Paris
Art & Public Geneva
Galerie Daniel Blau Munich
Peter Blum NY
Blum & Poe Santa Monica
Marianne Boesky Gallery NY
Bonakdar Jancou Gallery NY
Rena Bransten San Francisco
Galeria Camargo Vilaça Sao Paulo
Galerie Gisela Capitain Cologne
Marta Cervera Gallery Madrid
Cheim & Read NY
Sadie Coles HQ London
CRG Gallery NY
D'Amelio Terras NY
Deitch Projects NY
Galerie Eigen + Art Berlin - Leipzig
Thomas Erben Gallery NY
Feature Inc. NY
Feigen Contemporary NY
Ronald Feldman Fine Arts NY
Galerie Franck + Schulte Berlin
Jessica Fredericks Gallery NY
Stephen Friedman Gallery London
Barbara Gladstone Gallery NY
Marian Goodman Gallery NY
Gorney Bravin + Lee NY
Greenberg Van Doren NY
Galerie Hauser & Wirth Zurich
Pat Hearn Gallery NY
Galerie Max Hetzler Berlin
Rhona Hoffman Gallery Chicago
Jablonka Galerie Cologne
Jay Jopling / White Cube London
Casey Kaplan Gallery NY
Georg Kargl Vienna
Paul Kasmin Gallery NY
Kerlin Gallery Dublin
Anton Kern Gallery NY
Nicole Klagsbrun Gallery NY
Tomio Koyama Gallery Tokyo
Galerie Krinzinger Vienna
L.A. Galerie-Lothar Albrecht Frankfurt
Lehmann Maupin NY
Lisson Gallery London
Lombard-Freid Fine Arts NY
Luhring Augustine Gallery NY
Sprüth / Magers Cologne / Munich
Mai 36 Galerie Zurich
Lawrence Markey NY
Matthew Marks Gallery NY
Metro Pictures NY
Modern Art London
Mark Moore Gallery Santa Monica
Paul Morris Gallery NY
Galerie Vera Munro Hamburg
Galerie Nächst St. Stephen Vienna
Galerie Christian Nagel Cologne
Neu Gallery Berlin
Galerie Nathalie Obadia Paris
Roslyn Oxley9 Gallery Sydney
Patrick Painter Inc. Santa Monica
Maureen Paley / Interim Art London
Parkett Editions NY
Galerie Emmanuel Perrotin Paris
Friedrich Petzel Gallery NY
Produzentengalerie Hamburg
Galerie Almine Rech Paris
Regen Projects Los Angeles
Robert Sandelson London
Julie Saul Gallery NY
Scalo Zurich - NY
Galerie Aurel Scheibler Cologne
Schipper & Krome Berlin
Brent Sikkema NY
Holly Solomon Gallery NY
Gian Enzo Sperone Rome
Stefan Stux Gallery NY
Leslie Tonkonow NY
Henry Urbach Architecture NY
Bob Van Orsouw Gallery Zurich
Galleri Nicolai Wallner Copenhagen
Gitte Weise Gallery Sydney
Donald Young Gallery Chicago
Zeno X Gallery Antwerp
David Zwirner NY
303 Gallery NY

.AZZO DELLE PAPESSE
Centro Arte Contemporanea

18.12.1999 » 05.03.2000 h. 12.00 » 19.00

COLLEZIONISMI

the Collection of the
Fondation Cartier pour l'art contemporain

BILL VIOLA
VIRXILIO VIEITEZ
WOLFGANG TILLMANS
HIROSHI SUGIMOTO
ALAIN SÉCHAS
THOMAS RUFF
MARKUS RAETZ
BERNARD PIFFARETTI
VIK MUNIZ
MARIO MERZ
WOLFGANG LAIB
UDOMSAK KRISANAMIS
BODYS ISEK KINGELEZ
SHIRLEY JAFFE
SIMON HANTAÏ
DAVID HAMMONS
PETER HALLEY
RAYMOND HAINS
NAN GOLDIN
SAM FRANCIS
HUBERT DUPRAT
THOMAS DEMAND
MARC COUTURIER
JAMES LEE BYARS
CHRISTIAN BOLTANSKI
BEAURIN DOMERCQ
MATTHEW BARNEY

ONTRAPPUNTI BURRI BACON BEUYS

MARCO VENERI

COMUNE DI SIENA Assessorato alla Cultura
Siena arte contemporanea progetti opere eventi
MONTE DEI PASCHI DI SIENA Istituto di diritto pubblico fondato nel 1472
THE CHARMING HOTELS INDEPENDENT LUXURY HOTELS
CREDIT SUISSE FIRST BOSTON

via di Città, 126 53100 Siena Italy office: phone/fax ++39 0577.42093 press office: phone/fax ++39 0577.226121 e-mail: papesse@comune.siena.it

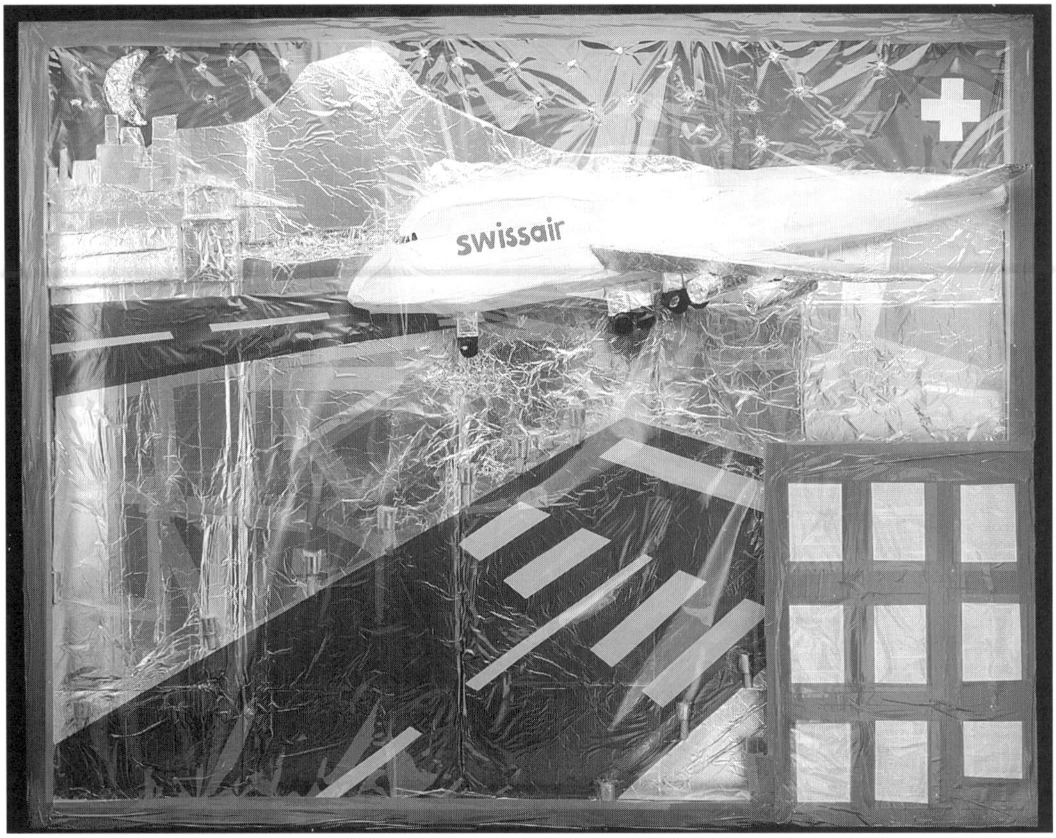

THOMAS HIRSCHHORN

Over the last five years, Swiss artist Thomas Hirschhorn has developed one of the most idiosyncratic and original sculptural vocabularies of his generation, establishing him as a major international artist. Hirschhorn forms his sculptures from the detritus of urban life, ranging from scraps of wood, tape, and plastic, to aluminum foil. The results are seemingly casual, chaotic, obsessive, and excessive environments informed by the artist's unique sense of materials, wry wit, and profound commitment to issues of social justice.

Presenting his most recent piece, "World Airport," as well as an entirely new installation, this book features essays by curators Okwui Enwezor, James Rondeau, and Hamza Walker, that explore the conception and construction of these works and situate them in the artist's œuvre and beyond. The Art Institute of Chicago and the Renaissance Society, Chicago, are cooperating in presenting this catalogue and museum exhibition, Hirschhorn's first in the United States.

Published by The Art Institute of Chicago and The Renaissance Society
ISBN 0-86559-181-4
US $19.95

To order and for a free catalogue

North and South America
D.A.P.
800 338 2665 tel
212 627 9484 fax

Europe
IDEA Books
+31 20 6226154 tel
+31 20 6209299 fax

d.a.p.
distributed art publishers

Art | 31 | Basel | 21–26 | 6 | 2000
The Art Fair

Art 31 Basel, P.O. Box, CH-4021 Basel
Tel. +41 61 686 20 20, Fax +41 61 686 26 86, E-Mail: Art@messebasel.ch, www.Art.ch

Messe Basel.

sponsored by UBS

1. – 9. APRIL 2000

kunst KÖLN

2000

Internationale Messe
für Editionen, Art Brut
Kunst nach 1960

weitere Informationen:
KölnMesse GmbH
Postfach 210760, D-50532 Köln
tel. (0)221/821-32 15, fax (0)221/821-37 34
www.koelnmesse.de

KölnMesse

Die Messe zum Thema Kunst ***Moderne Kunst von den 60er Jahren bis heute – Halle 1.2, New Attitudes: Junge Galerien und Kunst der 90er Jahre, ArtKino, Multiple District, Künstlerbücher – Halle 1.1. Messegelände Eingang City, täglich 11 – 19 Uhr, Eintritt inkl. Katalog: Tageskarte 25 DM, Abendkarte 12 DM, Infoline 069-75 75 66 64, Internet www.artfrankfurt.de, Messe Frankfurt GmbH, Ludwig-Erhard-Anlage 1, 60327 Frankfurt am Main*** ***The fair that keeps to the subject of art*** ***Modern art from the Sixties until today – hall 1.2, New Attitudes: young galleries and art of the Nineties, ArtCinema, Multiple District, Artist's Books – hall 1.1. Fairgrounds City entrance, daily 11 a.m. to 7 p.m., Tickets incl. catalogue: daily ticket 25 DM, evening ticket 12 DM, Infoline +49-(0)69-75 75 66 64, Internet www.artfrankfurt.de, Messe Frankfurt GmbH, Ludwig-Erhard-Anlage 1, 60327 Frankfurt am Main***

art frankfurt

Messe Frankfurt

24.–27. März 2000

SCALO Zürich – Berlin – New York

International Publishing Project for Photography, Art and Popular Culture
Internationaler Projektverlag für Fotografie, Kunst und Alltagskultur

Verlagssitz / Head Office
SCALO VERLAG AG
Weinbergstrasse 22a
CH-8001 Zürich
Tel. 01 / 261 09 10
Fax 01 / 261 92 62
publishers@scalo.com

Fax to: Nan Goldin

from: Walter Keller

Re: Your exhibition in Zurich
Zurich, December 18, 1999

Dear Nan

Welcome to Zurich!
We here at Scalo are all very much looking forward to your exhibition

Nan Goldin
NEW WORKS
January – March 2000

at our Zurich gallery space. It was great fun to do the selection with you in New York. There is no one who can paint with colors in photography like you do.

And let me tell you how proud I am to be the publisher of your books for almost a decade now. Let's start working on a new book as soon as possible!

Love
Walter
Walter

Vertrieb von / Distributor for
PARKETT (Deutschland, Österreich, Schweiz)
EDITION PATRICK FREY
ANDREAS ZÜST VERLAG
(Alle Territorien / All Territories)

SCALO USA
560 Broadway, # 301
New York, NY 10012
Tel. 212-334-9393
Fax 212-334-4290
publishers@scalo.com

Buchhandlung & Galerie / Bookshop & Gallery
Weinbergstrasse 22a
CH-8001 Zürich
Fax 01 / 261 92 62
Buchhandlung / Bookshop
Tel. 01 / 261 09 28
Galerie / Gallery
Tel. 01 / 261 09 41
Di – Fr 12 – 18.30 Uhr
Sa 10 – 16 Uhr

SCALO books & looks
BUCHHANDLUNG & GALERIE

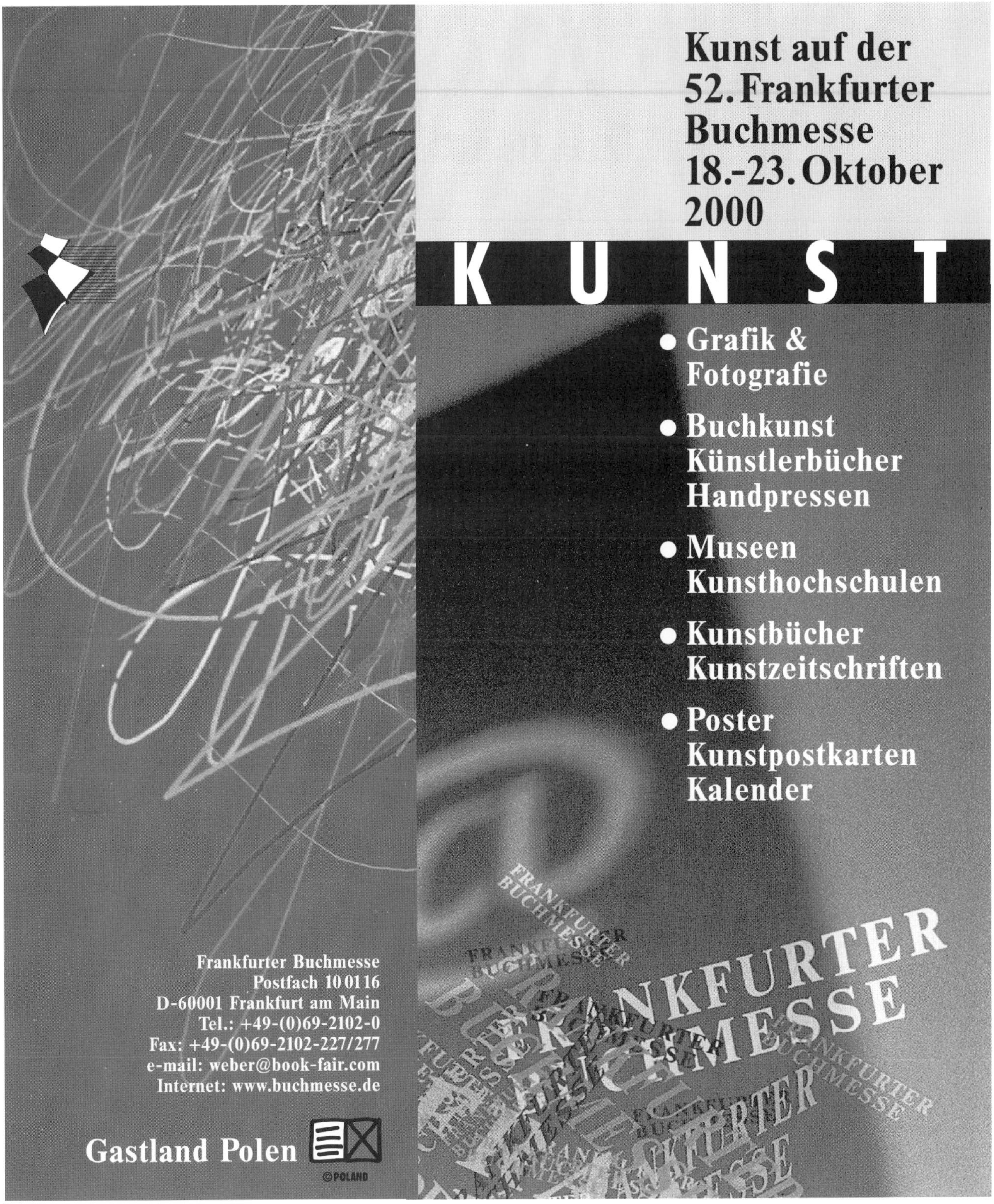
Kunst auf der
52. Frankfurter
Buchmesse
18.-23. Oktober
2000
KUNST
• Grafik & Fotografie
• Buchkunst
Künstlerbücher
Handpressen
• Museen
Kunsthochschulen
• Kunstbücher
Kunstzeitschriften
• Poster
Kunstpostkarten
Kalender
Frankfurter Buchmesse
Postfach 10 01 16
D-60001 Frankfurt am Main
Tel.: +49-(0)69-2102-0
Fax: +49-(0)69-2102-227/277
e-mail: weber@book-fair.com
Internet: www.buchmesse.de
Gastland Polen
©POLAND
FRANKFURTER BUCHMESSE

material

Die neue Kunst-Illustrierte

483g material* enthalten	
Perfect Day	69,2g
Bubblehouse	48,5g
Amsterdam, Köln, Berlin, Zürich	43,8g
Kopfball	41,6g
Lounging	39,9g
The Nuyorican Poets	37,1g
Tjoss May	34,2g
Nintendo	29,6g
viele Bilder von Carlos Amorales und Elke Krystufek sowie weitere Inhaltstoffe	139,1g

* Nr. 2 jetzt erhältlich

herausgegeben von
«migros museum» Museum für Gegenwartskunst Zürich

material ist käuflich
1 Ausgabe kostet am Kiosk
CHF/DM 14.–, ÖS 125.–
Abo 4 mal pro Jahr ins Haus geliefert
CHF/DM 50.–, ÖS 435.–

Bestellungen
per Telefon: +41 1 405 60 70
per Fax: +41 1 405 60 71
per E-Mail info@material.ch

Art On Paper

Vol. 4, No. 2
Nov.-Dec. 1999
US $10/Can $12

Prints

Ed Ruscha
Henri Michaux
David Hockney
Linda Schwarz

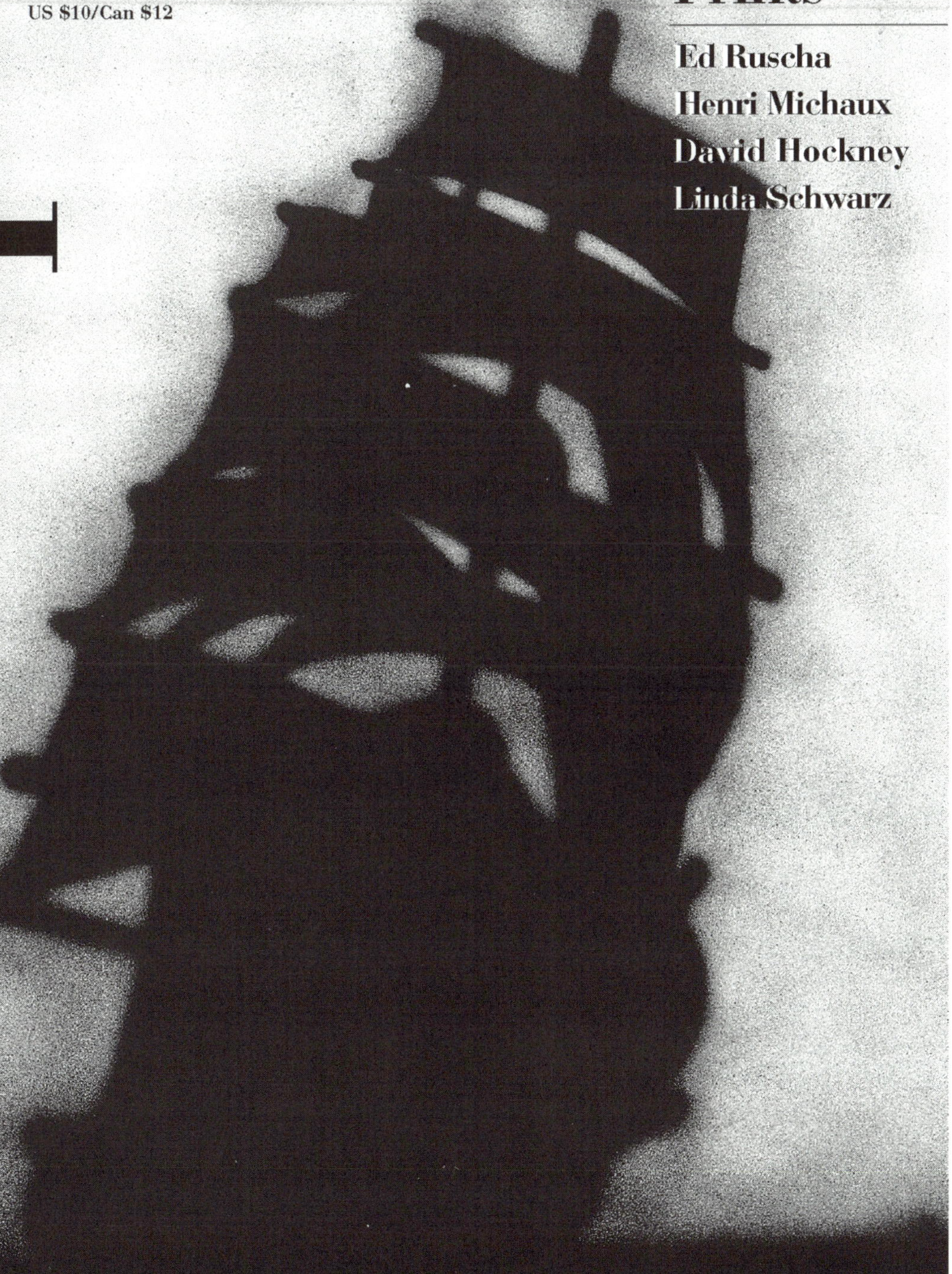

The International Art Magazine Dedicated to Prints, Drawings, and Photography

For Subscriptions & Information call: (212) 988-5959 or (800) 685-9777 • Fax (212) 988-6107

GustavKlugeEisenblicke

Eisenskulpturen
1985–1999
6.11.1999–14.1.2000

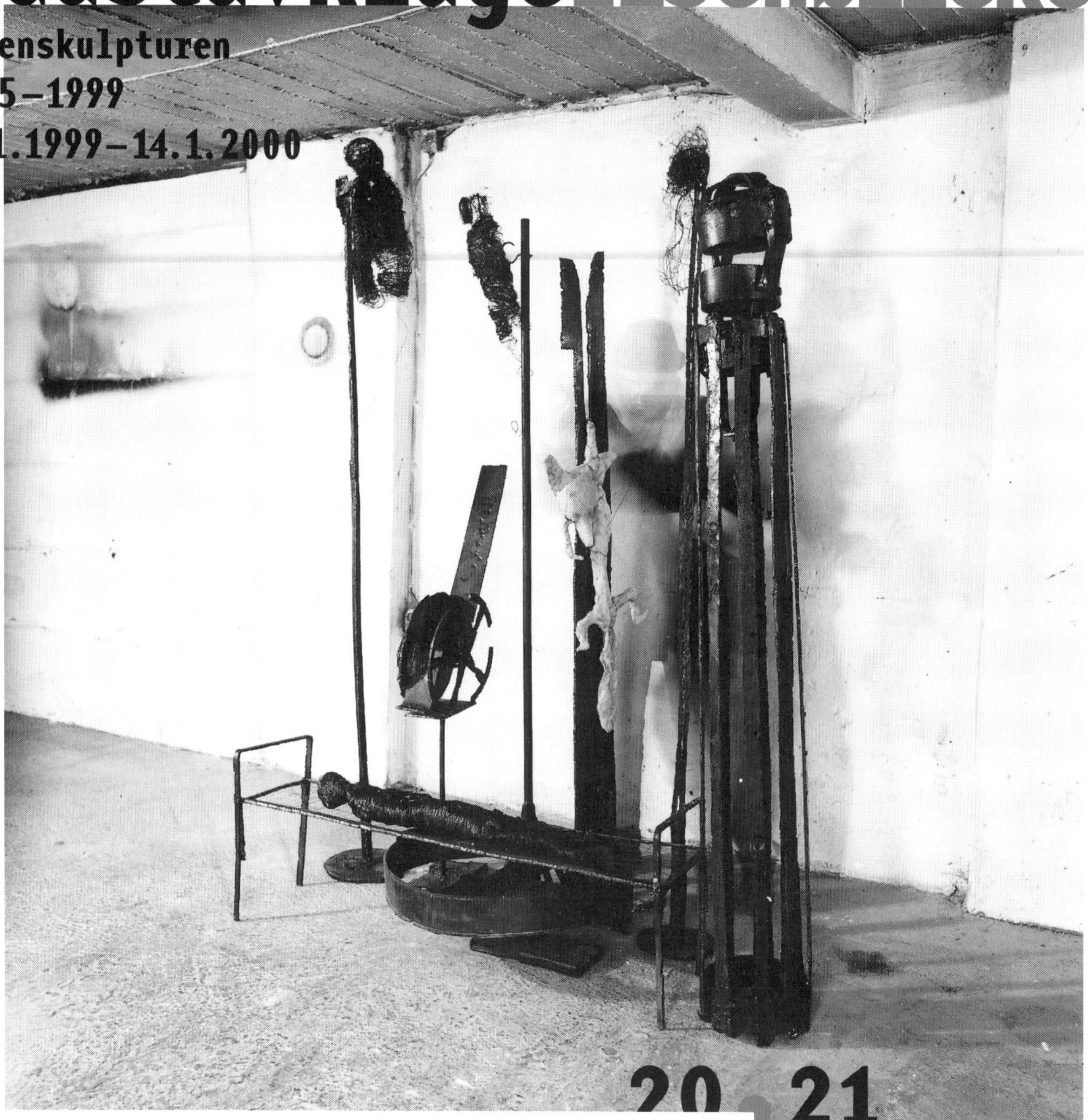

20 21
Galerie Edition Kunsthandel GmbH
Meisenburgstraße 169–173
D-45133 Essen
Tel. **+49 (201) 87100-0**
Fax **+49 (201) 87100-10**
Email INFO@2021ART.COM
http://www.2021ART.COM
Mi–Fr 14–19 · Sa 11–16
und nach Vereinbarung:
Sprechen Sie mit Irmgard Schnell.

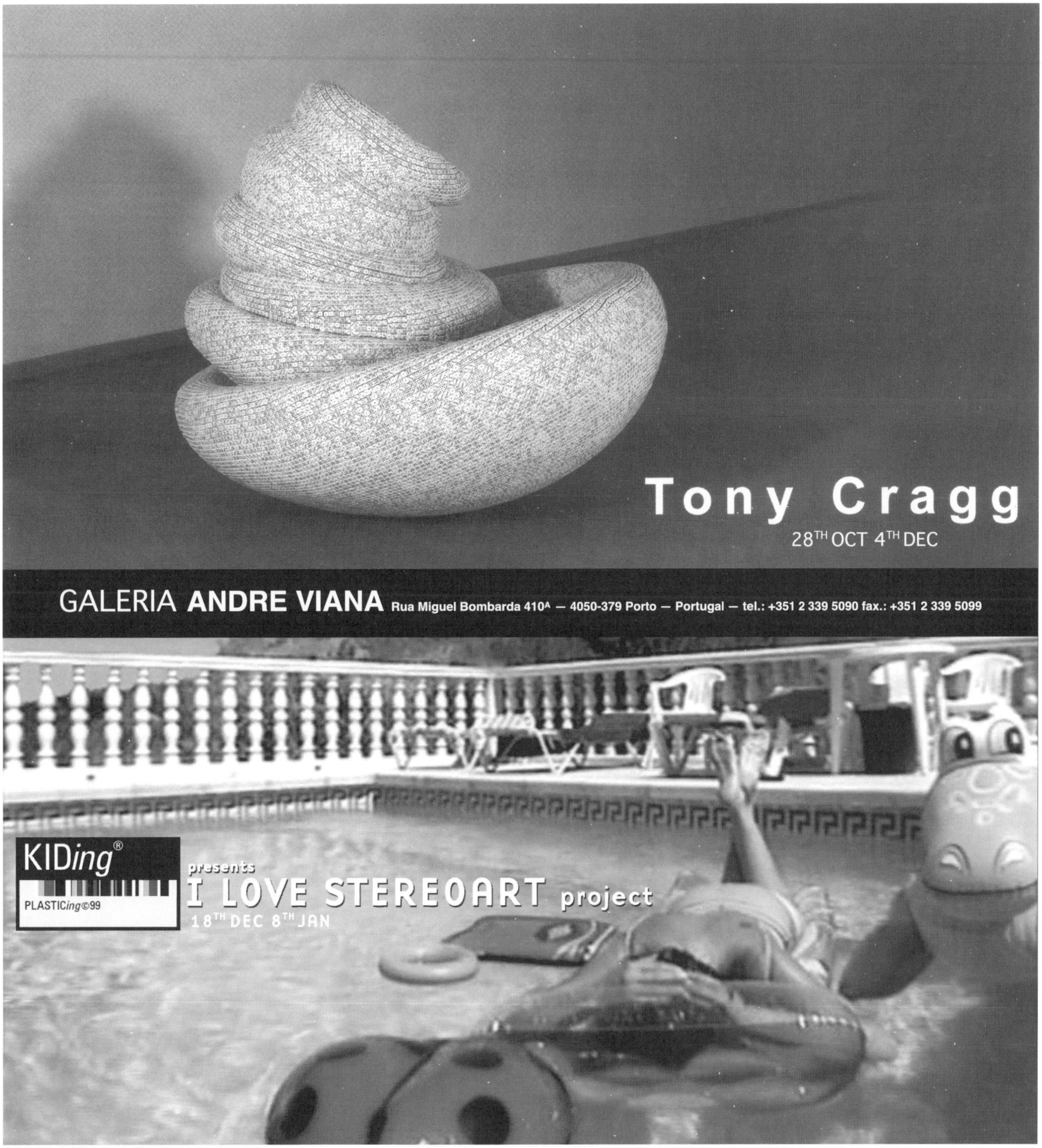
Tony Cragg
28TH OCT 4TH DEC
GALERIA ANDRE VIANA Rua Miguel Bombarda 410A — 4050-379 Porto — Portugal — tel.: +351 2 339 5090 fax.: +351 2 339 5099
KIDing®
PLASTICing©99
presents
I LOVE STEREOART project
18TH DEC 8TH JAN

Kunsthalle
Basel

Claudio Moser
Markéta Othová
29. Januar - 26. März 2000

Rot-Grau
29. Januar - 30. April 2000

Kunsthalle Basel, Steinenberg 7, CH-4051 Basel, Telefon 061/206 99 00, Fax 061/206 99 19, http://www.kunsthallebasel.ch
Öffnungszeiten: Dienstag – Sonntag 11 – 17 Uhr, Mittwoch 11 – 20.30 Uhr, Montag geschlossen. Führungen: Mittwoch 18.30 Uhr, Sonntag 11 Uhr

28. Januar – 9. April 2000

Dinge, die wir nicht verstehen

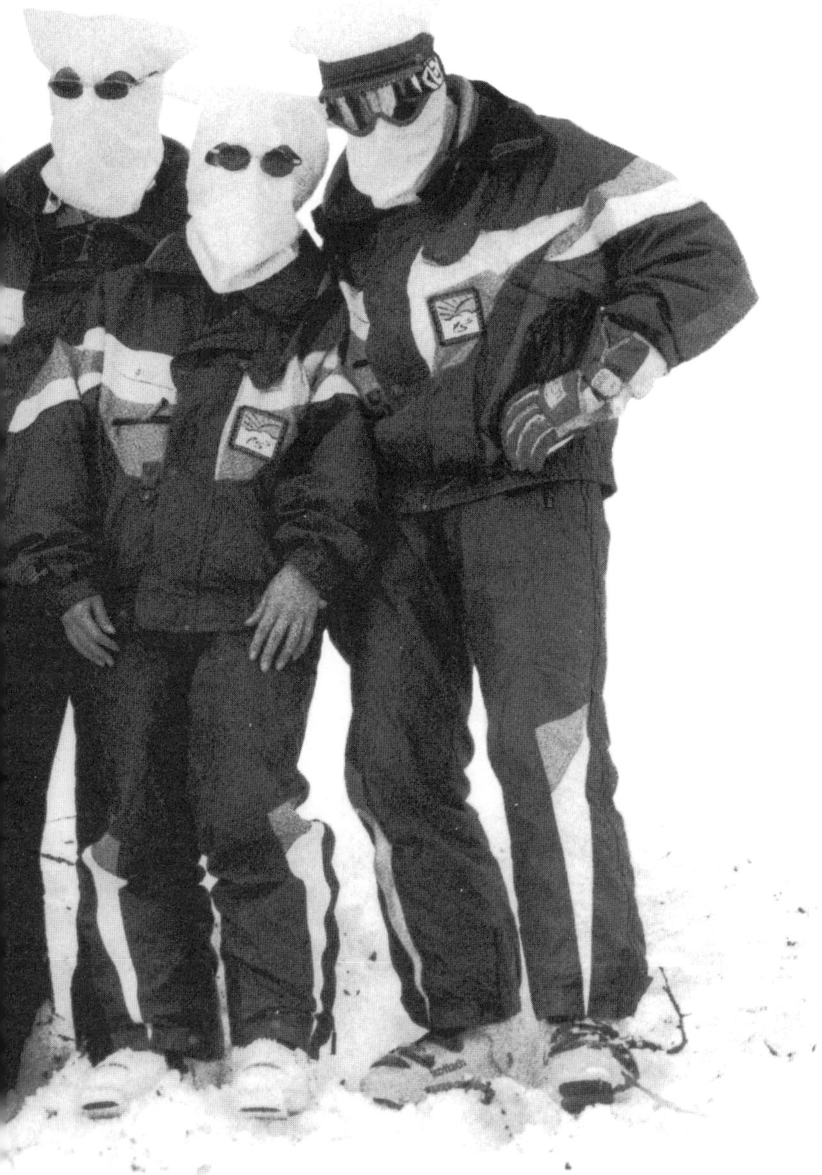

Eleanor Antin, Ines Doujak,
Harun Farocki, Peter Friedl,
Iñigo Manglano-Ovalle,
Nina Menkes, Alice Ohneland,
Alejandra Riera

Gastkuratiert von Ruth Noack
und Roger M. Buergel

Publikation erhältlich

GENERALI FOUNDATION

Generali Foundation
Wiedner Hauptstraße 15
1040 Wien, Austria

Tel. (+43 1) 504 98 80
Fax (+43 1) 504 98 83
found.office@generali.at

www.gfound.or.at

SEAN KELLY GALLERY

43 MERCER STREET
NEW YORK NY 10013
TELEPHONE 212 343-2405
FAX 212 343-2604
www.skny.com

Julião Sarmento

December 9, 1999 - January 22, 2000

Duchamp/Man Ray

January 22 - March 4

Christine Borland

March 9 - April 15

Ann Hamilton

April 20 - May 27

THOMAS AMMANN FINE ART AG ZURICH

IMPRESSIONIST & 20TH CENTURY MASTERS

SELECTED WORKS BY MAJOR ARTISTS

BACON
BALTHUS
BEUYS
BRAQUE
CALDER
CHAGALL
ERNST
GIACOMETTI
KANDINSKY
KIRCHNER
KLEE
DE KOONING
LEGER
LICHTENSTEIN
MARDEN
MATISSE
MIRO
PICASSO
RYMAN
ROTHKO
TAAFFE
TWOMBLY
WARHOL

RESTELBERGSTRASSE 97 CH-8044 ZÜRICH TEL. (411) 360 51 60 FAX (411) 360 51 61

www.ammann-fineart.ch

georg baselitz
nicola de maria
pia federspiel
karl gerstner
rebecca horn
jahanguir
catherine lee
alois lichtsteiner
ingeborg lüscher
darryl pottorf
robert rauschenberg
sean scully
richard serra
joel shapiro
frank stella

25 jahre galerie jamileh weber

through january 29, 2000

galerie jamileh weber
waldmannstrasse 6
ch-8001 zürich
telefon 01 252 10 66
telefax 01 252 11 32
email: jamilehweber@access.ch